100 YEARS
OF
AUSTRALIAN
FOOTBALL

Footscray rover Merv Hobbs flies high over Melbourne ruckman Trevor Johnson to take an outstanding mark in the 1961 Preliminary Final. Footscray captain Ted Whitten looks on in appreciation.

100 YEARS
OF
AUSTRALIAN
FOOTBALL

1897–1996

PENGUIN BOOKS

Penguin Books Australia Ltd
487 Maroondah Highway, PO Box 257
Ringwood, Victoria 3134, Australia
Penguin Books Ltd
Harmondsworth, Middlesex, England
Viking Penguin, A Division of Penguin Books USA Inc.
375 Hudson Street, New York, New York 10014, USA
Penguin Books Canada Limited
10 Alcorn Ave, Toronto, Ontario, Canada M4V 3B2
Penguin Books (NZ) Ltd
Cnr Rosedale and Airborne Roads, Albany, Auckland, New Zealand

First published by Penguin Books Australia Ltd 1996
This edition published 1997

10 9 8 7 6 5 4 3 2 1 0

Cover designed by David Lancashire Design
Cover illustration/artwork by Uncommon Characters

Printed by Southbank Book, 261 Salmon Street, Fishermens Bend, Melbourne, Victoria.

National Library of Australia
Cataloguing-in-Publication Data

100 years of Australian football.

Bibliography.
Includes index.
ISBN 0 14 026969 X.

1. Australian football teams – Victoria – History.
2. Australian football – Victoria – History. I. Title:
100 years of Australian football 1897–1996.
II. Title: One hundred years of Australian football.

796.33609945

ACKNOWLEDGEMENTS

Australian Rules Football is a big game with a big history, and we are grateful to many individuals and organisations who have been involved in the presentation of *100 Years of Australian Football*.

Firstly to advisors and readers, Col Hutchinson and Stephen Rodgers, men with a vast knowledge of the facts of the game, who were able to pounce on inconsistencies. And to Ross Oakley, Tony Peek, John Lauritz and Joanne Tregear, particularly, amid the general enthusiastic support of the AFL staff.

We read many books and list a bibliography with the index and photo credits. But particular reference must be made to the two 'bibles' of the AFL – *Every Game Ever Played* by Stephen Rodgers (Viking) and *The Encyclopedia of League Footballers* by Jim Main and Russell Holmesby (Information Australia). Similarly every illustration is credited, but acknowledgement is especially made to private suppliers John Barnaby, Tom Mahony, Rick Milne, Brant Atkinson, William Ellis Green (WEG), Peter Haby, Rennie Ellis, John Spooner, Ron Tandberg and Ian Kenins, Michael Leunig, Ken Dowd, Joel Williams, Nicole Lovelock, Ian Currie, Mark Knight, Beryl Frost and the families of Dan Minogue and Edward `Carji' Greeves. We are indebted to *The Age* and the staff of The Age Photo Library (particularly Susan Carabott, Kylie Moss, Monica Simpson, Graham Meade and George Gorsevski) and The State Library of Victoria (particularly Latrobe Librarian Diane Reilly, Latrobe Newspaper Librarian, Deidre Wilmott and library staff members Mario Frattin, Kim Wilson, Philip Carr, Michael Kosh, Sandra Sindici, Graham Barnett, Neil Munro, Steve Shannon and Andrew Nicholls) for their assistance in locating and supplying pictures. We have received valuable help and illustrations from the Australian Gallery of Sport and the Melbourne Cricket Club museum, and thank Graeme Atkinson and Judy Hansen for their assistance.

HOW TO USE THIS BOOK

100 Years of Australian Football begins with a general coverage of the foundations of the Australian game. From 1897, with the first season of the Victorian Football League (the antecedent of the Australian Football League), the coverage is year by year. The book is prepared as both a reading experience and an information system. Browsing in any part of the book can be done with satisfaction, but the order of presentation allows quick access to specific information.

The stories presented in each year are dated, according to the most reliable information. Where articles are part of a running story, or do not relate to a precise event within a year, dates most appropriate to the presentation of the story have been chosen. The book seeks to give immediacy to its stories by reporting events as they happen, like a newspaper. It seeks to avoid a foreknowledge of events to come, although in weighing the importance of stories for presentation the editors do allow themselves the benefit of hindsight. For instance, if we report the early games of Ted Whitten, Ron Barassi, Peter Hudson or Gary Ablett it is because we know we'll be hearing from them later. But we report only the facts known at the time, and use illustrations which were available at the time of the story.

Each year opens with a 'chronology' panel, which might note an event which has not been selected for an article, or a linked occurrence which precedes or follows an article. At the bottom of each panel the debuts and retirements of many significant League players are noted.

To link chronology items and stories together we have a cross-reference system which will lead the reader from one story to another. In this way a sequential story, a subject, such as uniform changes, or a player's career, insofar as it is mentioned in the book, can be followed. The system is a series of arrows and dates at the end of a chronology item or article. All arrows link events forwards, either within a month (→ 12), within a year (→ 12/6) or to another year (→ 12/6/66). If a cross-reference from a chronology item refers to the same event in an article it will be marked by an →.

We cannot show all connections which flow from a particular item, as many items could be given multiple connections which would confuse rather than inform the reader. To avoid such complexity, only one cross-reference appears at the end of an entry. The comprehensive index is devised as a more complete reference to everything covered in the book.

Throughout the book there are many essays on aspects of the game, and personalities on and off the field. These are generally within borders and do not have datelines. Unlike the news articles they are not constrained by datelines, and can roam at will across the subject. They are, unless written by a staff writer, under the name of the special writer.

The book is broken into eras, selected to introduce periods of change in the game, and each is preceded by a major illustration and a keynote essay.

Contents

What it's all about. Melbourne and Geelong players watch the raising of Melbourne's 1955 Premiership Flag at the Melbourne Cricket Ground.

100 Years of Australian Football

Editor in chief	John Ross
Executive editor	Garrie Hutchinson
Illustration editor	Michael Roberts
Researcher	Damien Cash
Production manager	Ron Duhengoh
Administration manager	Rosemary Braithwaite-Young
Writers	Kevin Childs, Peter Weiniger, Roger Dunn, Alex Hutchinson
Special writers	Geoffrey Blainey, Damien Cash, Noel Delbridge, Keith Dunstan, Martin Flanagan, Harry Gordon, Gillian Hibbins, Russell Holmesby, Col Hutchinson, Garrie Hutchinson, Garry Linell, Ross McMullin, Stuart Macintyre, Robert Pascoe, Michael Roberts, John Ross, Geoff Slattery, Robert Walls
Editorial services	Bill Donlevy
Index	Fay Donlevy
Photographic services	Sporting Pix Australia
Production co-ordination	Jacques Legrand s.a., Paris

Following pages:
Arthur Streeton (1867–1943)
The National Game *1889*
oil on cardboard, 11.8 × 22.9 cm
The Art Gallery of New South Wales

Introduction

Australian football has always had a hold on Victoria, where the game originated, and on the people of southern Australia. The pages of this spectacular history of the Australian Football League are testimony to the quality of the game and its star players, and the fever that gripped football followers from the earliest days in the fierce competition between the suburban based Victorian Football League clubs.

The game has always been full of great characters and champion players, and we meet them again in these colourful pages.

In the case of old time champions, many readers will discover why they were household names in their day, and how they played the game. Readers will also discover something of how the game was played a hundred years ago and how it has evolved through the decades to the highly skilled, action packed, professional sport that it is today.

It is fitting that, by this 100th season of top class Australian football competition, the AFL has grown to become a truly national league of clubs from five states.

The game has always had heart stopping matches, headline grabbing incidents and strange happenings, and this book, reporting them as if they happened yesterday, brings all these stories back to life.

In planning the Centenary season, the AFL felt that an essential element would be the publication of a history that captured the excitement, the great moments, the great players and great images of the game.

We commissioned Penguin Books to do that, and the result is something football followers, whichever team they support, will want to have near them through the Centenary year, and seasons to come. There's something fresh and fascinating on every page.

We are certain that *100 Years of Australian Football* will be of great interest to sports followers around Australia, and we know that millions will join us in celebrating the 100th year of the AFL's involvement in the great Australian game.

Ross Oakley
Chief Executive Officer
Australian Football League

A NEW AUSTRALIAN GAME

1858

The origins of our game

Australia is such a young nation and so many of its institutions have been borrowed from Britain that Australian Rules football came to be seen as primarily an imported game. In fact it is an Australian invention, indeed a chain of inventions.

It was first played on the parklands of inner Melbourne in the late 1850s, and the early players were nearly all born in Australia or the British Isles. There was a British influence on the first rules but that influence faded.

When the game began a wide variety of football rules was followed by English schools and by adult football clubs. What we now call rugby and soccer were played in an endless variety of ways. Some English schools such as Harrow and Eton played a soccer-type of game, while Rugby and Marlborough Schools handled rather than dribbled the football. Australian Rules football happened to be born at the time when the British rules of football were still fluid. The first Australian players selected rules from here and there.

Rugby was the most visible parent of Australian Rules but not the only parent. Tom Wills, the most influential of the early footballers and rule-makers, had sailed from Melbourne to England as a lad to attend the Rugby School, returning in 1856. And yet even in 1858 the early Melbourne games deviated from rugby football in many important ways – too many, in Wills' opinion. In 1865 he was still trying to introduce, with no success, a goal post with a cross-bar.

What we now call soccer had much less influence than rugby on the Victorian football paddocks; but we can glimpse just a touch of soccer in the first rules. Handling the football was restricted far more than it is today. To dribble or soccer the ball along the ground was a common approach to the goals. Round soccer-type balls were used in some of the early games though the oval rugby ball was ultimately selected.

The offside rule is almost the hallmark of today's soccer and two rugby codes. Even at its start, Australian Rules had no strict offside rule – so far as we can tell – though the games probably began with the two teams facing one another like opposing armies.

Australian football is also a product of cheap, abundant land. It was first played on huge arenas, which were oblong if they had a shape. On such big grounds four or even six dozen players could take part. The first rules imposed no limit on the number of players. Even in 1877 the official Victorian rules imposed no restrictions on the number of players. South Australia's rules of the same year stipulated 20 players to a side but allowed more if agreed.

Melbourne's parklands shaped the game that developed. That strip of Yarra Park between the present Melbourne Cricket Ground and the Jolimont railway station, and Albert Park and the Carlton parks on both sides of Royal Parade, provided those huge playing fields of the 1860s and 1870s. In Geelong and Ballarat the fields were probably smaller but they dwarfed – and still do – the football pitches of the international codes of football.

By the 1880s the main Victorian matches were increasingly moved from the rough parklands to the adjacent, fenced, cricket grounds. An oval or round arena replaced the oblong arena, without even calling for a rewriting of the rules.

Australian football was partly a reaction against the rough and tumble spirit of rugby. In Melbourne, Geelong and Ballarat – the first strongholds of the game – footballers playing on Saturday wished to be fit for work on the Monday. They resented the injuries arising from unturfed grounds that were hard, whereas those in England were soft.

Melbourne had a freakishly dry winter in 1858, and the hard gravelly grounds made most footballers decide that if at all possible they should avoid heavy falls and tumbles. That attitude affected the rules improvised for the games. Thus an early rule banned the tripping of opponents. The black eye was also frowned upon. Of course there was no send-off rule and, in the early years, no power to suspend a player.

Today there is a booklet full of rules, but initially only 10 rules were agreed to, and they could be written down on one sheet of paper. Soon some of those rules were disputed by clubs and players and new rules

Geelong play Carlton in 1881.

Caps and chamois leather shoulder pads are the fashion for the Blues, Geelong play in the familiar blue and white stripes.

The origins of our game (cont.)

were added. The fact that for so long the game was played in only one country meant that its rules could easily be changed.

Nearly all the rule changes came as the result of simple one-night meetings organised by clubs in Melbourne.

In contrast, to change one rule in international games like soccer and the two rugby codes is a slow, arduous task.

The distinctive qualities of today's game were not to be seen in the 1860s. Most were the outcome of Australian players and officials inventing and adapting.

Thus in the first half dozen years there was no sign of such features of the game as the high mark, the handball, the drop-punt kick, the flow-on play, and the starting of a match with the umpire bouncing the ball in the centre of the arena.

There was not yet a ban on grabbing an opponent by the neck or pushing him in the back. There was no division of the game into four equal quarters, no counting of behinds as well as goals in scoring, no limiting of a team to 18 men, and no throwing in of the ball after it went out of bounds. The high score was unknown. A match could extend until darkness without a goal being kicked.

For decades there has been argument about where the game came from? Some say Ireland, some say England, and some say the Aborigines. These theories overlooked a simple fact. The game did not descend ready-made on Victorian parklands.

It was not a once-only invention. It developed into a unique game through a procession of inventions some of them as recently as the 1990s.

Admittedly the game today has some uncanny resemblances to Gaelic football but Australia's is older than the Gaelic code whose formal rules were written only in 1885. None of the early rule-makers seems to have known of Gaelic football.

Irish or Catholic lads were not at first prominent as players. Melbourne Grammar, Scotch College and St Kilda Grammar – not Catholic schools – played in the first recorded matches in Melbourne in 1858.

The Irish towns were not the first in rural Victoria to take up the game. The Irish green was not to be seen in the colours of any major club.

So far no evidence has come to light to suggest that Gaelic football even influenced early Australian football, let alone gave birth to it.

The recent idea that Australian football stemmed from an early Aboriginal brand of football is more a wish than a fact.

A version of football was played by some Aborigines in prehistoric Victoria, using a ball made of possum skin, but versions of football were played in dozens of parts of the world stretching from China to Europe.

Irish-Australians and, recently, Aborigines have been wonderful exponents of the modern game, which helped to support myths that these peoples must have invented the game.

Australia has a very old tradition of spectator sport, and its senior Victorian football clubs are ancient by world standards.

Melbourne (1858) and Geelong (1859) are older than any clubs in the English Football Association, the father-league of world soccer.

Some of the slightly later Melbourne clubs such as Carlton and North Melbourne are much older than any senior football clubs in South America and in the United States.

Even great footballing nations such as Italy and Germany have no senior clubs as old as Essendon, St Kilda and Fitzroy. Whether there is another senior football club in the world as old as Melbourne and Geelong is open to doubt.

The only possible contender would be an old senior rugby club in the south of England.

The Australian game originated at the very time when English football was making its transition from solely a schoolboy game to a sport for young men.

The rules were astonishingly flexible when Melbourne, then Australia's largest city, seriously adopted football. So the first footballers made some of their own rules and borrowed others.

But if Melbourne had first fallen in love with football twenty years later, it would almost certainly have taken to either rugby or soccer.

Geoffrey Blainey

MELBOURNE

Melbourne Football Club has a unique place in football as the pioneer club of Australian football.

Thomas Smith and Tom Wills officially formed the club in 1859 at the Parade Hotel in Wellington Parade. Although 'Melbourne' had been mentioned as having played against South Yarra in 1858 it seems that members of the Melbourne Cricket Club played scratch matches between teams that were decided on the day of play, often under the direction of first captain, and Melbourne Cricket Club Secretary in 1857-58, Tom Wills.

The Melbourne Football Club and ground were sometimes called 'Metropolitans' at this time.

Despite the strong cricketing connection the football club operated separately from the MCC, playing its games on the paddock outside the cricket ground and holding its meetings at a hotel.

Melbourne and Carlton were the dominant clubs in the early years of the game and they attracted the biggest crowds of the time. Melbourne won the first Victorian championship in 1870 and the club also triumphed in 1872 and 1876.

Throughout these years Melbourne was unable to play matches on the MCG because the cricket club thought football would cause too much damage to the surface. A trial match was played against the police force in 1869, but 10 years passed before an official game was permitted on the hallowed turf.

By that time Melbourne had been in the newly formed Victorian Football Association for two years. In each of the first two seasons Melbourne came second to arch-rival Carlton.

After its early dominance Melbourne was gradually overtaken by younger clubs and in 1889 it reached its lowest ebb by running last on the VFA list.

In desperation the football club approached the MCC to seek help. The cricket club agreed to take over the football club's operations and for several years the team was even known as the MCC. On the field matters took a turn for the better and in 1892 the club finished fourth.

The club started sensationally in 1895 with eight wins on the trot, but could not maintain the form. A key player was the brilliant Fred McGinis, the ex-Tasmanian rover who was one of the game's early champions. He dropkicked magnificently, was courageous and determined in his approach for the ball. Those who saw McGinis play ranked him as one of the game's all-time greats.

The takeover by the cricket club appears to have been beneficial as Melbourne restored its reputation in the last four years in the VFA. Second placings in 1893 and 1894 were dwarfed by the all-conquering Essendon, but Melbourne still had many fine performers including the brilliant Dave Christie and heavyweight ruckman Herb Fry.

In 1893 Melbourne was the only club to seriously challenge the barnstorming Essendon and a clash between the two clubs late in the season drew 28,000 people. Melbourne went down narrowly in a game where one of its best, 'Goosey' Lewis, excelled.

Their form slipped unaccountably in 1895 and they were said to have been over-trained. One writer said they picked up towards the end of the season 'when the majority of them had practically ceased to train'.

Melbourne came a creditable fourth in 1896, but in many ways were considered a disappointment because they possessed more talent man for man than any other team in the competition.

GEELONG

There were evidently scratch football matches played before 1858 around the Corio area and Geelong lore states that around this time a Barwon team claimed to be the champions of Victoria and they were challenged by the Melbourne cricketers.

It appears that Melbourne's first captain Tom Wills had much to do with the beginning of Geelong football and that is supported by the fact that he grew up in the Western District. There is evidence that Geelong was formed at a meeting on July 18, 1859, before the official formation of Melbourne.

In the early days of the game Geelong was happy to adopt its own rules for football in the area rather than follow the ideas being used 50 miles away.

Melbourne and Geelong did not meet until 1860 when they struggled for three hours to achieve a scoreless draw. They played on the Argyle Square ground in Aberdeen Street near the Argyle Hotel. This was the club's home for some time until it moved to East Geelong then later to the Eastern Park site, known as the Corio Oval.

Geelong was the strongest provincial club in Victoria and could more than hold its own against the best teams from the city.

In one encounter with Melbourne in 1868 the game did not finish until 6.15 p.m., well after dark, when each side had scored.

Geelong won its second successive premiership in 1879, without a defeat in 17 games.

Over the space of a decade Geelong built a record that rates as one of the most sustained periods of dominance in the history of football.

In 11 seasons they won seven premierships, were runners-up three times and third in the other season. That run included hat-tricks in 1878-79-80 and in 1882-83-84. Geelong players topped the goalkicking six times and on five occasions were named Champion of the Colony.

So absolute was the Geelong dominance that in 1886 their players filled the top five places on the goalkicking list. There were no losses in their 27 games and only two draws. The Pivotonians had champions such as Arch Wilson, Harry Douglass, J.T. Kerley, Jack Julien, Dave Higinbotham, Tom Mullen, Ben Hall and the famed McShane brothers – Tom, Joe, Jack, Harry and Phil.

Another who led the side was Charles Brownlow, a man who would give his name to the game's most famous award.

Geelong's teamwork assumed the precision of a science. It started when a couple of Geelong players were criticised by their own barrackers for hanging out of the heavy clashes, but it soon became obvious that they were getting more of a share of the ball and the Geelong leaders developed it into a team tactic.

As with any era, it had to end and Geelong gave way to Essendon at the start of the 1890s.

It was Geelong, however, that ended a two-year winning streak by Essendon in 1894 when they used a strategy of having an extra defender play in front of the brilliant Albert Thurgood to cramp his movements.

Geelong was the first club to suggest a breakaway group of VFA teams. That 1894 notion did not get off the ground, but it planted the seed and two years later it would result in the formation of the VFL.

Oddly enough when the split came Geelong was unsuccessful on the field.

In their last year of VFA football Geelong ran 11th and of the eight new League clubs only Carlton finished lower on the list.

CARLTON

Carlton turned out for its initial match in 1864 on the sloping, pebble-strewn Royal Park near the spot from which Burke and Wills set off on their ill-fated expedition. There was little to distinguish opposing teams then and Carlton's started to wear a distinctive orange cap. Before long blue was added and the 'old dark navy blue' would dominate the club's uniform.

The Blues were dubbed 'the wild men of Carlton' when they fronted the lilywhites from the aristocratic South Yarra in a Challenge Cup match in 1866. The tag 'Bulldogs' was also used.

Carlton fielded teams that included some of the most talented players and officials. T.S Marshall, later Secretary of the VFA was captain in 1866. A theatrical entrepreneur, comedian, theatre builder and much else, George Coppin was President between 1867 and 1872.

In the early days of the game the matches which captured the imagination were those played between Carlton and Melbourne. The rivalry became even more intense when star players Harry Chadwick, Jim Byrne and Charles Forrester decided to cross to Melbourne in 1868 after an internal fight at Carlton.

A continuous problem for Carlton in its early years was its home in Royal Park and in 1868 several clubs declined to play there. Finding suitable venues for football matches was a constant worry in those days and one 1869 game between Carlton and South Yarra at Fawkner Park came to a sudden end when a park ranger stopped play because the footbal-

lers were damaging grazing land. Carlton and Melbourne games attracted huge crowds of 10,000 spectators in the 1870s.

Carlton won the Challenge Cup in 1871 losing just one game for the year and again topped the pile in 1873.

This was one of the greatest Carlton teams, with men like Billy Lacey ('the greatest centre player the Colony has seen'), Billy Newing ('the little wonder') and Jack Gardiner. To add to Carlton's delight the Blues beat Melbourne four times.

After the Melbourne City Council refused permission to enclose the Royal Park ground Carlton leased a site at Madeleine Street Carlton (now Swanston Street Carlton) where they played until the end of the 1877 VFA Premiership season.

The University Council then decided that the ground could not be used for football and Carlton had to shift back to Royal Park. The club suffered an uneasy tenure there until 1890.

From then until 1896 Carlton played its home games on a variety of different grounds.

Lack of a settled home did not make any difference to Carlton's playing performance. The club was able to produce a succession of champions, including George Coulthard.

Carlton slumped in the early 1880s, but rebuilt and a strong Blues team took out the Flag in 1887. Stars in that side were Jack Baker, 'Dolly' Batters, Sam Bloomfield, Tommy Leydin and Billy Strickland.

A highlight of 1888 was a match against a visiting English rugby team, which Carlton won before a crowd of 25,000 at the MCG. Carlton was runner-up three times in a row from 1889 to 1891, but then the Blues slid down the ladder to eventually hit rock bottom in 1894.

The old club's playing and administrative strength was harshly criticised in the press, but Carlton's reputation and following – and new ground at Princes Park – meant that they had to be part of the new VFL.

Wills starts a new game

The Melbourne Cricket Ground on 1 January, 1864: a Victorian cricket 22 bows to the visitors' greater experience and plays an English Eleven.

When Tom Wills suggested in a letter to the local sporting paper, *Bell's Life in Victoria*, that Victorian cricketers keep fit out of season by playing football, an astute publican promptly offered a football for practice near his Parade Hotel just north of the cricket ground. It was July 31, 1858 and, at this time, organised football barely existed.

There was no soccer. There was no rugby – in the sense of a game played between different sides from different areas; there was only Rugby School Rules for the game played at that English school.

A very few written football rules *did* exist but only at Cambridge University and at select Public schools in England – Rugby, Eton, Harrow, Winchester, and Shrews-bury, and they were peculiar to each institution, that is, only played within the school by the pupils but not between the schools.

Thirty years earlier schoolmasters had adapted English folk football – rough and ready games played by the yokels – to the limitations and peculiarities of their own particular school grounds.

So, of the many young colonials who turned out to kick the ball that July in Melbourne, some had experience of different school rules and some of no rules at all.

The result was conflict and chaos.

On the same day the same problem was experienced by the infant Melbourne Grammar School, which modelling itself on the English public school, played football against a number of men calling themselves the St Kilda Club.

The St Kilda-ites were frustrated by the agreed-upon rules, which evidently encouraged carrying the ball rather than kicking it, as they came mainly from Etonian-type football backgrounds which emphasised kicking and no ball-handling at all.

Fisticuffs brought the match to an end.

A week later Melbourne Grammar probably turned with some relief to Scotch College for an opponent. Tom Smith, the Scotch classics master, was an enthusiast and some oval Rugby School balls had been sent out for the boys at Scotch College. It would seem that the schools played under modified Rugby School Rules.

This famous three-day match, mistakenly thought to be the first Australian Rules match, was played on August 7 and 21 and September 4 in 1858.

The Melbourne Grammar and Scotch College game stimulated local interest and, during August and September, the Melbourne cricketers organised some impromptu football games.

One player wrote: 'three or four Saturdays of this kind of play sufficed to show that something must be done to reconcile the different codes of rules.'

Reservations about Rugby School Rules were expressed by the Melbourne *Herald* which said these rules 'might be altered for the better'.

14

Thomas Wentworth Wills returns to Australia from England in 1869.

Henry Harrison is elected a Member of the Melbourne Cricket Club.

The whole vexed question of football rules was put on hold as cricket began again.

So it was not until the autumn of 1859, on Tuesday May 17, that four men met in the Parade Hotel in Wellington Parade, Melbourne to tackle this confused football rules situation.

William Hammersley, from Surrey, England, was a descendant of the Spode pottery family and of the Hammersleys who were landed gentry. William, an excellent shot, athlete and cricketer, had been to Cambridge University and was working for *Bell's Life in Victoria*.

A journalist for the local *Argus*, James Boyne Thompson, was the youngest son of a large family who lived in York. Smart and scholarly, he also had attended Cambridge University and may well have met Hammersley there, as they were both accepted for the University in 1845 and were residents of Trinity College.

Although they were emigrants to the booming goldrush colony of Victoria, they both knew Tom Wills, the young colonial born in Parramatta who had come to Port Phillip as a little boy.

Son of Horatio Wills, a prominent pastoralist and politician, Tom had been to Rugby School in England where he excelled at sport.

Not long returned from playing county cricket in England, Tom Wills was regarded as the best cricketer in the Colony and was the Secretary of the Melbourne Cricket Club.

The fourth man, Thomas Smith, was Irish and had a peppery temper probably well tested by his pupils at Scotch College.

Smith's father, a prosperous storekeeper, had sent Thomas to Trinity College (not the Cambridge one), the University in Dublin.

He knew Wills because Wills had umpired the Scotch and Grammar football match in which Smith had been one of seven masters playing.

Wills, Hammersley and Thompson were celebrated Victorian cricketers and all of them were members of the Melbourne Cricket Club, and now of the Melbourne Football Club which the interested members of the Cricket Club had officially formed three days earlier on Saturday May 14, 1859.

They had been appointed to the new Football Club's committee and probably chosen to formulate some rules for football because they had some scarce expertise in that area.

An almost identical circumstance had existed when Hammersley and Thompson had been at Cambridge. There pupils of Rugby and Eton had found it impossible to play football together because their school rules were so different.

The Old Etonians 'howled at Rugby men for handling the ball' and complained especially about hacking – the practice of kicking the shins of one's opponent to make him release the ball. Common sense decreed a compromise and a committee at Trinity College the

Wills starts a new game (cont.)

same college attended by Hammersley and Thompson, had formulated the 'Cambridge Rules' in 1848 and football at Cambridge was played by these rules.

It seems likely it was this university precedent that recommended Hammersley and Thompson to their Melbourne Football Club committee positions.

The football played in Smith's time at Trinity College in Dublin, from the very slight evidence available, seems to have been influenced by undergraduates who had attended Rugby School.

Wills was all for adopting Rugby School rules that he had personally played but was overruled by the others who considered them too complicated.

The four men also looked at the written Eton College rules and those used at Harrow and Winchester. They hoped to combine the merits and exclude the vices of each. The Melbourne Rules should be, Hammersley suggested, 'short, very simple, easily understood and remembered'.

The other consideration was to rid themselves of the English practice of hacking.

Hammersley could show legs scarred by spiked boots and Thompson considered hacking was all very well for schoolboys with their lesser weight and lack of responsibilities but young businessmen wanting to make their way in the flourishing colony would not relish the thought of injuries.

'Black eyes don't look so well in Collins Street', the *Argus* said later.

So of the ten rules laid down, Rule 7 banned hacking altogether. It was a most important decision.

The first five rules laid out the measurements of the ground and the distances between the four goal posts, defined a goal, and gave the captains the toss for choice of goal, the losing side getting the first kick from the centre of the ground.

Rules 6 and 8 dealt with the crux of the game.

Rule 6 allowed for catching the ball directly from the foot, calling 'Mark' and having a free kick.

This was part of the Rugby School try at goal but not part of its general play. Harrow had a similar rule applicable all over the ground

allowing a run on three yards before the kick. Cambridge Rules allowed a free kick but no run and at Winchester you could catch the ball, run until stopped and then take your free kick.

Rule 8 was the compromise between the carrying game favoured by the Rugby School-style players and the kicking game favoured by the Etonian type of play.

It said the ball may be taken in the hand or carried when caught from the foot (a mark) or on the hop (bounce) but in no case could it be lifted from the ground.

This was soon to become the main bone of contention and a bouncing rule was brought in and refined during the next few years so that the footballers were required to bounce the ball at intervals while running with it.

It was probably Thompson who successfully promoted and publicised the new Rules through the *Argus*.

In 1866 the Melbourne Rules Football was accepted as Victorian Rules Football and much later as Australian – even Australasian – Rules Football.

Cambridge Rules did not last this test of time. Nor did Eton Football, Harrow Football, or Winchester Football develop into anything more than a game played within a particular school.

When English footballers came together in 1863 to decide on rules which teams all over the country could play, they formed the Football Association ('soccer').

Those in favour of carrying the ball and hacking, went their own way, taunting the non-hacking kickers with faint-heartedness. It took until 1871 for Rugby Union to get organised.

The aim, as in Victoria, had been one universal game of football but the English ended up with two.

If the English had not split over hacking, they might have one football game now, perhaps one like Australian Rules.

Or if Hammersley, Smith, Thompson and Wills had not agreed to ban hacking, then perhaps Australia might have gone the English way and had two types of football games.

Gillian Hibbins

ST KILDA

ST. KILDA

The name of St Kilda appeared on the football scene just three weeks after Tom Wills sent his famous letter to *Bell's Life* in July 1858. But that team soon faded from the scene and had no link to the St Kilda Football Club formed in 1873. It was a union between St Kilda cricketers and the remnants of the old South Yarra Football club.

St Kilda played its early games on a patch of ground near the St Kilda Railway station. It was known as the Alpaca Paddock because a herd of the animals had grazed there a few years earlier in an unsuccessful attempt to breed.

The new football club thrived in a way the alpacas never had. By its second season it was ranked as a senior team. Arthur Greenwood, the club's first captain, headed a talented band of players, which included Jennings, one of the greatest kicks in the game.

Shortage of players led to a brief amalgamation with University in 1875, but the union was disastrous and the team was said to have played without spirit or energy. The hybrid team lasted for just half a season and St Kilda resumed in its own right in 1876.

St Kilda elected to drop down to junior ranks in 1879 and there it remained for the next seven years. It rebuilt its strength and rejoined the Victorian Football Association in 1886. So had neighbouring Prahran and there were suggestions that they merge. Prospects looked remote when the two clubs met in 1886 and there was a succession of punch-ups on both sides of the fence. By early 1888 they managed to put

aside their differences.

It was a one-sided merger as St Kilda retained its colours, name and ground. Among the Prahran players who came across in the merger was the talented Wally Lockett and his teammate 'Jigger' Morehouse. They joined forces with St Kilda stars such as Alf Smith and the newly combined club did well at first.

One scalp that St Kilda added to its collection in 1889 was the unlikely one of the New Zealand rugby team on its way home from a tour of England. St Kilda had a great run home at the end of 1890 when it notched five wins and three draws from its last nine games. There was controversy when Alf Smith, the star rover, and skipper Rusden stole a march on its opponents North Melbourne by wearing 'illegal metallic projections in their boots'. At half time the pair was ordered to remove their primitive 'stops'.

The Saints lost a champion when Alf Smith retired in 1894, but the following year gained a new star when Joe Hogan joined the club from Wesley Collegians.

In an era when professionalism was spreading like wildfire the Saints were complimented on their lofty ideals. The *Australasian* said: 'Two classes of men play football. With one the pleasure of participating is more than sufficient recompense for defeat: the other class thinks that a win is above everything else. To the first class I think those happy, genial Saints belong.

St Kilda was invited to join the Victorian Football League at the end of 1896 because it was one of only two clubs located south of the city, with a well-appointed ground which was handily placed at the St Kilda Junction.

In their last season of VFA football the Saints ran ninth in the 13 team competition, finishing ahead of Geelong and Carlton.

But money was always a problem with the Saints. Five days after the club had registered white knickerbockers as part of its uniform the committee hastily changed to dark blue knickers. They weren't as expensive.

New game played in Richmond Paddock

On July 31, 1858 publican Jerry Bryant, knowing that an 'ounce of practice is worth a pound of theory', took a leather cased pig's bladder onto the Richmond Paddock, near the Melbourne Cricket Ground.

Bryant's Parade Hotel was just across Wellington Parade from the Richmond Paddock, an area of land that extended beside the Punt Road from the river to Wellington Parade, and towards East Melbourne's elegant mansions.

After this 'first' match, the players who included MCC Secretary Tom Wills, were to sit down over a beer at Bryant's to draw up a set of rules. Perhaps the game, or the beers, interfered because nothing further is heard of rules until 1859.

But more scratch matches and school games were played, including one between representatives of Scotch College and Melbourne

Grammar on Saturday August 7, 1858 umpired by Wills and Dr John McAdam, the Scotch College chemistry master.

J.B. Thompson, another signatory to the rules of 1859, was sportswriter for the Melbourne *Argus,* and wrote (August 16, 1858): 'Football seems to be coming into fashion in Melbourne, and as it is a most manly and amusing game we hope that it may continue to grow in favour until it becomes as popular as cricket.'

Grammar took exception to the imputation it had shown the 'white feather', in not turning up for week two of that match. They said the match had been postponed 'to a date to be fixed.'

Then, said the Secretary of Grammar, 'we hope to show we are not wanting in pluck'.

Play recommenced on 21 August but no goals were scored – and the

same was the case a fortnight later. The 'first' match took a month to play, but ended in a draw.

By next season Thompson could write in the *Argus* (April 18 1859): 'Football like cricket has become an institution in and about the metropolis, and it would not be surprising if the epidemic spread wider'.

The next month, May, saw the writing of the first code and the establishment of the first club at a meeting at Bryant's hotel.

The 10 rules provided for marking, tripping and pushing but not for hacking – kicking in the shins. There was no mention of offside.

In June the St Kilda Club objected to playing Hammersley's Melbourne Football Club because the rules did not allow hacking.

Hammersley later remarked that the absence of the rule did not prevent people kicking him.

'My shins now show honourable scars, and often have I had blood trickling down my legs. No wonder, for hacking was permitted, and no objection taken to spiked shoes.'

And on July 2, 1859 during a match between two sides of the Melbourne Football Club 'the practice of "sneaking" against which no law has been passed was in full force'.

Sneaking was the tactic of forward players lurking near the goals, rather than joining the scrummage.

And as for the state of the paddock? In August 1860: 'The ground was none of the best and left only one of two alternatives, either a hard and dusty road, or a soft and muddy swamp, a fall on either being anything but pleasing.'

But the seed of football had been planted and would grow into a mighty tree – in that very paddock.

An artists impression of the Richmond Paddock in 1866, with the Melbourne Cricket Club's pavilion in the background.

ESSENDON

ESSENDON

The force behind Essendon's formation was the McCracken family which had made its mark as the owner of a brewery and many hotels around Melbourne.

Essendon began in junior ranks in 1873 and played its games on the McCracken family's paddock in Ascot Vale.

The team wore its red and black colours from the beginning, but for the first two years it was in the form of stripes. The red sash on a black background was introduced in 1875 and by 1876 Essendon had established themselves as the best junior side in Victoria. Players like Herbert Bryant, George Robertson and Ned Powell helped Essendon gather a base of support.

At first they moved to a Flemington Hill site in 1878 then decided to accept the offer of the East Melbourne Cricket Club and move to their ground in Jolimont from 1882, which was close to work for the city gentlemen.

It may seem strange in retrospect that the club moved out of its own district, but it could have been partially due to Essendon's lack of a local cricket club connections, which other clubs had. The football club applied to use the Essendon Reserve, but was refused by the local council and there was said to be a feeling that cricket was the only game for gentlemen.

Essendon had its most successful season to that point by running second to Geelong. They played Geelong in the final round after a trip to Tasmania and their boat berthed at Queenscliff just before the game. Several players were too ill to take the field and

others were far below their best. Geelong agreed at first to rearrange the game for two weeks later, but backed out of the commitment, thus winning the Flag.

Essendon became the 'school tie' club as it attracted many players from the Melbourne University and the public schools.

Essendon ran second in 1884 and 1885. In that year South Melbourne went through the season apparently undefeated, but according to Essendon their draw with the Southerners should have been a win, with a goal wrongly credited as a behind.

From 1891 Essendon fielded one of the best sides ever seen in Australian Football.

The 1891 season was one of the wettest on record, but nothing could stop Essendon which lost only one game on its way to the club's first Premiership. By now Essendon was the pace-setter both on and off the field.

Essendon introduced a style in which there were specialists in each position, with recognised key men down the goal to goal line. They had big, fast defenders, clever wingers and forwards with natural goal sense.

Dr Ned Officer at full-back was not only a mighty kick, but was a fast big man who was a splendid high mark and was clever in ground play. They also had stars in Bill Chadwick, 'Tracker' Forbes and 'Joker' Hall.

On top of all this talent Essendon picked up a brilliant youngster Albert Thurgood in 1892 who immediately staked a claim as a champion. He booted 56 goals in his first season, the first man to top the half-century of goals, and set new standards.

Not surprisingly Essendon won the 1892 flag and in 1893 cruised through without a loss under captain Alick Dick.

By the end of 1894 Essendon had their fourth flag in a row and in 66 matches had only been defeated three times.

Essendon and Geelong had pushed for a group to break away from the VFA in 1894, and when the VFL formed two years later Essendon was in the van.

FITZROY

FITZROY

There were only 23 people at the initial meeting of the Fitzroy Football Club at the Fitzroy Town Hall in 1884 and one guinea constituted the entire finance of the club. It was handed to the Secretary Mr Simpson 'for promotion purposes'.

Most of them were Fitzroy Cricket Club members who had attended earlier meetings at the Brunswick Hotel, at 113 Brunswick Street, and played on the Brunswick Street Oval, where the football club would play.

It was decided that the club uniform would be a blue cap and knickerbockers, maroon cap and hose. When it was found that maroon material was unavailable locally the President John McMahon ordered special lace-up guernseys from England which featured a chamois leather collar.

Fitzroy was lucky enough to have as its captain Paddy McShane – an all-round sportsman who had been prominent with Essendon Football Club and was a good enough cricketer to play three Tests for Australia.

The club recruited well in its first season securing men like 'Dummy' Muir – so nicknamed because he was deaf and dumb, and Jack Worrall, a sturdy young player from South Ballarat.

Like McShane, Worrall would go on to play Test cricket, but first made a mark on the sporting world with his deeds as a footballer for Fitzroy.

A debut season placing of fifth was impressive by any standards and Fitzroy showed a high degree of resourcefulness from the start.

One instance was the game against Carlton when Fitzroy em-

ployed the tactic of tagging, or 'watching' as it was called.

Fitzroy established itself as one of the strongest clubs in the VFA, running fourth in 1887 and third in both 1890 and 1891.

The choice of Worrall as captain from 1886 was an inspired one and he revelled in it.

Tom Banks stepped into the leadership role after Worrall retired in 1892 and he proved to be just as effective as a captain.

Banks had been persuaded to come from Bendigo to Fitzroy by his friend Con Hickey, a longtime stalwart with the Roys. Hickey took on the role of Secretary while still serving as a player and he held the administrative post for more than 20 years.

Fitzroy's climb up the ladder wasn't without controversy. The club's innovative approach included building a gymnasium and paying a professional trainer to get the team fit.

Fitzroy was the only team to defeat the rampaging Essendon in 1892, finishing second. But the club slipped out of contention the following year.

The absence of Banks through injury was costly in 1894, but when he returned to the fold Fitzroy gathered in strength.

The team's path in 1895 was a difficult one and although it was on top with three matches to play, Fitzroy had to confront stiff opposition in Geelong, Essendon and South Melbourne. With many players injured Fitzroy managed to win one and draw two of the games and hang on to just pip Geelong for the Flag.

The battling draw against South sealed the Premiership for Fitzroy. Two men instrumental in the success were brothers Jim and Mick Grace, both footballers of the highest calibre who were matchwinners on their day.

The hero, though, was skipper Banks who announced his retirement after the final match. He would turn out again over the next couple of years, but his real influence was behind the scenes. Fitzroy finished fourth in 1896.

But the Maroons were to be a top team in the new VFL.

SOUTH MELBOURNE

SOUTH MELB

A team bearing the name South Melbourne did not come into being until 1874.

The area was known as Emerald Hill and a team sporting that name, and another called Albert Park, were prominent from 1864.

Albert Park won the South Yarra Challenge Cup in 1870 – a four-way series between the top teams in Melbourne. Albert Park would continue by merging with the Southern club (1875) and a team known then as North Melbourne in 1876.

Meanwhile on June 19 1874, 12 football enthusiasts met in the Temperance Hall, Napier St, Emerald Hill to launch a new club that could represent the area. Mindful of the previous bickering over the South Melbourne name they decided at first to name it the Cecil Football club.

The meeting decided to adopt the colours of 'a red and white cap with blue stripe from back to front, blue knickers, blue and white jersey and hose and a scarlet sash over the left shoulder'.

Three weeks later a meeting at Mr Evers' house on July 5 decided that the club would be named the South Melbourne Football Club and that F. Lightfoot would be captain and F. Evers vice-captain.

By 1877 the Albert Park club was in a parlous state and approached South Melbourne seeking an amalgamation. It was rejected by 28 votes to two at the annual meeting, but by January 1880 South agreed to accept Albert Park into the fold.

The club adopted the red and white colours and in its first season the new unit was runner-up

for the Premiership and in 1881 it took out the VFA Flag.

Home games were played at the South Melbourne Cricket Ground from 1878.

From its earliest days South had a strong link with the cricket club and Test cricketers Jim Slight and George Palmer were members of the 1881 football Premiership team.

South took another Flag in 1885 when they went through undefeated. Famous names in that side were 'Sonny' Elms – the 'Prince of captains', Peter Burns, Jim 'Diddley' Young, Harry Purdy, Fred Waugh, Ben Page, Jim Dunn and Archie McMurray, father of the umpire. One of the key players in this era was Peter Burns, a barrel-chested follower from Ballarat who was recognised as one of the best players in the game's early days.

In the 1880s South built a great rivalry with Geelong. It reached its zenith in 1886 when a huge crowd, estimated at between 30,000 and 40,000, crammed into the South Melbourne ground for the Premiership.

Although South lost, they had the nucleus of a team that would become one of the most dominant in the game's early years.

They won a hat-trick of Flags in 1888, 1889 and 1890 with a team structure based on small speedy wingers and flankers. During that period the side lost only six of its 57 games.

During 1890 South Melbourne not only won the VFA Flag but also found time to travel to Queensland, and NSW and, after the end of the local season, to Adelaide to play Port Adelaide for the 'Australian Premiership', which they lost by a kick.

South slipped in the early part of the 1890s, but by 1896 the club was back at the top and fought and lost the battle for the Premiership with Collingwood.

Observers believed that the teams were so close that the Flag should have been shared.

With a young team of local talent South Melbourne was well placed to take a leading part in the new VFL.

COLLINGWOOD

COLLINGWOOD

Collingwood was formed just five years before the start of the VFL, yet it entered the new competition as the premier football team in Victoria.

The 'junior' Britannia Football club is regarded as the father of Collingwood Football Club. That is not entirely true.

Britannia was a strong club and played at Victoria Park, but it also had links with Fitzroy.

Within the suburb of Collingwood there was a growing push for a senior football team to carry the district's name.

A group of citizens met in 1889 to form what they dubbed the Collingwood Football Club and then sought Britannia's assistance in arranging for a joint Collingwood-Britannia deputation to approach the VFA about possible admission.

Some of these early meetings were held in the Grace Darling Hotel on the Collingwood side of Smith Street.

Britannia's interest waned after the VFA rejection, but the Collingwood push continued even though they had a club in name only. They were thwarted by the dissension and squabbling in the VFA, but by early 1891 the VFA amended its rules to allow the admission 'of a prominent junior club'. Collingwood then asked if Britannia would be admitted as a Collingwood team if Victoria Park was upgraded to VFA standard, and was given the all clear. The momentum had started and the local parliamentarian announced that the team would soon win a Premiership and 'the very name of Collingwood would strike terror into the

hearts of opposing players'.

Britannia's colours of blue and white with a scarlet sash resembled Footscray's and for that reason the new Collingwood had to look for different colours.

According to club records a supporter had suggested the black and white colours after being impressed by the black and white magpie on the South Australian coat of arms.

Collingwood's debut in May 1892 attracted 16,000 people and, although they went down by two goals to Carlton's three, the new club showed enough to justify its inclusion in the VFA. By the end of the season they were able to beat Carlton.

Indeed it was a Carlton man that hastened Collingwood's ascent in the football world. Billy Strickland was already a star with Carlton and when he switched to Victoria Park early in 1893 he immediately became a lynchpin of the side. Within two weeks of his arrival Strickland was appointed captain and it was he who led the club to its early glory.

Collingwood's playing record improved in 1894 and the team lifted to eighth position.

Rigid discipline was the governing factor at Collingwood. Captain Strickland reported his star winger 'Buffer' Sime to the committee for swearing in one game and a brilliant youngster Dick Condon was hauled before the committee and made 'to obey the captain on the field without stopping to argue'.

By 1895 Collingwood had risen to fourth on the Premiership list and under Strickland's guidance they were said to have eliminated individualism and perfected teamwork to the highest degree.

The winger Charlie Pannam was rated as one of the best players in the competition and the side was strong all over the field. Even at this early juncture the aura of Victoria Park was gathering steam and the Magpies were said to be 'well-nigh invincible' at home after only losing one match on their home turf in 1895. Collingwood was now on target for the 1896 VFA Premiership.

The first football seasons 1858-1860

Bell's Life, July 31, 1858

We understand that a number of gentlemen interested in keeping the muscles in full vigour during the winter months, and also anxious for an occasional afternoon's outdoor exercise, have determined upon getting up a football club.

Mr Bryant of the Parade Hotel, on the principle that an 'ounce of practice is worth a pound of theory', will have a ball on the Richmond Park today at one o'clock. After the game a committee will be formed to draw up a short code of rules.

Herald, August 7, 1858.

A grand football match will be played this day, between the Scotch College and the Church of England Grammar School, near the Melbourne Cricket Ground. Luncheon at the pavilion. Forty a side. The game to commence at twelve o'clock.

Herald, August 9, 1858.

Richmond Park was unusually lively on Saturday ... the juvenile presbytery and episcopacy came out uncommonly strong ... and most jubilant were the cheers that rang among the gum trees and the she-oaks of the park when the Scotch College obtained a goal. The compliment was shortly reciprocated by the opposition. Evening's anxious shades cut short an amusement which to judge from the balanced scale of results, and the apparently inexhaustible physique of the combatants, must otherwise have been interminable.

Argus, April 18, 1859

Football like cricket has become an institution in and about the metropolis, and it would not be surprising if the epidemic spread wider. There are many well-grassed valleys and plains in the immediate neighbourhood of the various diggings, where the miners, cramped in their limbs with working in constrained positions, and whose lungs might enjoy themselves on Saturday afternoons in straining for goals of easier attainment than that which is the aim of their ordinary occupations. Mechanics, too, and artisans, would find their health much improved by a good game of football once a week ... The buzz in the various metropolitan and suburban hives, which promises to end in swarming to the open spaces about the city during the winter months, shows the necessity for exercise alluded to is fully appreciated ... Before the month is out we may on all favourable occasions expect to see every available portion of Richmond Paddock, and other 'lungs of the city' dotted by animated groups in full pursuit of the leathern sphere.

Herald, June 6, 1859.

The season for football may be said to have fairly set in and the game bids fair to become as great a favourite and outdoor amusement for winter as cricket is for summer. On Saturday afternoon the members of the (Melbourne) Football Club assembled outside the Melbourne cricket ground for the purpose of engaging in a little friendly strife. Sides were chosen by Messrs Bryant and Bruce, and the various combatants having fastened on their colours – blue and red – the game commenced in right earnest. After a good deal of shilly-shallying with the ball from one side to the other, Bruce kicked a goal for the blues (then) Bryant for the reds ... The ball was again put down, and the game fell to the lot of the blues, by a small boy kicking a goal, to the great risk of his own shins.

Herald, June 13, 1859

The game played on Saturday was considered the best of the season. Sides were chosen by Mr Hammersley and Mr Smith, but nothwithstanding all their exertions to urge their men on to the fight, victory did not smile on either party, though the game lasted three or four hours. As a compensation for no goal having been kicked, there was no lack of bruised shins.

Herald, June 20, 1859

We may soon expect a match at this same game between the St Kilda and Melbourne clubs, but the first named club objects to rule No. 7 of the Melbourne club, which provides for 'tripping' but not for 'hacking' whether over the ball or not. The St Kilda men are decidedly more discreet in not allowing this 'tripping' when away from the ball, as it may lead to serious quarrels between the members, and in our opinion is

A game of football in progress in 1877,

quite unneccessary.

Herald, July 4, 1859.

The usual hebdomadal game of football took place on Saturday in the Richmond paddock. Sides were selected by Mr T.W. Wills and Mr Smith. Play was continued for about four hours with the usual result – that of no goal being kicked. The new revised rule as regards 'tripping' was in force and no doubt was thought by many a great improvement. Next Saturday week the match with the South Yarra club is to come off.

Herald, July 11, 1859.

The long talked of match between the Melbourne and South Yarra clubs came off on Staurday afternoon ... 25 gentlemen contended on this occasion ... the first goal was won by the Melbourne men amid loud applause. Wills had caught the

A 'costume football match' between Opera House Players and Other Theatres.

20

...rst season of the Victorian Football Association. The umpire watches the play.

ball and kicked it to his outside man, Wray, who kicked the goal. After playing until a quarter past five, the game was postponed until next Saturday week. There were about 2000 on the ground to witness the match and among them a large contingent of the fair sex.

Herald, July 25, 1859.

The football match between the Melbourne and South Yarra clubs continued ... On Saturday, after a good deal of work on both sides, Mr Wray managed to get a second goal for Melbourne. As it was yet early, the South Yarra submitted that it should take the best out of five, as they did not want to commence the return match that day. This was agreed to, and the contending parties again went into the fray. After some few spills had occurred, and the shades of evening were very nigh drawing in, Mr J.B. Thompson, un-

willing to let South Yarra off with even one chance, kicked the third goal ... The arrangement of the ground on this occasion was a marked improvement on the other Saturday. The ground was well roped off, and a man placed at the gate of the pavilion to keep out those persons who do not subscribe.

Herald, June 4, 1860.

The match between Richmond and Melbourne took place on the ground of the former, Mr Wills and Mr J.B. Thompson the respective captains. It was amusing to the spectators to see the various 'spills' and 'scrimmages', which were numerous and varied. The new rule relative to taking up the ball was productive of some 'talk' and some two or three 'free kicks' were allowed for the infringement of the law. After the game had been carried on for some time a goal was kicked by

one of the Richmond men, but just as the ball was passing through the posts it struck a small boy on the head, and then glanced off touching one of the goal posts in its course ... Neither side kicked a goal.

Herald, July 2, 1860

Football has completely usurped the place of cricket, and as regularly as Saturday comes round are the votaries of this game to be found at their rendezvous in the Richmond Paddock. On Saturday, the Melbourne and the Richmond clubs again met, the ground of the latter being selected ... The ball having put in motion by Mr Wills, the game began in right earnest, neither party gaining much advantage, but at length Mr Wray, kicked the ball into the goal, and the Melburnites hailed his feat with an ecstasy which, alas, was only too soon to be dispelled. for the ball on passing touched Mr

Bruce who was keeping goal before it went through the posts.

Mr Wills the indefatigable captain of the Richmondites, tried a coup de main, and placing his men right down to the goal, by this means successfully landed the ball between the posts.

The hitherto 'unconquered whites' were not to be beaten yet, and the battle was resumed with greater vigour than ever; the 'tussles' became more frequent, the 'spills' less inviting, and the 'scrimmages' thicker and thicker; the whites and the reds everywhere in collision.

The spectators of which there were many did not escape scathless; many of them preferred standing in the middle of the field, and when a rush took place they were knocked over by the eager players, and were to be seen sprawling about in all directions.

Victorian Football Association kicks off

A meeting of the honorary secretaries of the senior Melbourne football clubs, Albert Park, Carlton, East Melbourne, Essendon, Geelong, Hotham, Melbourne and St Kilda, was held at Oliver's Cafe in Collins Street East, near Swanston Street, on Monday May 7, 1877 for the purpose of forming the Victorian Football Association.

Its aims, according to *The Footballer* of 1877 edited by the VFA's first Treasurer, Thomas Power, were: 'the promotion and extension of football throughout the colony; to have entire control over intercolonial contests; to act as court of appeal in all cases of dispute; to undertake, when required, the revision of the playing rules; and watch over generally and protect the best interests of the game.'

Country clubs could also join the VFA – provided they had a delegate residing in Melbourne and paid a guinea in advance.

Albert Park played games against Barwon, Castlemaine and Maryborough in the first season.

Another meeting was held, at Nissen's Cafe, 103 Bourke Street East (near Russell Street), on May 17, 'to arrange fixtures for the season'. The senior clubs played between 12 and 23 games with two or three of them 'at odds' especially early in the season when they were practice games. The odds saw some teams such as Victorian Railways or Excelsior having 25 players.

According to *The Footballer* the first work of the VFA was 'the revision of the playing rules' resulting in 'a few excellent modifications', such as outlawing 'slinging,' that is catching a player by or round the neck and throwing him to the ground, charging and knocking a player down when not near the ball; and stopping all attempts at scrimmages'.

These rules took time to filter through. A Melbourne 20 played and defeated a North Fitzroy 25 on May 26, 1877 by a goal to nil. The *Argus* reported: 'the new football rules came into force on Saturday, but no very remarkable dimunition of the roughness they are designed to check was perceptible ... the naughty hands forbidden to clutch an opponent's neck in order to pull him off his feet went thither not infrequently in the cause of the play.'

Until the establishment of the VFA the matter of who was the best team for the year in Victoria was something that was left to the opinion of barrackers and reporters.

Clubs regarded as 'premiers' were determined by consensus rather than any system.

The organisation of matches was left to individual clubs negotiating with each other and players moved freely between clubs, some lining up for two or three different teams in the same season.

Movement of players was curtailed by agreement between clubs in 1874 that a player could only represent one team per season.

Other arguments, such as one which flared over a disallowed goal in the 1876 Carlton and Melbourne game, degenerated into farce. Melbourne's annual report showed it as a win and Carlton listed the match as drawn.

After a dispute in a Challenge Cup game the umpire was required to make a statutory declaration to settle a point.

The arrangement of intercolonial matches was a matter of special interest to the new association and in fact that was the sole task listed in the formal constitution. Although Carlton visited Sydney and Melbourne and St Kilda both made trips to Adelaide, the idea of a Victoria versus South Australia match fell through.

Changes to the rules by the VFA were of long-term importance in defining the Australian game, particularly preventing the handing of the ball to a team-mate, and calling on the umpire to award a free kick or to throw the ball in the air in the event of a scrimmage.

It was generally felt that the rule changes made the game more attractive in 1877 although there were other issues that troubled observers of the time such as the lack of uniformity in team outfits.

The *Australasian's* writer Peter Pindar said that when watching a big game he was amazed at the mixture of designs worn by the one team 'when a player of what seemed the attacking force got a mark near goal my ideas got a severe shock at seeing him kick in a contrary direction'.

As for the notion of the VFA settling disputes it seems that its very existence prevented arguments having to be arbitrated.

There was still no Premiership Ladder in 1877 and a writer for the *Australasian* commented: 'I presume the premier position for 1877 must fairly be adjudged Carlton.'

Carlton played 21 games, won 14, lost three and drew four. One of the losses was under Rugby rules against Waratah in Sydney – Carlton won the return game against them under Victorian rules six goals to nil. Four games against Melbourne saw two wins, one loss and one draw.

Melbourne might fairly have disputed Carlton's award of the Premiership – having played 23 games, won 16, lost three and drawn four but apparently the two losses to Carlton weighed heavily in contemporary observers' eyes.

A system of awarding Premiership points would not be introduced for more than a decade.

A crucial advance in that first season was the enclosure of two grounds – Melbourne's, adjoining the MCG, and Carlton's temporary home at Madeleine Street – now the extension of Swanston Street beyond Victoria Street past Melbourne University.

This meant that clubs could charge admission and in time would build enough financial reserves to pay players in contravention of the VFA's principles of amateurism.

President of the VFA was W.J. (later Sir William) Clarke; Vice-presidents H.C.A. Harrison and Captain R. Robertson; honorary Secretary H. Hale Budd and honorary Treasurer Thomas P. Power.

The foundation clubs were Albert Park, Ballarat, Barwon, Beechworth, Carlton, Castlemaine, Geelong, Hotham, Inglewood, Melbourne, Rochester and St Kilda.

The cricket and football grounds of 1874. From the top, East Melbourne, St Kilda, South Melbourne and Carlton, No fences to keep spectators out.

Essendon kick for goal in the game against Melbourne on July 2, 1881. Essendon won the match, three goals to two.

The spread of the game

Following formation of the Melbourne Football Club in 1858, new clubs soon emerged in Richmond, St Kilda, South Yarra, and Royal Park. Limited competition led to made up matches, such as 'Australia v the World' and 'North v South'.

Wild games were held against soldiers from the 14th and 40th Regiments, mostly Irishmen stationed in Melbourne. The 'barrackers' had an unfortunate tendency to confuse opposition players with 'the enemy'.

As leading Victorian schools adopted the game, its prospects brightened. Melbourne Grammar and Scotch College had formed clubs by 1860 and within five or six years clubs began at Geelong College, Geelong Grammar School, Ballarat College, St Patrick's College and Wesley College.

The game reached major country townships early, starting at Geelong in 1859 and reaching Ballarat and Bendigo by 1861-2. As communications improved and Victoria's population became more settled, the pace quickened. Clubs emerged at Hamilton in 1867, Kyneton in 1868, and Belfast (Port Fairy) in 1869.

During the 1870s more than 60 senior clubs started in country Victoria. Over 40 junior clubs began in Melbourne alone. By the early 1880s at least eight clubs were playing regularly in Geelong, seven in Ballarat, and over 100 in Melbourne where big games drew crowds of 12,000 or more.

The Victorian Football Association (VFA), formed in May 1877, linked senior clubs under common rules. Despite a commitment to promoting the game in Victoria and elsewhere, the VFA and others failed in two important places: England and New South Wales.

In 1884 H.C.A. Harrison tried to interest English rugby and soccer authorities in an exhibition match of the Australian game. Touring English cricketers had brought back good reports, but the English football bodies were unimpressed, and told Harrison, as he recalled: 'This game of ours is 150 years old. If one has to adopt the other's game, the obligation is surely upon you, the younger people, to adopt our game.'

Around that time Harrison also went to New Zealand, only to be rejected by Rugby authorities who did not want to forsake forever the prospect of playing football with the 'old country'.

More vigorous efforts might have preserved Australian football in New Zealand, where the game was spread in the 1860s by the movements of bankers, gold seekers, soldiers and others who were familiar with football in Victoria.

Soldiers from the 14th Regiment took a version of the game to Perth in 1868, when a match was played against a WA team at the Bishop's Collegiate School. But soccer was then strong in WA and the Australian game grew slowly.

Various clubs emerged in the early 1880s, culminating in the formation of the Western Australian Football Association in 1885. Not until the gold discoveries of the 1890s brought large numbers of Victorians to the West did the local game kick ahead.

Communications with Victoria seem to be only a partial explanation for the spread of Australian football. Both South Australia and Tasmania had strong Victorian links, yet both played mixtures of various codes and local rules for much of the 1860s and 1870s.

In Tasmania's case, Jack Worrall notes the impact of W.H. Cundy's arrival from Victoria in 1879. Cundy found the locals playing rudimentary football on the side of a hill near Battery Point in Hobart. There was a house in the middle of the field.

Cundy brought with him a copy of the Victorian rules and had 50 copies printed for distribution. In 1880 he joined the Fitzroy player, Ted Rojo, and began to teach the game. Four clubs formed that year experimented with rugby, soccer and Victorian rules, voting by a slim margin in favour of the Victorian game at the end of the season.

On 5 July 1881 a southern Tasmanian team beat the senior Victorian club, Hotham. Tasmania adopted formal links with the VFA and its rules in 1882.

South Australia accepted the Victorian rules before Tasmania, in May 1877, when the South Australian Football Association was formed (at the same time as the VFA).

The game in South Australia received several early boosts. In 1877 the Melbourne and St Kilda clubs

THE ARRIVAL WITH S
THE START SO JOLLY COLD
AN INCIDENT NOT IN THE PROGRAMME
AS WE ENTERED THE FIELD
THE GAME WAS STOPPED A LITTLE WHILE BECAUSE

travelled to Adelaide, and the Adelaide 'Victorian' club (comprising Victorians living in SA) journeyed to Melbourne in 1878.

An intercolonial match was held in Melbourne in July 1879 and twelve months later Adelaide's Norwood club enjoyed a widely publicised visit to Victoria.

But in New South Wales, birthplace of H.C.A. Harrison and T.W. Wills, Australian football found barren ground. Both here and in Queensland, rugby union had built an early and well defended tradition. Victorian rules possibly reached

Queensland by the mid 1860s. A notable match was played in 1870 at Queen's Park, Brisbane between Ipswich and Brisbane Grammar Schools, but Brisbane had closer ties to Sydney than Melbourne and rugby maintained its hold.

In 1877 NSW rugby union representatives rejected VFA overtures to play a few games against Victoria under both rugby and Victorian rules. But the Sydney club Waratah came down to play Carlton in June 1877 and soon afterwards the Carlton champion George Coulthard went to Sydney to teach the Victorian game. The story goes that he lost interest in New South Wales after a fishing trip in which a shark pulled him off a boat as it took a bite out of his coat tail, which was dragging in the water.

The *Footballer* in 1881 speculated that the great objection to Australian football in New South Wales was that it was then styled as 'Victorian Rules.'

Who knows, but for that intercolonial rivalry, and perhaps a Port Jackson shark, the progress of Australian football might have been very different. **Damien Cash**

Henry Harrison 'as old as Melbourne'

Harrison often claimed to be as old as Melbourne for, although born in the colony of NSW, his birthday in October 1836 fell in the month Melbourne received official recognition. His full name was Henry Colden Antill Harrison but he was called Colden or Colly. His father was an accident-prone sea captain and his mother, Jane Howe, was the daughter of convict George Howe who became rich by printing, publishing, retailing and speculating in real estate.

Harrison's earliest recollections were of Port Phillip for he came overland with his parents when he was one. His father attempted squatting on the Plenty and the Avon Rivers before returning to Melbourne in 1850 where Harrison went to the forerunner of Melbourne Grammar School.

Father and son briefly joined the Victorian goldrush, again unsuccessfully, and in 1853 Harrison started work at the Customs Department, remaining until 1888 when he transferred to the Titles Office, rising steadily to become the Registrar-General and Registrar of Titles.

Harrison had a cousin, Tom Wills, who was a year older, and with whom he had in common a maternal grandmother, Sarah Harding (Sarah having married twice, first to Edward Wills and then to George Howe). When Tom Wills returned in 1856 from Rugby School in England where he had played school football, he immediately achieved fame playing cricket for Victoria. He and three others formulated the Melbourne Club Football Rules in 1859 to enable young men to play winter sport.

As a cousin of Wills and as a cricketer, Harrison was drawn into this group of young men, and in 1862 he married Tom's sister, Emily. Encouraged towards the end of 1859 to try his luck at footracing, he became the 'pedestrian' or amateur sprint champion of the Colony.

By 1867 when he retired from running, Harrison had built up a formidable reputation, taking on the professionals, and claiming to have run the quarter mile in 50 and a quarter seconds.

At the same time Harrison became involved in football, first playing in scratch sides, then briefly playing for Richmond before captaining the Melbourne Club (except for a year playing for Geelong when transferred to the Geelong Customs).

Harrison's fearlessness and his speed made him a much-respected opponent.

After 1862 considerable latitude was given to the players to run with the ball for 40 or 50 yards without being required to bounce the ball. It was, however, the most common source of conflict, being acknowledged as a Rugby School practice and not in accordance with the Melbourne rules.

In 1865 in a match between the Melbourne Club and the Royal Park Club, the captain of the latter decided to test the rule fully. He told his swiftest player not to bounce the ball and to run as far as possible. This

the player did and kicked a goal. Harrison, who was not averse to using his own speed to run 40 yards or so without kicking or bouncing the ball, was captaining the Melbourne side and questioned his opponent's action.

When it was explained that the matter needed to be settled, it was agreed that the ball should be bounced at least every 10 yards.

The distance was shortened to every five or six yards in the modified rule incorporated into the 'Rules' by a meeting which approved the draft prepared by Harrison, a Melbourne Club delegate. By 1870 such ball-handling was recognised as integral to the game.

In 1872 when he was 36 years old, and after 13 years as a player, Harrison retired from playing but his outstanding football skill, his fame as a runner, and his administrative ability had earned him considerable acclaim.

In 1875 the new sporting paper, the *Footballer*, mistakenly credited him with formulating the first football rules in May 1859 and, although this was corrected by Tom Smith, one of the original rule-framers, this error has been reiterated down the years.

It was perhaps understandable that, in view of Harrison's early as well as long participation in football, the *Footballer* was to claim him in 1876 as 'the father of Victorian Football'.

The year after, when the Victorian Football Association was formed, it was Colden Harrison who was made a Vice-president when William Clarke, the largest landowner in the colony, became the President.

In 1905 when the first Australian Football Conference was held in Melbourne, Harrison was elected Chairman. The Australasian Football Council was established and its inaugural meeting did Harrison the honour of electing him the first Honorary Life Member 'for special services rendered to Australian football' and also designated him 'Father of the Game'.

Harrison was elected to the Committee of the Melbourne Cricket Club in 1871 and in 1892 became Vice-president. The Club was one of his 'life's hobbies' and in 1906 the new stand at the MCG was named after him as was the VFL headquarters in 1930.

Sport was the preoccupation of Harrison's life and he valued most highly the characteristics of endurance, self-control and courage. In his autobiography, *The Story of an Athlete*, written six years before his death at the age of 93 in 1929, he bequeathed 'my fatherly blessing on all true footballers; expressing the hope that they will always do their utmost, not only to excel in the game, but to keep it a clean sport.

I feel sure that my love for it and all that it means in the development of a true and honest manliness, will never die, and that my spirit will preside at many a good, rousing game, even after I am gone'.

Gillian Hibbins

Inventing football's equipment

A football was probably rarer than gold in 1850s Melbourne.

Tradition has it that the pioneers of 1858 could not find any football at first, and there was 'wild excitement' when a rugby ball made by William Gilbert of London was unearthed in a heap at the back of an old clothes store.

The 'leathern sphere' described by writers of the time was usually made from a preserved pig's bladder, stretched and blown before being encased in leather by a shoemaker. The natural shape of bladders influenced the shape of footballs, and those used in the 1850s at least tended to be round rather than oval.

When an oval ball was used in Melbourne in May 1860, the *Argus* newspaper described it as 'objectionable'. The oval ball could be kicked further, but was considered less accurate than a rounder type. Australian football rules did not specify the oval 'rugby no 2' ball until 1877.

Rugby league historian Geoffrey Moorhouse notes that rubber football bladders were invented in 1862. Common use of pneumatic rubber bladders in Australia by the late 1870s is suggested by advertisements for 'Macintosh's best bladders' and 'air inflators'.

Most footballs were imported from England. In the 1860s T.A. Burrage and Marshall's Cricketing Depot sold footballs in Melbourne. H. King and Boyle and Scott were prominent in the 1880s and 1890s. London makers, like J.Davenport, Feltham & Co. and J. Bryan, also advertised in Victorian publications.

In the Melbourne suburb of Carlton, Hatsell King sold locally made footballs from 1879. A few years later Tom Sherrin commenced in Wellington Street, Collingwood and by the turn of the century his 'Match II' footballs were being used throughout Australia.

Footballs were not cheap. In 1881 King sold Gilbert's Match II balls for 17/6 each, a shilling more than the cost of a complete outfit of football clothing. Senior footballers had to buy their own uniforms, boots and knickers in those days, and the results were anything but uniform.

During the 1880s uniforms were readily available in Melbourne from mercers and outfitters such as John Lang and Callaghan & Co., but in the early years coloured caps were often the only distinctive items worn.

When the Melbourne team adopted a magenta uniform in May 1861, some of its players still wore plain white shirts. Contemporary illustrations show footballers in long trousers, often tucked into their socks. Some are in sleeved shirts, some sleeveless, and some have long sleeves rolled up to their elbows.

Woollen knickerbockers, wide belts, and long socks or stockings were popular by the early 1870s. And by the 1880s many players had adopted tight-fitting, short laced vests or 'guernseys', often strapped with leather and designed to be slippery and difficult for opponents to grip. They were also easily torn. Billy Freeman, a champion sprinter known as the 'eel' from his talent for squirming through packs, once went through five guernseys in a match.

Boots were an everyday item of dress in the 19th century and all a footballer needed was a shoemaker to insert some small leather blocks or 'stops' in the sole to prevent slipping. Iron spikes were used in the early years. An 1880 picture of Carlton's George Coulthard shows high boots protecting not just his ankles, but most of his shins as well.

When Coulthard officiated as an umpire in a match between Melbourne and the SA club Norwood, in July 1880, he wore all-white. Before then, the person we now know as 'the man in white' was just as likely to be the man in the striped flannel trousers, dark jacket, necktie and hat.

Goal umpires are mentioned in the 1874 'Victorian Rules', and there was talk of them operating earlier elsewhere, such as at Kapunda in SA. Signalling of scores with white flags came to Victoria in June 1886. The system was used in Tasmania from 1884.

Goal posts were not always white, and they probably weren't even posts in the beginning, just trees. Jack Worrall recalled early goal posts painted in club colours with emblems proudly waving from small flags on top.

Boundary lines on the Richmond Paddock or 'gravel pits' evolved from gum trees in the 1850s to a makeshift, moveable fence of short posts in the mid-1870s. Crowds would often encroach on to fields, sometimes reducing playing widths to 25 metres or less.

Many clubs had dressing rooms by then, but training equipment was simple. The 1880s champion Peter Burns recalled that players didn't even handle a football between matches: 'if we did mid-week training it consisted in a bit of a run or a skip, or a turn on the punch ball.'

Trainers used eucalyptus oil on stiff joints and bruises, and players dipped their hands in resin to improve their grip.

Before a game in 1888 the Carlton players were given 'brown, bilious looking' herbal mixtures to keep their mouths moist. They took their medicine. Football was no longer a run in the paddock.   **Damien Cash**

Flying shot for Goal, *Australasian* 1888

A shot for goal looks like going 'behind' in a game between Carlton and Geelong in 1888.

Football takes to the sky

A mark is called,
some look appalled,
And the straining of many eyes.
What a shout!
from that numerous rout,
As through the goal it flies.
(The Footballer, 1876)

What distinguishes Australian football from the more earth-bound varieties – apart from the democratic spread of players all over the ground as a result of no offside rule – is the mark, especially the high mark, the spectacular grab.

But aerial work was not always a feature of Australian football. It was something that evolved in the experimentation and bravery of a handful of players in the mid-1880s which, in turn, was permitted by rule changes and developments in kicking techniques, the actual footballs, and football grounds themselves.

Football, in particular the Melbourne and Carlton clashes were fashionable, free attractions with crowds of 10,000 in the 1870s.

According to Thomas Powers' annual *The Footballer 1875* the crowd were 'steadily pressing for-ward and narrowed the playing space, rendering the game anything but a free and open one.'

A wire fence was erected for the next game at the ground Melbourne used outside the MCG, in an attempt to keep the crowd off the ground. Right through this period commentataors remark on people getting in the way of shots for goal, and the ineffectual nature of 'crowd control'. Carlton's leasing and development in the grounds of Melbourne University in Madeleine Street in 1876 was the first purpose-built Australian football ground, and admission was charged.

The Footballer 1876 saw Carlton veteran 'Lanty' O'Brien 'not far from the tree so familiar with his fame for flying marks stops the progress of the ball by a splendid catch'.

Carlton's George McGill 'makes a splendid mark within easy kicking distance, but far and wide past the posts the ball is madly propelled'. McGill was one of a number of renowned long kickers – roosting a pneumatic football 60 yards in an 1875 kicking competition.

Developments in marking had not only to do with jumping up – they also were about using the rules.

'Tom Jones in the 1875 *Footballer*, amongst other sage advice on how to play football said "Jumping for marks is dangerous, I pray you avoid it".'

At the first Carlton and Melbourne game in 1876 at the new ground at Madeleine Street 5000 fans paid £115/11/4 after expenses.

They saw the ball kicked forward, where Harry Nudd and Fred Baker, motionless, awaited it. Baker, who stood behind Nudd, pushed him forward and took the ball over his head, upon which a dozen Carlton throats shouted 'How's that, Umpire?' and he replied 'No mark,' intending to follow it up with 'Free kick for Carlton'.

'But Baker did not wait an instant, and had the leather through the posts like lightning, the goal umpire awarding a goal for Melbourne. The Carlton players clamoured around the field umpire to get him to give Carlton a free kick, thereby annulling the goal; but he got a little confused, and very much annoyed at some of the language being used, left the ground in disgust, and the game continued with another umpire.'

A sea-change in marking styles arrived in the 1880s when some players, chief among them Essendon's Charles 'Commotion' Pearson who was Champion of the Colony in 1886, started to jump high in the air on the backs of other players to take marks overhead.

The *Argus* records that in a game between Essendon and Carlton on July 16, 1885 Pearson was awarded a mark after being 'amongst a number of players who jumped to obtain the ball' – an overhead mark in a pack.

Another early high mark was Geelong's Dave Kerley whom Jack Worrall recalls as 'the first man to my knowledge that soared into the air with a flying leap'.

Pearson was nicknamed 'Commotion' by barrackers after his uncle William's 1884 Melbourne Cup runner-up, and third place getter in 1883, Commotion. William Pearson was pastoralist, VRC committeeman and MP.

The *Argus* saw his spectacular marking this way: 'At East Melbourne ground on Saturday Mr Pearson, who was the outstanding player for Essendon, gave spectators many thrilling moments with his phenomenal leaps skyward. Ladies in the pavilion screamed for fear Mr Pearson would cause some serious injury to himself when he caught the ball high above himself but toppled down head first among the bunch.

'While Mr Pearson takes risks with his rocket like leaps into the air, who knows but that this may be a new revolution in high marking. What a thrill the game would become as a spectacle if all players tried out this new idea. Perhaps in years to come we will see players all over the field sailing into the air in this Pearson like fashion.'

Pearson's team-mate Alf Young said that Pearson also had a magnificent 16 stone physique, and great speed. He played in flashes, 'a veritable meteor in the field'.

Pearson was the man who was Australian football's first aerial artist. Long before manned flight, he was a man who flew – for marks.

Garrie Hutchinson

Football in 1896: a high mark; a pack; the captains of South Melbourne and Essendon, Williams and Sykes.

A Great Football Match 1888

June 9, 1888

The *Australasian* on June 23, 1888, reports on the off-field activities at the football in Australia's centenary year, between old rivals, Carlton and Geelong.

The Melbourne Cricket Ground is something of a great octopus, stretching out its arms to gather in the thousands along the tentacles down Flinders Street, through the Fitzroy Gardens and out of its south-east gate, and along Powlett Street.

Inside the ground the Ragamuffin Troupe of acrobats and tumblers entertain the gathering crowd, one taking a collection in a ragged cap. A policeman tries to contain them in order to shepherd them outside the ground, but might as well direct a mob of rabbits.

While the huge crowd assembles, the Carlton and Geelong teams ready themselves for battle.

Inside the Carlton rooms.

An overwhelming odour of euca-lyptus oil, with which several players are generously anointing them-selves. They are patriotic in their choice of unguents, and the room smells like a dense gum forest on one of those dull dewy mornings when the sun has not begun the work of distillation.

The bustling little man who has the honour of being the trainer of the Carlton team is now rubbing down a player with a pair of hard-flesh gloves, and now handing each player a wine glass of a brown her-bal mixture – not an intoxicant he maintains but a 'reviver' designed to keep the mouth moist.

At one end of a bench seat the club shoemaker is fitting to the boots of the players small leather blocks to prevent their slipping — spikes are not permitted.

At the other end of the bench is a heap of glistening yellow dust – the powdered resin into which each player rubs his hands.

There is a great deal of harmony in the uniforms, and the physiques of the players. Several wear small blue skull caps, but the majority play bare headed. Every man has the shoulders of his jacket – for it is no longer the jersey of olden times — strapped with chamois leather.

Once the jerseys might be pulled over the head, and were often torn to ribbons in a match, but the sleeve-less dungaree jacket is now tight-laced, and opposing hands glance over it without finding a hold. It is the battle of ships and guns again. A player puts on a jacket which he claims cannot be held, and rubs upon his hands a preparation war-ranted to hold anything.

The Carlton team are wonderfully alike in build. There is no tall man among them, and but two to whom the descriptions small or slight may apply. They may be correctly descri-bed as little-big men.

The Geelong team.

Geelong methods are not exactly those of Carlton. Each player, for example, after coating his hands with the powdered resin, pours upon it a few drops of liquid from a small vial which smells strongly of ammonia. It makes the resin stick, and apparently has the effect desi-red for the team have the reputation of being holders.

Before going out each player in turn stands erect with the arms ex-tended aloft, at an angle of 45 de-grees between the line of the head and shoulders. Then, standing in front of him, the trainer drums on the player's chest pretty vigorously with his open palm.

Then the trainer stands towel in hand, watching the players go out, very much as you may have seen the horse trainer in the birdcage at Fle-mington send away his Cup horse with a last flick of the towel at an imaginary speck of dust upon its glossy skin.

Coming out.

A cheer taken up all round the ground announces the appearance of the Geelong twenty. Close behind them is the umpire in white cricke-ting flannels and Cambridge-blue cap, the hardest worked man, per-haps, of the whole forty. A still wil-der cheer announces Carlton.

Not many years ago the captain would have moved about, paper in hand, placing his men and instruc-ting them. 'You play back and watch the goal-sneak. You keep just out-side the ruck. You go forward on the right and play to so-and-so.'

Such were the orders given by skippers of old. Now every man knows his place, and experiments in the way of changing are rarely made in a big match unless there is good reason for it. Even the coin is spun in the dressing-rooms. The losing side places the ball in the centre of the ground, the partisans of both sides unite their voices in a swelling roar of excited encouragement, and the game has commenced.

In the crowd.

The fascination of the game can only be realised by moving amongst the crowd.

Here us a youth of 14, perhaps, hanging half over the front of the grandstand. His face is a mirror, in which every change in the game is faithfully reflected.

In the one instant there is gloom – Geelong are forcing it up the ground – then a spasm of joy, Carlton has turned the attack.

All the badges worn are blue and white today. The colours displayed in hat, scarf, or button hole are of three styles. First the sixpenny badge of superfine silk, then the threepenny favor, hardly so good in quality, and last, the penny card-board, generally worn by a boy in the band of his hat. Had it cost a guinea, it could not be the symbol of a keener partisan.

A delicate looking boy, not more than eight years old, is talking foot-ball to a friend. 'I've been a suppor-ter of Melbourne for three years,' he says in a melancholy tone as though venturing the hope that such devo-tion must some day have its reward.

'The South Melbourne push' we learn, are pretty good, and another team are 'nearly all butchers' whe-ther by occupation or inclination is not made clear.

For the time being all the onloo-kers are but boys of large growth.

The highest official of the Carlton club is even more illogical than the rest and all through the play conti-nues to assert things just as firmly in the one instant as he denies them in the next. A Carlton player has the ball now, and the President ap-plauds vociferously. 'Well played Johnnie. The best man in the team,' he continues in a tone that chal-lenges contradiction. Then the player bungles it sadly, and all the praise is taken back again with an indignant 'Pooh! he's not fit for the second twenty.'

Carlton won the game five goals with four behinds to Geelong three goals and five behinds.

The 'fairer sex' formed a large proportion of the football crowds.

There were giants in those days

Dec. 30, 1896. Albert Thurgood, the Essendon champion, is regarded by most observers of the game as the greatest player ever to lace up a jumper in the first 40 years of Australian football.

Essendon hardly lost a game when he was playing in the early 1890s. 'Observer' of the *Argus* (former Essendon player Donald McDonald) wrote of him: 'A champion he was most emphatically, for he could do what no other footballer ever did in Melbourne. I have seen him, when his side wanted three goals and had but five minutes to play, leave his post up forward, go into the ruck, and carry the whole game on his back with such marvellous success that he has made his own opportunities, and practically, by his own unaided acts, gained the goals necessary to win the match.'

But as Jack Worrall, champion Fitzrovian in the years before Thurgood, from 1884 to 1892, says: 'The old stagers amongst us, fine physical specimens every one, and living examples of judicious indulgence in athleticism, like veterans the world over, commiserate on the fact that 'football is not the game it used to be'. And truth to tell it is not. Yet there were giants in the land in those glorious days of of long ago.'

'Markwell' (John Healy) of the *Argus* says of Worrall the player: 'In his best days, he had the art of roving perfected. Indeed it is a moot point whether any player, before or since his time, excelled him as an all-round player.'

While the champions still playing, such as Thurgood, loom large in the mind's eye, there were others, going back to the very beginning of the game in the Richmond Paddock who dominated the game as it was played in their time.

The tragic figure of Tom Wills is one. He was the man who, by playing the game as he was chief among those inventing it, created tactics, dodges and physical feats to guide the rules he helped write.

Henry Harrison, Wills' cousin and speedy pedestrian athlete played from 1860 to 1872. Markwell says: 'He was the mightiest warrior of his day. When he heard a charge, his pace, his weight, his pluck and his power seemed irresistible. I have seen him lead old Melbourne against old Carlton on the old convincing ground outside the MCG times out of number, and seen the fire, the forcefulness and the tact with which he repelled the fiercest onslaughts on his citadel. On these occasions his flashing eye as much as his fine physique overwhelmed his adversaries.'

George Coulthard looms large in the football records of the late 70s and 80s, when he was the best all-round player of Carlton. He could not be misplaced. His clever handling, his pace, his expertness in dodging, his sureness in the air and his masterful kicking proved invaluable to his team.

Coulthard was the brighest star in a Carlton galaxy that also included Jack Baker, who played between 1882 and 1890.

Baker was a graceful breezy player who carried the ball along with a rhythm that moved like music. How smoothly he glided past opponents, and how surely did he pick his man and kick to him. He was a beautifully scientific, fast and manly footballer.

George Robertson played for Carlton at the same time as Coulthard and was captain in 1880 and 1881. He was a player blessed with magnificent development, remarkable activity for a burly man, and limitless staying power. Robertson was a fine judge of a player, but he always had a prejudice against narrow-chested men. He would not have a weed on his side no matter how skilful. There was something of Julius Caesar about Robertson. He wanted fat men about him.

Peter Burns is the best man among many great men to have come from Ballarat. His years of masterful service at South Melbourne from 1885, where he was always head and shoulders above his associates, made him the idol of Emerald Hill.

Burns was a grand mark and was a wonderful long place kick. In one game in 1888 the Carlton crowd brought a coffin to the ground to bury the South Melbourne foe who was to be left dead and dying in the field, but Burns won the game with a remarkable effort.

Archie MacMurray took a mark with seconds to go, about 90 yards out. He carefully placed the ball, and as he walked back to take his kick, Burns sauntered from the centre towards the goal. MacMurray ran to the ball, picked it up, passed to Burns, who calmly kicked it through from 70 yards – and South Melbourne won the game.

Billy Hannaysee came to South about this time from Port Melbourne. He was an expert 'potter' of goals from 30 or 40 yards. It was said that from his doorstep in Clarendon Street he could drop kick a ball straight into the glass top of a lamp across the street. Hannaysee was not a great mark in a crowd, but was dashing and tricky in the extreme. He was the first player to bring into vogue dodging the man on the mark to have a shot at goal.

Other players among dozens include Geelong's Dave Higinbotham, who was, in Worrall's opinion 'the finest centreman that ever graced the game during my connection therewith. He was fast, wiry, indefatigable and an exceptional kick.

Another Geelong great was Hugh McLean, says Worrall, 'a finished artist, bringing a factor into half forward play that had never been exploited. So elusive and clever was he at turning, and such a fine drop kick, that he would bring the ball from the centre and kick a running goal or pick out a man at will. He was one of the most graceful players the game has known'.

(2) **H. ELMS**, 1882-94.
SOUTH MELB. FOOTBALL CLUB.

(11) **W. STRICKLAND**, 1882-89.
CARLTON FOOTBALL CLUB.

(1) **P. BURNS**, 1885-91.
SOUTH MELB. FOOTBALL CLUB.

(3) **J. WORRALL**, 1883-91.
FITZROY FOOTBALL CLUB.

Charity games expose VFA problems

June 6. A paper read last month by VFA secretary T.S. Marshall on the crisis facing football bore first fruit in a series of matches which were played for the Charity Shield at the Melbourne Cricket Ground today.

This set of shortened games between Essendon and Collingwood, Port Melbourne and South Melbourne saw a win in the final to the Same Old over Port Melbourne.

The interest in the football itself was evidenced by the poor crowd of just 8000. It appears that the public is sick of the game's overcrowded and confused play.

However, the two 'experimental' rules introduced were seen to be moderately successful.

Using boundary umpires to throw the ball and allowing players to hit it while the ball is in midair gave the central umpire a better view of the game, and also helped spread the packs that dwell usually at the bounce of the ball.

The experiment of not allowing the notorious 'little mark' might take some time to understand.

The current habit of players barely touching the ball off the boot, almost passing to each other, is a blot on the game, but umpires will need practice in judging five yards before blowing the whistle for a mark.

But anything which lessens over-umpiring and the violent consequences must be welcomed.

VFA football has gone flat with its crowded packs and little marks.

Webb alleges professionalism

June 11. The VFA, struggling to improve the quality of matches and arrest falling attendances, has been dumbfounded by a letter from a former Essendon player, R. Webb, which states that he was paid for his games at the club.

There have been widespread calls for a full investigation into suggestions of professionalism – of 'veiled and underhand' payments in what purports to be an amateur game. Essendon and Melbourne are most under suspicion.

The *Freelance* says that the VFA, in the throes of trouble over 'professionalism', seems to be as 'helpless as a moonstruck codfish on the sea-shore'.

Bill Proudfoot felled by larrikin mob

Proudfoot: pride of Collingwood.

July 25. At Arden Street ground on Saturday a mob of ruffians invaded the field and attacked Collingwood ruckman Bill Proudfoot, after he went to the aid of the umpire.

Proudfoot, a policeman, was almost knocked unconscious by a savage blow to the head. He was later trampled on by the rioting mob.

Knives, a metal rod and other weapons were produced as rowdies set upon the goal umpires.

The match, narrowly won by Collingwood, was a thriller and in a fiery last quarter umpire Roberts elected to keep the game flowing, thus earning the enmity of the North barrackers. Were it not for the efforts of Proudfoot and a few like-minded men, Roberts could have been torn to pieces.

Angry umpires boycott Arden Street ground

Aug. 6. A special meeting of the VFA was convened at Young and Jackson's Hotel tonight to consider the threat by umpires to refuse to officiate at games at North Melbourne in future.

The umpires are angry over the cowardly treatment meted out to umpire Roberts by the mob at the match between North Melbourne and Collingwood a fortnight ago.

Roberts told the meeting that except for the action of the players, including Magpie Bill Proudfoot, he would have come out badly.

Goal umpire Wallace said that a North Melbourne barracker had threatened to put a knife into him.

Another barracker had a bar of iron in brown paper, known to the 'Push' as a 'Ben Bolt'.

The VFA decided to close the ground to football for the remaining four matches, and to insist on better protection of umpires by the club in the future.

The umpires then withdrew their strike threat (→ 15/4/05).

Will it come to this at Arden Street? The perils of the mob caused an umpires boycott, and the ground is closed.

Doctor finds football brings out 'animal'

July 24. Football may reduce man to the primal elements of our tree-climbing ancestors, according to Dr P. Maloney in his recent learned lecture on 'Sport'.

Dr Maloney opined that the cricket ball represented the fruit which the tree climbers tossed to their young. The best catch would have the most food.

'Football, perhaps, is also a survival of a very remote scramble for the larger fruits (which are so dear to the anthropoid ape), such as the durian and jack and bread fruits, which are about the size and shape of a football'.

Dr Maloney talked of the primal elements of a few intense emotions, and a small, savage vocabulary.

'The cheer, the jeer, the howl, the bawl, the yell, the scream, the boo-haa-haa are as unavoidable as the notes in an octave'.

'To demonstrate the savage in our blood we need only to look at the barracker – the most offensive parasite that has ever battened on a manly game.'

A change of style for some players as they conduct a footballers theatrical night. From left are Leon Caron, Howard Vernon and Wallace Brownlow.

Blues in big blue over rules blunder

July 1. The new 'little mark' interpretation introduced by the VFA last week had an unfortunate outcome at the Carlton versus St Kilda match on Saturday.

Under the rules now played the ball must leave the hand before it can be kicked and marked, with no specific distance required.

It must not simply be placed on the boot and passed to the next player over a tiny distance.

Four Carlton players were reported for having misconducted themselves because of the rule.

This mainly involved the use of forcible expressions, but also in putting up hands and expressing a desire to fight the umpire.

The Carlton quartet's defence was that no offences occurred.

But if they did it was because of the umpire's bias, in that he briefed the St Kilda team on his interpretation of the little mark and not Carlton, thereby causing the Navy Blues to be continually 'free kicked.' The players were reprimanded, however, and suspended (→ 15/5/97).

Breakaway meeting forms new football league

Oct. 3. On the eve of the Grand Final match between Collingwood and South Melbourne a decision by a 'select circle' of top clubs to form a new Victorian Football League was taken at a meeting at Buxton's Art Gallery last night.

Six of the strongest and oldest VFA clubs will start a new competition next year, and have decided to invite two other clubs with a long tradition to join them.

The meeting rejected the idea of reforming the VFA into A and B sections, instead deciding on a new competition, with some new rules, and the best clubs competing against each other through the season.

This breakaway has been widely rumoured in recent months.

The six clubs represented at the meeting were Collingwood, South Melbourne, Essendon, Melbourne, Fitzroy and Geelong.

These are the most financially secure of the clubs and best performed teams this season.

Geelong, it was decided, had done so much for the game that recent form should be discounted.

The clubs have unanimously invited St Kilda as another representative club from south of the Yarra, and Carlton if it can reassure the new league that it possesses an appropriate ground.

Each club will play the others twice, the top four playing off for the Premiership in a series at the end of the season.

The meeting did not decide which rules would be altered, but the controversial 'little mark' seems sure to be abolished, replaced with a ten yard rule for a mark, and also scoring six points for a goal and one for a behind, with total points counting towards the score (→ 5/2/97).

T.S. Marshall: stalwart of VFA.

Collingwood win their first and last VFA Flag

The deadlock is broken and Collingwood win the Grand Final as Danny Flaherty goals from a free kick to snatch a one goal victory over South Melbourne.

Bill Strickland: shrewd tactics brought Collingwood Flag.

Oct. 3. Collingwood won the 1896 Premiership – its first ever – by the barest one goal margin, 6 to 5, in an exciting contest against a valiant South Melbourne, watched by 12,000 spectators at the East Melbourne Cricket Ground.

Collingwood captain Bill Strickland used shrewd tactics in telling his players to go slow in the third quarter knowing that their superior fitness would tell in the uncommonly hot conditions.

This proved to be the case as the Collingwood defence held out in a desperate finish against the determined, but visibly tiring, men from South Melbourne.

Few gave Collingwood much chance as the teams lined up for the final stanza, but South Melbourne have only themselves to blame as they wasted their early superiority by poor kicking for goal.

For much of the tense last quarter it seemed that the teams would be compelled to play an extra 20 minutes to decide the outcome, but a free kick to Flaherty, who had been unfairly flung to the ground only 20 yards from goal in the final minutes, broke the deadlock.

The turning point came ten minutes into the last quarter when Strickland reshuffled his pack sending Jack Monohan into the forward line where he marked three times in quick succession.

Although Monohan failed to goal, the Collingwood team had regained the ascendancy.

The experiment of filling the ball with hot air to lighten it failed, as it burst during the game (→ 10/7/02).

1896 Statistics

Final: Coll def S. Melb 6.9 to 5.10
Champion of Colony:
W. Strickland (Coll)
Most goals: N. Waugh (Ess) 29

Ladder:	W	D	L	pts
Coll	14	1	3	58
S. Melb	14	1	3	58
Ess	14	–	4	56
Melb	12	–	6	48
Fitz	12	–	6	48
N. Melb	8	1	9	34
Port Melb	7	3	8	34
W'town	7	3	8	34
St K	6	1	11	26
Foots	5	3	10	26
Geel	4	3	11	22
Carl	2	2	14	12
Rich	3	–	15	12

OLD TIME FOOTBALL

1897

Feb. 5. VFL accepts offer from proprietor of the Port Phillip Club Hotel in Flinders Street, City, to rent clubrooms at 15/- per year.→

May 10. Good crowds at opening round VFL matches, and spectators reported delighted at more open play. Return of drop-kick predicted by 'Observer' in *Argus*.

May 14. League amendment abolishes rule against pushing from behind while player in rapid motion. Reduced umpiring interference reported.

May 22. Quality of play and crowd-pleasing spectacle at Geelong and Melbourne match show the improvement in football. Melbourne win 9.10 (64) to 3.1 (19).

June 12. Reported reluctance of Melbourne Cricket Club to offer pavilion facilities to League delegates results in VFL versus Ballarat match being played at Fitzroy.→

June 19. Flags at half mast at Collingwood and Melbourne game to mark death of old footballer Fred Pleasance. Melbourne win 5.3 (33) to 3.8 (26).

June 22. Carlton's new ground at Princes Park opened on Diamond Jubilee holiday. Monohan and Condon steer Collingwood to victory 6.4 (40) to 5.6 (36).

July 3. Princes Park ground in need of improvement, but inadequate funds available.

July 3. Fitzroy rover Billy McSpeerin weaves and bounces length of the ground to score goal against St Kilda. Fitzroy win 9.21 (75) to 2.6 (18).

Aug. 8. Fitzroy make unsuccessful protest at disputed goal following one point loss to South Melbourne, 4.5 (29) to 3.12 (30).

Aug. 17. League accedes to the demand of Geelong Football Club to play its first final game against Essendon at Corio Oval.

Aug. 21. Collingwood and Melbourne finals match described as best of year. Fred McGinis and Jack Leith best on ground for Melbourne but Collingwood win 7.9 (51) to 7.5 (47).

Sept. 30. Eddy James of Geelong is League's leading goalkicker with 27 goals. Next are Jack Leith (Melb 26) and Norm Waugh (Ess 23).

VFL age dawns to barrackers' delight

The first round of VFL and a big crowd is at the Lake Oval for the Melbourne-South Melbourne match.

May 8. The opening round of matches in the Victorian Football League was played today.

The new regime was greeted with enthusiastic crowds and, with the rule changes, more open football.

The abolition of the 'little mark' has passed without causing any trouble at all – except to South Melbourne whose game in recent years has been built on close foot-to-hand passing of the football. It was noticable today that the game was more open, with longer kicking fostering position play and the marking skills that make the game so interesting.

Longer-kicking Melbourne comfortably beat South, last year's Grand Finalist, 6.8 (44) to 3.9 (27) South will need to adapt to the new ten yard rule or fall behind.

Collingwood had no such problem, easily disposing of St Kilda 5.11 (41) to 2.4 (16)

The main entertainment of the day at Victoria Park involved the stubborn refusal of last year's Flag to unfurl before the game.

A final heave given by a local councillor nearly snapped the flagstaff, but did break the rope and unfurled the final old VFA Flag.

A topic of conversation was the bizarre decision of the VFL to abolish the push-in-the-back rule.

Most onlookers thought this a problem and a danger to players running close to a fence, or waiting under a high ball.

McCracken named VFL President at first official meeting

April 12. At a meeting at the Port Phillip Club Hotel tonight the Essendon delegate, Alexander McCracken, was elected to the Presidency of the recently formed Victorian Football League. Mr E.L. Wilson of Collingwood has been chosen as the first Secretary.

Mr McCracken, head of the McCracken Brewery, is a genial figure who mixes well with people. He is a leading sporting figure in Essendon, having founded the rowing club and lent his patronage in the district to cricket, tennis, golf, bowling, athletics, cycling and lacrosse.

He is a 'sportsman' in the real sense, and enjoys riding to hounds at the Oaklands Hunt Club.

He has been Chairman of the Victoria Racing Club and one of his horses, Knight of the Garter, won the Grand Annual Steeplechase at Flemington in 1893. (→ 10/7/08).

Minutes of Annual General Meeting of Victorian Football League held at Port Phillip Hotel on Monday the 12 April 1897 at 8 p.m.

The Secretary read the notice of meeting

Mr R McLeod was voted to the Chair

Communications were read and received from the various League clubs announcing that the following gentlemen had been elected delegates for the year

Carlton Messrs J. Melville and A H Shaw
Collingwood Messrs W D Beazley, MLA and W Strickland
South Melbourne Messrs J Sloss and H A Godling
Fitzroy Messrs C M Huckey and T Banks
Melbourne Messrs J. McLaughlin and R H McLeod

From the Minute Book recording proceedings at the first official VFL meeting.

Fred McGinis named finest in colony

Sept. 6. 'Observer', football writer for the *Argus*, has named his best players for season 1897, and joined the general feeling that Melbourne rover Fred McGinis was one of the best to pull on a boot.

Joe McShane of Geelong, 'Tracker' Forbes of Essendon and Dick Condon of Collingwood were next.

McGinis came to Melbourne from Tasmania in 1894, intending to play with Essendon.

But with George Vautin starring it was felt that McGinis would have little chance of breaking in – and he was snapped up by Melbourne.

Early in his career it was said of the little Tasmanian 'if the play of McGinis is the island's idea of football, then they can teach us something here on the mainland'.

McGinis beat Essendon on his own in one game in 1895 – which was just Essendon's fourth loss in five seasons.

Hampered by a knee injury last season, he has been back at his scintillating best. 'His splendid drop kicking, pertinacity in redeeming a mistake, determination in getting the ball, and coolness and quickness in passing it on to a team-mate place him in a class above his contemporaries', said Observer.

Ruckman Joe McShane first played at the Pivot in 1885 and was captain in 1895. He is one of six brothers who have all played for Geelong.

Although Joe is feared as a rough and tough player, he is also fair – as was seen in the game against Collingwood on Saturday where he intervened to stop a brawl.

The *Australasian* reported that 'The summary fashion in which he ejected his brother Henry from a crowd into which the latter had dashed with hostile intent clearly indicated that he was determined to exercise in the interest of peace his authority over the younger members of his family'.

Of Essendon's endearing ruckman Charles 'Tracker' Forbes a book could be written – suffice to say that he is universally acknowledged as one of the best footballers in the best team in the competition.

Tracker first played with Essendon in 1885. Hounded by all club secretaries Tracker turned up at a Melbourne and Essendon game at the EMCG with his football togs (he calls it his 'wardrobe') wrapped in brown paper.

The doorman turned him away saying 'Your name is not on the list', but luckily an Essendon man recognised him and took him to their room where a selected player stood down so Tracker could play. The rest is football history.

Dick Condon of Collingwood is the fourth player – a gifted player, the 'football acrobat' of whom it might be said 'the best is yet to come'.

Fred McGinis: a cut above.

Joe McShane: tough but fair.

'Tracker' Forbes: best of the best.

Dick Condon: football acrobat.

Old push-in-the-back rule is back, to the relief of players

May 15. The experiment of abolishing the push-in-the-back rule has been abandoned after just one week.

Although the change sprang from a desire to minimise the role of the field umpire, it has been generally regarded as a failure.

While many agreed with South Melbourne that 'The most conspicuous man on the ground for many a long day has been the field umpire', this change was not right.

Umpires have been re-directed to pay a free to a player pushed in the back on the ground, and when pushed in any direction while in the air.

They have also been directed not to interfere unnecessarily in play, and to overlook merely technical infringements, especially when players are contesting the ball (→6/8/10).

The despised 'little mark', shown here, is now off the agenda for VFL play.

Ballarat humbles pride of the VFL

June 12. There is a saying: 'A champion team will beat a team of champions.' The adage was no better demonstrated than in the drubbing handed out today by the Ballarat team to an all-star team from Melbourne's League clubs.

The Ballarat team has always been hard to beat at home, but its victory in Melbourne is humbling for the League.

Ballarat were quick, they worked together and used the ball wisely. The League men had not trained together, and there were six last minute replacements in the selected side. The final score of 13.11 (89) to 8.6 (54) is an indicator that the local men were all at sea (→27/6/63).

Pivot pressure brings Corio final

Aug. 21. Geelong's desire for a finals game to be played at 'home', as the agreement forming the League implied, was eventually granted after they threatened not to play.

However, Geelong still lost to Essendon – 3. 11 (29) to 5.5 (35).

As a prominent Melbourne cricketer said last week: 'It was very unfair to Geelong to alter the conditions at a time when they must necessarily be the losers by it.'

A large crowd attended the game, many seated in carriages around the perimeter of the ground, and in country style took a drive around the oval at half time (→ 30/9/99).

1897 Statistics

Leading Goalkicker:
Eddy James (Geel) 27
Champion of Colony:
Fred McGinis (Melb)

Finals Ladder:	W	L	%	pts
Ess	3	0	177.6	12
Geel	2	1	105.8	8
Coll	1	2	76.3	4
Melb	0	3	82.9	0

Ladder:	W	L	D	%	pts
Geel	11	3		184.3	44
Ess	11	3		159.0	44
Melb	10	4		144.8	40
Coll	9	5		113.9	36
S. Melb	8	5	1	138.1	34
Fitz	4	9	1	104.7	18
Carl	2	12		51.2	8
St K	0	14		29.1	0

A flannelled fool joins muddied oafs

June 26. To the applause of his teammates, Essendon ruckman August Kearney made a surprise appearance against Geelong today.

Kearney, a former Victorian tennis champion, was scheduled for a tennis match at Albert Park when heavy rain intervened and cancelled the game. Kearney arrived at the ground minutes before the match was due to start.

Despite Kearney's presence and his strong play, Essendon were no match for the competition leaders Geelong, who won convincingly, 8.9 (57) to 5.2 (32).

A new Flag for 'Same Old' Essendon

An Essendon mark in the goal square on the way to a Premiership win in the low-scoring match against Melbourne.

Sept. 4. Essendon today won its third match in the round-robin finals series to take the Premiership Flag, but it was a peculiar game in which it scored only 1.8 (14) to Melbourne's eight points.

Had Melbourne won there would have been a play-off next week between Essendon and Geelong, but the hapless Fuchsias hit the post three times.

Essendon, too, had its share of luck in the match at the South Melbourne Cricket Ground. In the third quarter 'Tracker' Forbes had what seemed to be an easy shot for goal – so easy that all the players had returned to the centre for the ball up. All, that is, but Don Edgar Croft, who lingered in the forward pocket and was unattended as he marked Forbes' shocking miskick and scored the goal.

Geelong, who finished at the top of the ladder after the home-and-away series, went down to Essendon in the first final week, and the showed in the other two matches that they were unlucky losers. The Pivots kicked themselves out of contention, however, scoring 3.11 (29) to Essendon's 5.5 (35).

Despite the brilliance of Fred McGinis, Melbourne lost all three finals matches, while Collingwood had only one win (→ 18/3/98).

Fitzroy's Thomas Banks, a VFA champion who is still playing.

Finals system cops blast from critics

Sept. 11. Essendon are worthy Premiers, and the new finals system, in which the four leading clubs play off the Premiership all starting on level terms, worked well. However, the system has problems and the potential for injustice remains if a lowly club succeeds at the end.

For example, if Collingwood had won their three finals and Essendon had only won two, Collingwood would have been Premiers with a season's record of 12 matches won and 5 lost. Essendon would have been second with a better record of 13 wins and 4 losses (→ 14/5/98).

Waugh loses heart: South loses Waugh

July 10. An affair of the heart was the reason Fred Waugh failed to turn up and take his place in the South Melbourne team today.

Waugh, 25, had attempted suicide after being spurned by the object of his desires. He had been disconsolate for some days and his family were concerned that he might harm himself in some way.

This morning his mother found him in his room covered in blood. He had cut his throat with a blunt knife. Luckily, he had missed blood vessels and the windpipe and a doctor was able to repair the wound.

1898

March 18. League Chairman A.H. Shaw presents Premiership caps for season 1897 to Essendon Football Club at EMCG.→

May 21. Internal club troubles keep Mick Grace and Sam McMichael out of Fitzroy side, and they are beaten by Essendon, 10.10 (70) to 2.5 (17).

May 24. Eddy James kicks seven goals and Firth McCallum goals after eluding 12 opponents as Geelong beat St Kilda, 11.19 (85) to 2.5 (17).

July 22. Dawson's Whisky company advises VFL Secretary it wishes to present trophy to £50 value, at the disposal of the League.

July 23. A weakened Essendon side kicks seven goals straight in first half against St Kilda and wins, 10.11 (71) to 1.9 (15).

Aug. 12. League field umpires banned from playing in football matches after umpire Hood played in Footscray v. North Melbourne VFA match on August 6.

Aug. 20. Collingwood second to Fitzroy on Minor Premiership ladder, after count of points for and against.

Aug. 27. Fitzroy's Jim Grace gives away important free kick in Premiership round match against South Melbourne by arguing with man on mark. Michael Grace, with head in bandages, saves match for Fitzroy, 6.11 (47) to 5.3 (33).→

Sept. 10. Despite having announced his last game enigmatic Dick Condon turns out and beats Fred McGinis as Collingwood win Premiership round 7.13 (55) to 6.5 (41).

Sept. 17. Collingwood, wearing all-black socks, go to their own funeral as Fitzroy win the Semi-final 2.10 (22) to 1.5 (11).

Sept. 30. Geelong's Teddy Rankin has missed season because of typhoid fever.

Sept. 30. Soldiers on Boer War service in South Africa are playing Australian Rules behind the lines.

Debuts
Vic Cumberland (Melb)
Matthew Fell (Coll)
Fred Fontaine (Fitz)
William 'Newhaven' Jackson (Ess)

Retirement
August Kearney (Ess)
George Vautin (Ess)

Collingwood receive unnecessary incentive

Collingwood heading for victory over Geelong in the first match of the season.

July 30. You could ride a bike between the Collingwood and Fitzroy football grounds in five minutes, but the neighbouring suburbs might be different countries, as far as their football supporters are concerned.

The second round of the annual battle has just been completed at the home of the Magpies, Victoria Park, where the roar of the Collingwood faithful can be frightening.

Even more disconcerting to Fitzroy was the news this week that the Collingwood Council had promised its players £10 each if they won.

Fitzroy came with the memory that they had a two goal win at the teams' first meeting this season, and began the match confidently. But Collingwood, superbly led by Bill Proudfoot, and with Dick Condon, Charlie Pannam and Fred Leach at their best, started to get most of the ball in the second half.

Despite everything Collingwood nearly lost it, as they racked up a lot of points, the winning score being 4.11 (35) to 3.5 (23).

Dons show new system of football

Aug. 1. After a dozen games Essendon have shown us precisely why they are favourites for this year's Premiership Flag.

Their machine-like efficiency against Melbourne on Saturday showed just how the game has changed since the disappearance of the little mark.

The final score, 11.9 (75) to 2.8 (20), was a measure of Essendon's superiority in thinking and playing – what might be called teamwork, rather than individual play.

Instead of the crushes of old, or the kick-it-forward-any-old-how school of thinking, Essendon played their usual hand-to-hand game, almost always to a man in position.

Melbourne players were often nowhere near their own man, to the point that Essendon frequently seemed to have extra men on the field.

The *Argus* said 'Time after time the ball was played just where it should have been, and there was always a comrade to help an Essendonian in distress.

'The rapid exchanges from man to man were very pretty, and quick as lightning.'

Once the ball went from Hugh Gavin at fullback, with six passes in the twinkling of an eye, finishing with Tod Collins for one of his rare shots at goal.

Planning to play as a team, and precise hand passing and kicking are welcome signs (→1/8/05).

VFL forces prodigious prodigal out until the next season

July 1. Essendon champion Albert Thurgood has been refused permission by the VFL to play for the Same Old this week.

Thurgood must stand out of football for 12 weeks to fulfill the League's residency rule.

Essendon supporters are of the view that if Thurgood wanted to play for any other team he would have had the residency rule waived.

'I have come back to play with the Same Old Essendon. If I am not allowed to play with then I will play nowhere else,' Thurgood said.

Thurgood has always been a loyal clubman since he joined Essendon in 1891. In that year he was selected to play in a St Kilda team, but he refused to turn out for them.

He is widely regarded as the most prodigiously talented player of his generation, and was crucial to Essendon's string of Premierships in the VFA in the early 1890s.

A renowned long kick, and goalkicker, Thurgood's skills will surely not have deserted him.

He has kicked over a hundred yards on a number of occasions, and in one game in 1893 he kicked 12 of 14 Essendon goals.

He went to the gold fields of Kalgoorlie in 1896, and his return to Essendon can only be a bonus.

If he cannot play this year it must only mean Essendon will be stronger in years to come (→22/7/99).

Albert Thurgood: on the outer.

Profs seek tenure in Football League

July 18. Perhaps the roars from Princes Park that filter into the University's corridors on Saturday afternoons have aroused the academics. They are seeking to have a League team.

Dr Martin (physiology) and Professor Lyell are leading the move, and they have 700 students from which to draw a team. They have also been promised the playing support of students Colin Campbell and August Kearney (Essendon), Joseph Hogan (St Kilda) and Edward Greeves (Geelong) (→ 9/5/08).

VFL tries another Premiership system

May 14. The League has introduced a new Premiership system to foster greater interest in the competition.

The eight teams will now play two matches against each other, for the Minor Premiership

After this round, the clubs will be divided into two groups of four with every club in each group playing the other three. The top clubs in each group then play off for the Major Premiership, with the Minor Premiers having the right to challenge if they don't win through.

To ensure that the Minor Premier takes the finals seriously, that club will have to gain at least eight second round points to have the right to challenge (→ 30/4/02).

1898 statistics

Leading Goalkicker:
Archie Smith (Coll) 31
Champion of Colony:
Dick Condon (Coll)
Minor Premiers: Essendon 11 wins, 3 losses, from Collingwood 10/4, Fitzroy 10/4, Geelong 9/5.
Finals: Section A Fitzroy 3 wins 0 losses, from Essendon 2/1.
Section B Collingwood 3/0 from Geelong 2/1.
Thus, **Semi-final** Fitzroy 2.10 (22) d. Collingwood 1.5 (11) giving Fitzroy right to challenge Essendon as Minor Premiers in **Grand Final** Fitzroy 5.8 (38) Essendon 3.5 (23).

Fitzroy open VFL Flag account

Jim Grace of Fitzroy emulates his brother Mick and marks brilliantly to set up another forward move.

Sept. 24. Fitzroy began the second season of VFL football with a humiliating defeat at the hands of Essendon, but fought their way up the ladder to finish third to the Same Old and Collingwood after the minor round, and have now won the Premiership. They beat Essendon 5.8 (38) to 3.5 (23).

The Maroons have become famous for 'steamrolling' last quarters to overwhelm the opposition.

Fitzroy had to beat Essendon, South Melbourne and Carlton to win the A section round robin – then beat the winner of B section, for the right to challenge Essendon, the Minor Premiership winners.

Fitzroy did just that and then faced up to Collingwood in the semifinal match.

Before the game lots were drawn for the venue. Fitzroy won the toss, and then the game, which was played at Brunswick Street, with a score of 2.10 (22) to 1.5 (11).

Collingwood played in black rather than black and white hooped socks for first time at the suggestion of former Fitzroy star Jack Worrall.

A large crowd of 15,000 were at the St Kilda Ground for the Grand Final against Essendon.

Players 'skated a good deal' on some parts of the ground – for want of something to 'stop' them, but Fitzroy created the better scoring chances in the first three quarters.

Essendon tried to spread the game as a tactic against Fitzroy's tough bustling tactics.

Fitzroy champion Mick Grace brought off the mark of the match, flying high over the pack to find the ball sticking to his fingers. He capped it off with a long distance goal.

In a relentlessly defensive last quarter Fitzroy did not score a goal, but equally Essendon were unable to bridge the 16 point gap (→ 16/9/99).

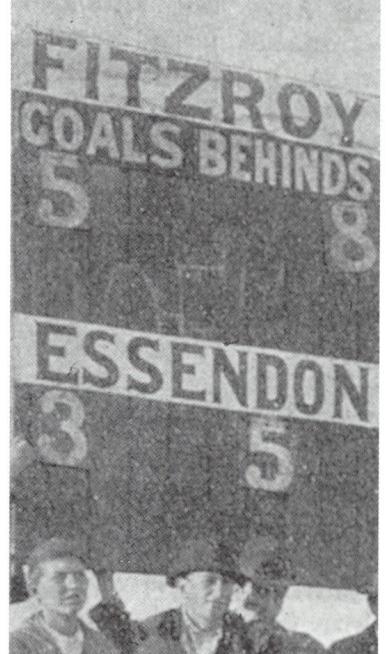

The scoreboard tells the story.

Grace brothers moving force for Maroons in painful win

Sept. 24. The heroic efforts of the brothers Grace in Fitzroy's win over South Melbourne in the first round of this year's Finals, was a reminder of the great service they have given the Maroons over the years.

Jim and his younger brother Mick were instrumental in winning Fitzroy's first ever Premiership in the VFA in 1895, and they remained the driving forces of the team this year.

Jim was leading goalkicker in the colony in 1890 and 1891 but has increasingly been used as a follower in recent seasons.

After sorting out some 'matters of mutual concern' early in the season

Jim came back to form, enthusiastically charging through packs.

Mick is the sticky-fingered follower and forward whose long kicks are the despair of the opposition.

Mick should not have played in the South Melbourne game, as he was suffering a terribly painful tooth abcess. But he appeared, his head swathed in bandages, and was probably best man on the ground, kicking two goals himself to seal the game, 6.11 (47) to 5.3 (33).

The Grace brothers are proof of the influence of former Fitzroy captain Jack Worrall on the style of today's Fitzroy teams (22/9/06).

Jim Grace: back in top form.

April 14. Dawson's Whisky trophy presented to Essendon for being runner-up last year.

May 24. Collingwood win morning match with St Kilda on Queen's Birthday, 13.9 (87) to 2.6 (18).

June 3. 'Extraordinary fog' blankets Fitzroy and Melbourne match, and 12,000 crowd sees only patches of play. Melbourne win 4.11 (35) to 3.6 (24).

June 10. Albert Thurgood makes his long-awaited return to the Essendon team.

June 17. Teams lectured on rough play and the evils of betting, in wake of Mayor of Melbourne's comments to visiting rugby team.

July 29. Carlton's hopes, centring on new captain William Stuckey, are dashed when Collingwood defeat them 5.13 (43) to 4.3 (27).

Aug. 5. Fitzroy captain Alex Sloan's offer of a fresh football at half time (the old one greasy), is declined by Magpie skipper Dick Condon. Collingwood win 5.7 (37) to 3.7 (25).

Aug. 12. Fitzroy win Minor Premiership by beating Carlton, 5.9 (39) to 2.4 (16). Umpire sets pattern by giving first seven kicks of game as free kicks.

Sept. 8. Concern expressed that, under the new finals system, places could be affected by percentage via the extent of St Kilda's losing scores.

Sept. 8. Calls for VFL Second Division including VFA teams.

Sept. 9. South Melbourne defeat Essendon, 3.10 (28) to 2.1 (13), to ensure top place in Section B and the right to play Fitzroy (Minor Premiers and winners of Section A) in the Grand Final. Essendon captain George Stuckey toasts the winners with a glass of wine.

Sept. 16. Promising giant cricketer Warwick Armstrong plays in ruck in South Melbourne's Grand Final loss.

Debuts
T 'Tammy' Beauchamp (Fitz)
Fred 'Pompey' Elliott (Melb)
William Griffith (Ess)
Harold Lampe (S. Melb)
Ted Lockwood (Geel)
Robert Rush (Coll.)

Retirements
Edgar Croft (Ess)
Jim Grace (Fitz)
George Moysey (Melb)
George 'Sugar' Sparrow (St K)

Grovelling Mayor lectures Aussies on violence of football

June 13. The Mayor of Melbourne, Cr McEacharn, has chosen a reception for a visiting English rugby team as an occasion to pour scorn on Australian Rules football.

'It is something really appalling,' he remarked, with the fine use of language which must have impressed his genteel visitors, 'to attend a football match here. It is disgusting to come home in a tram or train with those who have been attending the game – men who don't know anything about the game, and have attended it simply for the brutality they see in it.

'They attend there either to hoot or create trouble. If you want to keep football clean you must do away with the betting that exists.'

The mayor's remarks, seen as a prime example of forelock tugging before the noble English, met with many cries of dissent from the audience at the reception.

At a VFL lunch for the visitors later William Beazley MLA protested at the mayor's remarks. He said most footballers played a 'straightforward, manly game'and that betting was most uncommon.

Football with savoir faire, as the Mayor of Melbourne might like it, rather than the 'disgusting' and 'appalling' aspects he mentioned in his speech.

Some ladies like to go to the football, and football is starting to have its influence on winter fashion. The horizontal striped jumper is combined with pantaloons, stockings and boots. Jaunty caps complete the charming ensembles.

Message for umpire fails to find target

July 15. Umpire Ivo Crapp was in charge of today's match at Fitzroy, in which the Maroons lost 8.10 (58) to 3.5 (23) to Geelong.

Observers noted that umpire Crapp was strict but fair, and his performance would hardly have rated a mention but for a curious incident involving a telegram boy.

The lad ran onto the field, bearing a telegram. He dodged among the players, clearly seeking someone in particular – but who?

After a while the boy left the field, apparently with his quest unsatisfied, and appeared in the press box.

The telegram was for Mr J.J. Trait, the famous umpire, and the boy apparently believed that if Mr Trait was at the ground he must have been the whistle-man.

Unhappily for the telegraph boy Mr Trait was elsewhere. It is unknown what was so important that it needed to be said to an umpire on a Saturday afternoon.

Thurgood returns and kicks ball-burster

June 22. Albert Thurgood demonstrated that he was well and truly back in town today at the East Melbourne Cricket Ground during an Essendon training run.

Using a place-kick he sent the ball 107 yards, two feet. The distance was measured by astounded Essendon officials, and representatives of *The Age*, the *Argus*, the *Herald* and the *Australasian*.

No one has ever been known to kick a football as far as this before.

Thurgood might only have played a single game for the Same Old this season, but with kicking like that he shows that he will be a powerful weapon for the club in the future.

During his return game against Melbourne two Saturdays ago he was punting better than he was placing, but still managed a goal and a behind. Even with the great Albert, practice makes perfect (→ 23/5/00).

McShane kicks bag in thrashing of Saints

Sept. 9. Geelong, spurred by its hope of a place in the Finals, crushed a pathetic St Kilda side in the B Section final round today. The score of 23.24 (162) to one point was a League record score and the highest winning margin recorded. Full-forward Jim McShane also scored a record in kicking 11 goals – the most by a player in a match.

Geelong had to beat the Saints by more than either Essendon or South Melbourne to make the Final, and additionally it had to rely on Essendon to beat South Melbourne.

The Pivotonians fulfilled their mission, but the initial joy at Geelong was dampened with the news that Essendon had failed and that South Melbourne would be playing Fitzroy in the Grand Final.

Geelong was as gallant and skilled as St Kilda was fumbling and lacklustre. 'Old Boy' of the *Argus* says the League will have to look hard at St Kilda's tenure in the League. The Saints have not won since 1896.

Among its many dismal losses this season St Kilda went down to Geelong by 119 points to two in the final home-and-away round.

The Saints ran onto the muddy

Jim McShane: record goalkicker.

Geelong ground determined to do better, and seemed to be succeeding for a time, but a nine goal burst by Geelong, including six to McShane, took the heart out of them.

It was a McShane day, as Jim's brother Joe was judged the best man on the ground.

SA wet ball wiles fail to stop Burns' Vics

July 1. Geelong veteran Peter Burns captained Victoria against South Australia at the MCG.

Conditions were atrocious after continual morning rain, but a hardy band of 8500 barrackers saw Victoria win an interesting game 8.10 (58) to 3.6 (24).

As the League had guaranteed a substantial amount to the South Australians for expenses in coming to Victoria, the gate of £163 was welcome.

Barrackers for particular League teams found it hard to recognise their heroes as the Victorians wore the unfamilar plumage of the Melbourne Football Club.

The Victorians all wore long sleeves, and the South Australians short sleeves, which proved an inappropriate choice in the conditions.

Victoria teamed together better, while the South Australians, including the 1899 Stawell Gift winner N.Clarke, had little chance to show their individual pace and skill.

One innovation the Croweaters

Peter Burns: winning skipper.

tried was a home town interpretation of the bouncing-the-ball rule. On a wet day in Adelaide they tap or throw it to themselves as they run along instead of touching the ball to the ground. Not in Melbourne.

Corio champions cheer country crowds

Front row view at Corio Oval.

Sept. 30. Country Victoria, particularly the Western District, seems to have taken the Geelong team for its own. The big towns of Ballarat and Bendigo have a lot of football enthusiasts and their own strong league, but see Geelong as representing their interests against the city teams. The people at places like Horsham and Hamilton, Stawell and Ararat feel the same way.

When the football trains leave Melbourne to bring the visiting teams from the city and their armies of supporters, they are also coming in from the north and west and the colours of blue and white are seen to be adorning those who alight.

Buggies, drays and buses also start to move in from the country towards the Corio Oval, and there is no shortage of local citizens to swell the ranks around the ground.

This season the Pivotonians have carried their supporters hopes brilliantly, only to fall at the last hurdle. They were second on the Minor Premiership ladder, but were just beaten by South Melbourne for a place in the Grand Final, despite their record-breaking 161 point win over the hapless St Kilda.

The favourite of the Geelong crowds is Peter Burns, who started his career with Ballarat Imperials and played with South Melbourne in the VFA before joining Geelong. His ruck work is well read by the nippy rover Teddy Rankin.

Ted Greeves and Arch Thompson have done well across the centre all year while the three McShanes have been a backbone of the club. Henry has left to go to Carlton, but Joe has worked superbly in the ruck all year and Jim has been brilliant up forward, particularly on the day he created a League record of 11 goals against St Kilda.

But the most consistent forward has been Eddy James, who has topped the VFL goalkicking list again with 32 goals (→ 17/9/00).

Teddy Rankin: great rover.

How Fitzroy train for success

Sept. 30. Premiers two years in a row: The Fitzroy Football Club must be doing something right.

Is it their training methods?

Since the improvement in economic conditions in recent years, most footballers are now employed and have arranged to practise together twice a week, on Tuesdays and Thursdays.

A visit by the magazine the *Australasian* to a Fitzroy training session showed some of the techniques they use to get fit.

'Perfect condition is an absolute necessity for the football player. To attain this means very hard work and strict attention to diet and abstemiousness.

'The means used are skipping (which stops cramp in the leg), ball punching, clubs and field practice with the ball.

'The shower bath and rubdown are also necessities, followed by a good oiling, generally with eucalyptus. Oranges only are allowed as thirst quenchers.'

Dumbbells to build muscle and skipping to get that extra yard of pace.

A whack at the medicine ball.

A trainer checks an injury.

South marooned in Grand Final rain

The Maroons win their second VFL Flag.

Sept. 16. Justice has been done in Fitzroy's nerve-wracking one point Grand Final win over South Melbourne – 3.9 (27) to 3.8 (26). Fitzroy has been best all year and headed the home-and-away ladder.

South worked its way up from sixth, having been beaten at least once by all sides except St Kilda.

The fact that the teams were playing at all for the flag is the fault of the odd finals system, which gives all eight sides a second chance, through the round robin sectional finals. South made a late revival to have their chance today, and were in touch with glory until the end.

The game was played in wind and rain at the St Kilda Cricket Ground, and South made it clear that they would prefer a postponement. But Fitzroy was determined to play.

They may have regretted their bravado as South had the wind in the first quarter and their rushes at Fitzroy's goal brought two goals from Harold Lampe.

South's tactics against the wind bottled Fitzroy up, as they kept sending the ball out of bounds on the St Kilda Road wing. But Fitzroy found its feet and had goals from Mick Grace and Fred Fontaine.

South edged ahead in the third quarter and appeared to have the game despite Pat Hickey's herculean efforts in defence for Fitzroy. Then Billy McSpeerin nipped in for a goal to Fitzroy 15 minutes into the last quarter.

Lion king Hickey crowns season

Sept. 18. How the wheel of fortune turns in football. Only ten days ago Fitzroy's Pat Hickey's tough play in defence caused an umbrella attack from one of Collingwood's most vocal supporters, the mother of Collingwood player Jack Monohan.

He weathered the storm calmly as he headed for the changing rooms, but then had to dodge about 150 larrikins, who were waiting to settle with him outside the ground.

Since then he has enhanced his hero status at Fitzroy. He was best afield in Fitzroy's winning Grand Final, and has been named player of the year by 'Old Boy' of the *Argus*.

1899 Statistics

Leading Goalkicker:
Eddy James (Geelong) 31.
Champion of Colony:
Mick Grace (Fitzroy).
Finals. A: Fitz (3); Coll (2); Carl (1); Melb (0). **B:** S. Melb (3); Geel (2); Ess (1); St K (0). **Final:** Fitz 3.9 (27) S. Melb 3.8 (26)
Minor Premiership

	W	L	%	pts
Fitz	11	3	153.3	44
Geel	10	4	177.2	40
Coll	10	4	135.3	40
Ess	9	5	140.2	36
Melb	8	6	136.7	32
S. Melb	5	9	105.2	20
Carl	3	11	53.1	12
St K	0	14	28.0	0

May 11. The VFL outlaws payment to players and forbids players to wear felt hats and also caps of colours 'other than the registered colours of the club' (→ 2/5/03).

May 19. League matches postponed due to adverse weather. Games to be played after Round 14.

May 23. Albert Thurgood of Essendon is reported to have kicked a place kick 102 yards, 2 feet at the East Melbourne Cricket Ground. Essendon 13.7 (85) beat Collingwood 2.4 (16) (→ 27/7/01).

June 2. Carlton finally defeat Collingwood at Princes Park with a score of 4.1 (25) to 0.9 (9) Jubilation ensues.

July 10. Geelong player Jim D'Helin retires and is appointed to the central umpires list.

July 14. Fitzroy players are jostled by the crowd as they leave the South Melbourne ground after beating South 5.9 (39) to 4.9 (33).

Aug. 11. Best 10 minutes passage of play for years, says 'Old Boy' of *Argus* in magnificent match as Geelong beat Fitzroy 8.9 (57) to 1.6 (12).

Aug. 18. Fitzroy are Minor Premiers at end of home-and-away, ahead of Geelong, Essendon and Collingwood.

Aug. 26. 1000 points kicked against St Kilda after home-and-away series and first sectional round.

Aug. 25. Harry Lampe kicks entire South Melbourne score in first section final, as Essendon win 9.5 (50) to 3.1 (19).

Sept. 1. Cycling star and footballer W.C. 'Newhaven' Jackson returns to Essendon side after missing most of year through cycling accident.

Sept. 1. *Argus* sees Essendon v. Fitzroy second section final as 'match of year'. Essendon win 6.3 (39) to 5.6 (36).

Debuts
Lou Barker (Fitz)
Gerald Brosnan (Fitz)
Fred Hiskins (Ess)
Ernest 'Bung' Newling (Geel)
Charlie Roland (Carl)

Retirements
Warwick Armstrong (S. Melb)
Joe Grace (Fitz)
Jim D'Helin (Geel)
Eddy James (Geel)

Mafeking relieved with football gala

The crowds gather to celebrate a great day for the British Empire.

May 24. The eruption of patriotic sentiment following the relief of Mafeking a week ago brought a special flavour to the matches played yesterday – a holiday to honour General Baden-Powell and his gallant men in South Africa – and today, the Queen's Birthday.

The muddy football fields of Melbourne may seem a far cry from the dusty Transvaal, but the joy flowing across the Empire has no doubt been expressed in odder ways than in playing and watching football.

Following the recent postponement of a round due to bad weather, the Government's proclamation of Mafeking Day was made to order, and the holiday spirit brought huge and happy crowds to the matches between Essendon and Collingwood (yesterday); Fitzroy and South Melbourne, Carlton and St Kilda and Geelong and Melbourne (today). Many were carrying flags and red, white and blue streamers.

Fitzroy came out wearing red, white and blue sashes and rosettes, but took them off before play. The Collingwood team played with Union Jacks sewn on the back of their sweaters.

At each match there was a loyal demonstration – three cheers and God Save the Queen.

Essendon, Fitzroy and Geelong won handsomely, while Carlton had to struggle to defeat St Kilda.

VFL soothe Saints over sore point

May 11. St Kilda won their first game in over three years last night, when the VFL changed the result of last Saturday's match against Melbourne. The final score is now St Kilda 10.8 (68) to 9.13 (67).

This game ended as a draw – but St Kilda disputed a behind allowed at the end of the third quarter.

Arthur Sowden of Melbourne passed the ball to team-mate Dick Wardill, but the bell rang as the ball was in flight, and before Wardill took the mark and kicked a behind.

As both teams agreed to these facts, the VFL was able to make the unusual decision to alter the result of a game – to the jubilation of the struggling Saints (→ 15/6/07).

Secretary strips for depleted Essendon

July 21. The absence of nine injured Essendon regulars, including Thurgood, for the game against Collingwood saw anxious officials button-holing everyone they could in order to field a complete team.

Secretary of the club William Crebbin was forced to play his first game for the Same Old since 1896.

Hugh Johns, an Essendon barracker through 'thick and thin', realised every boy's dream by being called upon to play – and kicking two goals. Essendon's makeshift team performed creditably, losing 4.5 (29) to 6.14 (50).

Geelong and South at odds over the ladies' privileges

Sept. 17. The most trivial of disputes, arising over access of Geelong lady members to free entrance at South Melbourne, has dragged on for months now and threatened Geelong's membership of the VFL.

First South refused the ladies, and then Geelong refused all South members as a pay-back. The League demanded Geelong pay South £6/1/- in compensation. Geelong refused to pay and copped a £20 fine, which they also ignored.

Now the Geelong President J. MacMullen has resigned and the affair has been settled with the old practices maintained (→ 31/7/05).

The civilising side of football: ladies in the grandstand at Geelong.

Dick Condon gets life

Dick Condon (rear) seems about to protest to the umpire in a match at Fitzroy.

Sept. 17. Collingwood's most brilliant player Dick Condon has been rubbed out for life by the VFL Investigative Committee.

The man who invented the stab pass, and who has all the football skills built in to his wiry frame, can spend the rest of his days thinking about the joy and glory of his lost future in the game.

The Collingwood club has made no attempt to rescue him from the football wilderness.

Although he has been a great player – perhaps the greatest – since he began in 1897; although he is a local boy who might say that his love of the club has led to his actions; although he has often demonstrated the attributes of a leader – Collingwood has turned away from him. Club discipline has outweighed any sympathy for a fallen hero.

Condon, made captain half way through the season, has not endeared himself to the club with his turbulent behaviour this year. He is not able to stand failure, and when the tide has turned against the Magpies his temper has got out of control.

The 'victims' are usually umpires, and he begins to give them a tongue-lashing every time a decision goes against his club. So unruly was his behaviour in the July 7 match that he received a three-week suspension from the League and was also censured by his own club.

On that day Condon just kept swearing at the umpire until he had no option but to suspend him.

Two weeks later Condon's tem-per turned inwards on his own team at three-quarter time and he came to blows with his team-mate, ruckman Arthur Robson.

On September 1, in the second round of the sectional finals, Condon became so incensed with the umpiring in the last quarter of a match against Geelong that he stormed off the field, and beckoned his bewildered players to follow him.

He demanded that the committee order Collingwood off the field, but committee members ordered him to go out and defend the one point lead they were holding. The incident did not help the team's composure and it did not score again, while Geelong added two goals. In hindsight, Condon's action probably cost Collingwood a place in the finals.

The last straw came in the third final match against Melbourne, umpired by an experienced man in H. 'Ivo' Crapp. Condon would not leave Crapp alone all day. He sealed his fate when he was free-kicked for tripping a Melbourne player in the second quarter and said to Crapp: 'Your girl's a bloody whore.'

We may be left only memories of this man who made a speciality of twisting in mid-air as he took a mark, hitting the ground running towards goal. He could pick the ball up with each hand with equal sureness, and kick accurately, short or long, with both feet. He was fast, had tremendous balance, and was the best man in the game at getting out of trouble – except with his mouth (→ 10/5/02).

Fuchsias filch Flag in farcical Finals

Sept. 22. Melbourne certainly deserved to beat Fitzroy today, in yet another heart-stopping Grand Final. But the fact that Melbourne was in the match at all casts the finals system in a bad light.

Melbourne won only ten games for the whole season, including four finals. It lifted itself from sixth on the ladder to head Collingwood and Geelong off for the right to meet Essendon in the Semi-final play-off. It then went on to beat Essendon by two points and Fitzroy by four points today, 4.10 (34) to 3.12 (30).

The celebrations in the Fuchsias' dressing room reached a peak when the Fitzroy captain Alex Sloan visited and said that, next to Fitzroy, he would sooner see Melbourne Premiers than any other club.

The game, before 16,000 people, was a hard fought and close affair to half time, but Melbourne had a brilliant third term, scoring 2.3 to nothing. Ruckman Richard Wardill gave an armchair passage to rover Fred McGinis.

Melbourne tried to bottle the game up in the final quarter. Fitzroy stormed forward with Mick Grace and Pat Hickey leading the charge but they kicked badly and their 1.5 to Melbourne's two points saw them plunge to a shock defeat.

Their carriages, decorated in maroon and blue and emblazoned 'Fitzroy – Premiers 1900', drove forlornly from the East Melbourne Cricket Ground (→ 21/8/06).

The Melbourne team who worked their way to the Flag from sixth position.

Dick Wardill of Melbourne and Alex Sloan of Fitzroy toss for ends before the start of the Grand Final.

1900 Statistics

Leading Goalkicker:
Albert Thurgood (Ess) 25
Champion of Season:
Fred Leach (Coll)
Finals:
Semi-final Ess 5.13 (43) Melb 7.3 (45) **Grand Final** Fitz 3.12 (30) Melb 4.10 (34)

Ladder:	W	L	%	pts
Fitz	11	3	168.0	44
Geel	9	5	150.9	36
Ess	8	6	137.3	32
Coll	8	6	116.1	32
S.Melb	8	6	90.4	32
Melb	6	8	101.7	24
Carl	5	9	70.6	20
St K	1	13	39.1	4

Collingwood feather new nest for lady Magpies

Victoria Park, Collingwood.

The new grandstand at the Collingwood ground will provide some comfort and privacy for the club's 600 lady members.

May 11. The Collingwood Football Club today acknowledged the large proportion of women among its supporters and members by opening a new grandstand especially for them at Victoria Park.

About a third of Collingwood's approximately 2000 members are women, and it has long been apparent that they might require separate accomodation on match days.

While the new Ladies Pavilion is of a somewhat makeshift appea-

rance and cost just £80 to build, it at least keeps out the rain.

Some observers have suggested that it also protects some of the more delicate members from the umbrellas and worse of the women.

The original 1892 grandstand nearby was designed and erected free of charge on the foundation of the Collingwood Football Club, by architect William Pitt, a patron.

'Billy' Pitt was a Collingwood City councillor between 1888 and

1894, and mayor 1890-91. He is now MLC for North Yarra, and the noted architect of the Princess Theatre, Gordon House in Little Bourke Street, Queens Bridge, the Melbourne Stock Exchange, and the Brunswick Town Hall, as well as Markillies Hotel in Flinders Street.

Billy Pitt is hard at work as architect and politician as he recovers from the Depression, and losses on some speculative projects in the Kimberleys (→9/6/09).

Has great forward kicked last goal?

May 16. Last season's leading goalkicker, Eddy James, may have scored his last goal after seriously injuring his knee.

The tall and talented forward topped the goalkicking last year for the second time with 31 goals. In 1897 he top scored with 27 goals.

At only 26 years of age, James will be a great loss to the game. He was a fine sportsman who, despite his height and power, refused to resort to violence on the field, although he was frequently the victim of unfair and rough-house tactics by some of his opponents.

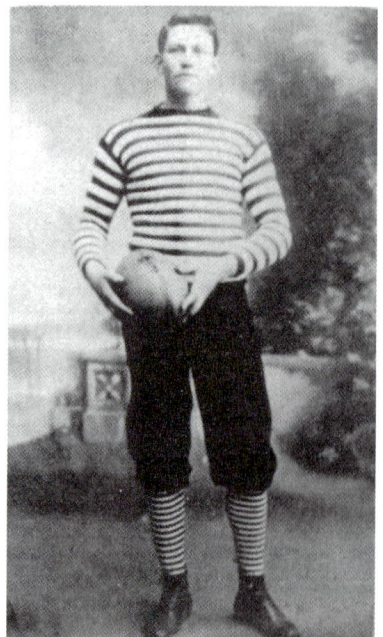

Eddy James: a great loss.

A TUSSLE ON THE WING

A tussle on the wing in the round eight match between Fitzroy and Collingwood this year. Fitzroy won to reverse their loss to the Magpies in Round One.

1901

Official blunders have been a mixed blessing for Magpies

July 20. Collingwood has been caught up in some great blunders by umpires in recent matches. The first on July 6 cost them the game against Melbourne, and the second, today, brought a win over Fitzroy.

Melbourne won the earlier match by a point, 5.6 (36) to 4.11 (35), but there were two obvious mistakes by the goal umpires. In the first quarter a shot from Melbourne rover Frank Langley clearly went through for a behind, but was signalled a goal.

In the second quarter Collingwood captain Bill Proudfoot punched a Melbourne shot away, right on the goal line. Under the rules and as a clear matter of logic the goal umpire had either to award no score or a goal, but he signalled a point, to the outrage of the Collingwood crowd, this time justified.

In today's match Fitzroy were in attack and five points behind when the bell went five minutes early. The players stopped momentarily, loo-

Bill Proudfoot of Collingwood (second from left) goes for a mark.

ked at the clock on the stand and resumed, to be met by a further furious ringing of the bells.

It transpired that the chronometer of Fitzroy's Mr Del Zarte had broken down, and he agreed to accept the time of his fellow official, Mr Manning of Collingwood.

A furious crowd of Fitzroy supporters, brandishing their timepieces, surrounded the time-keepers and made many choice suggestions to them, but the score stands, 3.6 (24) to 2.7 (19).

Return of Fred McGinis: 'the most brilliant player of all'

July 27. Melbourne's champion rover Fred McGinis returned to the field today after recovering from a severe ankle injury, and immediately stamped an impression on his team's fortunes by starring in the win over Fitzroy.

Melbourne won a low-scoring game 4.5 (29) to 2.11 (23).

This ensures the Fuchsias a top four place in the first of the sectional matches, where they will meet the rampaging Collingwood.

McGinis was injured by a kick to the ankle that laid bare the bone in the game against Collingwood a fortnight ago – a game which Melbourne won by a single point.

This incident had a sporting aftermath when Collingwood's Robert Rush, who had launched the kick, went to the Melbourne rooms after the game and apologised for unwittingly maiming his opponent.

'That's all right, old chap,' said Fred 'I know it was an accident.'

As Robert Rush was leaving the Fuchsias' dressing room, McGinis remarked that he was 'one of the fairest men playing football'.

The return of McGinis to the side makes a repeat of last year's Premiership win for Melbourne more of a possibility (→ 6/6/03).

Fred McGinis, superb athlete and fine sportsman, gives Melbourne a chance.

Thurgood's year, and Same Old Flag

Boroondara boy is Federation Champ

Fred Leach: mercurial genius.

Albert Thurgood is standing left of the Essendon team as they rest during 'lemon time' in the Grand Final at South.

Sept. 9. Fred Leach the Collingwood centreman was today named Champion of the Season by 'Old Boy' in the *Argus* – despite taking three games off in the middle of the season for a holiday in Brisbane.

But that is the measure of Leach's mercurial genius.

As one opposition barracker remarked last year, 'If we had Fred Leach we'd lick creation. He's the wonder of the age'.

Leach has played the centre position in a new way.

Traditional centremen have stayed 'placed' in or around the centre, but Leach goes with the ball, one observer noted, and is really a roving place man. 'That sort of thing is only possible with a very good or very cute player.'

Leach, he said, is 'the perfection of artistic cleverness'.

Of a winning match against Fitzroy this year, the *Australasian* said: 'Fred Leach played the finest individual football of the match and his pace to the ball, his good marking and his uncommon capacity for getting through with the ball gave Fitzroy no end of trouble.'

Leach was recruited four years ago from the quality non VFA or VFL club Boroondara (now playing as Hawthorn) in 1897 after an outstanding display in a warm-up game against Fitzroy. He is six feet tall and 13 stone and can run a hundred yards in even time.

These elusive and athletic skills have made him the best player in Victoria this year, and perhaps the best Collingwood player thus far.

Sept. 7. Essendon would not have won its second VFL pennant without Albert Thurgood. He has kicked 19 of Essendon's 45 goals in the last five games of the season, including three in the Grand Final against Collingwood.

When he didn't play during the season, Essendon lost four of its five games – briefly landing in the cellar.

The other Essendon loss in the season was to their Grand Final opponents, Collingwood, when Thurgood was held goal-less.

His opponent then was 'Lardie' Tulloch, who also played well in the Grand Final, but was unable to stop Thurgood from contributing strongly to Essendon's 6.7 (37) to Collingwood's 2.4 (16).

Since his return to Victorian football from Fremantle last year, Thurgood has worked to lead a return to the dominating form that the Same Old had in the early nineties.

His long kicking, his high marking, his speedy running and body work were all in evidence again.

Perhaps he will have the opportunity to win a game with one of his prodigious place kicks - such as the one of two years ago measured at 107 yards 2 feet 1 inch.

The old Brighton Grammarian joined Essendon in 1892, and is a genuine six feet tall, playing at a touch over 12 stone.

Thurgood was Champion of the Colony in 1893 and 1894, and top goalkicker 1892-94 (→ 7/6/02).

Charles Pannam marks for Magpies.

Alex Sloan puts oar in for Fitzroy victory

Aug. 24. Fitzroy secured a place in the finals by beating Melbourne 4.13 (37) to 3.6 (24) in the last of the Section B round robin games.

A Melbourne win would have seen them into the 'final four,' but Fitzroy, who were without goalkicker Gerry Brosnan, overturned the result of last year's Grand Final.

The Maroons did have former captain Alex Sloan proving to be almost impassable at half back.

Sloan's renowned athleticism – he is the stroke of the Victorian eight – belied his veteran status, and he seemed to be everywhere on the back line to keep Melbourne out.

He is a tremendous runner on the football field, and when he is not in possession he is moving to block an opponent or create an opportunity for a team-mate.

Fitzroy supporters will remember this love of sport and fitness, for in 1898 he 'caught the cycling craze' and missed a game because he was pedalling to Adelaide.

The game was played in sporting spirit – before the match Fitzroy Secretary and old player Con Hickey had invited both teams back to the Maroon rooms, saying 'Win or lose, will you come in afterwards?'

Melbourne did, and all players toasted each other, and even the umpire, with glasses of whisky.

Rover Fred McGinis was Melbourne's best player.

1901 Statistics

Leading Goalkicker:
Fred Hiskins (Ess) 34
Champion of Colony:
Albert Thurgood (Ess)
Finals: First Semi-final Ess 6.10 (46) Fitz 6.9 (45) **Second Semi-final** Geel 3.6 (24) Coll 6.9 (45) **Grand Final** Ess 6.7 (43) Coll 2.4 (16)

Ladder:	W	L	D	%	pts
Geel	14	3		142.9	56
Ess	12	5		186.4	48
Coll	12	5		158.4	48
Fitz	9	7	1	131.7	38
Melb	9	7	1	117.4	38
S. Melb	8	9		99.6	32
Carl	2	15		47.0	8
St K	1	16		32.1	4

May 10. Carlton have a second round shocker, being beaten by South Melbourne 8.13 (61) to 0.8 (8).

May 10. Dick Condon returns to Collingwood. Ted Rowell plays brilliant game for Collingwood in win over Melbourne, 8.10 (51) to 4.10 (44) (→1/8/60).

May 30. League called upon to ensure games start on time, and that half time be kept at 10 minutes rather than extending more than 20.

June 7. 'Well dressed larrikins' at Princes Park kick umpire in Carlton thrashing by Fitzroy, 9.14 (68) to 4.6 (30).

June 7. Albert Thurgood Essendon's best player as they thrash Collingwood in rare Victoria Park win, 11.10 (76) to 6.15 (51).→

June 14. Former Geelong player Joe McShane brilliant in Carlton win against old club, 7.5 (47) to 6.7 (43).

June 14. Collingwood kick 4.26 (50) to 1.8 (14) in a shocking display against South Melbourne.

July 12. Geelong VFA and VFL veteran Peter Burns retires after 20 years in the game.

July 19. Collingwood kick hard and burst two footballs in 19 goal thrashing of St Kilda, 19.13 (127) to 1.4 (10).

July 26. Governor Sir John Madden saw his first game of Australian football today at the EMCG as Collingwood defeat Essendon, 7.5 (47) to 5.6 (36).

Aug. 16. 'Day of disasters' as Melbourne beat Carlton 7.5 (47) to 1.7 (13) to end Blues' run at Flag.

Sept. 30. Fred Hiskins leaves Essendon for Western Australia. Doubts have been raised over his 'loyalty'.

Debuts
George Angus (Coll)
Vince Coutie (Melb)
Bill Eason (Geel)
Harvey Kelly (S. Melb)
Jim 'Bull' Martin (Carl)
Bert 'Boxer' Milne (Fitz)
George Topping (Carl)

Retirements
Peter Burns (Geel)
Charles 'Tracker' Forbes (Ess)
Archie Smith (Coll)
George Stuckey (Ess)

Grand old men recall grand old days at city smoke night

April 25. The grand football smoke night has been a great success, with songs, recitations and stories variously described as classy, humorous and enjoyable.

Chief among the battery of speakers was Henry Harrison, Vice President of the VFL.

Vice President of the VFA T.S. Marshall said Harrison was a great sprinter, 'the grandest athlete Victoria ever had'. He also declared 'That's the man who made football in Victoria,' and recalled the great games that Harrison had played on the Richmond paddock more than 40 years ago.

Marshall said that in one game in 1862 Harrison had captained Native Born Victorians, and Marshall had captained the Rest of the World.

In those days, and later, a game was decided by the first team to get two of three goals.

Harrison recalled games decided in ten minutes, and others which lasted three weeks, and yet others played in kilts – over which he drew a dark shade.

Harrison said he was of the view that manly sports go a long way towards strengthening a nation.

The grand scene at the smoke night in the Masonic Hall, Collins Street.

'It is the duty of men in high places, such as the Members of Parliament, to help and foster the game in every way, because it is the national game. It is the national games of old England which have made England the country she is.

'I think the day will come when Members of Parliament will find it in their interest, and in the interest of their country, to show a little more interest in the national sports.'

However, Harrison concluded, if any government ever dared to bring in a tax on the sports of the people, then that government would be out within 24 hours.

The assembled football crowd toasted Henry Harrison as the great man he is.

Cricket champion coach at Carlton

July 19. Carlton's win over Essendon today marks the progress the team has made under new secretary and coach John 'Jack' Worrall.

Worrall has instilled a new discipline and cohesion into Carlton's play, and the Old Dark Navy Blues look like soon rising from the bottom of the ladder.

He is the first coach to personally take charge of training, donning football togs and instructing the players on the field.

He is a strict disciplinarian. 'Boys! Booze and football don't mix. Players who prefer beer to eucalyptus will be struck off the list.'

Worrall played for Fitzroy as a skilful nuggety rover from 1884 to 1892, and was named Champion of the Colony in 1887 and 1890.

Jack Worrall is also a fine cricketer, representing Australia in 11 Test matches and Victoria 65 times, and hit 417 not out for Carlton in 1896, an Australian record (→7/5/04).

Collingwood's forward Archie Smith is recognised with a club certificate.

Collingwood discover short game in snowy Tasmania

July 5. Collingwood have returned from Tasmania with a new and possibly lethal weapon – the short game. They tried it out on Geelong today with devastating effect.

The Magpies arrived back from Tasmania in a sorry state, as Bass Strait seems to have taken revenge for their humiliation of the weaker Tasmanian teams.

As they tried to recover from the misery of seasickness they delayed the departure of their train from the city to Corio, where they were to step into the fray against opponents worthy of their well-tried skills.

Eighteen pale men in black and white ran on to the ground, but they started as if they wanted to get a lead early before they all collapsed again, and soon had the game in their command. The short and snappy foot passing, quick handball and playing to position seemed to bamboozle the Pivotonians as much as it had the Tasmanians.

Edward Lockwood and brother George, both former Geelong men, Dick Condon, 'Lardie' Tulloch and Jack Monohan all took pleasure in displaying their skills, but Charlie Pannam was the best and made one bouncing run that thrilled followers of both sides. Collingwood won the

The Collingwood team photographed in the snow at Mt Wellington, Hobart.

match easily, 12.12 (84) to 6.8 (44).

The basis of the short game is teamwork and passing skills, and the Collingwood men were able to work on it in Tasmania, where the opposition could only stand and watch in frustration, humbled before the big home crowds.

The Magpies were, however, well entertained by the Tasmanians, and had the novel experience of training in the snow at the top of Mount Wellington. They left Melbourne with three straight wins behind them and now look the favourite for the Premiership (→ 20/9/02).

Thurgood is outed; but Goodthur plays

Goodthur: A familiar face?

June 16. The Essendon Football Club have protested that their champion, Albert Thurgood has been wrongfully suspended for striking St Kilda's Alf Trevillian in the match which Essendon won 10.4 (64) to 6.4 (40).

According to the club, the central umpire, Mr Franks, says that he did not see an incident, and heard no complaint until after the game.

Thurgood has signed an affidavit declaring his innocence. Meanwhile a dark haired, elderly recruit named Goodthur lined up for Essendon on Saturday (→ 16/6/06).

T.W. Sherrin and the Football. The manufacture of standard Australian footballs, especially by the Collingwood firm of T.W. Sherrin, around the turn of the century, has had a profound effect on the kicking styles of players. Sherrin was a keen football man and studied the requirements for the Australian game. His footballs were blunter at the ends than the rugby balls imported from England. The drop kick and the stab pass required absolute timing in contact between boot and ball, just as the ball lands on the turf, and the blunt end made the ball 'sit up' for a fraction of a second.

A rugby ball could not be sent on the low skimming and spinning trajectory achieved with the stab pass. And despite the reservations of some critics the new balls did not diminish the glorious feats of prodigious punters and placers such as Albert Thurgood and Dave McNamara. Heavy boots sent heavy balls vast distances and this long kicking thrilled the crowds at early games. Albert Thurgood's wind-assisted place kick of 107 yards two feet one inch took place at the slightly downhill East Melbourne Cricket Ground. It was roosted at practice on June 22, 1899.

Ted Rowell 'tank' talk

What shadowy forces are shackling the footballers' natural ability?

June 28. Collingwood's centreman Ted Rowell was virtually accused of 'tanking' in his club's losing match against Fitzroy on May 24. Today he reacted to weeks of innuendo and bad feeling around the club, and some stigmatising in the press, by offering his resignation as a player.

This was refused, and Rowell was no doubt given some assurances about the club's feelings towards him, as he went out and played a 'blinder' against Carlton and saw his team win 8.11 (59) to 3.3 (21).

There is no doubt about Rowell's brilliance. In only his second year since he came across from the Kalgoorlie goldfields he has stamped himself as one of the most exciting players in the Leage. He is amazingly fast, an accurate kick and has fine judgement in both marking and ball handling.

As Fitzroy 7.13 (55) beat Collingwood 3.4 (22) the *Argus* writer 'Old Boy' pulled no punches in his report and fuelled the fire already burning among spectators.

He described Rowell's form as 'too bad to be true' and went on: 'Collingwood are to be sympathised with. Just when they want Rowell most he fails them most.'

Old Boy said that in other matches: 'Rowell did his work so well that Collingwood to a man – and a woman, too – swore by him. On Saturday he failed just as he did in the final game last year and Collingwood to a man (and woman?) swore at him.'

Rowell's on-field response to this criticism has been to play superbly in games against St Kilda and Essendon, but his efforts have only served to increase the whispers that he must have been playing 'dead' against Fitzroy. His confrontation with club officials may now settle the matter (→ 5/5/06).

Tracker Forbes hits the wallaby track

Sept. 29. The Same Old Essendon will never be the same now that its redoubtable ruckman Charles 'Tracker' Forbes has retired after 52 games in the VFL.

Forbes has been known as Tracker since he was a boy growing up in West Melbourne, where he still lives, and every Forbes ever since has been called Tracker as well.

It's well known that Tracker came to Essendon by accident, when as a young star for the North Park team in 1889 he was courted by every Secretary and turned up to play for Melbourne but was not recognised and turned away.

The Fuchsias' mistake was the Dons' opportunity.

Tracker was a star from the beginning – in the VFA Premierships of 1891-1894 and the VFL Flag winning team of 1897. He was Champion of the Colony in 1891.

One of the strongest, fairest players ever to pull on the red and black, Tracker used to say to young players wanting to play dirty 'Turn it up lad, it's bad for the eyesight'.

Off the field Tracker has something of a reputation as a comedian, and at his regular station outside Miller's feather shop on the corner of Bourke and Swanston Streets most evenings he would regale a crowd of admirers with his comments and quips.

Tracker said of one recruit 'No good, he's got a chest like a chicken's forehead'. He would say of himself that his eyes were 'lamps', his arms his 'wings', his football kit his 'wardrobe' and his dress suit his 'singing coat'.

R.W.E. Wilmot says of these gatherings that 'In that circle the politics of football were freely discussed. Tracker had no time for the slacker or pointer, and he detested a man who was disloyal to his country or his club'.

Tracker will be missed by friend and foe (he had none) on the field, but not, yet, off it.

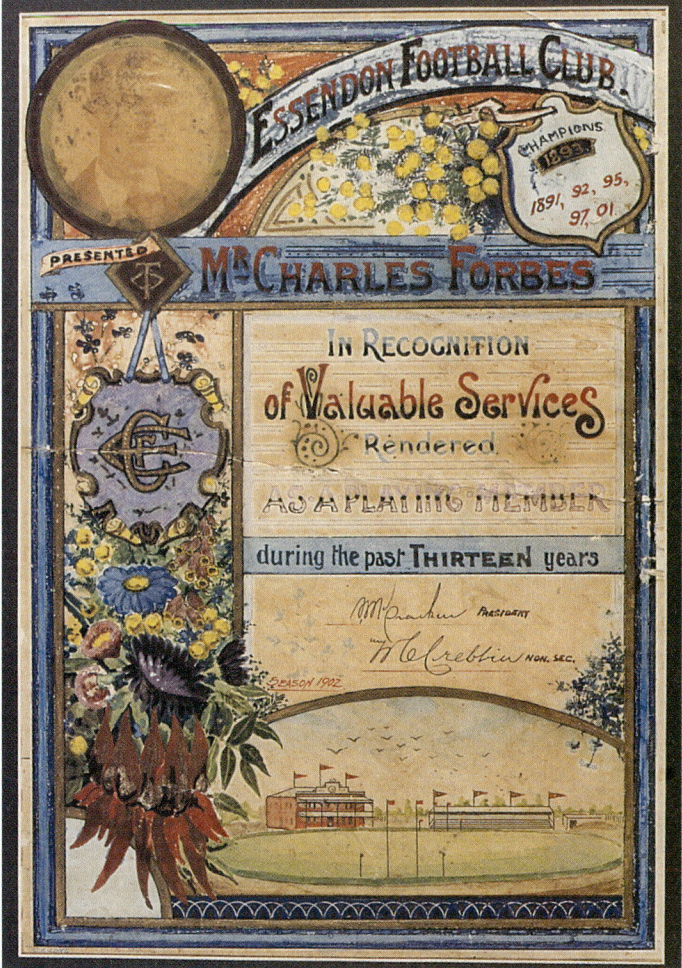

A tribute to the great Tracker Forbes: off the field comedian and raconteur.

Collingwood clinch first VFL Flag

Charlie Pannam ton and temper up

Sept. 6. Charles Pannam this year became the first VFL player to play 100 games and racked up 104 in Collingwood's loss to Fitzroy in the Semi-final, 6.12 (48) to 9.10 (64).

As Collingwood have only played 106 games since 1897, this is a great feat of endurance.

During all this time Pannam's wandering wing play has been a revelation to others, as he has been fit and skilful enough to be found in the forward line and kick goals.

His foot-passing is accuracy itself. Perhaps he is a trifle fortunate in not having to wait until next year for his century of games – as he was party to a most unsavoury incident, also against Fitzroy, in July.

Pannam was unable to control his temper and responded to what was admittedly great provocation from a particular barracker, and jumped the fence to punch him.

The man assaulted was urged by fellow Fitzrovians to charge Pannam with assault, but cool heads prevailed and further barracking of Pannam sufficed as revenge.

While observers regard Pannam as a very fine player it was also noted that 'Pannam exasperates every man who plays against him with his sly and spiteful tricks, yet watches the umpire so carefully that he never gets into trouble'.

Charlie Pannam: feat of endurance.

Bob Rush and Charles Pannam seem to have the ball in their keeping during the Magpies winning Premiership effort.

Sept. 20. Before a record crowd of 35,000 at the Melbourne Cricket Ground, Collingwood overran Essendon after half-time to win their first Victorian Football League Premiership. Final scores were Collingwood 9.6 (60) to Essendon 3.9 (27).

Collingwood, with first use of the wind, went straight into attack. With Charles Pannam and Frank 'Charger' Hailwood in full flight, the Magpies had Essendon defending grimly. With players crowding the centre, scoring was difficult and ten minutes passed before the first score – a point by Fred Leach of Collingwood – was registered. Ted Rowell kicked the first Collingwood goal on the run after an Essendon miskick.

Essendon finally scored when Fred Hiskins shot truly from a place kick. The quarter ended with Essendon leading by a point.

The second half was all Collingwood, scoring 6.4 to Essendon's paltry 1.2. Collingwood played with such system and verve that Essendon were unable to take advantage of the wind in the final quarter.

In an even side, Pannam stood out for Collingwood, along with Hailwood, Jimmy Allan and Bill Proudfoot, while centre-halfback Hugh Gavin was a gallant skipper for the losing side. Albert Thurgood had a quiet day (→ 12/9/03).

The Collingwood member's card.

VFL tries new Argus finals system

April 30. The VFL is trying, again, to discover a Finals system that is fair to the team which finishes on top of the home-and-away matches, as well as giving the other finalists a reasonable chance.

Last year's alteration which gave the four finalists, after the completion of the A and B section games, an equal chance to play off in the Grand Final was unsatisfactory.

It failed to give Geelong, the team which finished first after both the minor round and the Semi-final round, the right to challenge for the Premiership.

The Pivotonians lost one Semi-final and were out, despite having won most matches for the year.

This system improved on the pre-

vious one, which gave Melbourne the 1900 Flag, despite having a lamentable home-and-away record.

There will now be a section A and B Round, in which all teams, four in each section, will play a series of three 'round robin' matches.

The top four teams after these sectional matches will then play in two Semi-finals. The winners of these games will play in the 'preliminary' Final.

If the Minor Premiers lose in their Semi-final match, or the preliminary, they will challenge the winner of the preliminary Final for the Flag, in a Grand Final.

This new system was mooted by the *Argus* newspaper and is called the Argus system (→ 9/4/24).

1902 Statistics

Leading Goalkicker
Ted Rowell (Coll) 33
Champion of the Season:
Ted Rowell (Coll)
Finals: First Semi-final Ess 9.7 (61) Melb 7.9 (51) **Second Semi-final** Coll 6.12 (48) Fitz 9.10 (64) **Final** Fitz 4.10 (34) Ess 6.9 (45) **Grand Final:** Coll 9.6 (60) Ess 3.9 (27)

Ladder:	W	L	%	pts
Coll	15	2	199.5	60
Ess	13	4	141.6	52
Fitz	10	7	125.9	40
Melb	9	8	108.8	36
S. Melb	7	10	99.4	28
Carl	7	10	77.1	28
Geel	7	10	76.8	28
St K	0	17	41.9	0

Maroons and Magpies fight for points in Sydney

A tense moment in Sydney is watched by the bowler-hatted goal umpire as Fitzroy and Collingwood vie for a mark.

May 23. A crowd estimated at 18,000 saw Fitzroy down Collingwood, 7.20 (62) to 6.9 (45), at the Sydney Cricket Ground today.

In a game played in the presence of the Governor-General, Lord Tennyson, both clubs fielded their strongest available line-ups.

Collingwood started brightly, kicking into a slight breeze, with their marking a feature of the game as they went into the first break with an 11-point lead.

Fitzroy hit back in the second quarter, but their all-round superiority was marred by some woefully inaccurate kicking by their key forwards. Although both teams played with great determination, it was Fitzroy who were consistently first to the ball and stronger in the ruck.

Sadly, the game deteriorated as spectacle in the last quarter with teamwork abandoned for individual efforts. This would not have been what the League had in mind when it decided to promote the game interstate.

Fitzroy maintained their superior ground play, and in Lou Barker they had the best follower on the field. Collingwood fought out the rugged encounter to the very end. They were well served by Bill Proudfoot, whose kicking out from goal was a feature of the day.

Plod Proudfoot's nom de game

Sept. 17. A strange name but a welcome sight has greeted Collingwood barrackers during the Finals.

The name is Wilson, but the sight is definitely Proudfoot.

Big Constable Bill Proudfoot was forced to retire from football half way through the season by the Police Commissioner, but someone looking awfully like him is still playing for the Magpies.

The Commssioner thought that a policeman should not be involved in a game that tolerated flagrant assaults on and off the field – even though Proudfoot's presence has often stood bravely between the mob and its intended victim.

Just ask Umpire Roberts if he remembers 1896.

James Sharp: Fitzroy champion.

No ball up with Same Old balls-up

July 18. Geelong and Essendon players and supporters froze for 25 minutes today as they waited for a new ball to arrive at the Corio Oval at Geelong.

The delay was instigated by Essendon, and it may not have helped the club, as a determined Geelong easily beat them, 13.11 (89) to 6.8 (44), reversing the result of their match in May.

The Essendon captain Jim Anderson objected to the fact that Geelong had kicked the ball around before the match, and demanded that a new one be found for the match. But a search revealed that there was no such object at the ground and a messenger had to rush to the city to make a hasty purchase.

Saints break drought with three in a row

A mark is hotly contested in the match between St Kilda and Geelong.

June 13. St Kilda has avenged its first round loss by defeating Geelong and recording its third successive win for the season.

When the season started, St Kilda had the unenviable record of having won only two of the first 100 games it contested in the League. The win against Geelong sees St Kilda replace Geelong in the top four.

St Kilda's much-improved form has been a long time coming, and after some familiar big defeats early in the year they have finally started to win games and establish themselves as a force in the competition.

After an even first half, St Kilda turned on a brilliant display to wipe out a 15-point deficit at the break and go on to win convincingly, 7.13 (55) to 5.9 (39).

St Kilda showed such determination in the second half that Geelong were outplayed in almost every part of the field. Geelong tried hard to come back in the final quarter, but they lacked the pace, judgement and stamina of their opponents who, had they been more accurate in kicking for goal, might have almost doubled Geelong's final score.

St Kilda's victory was not unexpected, for their recent form has been very good and Geelong, although playing at home, were forced to take the field without their captain, Henry Young. It was an even performance by a very determined St Kilda team and the club now seems to have, at last, got onto the track that leads to success.

The win demonstrated that St Kilda is no longer a team to be taken lightly.

After the game there was much jubilation in the St Kilda dressing rooms as players and supporters celebrated (→ 15/6/07).

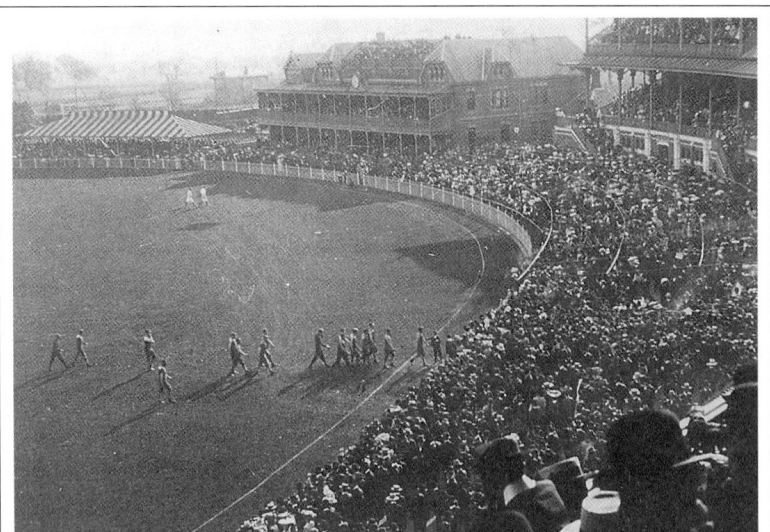

Finals time in perfect Spring sunshine. The big crowd looks on at the Melbourne Cricket Ground as the teams leave the ground at half time.

Scientific football wins Magpies Flag

Sept. 12 Earlier in the season, watching Collingwood beat South Melbourne, an observer in *The Age* wrote: 'By making football a science, Collingwood will probably win this season's Premiership. As the game is now played, individual excellence unbacked by perfect system has no chance of achieving success.' So it happened.

Collingwood's system of short passing eventually overcame Fitzroy in a close and hectic Grand Final – despite the individual efforts of many of the Maroons. The final score was Collingwood 4.7 (31) to Fitzroy 3.11 (29).

For the first time in VFL history the result of the Grand Final rested with the final kick of the day. The usually accurate Fitzroy captain Gerald Brosnan missed the goal and Fitzroy lost by two points.

One player said that Brosnan's shot was so close that a lace brushed against the post in passing.

A crowd of 32,363 were kept at fever pitch by the close scores. But football justice was perhaps done, as Collingwood's systematic work has brought a new dimension to the game (→ 26/11/06).

The Premiership game reaches its thrilling climax at the MCG.

Victoria's record win over Ballarat

June 27. On the same afternoon that Victoria beat South Australia another Victorian team made the traditional annual pilgrimage to Ballarat.

These games have gone either way in the past, but the 'seconds' team showed the current differences in strength between the city and country competitions.

In Ballarat the biggest crowd in the history of these matches saw a goalkicking feast, with the Miners kicking a record total of goals against the League, but still losing. The scores were Victorian League 17.7 (109) to Ballarat Association 12.11 (83) (→ 18/6/04).

1903 Statistics

Leading Goalkicker:
Edward Lockwood (Coll) 35
Champion of Season:
Hugh Gavin (Ess)
Finals: First Semi-final Fitz 11.15 (81) Geel 4.5 (29) **Second Semi-final** Coll 4.3 (27) Carl 3.5 (23) **Grand Final** Coll 4.7 (31) Fitz 3.11 (29)

Ladder:	W	L	D	%	pts
Coll	15	2		159.4	60
Fitz	14	3		171.6	56
Carl	11	6		136.0	44
Geel	9	8		120.7	36
St K	7	9	1	76.4	30
Ess	6	10	1	78.6	26
Melb	3	14		64.1	12
S. Melb	2	15		54.9	8

Barrackers develop language of football

'Center' in *Melbourne Punch* **characterises football barrackers:**

The football barracker is a wonderful personality. The worthy censors of public morals frequently find fault with him for indulging in innocent mirth, like hitting visitors over the head with pickets or showering blue metal at their cabs, but he really means no harm in the world.

Horribly impartial people would complain that he is one-eyed; of course he is – he wouldn't be a barracker if he wasn't. He would be merely a disinterested and wearisome spectator.

Whenever you hear anybody boast that he sees the good play on both sides you can be perfectly sure he doesn't see anything at all...

Each team has its following and, though victory naturally swells the numbers, there is a section in every crowd that remains staunch to its team through all the evolutions and revolutions of fickle Fortune.

The Collingwood man takes a scientific view of the game. This is owing to the system for which Wood are so celebrated. Every Collingwood man swears by the system; he may not know exactly what it means, but he swears by it all the same. 'That's what they call breaking of our system, is it?' he says in a superior tone when Wood are going strong. 'It seems as strong as a brickhouse today, anyhow.'

He has a take it for granted expression and patronises the other teams. 'Yes they played a real good game. With a bit more system...' and so on. He seldom praises his own team. He always expects them to win easily.

The Roy following has more vigour. Great faith is expressed in the team, and it is always expected to come when wanted – to rise to the occasion, however high.

That is not the high seriousness of the Carlton barracker. The Blue and White contingent take football with deadly earnestness, though their ruling passion is a monumental confidence.

At the beginning of every season Carlton are sure to win, and no untoward combination of circumstances can shatter their faith by the end of the season that Carlton 'should' have won.

The Dons are also confident, and fully expect to collect the pennants this season. Their barrackers are keen, excellent in victory, but particularly bitter under defeat. They are particularly severe on their own men, and when things are going against them advise half their players to get into the Morgue or otherwise lose themselves. 'Oh! you wooden cart horses.'

South probably divide with Carlton the honour of the most strenuous and numerous following, and when they meet the barracking gets very wild and woolly.

South have a giant team and barrackers cry: 'Don't be frightened to 'urt 'em, South! Rip 'is bloomin' sideboards off! Push 'is neck in!'

Then when somebody bumps a Southerner the cry: 'You low cur – why can't you play football? South never begin the rough play – but if necessary –!'

On the South ground may also be seen a beautiful assortment of colours, hats and rosettes, flags, red and white 'brollies'.

The Geelong crowd is perhaps the most pleasant. Though proud of their team, they are not arrogant, and they recognise the good play of their opponents.

When they come to Melbourne they come to have a good time – the match is but a pleasant interlude – so if they win they enjoy themselves royally, and if they lose – 'Well, it was a good game; come and have a drink' and will have a good time all the same.

Melbourne have many barrackers, but the most characteristic is the Johnny in the Ladies Reserve, who refers to 'Our Boys', without probably knowing any of them, and the fashionable young lady who thinks the Redlegs seem so 'cosy' and if they get beaten remarks 'anyway they looked the prettiest'. The old sport on the steps who remarks 'Played Horry, admirable!' deserves honourable mention.

Though sore stricken by evil Fortune, the Saints have a staunch body of barrackers. There are exceptions, however: One local resident only gave two goals in against Wood: 'I didn't like to do it, you know – didn't like to bet against Saints – but it was too good: couldn't resist it, and I needed the money, I'm going fishing next week.'

But the average St Kildaite is quite satisfied. 'Wait till next year,' he says, 'just you wait.'

And, after all, it is good to have a big stock of hope; none of us can tell what will happen next year.

THE FOOTBALL BARRACKER

1. "Go it, East, you beauties!"

2. Goal for West.

3. "Goal for East! – No! D— hard luck : hit the post!"

4. "Garn! Of course it's a free kick to East!"

Result :— West . . . 1 Goal

A day in the life of the football barracker when 'East' meets 'West'. One-eyed but not blind.

Blues wrangle as season opens; Worrall on merry-go-round

May 7. The final act in the pre-season drama at Carlton was played out at Princes Park today.

New President, and Attorney General in the Federal Labor Government, is Henry Bournes Higgins.

Mr Higgins was presented to the players on the ground before the Fitzroy game to hearty cheers.

It was said that the smell of eucalyptus in the dressing room would have overwhelmed Mr Higgins' somewhat delicate constitution.

Mr Higgins said it was an honour to have been elected President of such an old body as the Carlton club, the first ball for which had been kicked by that entrepreneur and theatre legend George Coppin.

He looked forward with confidence to a new era for the Blues, and intended to bring the club together after the Worrall affair.

Coach and secretary Jack Worrall was sacked by the Committee for what were described as unorthodox accounting methods when he paid some match receipt cheques into his bank account before passing the money on to the club.

There was no hint of dishonesty, rather it was an excuse to get rid of the coach.

The Committee voted 16 to 7 to sack Worrall, but the Carlton players ran a successful 'ticket' at a Special General Meeting, opposing all who opposed Worrall, and were successful. Worrall was reappointed last week (→26/7/09).

There's eucalyptus in the rooms and King Football is back on his throne.

Scenes from the Melbourne and Essendon match in Sydney on May 28. The crowd; three cheers; the casualty.

Trotter cog in Fitzroy's winning machine

Sept. 19. Fitzroy followers can thank their champion rover Percy Trotter for their great results this year, and his fine Grand Final efforts. The clincher in the Grand Final was the sixth Maroon goal, scored by the little champ Percy after a long run and kick by Fred Fontaine.

Trotter was by far the most conspicuous player on the ground.

Umpire Jack Elder says of Trotter that as an all-round champion he is unchallenged, and as a rover the most accomplished player he has seen in that position. He has never seen a more versatile player.

There is Trotter the rover who kicks long with either foot, the Trotter who could dominate a wing at a moment's notice, the Trotter whose magnificent marking, kicking and ground play at half back could dominate the opposing line, and the Trotter who can be flung into the fray in any part of the field to overwhelm the opposition.

What a grand player he is! He can pick up the ball with one hand on the run, bounce it and let go his kick seemingly in one action.

Opponents hurl themselves at him to find he is not there. They reel past that swift turn away and finish on the grass.

Fitzroy's champion Percy Trotter kicks over the Magpies' Dick Condon.

Ostracised Kiernan plays for Brighton

June 11. The former Fitzroy player Chris Kiernan, whose clearance to Collingwood has been blocked by League delegates, played his first game on Saturday for the Brightonians, who have appointed him as their vice-captain.

Kiernan's case, and his treatment by the League, has aroused the indignation of football followers. Kiernan, who has fallen out with the Fitzroy committee, made a statutory declaration denying all charges against him. The charges, which have not been substantiated by the League, include professionalism and a claim that he did not give wholehearted effort in a game.

Vic Cumberland of St Kilda.

'Reject' Brosnan leads Maroons to Flag

Carlton rover Arch Snell and Fitzroy's Ernie Jenkins race for the ball.

Sept. 17. Gerald Brosnan, rejected by two League clubs, today led Fitzroy to a Premiership win over Carlton. The final score was Fitzroy 9.7 (61) to Carlton 5.7 (37).

Brosnan, who is idolised by the Fitzroy followers, showed his great leadership qualities as he dominated the centre-half-forward position and kicked two of Fitzroy's nine goals.

He was well supported by a strong halfback and centre line and brilliant roving by Percy Trotter and Bill McSpeerin. Carlton's champion follower Fred 'Pompey' Elliot was best in a side which worked manfully and led at half time.

The Blues were let down in the third term when they could only manage five points to two straight goals by Fitzroy.

A sensational mark to Carlton was disallowed by Umpire Crapp, who said a Fitzroy player was kneed in the back. This incident spurred Fitzroy to a four goal run in the final term and a 24-point win.

Brosnan tried out at both Geelong and Essendon without success, but his subsequent form in the strong Ballarat competition attracted Fitzroy's attention. He was made captain last year.

His two goals today help to make up for the vital shot he missed in last year's Grand Final (→ 13/9/05).

Savagery at South: three disqualified

Aug. 17. Bill Gent of South Melbourne has been suspended until the end of next season for virtually running amok with his fists during last Saturday's match, which Fitzroy won 8.10 (58) to 5.16 (46)

A VFL Investigating Committee also gave Henry Clarke of Fitzroy and Bill McGee of South three weeks suspension each for striking.

But it was Gent who was seen as the instigator. He was described as charging at players in the first quarter and 'getting into their faces with his fist'. He struck both Bill McSpeerin and Bill Walker. Gent said that he was provoked.

1904 Statistics

Leading Goalkicker:
Vince Coutie (Melb) 39
Champion of Season:
Vic Cumberland (St K)
Finals: First Semi-final Carl 6.7 (43) Ess 6.4 (40) **Second Semi-final** Fitz 9.7 (61) Coll 7.8 (50) **Grand Final** Fitz 9.7 (61) Carl 5.7 (37)

Ladder:	W	L	D	%	pts
Fitz	12	5		128.2	48
Carl	10	6	1	105.5	42
Coll	10	7		117.0	40
Ess	10	7		113.1	40
S. Melb	10	7		108.5	40
Melb	8	9		112.7	32
Geel	4	12	1	77.2	18
St K	3	14		62.1	12

1905

Essendon end Magpies great run of 12 on the trot

Fitzroy and Collingwood meet at the opening of the season and watch the unfurling of Fitzroy's Premiership Flag.

Aug. 18. They have been calling Collingwood the greatest football team to have ever run onto a field. The critics have declared them a 'monte' for the Premiership Flag as they notched up 12 wins in a row. But Essendon have put a dent in their pride at Victoria Park with a 10.6 (66) to 7.11 (53) win.

That fiery football genius Dick Condon took over from Collingwood's first ever coach Bill Strickland at the beginning of the season.

His combination of fire-and-brimstone oratory and skilful tactics had still seen the Magpies finish the season two and a half games clear. But the Same Old's exposure of the Magpie mortality will give all the other teams hope for the Finals.

Essendon's champion player was their forward George Barker, who kicked seven goals and made a reliable target for the powerful centre line of Harry Davis, Bill Sewart and Ben Baxter.

The game was a see-sawing affair in the first half, with Collingwood's much vaunted system breaking down against Essendon's powerful defence, led by Michael Madden.

An amazing aerial sequence between Collingwood centre-halfback Jack Monohan and his counterpart Madden may have been the turning point in the game. They marked and kicked to each other in a series of eight before Monohan, realising that he could not get past the Essendon man, kicked to the flank. Essendon's dominance of the game began at around that time (→ 4/10/12).

McNamara makes stunning debut

Aug. 10. A six-foot-three country boy from around Benalla made a notable debut in St Kilda's hard-fought win over lake rivals South Melbourne, 5.11 (41) to 5.9 (39).

Dave McNamara is a strapping lad, filling a pair of shorts like wheat overflowing a silo: which object he seems able and willing to kick a football over.

Playing in defence when South kicked with a big breeze, he took mark after mark, and kicked the Saints back into attack.

South might have had McNamara but turned him away – to the other side of the pond (→ 25/04/14).

The evolution of the perfect footballer is traced in 'Punch' as modern man finds new physical aids with which to leap for the flying football.

Finish of all finishes gives Pivots hope

Sept. 2. Geelong's extraordinary sectional match win over Fitzroy keeps the Pivotonian hopes alive for another week. It has been called 'the finish of all finishes in the history of Geelong football'. The final score was 10.8 (68) to 9.12 (66).

Fitzroy hit the front with seconds to go, but Geelong captain and hero Henry Young, not giving up, rushed the ball to their end of the ground where he received a free, and goaled as the bell rang.

Young was chaired off the ground as all around Corio hats and sticks were thrown into the air.

Manager will see wooden spoon well

Sept. 9. Melbourne seems likely to remain in the football abyss, judging by today's drubbing at the hands of Carlton 18.17 (125) to 5.8 (38).

The spirit of amateurism is affecting the Fuchsias on the field (this team contained many untried players from amateur teams), but it creates a fine atmosphere.

At half time the team presented their manager, Mr A. Northcott, with gold spectacles – one set for reading and the other for distance. Maybe they are asking for him to pay more attention, both to team lists and far-sighted planning.

A new uniform at South.

Fitzroy stick it out to win in mud

The players stream towards the ball, and umpire Ivo Crapp watches intently, during the Grand Final.

Sept. 30. Fitzroy, which beat Collingwood in the first round, showed they really had their measure to win the Flag today, 4.6 (30) to 2.5 (17)

Markwell in the *Australasian* says of the Maroons: 'They have fought their way through the most severe campaign on record.'

Collingwood lost captain Dick Condon at half time and their hopes seemed to go with him, as Fitzroy slammed on 2.2 to one point.

Best for Fitzroy was charming Barclay 'Titch' Bailes, the brilliant first year winger. Champion rover Percy Trotter, centreman Tammy Beauchamp and follower Bert 'Boxer' Milne also took control in the third quarter.

Fitzroy closed out the game by having every player on the ball in the last quarter, denying the Magpies any room to move. It was not pretty, but effective (→ 27/9/13).

A birds-eye view of the match for these young supporters at the MCG.

Melbourne teams make bush visits

Aug. 14. The midwinter break has the barrackers of Melbourne clubs wondering how to get through the weekend, while most of the footballers are playing in the country. It is a chance for players and officials to enjoy the air and the lavish hospitality which goes with such visits.

A mixed League team went to Ballarat, but the sturdy miners had a good win over them 10.12 (72) to 7.10 (52). Collingwood beat Broken Hill 7.7 (49) to 2.9 (21), Melbourne beat a Gippsland team at Traralgon 10.14 (74) to 5.7 (37), while Fitzroy had a hard time beating Bendigo 11.12 (78) to 10.9 (69).

Geelong blizzard keeps team in

July 31. *The Age* says it would be interested to know what sort of 'adverse weather' would be sufficiently 'adverse' to cause the League to put off a round of matches.

Obviously, much worse than the worst Saturday for rain, sleet and snow that anyone could remember coming to Victoria, which has its fair share of miserable weather.

Conditions were so 'adverse' down at Geelong that the home players were virtually cowering in the pavilion, reluctant to leave the shelter. They soon warmed up, but were beaten by Carlton 6.11 (47) to 6.5 (41).

1905 Statistics

Leading Goalkicker:
Charles Pannam (Coll) 38
Champion of Season:
Percy Trotter (Fitz)
Finals: First Semi Fitz 12.7 (79) Ess 4.12 (36) **Second Semi** Coll 4.6 (30) Carl 11.10 (76) **Final** Carl 6.9 (45) Fitz 11.6 (72) **Grand Final** Fitz 4.6 (30) Coll 2.5 (17)

Ladder:	W	L	D	%	pts
Coll	15	2		175.0	60
Fitz	12	4	1	135.4	50
Carl	11	6		127.4	44
Ess	9	8		114.4	36
S. Melb	7	9	1	83.7	30
Geel	6	11		79.0	24
St K	4	13		64.1	16
Melb	3	14		70.9	12

May 5. Henry Young is made captain of Geelong, but is not playing in the opening game because he is on holidays.

May 5. Ted Rowell makes his return for Collingwood against Geelong, kicking four in their 12.19 (91) to 5.7 (37) win. Rowell had to stand out of football in 1905 after his return from Kalgoorlie (→4/5/12).

May 12. A number of visiting Japanese naval officers watch Fitzroy 10.13 (73) defeat Melbourne 8.5 (53). The 'father of the game', Henry Harrison, leads cheers and is greeted with 'banzais' (→2/2/29).

May 26. Small dog on field is patted by Jack Purse of Melbourne and follows him around until it trips another player, and is removed. Melbourne beat South 5.9 (39) to 5.4 (34).

May 31. 'Center' in *Melbourne Punch* waxes eloquent over 'Pompey' Elliott's play against Collingwood. Carlton win 8.9 (57) to 4.13 (37) (→17/6/22).

The gong found him still going strong and he returned to his corner covered with mud and glory, while a cab waited outside, loaded with peanuts, cork screws, ginger ale and Victoria Park crosses...

June 16. The players of Essendon advertise in the *Argus* that charges of improper conduct laid against Albert Thurgood in 1902 cannot be sustained, and he should be eligible to play.→

June 23. A League team defeat Ballarat 17.13 (115) to 10.10 (70) in 'an exhibition one would have liked to display to foreigners' (→7/7/37).

Aug. 6. The barracking of 'younger patrons' on the hill at Geelong described as 'deplorable' by the *Argus*.

Aug. 11. Victoria 14.19 (103) beat South Australia 13.9 (87) on a day where more interest is in the postponed Carlton and Fitzroy game. Critics claim it was only changed because of boredom with interstate football. Fitzroy win 5.14 (38) to 5.3 (33).

Debuts
Fred Jinks (Carl)
Alex 'Bongo' Lang (Carl)
Walter H. 'Dick' Lee (Coll)
Charles Ricketts (S. Melb)

Retirements
Bill Proudfoot (Coll)
Albert Thurgood (Ess)
Percy Trotter (Fitz)

Big crowd enjoys 'Wale' of a game

June 4. The Prince of Wales Birthday split round drew immense crowds to today's games, especially to the match between Carlton and South Melbourne.

The tram service was overwhelmed by the numbers, and thousands of South Melbourne supporters were forced to walk across the city to Princes Park.

An estimated 35,000 people packed into the ground before the gates were locked, a football assembly larger than anyone could remember at the Carlton Oval.

The Blues made it five in a row in an impressive start to the season holding out South to win 10.9 (69) to 10.5 (65), Mick Grace kicking four goals for Carlton.

Mick Grace and Charlie Hammond of Carlton have the ball under control.

New Magpie song is out of tune

Sept. 26. 'Good Old Collingwood forever. We know how to play the game' may well be the stirring opening lines of the new club song, but harmony is sadly lacking at Victoria Park following the sacking of the coach, Dick Condon.

Although Collingwood finished in third place, it has been a season marred by dissension and poor team spirit. By the end of the season, two captains, 'Rosie' Dummett and Jack Monohan had resigned.

The dismissal is the latest incident in Condon's colourful and controversial career, both as a player and as a coach. It became clear from the start that all was not well when Condon was suspended by the Committee for three matches. The Committee considered him to be a cause of dissension within the team.

Whatever happens to Condon from now on, no football supporter will forget his exceptional skills and inspirational leadership qualities on the field. His sacking comes a year after he won Collingwood's best player award.

Condon, with his headstrong ways and sharp tongue, has had continual problems with discipline. Who could forget his clash with umpire 'Ivo' Crapp, which cost him a long suspension. Nevertheless, few would deny his deep knowledge of the game (→18/11/09).

Amateur Melbourne gents too nice to win

Aug. 27. The red stockings of Melbourne are down around their ankles, and there is gloomy talk in the pavilion as the Fuchsias complete a truly disastrous season.

Saturday's match against Fitzroy was rock bottom. Having finished last on the Premiership ladder with only one win, they played the first final round match, and were beaten 17.18 (120) to 2.1 (13).

After 15 games they have had 1218 points kicked against them to 597 in their favour. Only family and committee members are bothering to turn up regularly to watch these terrible drubbings.

The problem seems to rest squarely with the principles of the club, built around amateurism and fair play. The club supporters say that they follow the strict rules of the League and don't pay players.

'How can you expect a team that costs £300 to beat one that costs £1500', a former player complained to the *Argus* on Saturday.

The *Argus* today throws the question back at Melbourne and their grumbling committeemen. 'Either the players in the leading teams are paid or not. It they are then the managers of the Melbourne team, who know what expenses are legitimate, should bring the matter before the League. It is idle for men to talk in the MCC pavilion unless they follow it up with the VFL.' (→17/5/13).

Official greetings to the Japanese Fleet, here for the football.

Red hot Navy Blues flatten the Maroons

The huge crowd at the Melbourne Cricket Ground for the Grand Final watch a tense passage of play as the Blues take the road to victory over Fitzroy.

Sept. 27. Carlton has won its first Flag of any kind since 1887. 'Center' in *Melbourne Punch* has been moved almost to poetry in his report after the Grand Final was won by the 'Brewers' 15.4 (94) to Fitzroy 6.9 (45). The record crowd of 44,437 seemed on Carlton's side.

'Carlton.. ain' they blithrers.'
'Would have won if it had snowed.'

'On Saturday's dewy eve such scraps of dialogue were heard all over this great, great city. No matter where you turned even in the pub, your eardrums were tickled with 'Grace', 'Great game', 'Should 'ave

'ad his shot', 'Jack Worrall', 'Bongo' and other classic sounds that pattered like a rain of Grand Italian Opera.

'Everybody was decorated with blue and white ribbons. Their talk was blue. Everybody wanted to get into the blue tram and have a ride. At the finish they were drinking blue beer...it tasted blue anyhow. The pubs dispensed free beer. Free Beer. Think of it, free beer in Carlton.

'After a grand Fitzroy fight-back in the third quarter they had little left in the last. Carlton put on six sixers accompanied by wild warcries

and chants of triumph, and waving of hats, scarves, brollies, other people's tall hats, bits of fence, husks of grandstand and anything else lying handy.

'After 19 dormant years the Old Blues were sailing gaily up the happy harbour, for home and beauty. The globule had been sent through the sticks so often that it seemed to know the way.

'By the end they were actually handballing, handing the orb round like it was a cheese sandwich, passing like passengers through turnstiles, all in turn, and shoving it right

through the gaudy uprights without frightening the children.

'Carlton broke all the records, attendance, goalkicking, artistic finish, Maroon superiority, most of the fence and heaps of other things.

'The Blues put up one of the finest exhibitions this wondering world has ever seen. It was a greater and finer exhibition than the Pyramids, or the Crystal Palace or the Taj Mahal or the Melbourne Waxworks. The Brewers played team ball like a well oiled clock, shining in clusters rather than as bright particular stars.' (→21/9/07).

Amazing Grace the first to fifty goals

Sept. 22. Mick Grace has capped Carlton's great year by topping the goalkicking list. The veteran forward kicked three goals in the Grand Final today to take his tally for the season to 50. This is, to date, the highest seasonal tally in League football.

Grace has long been one of the great marks in football. The height and bulk that carried him through years as a ruckman give him a decided edge as he flies for the ball on the forward line, and he applies vigour with the judgement that comes from experience.

He began his football with Fitzroy in 1897, and was regarded by football writers as Champion of the Colony in the next year. After a two-year break he crossed to Carlton in 1903, following his mentor, the Carlton coach Jack Worrall.

Mick Grace: a towering figure on the field for the Blues this year.

Champ leaves: sore knee and sad note

Sept. 15. An injured ankle during the Semi-final against Fitzroy has ended the career of Essendon's 'Albert the Great' Thurgood.

It was a sad finale. The year started on a controversial note for Thurgood, who had to overcome considerable hostility from the Essendon Committee as he sought to make a comeback with the club he left in 1902. Then, having been refused a clearance to Collingwood, he wrote an open letter to members complaining of 'personal animosity' by the Committee.

Ironically, Thurgood wanted to retire after the home-and-away games, and had to be talked into taking to the field for today's eventful Semi-final, which Essendon lost 10.12 (72) to 5.6 (36) (→6/09/27).

1906 Statistics

Leading Goalkicker:
Michael Grace (Carl) 50

Champion of Season:
Jack 'Dookie' McKenzie (Ess)

Finals:
First Semi-final Fitz 10.12 (72) Ess 5.6 (36); **Second Semi-final** Carl 9.10 (64) Coll 8.6 (54); **Grand Final** Carl 15.4 (94) Fitz 6.9 (45)

Ladder:	W	L	%	pts
Carl	14	3	153.5	56
Fitz	13	4	153.3	52
Coll	11	6	140.3	44
Ess	10	7	115.1	40
S. Melb	8	9	99.9	32
St K	6	11	88.1	24
Geel	5	12	64.3	20
Melb	1	16	48.7	4

1907

The season proceeds with new jerseys and knees up

Len Mortimer in South uniform.

Collingwood won their opening game with Fitzroy, but are outmarked here.

June 15. Collingwood have been taking to the field with bare knees this year, and it seems that footballers are going to become less and less encumbered with clothing. Collingwood's new appearance brought a buzz of surprise from the crowd when they ran on to the field.

Over the years the caps and hats, knickerbockers and stockings have been swept off the football field in favour of lighter weight clothing.

Collingwood picked up the uniform style used in rugby – short, loose knickers and bare knees with long socks. 'Observer' of the *Argus* reported that 'they looked smart and workmanlike – in all respects a team of thoroughbreds – and the new style gives the impression of increased height and weight'.

South Melbourne have made a fundamental change to their uniform, adopting a white jersey with a red sash over the left shoulder. The old laced-up jerkin of horizontal red and white stripes now looks old-fashioned and hard on the eyes.

Carlton, too, have made a uniform change, to a jersey that is totally dark blue. The previous dark blue lace-up had a chamois coloured yoke (→ 11/5/18).

Saints stumble at home after their best run of wins

June 15. St Kilda's runaway start of six wins was halted today at the hands of South Melbourne in a rough, slogging game in the rain. South won 7.2 (44) to 4.8 (32).

St Kilda's winning streak and the play of Dave McNamara and Vic Cumberland have been the talk of Melbourne recently. The Junction Oval was packed with 27,000 spectators, including the Lieutenant-Governor, Sir John Madden, the Mayor of St Kilda, Cr Gibbs, and various other dignitaries.

But St Kilda showed none of their recent brilliance, and it seems that they were knocked off their game by South's ferocity. So hard were South that they conceded eight free kicks in a row in the first quarter.

St Kilda led by six points at the last change, but seemed rattled by South's persistence and wasted opportunities to score.

All eyes are on the ball in the goal square, with St Kilda on the attack.

Mainly trains on the Werribee plains

June 29. Geelong have been nearly as concerned with transport as they have with football in recent weeks.

Today, to ensure victory over Carlton, the Pivotonians sent a motor-car to fetch teacher Alex McKenzie from Keilor where he was on a nature study excursion. Geelong won 7.4 (46) to 5.9 (39).

The 'special' football trains to and from Geelong often take their time. In the game at Fitzroy in May they had to start 20 minutes late. However, a rested Geelong won, 12.5 (77) to 9.10 (64).

Coaches cheer clubs with no beer

June 8. The theory that drinking plenty of beer is good for a footballer's condition has been disputed by a club captain who recommends moderation in all things as the recipe for success.

The League captain, who prefers to remain anonymous, challenged the traditional view of trainers that a man should drink plenty of beer and work it off during training. 'Personally...the less a man drinks of beer or spirits, the better for his training,' he said.

Navy Blues raise another Flag

Sept. 21. Carlton has won its second successive Premiership, just beating South Melbourne in a hard-fought match, and on a softer MCG than might have been expected.

The League had decided, after representations from the two clubs, that the MCG should be watered if no rain fell before the Grand Final. The Semi-finals were plagued by a rock hard surface and raised dust.

A committee of three old players last night consulted the oracular groundsman Mr Baracchi as to the prospect of precipitation. On his advice they decided, correctly, to water the ground.

Carlton were overall taller and heavier than South Melbourne and this told on the 'Lagoonites' in the end. Carlton withstood a Southern fightback in the last quarter to win 6.14 (50) to 6.9 (45).

Appropriately 'The Silver King,' Frank Caine, was shooting for goal as the bell rang, and thousands of spectators swarmed on to the field.

Jim Flynn modestly gave the laurel to coach Jack Worrall, but his own role was substantial, as he had returned for the Finals after a mid-season retirement.

And Mallee Johnson, named by the *Australasian* as the player of the season, was the biggest and best big man on the ground (→ 26/9/08).

Carlton stalwarts Norman Clark, Fred Jinks (with ball) and Rod McGregor.

1907 Statistics

Leading Goalkicker:
W. 'Dick' Lee (Coll) 47
Champion of Season:
David J. McNamara
Second round wins: Section A: S. Melb 3, Carl 2, Ess 1, Melb 0; Section B: Fitz 3, St K 2, Geel 1, Coll 0
Finals:
First Semi S. Melb 12.10 (82) Coll 6.12 (48); **Second** Carl 13.13 (91) St K 4.11 (35); **Grand Final** Carl 6.14 (50) S. Melb 6.9 (45)

Ladder:	W	L	%	pts
Carl	13	4	155.7	52
S. Melb	11	6	118.4	44
St K	9	8	117.5	36
Coll	9	8	110.4	36
Fitz	7	10	85.5	28
Geel	7	10	85.3	28
Melb	7	10	81.1	28
Ess	5	12	74.0	20

Walter 'Dick' Lee of Collingwood is making a name for himself with big marks like this one at South Melbourne.

Richmond win their first game

May 2. There are yellow and black banners waving and cheery faces around the watering holes of Bridge Road and Swan Street tonight, as the Richmond team have marked their debut in the Victorian Football League with an 11-point win over Melbourne – 8.14 (62) to 7.9 (51).

The other new club, University, elevated from the Metropolitan League, seemed overawed in their encounter with the well-tried Essendon side, and could manage only 3.11 (29) to Essendon's 14.11 (95).

Richmond, a big name in the VFA, also seemed at sea early, despite the support of the partisan crowd at the Punt Road Oval. Melbourne raced to 3.1 at quarter time, while Richmond, having a lot of ball but little luck, could get only 5 points into the wind.

Richmond seemed to be suffering from the VFA convention that the ball should not be kicked from a ruck of players, but moved along until a player could pick it up and pass it by hand. Melbourne did not bother about this, giving the ball a hefty kick from the ruck when an opportunity presented itself.

Melbourne were weakened by the absence through injury of senior players, star forwards Vince Coutie and Jack Strong and sturdy defender Herbert Parke, while Richmond were boosted by former Collingwood champions Dick Condon and Charlie Pannam. Condon's dazzling skills around the centre and Pannam's pace and accurate kicking

Richmond, ready to play in the big league, before the opening bounce.

have given Richmond a big engine.

Richmond finally got into their stride late in the second quarter and kicked three quick goals.

Condon, the coach, told his men to go straight down the centre in the hard-fought third quarter, and they forged a 10-point lead. They lasted better than The Reds, and Bill Schmidt gave their forward work some focus with four goals.

University, at their East Melbourne ground and a long way from their cloistered precincts, seemed unready for this new, hard company. They have been a persistent applicant to join League ranks and, having met Essendon, now know what the 'big boys' will throw at them every week. Their best was the ruckman Leo Seward (→6/6/14).

Profs supporters far too polite

July 24. The new University team, dubbed by its supporters 'The Professors', is suffering from a lack of supporters and verbal vigour.

The new chums lack a natural suburban support base, and the feeble cries of the few are not helping their on-field efforts.

One critic from South Melbourne was overheard to say at an early encounter 'I thought these was the kind of blokes what cleaned their teeth and wore pyjamas'.

The Profs play in a democratic spirit with a sufficient measure of slam and brawn and bump, but do not attract genuine barrackers.

The football kookaburras of other clubs are developing the Australian language. Such words as 'bonzer' and 'blitherer' are being used freely, and everyone knows that they have a football-specific meaning.

At present if one were to ask for a definition of either of these words, the meaning would depend on the club barracked for, but all would be at a loss without using a surname.

A South Melbournite would say 'I don't now what it is, but Ricketts is one'. Essendon would fill in the blank with the name of Busbridge.

Barrackers know no reason and allow none to influence an argument, deriding their own team after a loss, but having few adjectives when they win. This is where the Profs could shine (→2/7/10).

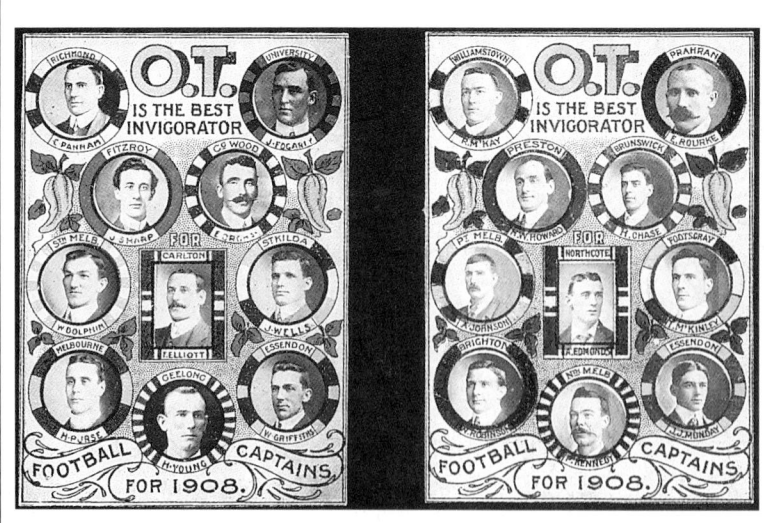

The finest footballers in the land keep OT cordial in their larder.

Football jubilee toasted

Aug. 31. Victoria have triumphed at the football jubilee, billed as 'the greatest sporting event in the Southern Hemisphere', on the fields where the game was first played. But the game of football was deemed to be the real winner.

The Prime Minister, Mr Alfred Deakin, who played in his youth, toasted 'The Australasian Game' at the Smoke Concert in the Melbourne Town Hall last Thursday night. 'I have yet to find a game which carries as much pleasure, as much harmless excitement, as much stimulus', he said. (Cheers!)

He spoke of a time when the game would be played 'wherever the sea washed the shores of Australia, and all the interior between'.

The *Argus* commentator 'Old Boy' went so far as to say: 'There is a drawback perhaps, and it is a big one, that the rest of the world does not play our game. But that is soon to be overcome.'

The Carnival teams, and their colours, were Victoria (dark blue with white V), Tasmania (green, rose and primrose), SA (brown with turquoise and blue facings), WA (green with a gold swan), NSW (royal blue with a red waratah), Qld (maroon with a white Q) and New Zealand (black with a gold fern leaf).

The first two games did not impress the critics, for NZ did not seem to know how to play, and their NSW opponents were even worse, losing by a point. Tasmania, old hands at the business, put paid to any pretensions that the game had got a grip in Queensland. Tasmania won 22.22 (154) to 2.2 (14).

Victoria could probably have doubled their score against NZ, but chose to show the 'All Blacks' the latest methods and were content to win by a margin of 131 points.

It became clear as the ten-day Carnival progressed, that on-field affairs rested with the four 'football states'. SA and WA showed this with a skilled and desperate battle, which WA won 8.11 (59) to 8.5 (53). After all this the WA versus NSW match attracted so little interest that only £30 was taken at the Melbourne Cricket Ground gate.

Victoria's only two 'serious' games were against SA and WA and won handsomely. They did not play Tasmania, but that side was thrashed by SA, so it can be assumed that Victoria were the top side.

Meanwhile the officials enjoyed both entertainment and official meetings, at which it was decided to employ a 5-foot circle in the centre of the ground to prevent scrambling. Players who entered the circle at the bounce would be free-kicked. A motion that the ball be thrown, rather than punched, was defeated.

Come to the Carnival – an enticing programme of the best of the game.

The teams line up for the opening of the football jubilee by the Governor of Victoria, Sir Thomas Gibson-Carmichael.

Some don'ts for the players of 1908

July 16. *Melbourne Punch* records some of the don'ts for footballers this jubilee season:

Don't run amok! If you do you're sure to cop.

Don't 'chew' if the umpire holds his finger up and says 'Now, Sonny, stop'.

Don't tell him to go to Warracknabeal or some other hot locality. You might get a month.

Don't funk it. Go in with your head down, or stop training and wasting the eucalyptus.

Don't play to the forwards. They are only ornaments, and put there to watch you kick goals.

Don't go dead. You'll never come to life if the club finds out.

Superior coaching wins Blues' third Flag

Sept. 26. Carlton's record before today stood at 18 wins and one loss. But that defeat in round 12 was no prediction of the Grand Final result against Essendon.

The mud and wintry rain that prevailed at the East Melbourne Cricket Ground on July 11 had become firm springy MCG turf by a windy Grand Final day.

Coach Jack Worrall, in coaching the Dark Navy Blues from 1902, has developed a style and system that has already won Premierships in 1906 and 1907.

Captain 'Pompey' Elliott's long kicking and marking, combined with the pacy centreline of George Bruce, Rod McGregor and Jim Kennedy, allowed the Blues to dominate the first half of the game.

Marking by 'Mallee' Johnson for Carlton and Essendon's Bill Busbridge was a feature.

Defending grimly and crowding out play in the much windier second half, Carlton held Essendon out.

Final score: Carlton 5.5 (35) Essendon 3.8 (26). The crowd was a huge 50,261.

What are the secrets of the coach? Worrall stresses the importance of 'harmony' between Committee and players through the go-between Secretary or coach.

'Footballers are like soldiers the wide world over. They require leading and instructing', he says.

Carlton captain 'Pompey' Elliott.

'There must be discipline. It is no use telling players what they should not do, unless it can be clearly demonstrated what should be done.'

Worrall says that players must know the 'intricate' rules, be fair-minded and self-disciplined.

He stresses bringing a team to a peak of fitness for the most important game of the year (→ 26/9/14).

Memories of a glorious year will live on in Carlton's Premiership Shield

1908 Statistics

Leading Goalkicker:
W. 'Dick' Lee (Coll) 54.
Champion of Season:
Bill Busbridge (Ess)
Finals: First Semi-final Ess 9.14 (68) Coll 5.3 (33); **Second Semi-final** Carl 12.12 (84) St K 3.8 (26); **Grand Final** Carl 5.5 (35) Ess 3.8 (26)

Ladder:	W	L	%	pts
Carl	17	1	169.4	68
Ess	14	4	142.5	56
St K	10	8	101.4	40
Coll	10	8	97.0	40
S. Melb	9	9	101.4	36
Univ	8	10	96.0	32
Fitz	7	11	109.4	28
Melb	7	11	87.0	28
Rich	6	12	73.7	24
Geel	2	16	68.6	8

Umpire stoning a blot on the game

June 6. After the unsavoury incident at the Fitzroy and South Melbourne at Brunswick Street, when the umpire was hit in the head by a stone, there was more mayhem at the same ground today.

Many Fitzroy fans were upset by the umpiring, and the injury to young George Holden, venting their anger at the Essendon team.

Some Essendon players were bashed as they left the field, and a mob waited outside the ground.

Former Collingwood Premiership player Constable Bill Proudfoot protected Essendon ruckman Alan Belcher – of particular interest to the Maroon mob – as they escaped via the tennis courts (→ 2/5/14).

The umpire reels as he is hit by a stone flung by a Fitzroy supporter.

RICHMOND

RICHMOND

The first mention of a Richmond team dates back to 1860 when the 'Richmondites' were recorded as playing against Melbourne. The Richmond tactics of using players 'in a goal to goal line' was said to be a novel and successful ruse.

Richmond, as it emerged as a VFA team in 1885, may have been only a couple of kicks away from their famous and opulent neighbour, but the gulf between the two clubs in terms of wealth and attitude has always been enormous. Richmond compensated with a mix of grit and cunning that has been a constant.

When the new Richmond team took the field for the first time in 1885 its famous yellow and black colours were restricted to the caps, and the guernsey was actually an all-blue affair.

From the outset Richmond was prepared to stand up, regardless of challenge and controversy. In one incident in 1887 Prahran supporter tore a picket off the fence and hurled it at a Richmond player. He missed the target and hit one of his own men!

By 1888 the Richmond team was in the yellow and black striped guernsey. Even at this stage there was an 'us against the world' attitude.

Richmond desperately clawed its way to respectability in the early 1890s. It then lost its way, even to the point of talk, in the upheavals of the time, of a merger with Collingwood.

When the VFL breakaway eventually came in 1896 Richmond was in no position to stake a claim. Even in the reduced VFA competition of 1897 Richmond

did not make a great impact.

By 1901 the Punt Road men had turned the situation around and they sat at the top of the Ladder for most of the year before being pipped by Port Melbourne for the Premiership. One great discovery was a man reputed to have kicked a bag of spuds across the Murray River. That part of 'Mallee' Johnson's story may have been folklore, but the fact that he was a star was indisputable, as shown in his great years with Carlton.

In this era the head-on clashes between Richmond and Port Melbourne were legendary. The intensity between the two clubs extended over the fence and it became customary for police to attend the games in numbers.

In 1902 the Tigers were irresistible and surged to their first ever Flag, then awarded for the team with most home and away wins.

The VFA decided that for future years it would introduce a finals system. Richmond's first experience of the finals system would end on a bitter note when they were rolled by North Melbourne in a vicious game.

The enmity with North Melbourne spilled over into the next season when Richmond asked field umpire Allen to check the boots of North's players as the Richmond men had received bad gashes. He refused and Richmond was incensed.

The club said it would not play in the Finals match against North if Allen was appointed umpire. The VFA would not be dictated to and Allen was the one it nominated. Richmond stuck to its guns and forfeited the Premiership.

Not for the last time Richmond thrived on the anger directed at it and bolted away with the 1905 Flag. Over the next two seasons Richmond was in contention for the Flag, but did not take off the ultimate prize.

Early in 1907 Richmond defied an edict that no club should play a practice match against a VFL side. In October the club applied for admission to the VFL. Nine days later the application was accepted. **Russell Holmesby**

UNIVERSITY

UNIVERSITY

Melbourne University's involvement with Australian Rules Football stretches right back to the earliest days of the game.

Details of University's initial games are sketchy to say the least, but it is recorded that by 1868 University was regarded as being among the top six or seven clubs in the metropolitan area.

A team bearing the University name had first appeared in 1860. In 1862 the Caledonian Society offered a Challenge Cup for the best football team, and when the challenger won it had to confront other challengers in the same team. University met Melbourne in a challenge game in 1863, but it seems that the students got their arithmetic wrong as the Melbourne captain called for a count and it revealed that University had five too many men on the field!

It is clear that by 1875 things were not travelling smoothly for the Varsity boys. Late in June, University merged with St Kilda and the hybrid creation played out the rest of the season under the unusual title of St Kilda-cum-University.

Observers were unimpressed and one wrote that the merger had made little difference, 'the amalgamation not improving the play of St Kilda or University from that exhibited by them under their own distinctive banners'. The union was a disaster and the combination went winless for the rest of the year.

By the start of 1876 St Kilda had reverted to its solitary existence.

University seems to have slipped into the background for

many years after that, and was not mentioned in reports of senior competition. The University name re-emerged in the Metropolitan Football Association in 1905 and the team had great success. It lost only one game, to Hawthorn, in 1906 and charged to a premiership. Although pressed hard by Brighton, University took out another Flag in 1907 before a crowd which included the Premier, Thomas Bent, and other dignitaries such as Professor Baldwin Spencer.

Spencer was a key figure in pressing University's claims for inclusion in league ranks as he headed the Melbourne University Sports Union. Spencer was to become President of the VFL in 1919.

It is part of University's footballing folklore that Spencer persuaded the students not to return to VFL competition after World War I because the commitment for football at that level was too great. They were students first and footballers second.

Even in those long-gone days they struggled to match the fitness level of the other League teams. University was admitted to the VFL by a unanimous vote on October 7 1907 and a fortnight later the League met to decide between Richmond and North Melbourne for the remaining place. Richmond was given the nod.

University began the 1908 season in the VFL by unfurling the flag it had won in the previous year's Metropolitan Football Association. The ceremony was completed by Mrs E.J Cordner, the matriarch of the famous clan that started with her son Harry, University's centreman.

Expectations were high for the new club and The *Australasian* predicted that the superior intelligence of the University men 'would tell in time.' All players representing University needed to have the Matriculation certificate or higher degree.

The VFL team ran out on to the East Melbourne Oval in 1908, wearing black guernseys with blue V collars. **Russell Holmesby**

1909

April 3. Geelong Secretary Charles Brownlow advertises for a football coach, at a salary of £1 per week (→ 25/5/17).

June 5. At the South and Richmond game Frank Paxton, a little boy wearing the red and white, is injured internally when the fence collapses, and taken to the Melbourne Hospital.

June 9. South Melbourne blames its loss to Richmond, 8.10 (58) to 10.11 (71), on the smallness of the Punt Road oval. Richmond says it is two yards shorter than Victoria Park and seven yards wider.

June 12. Melbourne 8.7 (55) defeat Fitzroy 5.12 (42) in a game marred by numerous episodes of foul play, and a melee among spectators at the end of the game.

June 18. A new grandstand opened at Princes Park, built at a cost of £2500 and seating 1400 with 400 standing in front.

July 24. A riot follows South Melbourne's loss to Fitzroy 4.6 (30) to 5.14 (44) at South. When a constable appeals for Umpire Bunce to be allowed to leave, a burly larrikin says 'He's not a man at all, we want pieces of him'.

July 31. When a fight seems likely to break out between players in the game won by Collingwood 8.6 (54) over South Melbourne 6.7 (43) the timely appearance of a policeman on the field has the effect of cooling things down.

Aug. 7. Dick Lee's father Wal Lee presented with a purse of 25 sovereigns in recognition of 27 years devotion to local Collingwood football – before the Magpies lose to Essendon, 6.6 (42) to 14.14 (98).

Aug. 21. University and Collingwood draw on 5.9 (39). The students have played well in the wet throughout the season, with Ted and Harry Cordner prominent.

Aug. 28. Richmond advise their captain-coach Dick Condon, and players Herbert Hill and Tom Heaney that their services will not be required by the club next year.

Debuts
Jim Caldwell (S. Melb)
Alex 'Bunny' Eason (Geel)
Wellesley Eicke (St K)
Percy Parratt (Fitz)

Retirements
Gerald Brosnan (Fitz)
Fred Jinks (Carl)
George 'Mallee' Johnson (Carl)

Agitation at Carlton sees Worrall resign

July 26. Jack Worrall, the man regarded as the 'Napoleon of Victorian Football', has resigned as coach of triple Premiers Carlton.

Players had not been attending training, and Worrall himself had not been donning football togs and giving instruction.

Player dissatisfaction had resulted in letters to the Committee, and to Worrall writing 'For the sake of the club and for peace and quietness, I consider it better to resign...'

Captain 'Pompey' Elliott will take training, with Worrall as Secretary for the duration. Carlton's on-field success continues (→ 1/4/10).

Burns wins match with Lazarus act

May 8. An hour after being carted from the ground, concussed, Richmond follower William Burns took the mark of the day and then kicked the winning goal against University. The score was 6.6 (42) to 5.7 (37).

After kicking an early goal Burns was heavily bumped and, still groggy, carried from the field. Doctors feared he might have had abdominal injuries. Burns had changed and was waiting to go to hospital, when he heard the scores were level at the last change. He changed back and returned to the fray to perform his heroic deed, and was carried shoulder-high from the ground.

Saints win match but lose points

June 9. St Kilda, languishing at the bottom of the ladder, have had a memorable one-point win over Geelong snatched away by a League ruling on a player's eligibility.

The Saints won 6.13 (49) to 6.12 (48), but Geelong protested that they had played William Stewart while he was under suspension for striking in a Bendigo match.

St Kilda claimed that the League had not been notified of the suspension until after the match. The League has ruled that the time did not matter, and that St Kilda knew of Stewart's position (→ 8/8/11).

Crapp off after umpiring 291 games

An umpire's lot is not a happy one, as Umpire Harry 'Ivo' Crapp knows.

Sept. 30. Popular umpire Harry 'Ivo' Crapp has hung up his whistle after officiating in 291 games of League football.

Crapp umpired Finals in both Victoria and Western Australia, and was responsible for at least one rule change. This came after an incident during an exciting stage of the 1904 Fitzroy and Carlton Grand Final.

Carlton was getting a run-on when one of their forwards took a 'screamer', marking by placing his knees in the back of a Fitzroy defender. Crapp penalised the player for interference and gave the ball to Fitzroy, which steadied and went on to win the game by 24 points.

The decision aroused such controversy that the rule was quickly amended to allow 'unintentional interference'.

Another famous incident took place in a WA Grand Final. Perth, who lost the game by five points to East Fremantle, protested that a goal-scoring player had actually marked the ball after the half-time bell. Crapp insisted that he clearly heard the bell after the mark. His evidence was overruled and the Premiership was awarded to Perth.

Some more thoughts on the equipment needed by a football umpire.

Secretary arrests fan at Collingwood

Sept. 4. Around the traps it was being alleged that Collingwood would not be too disappointed to lose to Melbourne, as they would prefer the Red Legs to be in the Finals rather than Essendon.

But Essendon had to beat Carlton for this idea to work, and that was never likely to happen. Carlton 6.13 (49) defeated the Dons 4.10 (34).

In the event 'Snowy on the trams' was way off the mark because the Magpies easily beat Melbourne 15.18 (108) to 9.12 (66).

Dick Lee kicked five more goals, continuing his usual successful season. The game was played in a strenuous but fair manner, with the number of backhanders not too high.

That made an incident at the end of the game somewhat surprising.

A pair of players were scruffing each other, when a young Collingwoodite jumped the fence and punched the Melbourne player.

On seeing this the Secretary of Melbourne, Mr J.A. Harper, stormed on to the ground, and grabbed the perpetrator. The surprised youth seemed stunned by this intervention, and Harper easily handed him over to a police constable on the boundary line.

Neither event caused a riot, which they might well have done had Collingwood been losing.

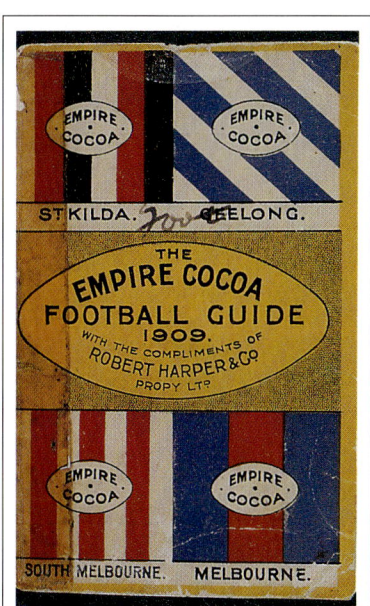

Hot cocoa is just the drink for a cold afternoon at the football.

Crowds out of tree at rough Fitzroy football matches

May 22. The vast crowds that attend the football, now that we have a general Saturday afternoon holiday, had an unfortunate consequence at the Brunswick Street oval.

Some 30,000 were estimated to have turned up at the Fitzroy versus South Melbourne match. As usual, some who could not get in were perched in trees around the ground.

South easily won the match, keeping the Maroons to one goal for three quarters. The 'Lagoonites' won 11.10 (76) to 5.7 (37).

The poor performance by Fitzroy must have had some effect on the swelling crowd which overflowed the ground and broke down the fence. Three supporters were crushed and had to be taken to hospital.

This occurred despite the Brunswick Street oval being one of the better appointed grounds in the competition.

Under the supervision of Secretary W.H. Banks grassy terraces and splendid grandstands have been constructed to offer most patrons an excellent view.

Many other grounds including Collingwood and Carlton are having stands and standards raised – but sometimes no ground will hold everyone who wants to attend.

When the going gets rough on the ground sometimes it's safer up a tree.

Grand new stands opened for huge crowd comfort

June 19. The big football crowds have put ground managers under a lot of pressure, and Carlton and Collingwood have responded with new grandstands.

The Carlton stand, which will seat 1400 people, was opened today by the Lord Mayor of Melbourne, Cr James Burston, before a group of dignitaries and the big crowd who had come to see the Carlton and Essendon game, which Carlton fittingly won, 6.14 (50) to 4.9 (33).

The President of Carlton, John Urquhart, said Carlton was the second oldest club in Melbourne and had a membership of 5000. It was surprising that it had been without a grandstand for so long.

The foundation stone of Collingwood's stand was laid by its instigator, Cr William Rain, amid festivities which included a man being shot from a cannon to land in Roseneath St. The design is based on a stand at Maryborough (→ 9/8/13).

The new stand at Carlton is declared open in a pre-match ceremony.

Oxygen fails to spark Magpies

Oxygen is not quite the answer.

Sept. 18. Despite a plan by the Collingwood medical staff to provide an oxgyen boost to players at the half-time break, the Magpies lost their Semi-final against South Melbourne 6.11 (47) to 10.8 (68).

The plan may have had its merits, but was probably before its time, and with Collingwood leading by two points at the long break the players must have thought they could do without the oxygen lift. All but one declined the offer.

This was a game Collingwood were determined to win well, as the club has had some close calls this season, including two draws, and has lost four matches. The windy conditions gave them hope as they had kicked 3.5 to nothing in the second term. Alas, it was not to be.

Upon resumption of play, South immediately took the initiative and raced to a commanding lead, shattering Collingwood's dreams of the Premiership Flag.

As the Collingwood players trudged back to the dressing room they would surely have noticed the cylinder standing there, still full of oxygen. They may have wondered whether the outcome would have been different had they taken a puff, as advised, at the interval.

If it is of any consolation, the only player to avail himself of some deep inhalation was Jack Shorten, and he failed to rate a mention among Collingwood's best (→ 18/10/10).

South have dream win

South's marvellous ruckman Vic Belcher flies high in the Grand Final.

Oct. 2. South Melbourne and Carlton were the best teams of the season, and had played three tough games before the Grand Final.

South won in round two 7.3 (45) to 4.4 (28) but Carlton reversed the result in round 11 with a brilliant barnstorming quarter.

The score at half time was Carlton 0.11 to South's 4.4 – but the Blues put on nine goals to none in the third quarter in what one scribe called the 'most marvellous exhibition of resistless attack ever seen on a Victorian football field'.

That made Carlton warm favourites for the 'preliminary' final, which they won 10.9 (69) to 7.5 (47).

But under the present finals system South Melbourne, as the Minor Premiers, had the right of challenge – resulting in today's Grand Final.

'Observer', in *The Age*, said that if 'instead of knocking opponents about South Melbourne players devoted their attention to the ball' they might do better against the Blues.

South seemed to heed the advice, 'and in consequence they gave the vast multitude assembled a splendid and exhilarating entertainment, and won the Premiership after having striven unsuccessfully to do so for 19 years.'

They can thank their rucks, tough and unpredictable Albert Franks, the tireless Vic Belcher and roving captain-coach Charlie Ricketts.

The score was South 4.14 (38) to Carlton 4.12 (36) (→ 10/8/18).

Argus votes Bill Busbridge Champion of Season

Sept. 30. Essendon's Bill Busbridge has been named by the *Argus* as the Champion Footballer of Victoria this year. Busbridge – 'Bussy' to supporters – is also the club champion for the second year running.

He is a strong marking centre-halfback who caps off his aerial work with hard defensive play and long kicking. Bussy is a local boy and has been with the club for five years, having been recruited from the Essendon VFA team. He played his first League game a few weeks before his 17th birthday, and immediately established himself in the Dons' defence. Busbridge is also big enough to be used on the ball when the occasion demands and his bullocking work has helped to turn many games.

The men from the 'Argus' count the 105,000 votes for the champion player.

1909 Statistics

Leading Goalkicker:
W. 'Dick' Lee (Coll) 58
Champion of Season:
Bill Busbridge (Ess)
Finals: First Carl 14.8 (92) Ess 9.2 (56); **Second** S. Melb 10.8 (68) Coll 6.11 (47); **Final** S. Melb 7.5 (47) Carl 10.9 (69); **Grand Final** S. Melb 4.14 (38) Carl 4.12 (36)

Ladder:	W	L	D	%	pts
S. Melb	14	4	-	168.9	56
Carl	14	4	-	146.8	56
Coll	12	4	2	130.3	52
Ess	11	7	-	121.7	44
Melb	10	7	1	106.3	42
Fitz	8	9	1	101.6	34
Univ	7	9	2	100.1	32
Rich	6	12	-	64.4	24
Geel	3	15	-	65.5	12
St K	2	16	-	59.3	8

1910

Carlton's 'Big Four' walk out on club

April 27. Repercussions from the Worrall affair surfaced at the meeting of the Permit and Umpire Committee of the League.

Applications from great Carlton stalwarts and former coach Jack Worrall loyalists 'Mallee' Johnson, Frank 'The Silver King' Caine, Fred Jinks and Charlie Hammond to play for North Melbourne had been refused by the Carlton club.

The Committee said appeals would be heard next week, but as Johnson, Jinks and Hammond had been granted tranfers by the VFA they would be released (→ 20/5/11).

'Silver' Caine: walked out.

Call for longer boundary throw-ins

Aug. 6. 'Observer'in *The Age* notes that calls for rule changes often serve as an excuse to 'tinker with a thing that is a gigantic success'.

But one alteration does find favour, and that is with the method of bringing the ball back into play after it has gone out of bounds.

'Observer' believes, along with many in the League, that it would be best if the boundary umpire stood with his back to the field and threw the ball in as far as he could.

He says the game could do without the little throw-ins, which cause crowding, and without the suggested free kick against the last player to touch the ball (→ 23/1/15).

Disgraceful ruffianism

Football in hell. How 'Punch' sees the season progressing so far.

July 2. This football season has been the roughest yet, and violent incidents on and off the field are causing concern to football administrators and even the Government.

The Premier, Sir John Murray, has been sent some samples of the foul language among the crowds, and has said that he will arrange for plain clothes police to be at matches.

Perhaps the worst display occurred at the South Melbourne and Carlton match on May 28, when the game degenerated into a series of scrimmages, notwithstanding Carlton's win, 6.13 (49) to 4.8 (32).

The worst incident occurred towards the end of the game when George Topping of Carlton felled Albert Streckfuss. People from the crowd surged over the fence and milled and jostled around the felled player, while Andy MacDonald picked up the ball and kicked Carlton's sixth goal.

Topping has been disqualified for two seasons over the incident.

On the same day Fitzroy's William Walker had to be escorted from the ground by police as a howling mob of Richmond supporters tried to 'get to him' after the match. Walker was described by *The Age* as having been 'abnormally supple in the elbow joints'. Richmond won the match 7.19 (61) to 4.8 (32).

At St Kilda Umpire Pierce, who had presided over Melbourne's 8.6 (54) to 7.9 (51) win over the home side, had to sneak away through the tennis courts to avoid a hostile crowd who vowed to 'deal with the rotter'. Pierce had disallowed a St Kilda goal just before the bell, saying the ball had been touched.

Similar incidents have occurred over the weeks and the University and St Kilda match at the East Melbourne ground today was stopped for some minutes after Arthur Thomas of St Kilda was 'dropped'in the last quarter (→ 17/8/18).

Blues lose to Pies in big Grand Final barney

Oct. 1. After a long series of losses in Finals, Collingwood has endured to defeat bitter rivals Carlton by 14 points in a hard, fast and strenuous game. The match was marred by an all-out brawl in the last quarter, which resulted in four players reported by the umpire.

Despite the ugly scenes, Collingwood played the better football and deserved their Premiership.

At various stages of the game three Collingwood ruckmen, George Angus, Percy Wilson and David Ryan, were injured and left the ground, only to bravely return and help their side on to victory.

The win was all the more sweet for Collingwood as they had lost 13 of the previous 14 encounters with Carlton.

At the end of the first quarter Collingwood were ahead by 19 points. They played clever, cool and systematic football, while Carlton were unusually loose and disorganised. Against the run of play Carlton, aided by some good fortune and a few mistakes by Collingwood, fought back in the second quarter to reduce their deficit to only 15 points at the half-time break.

Collingwood reasserted their superiority in the third quarter, frequently reducing their opponents to frustration and desperation as they fought to stay in the contest. Dick Lee was in great form, kicking four goals for Collingwood.

Collingwood went into the final term with a 20-point lead, which Carlton had reduced to 16 points when the melee erupted. Punching and brawling continued until trainers and police intervened to separate the combatants. Umpire Elder reported Jack Bacquie and Percy Sheehan of Carlton and Tom Baxter and Jack Shorten from Collingwood. The bell finally rang with Collingwood in control, 9.7 (61) to Carlton's 6.11 (47) (→ 22/9/17).

1910 Statistics

Leading Goalkicker:
W. 'Dick' Lee (Coll) 58
Champion of Season:
W. 'Dick' Lee (Coll)
Finals: First Semi-final Coll 14.11 (95) Ess 5.7 (37); **Second Semi-final** Carl 6.17 (53) S. Melb 10.5 (65); **Final** S. Melb 6.8 (44) Coll 8.7 (55); **Grand Final** Carl 6.11 (47) Coll 9.7 (61)

Ladder:	W	L	D	%	pts
Carl	15	3	-	160.1	60
Coll	13	5	-	122.3	52
S. Melb	12	6	-	122.2	48
Ess	12	6	-	115.6	48
Geel	10	7	1	105.9	42
Univ	10	8	-	101.5	40
Rich	7	10	1	102.6	30
Fitz	5	13	-	90.8	20
Melb	4	14	-	59.5	16
St K	1	17	-	62.3	4

What it's all about. A memoir of the Magpies' great Premiership win.

Not without pain. A Collingwood casualty is removed from the scene.

Cordners give Profs chance at finals

July 2. University today reached the pinnacle of their success in the Victorian Football League so far when they defeated Geelong at the EMCG 8.13 (61) to 5.8 (38).

The only note of caution to be sounded here is that they have lost to League powerhouses Carlton, Collingwood and South Melbourne, and will have to step up a notch to reach the Finals.

Principal architects of The Professors' success are the medical doctors Harry and Edward Cordner, and slick Martin Ratz.

University's best win of the season was the battle of the co-tenants at the EMCG a fortnight ago, when they downed Essendon 11.9 (75) to 8.9 (57) (→ 15/4/11).

The University's proud colours.

Bribery scandal hits League

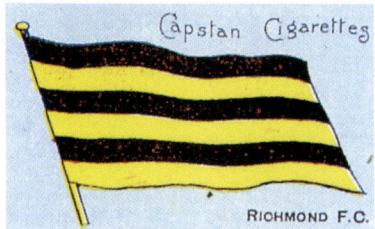

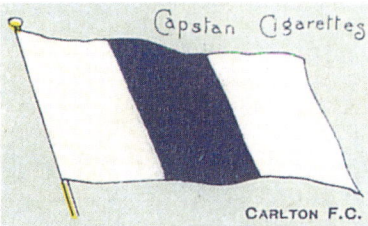

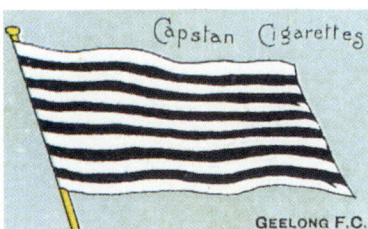

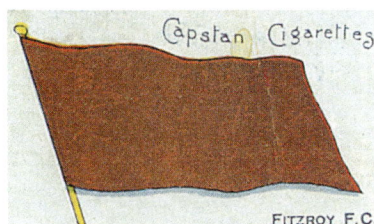

Sept. 30. The VFL inquiry into allegations that certain players were paid to play 'dead' has ended.

The Carlton players accused were not selected in the team which lost the second Semi-final to South Melbourne a fortnight ago.

They are Doug Gillespie, fullback in the 1906 and 1907 Premiership wins, who is famous for having been picked up by coach Jack Worrall after booting a ball back over the fence at training.

Also accused are rover Alex 'Bongo' Lang who played in the 1906-08 Flag wins and was the *Australasian's* Player of the Year last season, and first year player Doug Fraser.

Carlton's own inquiry has exonerated Gillespie, but the two others were subject of a closed door investigation by the League.

Lang and Fraser have now been suspended for five years.

This scandal comes hard on the heels of the player rebellion and the removal of coach and Secretary Jack Worrall at the end of last season, the defection of four players to North Melbourne, and the recent suspension of George Topping for two years on a striking charge.

It is quite remarkable that Carlton are to contest tomorrow's Grand Final against Collingwood, their fifth in a row.

Allegations that 'it is well known that there was more than one Carlton "stiff'un" in the final last season' were again raised in a letter to *The Age* last week.

This game was against South Melbourne, as was the match involving the five Fitzroy players allegedly offered £5 'to go dead'.

These charges were found not to be proved, as the players concerned treated the offer from a 'red headed

It seems the stench of illegal betting has invaded the football field.

man in the fish market'as a joke.

In another match South rover Alex 'Bubs' Kerr was supposed to have said to Melbourne's Harry Brereton words to the effect that 'You need not play so hard. Why don't you pull out of it?' but not to have made an offer. Asked whether he followed this advice Brereton said 'No, I kicked a goal'.

Illegal betting on football is conducted on a large scale, according to 'Follower' in *The Age*, and that everyone knows who and how, except, apparently, the police.

'Follower' warns that 'Rumours

of crooked play may be unfounded in some cases or exaggerated in others, but the fact remains that public suspicion concerning the bona fides of the game is increasing.

'It is the duty of the responsible controllers of football to allay that suspicion as promptly and effectually as possible.'

Otherwise football might go the way of cycle racing where 'the public became aware that they had been bestowing their patronage and enthusiasm on a thing that was a fraud', which signed the 'death warrant of cycle race meetings'.

1911

April 15. The University Football Club will be co-tenants with Melbourne at the Melbourne Cricket Ground this year (→ 19/9/14).

April 21. Arthur 'Shooter' Ford is alleged to be still acting as Secretary of the Carlton Football Club despite last year's disqualification.

April 21. A motion at a VFL meeting to rescind Rule 29, suspending players who receive payment, amended to allow a maximum of 30 shillings per week – and then lost (→ 15/5).

May 27. Joint conference of representatives of VFL and VFA recommends amalgamation of the two bodies from July 2 this year.

June 9. The VFL decides to drop amalgamation proposals with the VFA and instead agrees to 'advisory board' to discuss matters of common interest (→ 18/4/14).

June 17. South Melbourne, second on the ladder, defeat the formerly unbowed Essendon 6.8 (44) to 5.11 (41) after a titanic struggle in the slush of the Southerners' home lagoon.

June 23. The VFA has introduced a scheme to share profits with the players.

June 24. The League defers the question of whether to grant appeals for clemency from two players to mark the Coronation of George V. Many delegates deride the proposal.

July 15. Former Essendon player James Martin convicted in Court of Petty Sessions for assaulting Fitzroy player George Holden in a match.

July 29. Essendon centreman William Sewart leaves the ground to change his knickers. Geelong fail to take advantage of Essendon playing one short and lose 9.7 (61) to 4.11 (35).

Aug. 5. The Second Australian Football Carnival is staged in Adelaide. Victoria beat WA, Tasmania and NSW, but lose the championship when beaten by SA 11.11 (77) to 5.4 (34).

Sept. 3. For the third successive year the finalists are the same – Carlton, Collingwood, South Melbourne and Essendon.

Debuts
Roy Cazaly (St K)
Danny Minogue (Coll)
Mark Tandy (S. Melb)

Retirements
Vince Coutie (Melb
Fred 'Pompey' Elliott (Carl)

Collingwood players look on with pride as hopes of another great season go up with the Premiership Flag.

Shamateurism ended: League approves player payment

May 15. After years of shillyshallying, the VFL has ended the sham of amateurism.

Players have been entitled to receive reimbursement for expenses, but the rule now deleted has been that 'any player receiving remuneration for playing, either directly or indirectly, shall be disqualified', and that clubs paying their players 'shall be dealt with'.

The result of this rule has been a situation where many players have been paid 'under the lap' by clubs or by supporters of the club.

'Follower' in *The Age* says 'What the ultimate result may be remains to be seen, but it is at least gratifying to know that secretaries, treasurers and committeemen will no longer have to experience the degradation of cooking balance sheets in order to disguise the fact that they have been wilfully abrogating a rule of their own making and which they were pretending to observe'.

Payment of players can now be conducted in the open, with the value a matter of negotiation between player and Committee. Any player preferring to be amateur – as many do – will be free to do so (→ 9/6).

The end of the backhander comes with the new rules on player payments.

Jack Worrall comes back to Essendon coaching position

May 20. The masterly coaching hand of John Worrall was seen today as his new team, Essendon, had an overwhelming win over Collingwood 21.12 (138) to 7.11 (53).

The Dons have now breezed through three games after a drawn first match, and are already considered favourites for the Flag.

The former Carlton coach, winner of three Premiership Flags, inherited a great team of players at Essendon and has concentrated on keeping them fresh and keen to play through the long season ahead.

He has also worked on passing and teamwork, to the point that they ran rings around the sluggish-looking Collingwood side and kept up a blistering pace.

They kicked 12 goals straight during the third and final quarters.

Collingwood suffered from being without their full-forward Dick Lee, but they were slower all over the field and seemed lacking in skill. However, they may have a Premiership hangover (→ 23/9/11).

The badge of the 'Same Olds'.

Horse puts player on the injury list

June 17. Fitzroy back and policeman Bill Marchbank was refused leave to play against Richmond today, instead being assigned as mounted constable to the South Melbourne and Essendon game.

As South passed Essendon's score, a crescendo of noise caused Marchbank's horse to rear and throw him against the iron fence – fracturing his knee.

A sympathetic barracker said: 'That's a cow of a horse to do a thing like that'. South Melbourne won the game 6.8 (44) to 5.11 (41).

Rules in USA

Feb. 19. America had its introduction to Australian football when Harry Bromley bounced a Sherrin on the east coast.

Mr Bromley, who is representing Australian football in America has been busy discussing the game with sporting folk in that country. He has also witnessed games of American football and interviewed several of their leading players.

Mr Bromley found the quality of the Sherrin superior to that of the American variety.

Martin Gotz appeals against on field assault conviction

Aug. 29. The case of Martin Gotz has dragged itself out of the courts, leaving the Carlton player free of conviction for an on-field assault on Victor Trood of University.

In a match on May 20 there were reports of a brutal assault on Trood by an unnamed Carlton player, but there was no report by the umpire.

Soon afterwards University wrote to the Carlton Committee saying that they would refuse to play in the return match on July 15, unless 'certain players' were omitted from the Carlton team.

The Carlton Secretary, Mr Arthur C. Ford, responded that he did not know what to do with the letter as no players had been named. He added that football was not a child's game and some hard knocks were unavoidable.

The answer on 'names' was soon forthcoming. By the Thursday after the match University had arranged to issue a summons for assault.

Within a month Gotz was convicted of assault by the Melbourne District Court and fined £10, with £5/5/- costs. However, at the appeal, in which some witnesses said they saw Gotz strike Trood and some others said that Gotz was nowhere near the incident, the conviction was quashed.

The 'Herald's' view of players being hauled into court for on-field incidents.

The St Kilda Committee suspends players, loses games

Aug. 8. Turmoil continues at St Kilda with most of its senior players on strike against the club Committee.

Thus, a depleted St Kilda side, fielding only seven regular senior players, were thrashed by Essendon 23.20 (158) to 5.8 (38). So dominant were Essendon that for them the match was rarely more than a practice run, although at times their strike-stricken opponents displayed signs of spirit as well as skill.

Indications are that the dispute at St Kilda will not be resolved until the election of office-bearers at the annual general meeting. Saturday's display served only to further emphasise the club's impotence on the playing field as long as this stand-off continues. St Kilda has dropped to second last.

One positive sign for St Kilda is the form of younger players like Roy Cazaly who will make up the future of the club (→ 26/7/13).

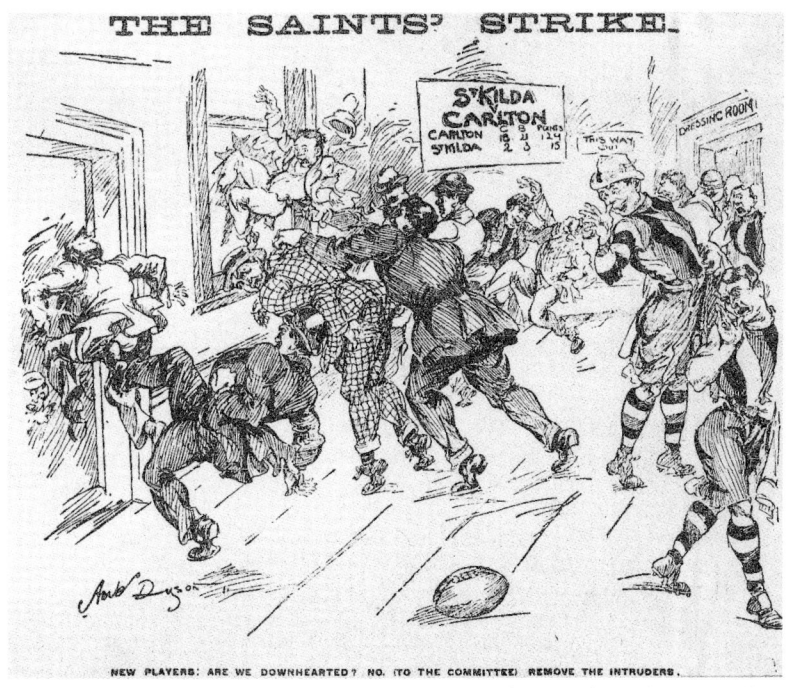

St Kilda's baby brigade show their spirit, despite the crippling players' strike.

Manly Vince Coutie accepts big purse

Sept. 2. Veteran Melbourne captain Vince Coutie was chaired from the ground today, after his last game for the Red Legs which they lost to Carlton 9.8 (62) to 8.6 (54)

Coutie was captain in 1907 and again in the past two seasons, and was Melbourne's leading goalkicker in 1903, 1904 and 1908.

He kicked eight goals against Geelong in 1904, and another bag of eight against St Kilda in 1908. Since 1902 he has played 152 games.

Coutie was married in June and after this season's home match against Geelong he and his wife were presented with a purse of 50 sovereigns, subscribed by the club and his supporters.

After testimony from all and sundry as to the worth of Coutie, he responded, in his typical way, with a few brief but manly sentences.

Croweaters turn on waterworks at Carnival

An invitation to the Carnival.

Aug 20. South Australia has put its stamp on the interstate football scene, handing out a huge drubbing to the fancied state, Victoria, 11.11 (77) to 5.4 (34).

The climactic game of the Carnival for teams from all over Australia this weekend was an added humiliation for Victoria, as the match was played in the wet conditions so prevalent in a Melbourne winter.

The Adelaide Oval was so dry during the week that the curator poured 250,000 gallons on to the ground to soften it on the evening before the match. Unfortunately it then rained for three solid hours.

South Australia's win suggests that they take these interstate matches more seriously, and their players train together for some time. Victoria's players looked as if they hardly knew each other.

The interstate Carnival opened in perfect weather in front of a crowd of 20,000, which included the Premier, Mr J. Verran, who hailed football as the means of keeping hundreds of young fellows away from liquor during the winter.

Two matches were played on the first day. Victoria disposed of Tasmania, 8.22 (70) to 6.3 (39), having kicked 4.6 to nil in the first term.

The second game of the day saw South Australia demolish Western Australia 13.18 (96) to 3.5 (23). In a one sided-affair, the home state had too much skill in the air and speed for the visitors from the West who battled gallantly until they lost heart in the second half.

The performance by the South Australians was appreciated by the vociferous local supporters who crowded the ground.

The Carnival programme.

Gardiner blooms as Carlton goalkicker

Gardiner (left): freakish forward.

July 29. Carlton full-forward Vin Gardiner kicked a freakish ten goals 11 behinds in the Blues' romp over strike-depleted St Kilda at Princes Park.

This was the first double digit score by a Blue, beating 'Silver' Caine's eight in 1907.

Carlton beat the hapless Saints 18.21 (129) to 2.3 (15).

Younger brother of Jack Gardiner, Vin moved the opposite way to him, and crossed from Melbourne to Carlton in 1907, and played in the 1908 Premiership.

Worrall flies Same Old Flag again

Sept. 23. Essendon only just held on to beat an extremely combative Collingwood and take the Premiership Flag in today's Grand Final. Essendon won 5.11 (41) to 4.11 (35).

Collingwood had their chances and there were grumbles about rover Tom Baxter, who twice kicked into the man on his mark, when shooting for goal at the end.

Essendon have had a mixed season, with a brilliant start and then some patchy efforts. South Melbourne emerged as the strong team in the League, while Collingwood have had to lift after a bad start.

Collingwood surprised in the first Semi-final to knock out South, 11.11 (77) to 6.11 (47).

John Worrall had the satisfaction in the second Semi-final of coaching Essendon to a comfortable win, 9.15 (69) to 6.12 (48), over Carlton, the team he took to three Flags.

This win seemed to instill in the Dons the confidence to go on and grasp the Flag.

Essendon's centreline of Sewart, O'Shea and Chalmers was on top all day, while Baring and Walker were strong in the ruck and Armstrong and Kirby did well up forward.

Collingwood was well served by Sharp at halfback, McHale in the centre, and Ted Rowell, the best forward in the game. Collingwood lost forward hope, captain Dick Lee, with a leg injury.

The Essendon and Collingwood ruckmen compete for the knockout.

1911 Statistics

Leading Goalkicker:
Vin Gardiner (Carl) 47
Champion of Season:
Bruce R. Sloss (S. Melb)
Finals:
First Semi-final S. Melb 6.11 (47) Coll 11.11 (77); **Second Semi-final** Ess 9.15 (69) Carl 6.12 (48); **Grand Final** Ess 5.11 (41) Coll 4.11 (35)

Ladder:	W	L	D	%	pts
Ess	15	2	1	177.5	62
S. Melb	13	4	1	140.4	54
Carl	12	4	2	142.0	52
Coll	12	6	-	124.4	48
Fitz	10	8	-	113.6	40
Geel	8	9	1	99.9	34
Melb	7	10	1	98.6	30
Rich	7	11	-	91.2	28
St K	2	16	-	48.2	8
Univ	1	17	-	52.1	4

1912

April 20. Club season tickets, which allow admittance to all Finals, introduced by the League.

April 27. Harry O'Bern, a goal umpire since the League's formation in 1897, announces his retirement.

April 27. Mrs W. Crichton, wife of the Essendon President, unfurls the 1911 Premiership Flag before the game against University at the EMCG. Essendon win 17.14 (116) to 6.6.(42).

June 22. Calls for an umpires' instructor, for training and consistency in interpretation between umpires.

July 27. Collingwood defeat Richmond 'The Wasps' 10.15 (75) to 6.4 (40), despite a hollow in the Punt Road ground which has become a bog.

Aug. 10. The League's balloting method of selecting umpires for matches has led to one club having the same umpire six times this season.

Aug. 10. South Australia again defeat Victoria at the Adelaide Oval 9.8 (62) to 6.7 (43). Other composite League teams beat Ballarat and Bendigo at South Melbourne double-header.

Aug. 31. Clubs call for an independent body to hear allegations of foul play and dispense penalties.

Sept. 21. Ern 'Ginger' Cameron breaks his shinbone in Essendon's Final win over Carlton. Essendon, with 17 men, win 7.10 (52) to 6.12 (48) before a huge crowd of 47,356 (→ 12/10/12).

Oct. 4. The journal Sport complains that, despite Essendon fullback Bill Griffith landing the ball in the centre with every drop kick in the Grand Final, this form of kick is 'becoming something of a lost art'.

Oct. 12. Jack Worrall applauds the VFL Final system which produces a Grand Final, as long as the 'Minor Premier' has a double chance. 'The League is a public entertainer and it is its bounden duty to cater for the public.'

Debuts
Jim Freake (Fitz)
Roy Park (Univ)

Retirements
Bill Busbridge (Ess)
Ern 'Ginger' Cameron (Ess)
Norman 'Hackenschmidt' Clark (Carl)

New football publication solves all match day mysteries

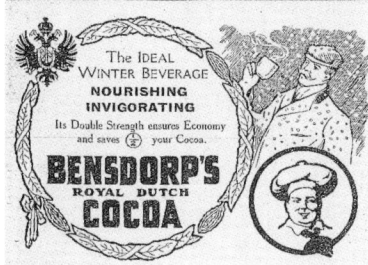

On the cover of the 'Record'.

April 27. The first issue of *The Football Record* was published today. The journal is under the patronage of the Victorian Football League and will sell at all the League grounds on match days.

One of its most interesting features will be the exclusive publication of player numbers each week. There will also be diagrams of the football fields with the players' names in their positions.

The motto of the *Record* is 'fair play is bonnie play'. The news it carries 'will be up to date, and presented in a smart crisp fashion that cannot fail to meet with the approbation of readers'.

'Read the *Record* regularly', it asks, 'and so obtain a respite from the week's worry of business. Carry the glad tidings home and read them aloud to mother.'

The Football Record.
"Fair play is bonnie play."

OURSELVES.

In producing the "Record" the proprietor approaches the task with a feeling of confidence that the public will appreciate his efforts to keep it posted with every point of interest in the football world.

The "Record" will fill the bill in this respect. Its news will be up-to-date, and presented in a smart, crisp fashion, that cannot fail to meet with the approbation of readers. No effort will be spared in obtaining for the general information matter of value. The chief aim will be to give our readers the very latest items of intelligence, and in all that will be published the motto of the "Record" will be observed, and that is "Fair Play is Bonnie Play."

While the "Record" will be widely read on the football grounds it will possess features that will lead to the preservation of each number, and consequently the little publication will go into the home—a recommendation which of itself will appeal to Advertisers.

A special feature of the "Record" will be the diagrams of the football field, with the picked teams for each Saturday's match, in the positions they will occupy at the commencement of their respective games; and, in addition, photographs of leading exponents of the game will be published weekly.

All about the 'Football Record'.

McHale appointed playing coach

April 27. Jock McHale, has been appointed playing-coach of Collingwood. The brilliant centreman, now in his ninth year with Collingwood replaces George Angus, who last season narrowly failed to win back-to-back Premierships for the club.

McHale had his first taste of coaching as assistant to Angus. As a player there are few better at reading the game and assessing the opposition than McHale, whose qualities of leadership and self-discipline are highly regarded (19/05/23).

Football stewards to curb rough play

April 27. As a result of the increasing violence on the football field, and the inability of one umpire to be everywhere and see everything on the field of play, the League has decided to appoint two Stewards to each match.

The Stewards will have the power to report incidents of over-rough play and each be paid 30 shillings.

They will be on patrol on the ground, wear all-white uniforms, with the word 'Steward' in red on their breast.

Rugby and Rules union discussed

April 26. The Victorian Football League has entertained the New South Wales rugby team on its way home from touring England, and again there have been discussions on whether there can be a new game adapted from the two codes.

An article in *Sport* suggests that if the off-side rule of rugby was abandoned, and the Australian game gave up bouncing the ball, were able to throw it and introduced a bar on the goalposts a whole new game might emerge.

The Cobb and Co. coach is doing a good trade taking passengers from the station to Corio Oval.

Rowell's game down the drain

May 4. Collingwood legend Ted Rowell added to his reputation for unusual feats on the football field when, in the game against Essendon, he caught his foot in a drainpipe, was unable to extricate it, and was mortified to see his opponent pick up the ball and goal. Essendon won 10.10 (70) to 6.17 (53).

Barrackers recalled that last year, at half time against Fitzroy, Rowell ran the world 100-yard champion Jack Donaldson to within inches off eight yards – then played the rest of the game brilliantly as usual.

Too few sent to play South Australia

Aug. 8. Victorian selectors have been ridiculed by the press for their niggardly action in sending only 18 players to Adelaide. Not surprisingly, the state team were beaten by South Australia, 9.8 (62) to 6.7 (43).

Worse still, while they were mean about the players, they found the wherewithal to send four delegates to witness the game.

Such attitudes are seen as diminishing the importance of interstate games and Victoria's football status. The selectors appear to have turned a honour into a perquisite.

Dons peak to win back-to-back Flag

Oct. 4. Unfancied Essendon beat favourites South Melbourne by 14 points today, to record their second Premiership in a row.

The victory was a tribute to their controversial coach, Jack Worrall. Essendon's form coming into the Finals had not been good, but the old master had them in top shape.

South, on the other hand, had left their good form behind them and were never really in the game. Only poor kicking for goal by Essendon kept the scores close.

The record crowd of 54,463 at the Melbourne Cricket Ground – the biggest crowd to attend a sporting event in Australia – witnessed a dour, rather than brilliant, game.

After an even first quarter, Essendon soon asserted their superiority with their small men dominating the packs and opening up the game. South looked slow, tired and awkward and lacked a reliable mark up forward, while their defence played without much system or cohesion. It seemed they had spent their force getting to the Grand Final and had run out of inspiration.

Essendon went to an 11-point lead at half time. South had no answer to the swift-flowing Dons, and when South did go forward, the Essendon backmen were virtually impassable.

Essendon maintained its superiority in the third quarter and should have put the result beyond doubt, but for stray kicking for goal. Although they had only scored four goals from 18 scoring shots, Essendon went into the final quarter 20 points in front.

With the strong wind at their backs, South still believed they had a chance and massed their players on the forward line. The tactic only served to crowd the play and help Essendon to hold the lead.

South made a brief rally in the last quarter to kick two quick goals, but then the Essendon defence held firm. The game was sewn up with a brilliant piece of individual play by Essendon when their centreman, Bill Sewart, sent a 60-yard drop kick to Fred Baring near the centre of the ground. Baring set off for the goal dodging three defenders – the last one by knocking the ball over his head – and running into the goal square to score. Final scores: Essendon 5.17 (47) defeated South Melbourne 4.9 (33) (→13/10/21).

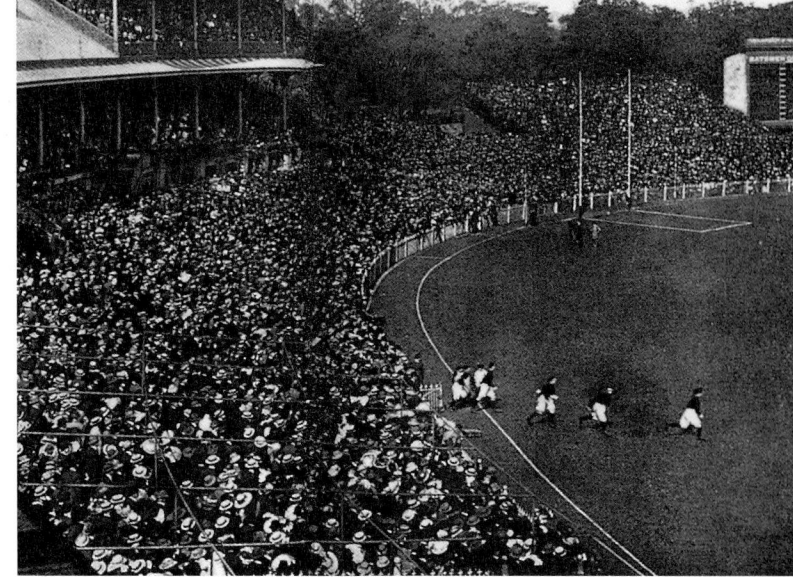

The magnificent scene as a record crowd attends the Grand Final match.

1912 Statistics

Leading Goalkicker:
Harry Brereton (Melb) 56
Champion of Season:
Ernie J. Cameron (Ess)
Finals: First Semi-final Carl 10.11 (71) Geel 4.19 (43); **Second Semifinal** S. Melb 6.6 (42) Ess 7.12 (54); **Final** Ess 7.10 (52) Carl 6.12 (48); **Grand Final** S. Melb 4.9 (33) Ess 5.17 (47)

Ladder:	W	L	%	pts
S. Melb	14	4	157.0	56
Carl	14	4	131.2	56
Ess	12	6	114.9	48
Geel	11	7	126.7	44
Fitz	10	8	108.5	40
Melb	9	9	98.9	36
Coll	9	9	91.7	36
St K	7	11	100.4	28
Rich	3	15	64.7	12
Univ	1	17	57.0	4

Dave McNamara has been having a football feast since he transferred from St Kilda during the players' dispute with the Committee last year. He has kicked 107 goals for the season for the Association club, Essendon, including an amazing 18 goals in one match from centre half-forward.

Ginger Cameron season's hot player

Ernie Cameron: fast and clever.

Oct. 12. Essendon's Ernie 'Ginger' Cameron has received the palm from the *Australasian* as the player of the year. The award may be some compensation for the gallant Essendon rover who broke his leg in the dying minutes of the Preliminary Final against Carlton and was unable to play in the winning Grand Final team.

The *Australasian's* football commentator John Worrall, who also happens to be Essendon coach, said that there could be no question among all fair-minded judges of the game that Cameron was the player of the season.

Worrall said: 'His great strength is his versatility, being equally at home in any part of the field.'

Cameron, who is noted for his speed, clever play and quick, accurate kicking, began playing for the Dons in 1905 at the age of 16.

In the game against South Australia this year it was obvious that the SA ruckmen were so conscious of his ability that their sole aim was to palm the ball away from him, rather than look for their own rovers.

Cameron won the admiration of football followers in the final. Lying on the ground with a broken leg he urged his team-mates on and refused to be carried from the field until the siren sounded.

Jack Worrall first King of Coaches

John Worrall, the super coach, is in the back row, flanked by players of Carlton's 1906 Premiership team.

John Worrall as player, coach and football writer was one of the most influential voices in Australian football from the 1880s through to the 1920s at three clubs, and in the pages of the weekly paper the *Australasian*.

Worrall, known universally as Jack, was born at Chinaman's Flat near Maryborough, Victoria, on 21 June 1861.

As a promising footballer in the strong Ballarat competition he was 'induced' by the Fitzroy Secretary to come to Melbourne to look after 'business interests' and play for the Maroons in 1884 under the captaincy of Paddy McShane. It seems likely that Worrall was being paid to play football, and perhaps cricket as well. His twin skills were soon well evident to McShane.

McShane played three cricket Tests for Australia between 1884 and 1888, and Worrall eventually played 11, between 1885 and 1889, with a batting average of 25. He played 65 matches for Victoria and had one innings of 417 for Carlton, then an Australian record.

Worrall captained Fitzroy for seven seasons until 1892. He was Champion of the Colony in 1887

and 1890. *The Leader* described him in 1890 as 'A veritable wonder whose remarkable kicking is only equalled by his dexterity in securing opportunities'.

He was appointed Secretary-manager of Carlton Football Club in 1902 – becoming the first official coach of a VFL team.

He set about recruiting fast big men from the bush, and instituted training, famously 'donning football togs' to conduct it.

Under Worrall's methods, Carlton rose to third in 1903, then a hat trick of Premierships in 1906, 1907 and 1908.

His fair-mindedness, rigorousness and straight talking sometimes got him into trouble.

In England in 1902 Worrall was alleged to have said that Australian bowlers Monty Noble and J.V. Saunders were 'chuckers', which copped him a ban from the Victorian Cricket Association.

And in 1904 Worrall was in hot water at Carlton when he paid some match receipts into the club via his own cheque account. It took a player revolt to prevent him being sacked – it never seemed to occur to him that this form of accounting could be seen

as a problem.

Nor could he see that by 1909 his rigorous management and coaching style would lead to another players' revolt – this time against him.

Worrall resigned when accused of slack training methods, but really over his dropping of players who had refused to play unless they were paid more.

1910 saw him briefly appointed VFL umpires instructor; he had strong views on the standards required of the men in white.

In 1911 he became coach of Essendon, and had immediate success, winning the Premiership.

'Follower' in *The Age* said 'The victory of Essendon emphasises very strongly the previously well-demonstrated fact that any team enjoying the benefit of J. Worrall's instruction and coaching has an immense advantage over all its rivals'.

The 'Same Old' won the Flag again in 1912. Worrall had won five Flags in five seasons.

He continued after Essendon's wartime recess, retiring at the end of 1920, and took up more regular writing on football and cricket in the *Australasian*. John Worrall died in 1937 (→ 16/6/92).

1913

April 26. The VFL has formed an independent tribunal to hear complaints against players, on the motion of Carlton delegate Mr Kennedy (→18/6/29).

May 3. Collingwood, the only team to win their first two matches, head the ladder.

July 5. The VFL decides to send only six, rather than 10, teams into the country for educative purposes, for want of sufficient funds. At the same time it votes £5 for each of 19 League delegates to accompany the interstate team to Adelaide.

July 12. Victoria defeat South Australia 10.9 (69) to 7.15 (57) in Adelaide.

July 26. Season surprise packet St Kilda's run of success continues with a win over Melbourne 9.17 (71) to 5.5 (35) (→9/8).

July 26. Stewards come in for criticism after the wrongful reporting of Essendon ruckman William Walker in the Dons' 4.12 (36) to 7.12 (54) loss to Fitzroy. Stewards are said to be continually nagging players for information, rather than trusting their eyesight.

July 30. The League says it is unable to agree to the proposal to play a benefit match against the VFA at the end of the season. Proceeds were to be for travelling scholarships for military cadets.

Aug. 9. St Kilda, enjoying unprecedented support this season, decide to build a new grandstand to cope with the crowds.→

Aug. 16. Victoria easily win the return match against SA at the MCG 16.12 (108) to 6.17 (53). SA Captain Richard Head plays 'brainily' in defeat.

Aug. 23. Fitzroy lose their Premiership pennants in a fire which destroys half the cricket pavilion at Brunswick Street.

Aug. 23. Revealed that the VFL and South Australian League met informally after the recent game to discuss alterations in the laws of the game.

Aug. 23. Worrall in the *Australasian* suggests abolishing behinds and awarding three points for a goal.

Debut
Paddy O'Brien (Carl)

Retirements
George Bruce (Carl)
George Morrissey (St K)
A.M. 'Joe' Pearce (Melb)

Saints supporters enjoy a heavenly start to season

June 30. As the season nears the half-way mark, perennial wooden-spooners St Kilda finally look like fulfilling the promise that internal conflict and lack of discipline has denied them for so long.

The Committee has built on the progress made last season and assembled a talented team.

They have already downed a top team in Fitzroy along with some less competitive sides, like University and Melbourne, and are now bidding for a place in the Final Four.

Although still unable to secure the transfer of Dave McNamara back from the VFA, they have, in Vic Cumberland, Ernie Sellars and Billy Schmidt, players of strength and brilliance. At last the long-suffering St Kilda supporters may have something to cheer about (→17/4/15).

St Kilda's one-point win over Carlton in round 15 had the crowd gasping.

Maroons and Pies back in business

Dick Lee (left), a face in the crowd.

April 26. Fitzroy and Collingwood, after missing the Final Four last year, have worked hard during the off-season to ensure that they will again be Premiership contenders.

Fitzroy have gained the services of North Fremantle's best player, forward flanker Jim Toohey. He is noted for his low, accurate passing. Ted Buist and George Holden have returned in the quest for glory.

Collingwood, with the ever reliable centreman Jock McHale as captain-coach, will have Percy Wilson back from injury. They have added Alan Cordner from Geelong to their squad for today's opening match against Melbourne.

Chucking throws critics off game

July 12. Umpires have been turning a blind eye to players 'chucking' the ball to such an extent that the throw is almost universally employed by some teams.

Those who still, on instruction from their coaches, follow the letter of the law are now beginning to be disadvantaged by the lawbreakers.

The law says: 'Throwing the ball is strictly prohibited. Where there is any doubt that the ball has been handballed fairly it must be considered a throw, and the free mark awarded accordingly.'

Most umpires seem to be ignoring this dictate, and crowds and players alike are becoming bewildered and angry over the inconsistencies.

Essendon coach John Worrall says that in recent games he has seen players throwing the ball over their shoulders with both hands, with the umpire looking on. On two occasions he saw goals resulting from the action, with the umpire watching imperturbably.

He describes the situation as a 'scandal', with the side that obeys the law becoming seriously handicapped and becoming obliged to break the law as well.

The question is now before the VFL. Has it allowed umpires to allow the throw as a prelude to legitmising it in the rules? Or will it heed the criticisms and instruct umpires to crack down on the 'chuckers'?

Fuchsias revolting

May 17. The Melbourne President, Dr W.C. McClelland, had to order some of his senior players on to the football field to play Fitzroy today.

The striking players are angry that the club did not support a player, as yet unidentified, when he was charged by police with hitting a Carlton player last week. Dr McClelland found them untogged and said: 'Unless you fellows come to your senses you will never play League football again.' The strike was quickly over and Fitzroy won, 7.11 (53) to 4.7 (31).

Long and short of League players

Sept. 13. Fitzroy and Collingwood, who played a Semi-final today, were almost evenly matched in height and weight. The Fitzroy team averaged just under 5ft 9 1/2in in height, while Collingwood were just over 5ft 9in. The Fitzroy combination averaged 11 stone 3 pounds in weight, while the Collingwood players were only two pounds less.

Allowing for the factor that the ruckmen in each side are big and heavy men of around 6ft and 13 to 14 stone, and allowing that the rovers and wings of each side may be as small as 5ft 5in and weigh as little as 8 stone, the heights and weights of the 'standard' players in the team – the forwards and backs – are around 5ft 8in and 10 stone.

The Collingwood combination looked bigger and stronger than the Fitzroy men, no doubt helped by the vertically striped uniform, but it did not help their cause. Fitzroy had a wonderful third quarter and won the game easily, 11. 14 (80) to 6.7 (43).

The Collingwood faithful were dominant in the crowd of 43,500 at the Melbourne Cricket Ground. They were hoping that a Final would bring them back to form, but the display was as indifferent as in the past few matches.

Park kicks goals in Profs' losing scores

Sept. 30. If there were more student players like Roy Park, University would be a force in the League, rather than the chopping block. They would not have gone two seasons without a win.

Although only nine stone, Park, a medical student, kicked 53 goals to be the leading goalkicker at the end of the home-and-away games. Only Jim Freake's goals for Fitzroy in the Finals stopped Park winning the year's goalkicking honours.

Park's endeavours are even more commendable considering that University kicked a total of only 115 goals all season and finished in last place on the ladder.

For this goal-sneak, however, the season has not been a total waste, as he was selected at full-forward in the state side (→ 7/8/15).

Saints fall just short of Pearly Gates

Drama in the goal square during the exciting Premiership game between St Kilda and Fitzroy.

Sept. 27. Fitzroy denied St Kilda its first Premiership today when they defeated the gallant Saints by 13 points.

In perfect conditions at the MCG, Fitzroy, after leading all day, withstood a late rally by St Kilda to take out the Premiership.

After seeming well beaten just after the final break, the Saints got within one point late in the game when George Morrissey kicked their fifth goal. Then Des Baird marked in the goal square. With players of both teams milling around him and the crowd of 54,479 in full voice, Baird handpassed to Morrissey who scored only a point.

The miss seemed to deflate St Kilda, and Fitzroy swept forward to kick two late goals and wrap up the Final. The Maroons are worthy champions, having headed the competition for most of the year. Their vigorous play proved too forceful for the Saints on the day.

Were it not for some wayward kicking by St Kilda, they would now be enjoying the romance of winning their first Flag and bringing rapture to their supporters. Final scores: Fitzroy 7.14 56) defeated St Kilda 5.13 (43) (→ 2/9/16).

1913 Statistics

Leading Goalkicker:
J. Freake (Fitz) 56
Champion of Season:
Vic Cumberland (St K)
Finals:
First Semi-final S. Melb 6.15 (51) St K 12.12 (84); **Second Semi-final** Fitz 11.14 (80) Coll 6.7 (43); **Final** Fitz 6.9 (45) St K 10.10 (70); **Grand Final** Fitz 7.14 (56) St K 5.13 (43)

Ladder:	W	L	D	%	pts
Fitz	16	2	-	144.3	64
S. Melb	14	3	1	128.6	58
Coll	13	5	-	117.7	52
St K	11	7	-	106.3	44
Geel	10	8	-	124.4	40
Carl	9	8	1	100.9	38
Rich	6	12	-	94.9	24
Ess	6	12	-	93.4	24
Melb	4	14	-	71.4	16
Univ	0	18	-	57.6	0

Sport or war? Trouble looming in Europe is taking eyes off the ball.

1914

Prime Minister sees a shame of a game at Punt Road Oval

June 6. Richmond's pride at the opening of a new grandstand by the Prime Minister turned to shame today as they lost the match, and their tempers, against South Melbourne.

The game got out of hand early when Umpire Davies, controlling his first League game, was hit on the head by a stone. From then on his nerves seemed shot, and players began to dictate to him. They also began to charge at each other like bulls, and hit each other openly.

Richmond were getting the worst of the game and running riot in an attempt to square off supposed injustices. At the last change Committeemen R.T. Kelly of Richmond and L.M. Thomson of South Melbourne went to their players and told them to play like men and not bring the game into disrepute.

What Prime Minister Andrew Fisher, a Queenslander, thought of all this is unrecorded (→ 8/5/20).

The umpiring incident at Richmond sparked this suggestion in the 'Herald'.

Belt from Belcher

July 25. The Essendon captain Alan Belcher, a vigorous but fair ruckman, has been brought undone by a spectator.

In an extraordinary scene in the match against South Melbourne a spectator ran on to the ground, unnoticed by the players.

He hit Belcher behind the ear, and the startled ruckman turned round, chased him and struck him. He has been reported for unseemly play. Essendon beat South 15.14 (104) to 4.8 (32) (→ 12/6/19).

Cumberland gets the chocolates.

Dick Lee the highest flying Magpie

July 18. Collingwood's goalkicking hero Dick Lee wrote his name into the record book with 11 goals today in Collingwood's 15.13 (103) win over University 3.5 (23.)

This equalled Jim McShane's VFL record total in the infamous 161-point win over St Kilda in 1899.

Although Lee was 'fed', his kicking and marking were exceptional in the slimy and treacherous conditions. He kicked seven goals after half time, which was the whole of Collingwood's goals score.

As usual the crowd was shouting 'Dick – Dick Dick – eeee' in a crescendo as he rose high to take one of his impossible marks.

One of them no doubt was the small boy overheard when the Coronation honours list was announced in 1911 saying, 'Wot! Dick Lee not knighted?' He is already King of Collingwood (→ 12/6/15).

Another great mark by Collingwood's acrobatic full-forward Dick Lee.

McNamara, Victoria kick goals at Carnival

Aug. 15. Long distance kicker Dave McNamara not only starred in Victoria's great wins in the Carnival at the Sydney Cricket Ground, but also upheld the honour of the Australian game in a head-to-head kicking contest with the jewel of rugby's crown, 'Dally' Messenger.

McNamara, who has been known to kick over 90 yards, easily won the place kicking competition, with a kick of 67 yards, 8 inches, and later kicked 76 yards, 8 inches.

Dally Messenger, who crossed to Rugby League from Union seven years ago and captains New South Wales and Australia, kicked well but not as far.

When it came to accuracy it was a different matter, with Messenger easily winning a goalkicking contest from H. Limb of Western Australia.

McNamara captained the Victorian side which defeated South Australia in a final Carnival match, 11.11 (77) to 5.10 (40). The match was watched by a small crowd.

Victoria thus regained top football perch from the Croweaters who had won the last Carnival.

Poor crowds saw rich football and a leap in standard in the play of Victoria, SA and WA. Victoria booted 29.14 (188) against hapless Queensland's 12.18 (90) with every Victorian player goaling.

The Carnival has been a football success, but it has held little interest for the people of Sydney. Victorian officials say that receipts have been only half of expenditure (→ 25/5/18).

Dave McNamara's long place kicking came from a classic style with a strong take-away and massive follow through.

Critic slams umpires and stewards

Aug. 29. John Worrall, writing in the *Australasian*, reports that the League's experiment with stewards is having less of an effect on players behaviour, and the public is losing confidence in the whole system.

Worrall says that players are taking less and less notice of umpires and stewards. 'The game was never so foul as it is at present, the indiscriminate use of the elbow and the whirling of flying fists being common occurrences.

'In almost every match this year men have been deliberately and openly punched right before the eyes of the umpires and stewards, yet scarcely any notice has been taken, except at times a mild reproof from the umpire, such as "Steady there, old chap, you are making it a bit too willing".

'In a match between Essendon and South Melbourne this season, a player with the ball was stopped fairly with the open palms, when the steward – who had evidently never played the game – rushed up and said: "Any more of that and I'll send you up."

'The man in astonishment replied, "What do you mean, it was perfectly fair." "So it might be," replied the steward, "but the crowd are going crook, and you must take notice of them." ' (→ 14/5/15).

One Flag, One Destiny, One Football Game

Aug. 8. The Australasian Football Council was established this week during the Third Australasian Championships being held in Sydney.

The originators of the Council are imbued with the idea of having only one code of the Australian game in existence throughout the length and breadth of the land, and making the pastime national in character as well as in name and origin.

Jack Worrall of the *Australasian* commented from Sydney that there was now an overseeing body that would make all major decisions in relation to the conduct of football, and co-ordinate the efforts of the state organisations. He said this was fitting, 'for it is the only brand of sport that is of native birth'.

The AFC will meet every three years at the Carnivals, and will comprise delegates from all the Australian Rules football bodies. But there will be regular communication between delegates.

Worrall went on to say of this 'happiest of events' that 'there should be no room for doubt among the football public that neither the League nor any controlling body of any state has the power to make, alter or amend any law of the game. That prerogative belongs to the Council'.

War takes football's eye off ball

There's a new and bigger game ahead for these young men off to war.

Sept. 5. The war, the weather and rising ticket prices have all combined to account for a dramatic fall in attendances at today's Semi-final. Only 24,846 onlookers turned out to watch the clash between Geelong and South Melbourne. Last year's Semi-final attracted a crowd of more than 40,000.

The extra sixpence charged by the League has been resented. Already workers in every factory and place of business are giving weekly subscriptions to the Lord Mayor's patriotic fund.

A hot north wind blew across the ground, and the turf was hard and looked as slippery as glass. The standard of play was nothing to enthuse over. Many players have enlisted in the armed forces and their absence has been noticeable throughout a mediocre season.

Play all round was far below Premiership form with players guilty of much nervous fumbling and uncertainty, particularly by the fancied Geelong team, which allowed South Melbourne to win 5.14 (44) to 5.8 (38).

Profs fail exam, merge with Melbourne

Sept. 19. After completing their second consecutive season without a win, University have succumbed to the inevitable and will merge with the Melbourne Football Club.

The move to join forces with Melbourne was not unexpected. After 51 consecutive defeats, it had become common talk that the students' future was limited.

Although the experience must have been disheartening for the students, they fought each game out. The planned merger should create a strong club. Properly managed, the combined team will have every chance of being competitive given their strong recruiting base among schools and the University.

The decision was taken at a special Committee meeting of University and the next step will be to gain the support of the majority of the members, some of whom may be contemplating joining other organisations. Had University not taken the step themselves, the League would have been forced to intervene to resolve the issue.

Association Premiers, North Melbourne are favoured to fill the vacancy, although Prahran and Brunswick are expected to press their claims as well.

Boys of the Varsity. Gentlemen all, but losers in League football.

Carlton win third Jubilee Flag, despite mid-year blues

Carlton take the football prize with their Jubilee Flag win over South.

Sept. 26. Despite Carlton's 'annual upheaval' where the President and other office-bearers were replaced mid-season, the Blues have completed a hat trick of 'Jubilee' Premierships, beating South Melbourne 6.9 (45) to 4.15 (39), 50 years after the foundation of the club in 1864.

Carlton also won in 1908, the Jubilee of Australian football, and in 1887, Jubilee of Queen Victoria.

Half the Carlton Premiership side were first year players.

The preoccupation with the war did much to keep the crowd down to 30,427, half that of last year.

Like many sporting teams, Carlton are somewhat superstitious, and took strange steps when they lost the toss for the use of dressing rooms. Rather than use the gymnasium, and unable to use the dressing room near the skittle alley, they changed in the cricket room under the Grey Smith stand – to good effect.

The game was a contest between the speed of South Melbourne and the weight of Carlton.

John Worrall in the *Australasian* has written: 'Taking him all round, the footballer is not a thinking animal, for, if so, he would recognise that the possession of dash is not to enable a man to run from one end of the ground to the other, but to give him first handling of the ball, and then to use his brains.'

South did not observe this football fact, and despite a splendid fight back, fell short and kicked badly under the weight of Carlton's sterling defence. Blues defender and captain William Dick was best on the ground (→ 18/9/15).

1914 Statistics

Leading Goalkicker:
W. 'Dick' Lee (Coll) 57
Champion of Season:
David J. McNamara (St K)
Finals: First Semi-final S. Melb 5.14 (44) Geel 5.8 (38); **Second Semi-final** Carl 9.8 (62) Fitz 5.12 (42); **Final** Carl 3.6 (24) S. Melb 5.13 (43); **Grand Final** Carl 6.9 (45) S. Melb 4.15 (39)

Ladder:	W	L	D	%	pts
Carl	13	3	2	129.7	56
S. Melb	12	5	1	109.4	50
Fitz	12	6	-	137.2	48
Geel	11	6	1	128.4	46
Coll	10	7	1	120.0	42
Ess	9	7	2	120.7	40
St K	9	8	1	118.2	38
Rich	8	10	-	100.6	32
Melb	2	16	-	61.3	8
Univ	0	18	-	47.0	0

1915

Jan. 23. A crossbar on the goalposts, throwing the ball backwards and a stronger tackling rule are proposed by the SA League, to be considered by the Australian Football Council (→ 5/7/19).

March 12. A vote at a meeting of the VFL defeats a motion to suspend the 1915 season, 13 votes to four.

March 12. VFL President Alexander McCracken notes that £2257 has been paid by the VFL to patriotic funds since September 1914 (→ 26/6).

March 12. VFL President McCracken notes that proportionally many more footballers than men from the wider community have volunteered for war service.

May 14. At instigation of SA League interstate matches have been abandoned for the season.

May 14. League insures 60 umpires under the Workman's Compensation Act at a premium of 10/- each for the season (→ 3/6/20).

May 14. League decides quarter-time break should be no longer than required to change ends, half time limited to 15 minutes, and three-quarter time to five minutes.

June 12. Collingwood's Dick Lee takes 'one of the most brilliant marks ever seen' according to the *Australasian*, as the Magpies beat Fitzroy 11.8 (74) to 6.14 (50). However, Umpire Rawle awards a free kick against him – against the long-standing League interpretation (→ 4/9/16).

June 26. After today's Patriotic Day collection the League says that 10 % of net proceeds from July 26 to August 21 will be for patriotic funds (→ 14/8).

Aug. 14. Over 10,000 people attend a Patriotic match between St Kilda and VFA team North Melbourne.→

Aug. 25. Alexander McCracken, President of the League from its inception in 1897 to his retirement a few months ago, died today.

Sept. 4. Arthur Jones, who played seven games in the ruck for Fitzroy last year, has been killed at Gallipoli.

Debuts
Bill Cubbins (St K)

Retirements
Bill Eason (Geel)
Ted Rowell (Coll)
William Sewart (Ess)

Saints new colours in patriotic style

April 17. The St Kilda Football Club has changed its traditional colours of red, white and black, which also happen to be those of the dreaded Hun, to the new colours of red, yellow and black which correspond to those of Belgium, an ally.

The colour change also acknowledges the patriotism of those St Kilda players now serving with the forces in Belgium. Among them are Stan Brady, Clarence Roberts and Vern Couttie, who only played a handful of games between them before they answered their country's call (→ 10/5/19).

The Saints' patriotic new colours.

Jockey places then wings it to footy

May 29. The staying ability of Cyril Gove, the Essendon wingman, as an amateur steeplechase jockey and footballer was put to the test today. He had to ride and play football on the same afternoon.

Gove had a ride on Menthe in the 2 p.m. Springbank Corinthian Hurdle at Moonee Valley.

They came a creditable third.

Gove was then transported by fast cab down the Mount Alexander Road to the EMCG where he played a zippy game for the 'Same Old' in their 8.7 (55) to 8.16 (64) loss to South Melbourne.

If Gove's team does as well as his horse this season he will be lucky.

Round one at Gallipoli as football begins

Still battling on. The scene at Carlton at the opening of the season.

May 15. The news has reached Melbourne that on April 25, just one day after the opening of the football season, Australian troops were going ashore at Gallipoli in Turkey in a great invasion of allied forces under British command.

There are many footballers in the ANZAC, as the combined Australian and New Zealand troops are called, and it is certain that many more will be joining up. Only recently the Melbourne Football Club conducted a Sportsman's Night at the Melbourne Town Hall, attended by 2000 young men.

At the meeting the President of the Victorian Cricket Association, Mr Donald Mackinnon, said that sportsmen who volunteered would fight together in their own unit.

The President of the club, Dr W.C. McClelland, told Melbourne members that it is 'the duty of many of our footballers to enlist. Footballers should make admirable soldiers'.

With news of the campaign and the big casualty lists dominating life, questions are being asked about whether the League season should be abandoned.

There are feelings expressed that it is anathema for sport to be played at home while young men are giving their lives for their country, and that all young able-bodied men should be enlisting for war if their country can spare them from essential tasks.

John Worrall, writing in the *Australasian* takes a widely held opposing view that football should go on.

'The idea of what constitutes a moral duty depends almost entirely on the individual, and the abolition of football would drive more men to drink than to war.

'The war news has more intense interest now that our brave boys are giving up their lives for the cause of freedom, rendering it more than

Joe Pearce: Fuchsia at the front.

ever necessary that there must be some relaxation from the mental strain of poring over the news from the seat of war.

'It would be a sign of decadence and funk to show the white feather in stopping all sports and amusements at this critical part of our nationhood, for sport and war go hand in hand, and the best soldiers are athletes.'

There is talk of using some of the gate takings from football to help the patriotic cause. Meanwhile the games are going on, and the crowds are not yet noticeably down. Those scanning the casualty lists may be primarily concerned for family and friends, but may also be watching ut for their football idols (→ 25/9).

VFL resolves to 'carry on' with season

Sept. 25. The football season has dwindled to a close, with attendances down and a lot of rancour over whether games should have gone on at all while young Australians are at war.

The Victorian Football League resolved on July 21 to continue with the season, defeating a proposal that it be cut by five weeks.

The League had on its side the sentiments of the Premier of Victoria, Sir John Madden and the Prime Minister, Andrew Fisher. Mr Fisher said that 'healthy outdoor sports may be regarded as preparation for the serious business ahead'.

But there have been those who have found it distasteful that play continues. 'Old Boy' of the *Argus* says: 'Day by day we scan the ever-growing casualty lists, and we hear the appeals for men, and we see our finest athletes deaf to the call.'

But it must be said that many footballers are joining up. All the clubs are losing men and their conversation in the dressing rooms is more about war and duty than about the Premiership.

The decision to continue the season revolved around pragmatic club interests. For instance, the Collingwood delegate, Mr E.W. Copeland, discussed the loss of club revenue, and of income for gatekeepers and other ground attendants. He also said: 'This is the working man's re-

Something to steady the nerves.

laxation for his half holiday. It is cheap amusement for thousands of people.'

The move for curtailment came from Geelong, who were seconded by Melbourne. It was supported by Essendon, St Kilda and South Melbourne. Voting for continuation were Carlton, Collingwood, Fitzroy and Richmond. As a three-fourths majority was required to rescind the original arrangements, the motion was lost.

However, the League has given 10 % of match proceeds to the war effort (→ 20/1/16).

Park suspended and retires in disgust

Aug. 7. Dr Roy Park, a great full forward for University and then Melbourne, joined the army on July 31, the day after playing for Melbourne against St Kilda. It was a fiery game and Park was one of a number of players who were 'laid out' in the last quarter.

Now Park finds himself, on the evidence of a steward, guilty of striking Gerry Balme of St Kilda, despite evidence from three witnesses that he was nowhere near that player when he was felled.

Dr Park has been given four weeks suspension – something for him to ponder as he goes about his military duties. He had previously played 80 games without being charged.

1915 Statistics

Leading Goalkicker:
W. 'Dick' Lee (Coll); Jim Freake (Fitz) 66.
Champion of Season:
W. 'Dick' Lee (Coll)
Finals:
First Semi Carl 11.12 (78) Melb 10.7 (67); **Second Semi** Coll 4.12 (36) Fitz 9.16 (70); **Final** Fitz 5.8 (38) Carl 6.18 (54); **Grand Final** Coll 6.9 (45) Carl 11.12 (78)

Ladder:	W	L	D	%	pts
Coll	14	2	-	166.1	56
Carl	13	2	1	143.9	54
Fitz	11	4	1	149.4	46
Melb	9	7	-	99.2	36
S. Melb	8	8	-	106.2	32
Rich	5	11	-	77.8	20
St K	5	11	-	75.9	20
Ess	3	13	-	70.3	12
Geel	3	13	-	68.0	12

Carlton fly war Flag

Sept. 18. The battles between the year's two best teams climaxed today in the Grand Final, when the Blues met the Magpies for the third time, and won 11.12 (78) to 6.9 (45).

The first game drew to Princes Park an extraordinary wartime crowd of over 30,000 who saw Carlton win 11.9 (75) to 10.13 (73), with Dick Lee responsible for nine of Collingwood's goals.

At Victoria Park there were 25,000 to watch Carlton surge home, kicking 3.1 to four behinds in the last term to win by a point, 9.9 (63) to 9.8 (62).

The Grand Final began with the news that the incomparable Ted Rowell would play his first game for the season with Collingwood.

Then there was the bizarre intelligence that two Magpies, Paddy Rowan and 'Doc' Seddon, had been fetched by Secretary E.W. Copeland in a motor car from the army camp at Seymour, after initially being refused permission to play.

They had done a ten-mile route march on the morning of the match.

Carlton were 16 points up at half time and looked likely to win – but Collingwood came to life, only managing one goal seven but keeping the Blues to two points.

The one goal was a Dick Lee special in which he dispossessed the Carlton fullback who had kicked a little mark to himself.

In the last term Lee marked and goaled to put Collingwood ahead. Then a dubious mark was paid to Carlton's Herb Burleigh, who put the Blues back in front. They then kicked four goals (→ 30/7/23).

The scoreboard tells the story as Carlton move ahead in the second term.

Honours even in a ruck contest during the Grand Final at the cricket ground.

Game continues with war damage

May 6. The VFL has been reduced by the war to a somewhat farcical season in which four clubs will play each other four times.

Carlton, Collingwood, Fitzroy and Richmond will play in a season likely to become monotonous.

There is obviously great division in the community over the morality of playing football while the war continues to take such a tragic and savage toll of young Australians, including many footballers.

One writer to the *Argus*, 'Duty' of Jolimont, is especially distressed to listen to the 'boohooing and boisterous acclamation' of 'loud voiced shirkers' at the MCG when she has two boys serving at the front.

But others argue that 'the public have to go somewhere' and that if Saturday afternoon football is banned, what about racing, theatre and reading books.

The feeling that 'football has proved a great military asset', as well as the great numbers of footballers joining up, seems likely to ensure that the game will continue through this season at least.

If the amount that the receipts from games will contribute to Patriotic Funds is published the public may be additionally reassured.

The lower standard and repetitive nature of a four-team season could prove more deleterious (→ 12/5/17).

A Pioneer Football Match in London, organised by Lt Frank Beaurepaire.

Football players heed the call to bigger field of action

Dan Minogue: rousing send off.

June 24. What it is to be a soldier! The crowd at Princes Park showed their appreciation of footballers who are leaving for the war when they cheered Danny Minogue today.

The Collingwood captain gained leave from his military camp to play his last game and, as usual, he acquitted himself well, despite Carlton's win over Collingwood, 9.11 (65) to 7.11 (53).

Many of Minogue's comrades came to watch the match, and they invaded the ground at the end to carry him off the field, shoulder high, to the applause of the crowd.

It was a fine tribute to the former Bendigo miner, who has always played a hard and fair game. When he first announced his departure in May he was presented with a wristlet watch from the club, suggested 'for use when serving the Empire'.

As the League season struggles on, and the casualty lists from the war are making tragic reading in the newspapers, more and more footballers are responding to the call to join the forces.

Many of the clubs that have pulled out of the competition did so not only because they were losing players, but also because those who could not go did not want to cheapen the war effort by playing games at such a time.

Among other notable departures, Hughie James, the champion Richmond ruckman, recently received a money belt when he announced he had joined up. Fitzroy rover Clive Fergie was given a gold fountain pen and a silver cigarette case at a farewell function.

Wasps stung in first Final match

Aug. 19. Richmond, despite a brave and desperate finish, fell four points short of defeating Carlton and notching a victory in their first Finals appearance in the League .

Richmond were far from disgraced and could have won the game, but for some wayward kicking for goal in the first three terms of the Semi-final clash. The closeness of the encounter and the fierceness of the contest had the big crowd cheering wildly as Richmond stormed home and just failed to overtake Carlton which had led all day.

In the final minute, George Bayliss received a free kick in front of goal, but the occasion seemed to overwhelm the young player, and he kicked only a point, when a goal would have given Richmond an historic victory and a berth in next week's Grand Final against Fitzroy.

Although they will be greatly disappointed, Richmond supporters can take solace from the way the game was played, and that it was undoubtedly the match of the year in terms of skill, courage and competitiveness. Both sides play similar uncompromising styles, Richmond having modelled their game on Carlton's successful formula.

Despite the loss, the game confirms Richmond's emergence as a force in the competition. Final score: Carlton defeated Richmond 10.15 (75) to 10.12 (72).

Dick Lee's goalkicking spree

Dick Lee: dazzling leads.

Sept. 4. Collingwood might not have featured in the Grand Final this season, but they do boast the League's leading goalkicker, for the seventh time, in the flying form of the irrepressible Dick Lee.

Lee has kicked 48 goals in three fewer games than his major rival, Vin Gardiner of Carlton, who scored 44 goals.

Richmond fullback Vic Thorp, himself one of the greats, said that Lee is more than just a good forward, he is a great footballer.

'You have to be on the watch for his dazzling leads but also for the dozen and one tricks he's likely to spring. His anticipation and sense of the game is uncanny.'

Lee first played for the Magpies in 1906, and has played for years with an injured shin (→6/8/21).

Fitzroy, last to first

The Fitzroy team is on parade before the Grand Final encounter.

Sept. 2. In this strange season of four teams, Fitzroy had the distinction of being the first team to finish last after the home-and-away round, yet win the Premiership. Due to wartime austerity, the team was not paid to play.

But 'to the victor go the laurels' and Fitzroy beat Carlton in the two games that mattered in terms of the Flag – the first Final, 9.11 (65) to 5.12 (42), and the Grand Final, 12.13 (85) to 8.8 (56).

Had the Blues won either of these games they would have been Premiers because they finished on top of the ladder, with 10 wins from 12 games, while Fitzroy only won two games for the whole minor round.

The Grand Final featured good football and bad temper in equal measure, but the injury-depleted Carlton side were also beaten by the fast start of Fitzroy, which led by five goals at half time (→14/10/92).

Veteran Fitzroy forward Percy Parratt has been with the club since 1909, but he still kicked goals in the Grand Final against Carlton.

1916 Statistics

Leading Goalkicker:
Dick Lee (Coll) 48
Champion of the Season:
Victor C. Thorp (Rich)
Finals:
First Semi-final Coll 8.9 (57) Fitz 9.9 (63); **Second Semi-final** Carl 10.15 (75) Rich 10.12 (72); **Final** Carl 5.12 (42) Fitz 9.11 (65); **Grand Final** Carl 8.8 (56) Fitz 12.13 (85)

Ladder:	W	L	D	%	pts
Carl	10	2	-	137.2	40
Coll	6	5	1	100.0	26
Rich	5	7	-	89.9	20
Fitz	2	9	1	81.6	10

A big turn-out at Victoria Park on August 5, where £500 was raised for the Returned Soldiers' Repatriation Fund at the Patriotic Carnival.

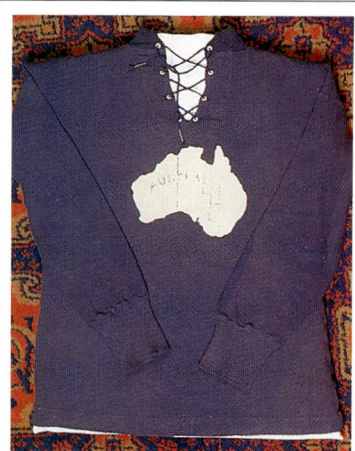

One of the football jumpers used in the Anzac match which was played in London on October 4.

Football weathers the storms of war

When visitors to Australia in the early years of this century set down their impressions, they found remarkable progress. The high standard of living, the experiments in democracy, the modernity of the cities and public amenities were all manifested in an obsession with sport.

Australian conditions – climate, space, time and money – favoured sport. Many played and many more paid to watch.

Boxing, sculling, swimming, athletics, horse-racing and cricket were all popular, and when the former British colonies came together in a federal Commonwealth, the celebrants sometimes boasted how they were l.b.w., or 'leading the bloody world', on the field as well as in other pursuits.

Sport had different meanings for different sections of society. Australian rules football had begun in Melbourne's private schools, where it was a training of body and character, developing chivalry and team-spirit.

By 1914 football was also a mass sport. A highly developed sporting press and an effective public transport system sustained a remarkably high level of supporters who paid to follow their team in the Victorian Football league. Some of the clubs that made up the VFL subscribed to the middle-class ethos of amateurism. Melbourne and the University team, for example, drew heavily on players from the private schools. Other clubs - and especially the inner - suburban clubs, Carlton, Collingwood, Fitzroy and Richmond - recruited from further afield and were prepared to pay for success.

The fact that Melbourne's middle class and working class shared the enthusiasm for football, and exchanged bumps and tackles on the same grounds, encouraged the popular belief in the egalitarian nature of Australian society. The First World War put that belief to the test.

The War began during the 1914 season. The VFL immediately voted £250 to the Lord Mayor's Patriotic Fund, and added a surcharge to the cost of admission to games. Attendance figures fell sharply and all clubs ended the season in debt.

The 1915 season was due to open on 24 April, the day before the AIF finally went into action. But even before the landing at Anzac Cove and the heavy losses that followed, there were moves to suspend the competition. The University Club had disbanded and St Kilda had changed its colours from the red, white and black of Germany to the red, black and gold of Britain and Australia's gallant ally, Belgium.

This was not enough for L.A. Adamson, the headmaster of Wesley College and outspoken

A recruiting officer addresses the crowd in the outer at the MCG in 1917.

champion of muscular Christianity. As president of the Amateur Football Association, he had previously condemned the VFL for its encouragement of professionalism and consequent debasement of sporting ideals. Now, on the eve of the 1915 season, he contrasted the large number of players from his association who had enlisted in the AIF with the small number from the VFL. For paid footballers, he declared, sport came first and the country second. If the VFL was determined to continue distracting young men from their duty, he asked, 'Why not Iron Crosses for the premiers instead of medals?'

Adamson's criticism widened a division that had already opened in the ranks of the VFL. Melbourne and Essendon had proposed to abandon the 1915 season but were defeated at the League's annual meeting by 13 votes to 4. By July 1915 the same proposal was favoured by five of the remaining nine clubs (Essendon, Geelong, Melbourne, St Kilda and South Melbourne) and failed only because it did not secure the required three-quarters majority.

By this time the lines of argument were well established. For middle-class patriots professional sport was a dereliction of national duty, while for the battlers the burden of the sacrifice fell unfairly. As John Wren's *Truth* suggested, it was a case of 'Toorak urging the toilers to go forth to battle to defend property interests'. *Truth* asked its readers, 'What about the golfing gawks and tennis toffs?'

Collingwood's president insisted that football was a 'poor man's sport'. It was not that his players shirked their duty - Collingwood lost the Grand Final in that year to Carlton in the final quarter, when two of its players had completed a ten-mile training march earlier in the day. All clubs contributed players to the AIF and all provided for recruiting officers to speak at their games.

Rather, these inner-suburban clubs objected to the principle of compulsion, just as the labour movement did during the 1916 and 1917 referenda over conscription for overseas service.

Before the beginning of the 1916 season, the five patriotic clubs of the VFL withdrew, leaving the four inner suburban clubs to continue alone. A similar pattern was evident in other sporting codes. In Sydney the middle-class rugby union competition was suspended while the working-class rugby league continued. Port Adelaide organised fixtures among teams from the industrial suburbs after the SA League abandoned play.

During 1916 Carlton, Collingwood, Fitzroy and Richmond maintained an abbreviated competition. In 1917 Geelong and South Melbourne resumed playing; Collingwood won the Grand Final that year after its former captain, Dan Minogue, sent back from the Western Front a lucky horse shoe.

Essendon and St Kilda came back for the 1918 season, won by South Melbourne. 1919 was a bumper season with 60,000 turning out to see Collingwood defeat Richmond in the Grand Final.

Yet the memory of the war, and its divisions, persisted. In 1919 some wanted the *Football Record* to place a star against the names of returned soldiers in the team lists. Some even suggested a special badge on the jumper to indicate the wearer 'had played the greater game'.

There were others in the outer whose memories went back to a rally at the Melbourne Cricket Ground on the eve of the second conscription referendum in December 1917.

The Prime Minister had received a warm reception from the members, while in the outer the air was thick with stones and bottles.

Football, in short, was a metaphor for national life and a microcosm of social division, bringing the people together and separating them into warring tribes.

Stuart Macintyre

March 31. Richmond membership declined last year from 2,200 to 428. The club had an income of £614 last year, of which £39 is left in the kitty.

May 12. Military recruiting officers visit League grounds and address crowds, bringing some heckling.

May 12. Last year's finalists Fitzroy and Carlton meet in opening round for a draw, 6.9 (45) all.

May 25. League President Mr O.M. Williams resigns. Meeting Chairman Mr Charles Brownlow says that Mr Williams probably had a very good reason, and will not ask him to reconsider (→ 18/8/23).

May 26. South Melbourne have now won their first three games despite awful kicking for scores of 9.18, 8.16 and 5.16.

May 26. Geelong wear black armbands in memory of 108-game player Joe Slater, killed in France, and lose to Richmond 14.6 (90) to 6.16 (52).

June 2. The League decides to punish clubs that flout ruling on paying profits to Patriotic Fund.

June 23. Collingwood-Carlton game is marred by behind the play 'incidents'. Collingwood win 13.14 (92) to 8.7 (55) to push Blues out of Four.

June 30. Collingwood and Fitzroy produce 'one of the most exciting finishes in the annals of the game'. Collingwood win 11.11 (77) to 10.14 (74).

July 21. Dick Lee kicks 500th goal in six-goal tally against Richmond, which Magpies win 11.19 (85) to 7.7 (49).

July 28. Geelong make last ditch effort to make the Four, but lose two of their best players, Harry Craven and Percy Ellingsen and Fitzroy prevail, 12.10 (82) to 10.3 (63).

Aug. 18. Carlton beat Geelong in rough match, 10.11 (71) to 5.8 (38).

Sept. 1. Fitzroy, well behind in fourth place with only six wins, shock Carlton to win first Semi-final, 6.17 (53) to 6.8 (44).

Sept. 15. Fitzroy beat Magpies 8.10 (58) to 7.10 (52), to set up second Finals clash with Collingwood.

Retirements
Vin Gardiner (Carl)
Alex 'Bongo' Lang (Carl)

Clubs return from war suspension

May 12. Geelong and South Melbourne, who have both just rejoined the competition after suspending operations last season as a patriotic gesture to the war effort, met in the opening round.

They had felt that playing football might prejudice military recruiting, but have changed their minds after learning that recruiting actually dropped last year, compared to the previous year when all nine clubs competed. Geelong, however, have returned as amateurs so that net proceeds from their games can be donated to war funds without deduction of player payments.

There was a lot of interest in the match, but the large Geelong contingent who travelled down on the special train was split between the football, the Head of the River boat race and the funeral of Roman Catholic Archbishop Thomas Carr.

After an even first half, South Melbourne, fielding 13 of their old players, easily defeated Geelong, who had 16 former players participating, 9.18 (72) to 4.14 (38).→

Clubs fail to hand over money for war

June 17. The failure of some League clubs to deliver money promised to the State War Council from 'patriotic fund raising' has led to censure from the Council.

From now on the Council will require a committee to be appointed to oversee any fund raising effort, to submit estimates and guarantees to it before any event.

Clubs have apparently been finding that the 'expenses' involved in fund raising has left nothing for the patriotic pot.

With crowds down and football limited the clubs have been struggling to make ends meet, even though they have only been paying expenses without player payments.

But returns from the clubs from last year fall far short of promises. In round terms Fitzroy found £152 for the war from receipts of £918, Collingwood found £40 from £664, Richmond £90 from £614 and Carlton couldn't raise a copper from £884 (→ 21/3/19).

How to kick a goal: Jack Worrall tells

A fine goalkicking example, from Collingwood ruckman Harry Curtis.

June 16. South Melbourne are beginning to despair over their inability to kick goals. They will give you any number of points, as the scores in the first five matches show, but when it comes to bisecting the uprights they are all at sea.

The collective score for the first four matches was 28.59, and there was much hanging of heads in the forward line and derision from over the fence. Only the fact that they won three of them has kept morale on a steady plane.

But a week ago, against Fitzroy, they did it again, kicking 5.20 (50) and losing to Fitzroy's 8.7 (55). They played dashingly, beating Fitzroy for pace and method, and with some fine marking. But, oh, that kicking! The first quarter was the worst when they had all of the play but kicked eight straight points, while Fitzroy scored 1.3 from its few forward moves.

South continued to look full of class and running in the second quarter, but only managed 2.6, while Fitzroy stayed in touch with the lowly effort of 1.1.

John Worrall, a sage of the game who writes for the *Australasian* has found himself bound to give a public kicking lesson to the miserable Southerners, and to all those who will take heed.

Worrall gives this view: 'The forward organisation is a vital part of the whole, and the side deserved to suffer through the remissness in straight shooting. In many cases the misses were the result of lack of method and coolness.

'The ball would be anywhere in front of the sticks, wild and hurried shots bringing their due reward. There are not many men who know how to kick for goal. The prevailing and wrong custom is to watch the goalposts while kicking instead of the ball.

'It is essential for the foot, body, and eyes to act in unison in football as it is in golf, and the failure to kick properly is too frequently attributed to bad luck.

'South had enough chances to make the game safe at almost any stage, and their slackness, or want of finish, to their otherwise excellent play gave those northern bulldogs their one remaining chance, and when they got their grip they hung on to the end'. (→ 5/11/32).

Australian football on fields of France

May 10. Lieut L.G. Short formerly of the *Argus* has written to his old paper a football match held during the past winter in France, on a snow-covered, shell-pitted patch of ground won from the enemy and still within artillery range.

The Officers of '–' Battalion, wearing sheepksin jerkins, lost 2.2 (14) to 6.0 (36) to the NCOs, in a uniform of cardigans.

The centre of the ground featured large shell holes with two unexploded 5.9 shells in the bottom, and behind the goalposts at one end was a small heap of earth – the grave of dead soldiers. Still, great fun was had before a return to the front line.

A lucky horseshoe for Magpies.

Recruiting for the grander game of war halts football

Aug. 4. Football was suspended today at the request of the State War Council to enable recruiting meetings to go ahead as 'all hindrances to the success of recruiting campaigns must be removed'.

One recruiting sergeant was asked to attend a Fitzroy game and speak to the crowd at half time.

He complained: 'The committee gave us no assistance, bar admitting us to the grandstand. The majority of the public were averse to us speaking and hurled personal insults at us. When coming down the stairs of the grandstand we were attacked by many men and women, which necessitated our leaving the ground. I am not keen on being called upon to attend these matches.'

Fitzroy said they had not known that he would be at the ground.

This recruiting drive is going on at the same time as the argument is reaching its height for next month's second conscription referendum, over which the community is sharply divided.

The first referendum last year was lost. *The Age* has published editorials suggesting players were either unpatriotic or cowards for not joining up and that 10 out of 15 players

Lieut Dangerfield talks to the crowd during the Geelong and Fitzroy match.

are fit for overseas service.

However, all VFL clubs have been affected by players enlisting. All clubs are mourning the deaths of former football heroes.

For instance, Carlton supporters have lost a favourite in Sergeant George Challis, who played in Carlton's 1915 Premiership team. He

was killed at the same time as the 1916 Finals series.

At Fitzroy 15 players and former players have joined up. Arthur Jones was the first and was the first to be killed, at Gallipoli in 1915.

Jack Cooper, who captained Victoria in 1912, was also killed in the fighting at Gallipoli.

Magpies stop Fitzroy's fighting Finals campaign

Sept. 22. Collingwood led all day to take out the Grand Final and comprehensively destroy Fitzroy's Premiership hopes, winning 9.20 (74) to 5.9 (39).

From the outset Fitzroy were unable to match their opponents in speed, teamwork and man-on-man contests for the ball. Their marking, usually a strength, was nullified around the ground, and their star forward Tom Heaney failed to take

one clean grab.

In a scrappy opening, it was obvious that players from both teams were feeling the pressure and some rough play ensued. Collingwood, however, settled down more quickly and went to a 12-point lead at the first break.

If Fitzroy were expecting a Collingwood fade-out they were to be disappointed as the Magpies added more goals before the end (→ 11/10).

1917 Statistics

Leading Goalkicker:
Dick Lee (Coll) 54
Champion of Season:
'Paddy' J. O'Brien (Carl)

Finals: First Semi-final Carl 6.8 (44) Fitz 6.17 (53); **Second Semi-final** Coll 13.17 (95) S. Melb 3.17 (35); **Final** Coll 7.10 (52) Fitz 8.10 (58); **Grand Final** Coll 9.20 (74) Fitz 5.9 (39)

Ladder:	W	L	D	%	pts
Coll	10	4	1	133.4	42
Carl	9	5	1	116.4	38
S. Melb	9	6		118.0	36
Fitz	6	8	1	86.4	26
Geel	6	9	-	79.3	24
Rich	3	11	1	79.8	14

Collingwood, in front all day, lead in the race for the ball on the wing. The Magpies' 'right of challenge' finally put paid to Fitzroy's Finals campaign.

May 4. Ranks of experienced footballers depleted by enlistments for military service.

May 11. Geelong brighten up uniform with the addition of red socks (→ 30/4/21).

May 18. Richmond defeat Carlton for the first time, after 24 losses since 1908. Richmond win, 7.16 (58) to 8.5 (53).

May 16. VFL meeting decides to abolish use of stewards to monitor matches. Stewards have been often criticised for incorrect or 'hearsay' reports.

June 3. St Kilda stop South's three-match winning streak with a courageous win, 6.13 (49) to 6.8 (44).

June 8. A great game between South and Carlton. South finish superbly against the wind with three quick goals in the dying stages to win, 11.10 (76) to 10.12 (72).

June 8. Advertisement by Alcock & Co. lists seven different brands of footballs on sale.

July 13. A rare coincidence, as first plays second, third plays fourth, fifth plays sixth and seventh plays eighth.

Aug. 10. South come close to a perfect season, finishing home-and-away rounds with only one loss. In the final game they beat a pumped-up Richmond, 7.17 (59) to 7.12 (54).→

Aug. 10. St Kilda, safe inside the Four, rest six players against Geelong and are beaten 10.27 (87) to 6.6 (42).

Aug. 10. Geelong and Essendon, still suffering from the depletions of war, finish with only three wins each. Essendon are the wooden-spooners.

Sept. 7. Good attendances at Finals matches, including 39,168 at Grand Final, refect better spirits over war news from France.

Sept. 14. John Worrall profiles umpire Jack Elder in the *Australasian*. Says he is one of only three umpires in 30 years to have the complete confidence of managers, players and the public. Elder has umpired over 500 matches in 12 years service.

Debuts
Tom Fitzmaurice (Ess)
Bill Twomey (Coll)

Retirements
Charles Hammond (Carl)

As war cripples League junior football gets more attention

Sept. 30. Four years of war have reduced interest and vitality in the League competition, but the game is alive and well in the church, school and district teams of the suburbs and in the country.

The crowds are often there too, not only parents and friends, but locals who can't resist a game of football, at any level.

Talent scouts may be seen, looking for youngsters who will step up to the League.

Each club has its stronghold under League zoning. Collingwood gets the boys from Ivanhoe out to Eltham, while Carlton has Brunswick and Coburg tied up, and Fitzroy looks to Northcote and Preston.

Geelong, St Kilda, and South Melbourne have their own local territories, while Melbourne stretches its tentacles through South Yarra, Toorak, Hawthorn Kew and Camberwell.

Essendon operates locally and and also recruits through Maribyrnong and Flemington, while Richmond works into the Malvern area and beyond.

What the youngsters are getting up to on the suburban playing fields.

Big David a Goliath in lagoon battle

June 3. St Kilda hero Dave McNamara was everywhere on the St Kilda ground today as the Saints recorded a memorable victory over Premiership favourites South Melbourne in the Battle of the Lagoon.

The big man kicked three goals in Saints' 6.13 (49) to 6.8 (44) victory.

The *Australasian* said it was a game 'full of fire and with all the spectacular parts of the game in evidence' mainly from McNamara, and from South's 'Chook' Howell.

St Kilda's game plan was simply to kick the ball high towards the long arms of McNamara, and why not. He pulled down some towering marks, and kicked his three lovely goals in the first quarter.

South got to the front in the second quarter kicking five goals to lead 6.3 to 6.7 but failed to kick another sixer for the game.

This was mainly due to McNamara who, like an aviator, flew quickly all over the trenches in defence, marking, kicking, supervising and generally patrolling the game. From then on he only had an occasional flight into attack (→9/9/22).

David McNamara, who seems to be playing at the height of his powers. He joined St Kilda in 1905, but left in 1909 after a dispute and resumed service in 1914, only to see his club go into recession during the war.

Things aren't what they used to be

Sept. 7. A sportsman who calls himself 'The Autocrat' has written to the *Australasian* with some reminiscences about football, which he hadn't seen in 25 years.

He notes the 'imaginary punch' in hand passing, 'vim and vigour' of the play, and the excessive number of free kicks.

'Autocrat' was perhaps recalling the days of yore when former Carlton great George Robertson had become a tough leading umpire.

It is said that one day in a match between Carlton and Melbourne a player took such a bad fall that he lay motionless on the gravelled ground for more than ten minutes.

Play continued, friend and foe alike having to jump over him. After a while, one of the players said to Roberston: 'Umpire, umpire, stop the game, the man is dead.'

He replied: 'Remove the dead; let the game proceed. Fancy stopping a grand game for such a trifle.'

Soon the bleeding player was on his feet and playing strongly.

Smashing time in MCG beer booth

Aug. 17. The League may have to reconsider its pricing policy after larrikins in the outer went on a rampage and wrecked a beer booth during the first Semi-final between Collingwood and St Kilda. They smashed every glass on the premises, with the exception of two, and inflicted damage in excess of £10. The barman is said to have retreated to a place of safety.

Their actions were an angry response to the League's decision to increase the price of beer at the ground to sixpence a glass.

The incident raises a number of issues. Although beer booths at sports grounds are, no doubt, a source of income to the League and refreshment to patrons, they are also capable of inciting riot and endangerment to the non-drinking public.

It is notable that the colourful language and riotous behaviour that sometimes erupt at football matches can usually be traced to the area around beer booths.

If the League decides it cannot lose income by closing them down, it will have to ensure that the drinking is policed and that the public are not harmed (→ 30/8/19).

South Flag in nearly perfect Season

The big crowd at the MCG were in great voice as Collingwood and South Melbourne struggled for the upper hand.

Sept. 7. South Melbourne won its second VFL Premiership with a remarkable last kick win over Collingwood, before a crowd of 39,168.

The VFL had reserved a part of the Eastern grandstand for returned soldiers in uniform, and some 400 came from military hospitals.

The win by the red-and-whites was close but just. They had only lost one game for the season, although they had many close finishes.

South beat Carlton 8.10 (58) to 7.11 (53) in the second Semi-final. This game had been postponed a week because of rain.

By the half-time break Collingwood, through Les 'Flapper' Hughes and 'Snowy' Lumsden, and Dick Lee forward, had dashed to a lead of 4.9 (33) to 2.5 (17).

After an even third quarter South, with Jack 'Chook' Howell, Tom O'Halloran and the wandering fullback Sam 'Chip' Turner, fought back to level the scores with just a few minutes to go.

Dick Lee passed to Snowy Lumsden, whose placer scored a behind.

After clearing the ball, Flapper Hughes gained possession, had a shot, which was cleared but only as far as Dick Lee – on an acute angle. His kick only travelled 15 yards, and was marked by South's Vic Belcher.

His kick went to winger Mark Tandy who dodged three, shot at goal, and Chris Laird kicked the winning goal off the ground just before the bell (→ 30/4/21).

Laing turns back tide at EMCG

June 29. Essendon would have lost by an even greater margin to Richmond at the EMCG but for the work of defender Roy Laing.

The ground was covered in a sheet of water, and the game ended in darkness, Richmond prevailing 5.15 (45) to Essendon 3.4 (22).

Laing's performance in the conditions was one of the finest anyone could remember seeing, and he received an ovation on leaving the ground. He had taken mark after mark to hold up the persistant Richmond attacks.

Essendon were undermanned, with Alan Belcher alone carrying the ruck, at the end.

Bill Twomey swoops on the ball.

1918 Statistics

Leading Goalkicker:
Ern Cowley (Carl) 34
Champion of Season:
Jack E. Howell (S. Melb)
Finals:First Semi-final Coll 7.16 (58)
St K 7.7 (49); **Second Semi-final** S. Melb 8.10 (58) Carl 7.11 (53); **Grand Final** S. Melb 9.8 (62) Coll 7.15 (57)

Ladder:	W	L	%	pts
S. Melb	13	1	143.1	52
Coll	10	4	145.1	40
Carl	8	6	116.5	32
St K	8	6	92.2	32
Fitz	6	8	98.7	24
Rich	5	9	87.7	20
Geel	3	11	75.8	12
Ess	3	11	64.2	12

League asked to put up for Dookie

Aug. 31. 'Dookie' McKenzie, the former Essendon captain, has fallen on evil times, and a fund has been started to help him get his life back in order.

He has been left with six children to care for following the death of his wife, and is also out of work.

The Victorian Football League has donated £20, while Essendon and Collingwood have also responded handsomely.

'Dookie' left Essendon in 1906 and played in the VFA, but he came back as captain-coach of the Melbourne club in 1915 and got the team into the finals. He has also played cricket for Victoria.

March 21. Members' tickets rise from 5/- to 5/6 for the season. Reserve entry 1/3 and outer 7d.

March 21. League has donated £9,436 to Patriotic Fund to assist the war effort, since the start of the conflict.

April 19. Letter to *The Australasian* from C.C. Mullen says fixtures should be recast, as October 4 is far too late to finish season.

May 3. The League appoints a committee to select a President. The position has been vacant since 1917, when O.M. Williams resigned.

May 10. Chris Laird of South Melbourne kicks seven of his team's 10 goals against Melbourne as they win 10.19 (79) to 3.10 (28).

May 10. St Kilda field scratch team in round two because of influenza, but beat Collingwood 5.18 (48) to 5.15 (45). It is the Saints' first win at Victoria Park in 25 attempts (→ 31/5).

May 31. St Kilda hold Geelong goalless as they win 6.10 (46) to 0.18 (18).→

May 31. A collection is taken up for the widow of ex-Geelong player Jack Quinn, who died while trying to rescue workmen in a sewer.

June 28. Richmond captain Bill Thomas breaks leg in collision with teammate. Then star Carlton rover Lyle Downs leaves field with 'badly strained heart'. Richmond win 14.11 (95) to 9.15 (69).

Aug. 2. Interstate matches resume and Victoria win season's second match against SA, 11.8 (74) to 10.8 (68) at MCG. Victoria won Adelaide match 9.8 (62) to 8.8 (56).

Aug. 18. Victorian Cricket Association rejects VFL request for future cricket seasons to end before April so that football matches can get underway. (→ 30/8).

Sept. 26. League sets aside funds to begin a provident fund for players on retirement.

Nov. 21. League, in search of an earlier start to the season, puts its case for April start to Cricket Ground management committees.

Debuts
Newton Chandler (Carl)
Fred Fleiter (S. Melb)

Retirement
Jim Caldwell (S. Melb)

Resurrected Saints fall from grace after good start

July 26. South Melbourne today had sweet revenge on St Kilda, who inflicted their solitary defeat in last year's Premiership season.

South beat St Kilda 29.15 (189) to 2.6 (18) and established several records: highest score, greatest winning margin and highest scoring last quarter – 17 goals 4 behinds.

Harold Robertson's 14 goals give him a VFL record individual score.

South played beautifully, and it is hard to credit that St Kilda were in the Four a couple of weeks ago.

They are an occasionally brilliant but rather unstable team. They were down to 15 fit players in the last quarter, and a few others walked off in disgust (→ 30/6/20).

A classic marking duel between early favourites, South and Collingwood.

Broken foot stops Belcher's career

FOOTBALL CHAMPIONS No. 5.

YOUR CHAMPION
FOOTBALLERS
All know that
THE LEVIATHAN
Keep the best stock of
Shirts, Ties, Underwear, etc.

Alan Belcher: unhappy ending.

June 12. Lady Luck has rarely been kind to Essendon follower Alan Belcher and late last month she dealt him a further blow when he broke his instep against St Kilda. He has had to retire from the game.

The big follower, who was Essendon's acting-captain, will be missed for his lion-hearted displays. He started with Collingwood but moved to Essendon after a season. There, his high marking and strong play in the packs lasted for 13 seasons. Injury kept him out of Essendon's 1911 Premiership side, but he starred in the 1912 Flag team.

Melbourne back again, and the Seconds

May 3. With Melbourne resuming the League now has its full complement of nine clubs playing again. With many players eager for the fray the League has also introduced a Seconds competition.

The number of players wanting to get into League ranks is particularly high, because players are free to the highest bidder. The League and Association have admitted that their normal controls over players have lapsed during the war, and there is a virtual amnesty this season until things are sorted out.

The previous agreement was tentative, and honoured by clubs from both competitions more as a convention than a binding arrangement. The district leagues were the accepted places for prospective League players to enter the ranks, while the Association clubs have been able to gather their players from any source.

The League and the Association previously threatened life disqualification for any player who crossed over without permission, but the number of defections made the rule difficult to enforce. There was bitterness, but little will for a full-scale fight between the two bodies.

Now the players have the upper hand until some genuine and enforceable rules are created.

The Seconds competition will give the clubs the benefit of blooding young players under the eyes of the selectors, and give those dropped from the senior team something to do on a Saturday (→ 9/10/26).

After sticking with the game through the war years the Richmond Football Club is looking forward to a full and varied year of football.

Footy tribes a new puzzle for VFL chief Baldwin Spencer

May 2. Sir Walter Baldwin Spencer has been elected President of the Victorian Football League, a position which had been left vacant 'for the duration' after the resignation of banker O.M. Williams in 1915.

The League Vice President Charles Brownlow has been 'acting' in the position for three years.

Sir Baldwin Spencer has recently retired as Professor of Biology at Melbourne University.

He is a world famous anthropologist, having performed legendary journeys in outback Australia, studying and recording on film and wax cylinder traditional Aboriginal societies, their language and music.

His interest in tribal societies has clearly extended to the suburban

Spencer: head of football tribe.

football tribes – where he has some experience, having sponsored University's entry into the League in 1908, and as foundation President of the Melbourne University Sports Union. Since University's demise he has become a Carlton supporter.

Although born in Lancashire, England, in 1860, Sir Baldwin has become an enthusiastic Australian, throwing himself into all kinds of cultural activities. He is the 'embodiment of controlled energy'.

He enjoys convivial company, is a friend of artists and patron of the National Gallery of Victoria. He clearly regards the VFL as an institution of substance.

Unruly crowds at peacetime football

A dangerous situation, as the Melbourne Cricket Ground is packed to the rafters and beyond with spectators.

Aug. 30. Huge crowds are now turning up to League football matches, stretching the capacity of grounds and the patience of officials and police to the limit.

Perhaps it is the excitement of this year's competition, compounded by a freer attitude from the war years, but the crowds are definitely unsettled and more unruly this year.

John Worrall of the *Australasian* says the poor umpiring has a lot to do with the anger pouring from the spectators' side of the fence.

At a Richmond match recently he witnessed the extraordinary sight of the umpire being assaulted by some women and boys.

League delegates have acknowledged they are at their wits end about the standard of umpiring. They have been trying many new men, who come to them with references and credentials from various associations.

Once they are given a match, however, they seem to forfeit any knowledge of the rules and become rattled by the crowds.

Worrall says the players have been showing admirable restraint over shocking decisions, but may soon take matters into their own

An anxious looking little boy is surrounded by the lads on the fence.

hands and cause serious trouble.

'The game is too grand to be ruined by inefficient umpiring, and if anything serious happens the League will certainly be the responsible party', he says.

One agonising umpiring decision had the crowd on tenterhooks at Victoria Park. Fitzroy staged a superb last quarter comeback in this round 9 match, kicking three goals in three minutes.

The ball shot from the pack and through the Fitzroy goal on the siren, and umpire Elder and the goal umpire had a long conference on whether it came from above or be-

low Tom Heaney's knee.

A goal was finally awarded and a great roar went up, with many spectators coming on to the ground to try to give their opinions to the umpires. Fitzroy won 10.11 (71) to Collingwood's 9.14 (68).

Meanwhile the big crowds are having their own troubles. There have been many instances of fences giving way before the crush of the crowd and injuries from the weight of bodies collapsing forward.

The Richmond ground is notorious, and matters are not helped by the fact that Richmond has done so well this year (→ 12/6/20).

Bullocking of champs unfair

July 5. Unfair tactics are again marring the game, particularly the practice of 'bullocking' in ruck play.

Critics feel it is unsporting, and ugly to watch, when players jostle each other as the ball is thrown in. Worse still, players are turning their backs on the boundary umpire with the sole intent of stopping an opposition player getting the ball.

Umpires are being urged to ensure that all players are given a fair go. Champions, too, should be free from players who dog their footsteps all day (→ 25/9/22).

Ex-soldier team mooted for League

Oct. 4. Five VFA clubs and Ballarat have applied to join the Victorian Football League.

With nine clubs (University dropped out in 1914) the League has to play with a bye every week, and is looking for a club which will attract a supporter base and have success.

There has been talk of an Ex-Servicemen's Club and even of a Public Service Club, but those with their hats in the ring are North Melbourne, Footscray, Brunswick, Hawthorn, Prahran, and the Ballarat League.

1919 Statistics

Leading Goalkicker:
Dick Lee (Coll) 56
Champion of Season:
Victor C. Thorp (Rich)
Finals:
First Semi-final S. Melb 9.5 (59) Rich 10.13 (73); **Second Semi-final** Coll 9.10 (64) Carl 6.10 (46); **Final** Coll 6.9 (45) Rich 10.14 (74); **Grand Final** Coll 11.12 (78) Rich 7.11 (53)

Ladder:	W	L	D	%	pts
Coll	13	3	-	162.3	52
S. Melb	12	4	-	158.7	48
Carl	10	6	-	127.6	40
Rich	10	6	-	118.2	40
Fitz	9	6	1	125.3	38
Ess	7	9	-	94.6	28
St K	7	9	-	70.6	28
Geel	3	12	1	73.4	14
Melb	0	16	-	43.0	0

Magpies remove the wasp sting

A stirring ruck contest in the Semi-final between Richmond and South.

Oct. 11. Richmond, known to some supporters as the 'Wasps', have certainly stung a few teams this season, as they have buzzed up the ladder and into the Finals.

That being said, Collingwood have been the dominant team, only losing three home-and-away games, and finishing a game clear of South Melbourne on top of the ladder.

Richmond lost their last game of the season to Carlton (third) 5.12 (42) to 7.19 (61), and only made it into the final Four because Fitzroy capitulated in the last quarter to the Magpies. The Maroons only scored a behind in the final term in losing 6.10 (46) to 9.10 (64).

As it happened South also lost to Geelong who scored their third win of the season, 6.14 (50) to South's 3.8 (26).

Form was no guide to the Wasps behaviour in the Finals where they proceeded to easily beat South 10.13 (73) to 9.5 (59) in the First Semi, and then thump Collingwood 10.14 (74) to 6.9 (45) in the Final.

As Collingwood were Minor Premiers they had the right of challenge, and burst the Richmond bubble with a 25-point win, 11.12 (78) to 7.11 (53). Richmond gave away some costly free kicks in front of goal in the third quarter.

The better side of the season won on the day, with defender Alex Mutch attacking, rover Charlie Laxton stab passing, Con McCarthy and Bill Walton palming the ball and in defence the most prominent of the Magpie stars.

Best for Richmond was fullback Vic Thorp who kept Dick Lee to just three goals. Andrew 'Max' Hislop, the sterling centre-halfback, was injured for much of the game. George Bayliss and Donald Don were prominent near the goals (→ 25/9/28).

A Collingwood Flag again, with all the fun of the big Grand Final game depicted in the 'Leader' cartoon.

Heyday of the larrikin spectator

By the formation of the VFL in 1896, Australian football was well and truly entrenched as a cultural phenomenon in Melbourne. Crowds flocked to matches in extraordinary numbers even by international standards, and the spectators identified passionately with the fluctuating fortunes of their footballing heroes.

Sometimes, however, they were too passionate.

Exuberant and unruly supporters were involved in numerous unsavoury incidents during the League's first quarter-century, clashing on and off the field with umpires, players and other barrackers in a succession of disruptive episodes that the paltry police presence was powerless to prevent. The few constables at the matches tended to be more interested in watching the game than in controlling crowd behaviour. There were no barricades to protect players and umpires as they entered and left the arena. Ground enclosures were primitive; spectators in search of a vantage point frequently ignored the feeble or non-existent fences. Determined malcontents had plenty of scope for mischief.

The language of these larrikins was notorious. One magistrate, after convicting a Collingwood supporter for directing the 'most disgusting epithets' at the Essendon star 'Tracker' Forbes, declared that he did 'not believe a convict gang could coin or give utterance to such depraved and filthy language'. After adjudicating in a similar case in 1910, another magistrate decided to inform the Premier of the type of language being used, hoping to persuade him to introduce compulsory imprisonment or birching for such offences.

It was when the undesirable behaviour graduated from verbal to physical that middle-class commentators became most animated. 'Degradation of football: disgraceful displays of ruffianism' was *The Age's* headline above its report of a spiteful 1910 encounter between Carlton and South Melbourne that culminated in a last-quarter invasion of the ground by brawling spectators.

That same afternoon, *The Age* reported, there was also an 'unseemly' fracas at St Kilda, where furious Saints supporters reacted to a narrow defeat with a 'rush' towards Umpire Hastings as he left the arena. Lashing out to defend himself against the 'surging mob', Hastings struck an innocent bystander, which further inflamed the situation; in the ensuing scuffle 'a number of youths used their feet to the discomfort of the police and the more law-abiding citizens'.

For devoted supporters, in working-class suburbs especially, following their football club was a highlight of their existence. Life was tough; many of them were doing it hard. After five and a half days of strenuous, dreary toil in a factory, spirited barracking was a perfect outlet for accumulated aggression and frustration.

Since the notorious activities of 'Richmond larrikins' had been deplored as long ago as 1871, it was hardly surprising that the admission of Richmond and University into the VFL in 1908 underlined the differences between some of the League clubs (and their supporters). The fanatical commitment of the inner-suburban tribes contrasted with the more middle-class ambience of Melbourne and University.

Football success spread elation around working-class suburbs, boosting community morale and self-esteem. But a shattering defeat could engender a desire for retribution, especially if intense resentment had been fuelled by alcohol; typical targets were the man in white or an enemy enforcer, or both.

On 24 July 1909, for example, undesirable crowd behaviour was evident at three separate matches, and *The Age* again waxed eloquent in condemning these 'deplorable scenes'. St Kilda supporters responded to another home defeat by targeting a certain Melbourne bruiser for after-match harassment. A Richmond-Collingwood clash was such a 'degenerate rough and tumble' with 'many instances of foul and brutal play' that it was no surprise to the *Age* reporter that 'a section of the spectators – unregulated and irresponsible – should resort to violence'.

The most reprehensible misconduct on that July Saturday occurred at South Melbourne, where Umpire Bain was struck by one of many disgruntled devotees of the defeated home team as he walked off the ground at what should have been the conclusion of hostilities.

Afterwards there were further 'disgraceful proceedings'. As the persecuted umpire ventured to a waiting cab, he encountered 'a howling mob of hoodlums'. A solitary constable urged them to

Faces in the football crowd

give the man a chance. 'He's not a man at all, we want pieces of him', retorted a 'burly larrikin'. Resorting to the road metal that was the ruffian's staple weapon, he and his confreres showered the umpire's getaway cab with the stuff. The Fitzroy players emerging from their dressing-room then had to endure a veritable deluge of road metal from 'fully 2000' hooting hoodlums.

Lying in wait for departing players and umpires was a typical tactic of aggrieved barrackers intent on revenge.

More often, though, the retribution was not delayed and calculated, but hot-blooded and immediate. In fact, as that same 1899 game ended, a female spectator charged onto the oval as the players were leaving it, and whacked a Fitzroy player on the head with her umbrella.

The particular vulnerability of the umpire at the end of each game became increasingly apparent. At Princes Park in 1902 umpire Crapp encountered 'a crowd of well-dressed larrikins congregated at the gate'; not content with equating his refereeing with his surname, these Carlton supporters heatedly 'reviled' him, and 'one unmanly coward kicked him'.

By 1914 this sort of post-match conduct by vengeful home supporters had become flagrantly habitual. In May of that year, again at Princes Park, there was another of 'those blackguardly occurrences' when 'swarms of youths' who were 'chagrined at Carlton's defeat, ran amok.'

'It is a well-known fact', thundered the *Australasian*, 'that on certain suburban grounds visiting teams are unable to obtain fair play from umpires, owing to the hostile demonstrations of the home barrackers, who threaten all kinds of foul vengeance.'

There was some huffing and puffing from the VFL, but the problem did not go away. The following month an inexperienced umpire was struck on the head in the first quarter by a stone hurled by a spectator; evidently rattled, he lost control as the game degenerated into a vicious battle, and a calamitous riot was narrowly averted.

Later that same month of July 1914 – when events in faraway Europe were initiating the great madness that was to engulf Australian football along with so much else – a spectator at South Melbourne marched a long way across the ground during the game before clocking the Essendon captain from behind. The following week there was a brawl involving players and supporters at St Kilda, and ugly scenes at an intense Essendon-Collingwood struggle when disaffected Essendon barrackers mobbed the umpire after the Magpies' victory.

Ross McMullin

LOCAL HEROES

Local Heroes – How they played

The VFL between the Wars

The 1920s and 1930s saw the 12 team competition come to maturity. With the collapse of University in 1915 and the entry of the three ex-VFA clubs in 1925, the VFL now represented a broader cross-section of the population than the VFA.

Both leagues understood the intense tribalism of football and the importance of community links. As well, money was tight and clubs mostly recruited their talent from local junior competitions. So the traditional adulation of local heroes continued.

Melbourne: a social mosaic

The divide between the Catholic clubs (Collingwood, Richmond, North Melbourne) and the extreme Protestant clubs (Essendon, Melbourne, Hawthorn, Footscray) had been exposed by the conscription debate and the decision of some 'unpatriotic' clubs to continue to play during 1915, 1916 and 1917.

The most successful Protestant club was Essendon, which had a 'wowser' reputation. Essendon's supporters were old-school tie types who lived near its East Melbourne oval. But in 1922 the club was forced off this ground by the now Jolimont railway yards and moved to Windy Hill and this gave the club a new supporter base.

Essendon was already an affluent Protestant area, with a strong district football competition, and the team's success in the 1920s with its 'Mosquito Fleet' guaranteed a strong membership.

Melbourne, on the other hand, continued to suffer because its supporter base was not so well-defined. Its 1926 Flag was a remarkable achievement in this context. Indeed, to revive its footballing operations, the Melbourne Cricket Club in the 1930s imported several talented administrators from the Richmond Football Club.

Proletarian Footscray and bourgeois Hawthorn were also Protestant clubs, and their sup-porter bases were limited by geography too.

Social class divisions were very obvious, both between working-class and elite clubs, but also among the working-class clubs.

Carlton saw itself as representing the 'respectable' working class against the less respectable Collingwood. St Kilda and South Melbourne were also respectable working-class clubs, but they did not grow in membership.

Already there were signs that some clubs (such as Collingwood) were successful in signing up new members from outside the suburb, especially as people changed address (from Collingwood to Preston, Coburg, etc.) or as country districts adopted a metropolitan club allegiance.

Suburbs with little demographic movement (Fitzroy, Footscray, Hawthorn) were less successful. North Melbourne was a Catholic club but, more important, it was the starting-point for social and geographical mobility. Carlton benefitted from its role as a university area and more so from being an immigrant point of entry. Half a century later, many Lebanese, Italian, and Jewish supporters can trace their allegiance back to grandparents in Carlton in the 1920s and 1930s.

The crowds were always mixed. The larrikin pushes were colour-ful creators of football language (and numbered some players in their ranks in the working class teams), women were present in good numbers, and no doubt passed on the sense of team loyalty to sons and daughters. The members tended to be local businessmen and artisans.

Player recruitment

Clubs had begun recruiting players from country Victoria before World War 1, and the teams of the interwar period were sprinkled with bush lads. Players were billeted locally, however, and were found jobs in local businesses (Essendon at the Fire Brigade; Melbourne at Vacuum Oil or the ropeworks; Collingwood at the Council or the brewery, and so on). If they were not local lads by birth, they quickly became so by adoption.

In the 1930s Depression, what mattered to players was not so much the match payments, but the prospect of a guaranteed job. When Harry Collier lost his job at the Yarra Falls Knitting Mills, Jock McHale got him a spot at the brewery.

In 1940 the clubs with most lo-cal players were Collingwood, North Melbourne, Footscray and Geelong. Sixteen out of 23 senior Magpies, for example, were Collingwood bred. Already clubs like Fitzroy and Melbourne were mostly made up of country recruits: only five out of the 21 Demons were locals.

The making of football heroes

Who were these local heroes? The key playing positions down the spine of the ground were the prestigious roles, because the out-of-bounds rule which applied all this period (from 1922 to 1939) meant that teams mostly played down the centre. Boundary throw-ins returned to replace free kicks in 1939. Because attacking from the back-line was not yet common, it was also harder for the defenders to have their worth recognised. Heroes were general-ly the stand-out individuals, be-cause team-plays were not widely understood. One-on-one contests in relatively fixed positions were the order of the day. Coaches rarely moved a player during a match. The Nineteenth Man, in-troduced in 1930, only came on when a player went off with an injury.

Back pockets were utterly defensive in those days – only Kevin O'Neill of Richmond is remem-bered as a hero in that position. The most noted half-back flan-kers were also men of tough per-suasion, Charles Tyson (Colling-wood, North Melbourne) and Bob Chitty (Carlton).

The full-back was most impor-tant, but their heroism was of a dour variety. Players like Vic Thorp (Richmond), Jack Regan (Collingwood) and George 'Jo-cka' Todd (Geelong) needed to block and go the punch as well as mark.

They were facing the greatest assemblage of full forwards the game has seen in the likes of Dick Lee, Gordon Coventry and Ron Todd (Collingwood), Bob Pratt (South Melbourne), Harry Val-lence (Carlton) and Bill Mohr (St Kilda).

Centre-half-back was recogni-sed as the key defensive and play making position, and was occu-pied by such luminaries as Paddy O'Brien (Carlton and Footscray), Bert Chadwick (Melbourne and Hawthorn), the Brownlow Me-dallist Albert 'Leeter' Collier (Collingwood) and the Corio Bay institution Reg Hickey.

Centremen generally stayed at home and vied against each other, but picked up plenty of kicks around the congested centre areas. Some eye-catchers were Edward 'Carji' Greeves (Geelong), and the pack burro-wing Colin Watson (St Kilda), Charlie 'Chooka' May (Essendon), Alan Hopkins (Footscray) and Marcus Whelan (Collingwood).

The half-forward flank was a graveyard after 1922, and Percy Parratt and Gordon Rattray of Fitzroy were known as star expo-nents of the position in those ear-ly days, the 'swoopers' of a by-gone time. The wingmen flashed brilliantly into play and there were three great medallists, Wil-fred 'Chicken' Smallhorn (Fitz-roy), Stan Judkins (Richmond) and Herb Matthews (South).

Centre-half-forward was where the team often put its heroes on the line. It was where big Dave McNamara (St Kilda) let loose his famous 90-yard place kicks. It was also the scene for Horrie Clover (Carlton), four times Blues' leading goal-kicker, and for Laurie Nash (South Mel-bourne), the champion with a ra-king long kick off either boot, the durable Jack 'Skinny' Titus (Richmond, 1926-43) and the very talented Des Fothergill (Col-lingwood, 1937-40, 1945-47). In 1937 'Fother' was a Collingwood Technical School student.

He was rushed into the firsts for an intraclub match the same day he had starred in the seconds: this 16-year-old then proceeded to kick another 10 goals that afternoon.

There were many mighty men in the ruck, including the great team of Roy Cazaly and Fred Fleiter at South, the supreme utility player Ivor Warne-Smith (Melbourne), Tom Fitzmaurice (Essendon, Geelong and North), Syd Coventry (Collingwood), Percy Bentley and Jack Dyer at Richmond, and the Magpie institution Phonse Kyne.

And there was glamour as well as guts in the roving division with two triple Brownlow men in Haydn Bunton (Fitzroy) and Dick Reynolds (Essendon) among great players like Harry Collier (Collingwood), Percy Beames (Melbourne) and Jack Hale (Carlton).

The appeal of footballers

The interwar period saw the introduction of radio broadcast, daily newspaper photographs and the first coaching manuals. The players were thus more accessible to a wider audience, and they were public figures. The core values of Australian masculinity were modelled by these men. They were straight, honest-working, good-looking and durable men, not 'flash'.

Barrackers made up ditties about their heroes. After Moriarty was dropped by Essendon he became a firm favourite with the Fitzroy fans, who composed a song about his '...goog, goog, googly eyes'. Haydn Bunton was one of the first pin-up heroes. Bunton stood out because of his gazelle-like playing style, his good looks, and his white-collar occupation (he was a floor walker at a city store). Bunton was debonair at a time when most footballing heroes were rugged.

The style of football

Football was still basically a mark-and-kick affair, with some secret signals, agreed avenues to goal, and clever defensive ploys. The 1937 Grand Final between Geelong and Collingwood can be described in detail, as all its statistics are on record, and because it was regarded by contemporaries as a fine example of the way the game was being played at the time. Some heroes of the day were at their best in front of 88,540 fans at the MCG that afternoon. The ball in play went out of bounds only 11 times.

The ratio of kicks to handballs during this period was 10:1, as the handball was a purely defensive measure, or used to change the direction of attack. Over the game, a free-flowing affair, Geelong booted 291 kicks, took 122 marks, and executed 32 handballs, Collingwood 300, 109, and 35.

The scores were: Geelong 3.3 (21) 8.5 (53) 12.8 (80) 18.14 (122) – Collingwood 6.3 (39) 8.10 (58) 11.14 (80) 12.18(90).

The last Saturday in September, in the 40th anniversary of the VFL, promised everything football purists could hope for. Both clubs fielded their best teams, with all players at peak match fitness. Neither side would need to call in its Nineteenth Man.

Reg Hickey had his men kicking with their left foot at training that week; Collingwood's players trained with a quiet confidence. 'Pin your man down!''was the theme of Jock McHale's speech.

Collingwood captain Harry Collier won the toss and elected to kick with the breeze. Todd took some dazzling marks at centre half-forward, and Regan shone at full-back.

Collingwood coach McHale rarely made positional changes during a game. But his counterpart Hickey could feel the match slipping out of Geelong's grasp, and at quarter-time made several controversial changes, all down the spine.

This kind of wholesale change was regarded as panic, and Collingwood goaled again, through Kyne, to be four goals up early in the second quarter.

Then Geelong's new arrangement fell into place and a succession of goals to Coles, Evans and Metherall meant that the Cats were only 5 points down at half-time. The ball was delivered well to Coventry, but he failed to convert. At the end he had 7 behinds and only 3 goals from 11 kicks. He failed to meet his personal target of 1300 goals, even though he out-duelled Hickey on the day. There were high marks, long kicks, good bumps, and 'brilliant ground pace'. Les Hardiman was taking great grabs in the backline for Geelong.

The game rocketed ahead at great speed, fast and open, without any spite. Fothergill added one goal after running 18 yards (unnoticed by Umpire Batts), and Coventry kicked two more in the third quarter. On the bell Leeter Collier took a great mark, and set the ball for a place kick. He missed and the scores were level at three-quarter time.

In the final quarter wingman Laurie Slack cleverly sharked the ball out of the middle, threaded his way through the pack, balked, and fired a deadly pass to Jack Metherell.

Metherell ran on, dodged some backmen and kicked a goal which even the Collingwood supporters cheered. It was the first of several goals to Geelong, who won easily in the end as the Collingwood defence crumbled.

The only consolation was that Coventry kept ahead of Metherell in the VFL goal-kicking tally for that year, and that his last goal was his glorious 1,299th. Everyone knew it was a record which would stand for many years to come. No one, however, could guess that Jock McHale's barren years at Collingwood started on that fateful sunny afternoon.

Robert Pascoe

May 26. A St Kilda player tries to punch a team-mate, and is stopped by Essendon player. Essendon win the game 8.15 (63) to 8.6 (54).

May 29. Victoria 10.11 (71) beat South Australia 9.12 (66) in match before the Prince of Wales.

June 7. Harry Cumberland turns out for St Kilda at 43 years of age. Collingwood 12.11 (83) beat St Kilda 7.10 (52) (→ 6/8/27).

June 10. Geelong's Basil Collins, who has been labelled a 'scab' for working during a strike, stands out of football after a trade union threat to boycott matches he plays in.

June 12. Game at Brunswick St halted by invasion of hundreds of boys. Essendon 14.9 (93) beat Fitzroy 6.7 (43) (→ 28/8).

July 3. In round 10 Fitzroy halt Richmond's run of eight straight wins, beating them 12.6 (78) to 8.12 (60).

July 3. Umpires threaten to withdraw their services unless given police protection.→

July 10. Matches start at 2.45 p.m. instead of 3 p.m. or later, to avoid finishing in the dark.

July 17. Essendon's 185-game defender Len Bowe forced to retire with 'athlete's heart'.

Aug. 28. A record crowd of almost 50,000 for a home-and-away game see Carlton trounce Collingwood at Princes Park, 16.13 (109) to 7.15 (57).→

Aug. 28. South hit the post nine times, five times in the last quarter, as Geelong beat them at Corio Oval, 11.10 (76) to 8.25 (73). The result sinks South's finals hopes.

Sept. 4. Separated by percentage, Richmond and Fitzroy go hell-for-leather for the vital top spot in two games. Fitzroy 22.17 (149) thrash St Kilda 11.3 (69), but Tigers hang on by beating Essendon 15.14 (104) to 6.5 (41).

Debuts
Bert Chadwick (Melb)
Horrie Clover (Carl)
Gordon Coventry (Coll)
Bill James (Rich)
Greg Stockdale (Ess)
Colin Watson (St K)

Retirements
Vic Belcher (S. Melb)
Len Bowe (Ess)
Vic Cumberland (St. K
Rod McGregor (Carl)
Jock McHale (Coll)

Richmond's tigerish win is cubs coming of age

May 8. Playing in front of an enormous crowd of 30,000 at their home ground, Richmond stormed away in the last quarter to overwhelm Carlton and prove decisively that they have come of age as a force in League football.

So enthusiastic was the crowd that many broke through the fence at the lower goals end. Other parts of the fence also sagged dangerously. The Premier, Mr Lawson, had been expected to inspect the ground at the request of the Richmond Committee to assess whether the facilities were adequate. The incidents proved that the enclosure is at present too small for large crowds, such as the 30,000 that turned up today.

Richmond, despite a slow start, carried over their good form from the opening round when they disposed of Fitzroy in a thriller. As would be expected from two such strong combinations, the game was hard fought and fast throughout, but always fair.

The first half was all Carlton who opened brightly with some dashing passages of play. Richmond, on the other hand, were dour, but never let themselves be overwhelmed by their flashy opponents.

After half time, Richmond's game gradually improved as Carlton lost their early precision and accuracy. Although still behind at the last change, Richmond romped home, kicking 5.5 to one point to win 14.13 (97) to 9.14 (68) (→ 2/10).

The pack flies in the big game.

Collection allowed for Barrier strikers

May 13. Collections will be allowed by the League for the Broken Hill miners who have been out on the 'Big Strike' since last year, since the end of their wage determination under the Arbitration Commission award as well as some radical agitation on behalf of the One Big Union, 'Wobbly' movement.

This award had followed the famous 'Harvester Judgement' given by Mr Justice Higgins in 1906 – the same H.B. Higgins who was Carlton President in 1904.

League Secretary Mr E.L. Wilson attended a meeting of the Victorian Trades Council in Lygon Street and gave the assurance.

He explained that actual collections are in the hands of individual ground managers, but the League itself had no objection.

Some unions had threatened to boycott games, and to stop union member footballers playing, believing that it was the League which was preventing collections.

There was a pre-war League resolution that prevented collections being taken without direct application by the organisation concerned to the ground managers – and that was still the case.

Charles Brownlow for the Geelong club said that as Collingwood and some other clubs had allowed collections at their grounds, Geelong would also do so.

Clover sprouts after three weeks on ground

May 29. Carlton's young half-forward Horrie Clover has created a record by being selected in the Victorian state team to play South Australia at the MCG today after appearing in only three senior League games.

Recruited from Maryborough, Clover made a sensational start to the season when he kicked four goals in his debut against Richmond. It was this display that persuaded the selectors to pick the youngster, whose form in the other two games against Fitzroy and Essendon confirmed his abilities.

Clover is not only a capable young player, but a keen one as well, who used to travel from Maryborough by rail to watch Melbourne play and train (→ 14/8/26).

Clover: sensational start.

The King's Birthday parade of the Pageant of Youth at the MCG.

Saints strike over Billy Schmidt

June 30. The troubles at St Kilda continue to fester with most of their senior players threatening to go on strike rather than play with the out-of-favour Billy Schmidt, a champion centreman but a difficult character.

After much persuasion, all but four players – Eicke, Cubbins, Jory and Collins – relented and have agreed to play on. The Committee, concerned that the club might not be able to field a side, combed the district recruiting players and there are 50 juniors standing by in case they should be needed.

The strike threat is the latest incident to bedevil this strife-torn club. The irony of the Schmidt case is that St Kilda and Richmond have agreed to transfer the player back to the Tigers, but the League refuses to endorse the clearance insisting that Schmidt play the rest of the season out with the Saints.

The tragedy for St Kilda is that they have a talented squad, whose abilities are being wasted as the club tears itself apart (→ 30/7/23).

Grand crowds break fences and stands

Aug. 30. It has been another bumper year for football, with big crowds from the very start of the season. The glamour teams – Richmond, Carlton, Collingwood and Fitzroy – all have a big supporter base, and there have been some lock-outs.

Princes Park was overflowing with almost 50,000 on August 28 when Carlton and Collingwood played for an unassailable place in the Four. Carlton thrashed Collingwood, 16.13 (109) to 7.15 (57).

The tiny Punt Road Oval was host to 31,000 on May 26, when the unbeaten Richmond squeaked in against Collingwood by seven points, 11.12 (78) to 10.11 (71).

The excitement and foot stamping in the small grandstand was such that part of it collapsed, scattering bodies everywhere. There were a lot of scrapes and bruises.

After that, the practice of perching in the trees outside the grounds, adopted by many small boys, seems less dangerous than sitting in the stand.

Clubs recruit big boys from bush to get winning edge

May 8. As the intensity of the competition increases, so does the search for the kind of players who will give a team a winning combination on the field.

Breaking with convention, four clubs – Carlton, Melbourne, Fitzroy and Richmond – have set their sights on the boys from the bush and have been scouring country areas signing up promising recruits to boost their playing personnel.

Before the war, it was felt that country players were a poor football investment because they had too much to learn before they could hold their own in League ranks. Some also had problems in adjusting to city life.

Not so any more it seems. The latest crop of country recruits are already making their presence felt with their new clubs. One of the main advantages to be gained from country recruiting is size, as there has always been an abundance of big men from the bush. The improvement in their play must be attributed to their war service.

There, behind the lines in France, they joined their city cousins – many of whom had League and Association experience – in numerous keenly contested games of football, so that by the war's end they were not only battle-hardened, but footy – sharpened as well (→ 14/5/27).

Bert Boromeo, down from Maryborough, takes a big mark for Carlton.

Umpires ultimatum to League includes strike threat

The men in white may not always be right, but they are now protected from the boilover of partisan crowds, and even players, who take exception to their decisions. Police will be out in force at all League grounds, six on foot and two mounted, and umpires will be escorted to and from the playing arena.

July 3. The meeting held last night between the Umpires' Association, ground management committees and the VFL, chaired by Sir Baldwin Spencer, saw the League agree to the umpires' demands for increased police protecion for them, especially from the barrackers for losing home teams. The umpires threatened strike action.

Today's round of matches went ahead, and the effect was 'magical' at all grounds except South Melbourne and Richmond where invasions and assaults occurred.

The umpires say that the situation at South Melbourne is intolerable and they will not umpire there until the agreed conditions are met.

It is up to the ground management committee to request the required number of police (→ 30/5/21).

Tigers eat 'em alive in Grand Final

Oct. 2. Richmond has crowned its tremendous year of football by winning a hard-fought Grand Final against Collingwood, 7.10 (52) to 5.5 (35). It is the Tigers' first Flag in their 12 years in the League.

The Tigers have had the best team all year, and despite their Semi-final failing in the mud, when Carlton beat them 7.11 (53) to 4.6 (30), they deserved their second chance to take the prize (granted to them for being Minor Premiers).

Today they bounced out on to dry grass and a warm Spring day. They looked the fitter, racier side and the Collingwood men seemed less limber after their gruelling final against Carlton, which they won in the mud 12.11 (83) to 8.11 (59).

Both defences were on top through the tight, hard-hitting game, with Max Hislop, Jim Smith and Vic Thorp clearing repeatedly for Richmond, while Charles Brown, Gus Dobrigh, Harry Saunders and Tom Drummond were strong for Collingwood. Only two goals were scored in the first quarter, one an angle shot by Hugh James of Richmond.

Plenty of action in the Grand Final as the ball is loose in the centre.

Richmond had more of the play in the second quarter, but could not break away, and the game became a fierce battle in the third quarter, with both sides throwing in their weight. Collingwood's young full-forward Gordon Coventry showed his mettle here, and kicked two precious goals to help keep his side in the game.

But the gallant Magpies looked a spent force at three-quarter time, and seemed to rise reluctantly from the groundsheets, while the Tigers were up and ready to play.

Only the Collingwood defence held up, with its rucks, forwards and centres virtually extinguished. It was a tribute to the Magpies that Richmond did not win the Grand Final by much more.

It is an irony that the architect of Richmond's season, and their win today, was their captain-coach Danny Minogue, the former Collingwood hero and skipper. After nine years of football and war he has slowed a little, but he saw everything, read everything and made all the right moves (→ 15/10/20).

One game, one goal one Flag, one shot

Dec. 15. William James, the kid from Kyabram who replaced leading goal-scorer George Bayliss in Richmond's Premiership team, is unlikely to play again.

Bill James will be remembered as kicking the goal that was the final nail in the Collingwood coffin.

It was his first game for Richmond, in a big week where he also helped win a Flag for Kyabram.

Unfortunately for Bill, an accident while rabbit shooting has seen him badly wounded in the foot, shot by his mate.

Saint Cazaly heads south across lagoon

Sept. 10. Capping off an awful year for St Kilda, their captain and champion, Roy Cazaly, is joining lakeside rivals, South Melbourne.

Tired by the constant in-fighting at St Kilda, Cazaly had asked for a transfer to Carlton, but this was rejected by the Committee. It was eventually decided that he would be traded to South instead. The departure of the 27-year-old Cazaly is the latest blow to hit the troubled club in a season that has seen strikes by players, feuding between the Committee and players and a mere two wins on the football field (→ 15/9).

With standing room only at the MCG, these gentlemen found some temporary seating to get a perfect view.

1920 Statistics

Leading Goalkicker:
George Bayliss (Rich) 63
Champion of Season:
Roy Cazaly (St Kilda)
Finals:
First Semi-final Fitz 3.5 (23) Coll 4.17 (41); **Second Semi-final** Rich 4.6 (30) Carl 7.11 (53); **Final** Carl 8.11 (59) Coll 12.11 (83); **Grand Final** Rich 7.10 (52) Coll 5.5 (35)

Ladder:	W	L	%	pts
Rich	14	2	146.4	56
Fitz	14	2	143.2	56
Carl	10	6	128.7	40
Coll	10	6	112.3	40
S. Melb	7	9	108.6	28
Ess	5	11	87.8	20
Geel	5	11	84.4	20
Melb	5	11	74.2	20
St K	2	14	57.2	8

Essendon shunted from East Melbourne home ground by Railways

Geelong and the Dons compete with boat racing on the Barwon River.

Oct. 13. On September 10 Essendon played their last game on the East Melbourne Cricket Ground, a draw with Fitzroy, 10.14 (74) to 11.8 (74).

The EMCG is to be resumed by the Railways as a shunting yard, after having been used by the East Melbourne Cricket Club since 1860.

Essendon's first ground was in Flemington in a paddock behind President Robert McCracken's property, which is now occupied by a school opposite the Tramways Depot in Mount Alexander Road.

The 'Same Old' have unfurled four VFL and four VFA Flags on the EMCG in the 40 seasons since the team were first invited to play there by the prominent Committee of the EMCC in 1882.

The EMCC wanted year-round use of its first class facilities, and the revenue from football to further improve them.

While Essendon have seen great success at the EMCG they slumped to the wooden spoon in 1921.

They received offers of a ground from the Showgrounds, Victoria Park and North Melbourne, while the Essendon Council offered the Essendon Recreation Reserve. This latter offer has been successful.

There has been much controversy over Essendon's earlier decision to go to North Melbourne and amalgamate with the North Melbourne VFA club. The protests and legal action over this have concluded.

The wash-up is that the rump North will merge with the Essendon VFA club, and that Essendon VFL will gain some players and play, at last, at Essendon.

A flat punt

May 20. Essendon supporters and players are fretting over a goal allowed at the Punt Road Oval today.

Richmond kicked a point, and the ball came back from the crowd flat and punctured.

Essendon fullback Bert Day picked it up and kicked it idly over to Umpire Williamson for inspection, but not from the kick-off square. Richmond forward George Bayliss pounced on it and scored a goal, helping Richmond to win, 12.14 (86) to 10.11 (71).

Training tragedy

July 9. Carlton and Richmond players wore black armbands today in honour of Lyle Downs, the Carlton rover who died of a heart condition at training on Thursday.

Friends said he loved football so much that he played against doctor's orders. He would have been pleased that Carlton thrashed Richmond, 14.15 (99) to 6.12 (48).

Downs played 47 games of football after his debut in 1917, and averaged 57.8 in District cricket as leading batsman for the Blues.

South change gear

April 30. South Melbourne wore new guernseys of bright red with a white SMFC monogram on the breast for the first time today, replacing the old jumper of white with a red sash. South came home in the last quarter against local rivals St Kilda, winning by a point, 9.13 (67) to 10.6 (66).

This was Roy Cazaly's first game for South, having crossed the lagoon from St Kilda this season. Cazaly, rather than new guernseys, is likely to bring South good fortune.

The ladies of the Fleetwoods and Chorleys teams attracted a big crowd to their match at the St Kilda ground.

Donald Don dongs Blue Greenhill

Greenhill: sent far away.

Nov. 20. The Preliminary Final game where Carlton's Jack Greenhill was knocked unconscious has had its final result. Richmond's Donald Don has been suspended for six weeks by the VFL for the deed.

This finally concludes a match fought out by Richmond and Carlton in most unusual conditions.

During half time an amazing hailstorm covered the MCG in white.

The game was delayed, and Carlton waded to a three-point lead at three-quarter time, during which a behind post was knocked out of the ground and had to be replaced.

Richmond swam to the front, winning 10.7.(67) to 7.17 (59).

1921 Statistics

Leading Goalkicker:
Dick Lee (Coll) and Cliff Rankin (Geel) 64 **Champion of Season:** Horrie R. Clover (Carl)
Finals:
First Semi Rich 16.19 (115) Geel 6.18 (54); **Second Semi** Carl 9.11 (65) Coll 7.10 (52); **Final** Carl 7.17 (59) Rich 10.7 (67); **Grand Final** Carl 4.8 (32) Rich 5.6 (36)

Ladder:	W	L	D	%	pts
Carl	13	1	2	142.0	56
Rich	12	4	-	116.1	48
Coll	9	7	-	111.9	36
Geel	9	7	-	106.1	36
Fitz	6	8	2	103.9	28
Melb	6	8	2	95.4	28
S. Melb	5	10	1	84.6	22
St K	4	11	1	77.1	18
Ess	3	11	2	80.8	16

Tigers tame Carlton for second Flag

Oct. 15. Richmond convincingly won the 1921 Flag by beating Minor Premiers Carlton twice in successive weeks in battles described by one writer as 'Homeric'.

The team regarded as being one of the best fielded by the Blues in recent years had beaten Richmond twice during the season, losing just once, but finished the long year with nothing to show.

The Grand Final was also played in greasy and drizzling conditions, unpleasant but a lot better than the hail and mud of last week. However, Carlton's long-kicking and marking game seemed more effective in the first half, against Richmond's bustle and rush.

At half time Carlton had kicked three goals to one, and looked like going on with it. The lead would have been greater but for the solidity of the Tiger defence.

However, Richmond kicked a goal from the ball-up after the rainy

Richmond and Carlton fighting it out in the hailstorm Final game.

long interval without a Carlton player touching the ball. Tiger confidence soared, and they eventually ground out a win, 5.6 (36) to 4.8 (32). Black with mud, the two teams slugged it out in a tense last quarter.

Max Hislop the Richmond centre-halfback was best on the ground, and saved the game in the last seconds. The ball was flying towards Carlton's Alex Duncan, who looked certain to mark, but Hislop flung himself in the path of the ball.

Carlton's high marking Bert Boromeo was outstanding (→ 2/6/28).

The victorious Richmond team, as depicted by Sam Wells in his cartoon for Melbourne 'Punch'.

1922

Vics prove Croweaters no mudlarks

July 8. South Australia were literally buried in the mud against Victoria, losing the 28th of their 30 encounters with Victoria over the years, 9.10 (64) to 5.12 (42).

The South Australians are not used to the filthy winter weather that can prevail in Victoria. They ran on to the MCG with the rain slashing down, and with either pools of water or seas of mud as the playing surface. They started out well enough, but Victoria kicked 6.4 to two points in the second quarter and the game was virtually over.

The greatest drawback for SA was that they flew for the marks together, often putting the ball down in the path of a roving Victorian player. The best for Victoria were Dick Lee, Wels Eicke, Roy Cazaly and Mark Tandy.

Coming soon, a replay in Adelaide.

McNamara's ten a Saint first

Sept. 9. In one of the greatest goal-kicking exhibitions ever seen in the League, St Kilda's veteran champion, Dave McNamara kicked ten goals – nine of them from place-kicks and one from a punt-kick.

In a truly memorable display against a weakened Geelong, Mc-Namara showed he had fully recovered from a bad leg break, sustained last year, with strong marking and kicking for goal. In one instance the ball travelled 70 yards, while another huge kick bisected the goal-posts from 65 yards.

Even at 35 years of age, McNamara was unstoppable in the air. Never in his long and distinguished career has McNamara marked or kicked with such certainty and power. He deserves the honour of becoming the first Saint to bag ten goals in a League game.

Playing at centre-half-forward, McNamara had a total of 12 shots altogether, only missing the big sticks on two attempts as he led the Saints to a 55-point win.

It has to be noted that the opposition on this occasion was not too great with Geelong fielding an inexperienced line-up that was completely out of their depth until the final quarter, when they rallied to post five goals to the solitary goal kicked by a tiring St Kilda (→ 19/5/23).

Bugler stops game as funeral passes

June 17. There is not much that will stop a football match, but the game between St Kilda and Essendon today was brought to a sudden and solemn halt as a uniformed bugler marched to the centre of the arena.

Drawn up outside the ground was the funeral procession of Lieutenant James Bennett, the aviator who died in England with his pilot Captain Ross Smith, in a crash on the eve of an attempted round-the-world flight.

Bennett was born in St Kilda, barracked for St Kilda and was going to his grave in St Kilda. He had been lying in state in the Queens Hall at Parliament House before the State Funeral today.

Cyril 'Jazz Legs' Gambetta had just scored a goal for St Kilda with five minutes to go in the third term when the bugler appeared.

The players who were running to their places for the bounce stood stiff and motionless. A hush descended on the ground and every man in the crowd of 25,000 bared his head as the solemn notes of The Last Post sounded. The only sound was the engine drone of four Air Force planes which flew over in formation.

The bugler marched off, but the hush remained for a moment as the thoughts of a gallant life remained. And then the ball was bounced to a full-throated roar and Essendon went on to win a hard-fought match, 15.7 (97) to 13.11 (89).

Traffic in players causes concern

April 22. Con McCarthy, the champion Collingwood ruckman, has transferred to Footscray in the VFA for the unprecedented sum of £400.

Commentators don't blame the player: 'Why should McCarthy play for Collingwood when he gets a nice nest egg from Footscray?'

From the football point of view the 'curse of commercialism' and the buying of players could lead to the disappearance of the VFL and the VFA with a new competition formed from the best teams.

The financially weaker clubs like Fitzroy might be eliminated.

Fitzroy paid players £658 on an income of £2,313 compared to Carlton who paid £1,518 on an income of £3,746 in 1921.

The funeral procession of Lieutenant James Bennett leaves Parliament House.

Traditional style earns Maroons a Flag

The trainers of the Fitzroy team are on hand to help the players.

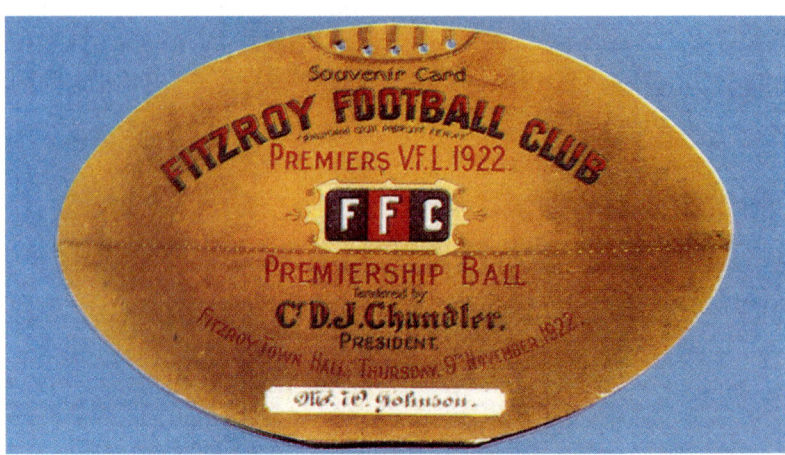

The fruits of victory. A Premiership Ball to honour the winning team.

Oct. 14. In a fine exhibition of Grand Final football a dashing Fitzroy downed a gallant Collingwood by 11 points.

Before an crowd of 50,054 at the MCG, Fitzroy surged ahead in the second half to take out their seventh Premiership Flag. The game was played in punishing conditions – hot, humid and dusty.

Fitzroy supporters were apprehensive, having lost to Collingwood twice this year, although they won the second Semi-final. But it was soon apparent that this was not only a contest between opposing teams, but also one between two contrasting styles.

Fitzroy's win proved to be a victory for tradition, with their direct,

The action is heavy on the Collingwood half-forward line half-way through the first quarter of the Grand Final.

long-kicking and high-marking game prevailing over Collingwood's short-passing, hand-balling and zig-zagging tactics. Among Fitzroy's best were follower Gilbert Taylor rover Clive Fergie, and forwards Jimmy Freake and Percy Parratt.

The opening stanzas were tense and tentative. Collingwood's forward line was on target early, but once Jim 'Snowy' Atkinson went to cover their star forward Dick Lee, their scoring opportunities were harder to come by.

Fitzroy led narrowly at the first change, but Collingwood went into the long interval five points ahead. The Maroons soon established their superiority with a dazzling five-minute spell in the third quarter. They hardly had a weak player, while too many top Magpies, like Bill Twomey, Maurice Sheehy and Charlie Pannam, were off form.

The Maroons were suddenly marking, passing, kicking and running to near perfection. Final scores: Fitzroy defeated Collingwood 11.13 (79) to 9.14 (68) (→30/6/34).

1922 Statistics

Leading Goalkicker:
Horrie Clover (Carl) 56
Champion of Season:
G 'Goldie' Collins (Fitz)
Finals:
First Semi-final Ess 5.9 (39) Carl 4.10 (34); **Second Semi-final** Coll 5.12 (42) Fitz 6.10 (46); **Final** Fitz 9.14 (68) Ess 6.9 (45); **Grand Final** Coll 9.14 (68) Fitz 11.13 (79)

Ladder:	W	L	D	%	pts
Coll	12	4	-	127.8	48
Ess	10	5	1	111.6	42
Fitz	10	5	1	108.8	42
Carl	10	6	-	112.8	40
Rich	7	9	-	92.0	28
Melb	7	9	-	88.9	28
St K	5	10	1	93.6	22
Geel	5	11	-	84.0	20
S. Melb	4	11	1	91.3	18

Umpiring's elder statesman retires

Oct. 21. Jack Elder blew his last whistle in the VFL to end the Grand Final last Saturday.

Elder, 37, has umpired 295 official VFL games since 1906, including ten Grand Finals.

Jack Worrall, a keen observer of umpires, said that Elder was 'our leading adjudicator'.

'To be a success an umpire must not see too much. He must overlook those trivial things which in no way interfere with the game's progress. Elder recognises that force, legitimately employed, is an essential to a rough and tumble game.

'He allows a certain freedom which makes for the enjoyment of all and it is only when the latitude is abused that a penalty is exacted.'

Elder did make mistakes, but his were the mistakes of omission for it is impossible to see everything.

Elder 'has been the outstanding figure in the umpire world, not only being above suspicion, but making a

Elder: has the respect of all.

name for himself in the pre-war world when the game was at its best and brightest'.

He has the respect of all players and other umpires and will make an ideal Umpire's Instructor, to which position the VFL are appointing him (→9/4/24).

Dick Lee the first high flying Magpie – a new kind of full forward

Dick Lee scored his 707th goal with his last kick, after 230 VFL games. It was the last Collingwood goal of the 1922 Grand Final which the Magpies lost by six points to Fitzroy.

Walter Henry Lee was born on 19 March 1889 into a Magpie nest – the son of the Britannia player and long time Collingwood trainer Wal Lee. The child was always known as Dick.

Lee first played for the Magpies in 1906 at 16, and was never sidelined, except through injury, until his retirement at 34.

He very nearly played two years before this, when playing for Rose of Northcote. Collinwood had promised him a run if a particular player did not turn up – but he did, and Lee rushed over to Northcote where he kicked six goals in three quarters.

Until his knee injury in 1911, Lee was given a roving commission, dropping back into the forward line in anticipation of taking

one of his spectacular marks.

Lee had the cartilage removed in 1912. He had the cartilage at home in a bottle. He played just six games in 1912 and 1913.

His other injury was the result

of a kick to the shin in 1908 which became infected from the dye in his footy socks. It was a terrible wound which kept opening up until eventually cauterised in 1912 and remained painful for

the rest of his career.

Dick Lee's courage in playing on at full forward through these debilitating injuries is only matched by the spectacular and crowd pleasing nature of his play.

In the words of Richmond's Vic Thorp, whom Lee thought the best full back he played against, 'He was an amazing mark. It did not seem to matter how he was herded off a mark, let him get a spring at the ball and he'd get his hands on it. He also had a trick of flying high into the air, as if miles too early for the mark. But he would stiffen himself and hang there as if suspended and down he'd bring the ball.'

Lee kicked straight too. He kicked at least one goal in each his 97 games between round eight 1910, and round ten 1918.

People of all football persuasions often came to watch the man who invented a new kind of full forward – a spectacular, high flying acrobat.

April Champions, chaff bags over the silo and other tall stories of football

Tall stories have been told about footballers since Tom Wills first roosted the pigskin into one of those big gum trees outside the MCG, and the ball was captured by a startled possum, and carried over the tree tops until it came to rest somewhere in the upper reaches of the Yarra.

Of course that was in 1858 when there were a lot more trees.

World record for the longest kick was one that was hoofed out of the MCG, or was it from Punt Road, and didn't hit the ground again for 232 miles.

Of course, that one landed in an empty wheat truck and was tipped out up at Nhill.

Plenty of blokes have come from up that way, especially in April, with big reputations.

All of them can drop-kick a bag of chaff over the local wheat silo; dodge a flock of rampaging sheep; fly for marks higher than an up-country goal post and ride a bump like a Rolls Royce traversing a country lane.

Of course, many an April champion has found the transi-

tion from Tangambaroopna to Tigerland somewhat difficult, as Melbourne is full of hard men who got there earlier.

These men will have their own collection of tall tales to tell.

In the matter of recruiting, for example. Half the dressing room will have been indulging in a bit of kick-to-kick in the park outside the Fitzcarlwood ground, while the great team was training.

A ball flew over the fence to land among the boys, whereupon the teller of the tale swooped on it, executed a perfect 70-yard droppie and was invited to train with the team, there and then.

Of course, he'd also had his Dad tell Snowy on the trams, who clipped the ticket of a bloke who's girlfriend worked in a pub where the bootstudder drank on Tuesday's after training – that his kid was worth getting in for a run.

His first game was, naturally enough, in the Grand Final that year, when the teller of the tale took an absolute sky-scraper of a mark in the dying seconds of the game, 99 yards out if it was an

inch, the ground covered in knee deep puddles, the ball as heavy as that stone Sisyphus had to push up the hill, his team five points behind – and the bell rings.

The Captain a tough but fair man, comes over and says, kick this one and you'll be a legend, miss it and I'll see to it you never pull on a sacred jumper for any team anywhere, ever again.

You could barely see the goals from where the umpire had a giant stand the mark. And then a blizzard swirled in from around the scoreboard as it went dark.

The teller of the tale pauses, to let the moment sink in. His team has never won a Flag, its supporters have grown old waiting. They need a reason to live on through the Depression.

The crowd hushes, the opposition players swear and throw clods of mud, but miraculously the sun comes out, the wind picks up the ball on the breeze like a feather bowled by Clarrie Grimmett – and it sails through.

And of course, the rest is football history.

The boys from the bush are eager to join the fray in the big smoke.

Jan. 23. The lapsed agreement between the VFL and VFA on transfers has been restored to control movements and prevent trafficking in juniors.

April 23. The appointments of former Collingwood player Charlie Pannam as coach of South Melbourne, and Fitzrovian Bert Taylor to Geelong raise questions of club loyalty in the minds of some observers.

April 30. Benefit match played in Hobart for former Melbourne champion Fred McGinis, now blind. McGinis played between 1897 and 1901.

May 5. Fitzroy Premiership pageant a bad day for Carlton as supporter hit by a falling post and another breaks his leg in a fall. Fitzroy beat Carlton, 11.13 (79) to 8.8 (56).

May 5. The new scoring boards erected by the *Football Record* at each League ground, indicating quarter by quarter scores at other grounds, are judged a complete success.

May 12. Carlton's call for umpires to be appointed by an independent committee, and return of stewards to monitor matches, rejected by League.

May 19. Collingwood coach Jock McHale recommends a glass of ale when players feel fatigued. 'There is no need for a man to wash himself in it, but a taste now and then is the best thing going.' McHale is celebrating 21 years at the club.

May 26. 'Charging' has become a matter of hot debate since round two when a South Melbourne player was wrongly given a free kick and nearly won the game. Fitzroy won 9.11 (65) to 9.9 (63).

May 29. An umpire states that a free kick for charging should only apply when the player who is contacted is standing still and not in possession of the football (→ 29/8/24).

June 9. John Worrall calls for the 'old cow bell' at St Kilda to be replaced by new time bell.

Aug. 18. Charles Brownlow, President of the Australian Football Council, Vice President of the VFL, and Secretary of Geelong, lies gravely ill (→ 23/1/24).

Debut
Edward 'Carji' Greeves (Geel)

Retirements
Frank 'Checker' Hughes (Rich)
Dave McNamara (St K)
Percy Parratt (Fitz)

Cartoon brings a Cat christening down at Geelong

A bit of whimsy from cartoonist Sam Wells, but the Pivotonians are now not going anywhere without their black cats.

July 7. What is a Pivotonian? The name derives from the city of Geelong being regarded as the 'pivot', or centre, of trade, but only people at Geelong seem to know or care. It seems that the clumsy nickname has a rival in 'The Cats'.

Occasionally the team is called 'The Seagulls' because of the closeness of the Corio Oval to the sea.

But the Association club of Williamstown got there first.

The idea seems to have stemmed from a Collingwood-Hawthorn Reserves match a month ago, in which the arrival of a black cat among the players at three-quarter time suddenly had them playing well and winning the game.

The *Herald* cartoonist Sam Wells took up the idea, with a cartoon suggesting that a black cat might help Geelong against Carlton. It did! After losing five of seven matches, Geelong beat Carlton, 13.15 (93) to 13.10 (98).

Now there are Cat replicas all around the club, and 'Carn the Pivots' is mingled with cries of 'Carn the Cats' (→ 10/10/25).

Off-field trouble for Saints and Blues

July 30. Three Carlton players and a trainer have been suspended for a punch-up after the Richmond game.

The suspensions follow that of St Kilda Vice President, A.D. Grant who incurred the wrath of the League for using the words 'we played you and the Collingwood team' against umpire A. Petrie.

In the Carlton incident, ill-feeling that has been prevalent in the club blew up as a Carlton Committee member and a player exchanged blows at a social occasion.

After considering the incident next day, the Carlton Committee suspended players Bert Boromeo, George Bolt and Jack Morrissey, as well as one of the trainers. The suspension might prove costly for Boromeo whose place in the state side must be in jeopardy.

The League, meanwhile, found the unrepentant Grant guilty, on his own admission, of improper conduct. He is suspended from holding any club office until he apologises (→ 20/5/25).

McNamara really sinks the slipper

May 19. 'Long Dave' McNamara certainly lived up to his reputation, and put paid to doubters in St Kilda's game against Collingwood.

Not only did the Saints win, 10.9 (69) to 6.12 (48), but McNamara dominated the match in defence.

He kicked two goals with such extraordinarily long kicks that the St Kilda Committee went out with a tape and measured the distances.

One was 75 yards, the other 84 yards and a shot that missed was measured from kick to the descent of the ball at 93 yards.

McNamara wrote an article in the *Sporting Globe* last month saying that kicking was easy and that anyone could learn the correct, simple techniques.

But no one kicks as far as consistently as 'Long Dave'.→

60,000 people saw Victoria beat SA at the MCG, 9.15 (69) to 4.5 (29).

Cazaly v. McNamara in Lake 'Premiership' epic

Sept. 15. A record crowd of almost 50,000 spectators went to the South Melbourne ground for the Lakeside challenge to determine whether South Melbourne or St Kilda would qualify for the Finals series.

It was to be a last home-and-away round like no other. As the crowd squeezed into the ground, sections of the fence broke. Hundreds of people sat on the verges and perched dangerously on the ridge of the footballers' pavilion. Another 10,000 supporters were unable to gain admission and some hoisted themselves on to trees outside the ground.

Mounted troopers kept the crowd from coming too close to the playing field. The drama in the crowd set the scene for an epic struggle between two traditional rivals and neigh-bours as well as a contest between two champions, St Kilda's veteran captain, Dave McNamara and South's brilliant Roy Cazaly.

Those expecting a close game were disappointed. St Kilda played poorly in the wet conditions and McNamara, in his last game, was hardly seen. Cazaly, on the other hand, was among the Southerners' best players.

St Kilda paid the penalty for experimenting with their line-up in such a crucial game, omitting regular fullback Bert Lenne and follower Jim Milne. Neither of their replacements played well and, after an even first half, South Melbourne took control to win comfortably and secure a position in the Finals. South Melbourne defeated St Kilda 8.20 (68) to 7.6 (48) (→ 30/9/27).

The huge crowd sought every vantage point inside and outside the Lake Oval.

Sensational Semi

Oct. 6. The League will inquire into the first Semi-final, in which Fitzroy beat Geelong, 14.13 (97) to 8.14 (62). Geelong started badly, as they dropped captain Bert Rankin, and his brother Cliff refused to play.

Among many incidents 'Snowy' Atkinson of Fitzroy and Lloyd Hagger kicked each other, Hagger slung Elliott to the ground breaking his collarbone, while Hagger was charged and hit from behind.

Mosquito Fleet captures the Flag

Oct. 20. The postponed Premiership has been won by Essendon's Mosquito Fleet on a day when sports lovers also had the Caulfield Cup to worry about.

The postponement of the Grand Final because of ground conditions has been much criticised.

Weather-conscious Melburnians recalled many games played in far worse conditions than those at the MCG last week, and were disgruntled that they had to choose between two favourite sports events today.

The Adverse Weather Committee met at 9.30 last Saturday, when it was still raining, rather than at the customary time of noon, when the MCG was drying nicely.

It has been said that they were more concerned with the 'shrinkage of the money take' than the rain.

However, there was no financial benefit in the postponement, as only 46,566 turned up today to watch Essendon's mosquitoes and a selection of taller high flyers defeat Fitzroy, 8.15 (63) to 6.10 (46).

Essendon went into the game rested because of the postponement, and having had a last round bye.

However, the bye did the Dons no good against South Melbourne whose Ted Johnson kicked a record seven goals to defeat them in the second Semi-final.

The small men are on the ball as Essendon go for the Premiership.

Having finished on top the Dons could challenge Fitzroy, who beat South in the Preliminary Final.

Essendon's Mosquito Fleet contains the 'little men' who have played a big part in the Dons' success this year.

George Shorten, 5ft 5in and a mozzie weight 7 stone 6 pounds was best on ground in the Grand Final

Charlie Hardy (5ft 1in) came from North Melbourne and played his first VFL game aged 34.

Other mozzies who played in the Grand Final were Jack Garden (5ft 5in), Vince Irwin (5ft 6in) and Frank Maher (5ft 6in).

Coach Syd Barker had blended these small players on every line with six-footers, including match-winning full-forward Greg Stockdale, halfback Tom Fitzmaurice and veteran fullback Fred Baring.

This was a quick and skilful side, who outran and outlasted Fitzroy. The highlight was the last goal which sealed the game when 'Tich' Shorten soared over Maroon captain Gordon Rattray to take a great mark, and ran on to goal (→ 27/9/24).

Jan. 23. Charles Brownlow dies.

April 9. A new finals system is re-introduced, in which the top four teams play each other, and the Premiership is decided on the results (→ 24/4/31).

April 9. The League decided that home sides will wear black shorts, while away teams will wear white shorts (→30/3/28).

April 9. Former umpire Arthur Norden replaces Jack Elder as VFL Umpires adviser. Elder, who last umpired in 1922, has retired because of ill health.

April 9. The Hawthorn Citizens' League campaign gains support of the Hawthorn Council for that team's quest for admission to the League. Council said the ground would be enlarged 'if necessary'.

April 26. Jack Worrall of the *Australasian* is critical of the Charles Brownlow medal. He does not think the League should give a medal, or that umpires are the proper people to make judgements on players.

April 26. Fitzroy defeat Carlton, 16.9 (105) to 15.13 (103). It is the first time each team has scored over a hundred points in a VFL match.

May 3. South Melbourne timekeeper Charlie Goding experiences auditory *deja vu* when, as in 1922, he tolls half time in the match against Fitzroy. This year South score a goal before the umpire hears the bell, but lose 7.15 (57) to 12.14 (86).

June 21. South Melbourne beat Geelong for the 19th year in a row at South, 7.6 (48) to 7.3 (45).

July 12. Public servants are agitating to play a team in the League next season, using the Friendly Societies Ground.

Aug. 23. The League decision to enforce hand passing with a clenched fist is widely aproved. Jack Worrall says: 'Less throwing means more kicking. After all the game is football'.

Oct. 22. A Smoke Night at the Melbourne Town Hall for many old time players and yarners raises £1,800 for the Lord Mayor's Hospital Fund. Among those present are Henry Harrison, Jack Worrall, George Robertson and Peter Burns.

Retirements
Fred Baring (Ess)
Newton Chandler (Carl)
Jim Freake (Fitz)

Free kick for kicking out of bounds rule

Aug. 29. At a meeting of the VFL a motion was lodged to refer the recent Australasian Football Council change of Law 11 back to the Council.

Law 11 has been altered to give a free kick to a player of the team opposite to the one forcing the ball out of bounds.

It appears that one of the VFL's delegates to the Council, Mr E.W. Copeland of Collingwood, voted for the amendment, against the express wishes of the League.

At the least it might eliminate the unseemly bullocking in the ruck at boundary throw-ins (→ 2/5/25).

Captain calls for the count – but can't

July 12. St Kilda captain Wels Eicke stunned the crowd during the second quarter of the game against Carlton when he demanded a count, claiming that there were 19 opposition players on the field.

Play was halted and the teams lined up in the centre as the umpires solemnly counted the players. At the conclusion of the count, the umpire called Eicke over and informed him that only the regulation 18 Carlton players were playing. Players were sent back to their positions and the game resumed with Carlton running out easy winners over the hapless Saints, 14.15 (99) to 8.8 (56).

Today's fast game is not a good game

May 24. The curse of modern football is that everything is sacrificed to pace, according to the leading football commentator John Worrall.

He says that with the majority of players the main idea is to run with the ball until it is lost, killing system and thoroughly disorganising the side.

'The game is faster decidedly than in the days of old, but to one mistake made 30 years ago there are 100 now,' Worrall writes.

'From a football point of view losing one's kick is a crime, but it is rather the rule than the exception.'

League censures quaking goalpost shakers

The League has acted quickly to stamp out this new football menace.

July 8. An epidemic of goalpost shaking has been cured by the League with the censure of two of the shakers, Arthur Hando of South Melbourne and Jim Spain of Richmond. But it ruled against awarding the June 21 match between Geelong and South to the Cats.

The practice of shaking, or swaying, the post came to light after that match between Geelong and South Melbourne, won by South 7.6 (48) to 7.3 (45).

Geelong claimed the match and several players testified that Hando was swaying the post two or three feet from the perpendicular when a shot by Arthur Pink hit it.

They also saw Hando wobbling the post as Cliff Rankin took a shot.

Post wobbling seemed to come into vogue with this incident. The next Saturday South were on their way to beating Richmond 9.7 (61) to 5.13 (43) when Umpire Cook reported Jim Spain of Richmond for the same offence while Ted Johnson of South was kicking.

Footballers' KNEE CAPS And ANKLETS

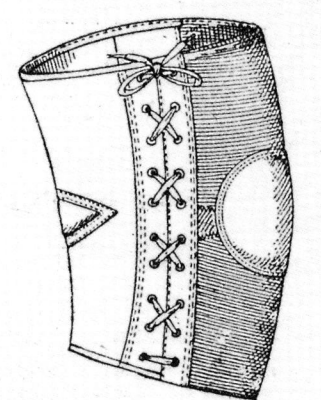

Just the thing for a dicky knee.

Moriarty breaks goalkicking tally

Aug. 30. A new goalkicking record was set today when Jack Moriarty of Fitzroy kicked eight goals against Melbourne, bringing his total for the season to 72 so far. This beats the 68 established last year by Greg Stockdale of Essendon, Moriarty's previous club. Fitzroy won 16.14 (110) to 9.13 (67).

Essendon will regret allowing Moriarty free to be acquired by Fitzroy. He began the year in fine style, kicking seven goals in each of his first three games with his new side. As several games are still ahead he seems certain to increase his record tally.

Essendon selectors have only themselves to blame for his departure, having played Jack Moriarty in their Seconds all last season.

MARK TANDY, STH MELBOURNE.

WELS EICKE, ST KILDA.

A. DUNCAN, CARLTON.

R. CORBETT, MELBOURNE.

J. FREAKE, FITZROY.

F. MAHER, ESSENDON.

CLIFF RANKIN, GEELONG.

H. G. SAUNDERS, COLLINGWOOD.

NORMAN McINTOSH, RICHMOND.

Victorian Football League Stars

Flag but no Grand Final

After the dull Finals, the Dons versus VFA leader Footscray match is attractive .

Sept. 27. The season has ended with a fearful anti-climax. Essendon has won the Flag despite losing today's match against Richmond, and there will be none of the excitement of a Grand Final next week.

The decisive match took place at South Melbourne in the third round of Finals. Richmond would have had to beat Essendon by more than seven goals to head the Finals ladder and so force Essendon (as Minor Premiers) to challenge in a Grand Final.

Richmond played very well, and there were hopes of a Grand Final at the first change, when they led 4.2 to 1.4. But while they sustained their edge, mainly in the ruck and in marking, they could only manage a 20-point win, 9.13 (67) to 6.11 (47). The dominant players were the leaders, Tom Fitzmaurice of Essendon and Danny Minogue of Richmond.

The whole Finals series has been poorly attended, with crowds averaging 28,000 to the six matches. Next year, and thereafter, the League will have to present a Finals series with a more fitting climax (→ 30/6/39).

1924 Statistics

Leading Goalkicker:
Jack Moriarty (Fitz) 82
Brownlow Medallist:
E. 'Carji' Greeves (Geel)
Finals Matches:

Ess 8.10 (58) : Fitz 2.6 (18)
Rich 13.7 (85) : S. Melb 9.3 (57)
Fitz 11.10 (76) : Rich 8.8 (56)
Ess 10.12 (72) : S. Melb 4.15 (39)
Rich 9.13 (67) : Ess 6.11 (47)
S. Melb 13.8 (86) : Fitz 10.13 (73)

Ladder:	W	L	D	%	pts
Ess	11	4	1	131.6	46
S. Melb	11	5	-	116.5	44
Fitz	10	6	-	112.1	40
Rich	10	6	-	102.5	40
Geel	8	8	-	107.2	32
Coll	8	8	-	96.0	32
Carl	5	10	1	92.3	22
Melb	4	12	-	83.3	16
St K	4	12	-	75.7	16

Final Placings:
(1)Ess (2)Rich (3)Fitz (4)S. Melb

Fitzmaurice quits over Dons loss slurs

Oct. 4. VFA Premiers Footscray ended VFL Premiers Essendon's season with a thumping win in front of 46,100 people at the MCG. Footscray won 9.10 (64) to Essendon 4.12 (36)

This was the first time the Premiers of the respective competitions have met.

The game, in aid of Dame Nellie Melba's Disabled Soldiers' Fund was a great success financially, contributing £2,800.

While the the game seemed to suggest that the standard of VFA football is more than a match for that of the VFL, rumblings inside the Essendon camp might indicate otherwise.

Essendon's champion centre-halfback Tom Fitzmaurice has said that he will never play with the Dons again.

He says that after the game a team-mate said to him 'Why grouch? You could have been in the cut up too,' a reference to allegations that some players had been paid off not to do their best, in the interests of a wager by a prominent Footscray football identity.

Only the persuasive powers of Canon Ernie Hughes could get some disgusted Essendon players on to the field after half time.

Fists are said to have flown in the Essendon dressing room after the game, as they did after the loss to Richmond which gave Essendon the Premiership under this season's farcical system.

Footscray are likely to join the VFL soon (→ 26/5/28).

The best and fairest, who will receive the newly inaugurated Brownlow Medal: Geelong's 'Carji' Greeves. The award is decided on umpire's votes.

1925

April 4. The phenomenon of football practice starting earlier and earlier each season was noted in the *Australasian*, as was the failure of 'March Champions' to prosper.

May 2. The new rule awarding a free kick against the player of the team last to touch the ball before it goes out of bounds has been a great success, resulting in a faster game, and eliminating boundary jostling by ruckmen (→ 13/4/28).

May 9. Footscray record their first VFL win, over South Melbourne, 10.10 (70) to 8.12 (60), at the Western Oval.→

May 30. Hawthorn Mayblooms' first win is at the expense of Footscray, 10.14 (74) to 8.10 (58).→

July 4. South Australia have a narrow victory over Victoria, 11.11 (77) to 11.8 (74), in an exciting game played at the Adelaide Oval.

July 11. Melbourne timekeeper of 37 years Walter Spry described as sitting dispassionately chewing a huge cigar like Madame Defarge knitting by the guillotine — waiting for the blade, or bell, to finish proceedings.

July 11. Geelong kick 11.4 (70) to South Melbourne's zero in a first quarter pounding, and then go on to win 18.13 (121) to 3.10 (28).

July 25. Victoria regain some pride by defeating Western Australia, 22.11 (143) to 8.10 (58). Cliff Rankin of Geelong kicks 10.1.

Aug. 6. Melbourne and Victorian wingman Gerald Donnelly has had his playing permit cancelled for the rest of the season. The League Investigations Committee has ruled that he is residentially bound to North Melbourne.

Aug. 22. St Kilda bring Geelong's remarkable run of 12 wins in a row to an end, beating them 9.8 (62) to 7.9 (51). (→ 30/6/33).

Aug. 22. Harry Davie, Melbourne's full-forward, kicks 13 goals, including eight in the last quarter, in Melbourne's 18.14 (122) demolition of Carlton 6.9 (45).

Sept. 7. A Port Melbourne official urges VFA clubs to resist 'siren song' of VFL inviting them to join League.

Retirements
Vic Thorp (Rich)

New teams do well in first VFL battles

The Shinboners colours on parade.

Mayblooms: carry Hawthorn hopes.

The Tricolours from the west.

May 2. Pleasant weather for the opening of the football season encouraged crowds at all venues. Cable cars were so packed they rolled along more painfully than ever, especially those heading to Fitzroy.

Three new sides were taking the field in the League competition. After long deliberations and tense meetings in January, decisions were taken to admit Hawthorn, North Melbourne and Footscray to the League. Footscray's inclusion had been expected, being the VFA Premiers last year, but North Melbourne's promotion came at the expense of Prahran.

At Glenferrie Oval about 16,000 people attended to watch Hawthorn's debut. Although failing to defeat the strong Richmond combination, they certainly justified their promotion from the Association. The result at Glenferrie was Richmond 11.11 (77) to Hawthorn's 5.8 (38).

North Melbourne created the surprise of the day by defeating Geelong, 9.13 (67) to 8.11 (59). The other newcomers, Footscray, proved their footballing value in an exciting tussle with Fitzroy, always a tough nut to crack at their home ground, losing by only nine points: Fitzroy 8.15 (63), Footscray 8.6 (54).

Teams disappointed in membership bids

May 2. The legal action threatened by the VFA over the VFL drawing away three leading clubs in apparent contravention of an agreement might be taken more seriously if there had not been such a rush by other VFA clubs to join up.

Individual VFA teams have made no secret of their desire to join the most powerful body in football.

Last year proposals were received from Brighton, Brunswick, Camberwell, Caulfield, and Prahran as well as the three successful clubs, Footscray, Hawthorn and North.

As for the League – its position in the selection reminded some of Lewis Carroll's poem:
'I weep for you', the Walrus said: 'I deeply sympathise'.
With sobs and tears he sorted out Those of the largest size...

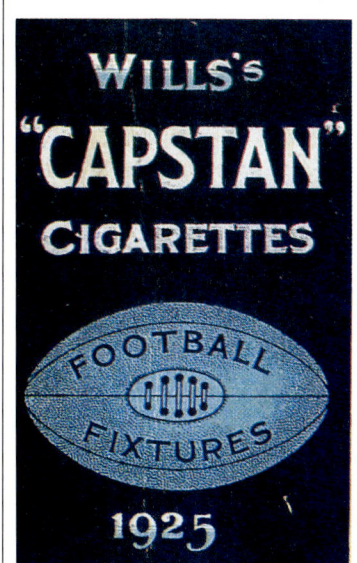

WILLS'S "CAPSTAN" CIGARETTES

FOOTBALL FIXTURES

1925

Some football barrackers like a cigarette, although the practice is reputed to stunt the growth. Wills supports the game with its handy guide to the 1925 footy fixtures.

MCC members sink to a low level

June 13. Melbourne Cricket Club members are partisan towards the Redlegs, and are vigorous barrackers, but their behaviour towards a Fitzroy player on Saturday went beyond the bounds of decency.

They assumed that the felling of the champion Melbourne player Dick Taylor by a Fitzroy man was deliberate, and subjected the Fitzroy man to a steady stream of abuse throughout the match.

Both Taylor and his 'assailant' were going fast when they clashed, and the members could not know if the blow to Taylor was intentional.

But they let out a mighty cheer when a Melbourne player met the Fitzroy man with a fair bump later in the game. An onlooker described their behaviour as being of 'a deplorably low level'.

FOOTSCRAY

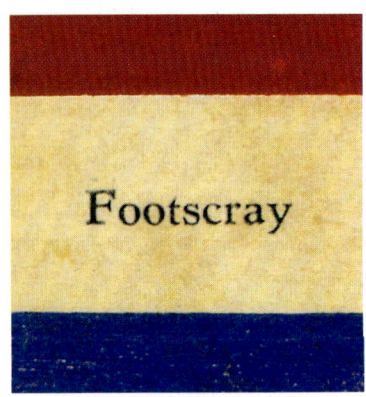

For a club with such strong working class links, Footscray Football Club had very regal origins. It was formed in 1883, the year of the death of the Prince Imperial and in its early days was known as Footscray Imperial.

Charlie Lovett, who would be appointed as Footscray's first captain, announced that Footscray had been accepted into the VFA, but there were still some difficulties.

The Western Oval had to be widened. It was also decided to move the pavilion from the Barkly Street end of the ground to the southern end, but it became bogged in the centre of the oval and every horse and person in the area was summoned to help move it! As in later years there was no shortage of people prepared to put their shoulders to the wheel.

Footscray's team was a tough, hard unit from the outset. Osborne (a Williamstown team) were reported to have left the ground in a game against Footscray 'as they did not want to participate in a free fight'. Men like 'Chunker' Considine, Jack Coward, 'Piggie' Kendall and Bob Dick kept the club's flag flying in those early days.

After eight clubs broke away from the VFA Footscray prospered, running third in 1897 then winning three Premierships of under the captaincy of Dave De Coite. The famed 'Ching' Harris and Joe Marmo were two of the shining lights, although the Tricolors struggled for a few seasons at the turn of the Century.

Footscray was notable for the longevity of some of its stars. Sam Hood retired in 1905 after 17 years of service and the durable Marmo notched up 20 years in the colors. He was part of the team that beat Brunswick before a record VFA crowd of 41,000 at the MCG during the visit of the American Fleet. Star of that team was full-forward Jack Hutchinson who in one match booted 16 goals to set a club record.

The Tricolors won another flag in 1913, but its greatest period of sustained success would come after World War I when it recruited strongly. The major acquisitions were former South Melbourne players 'Chook' Howell, a tireless follower , and the deadly forward Harry Morgan.

Footscray won the 1919 and 1920 premierships, but there was plenty of controversy along the way. At one stage there was dissension over pay involving Howell and in 1920 Footscray had to replay a final against North when the initial game was disrupted by the crowd invading the field before the final bell.

Johnny Craddock was a great leader as captain of those teams, and after his retirement Footscray gained leaders in Con McCarthy (Collingwood) and Alex Eason (Geelong). From 1920 to 1924 Footscray lost just eight home-and-away games. They had brilliant forwards in George Bayliss and Tom Mullins plus a champion youngster named Alan Hopkins.

A runaway win over Williamstown in the 1924 Grand Final gave Footscray its fourth Flag in six years and sparked calls for a charity match between Footscray and the VFL Premiers Essendon.

To this day the game remains shrouded in controversy with allegations that Essendon did not try their hardest. By day's end Con McCarthy's team had won by 28 points.

A few months later the League announced that it would accept Footscray into its competition. An incensed VFA refused to award Footscray the pennant and medals given to the Premiership team. The Dogs, by now, had their sights set on higher goals.

Russell Holmesby

HAWTHORN

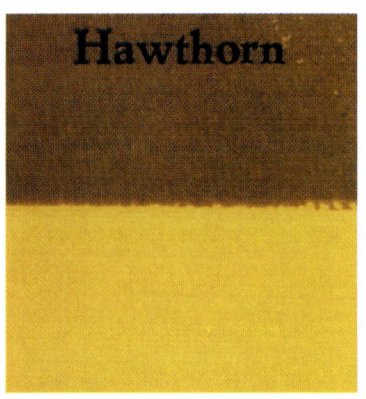

Hawthorn's pre-VFL history is the thinnest and most modest of all the clubs that form the League. Hawthorn's location was the vital factor, first in the VFA in 1914 and then in the VFL in 1925, as both bodies wanted to have a team from the eastern suburbs.

Hawthorn was nothing better than a mediocre Metropolitan Junior Football Association side when it joined the VFA and was only a mid-range performer in the Association.

Hawthorn was born in February 1873 at the Hawthorne Hotel in Burwood Road. It is believed that many of its early players were drawn from the nearby Hawthorn Grammar School.

By 1875 it appears that Hawthorn was established at Grace Park although it may also have played some games at nearby Meaney's Paddock. By the late 1880s Hawthorn was struggling to maintain its identity and in April 1889 it amalgamated with the stronger Riversdale club. Still the club meandered along and matters reached their lowest ebb in 1899 when Hawthorn scratched from the season.

The lack of identity was reflected in the uniform changes. The team had started in blue and white in 1873, then gone to yellow and black in 1889, red and blue in 1893, blue and white in 1902, then red and black in 1906. In its final two years of junior football Hawthorn wore blue and gold, but had to change in the VFA because those colours were already worn by Williamstown.

Hawthorn came last in its final year in junior ranks. The push to join the VFA came from the Hawthorn Council, the landlord of the Glenferrie Oval where Hawthorn had been based since 1906. Its debut was inauspicious, running second last in its opening year and last the following season.

It was a big, tough new world in the VFA and the home crowd was shocked by the ruffians from Port Melbourne who started a brawl when they were beaten at Glenferrie in June 1914. Hawthorn only made the VFA finals once and on that occasion it was bundled out of contention by Port Melbourne in the 1923 first semifinal. Its greatest glory came in 1922 when it kicked 30.22 to Prahran's 6.9, a record score which stood for 17 years.

The first suggestion of possibly joining the VFL came as early as 1919 and again the impetus came from the council. Meanwhile Hawthorn tried to make its mark on the field after recruiting men like Arthur Rademacher (South) and Jim Jackson (Collingwood). One of the more bizarre sidelights in football history came when Hawthorn secured Port Melbourne's Bill Walton as captain-coach, but Port Melbourne refused to clear him. He came to an agreement which enabled him to coach Hawthorn during the week, but then play for Port on Saturdays. Walton was finally cleared to Hawthorn and led the side into the Finals.

In what proved to be Hawthorn's last year of VFA competition, 1924, the team just missed the Finals, contrary to an oft-repeated story that the club finished in a blaze of glory. Another myth is that that Hawthorn was lucky to be accepted into VFL ranks in January 1925. Hawthorn and Footscray were the first two accepted, then North Melbourne was preferred to Prahran as the third club.

Thus, Hawthorn's entry to the top echelon had been brought about more by geographical factors and council pride rather than any sustained football performance. Success on the football field would be a long time coming.

Russell Holmesby

NORTH MELBOURNE

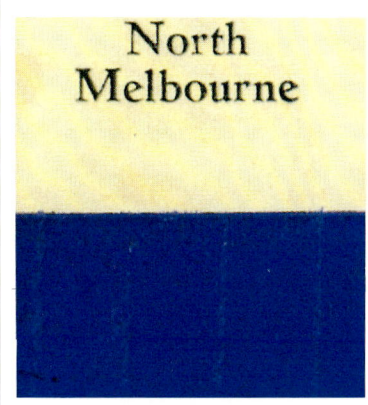

Over the years North Melbourne Football Club has built a reputation for resourcefulness and an enviable work ethic.

The way in which the club procured its first football says much about the North character. The money came from the sale of old roof iron belonging to one of the founders of the club, Tom Jacks.

Contrary to a popular belief, North Melbourne did not have its origins in the Hotham club. It began life as North Melbourne in 1869 and is believed to have originated from members of the St Mary's Church of England cricket team. Historian, Father Gerard Dowling has found that a separate team, Hotham, was playing games in 1870.

North Melbourne played its early games at Royal Park. It was a junior club in its early years, wasn't accorded senior status until 1874 and did not join the VFA until 1886, when it changed its uniform to vertical stripes to distinguish it from Geelong. It went to play at the Arden Street Ground in 1882.

The Town of Hotham was proclaimed North Melbourne in August 1887 and the club again became North Melbourne.

When the big split came in 1896 North could have reasonably hoped to have earned inclusion in the VFL as it had finished sixth of the 13 teams in the 1896 VFA competition, but there were several factors against it – it was not financially strong, had a reputation for hooliganism and was drawing players from the same territory as Essendon.

In 1903, under the leadership of Paddy Noonan, North broke through for its first VFA Premiership. It was a stirring and emotional win, in stark contrast to winning next year through Richmond's forfeiture.

North caused a sensation in 1907 when it proposed an amalgamation with West Melbourne, a fellow VFA club that shared the Arden Street ground, with the aim of joining the VFL.

The VFL admitted Richmond and University instead and angry VFA delegates voted to expel North Melbourne and West Melbourne. North Melbourne reformed as a 'new' club and took the field again in 1908.

By the end of 1910 the Phoenix-like Northerners had grabbed another Flag thanks to daring recruiting that netted Carlton champions 'Mallee' Johnson, Fred Jinks, Charlie Hammond and Frank Caine after an internal upheaval at Princes Park. It was a coup that remained unsurpassed for six decades, until the 10-year rule and Ron Barassi.

North won another Flag in 1914 and began an era of unprecedented success. The VFA suspended competition between 1916 and 1917, but North did not lose a game from August 1914 to September 1919, winning three Premierships. The champions were rover Charlie Hardy and ruckman Syd Barker.

The success heightened North's determination to join the VFL. In 1921 it announced that it would merge with Essendon (left homeless by the closure of the East Melbourne Cricket Ground), but the move fell flat when it was found that Arden Street oval belonged to the citizens of North Melbourne.

North did not play in the second half of 1921 and when it reformed it amalgamated with the Essendon Association team, but still it remained in the VFA.

Early in 1925 the admission to the League was finally achieved. Footscray and Hawthorn were first in the door and after much deliberation North was elected instead of Prahran. The men from Arden Street had made it at last. **Russell Holmesby**

Yanks to Nuts' nine: Attaboy Gordon

Aug. 1. Many Americans from the visiting fleet sampled Australia's style of football at the Collingwood ground today, where the home team met Essendon.

They were treated to a splendid exhibition of skill and cleverness by Gordon Coventry of Collingwood, who could do nothing wrong and kicked nine goals. His side dominated play from the first quarter and overwhelmed the opposition by 15.19 (109) to 4.5 (29).

The Americans were very taken with Coventry's shooting for goal. Yankee shouts of 'Attaboy Gordon!' were heard. One visitor in the Collingwood Committee's enclosure delighted his hosts with 'that guy Gordon is sure the snowy petalled marguerite' by which he meant 'isn't he a daisy'. (→ 22/8/27).

Coventry: a show for the fleet.

Blues in turmoil, coach O'Brien sacked

Paddy O'Brien: on the outer.

May 20. The Carlton club remains at a low ebb this season. A new Committee has failed so far to find a new direction. The latest example of confusion is the dismissal of Paddy O'Brien as coach. The Committee has felt 'obliged, reluctantly, to relieve him of his duties'.

O'Brien is known as one of the toughest and most dashing defenders in football, and is said to be an ornament to the game and a 'natural leader'. He was captain of the Blues last season, but his team-mates did not re-elect him this year, nor vote for him as their vice-captain.

The Carlton Committee believes that a coach who is not in either leadership role is in a poor position to perform his duties. They will now seek a replacement from outside the team (→ 28/8/36).

Shinboner Rutley gets life out of kicks

Aug. 6. A special tribunal has disqualified certain players reported by the umpires for deplorable behaviour in the Geelong game with North Melbourne on Saturday.

Sir Baldwin Spencer, President of the League, and Mr M.C. Duigan, decided that Fred Rutley (North Melbourne) would be suspended for life for kicking, during what had deteriorated into a vicious match won by Geelong 22.22 (154) to 9.5 (59).

To stand down until the end of next year's season are Stan Thomas and Arthur Coghlan, both of Geelong.

There is a grave doubt as to whether the real culprits were dealt with, and everybody who saw the game agrees that at least two other players were guilty of far worse tactics than any disclosed by the evidence before the tribunal. But an umpire's eyes cannot be everywhere.

Pride of Cats bring back Geelong's first Flag

The Geelong defence relieves a Collingwood attack in the Grand Final.

In the bag. Lloyd Hagger, Cliff Rankin and Keith Johns at lemon time.

Oct. 10. A record crowd of 64,288 saw Geelong hold off a fast-finishing Collingwood by ten points to win their first League Premiership Flag.

Geelong's last football title came in 1886, 11 years before the League was founded. They had great success in the early days, winning eight other Flags. The win was a triumph for this football-mad provincial town. All week Geelong has been at fever-pitch, with industries working until 6 p.m. so that both workers and employers could have a day off on Saturday. Some 8,000 made the trip down. Both Collingwood and Geelong have histories of failing to produce their best on these big occasions.

This time Geelong, despite the closeness of the score, were the superior team on the day. It was only in the last quarter that their defence came under sustained pressure.

Geelong went directly down the ground, while Collingwood chose to play a less-effective short-passing game that was all too often intercepted by opposing defenders. In near-perfect football conditions, Geelong started the game full of confidence and had two goals on the board in the opening ten minutes.

It was against the wind in the second quarter that Geelong really asserted their superiority. Playing in front and marking strongly all over the ground, they used their pace to be first at the ball. Geelong drove their advantage home to lead by 17 points at the half-way mark.

Although outplayed and, at times, looking somewhat clumsy, Collingwood hung on doggedly in the third quarter, but were still four goals behind at the final change.

The last quarter turned into a desperate struggle and with Collingwood kicking two goals in the first seven minutes the game became a contest once more.

Players threw themselves into the fray as Collingwood strove desperately to close the gap and Geelong fought manfully to retain the lead. With the huge crowd cheering them on, Geelong held out to win a thriller by ten points – 10.19 (79) to 9.15 (69). Captain-coach Cliff Rankin, kicked five goals (→ 10/10/31).

Saint's Brownlow, Cat's goalkicking

Oct 10. St Kilda has had one of its rare moments of triumph with the declaration of dashing centreman Colin Watson as this year's Brownlow Medallist. Watson played in only 15 games this year, but was voted best afield in nine of them.

Watson is a well-built, hard-hitting player and a tremendous worker on the field, and he can either kick the ball long or spear a stab pass to a team-mate.

He joined the club in 1920, from South Warrnambool and Port Melbourne, but the bickering at St Kilda in 1922 drove him back to the bush for a year.

Geelong's evergreen forward Lloyd Hagger has topped a great year for the Cats by becoming the leading goalkicker with 78 goals. Hagger started with Geelong in 1917, going from the lowly Barwon thirds to the Geelong senior team in two weeks (→ 30/4/35).

Colin Watson, the rugged centreman from South Warrnambool, has won this year's Brownlow Medal for St Kilda. He played 15 of 17 games but was best afield nine times.

Lady revives player with kiss of life

Aug. 29. Officials and police were too staggered to stop a young lady from crossing the field of play during the North Melbourne versus Essendon game today.

She was hurrying to the aid of a North Melbourne player who lay injured on the field, being restored by the trainers. Whether she offered a kiss or encouraging words, her treatment worked.

Not so fortunate were the North Melbourne team themselves. The Essendon backmen had little to do in a contest dominated by the 'Same Olds' after the first quarter. Their ruck and forwards had the better chance to shine.

George Shorten was particularly brilliant, kicking one goal but being responsible for at least six others. Final scores were Essendon 14.19 (103) to North Melbourne 6.9 (45).

1925 Statistics

Leading Goalkicker:
Lloyd Hagger (Geel) 78
Brownlow Medallist:
Colin Watson (St K)
Finals:
First Semi-final Ess 10.8 (68) Coll 12.6 (78); **Second Semi-final** Geel 13.8 (86) Melb 14.17 (101); **Final** Melb 3.8 (26) Coll 8.15 (63); **Grand Final** Geel 10.19 (79) Coll 9.15 (69)

Ladder:	W	L	D	%	pts
Geel	15	2	-	152.7	60
Ess	13	4	-	119.3	52
Melb	12	4	1	138.5	50
Coll	12	5	-	127.1	48
Fitz	12	5	-	125.7	48
St K	8	9	-	99.6	32
Rich	6	10	1	86.7	26
S. Melb	6	11	-	85.7	24
Carl	5	12	-	79.0	20
N. Melb	5	12	-	75.2	20
Foots	4	13	-	82.7	16
Haw	3	14	-	66.1	12

1926

Fists fly in the merry month of May

May 30. Five rounds have now been played, and already the tribunal has decided to suspend eight men, six of them for eight playing Saturdays. The rough play thus condemned included elbowing, punching the ball in a man's face, and fist fights behind the play. That such incidents are still occurring, despite the threat of such severe penalties, raises the question of whether punishment will ever eradicate the cowardly acts of violence that disfigure the game.

It is true that some players are provoked almost beyond endurance by mockery and rough-house acts. As one observer commented recently, 'A man begins as a fair player, but these kickers, trippers and elbowers soon make a fair man sick, and he has to get even'.

One interesting suggestion has come from an old player, who recommends that a committee of old players attends one game each week, as observers. They would later approach men they see offending, whether noticed by the umpires or not, to interview them concerning their behaviour. It is felt that this form of reproach, by men held in high regard, might have a better reforming effect on the pests than tribunal inquisitions.

Out: Shanahan (Coll), Shorten (Ess), Chesswass and Wilson (Coll).

Fitzroy full-forward Robert Merrick holds a mark against St Kilda.

The huge crowd at Collingwood are there for the football, but a hot meat pie is never out of mind as the vendor patrols the boundary for customers.

Dr McClelland in charge of VFL

McClelland: life of football.

May 5. Dr William C. McClelland has been elected President of the VFL upon the retirement of Sir Baldwin Spencer, who has been President since 1919.

Sir Baldwin, who presided over the successful return of 'King football' to Melbourne in the difficult years after the war, leaves because of ill health.

Dr McClelland brings a lifetime of football involvement to the job.

His career began at Brighton Grammar and Brighton juniors, before he made his debut with the Redlegs of Melbourne in one game in 1897 and then another in 1898.

During this time he was also studying at Melbourne University taking a B.A. in 1899, M.A. in 1900 and graduating in Medicine and Surgery in 1904.

Dr McClelland played for Melbourne in the 1900 Premiership team and was made captain the following season. He remained in that role until retiring at the end of 1904, having played 75 games, mostly on the halfback line.

While stationed at the Ballarat Hospital in 1906 and 1907, he played football for Ballarat.

'Doc', as he is universally known, was elected to the Melbourne Football Club Committee in 1909 and to the Melbourne Cricket Club Committee in 1910. He has been a VFL delegate and club doctor. Doc has as wide an experience as could be imagined (→ 19/3/30).

Horrie Clover on both sides of the fence

May 22. Plans by Carlton Secretary Horrie Clover to resume his playing career pose a unprecedented dilemma for the League.

Clover, one of the League's top players before a serious illness sidelined him, is also a member of the Umpire and Permit Committee.

Never before has a player held dual roles which could put him in a position of a potential conflict of interest. While there are no rules to prevent Clover from maintaining both positions, it would have to place considerable pressure on anyone's loyalties.

The point at issue is not whether Clover would place club (and employer) allegiance above that of the impartiality required as a member of the umpiring committee, but that Clover, like Caesar's wife, must be seen to be totally above any suspicion whatsoever.

In the circumstances, it appears that Clover can not do both. Undoubtedly he would be missed on the Committee where his extensive experience and vast knowledge of the game has been a great asset. But he would be missed most of all by football followers were he not to return to the playing field.

Clover is a spectacular footballer with his high marking and long kicking and the game would be much poorer were he to give up playing for he is an ornament to the game. Champions on and off the field are vital for all sports.

Clover: man in the middle.

Fuchsias bloom to take the Flag

Stan Wittman shoots for goal.

Desperate Collingwood defence as Melbourne try to scramble a goal.

Oct. 9. Melbourne's long years in the footlockers of football history came to a triumphant end today when they took the Premiership Flag from Collingwood with a 57-point win, 17.17 (119) to 9.8 (62).

The Fuchsias, so long used to a patter of polite applause from the Grey Smith stand, raised their arms in ecstasy as the full-throated roar of 59,362 people at the game acknowledged the win. The crowd, however, might have been diminished by then as many Collingwood followers left as they saw their hopes fading.

The proudest man there was the Father of Australian Football, H. C. A. Harrison, 96 years old and clad in red and blue as he watched the team he loved come out on top.

Both teams were below strength as Melbourne was without centreman Bob Corbett, KO'd last week, and Collingwood missed good players in fullback Charlie Dibbs and tough ruckman 'Kitty' Clayden. Melbourne covered Corbett's centre position with champion Ivor Warne-Smith and teamed new player 'Pop' Vine in the ruck with their towering trump card Bob Johnson.

Melbourne played with style and system in the first quarter, finding their forwards and shutting out Collingwood against the stiff breeze.

But the Magpies' gladiatorial spirit surfaced in the second quarter and they kicked 5.3 to be only nine points down at half time.

After that it was 'shut the gate'. The spirit of '26 surfaced and they ran through the Magpies with a 7.2 to 1.2 third quarter. Syd Coventry, rover 'Jiggy' Harris and Ernie Wilson were Collingwood's best.→

1926 Statistics

Leading Goalkicker:
Gordon Coventry (Coll) 83
Brownlow Medallist:
Ivor Warne-Smith (Melb).
Semi Finals: Geel 10.10 (70) Ess 17.15 (117); Coll 12.12 (84) Melb 13.17 (95); **Final** Melb 6.6 (42) Ess 5.9 (39); **Grand Final** Coll 9.8 (62) Melb 17.17 (119)

Ladder:	W	L	D	%	pts
Coll	15	3	-	149.3	60
Geel	15	3	-	145.2	60
Melb	14	4	-	146.4	56
Ess	12	6	-	124.3	48
S. Melb	12	6	-	118.9	48
Carl	11	7	-	106.5	44
Rich	9	9	-	92.0	36
Fitz	6	12	-	86.1	24
St K	6	12	-	75.8	24
Foots	4	14	-	69.9	16
Haw	3	14	1	66.4	14
N. Melb	0	17	1	73.7	2

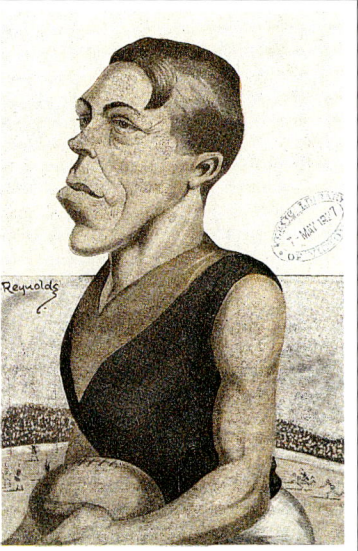

The Brownlow Medallist for 1926 is Ivor Warne-Smith, the Melbourne captain, a cool all-round player and the inspiration of the Fuchsias' Premiership win.

Substitute call as Corbett king hit

Oct. 2. Melbourne beat Essendon in the Preliminary Final 6.6 (42) to 5.9 (39) in a result that can only be described as football justice.

As the players were leaving the ground at half time Melbourne's centreman Bob Corbett was viciously attacked from behind, suffering a broken jaw. The Redlegs had only 17 men fit for the second half.

Melbourne increased their lead to nine points at three-quarter time, then had to defend a 'fightback'.

Just as it looked 'all up' a figure, its head swathed in bandages, emerged from the players race.

It was Bob Corbett. 'I just sneaked out to help my side,' he said.

This desperate action heightened calls to allow substitutes for injured players next season (→2/7/32).

Ivor Warne-Smith: led the Red Legs with character and example

Ivor Warne-Smith was considered by Victorian selector George Cathie as the most perfect footballer to play between the wars. 'He was fitted to fill any position, was well balanced in all he did, and was a two way player as well', Cathie wrote in 1949 in reviewing the 1920s and 1930s.

'He turned on his wrong (left) foot and used it just as well as he did his right. He used his left hand to handball, as well as his right. He was never at a loss.'

Warne-Smith is remembered as a superb high mark, a long kick and an exponent of opening up the game with handball. He played well, wet or dry, and could play any position.

He was six feet tall, lightly and strongly built and possessed great agility. His main role was as a defender, and yet he was often swung into the ruck, or forward, and kicked 100 goals in a 146 game career.

But leadership and character were probably the greatest strengths he brought to Melbourne. He had a natural 'presence' and an inspiring coolness and determination in play.

Melbourne's best year in his time was 1926. It won the Preliminary Final against Essendon with 17 men, after centreman Bob Corbett was 'king hit' and suffered a broken jaw.

Still Essendon could not make up the small margin between the sides, and Warne-Smith led the defence to hold them out. In the last few minutes, only just conscious and with his head swathed in bandages, Corbett came back on to the field, and his presence helped Melbourne to hold on and win. Next week Warne-Smith took Corbett's place in the centre as they annihilated Collingwood in the Grand Final.

In that year Warne-Smith won the Brownlow Medal, and two years later he won again, the first man to do so.

Warne-Smith was an excellent cricketer and athlete as a schoolboy at Wesley College, Melbourne, but war stopped any thoughts of sport as he enlisted at the age of 17 to serve in the A.I.F. at Gallipoli and in France.

By June 1919 he was playing for Melbourne, and he soon made his mark. The Fitzroy forward Bob Merrick was running riot, and had kicked 11 goals when Warne-Smith was sent to mind him. He shut the rampant forward down so well that some of the Fitzroy crowd sent a hail of stones in his direction.

Melbourne lost by 125 points, and did not win a game all season. They also lost the potential champion, as Warne-Smith went to start an apple farm in Tasmania and was away until 1925.

His career developed quickly from that point, and led him naturally to the captaincy and then to captain-coach or coach the team until he retired in 1932.

Warne-Smith wrote highly readable articles on football during the 1930s, published in the weekly magazine *Table Talk*. He combined this with a business career, and his abiding interest in Melbourne. He was on both the Melbourne Cricket Club and football club committees and was Chairman of Selectors during the build up for the great teams under coach Norm Smith in the 1950s.

I WARNE SMITH
Vice Captain

Warne-Smith: 'perfect player'.

Jock McHale: Prince of Coaches with a passion for Collingwood

McHale: heart of the Magpies.

In the Collingwood pantheon, one man stands alone as the greatest, most influential figure in the club's history – Jock McHale.

McHale was Collingwood.

He played 261 games, coached for more than 700 and was a part of 10 of the club's Premierships.

McHale was playing with Coburg juniors in 1902 when he first tried out with Collingwood, but he was rejected. A year later he was back at Victoria Park, playing for for a combined junior side in a pre-season match against the reigning Premiers.

His performance that day was good enough to put him in the Magpie side for the opening game of season 1903. From that moment, the names of McHale and Collingwood were inextricably linked.

Although not the most brilliant player of his day, McHale was a good centreman and a player of great cunning and nous. But it was his consistency that was most remarkable. He did not miss a match from the 13th round of 1906 to the third round of 1917 – 191 games in a row.

He took over the coaching role at Collingwood in 1912 and spent two seasons as captain-coach, four as playing coach and a staggering 32 as non-playing coach. In all, he was in charge for 714 games, during which time the club won eight Flags and finished runners-up a further nine times.

The Magpies were finalists in 27 of the 38 years in which he coached. Why was he so successful? He was not a good skills coach, leaving it to individuals to work on their weaknesses. His real strength lay in his ability to prepare and inspire players, and to instil discipline into the team.

He was a firm believer in players keeping close to their positions, and he used highly regimented training to reinforce his ideas and plans.

He was a master at training the team hard enough to be fit, but not so hard as to be stale.

His passion for Collingwood really shone through in his soul-stirring half-time addresses that could lift players to the heights.

A quiet man by nature, McHale would not yell at or abuse his players, nor denigrate them in front of their teammates. But he hated losing, and could not abide timidity on the field.

His players loved him, though few knew him well. Many only ever referred to him as 'Mr McHale' or 'Sir' That respect survived even after he finally retired as coach, just before the start of the 1950 season.

McHale died of a heart attack suffered the day after the Magpies had won the 1953 flag. For James Francis McHale, there could not have been a better send-off. **Michael Roberts**

April 30. North, who failed to win a game last year, beat Fitzroy in opening round, 9.21 (75) to 10.11 (71).

April 30. Geoff Moriarty, ex-Fitzroy player and father of present full-forward Jack, offers football lessons by post, at £2/2/- or 5/- per lesson, in advance.

May 2. Magistrate Mr W.G. Smith calls for abolition of bars at football, while convicting Stephen Brazil, a tanner, for having obstructed police.

May 14. Aggregate attendance of 330,000 for first three rounds this season is a record. Gate receipts £8623 (→ 24/8/29).

May 21. South Melbourne's idea of selling reserved seats in the grandstand is a great success with the supporters of the club.

May 21. During this holiday weekend, in a tough match in which Collingwood beat South, 16.10 (106) to 9.13 (67), 16 players are injured, eight on each side.

June 18. Death announced of former Essendon ruckman, Dr E.A. 'Neddy' Officer – 'so round he could not be held' who had most of his career in the VFA and retired in 1898.

July 2. Richmond halt Geelong's winning streak of eight games, scoring 9.15 (69) to 7.11 (53) on swampy Punt Road Oval.

July 2. Richmond Secretary Percy Page has his jaw broken in a fight which breaks out at a club dance after match.

July 9. Melbourne and Collingwood stage great game at MCG. Redlegs fight back to within a point after trailing by three goals, but rover Bill Libbis secures vital goal and Magpies win, 11.13 (79) to 10.12 (72).

Aug. 20. Gordon Coventry totals 27 goals in four matches to help Victoria dominate the Australian Football Carnival in Melbourne (→ 27/7/29).

Sept. 3. Vital games played in icy gale-force winds. Carlton hold out Richmond 4.6 (30) to 3.5 (23) to dash Melbourne's hopes for Finals.

Sept. 10. North, having won three of their first four games, lost the last 14. Hawthorn are last, scoring one win against North.

Debuts
Les Hughson (Coll)
Len Thomas (S. Melb)

Grounds go black in blue with League

Melbourne dignitaries watch H.C.A. Harrison raising the 1926 Flag.

April 25. Six League grounds have been declared 'black' and football followers have been asked to boycott games at these grounds until a dispute between the League and the Theatrical Amusement Employees Association is resolved.

The grounds affected are the Melbourne Cricket Ground, South Melbourne, St Kilda, Carlton, Essendon and Hawthorn. The dispute concerns the use of non-union labor and negotiations towards a settlement have broken down.

The union has distributed posters stating: 'Don't scab; this football ground will not employ unionists. Keep away.' Pickets will be stationed at the grounds, an official said.

The union wants those employed at the grounds to join the union because they are enjoying the benefits of award wages. Clubs could pay the fee and then deduct it from wages.

Duncan's 33 marks 'best ever'

June 25. In a game described by many as the greatest they had seen in many years, Carlton's Alex Duncan treated the crowd to a splendid display of the footballer's art, taking 33 marks. His aerial work was simply perfection, drawing applause from friend and foe alike.

Playing at centre-halfback, Duncan turned one Magpie thrust after another. His beautiful drop-kicking was as flawless as his marking.

If ever one man saved a game it was Duncan and, thanks to his work and captain Horrie Clover's leadership, the Blues won 14.11 (95) to Collingwood's 13.5 (83) in a game that was always hotly contested.

It provided a real test of Carlton's improvement since last season.

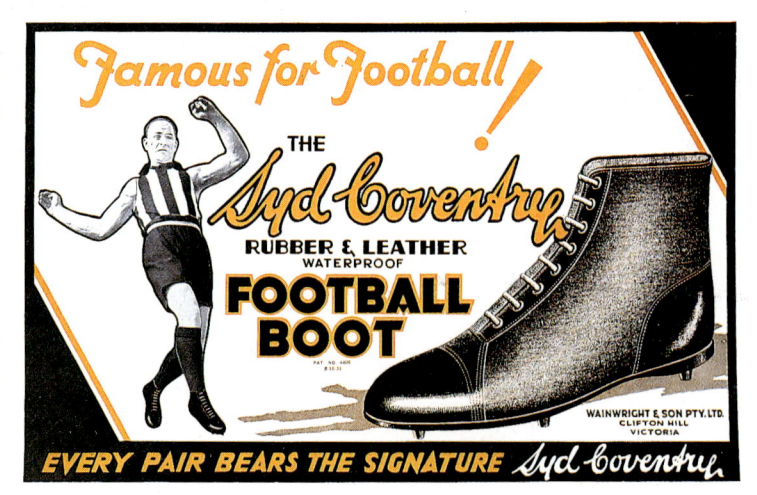

The great Syd Coventry puts his toe into the football boot business.

Radio man is kind to umpires

June 4. Geelong defeated St Kilda, which was not unexpected. The final score, 12.17 (89) to 11.4 (70), disguises the Saints' no-goal first quarter and six-goal last. Plus Lloyd Hagger's place kick after the bell to seal it.

The score also hides a display by the umpires which caused the barrackers near Rod McGregor, broadcasting on wireless station 3AR, to ask him to inform listeners of it.

Former Carlton great McGregor replied that while he did indeed have his own opinions he was not engaged to broadcast them. His duty was to give an account of the play.

Big V asked to set Magpies free

July 22. The League has rejected Collingwood's request not to select its players in the Victorian team to play Western Australia at the MCG.

Collingwood committeeman Mr Robert Rush said that Collingwood would be playing in WA at the same time as the interstate game. The game had been organised before the interstate match was announced and a depleted Collingwood team would be a great disappointment to Western Australians.

But the League has made it clear that the interstate match is of prime importance, far above the needs of an individual club.

Schoolboys scared by Tasmanian tigers

Aug. 15. A deplorable aspect of the All-Australian Schoolboys Carnival was the presence at the match in Hobart between Victoria and South Australia of a number of players from the Richmond Club, in Tasmania on holiday.

The Tigers jeered and hooted every decision against Victoria by the umpire, counting him out on several occasions.

The hooting frightened players of both sides, especially, it seems, the Victorians, who lost 4.6 (30) to 6.2 (38), The game was played on a freezing bog, which did not help.

Football wanderer Roy Cazaly up there with best

Sept. 30. Roy Cazaly has retired from League football after a long career, first at St Kilda where he played 99 games between 1911 and 1920 with a break for the war, and then at South Melbourne where he played another 99 between 1921 and 1924, and 1926 and 1927.

Cazaly spent 1925 coaching at Minyip for £12 per week, and it seems certain that he will not be lost to the coaching game.

One of ten children of Elizabeth and James Cazaly, Roy was born in South Melbourne on January 13, 1893.

His mother was a herbalist and midwife, and his father a champion oarsman and physical instructor.

James trained Roy and his brothers in a backyard gymnasium. While a teenager Cazaly rowed for South Melbourne in the Victorian Championships, and played cricket for Port Melbourne

From these childhood influences Cazaly developed a number of theories about physical fitness and football physics that would see him still able to play at the age of 34.

While at South he studied anatomy, Swedish massage, injury treatment and the art of breathing, with the club doctor and masseur.

Cazaly is a non-smoker and non-drinker, and says that a lungful of air at the moment he leaps for the ball gives him added levitation.

He also believes there is benefit in 'drying out' late in the week, eating little and sipping water sparingly.

Cazaly first played football for Albert Park School and Middle Park Wesley. However, in 1910 he was a Carlton supporter and had a few games for Carlton's junior team. A shoulder injury that wasn't looked after by the Blues resulted in his becoming disillusioned.

In 1911 he played his first game for St Kilda, ironically against Carlton, when the Saints, in one of their all too frequent upheavals, played a team of juniors instead of the striking senior side. Carlton won 18.21 (129) to 2.3 (15)

He said: 'I was a raw colt from the paddock. They came for me on Saturday at lunch time to play.'

In 1913 he was on the half-forward flank in St Kilda's first Grand Final side, that lost 5.13 (43) to Fitzroy 7.14 (56).

At St Kilda he learned a lot about

The great Roy Cazaly at his height, in the ruck for South Melbourne.

ruck work from Harry Cumberland, and about dodging and weaving from Billy Schmidt 'who would take me out in a park and and set me running full belt at a tree. Just as I was about to take the tree on the run I had to do a blind turn. After I had hit those trees once or twice I could turn on a threepenny bit'.

He won two best and fairests with the Saints, before moving to South Melbourne for the 1921 season, a gesture in support of Schmidt and against the infighting at St Kilda.

His career at South has been at an even higher level, resulting in Victo-

rian selection 13 times.

Although only five feet eleven inches tall, with rover Mark Tandy and blocking ruckman Fred 'Skeeter' Fleiter he formed the dominant ruck combination known as the 'terrible trio'. Skeet is the one who calls Cazaly in over the top with the famous cry 'Up there, Cazzer!'

Journalist Hec de Lacy said of Cazaly that 'He had skilled himself to be hard along with the hard. He matched an electric mind – a sense of split second imagination – against the more obvious tactics of the roughneck' (→ 28/4/43).

Umpire Kain is given bucketing

July 2. Umpire Kain was pelted by a shower of fruit and stones as he tried to leave the ground after Carlton's loss to Melbourne, 8.7 (55) to 10.10 (70). Kain was attacked for failing to award Carlton's Joe Kelly a free after a collision.

At the end of the game it took three attempts before Kain was able to reach the dressing room. On route, he was kicked and jostled and a policeman was punched in a brawl. One man was arrested and charged with throwing a missile. Several weeks ago, after a game, a supporter threw a bucket of water over the hapless Kain.

Deaths of great old football players

Aug 6. Two of the undisputed greats of football, ruckman Harry Cumberland and forward Albert Thurgood, have died this year, both as a result of motoring accidents.

Cumberland's career spanned 30 years, and at 43 he was the oldest man to play senior football. He played 176 games, for Melbourne and St Kilda, before going to Adelaide to win a Magarey Medal.

Thurgood is described by John Worrall as 'the greatest forward of all time'. A football wanderer, he appeared in over 200 senior games, but only 49 with Essendon. He was Champion of the Colony in 1901.

Jumpers swapped after State match

Aug. 20. Victoria won the Australian Football Carnival by defeating Western Australia in the final match 11.19 (85) to 10.12 (72) before a large crowd of 49,454 at the MCG.

The 'curtain raiser' to this match saw South Australia 20.23 (143) defeat Tasmania 14.24 (108).

Victoria won all four of their matches, over the two-week break between VFL rounds 15 and 16.

Peculiar incidents occurred after these final games where the players of each side swapped jumpers, and walked bare-chested from the ground carrying their heirlooms.

McHale's navy rules on Finals swamp

Oct. 1. Weather conditions for the Grand Final between Collingwood and Richmond were so atrocious that it could be said that Richmond's captain, Alan Geddes, elected to kick 'with the rain' on winning the toss. A crowd of only 34,551 braved the freezing cold and the rain that continued to drench the Melbourne Cricket Ground throughout the game. The city has been soaked for the past week, and only this morning did there seem any prospect of rain ceasing. Then it resumed torrentially after lunch, turning the centre into a quagmire, and making it impossible for any player to keep his footing around the wings.

No one was expecting any high scoring, and goals would be a miracle. This acquatic contest denied everyone what should have been a thrilling exhibition of football athletics between these evenly matched sides. The best entertainment for the spectators became the comedic spills of the unfortunate players as they slid and slithered around, attempting to gain possession of the slippery leather.

After the first quarter, Collingwood coach Jock McHale instructed his muddied men: 'Play soccer. You can't pick it up. Kick it along the ground, just get it forward.' As the rainfall grew yet heavier, both sides used this method for the rest of the game.

By match end, it was Collingwood the Premiers, 2.13 (25) to Richmond's 1.7 (13).

Tunnel ball at the Grand Final as the players struggle in the swamp.

Game not yet back to best, say veterans

May 28. Football memories rarely extend back more than a season or two, except in the mind's eye of the old-time players. In the golden light of nostalgia they never missed a goal, or dropped a mark. Every mistake they see today 'wouldn't have happened in my day'.

The view of veteran observers that football has yet to reach its glorious pre-war standards must therefore be taken with a pinch of salt.

Yet there are some aspects which point to deficiencies in the game of today. But perhaps these deficiencies were evident 'back then' too.

One is a lack of 'two-footed' players. John Worrall in the *Australasian* estimates that not one in a hundred players is able to use either boot to kick the ball.

The new out-of-bounds rule means many are being caught in a tight spot, and are unable to kick their way out.

In the game between Melbourne and Geelong, won by the Cats 12.13 (85) to 7.16 (58), at least one-third of the Geelong players tried to bounce the ball immediately upon gaining possession and just as quickly lost it.

And many Melbourne players simply kicked indiscriminately, causing the comment: 'Why worry? Kick the ball anywhere. Use your feet and give your brain a rest'!

Despite their failings Geelong were better at brain and footwork.

Goalkicking is one area that has improved – the most recent incident Gordon Coventry equalling his own and Dick Lee's record of 11.4, in Collingwood's 18.15 (123) win over Fitzroy 9.5 (59) on May 28.

1927 Statistics

Leading Goalkicker:
Gordon Coventry (Coll) 97
Brownlow Medallist:
Syd Coventry (Coll)
Finals: First Semi-final Rich 12.10 (82) Carl 11.10 (76); **Second Semi-final** Coll 16.18 (114) Geel 7.6 (48); **Grand Final** Coll 2.13 (25) Rich 1.7 (13)

Ladder:	W	L	D	%	pts
Coll	15	3	-	150.6	60
Rich	14	4	-	134.6	56
Geel	14	4	-	132.0	56
Carl	13	5	-	121.7	52
Melb	12	6	-	132.4	48
S. Melb	9	9	-	95.9	36
St K	8	10	-	75.3	32
Ess	6	11	1	96.8	26
Fitz	6	11	1	85.7	26
Foots	6	12	-	85.4	24
N. Melb	3	15	-	73.5	12
Haw	1	17	-	63.1	4

Great men of Collingwood come rain, hail or shine are captain and centre-half-back Syd Coventry and his brother Gordon, the prolific full forward. Another Flag to celebrate, as the Magpies sing in the trees this Spring.

1928

March 24. A new grandstand is opened at North Melbourne.

April 13. Umpires' new definition of holding-the-ball rule: that player with ball must be held, not bumped, clutched at or touched (→ 27/7/30).

May 26. Fitzroy kick an atrocious 2.27 (39) to lose to Geelong 19.8 (122).

May 28. Fire in Brownlow-Young stand at Corio destroys players' belongings. Appeal to crowd for football boots.

June 4. Fitzroy kick highest losing score, 17.13 (115), as they go down to Richmond, 19.6 (120).

June 9. Jack Baggott kicks 12 goals as Richmond beat South, 21.16 (142) to 9.12 (66).

June 9. Dull match between Hawthorn and Fitzroy has first-quarter hush pierced by astute comment from kookaburra on flagpole. Even players laugh. Fitzroy, 15.16 (106), beat Mayblooms, 10.12 (72).

June 23. A tenacious bulldog defies efforts to remove it from the Western Oval, and supporters say it typifies the 'bulldog spirit' of the Tricolours this year. But Collingwood win, 11.12 (78) to 9.10 (64) (→ 14/8).

June 30. Melbourne's Bert Chadwick and Jack Collins are hurt by an aluminium shield on a Footscray player's knee. Umpire says its legal (→ 15/3/29).

July 14. Collingwood's loss of two players against Fitzroy brings renewal of call for substitutes. Collingwood win 14.15 (99) to 7.12 (54).

Aug.1. Reports that some clubs living beyond their means. North run a drive for 60 life members at £10 a head.

Aug. 4. Footscray supporters are living on their nerves, following another close loss, to Fitzroy, 13.12 (90) to 12.17 (89). Footscray has now won five games and lost three by less than a goal (→ 6/9/30).

Sept. 1. Despite the fact that they are clearly at the top of the ladder, disgruntled Collingwood supporters boo their team off ground as they lose to Carlton, 12.15 (87) to 8.19 (67). Carlton's win keeps Essendon out of the Four.

Debuts
Bruce Andrew (Coll)

Retirements
Greg Stockdale (Ess)

Scoreboard saves Vics in drawn game

Bob Corbett gets a relieving kick for Victoria, against Alan Steward of WA.

June 16. The VFL had three combinations engaged today – against South Australia in Adelaide, NSW at headquarters, the MCG, and the third against the Ovens and Murray league at Wangaratta. None of the teams lost, although the South Australian game was not won.

The League beat Ovens and Murray 16.15 (111) to 15.14 (106). The team at the MCG had an easier time, winning 26.13 (169) to 14.11 (96). Horrie Clover kicked six for the Vics and Bill Mohr, a lad of 18 from Wagga, played well for NSW.

It might be deemed unfair that only six of the Vics were born in Victoria.

The South Australians, however, thought they had their game won when the bell sounded, with the scoreboard showing them in front.

Earlier, pretty stab-kicking and clever handpassing had looked good but not served the Croweaters well on the scoreboard against Victoria's straight ahead tactics.

With just a few minutes to go, the Vics were 15 points up, and spectators began to leave.

However, a change in tactics in favour of 'going straight through' saw South Australia kick a couple of goals and a number of behinds to get one point in front on the scoreboard. Sid Coventry wasn't paid a mark in front, and the bell sounded.

But the scoreboard attendant had made an error, said the goal umpires after conferring, and the game was declared a draw, the first in interstate football history.

Victoria 13.10 (88) drew with South Australia 11.22 (88).

New uniforms

March 30. When things are not going well at the club, when the players have bowed heads, and the supporters are hissing the coach and Committee there is only one solution – change the uniform.

Both Fitzroy and Carlton have been in the doldrums for some time, and the only hopeful thing that can be said is that they are 'rebuilding'.

But there is something fresh for the world-weary supporters to gaze upon. Fitzroy sweaters are sporting a blue monogram on their chests, bearing the letters FFC. Carlton have gone for a classic one-colour look and are now truly the 'navy blues', without the white collar and cuffs (→ 6/4/34).

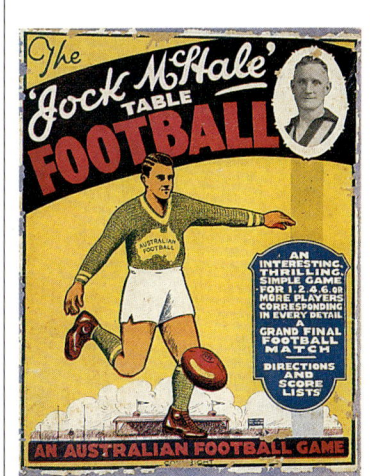

Collingwood's Jock McHale has invented a table top game to keep footy fans happy during the week.

Fitzmaurice shares his fee with Cats

May 26. Tom Fitzmaurice, the former Essendon great who has played with Geelong since 1925, was asked to take the position of coach at the Pivot at the beginning of the season.

Fitzmaurice accepted – but on one condition – that his £6 weekly fee be distributed equally among the players.

The Committee agreed to this unique form of player motivation.

To the relief, perhaps, of other coaches Fitzmaurice's sacrifice seems not to have worked.

But maybe it is changing. Geelong have won the last three of their first six games (→ 16/7/34).

Kittens in mittens for game in mud

June 2. Richmond defeated Geelong at the wet and slushy Punt Road Oval, 12.21 (93) to 13.12 (90).

Many people attributed the win to the fact that many Tigers wore mittens – fingerless gloves – which allowed them to grip the slippery ball.

Or did ex-Geelong player Henry Young have the answer: 'When we were leaving we could not help feeling sorry for our opponents. That supreme confidence lasted until Werribee. By then our opponents had just a chance. But by the time we reached Spencer St it had oozed out altogether.' (1/10/32).

Charlie Tyson, now at North, seems to be over his famous row with the Collingwood club.

Faulty bell gives Saints a victory

Magpies rule football roost

These men are at the pinnacle of football. The Collingwood team line up before the Grand Final bounce at the MCG.

The men for whom the bell tolls.

Aug. 21. Everyone now knows that Melbourne 'won' last Saturday's match against St Kilda, and that the Saints' forward Bert Smedley kicked the 'winning' goal at least seven seconds after the bell had sounded.

But the call was 'all clear', the flags were waved and the players left the field, accompanied by hooting and derision and the muted cries of joy from the Saints' followers.

But Umpire R. Devine told an inquiry that lasted two hours tonight at Harrison House that he had not heard the bell, even though timekeepers vowed they had rung it long and loud. They heard supporters say: 'Ring it again. They're still playing.' And on ringing it again, they received the umpire's acknowledgement. In the time between the bells, they said, the goal was scored.

But the verdict is that the score remains: St Kilda 12.10 (82) to Melbourne 11.15 (81), and Melbourne may have lost the double chance in the Finals.

Sept. 29. The season closed in a blaze of glory for the Collingwood Football Club today when the team kicked the highest score ever achieved in a Finals match to overpower Richmond, 13.18 (96) to 9.9 (64). Another record was set when the Magpie's champion full-forward, Gordon Coventry, wearing his favourite pair of old boots, kicked nine goals, the highest individual tally of goals in any Final.

Brilliantly led by Syd Coventry, Gordon's older brother, Collingwood excited even the Richmond supporters by their dash, determination and unfailing teamwork, which stamped them the outstanding side of the season. Richmond put up a vigorous opposition, but at no stage looked like the winning team. After three weeks of inactivity, the Tigers made mistakes, whereas Collingwood had been tightened by two

splendid struggles with Melbourne, and took to the field tuned to the last string.

The third quarter saw a heroic attempt by Richmond to save the game. They played like men possessed until, wilting under the relentless attack of the Magpies, they were beaten back.

The 50,026 spectators could not but be impressed by the superb play of the winners (→ 27/4/29).

Heartstoppers and Hawthorn horrors

Sept. 1. Hawthorn's miserable season concluded with a 56-point loss to Essendon, 16.22 (118) to 9.8 (62).

This loss capped off Footscray's 'if only' year as well.

If only Hawthorn could have won, and if only Footscray had not suffered another loss by less than a kick, and if only ladder leaders Collingwood had beaten Carlton, then the Tricolours would be in the Four and playing in the Finals.

As it was, Footscray finished seventh, two games out of the Four. Footscray lost to South, Essendon, Fitzroy and St Kilda, and beat Geelong (twice), St Kilda, Carlton and South, all by four points or less. Nine heartstoppers out of 18 games is enough to make any supporter lose his hair.

Alby Morrison kicked 50 goals 52 behinds in his first year – but no one blames him for the close results.

Alan Hopkins' game in the one-point win over Carlton is regarded by many Footscray supporters as the finest game ever played.

Hawthorn had one game where a goal kicked by a South Melbourne player well after the bell had sounded robbed the team of even one win for the year. They lost 14.11 (95) to 15.10 (100), having kicked seven goals in the last quarter.

But the Mayblooms took it on the chin. A club newsletter said: 'Incidents such as this are the very essence of our grand old game. This one is not quoted to excuse defeat – on the contrary, we accept our defeats like true sportsmen'.

A highlight for Hawthorn was the performance of Bert Hyde, who kicked 62 goals for the season, finishing third in the goalkicking.

Hyde did experience one win when he kicked six for Victoria in the first win ever over Western Australia in Perth (→ 13/9/30).

1928 Statistics

Leading Goalkicker:
Gordon Coventry (Coll) 89
Brownlow Medallist:
Ivor Warne-Smith (Melb)
Finals: First Semi-final Rich 17.15 (117) Carl 9.10 (64); **Second Semi-Final** Coll 9.8 (62) Melb 9.8 (62); **Second Semi-final (replay)** Coll 10.8 (68) Melb 9.10 (64); **Grand Final** Coll 13.18 (96) Rich 9.9 (63)

Ladder:	W	L	%	pts
Coll	15	3	134.6	60
Rich	14	4	133.6	56
Melb	14	4	122.2	56
Carl	11	7	121.4	44
Ess	11	7	113.0	44
St K	11	7	102.0	44
Foots	9	9	109.3	36
Fitz	7	11	88.4	28
Geel	6	12	99.5	24
S. Melb	5	13	85.5	20
N. Melb	5	13	67.7	20
Haw	0	18	61.6	0

1929

Coventry's 16 against hapless Mayblooms

COLLINGWOOD AGAIN !! THINGS DON'T SEEM TO HAPPEN ANYWHERE ELSE BUT AT COLLINGWOOD !!! THIS TIME 'NUTS' COVENTRY, COLLINGWOOD'S GOAL BIRD, HAS LAID A 'FEW' AT HAWTHORN'S EXPENSE, WHAT A HARROWING SIGHT IT MUST HAVE BEEN FOR THE POOR HAWTHORNITES TO WATCH THAT OUT — 16 OF THE BEST !!!

COCK A DOODLE DOOOOO — 16

OF COURSE IT HAD TO BE AGAINST US

The Magpie chorus is led by Gordon Coventry, with his litter of 16 goals.

July 27. By kind permission of Hawthorn, Gordon Coventry of Collingwood today kicked 16 goals to break the record for the most goals kicked in a League game. The record was previously held by South Melbourne's Harold Robertson, with 14 against St Kilda in 1919.

By winning against Hawthorn, 22.10 (142) to 7.14 (56), Collingwood have notched up an unbroken run of 20 victories, another VFL record, and few doubt that the Magpies are in the strongest position to win the Premiership again this year.

Gordon Coventry has had another great year, after heading the goal kicking list for the last three seasons, and being second in 1925. He seems able to kick the required number of goals whenever any team manages to threaten his side. He booted five in eight minutes when Carlton held a dangerous lead, and kicked another seven when Essendon looked secure (→19/7/30).

VFL incorporated at Harrison House

June 18. The Victorian Football League today took the significant step of becoming incorporated as a public company, registered at 'Football House'.

The decision to incorporate reflects the Committee's optimistic faith in the future of the League as a business concern. New revenue-raising activities can be expected, as the VFL will now be in a position to enter fields of business perhaps not directly related to football. That the VFL 'means business' became apparent with the purchase last month of their new three-storey premises, corner of Flinders Lane and Spring Street, for a sum believed to be as high as £20,000. Good rentals from tenants of 'Football House' will swell the revenue now flowing from the sixpence earmarked from every member's ticket (→28/8/31).

A habit-forming event. The raising of yet another Collingwood Flag.

Death of 'Father' of Australian Football

Sept. 2. Henry Colden Antill Harrison, given the title 'Father of Australian Football' by the Australasian Football Council at the Jubilee Carnival in 1908, has died at his home in Kew. Aged 93, he was Melbourne's longest lived resident.

Harrison, born in 1836 at Picton in NSW, was among that early group of athletes who played and propagated the Australian game through the 1860s.

Henry Harrison was present at some of the important developments in the game, notably in captaining Richmond in some early games, and helping draft the rules of 1866, as one of the founders of the Victorian Football Association and

Henry Harrison: friend to all.

the Victorian Football League.

He also captained the Melbourne and Geelong clubs in the formative years of football.

Having retired as a player in 1872, he was elected a life member of the VFA in 1889.

He also had a great career as a 'pedestrian', beating the Ballarat champion sprinter L.L. Mount in a famous series of races.

Harrison retained a spry fitness and in 1898 rode a bicycle from Melbourne to Sydney in ten days to watch the cricket.

'Every groundsman and official and member is a friend of his. He loves to loiter in the dressingrooms, where there is the reek of training oil and perspiration. It is the smell of powder to a war horse. Before the game starts, he has some advice to give both sides. It is to tell them to play the game, and to remember that football is a game.'

Magpies swoop to hat trick of Premierships

Finals fightback

Sept. 28. Collingwood today came back from their shattering defeat at the hands of Richmond in the Semi-finals to reverse the position, by winning 11.13 (79) to 7.8 (50).

The Magpies exulted in winning their third successive Premiership Flag before a crowd of 63,336.

The result was a coaching triumph for Jock McHale, who turned the tables on his arch-rival, 'Checker' Hughes. Hughes was out for revenge after two Grand Final losses to the Magpies, and he pulled off an amazing Second Semi-final win, with Richmond scoring 18.15 (123) to 8.13 (61).

On that day Hughes demanded a physical onslaught that completely winded the cocksure Magpies. So great were Hughes' demands that half-back Basil McCormack, normally a fair player, flattened Syd Coventry and George Clayden and has been suspended.

McHale's master stroke today was to use Gordon Coventry as a decoy. Every time he led he was besieged by Richmond backs, leaving the likes of 'Tubby' Edmonds (five goals) to mark unattended.

A great moment for Magpies, and captain Syd Coventry is chaired off the field.

Miss Kate Harrison, 'Queen of Football', tosses the coin.

Leeter Collier wins the Brownlow

Sept. 26. Collingwood defender Albert 'Leeter' Collier is the 1929 Brownlow Medallist.

Collier received six votes with Arthur Batchelor (Fitzroy), Ivor Warne-Smith (Melbourne) and Alan Hopkins (Footscray) all tying in second place with four votes apiece.

The brilliant centre-halfback had another dominant season after being shifted from the ruck to the backline. He was also centre-halfback for the Victorian State side.

Although he is still only 20 years of age, Collier has won just about every honour League football can bestow upon a player, since he made his senior football debut with the Magpies as a 15-year-old recruit from Ivanhoe.

A great team player, he has lived up to his nickname 'Leeter', a derivative of the word 'leader', which typifies the way Albert Collier always plays the game.

BOB MIRAMS —

A. COLLIER (Collingwood)

A triumphant year

Sept. 2. It has been a magnificent year for Collingwood, and the question must be asked: Is this the greatest team to have played the game?

The Finals are to come but the record is already amazing. The Magpies have gone through the home-and-away rounds undefeated - the first team ever to have done so in League history.

Gordon 'Nuts' Coventry is the first player to kick over 100 goals, and will certainly add to that. Whenever a threat has emerged Coventry has stepped up the pace and saved the day. He kicked a late goal to overcome St Kilda. Once Coventry gets in front it seems that no defender can get around him. His bulky body and his awkward gait seem to brook no interruption, and he never seems to drop a mark.

The supreme defender Albert Collier has won the Brownlow Medal. Add Syd Coventry, George Clayden, 'Tubby' Edmonds, Harold Collier and Harold Chesswass to name just a few, and you can understand why this side is so hard to beat. It has scored 1918 points and is set to top the 2000 (→11/10/30).

1929 Statistics

Leading Goalkicker:
G. Coventry (Coll) 124
Brownlow Medallist:
A. Collier (Coll)
Finals: First Semi-final Carl 12.9 (81) St K 11.7 (73); **Second Semi-final** Coll 8.13 (61) Rich 18.15 (123); **Final** Rich 15.7 (97) Carl 14.7 (91); **Grand Final** Coll 11.13 (79) Rich 7.8 (50)

Ladder:	W	L	D	%	pts
Coll	18	0	-	171.7	72
Carl	15	3	-	136.9	60
Rich	12	5	1	121.7	50
St K	12	6	-	130.3	48
Melb	11	6	1	105.5	46
Ess	9	8	1	96.0	38
Geel	8	10	-	109.6	32
S. Melb	7	11	-	84.8	28
Foots	6	11	1	86.6	26
Haw	4	14	-	76.9	16
Fitz	3	15	-	73.3	12
N. Melb	1	17	-	60.2	4

1930

Dropping the ball rule dropped: back to old ways

July 26. The Australian National Football Council has notified the VFL that the old holding or 'dropping' the ball rule is to resume immediately. Laws of the game cannot be changed by one member alone.

The change, outlined by umpires' coach Norden to a meeting of the VFL on April 9, provided that a player in possession of the ball had either to kick, hit or flick the ball as soon as he was held.

The change was designed to eliminate unseemly scrimmaging and bullocking by players who often did not obey the game's convention of keeping the ball moving.

Brutal play in the packs was a blot on the game.

At first the rule change was well received, because in concert with the kicking out of bounds rule open football resulted.

'The play maintained all its rug-

Under the new rule, now dropped, this was a 'free' to the tackler.

gedness, dash and determination, and as a result of the new law, in which nursing the ball is not allowed, there are fewer scrimmages... and less screaming at the umpire by ignorant, excited and biased crowds,' said the *Australasian*.

'The players recognise that in their own interests, as well as those of the side, the ball should be kept moving without delay.'

The return of the old law permitting 'dropping the ball' will, the paper says, 'naturally cause bunching, thus increasing scrimmages, with its consequent bullocking – a primitive sort of play adopted by the hired bravoes of the game' (→ 28/8/31).

Coulter Law on player payment

March 7. The VFL has agreed to the proposals from a committee on player payments, chaired by Melbourne official Gordon Coulter.

They provide for a maximum payment of £3 per week to players for Premiership matches. A scale of payment to injured and unemployed players was agreed to, with no payments to be more than £3.

Also agreed was a scale of penalties for clubs breaching the 'Coulter Law' on payments, including suspension for players, loss of Premiership points and expulsion from the VFL (→ 25/4/31).

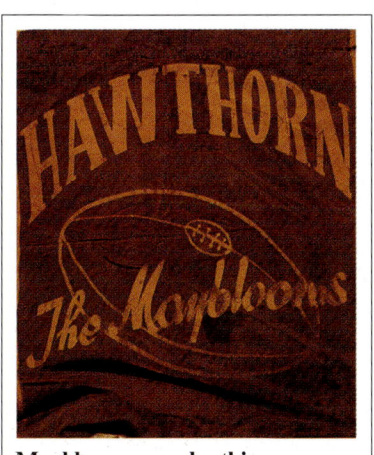
Mayblooms: maybe this year.

Ball for Mohr may end St Kilda strife

Bill Mohr presented with the 10-goal ball. A chance to heal wounds.

Aug. 23. In a grand sporting gesture, Collingwood President Mr Harry Curtis presented champion St Kilda full-forward Bill Mohr the football with which he kicked 10 goals against the Magpies when the two teams clashed on 21 June this year. Gordon Coventry also kicked 10 goals in that match, which Collingwood won 22.11 (143) to 14.8 (92).

The presentation took place before the start of the return game between the clubs, which Collingwood again won 17.13 (115) to 14.7 (91). Players from both teams lined up in front of the pavilion at the St Kilda ground, in a guard of honour to witness the presentation.

The fine form of Mohr has been one of the few consolations in another strife-torn year for the St Kilda club where players and Committee members have been engaged in public brawling.

Indeed, shortly after Mohr kicked his 10 goals against Collingwood, the Committee hauled the players before it, and informed them sharply that 'they entered into a contract with the committee and they are in the position of servants whose services may be dispensed with at any time'.

This show of strength by the Committee can hardly have helped to heal the rifts in the troubled club, although the players responded very positively a few weeks later by crushing North Melbourne by 75 points – Mohr kicking nine goals. The scores then were 18.15 (123) to 7.6 (48) (→ 5/9/36).

Hawthorn chop off Redlegs great run

Sept. 13. Hawthorn have had their finest hour. With nothing left to play for but pride they today sent a desperate Melbourne team plunging out of the Four.

Melbourne started with five wins and had a hard run at the Finals. Three weeks ago they had 11 wins on the board and an apparently assured place in the First Semi. They doubled Hawthorn's score in Round 11 and had every incentive to deliver another thrashing.

Melbourne lost to Richmond last Saturday, but were still in the Four if they won. Hawthorn changed all that and Geelong sealed it by downing Fitzroy and sneaking into the Four on percentage.

The wind was howling at the Glenferrie Oval and the Mayblooms had first use of it. They kicked 5.8 to 1.0 to set up the lead, but the Fuchsias came back and in the last quarter got to within four points.

But the brothers Sharpley came to the rescue. Keith at full-forward took advantage of a couple of breaks in play to score two goals, while his brother Jack at fullback held on as Melbourne threw everything at the goals. The final score was Hawthorn 12.18 (90) to Melbourne's 10.17 (77) (→8//5/31).

1930 Statistics

Leading Goalkicker:
Gordon Coventry (Coll) 118
Brownlow Medallist:
Stan Judkins (Rich)
Finals: First Semi-Final Carl 8.21 (69) Geel 13.11 (89) **Second Semi-Final** Coll 14.10 (94) Rich 14.7 (91) **Final** Coll 9.11 (65) Geel 12.19 (91) **Grand Final** Coll 14.16 (100) Geel 9.16 (70)

Ladder:	W	L	%	pts
Coll	15	3	144.3	60
Carl	15	3	141.6	60
Rich	11	7	124.7	44
Geel	11	7	118.7	44
Melb	11	7	104.7	44
Ess	10	8	105.5	40
SthM	9	9	100.0	36
St K	8	10	101.3	32
Fitz	7	11	89.2	28
Haw	6	12	77.3	24
Foot	4	14	75.8	16
Nth M	1	17	51.8	4

McHale in bed for ultimate victory

Oct. 11. An eight goal to none third quarter by Collingwood destroyed Geelong in the Grand Final, giving the Magpies the right to fly the Premiership Flag for the fourth year in succession.

This is unprecedented in the VFL. Essendon had a quartet of victories in the VFA from 1891 to 1894.

Collingwood achieved their win, 14.16 (100) to 9.16 (70) after a stirring speech at half time by former player and Treasurer Bob Rush. Coach Jock McHale was not at the ground for this history-making game, as he was confined to bed with what must have been a mighty dose of influenza.

The League's leading goalkicker, Gordon Coventry kicked a solid seven to complete the season with 118, and with brother Syd had an excellent afternoon.

Harry Collier, the brilliant rover, played up to the reputation that won him equal votes in this year's Brownlow Medal.

Aside from the third quarter it was Collingwood's steadiness and organisation rather than excitement that won them the game, as they won so many during the season.

Some commentators have called for a reduction in the number of players on the field to 16 to rejuvenate the game, which is said to be stagnating. Collingwood supporters do not agree (→12/10/35).

The heroes of the fourth Flag match go down in the Magpie annals.

League footballers in flight to catch smokers' delight.

Stan Judkins wins Brownlow after tie

Sept. 26. Richmond winger Stan Judkins is the surprise winner of the 1930 Brownlow Medal.

Judkins was part of a three-way tie with Alan Hopkins of Footscray and Harry Collier of Collingwood, brother of last year's medallist. Before a winner could be announced, the League had to overrule a recommendation from the Umpires Board that no award be made.

The League declared Judkins as the winner because he had played only 12 games – which was less than his two medal rivals. Collier had played 18 games and Hopkins made 15 League appearances.

There is a certain irony in Judkins' win as the reason he had played fewer games was due to being dropped for poor form.

Stan Judkins: only 12 games.

Norman Banks and footy on radio 3KZ

April 30. Mr Norman Banks called his first game over wireless station 3KZ today. He joins Mr Wally 'Jumbo' Sharland, a former VFA player who began describing games on 3AR in 1928. As with cricket and other sports the radio is bringing the game to the people.

There is no doubt that an exciting picture of the play in progress can be created in the mind by fluent words, the skill being in not allowing gaps of silence to frustrate the listener. Being able to follow a game although unable to attend is a boon for those who are infirm or recovering from illness (→ 29/7/32).

New Finals system looks the goods

April 24. There will be four Finals matches this year under a new system adopted by the League.

The changes were proposed by Richmond's Percy Page who said the new system would ensure that the Finals contests were genuine. The first Finals match will be between the third and fourth clubs; the second match is between the first and second clubs. The third match brings together the winners of the first and the loser of the second. The Grand Final will be fought out between the winners of the second and third matches (→ 4/3/33).

Brownlow system is overhauled

April 24. The system of Brownlow Medal voting, for the 'best and fairest' has been altered by the League, to widen the possibility of winning for consistently good players.

In the past the umpire has given one vote only for the best player on the ground. Now he will choose three players, and award three votes for the best, then two and one. This means that a player might win the medal with a mixture of first, second and third votes.

If votes are equal the player with the most 'best on ground' votes will win. Players disqualified during the season will be ineligible.

Fresh young talent in the League ranks

Early action. Terry Brain of South is too late to stop Footscray's Bill Cubbins.

May 9. On the evidence of the first two rounds of the season, 1931 looks like providing a vintage crop of new recruits.

Much has been written about young Albury rover Haydn Bunton, who made his long-delayed and long-awaited debut with Fitzroy.

Maroon supporters will hope that he plays a more dominant role than he has in his first couple of games. Bunton has played solidly without dominating, while Fitzroy search for the right position for him. The 19-year-old seems too tall to be an ordinary rover, and is more likely to be used as a centreman.

George Moloney, the former Western Australian and new Geelong full-forward has made an even greater impact, kicking seven and 12 goals (nine before half time) in his first two games.

Although Geelong lost the first game to Collingwood by five points, they trounced St Kilda, and look set for big things this year.

Even better was the performance by another Albury boy Doug Strang, brother of Gordon, who booted 14 goals 2 behinds in Richmond's record-breaking score of 30.19 (199) over North Melbourne 4.7 (31). Strang now has 18 goals.

Such was Richmond's dominance of this game that 19th man Jack Dyer, a rangy young local boy was not called on. Dyer is from De La Salle College, but has played with the local team known as 'the Richmond Hill mob.'

Ballarat rover Percy Beames, quick and solidly built, has made a good start at Melbourne.

Grandad changes character at the football. Drawn by Percy Leason.

Bell tolls last kick loss for Mayblooms

May 8. The Investigation Committee of the League has dismissed the complaint lodged by the Hawthorn Football Club concerning last Saturday's match against Footscray, who won by a point when the bell rang at the wrong moment. Hawthorn officials contend that their player Ted Pool was about to take a free kick in reach of goal when the timekeeper ended play six seconds ahead of correct time.

In evidence presented, the timekeeper for Hawthorn claimed that when he heard the umpire whistle, and saw him raise his hand, he announced 'time on' to the other timekeeper, who immediately rang the bell, perhaps hearing only the word 'time'.

The field umpire told the Committee he was amazed when the bell rang while he was signalling 'time on' but could do nothing because the crowd rushed on to the ground, excited by such a tense and close finish. Despite such evidence, the chairman, after brief consideration, announced that Hawthorn's protest had been dismissed.

At a full meeting of the League later, the President Dr W.C. McClelland was of the strong opinion that the umpire is always in supreme control, and should have insisted that the match be finished.

This will be of small satisfaction to the aggrieved Mayblooms, certain they could have won in the time stolen from them (→ 7/9/35).

Downs kicked out

The Downs incident, and implications that another boot was in the pack.

Aug. 28. The VFL went behind closed doors to consider the final appeal over the Tommy Downs case, and after lengthy deliberation decided to reject it.

Downs, the brilliant Carlton rover and vice captain on a number of occasions this season, was reported by a goal umpire for kicking Richmond captain Maurie Hunter in the game on July 25, won by Richmond 8.17 (65) to 6.12 (48).

Downs was suspended by the League for the rest of this season and all of 1932.

Downs has strenuously proclaimed his innocence of the charge, the worst that can be made in football, and has thousands of witnesses all willing to agree with him.

1800 Carlton members packed an angry meeting at the Brunswick Town Hall last week in protest, and asked the Committee to appeal once more to the League to re-open the case, citing a precedent from 1923.

Eleven of this number signed statutory declarations saying that it was not Downs' leg which came into contact with Hunter.

R.G. Menzies QC has provided advice that no further legal avenues of appeal are open. The popular player will have to wear the stigma.

Brownlow crowns dream season

Sept. 15. Fitzroy's boom recruit Haydn Bunton has won the Brownlow Medal in his first season, confirming the long-held faith of Maroons officials. Bunton has already had the honour of representing the State, against South Australia, where he was best on ground.

Bunton started the season fairly quietly as he adjusted to the city game and the selectors tried him in various positions.

He arrived as a rover, but he was tried in the centre and at halfforward, before the club decided to give him a roving commission.

He soon showed an uncanny ability to be at the fall of the ball, the speed and elusiveness to get the ball into the open, and great accuracy in both passing and long-kicking.

He won the Brownlow with 26 votes, one vote more than Footscray's Alan Hopkins, the Brownlow 'bridesmaid,' who was second also in 1929 and 1930. Despite Bunton's efforts, Fitzroy have finished 10th (→ 18/3/32).

Tricolours tripped in run for final Four

Sept. 5. Footscray's hopes of making the final Four were dashed today, even though they won against North Melbourne, 5.13 (43) to 3.16 (34). Their low scoring in a game of shockingly poor standard brought nowhere near the percentage lift they needed to reach the Four.

Perhaps players' minds were on developments in a game elsewhere, between Carlton and St Kilda. The Tricolours were fervently hoping for a sound victory by St Kilda here. A loss by Carlton would open Footscray's way into the Four. Their other opportunity for admission was dependent on a loss by Collingwood to Melbourne. But that too was unlikely, given Collingwood's unbroken run of home-and-away victories against the Redlegs since 1922.

So it went this time, with the Saints being crushed 13.12 (90) to 16.17 (113). Meanwhile at Princes Park a downpour may have assisted Carlton to overwhelm the visitors, 10.6 (66) to 6.12 (48). Footscray was out for another year (→ 19/1/35).

Members of the Old Veterans Teams.

The grand old players of yesteryear in fine fettle for the veterans match played for the Alfred Hospital at St Kilda.

Soapy slips eleven through in Semi

Cats top tame Tigers for second Flag

Oct. 10. The speedy Cats outran the high-flying Tigers to win Geelong's second Flag, and add another chapter to Richmond's heartbreak run of near misses.

Richmond have been runners-up six times since the war, and finished third last year, in addition to winning two Flags.

Both teams had lost just three games during the season, but two of the Tiger losses were to Geelong. They were clearly the best sides to play off for the Premiership – which used the much fairer Page Finals system for the first time.

Richmond reversed the home-and-away results with a handy win over Geelong in the Second Semi, 15.9 (99) to 10.6 (66), and took the easy route to the Grand Final.

Geelong defeated Carlton in a peculiar but very windy Preliminary Final. The Blues kicked 7.5 to nothing in the first quarter, but Geelong responded with 8.9 to 1.1 in the second, going on after an even second half to win the match when centre-half-forward Jack Collins kicked a goal with two minutes to go, 11.17 (83) to 11.11 (77).

The Grand Final, played under the influence of a strong south-westerly wind before 60,712 fanatics was a battle between the high marking power of Tigers such as Gordon Strang, and the running ability of Cats like tiny Jack Carney, in his bespoke size three boots. Remarkably both these players made their debuts this year.

Gordon Strang was in brilliant marking form on the backline and occasionally up forward, as was brother Doug who topped his work off with three goals.

In a way, Jack Carney was lucky to be playing. He was 19th man in round one, and when he finally came on to replace Carji Greeves, in the last quarter he was so enthusiastic that, not looking where he was going, he slammed straight into the biggest man in the VFL, North Melbourne's tough ruckman Johnny Lewis.

Carney's second quarter run from behind the centre line, dodging and outdistancing three opponents before passing to his captain Ted Baker in the pocket brought long applause and set the stage for Geelong's attacking win (→ 6/6/36).

Soapy Vallence hauls in a big mark.

Sept. 26. Before last Saturday's encounter the score stood at one each between Collingwood and Carlton.

The Blues were aggrieved by accusations that they had not done their best in the second game, which Collingwood won by ten goals, 20.15 (135) to 10.14 (74) on a very wet ground 'spangled with pools of water', as Hugh Buggy said.

The Semi was quite different. Stung into action 'Carlton reduced the Collingwood machine to a mere conglomeration of ineffective parts, made the Magpies look like sparrows, and left the crowd of 52,143 agape with surprise'.

'Soapy' Vallence kicked 11 goals, a Finals record, including six in the last quarter. The last kick of the day by Vallence hit the post.

Carlton's 20.10 (130) was also a record Finals score, as was the margin of 88 points. Collingwood managed a miserable 5.12 (42).

First year player 'Mick' Crisp played well, but this was balanced by the injury to veteran Horrie Clover, who might not play again.

The stars. Geddes and Hunter (Rich) and Baker, Moloney and Collins (Geel).

1931 Statistics

Leading Goalkicker: Harry Vallence (Carl) 86
Brownlow Medallist: Haydn Bunton (Fitz)
Finals: First Semi-final Carl 20.10 (130) Coll 5.12 (42); **Second Semi-final** Geel 10.6 (66) Rich 15.9 (99); **Preliminary Final** Geel 11.17 (83) Carl 11.11 (77); **Grand Final** Rich 7.6 (48) Geel 9.14 (68)

Ladder:	W	L	%	pts
Geel	15	3	151.4	60
Rich	15	3	141.1	60
Carl	12	6	125.1	48
Coll	12	6	124.0	48
Foots	12	6	110.2	48
Ess	10	8	99.2	40
S. Melb	9	9	99.1	36
Melb	8	10	91.7	32
St K	8	10	89.2	32
Fitz	4	14	86.0	16
Haw	3	15	82.1	12
N. Melb	0	18	50.8	0

Geelong were so keen they couldn't sit still for the Team photo.

March 18. Haydn Bunton receives his 1931 Brownlow Medal at Oriental Hotel after VFL meeting (17/9/32).

April 30. Essendon feature six players employed as firemen in a torrid win over Footscray, 15.15 (105) to 7.12 (54).

July 2. Melbourne return to the MCG, available after top-dressing, having lost previous three 'home' games played at the Motordrome, Swan St. The Redlegs celebrate with 12.13 (85) to St Kilda 10.14 (74) (→2/7/36).

July 8. South Melbourne goalkicking wizard Bob Pratt is cleared of striking Fitzroy hard man Frank Curcio to the delirious cheers of 300 supporters waiting outside Harrison House (→17/6/33).

July 16. After ten straight wins South Melbourne lose to Collingwood, 5.17 (47) to 7.8 (50), in a game spoiled by the curse of football, a cross-wind.→

July 29. Wireless station 3UZ publishes a plan in the *Argus* of the Punt Road Oval as a clock face, to assist listeners. 12 o'clock is north, putting the Punt Road goals at 2 o'clock.

July 30. A tremendous crowd watch Carlton 12.17 (89) defeat South Melbourne 11.14 (80) at South. The fence collapses and dozens of spectators are thrown to the ground and trampled upon. Two are taken to hospital (→23/6/36).

Aug. 27. Geelong's George Moloney kicks his 100th goal for the season. Richmond win, 13.8 (86) to 9.20 (74).

Oct. 17. The *Argus* reports on the number of top league footballers who also play District cricket. They include Richmond's Jack Baggott, St Kilda captain Stuart King, Footscray's Alan Hopkins, South's Austin Robertson and Fitzroy's Haydn Bunton.

Nov. 5. Jack Worrall, former Fitzroy player, coach of Carlton and Essendon, and football writer and critic for the *Australasian* is made a life member of the Australian Football Council (→17/11/37).

Debuts
Frank Curcio (Fitz)
Herbie Matthews (S. Melb)
Doug Nicholls (Fitz)
Keith Shea (Carl)
Norman Ware (Foots)

Retirement
Ivor Warne-Smith (Melb)

Cashed up Southerners get flying start on season

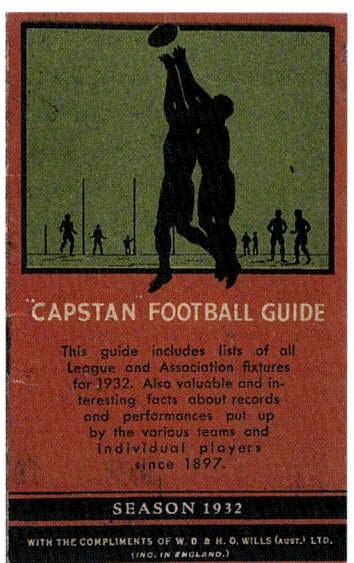

Its all here for the year.

July 9. South Melbourne defeated St Kilda by the barest margin, 9.16 (70) to 10.9 (69), and preserved their winning run at 10 games.

This is beginning to look like a quick repayment of President and grocery magnate Archie Crofts' investment in the Foreign Legion of South players.

Bill Faul is playing exceptionally well on the halfback line, Bob Pratt is starting to kick goals, and Herb Matthews, Jack Bissett and Brighton Diggins, before he broke his leg, are playing up to their reputations.

Crofts has 'made all things possible by *placing* each interstate and country player as he reached Melbourne'. South's membership has increased from 1900 to 4500 in two years (→29/7/33).

Peter Reville gets ready for season.

The trials and tribulations of the boom country recruit on his first match in the 'big smoke'.

'Skinny' Titus is glad of thick skull

Skinny Titus on a better day.

July 5. Richmond's star forward Jack Titus was a relieved man today when he learned that his skull was not fractured.

Titus was injured during last Saturday's game with Essendon when he accidentally collided with an opponent. He played on for a time but eventually had to leave the ground. Later he collapsed at his home in Swan Street, Richmond and was rushed to the Melbourne Hospital.

It was originally thought that Titus had sustained a fracture to the base of the skull, but later investigation showed that his injuries consisted of a bruise to the head, a bruised nose and a black eye. He is expected to be released from hospital in the next few days (→ 23/6/38).

Moloney's hundred, Bunton's second

Sept. 17. Haydn Bunton, Fitzroy's complete footballer, has won his second Brownlow Medal.

Bunton received seven more votes than Geelong sharp-shooter George Moloney, and South half-back Bill Faul.

Bunton is said by the *Australasian* not to be a 'champion in any branch of the game except fairness', but has a 'general all-round proficiency in all departments'.

Moloney is definitely a champion in one department – that is goalkicking. Despite Geelong's absence from the Finals ex-Claremont champion Moloney totalled 109 goals.

Moloney says that a goal sneak should not forget his other forwards – and should always kick for position if he can't goal (→ 24/5/33).

Moloney: 109 in home-and-away.

VFL says no to show game in America

Sept. 23. The Victorian Football League has turned down a proposal to send a team to play in the United States at the end of next season to promote the Australian game.

The idea was rejected on the grounds that the time was inopportune, and that the move would not help the game. Opposing the motion, delegate Mr G. Cathie said it was extremely doubtful whether grounds could be obtained that were large enough. Another delegate, Mr T. Rush, said it was too early and that when the time was right it

should be introduced by boys of the Young Australia League.

The idea of taking a team to America was first raised two years ago. It was revived this year by Mr Eric Cullenwood, a former Australian now resident in California who introduced the game to schools in San Francisco, calling it Field Ball. It was so popular that a half-day holiday was declared for the first game. When the Young Australia League boys visited San Francisco they played against a competent American team (→ 26/5/33).

Tigers triumph in classic

Charles Street of Carlton appeals for a free and gets one in the Grand Final.

Oct. 1. Richmond, playing desperately in the finish when all seemed lost, stemmed the Carlton tide today to win the Grand Final, 13.14 (92) to 12.11 (83).

The Tigers have been runners-up five times in the last 11 years, and perhaps the remembered pain of defeat gave them the steel to produce their final burst.

Richmond were seven points ahead at the last change and both teams had suffered from the bruising exchanges of the match. The record crowd of 69,724 had already had their money's worth (£3633/4/8) as players brought off wonderful pieces of play, and threw their bodies into packs to try to give their team a decisive break.

It was discovered later that one of Richmond's best, wingman Gordon Geddes, played the second half with a broken jaw.

As the last quarter progressed it was obvious that Richmond's big men, who had powered the drives out of the centre, were tiring. Carlton began to produce their streaming dashes down the ground and gained the lead for the first time.

But suddenly the Tigers took over again. They were fuelled by a superb relieving dash from back pocket by Kevin O'Neill, his link with centreman Eric Zschech and a drop kick of pinpoint accuracy to forward Gordon Strang. He goaled and then, with the crowd creating a continuous roar, the teams lined up for the last desperate minutes.

It was Richmond out of the centre again, through Zschech, and they charged in and made the Flag safe with another goal.

Richmond's best were defenders Jack Baggott and Basil McCormack, O'Neill, Zschech and both Gordon and Doug Strang (four goals) up forward.

Carlton's best two players were Gordon Mackie in defence and 'Mocha' Johnson, who was a power in defence and in the ruck and teamed well with rover Ansell Clark. Full-forward 'Soapy' Vallence kicked five goals, a great effort in a losing side (→ 10/10/34).

1932 Statistics

Leading Goalkicker:
George Moloney (Geel) 109
Brownlow Medal:
Haydn Bunton (Fitz)
Finals: First Semi Coll 17.12 (114) S. Melb 12.16 (88); **Second Semi** Carl 14.15 (99) Rich 18.16 (124); **Preliminary** Carl 23.19 (157) Coll 11.16 (82); **Grand Final** Rich 13.14 (92) Carl 12.11 (83)

Ladder:	W	L	D	%	pts
Carl	15	3	-	137.8	60
Rich	14	3	1	139.2	58
Coll	14	4	-	111.6	56
S. Melb	13	5	-	118.0	52
Geel	11	6	1	139.7	46
Ess	10	8	-	103.0	40
Foots	9	9	-	103.5	36
N. Melb	8	10	-	97.1	32
Melb	4	14	-	76.5	16
Fitz	3	15	-	76.2	12
St K	3	15	-	72.0	12
Haw	3	15	-	64.1	12

Football and the Depression

Football prospered during the 1920s along with most sports and leisure pursuits. Coming after the sacrifices of war, it was a period of expansion and pursuit of pleasure. The growth of population - there were a million more Australians by the end of the decade, and nearly a quarter of them settled in Melbourne – and the increase in wage levels encouraged new forms of commercial leisure such as cinema and the radio.

The VFL attracted nearly a hundred thousand fans to the six games each winter weekend after Footscray, Hawthorn and North Melbourne joined the competition in 1925. A record 64,288 watched the Grand Final in that year.

The game itself was still a mixture of popular pastime and business undertaking. It was relatively cheap (no more than the price a bottle of beer) and accessible. The players were heroes who earned less than basic wage for their efforts. The clubs were broad-based in their membership, yet closely tied to local businesses.

At the end of the 1920s the country fell on hard times. Export prices collapsed, the balance of payments swung into the red, overseas loans were refused, domestic sales fell and businesses went broke. By the early 1930s a quarter of the workforce was unemployed.

In this, the most severe economic depression in Australian and world history, sport retained its hold on the popular imagination. The interest in cricket was never higher. Football, too, maintained its appeal with just a dip in spectators occurring in 1937.

Yet the rigours of the depression touched football and footballers. At a time when job queues were long, and public assistance for the unemployed miserly, earnings from football became crucial.

The VFL had fixed maximum payments under its Coulter Law in 1930 a £3 a match, which was less than the basic wage, and most clubs paid less. But many players picked up additional earnings playing for the midweek business

league and other competitions, while others were found a job by their club bosses who now held the whiphand and used it to insist that players choose between work and football. Training didn't begin until 5, when most arrived by pushbike with their gear in a gladstone bag.

Jack Dyer began work in 1927 as a lad of 14 on 12/6 a week, playing for Richmond Hill Old Boys in the Metropolitan Junior League. On Wednesdays he supplemented his family's income with the Yellow Cabs team. When he made the Richmond list in 1931, he once recalled, his career almost ended before it began because he confessed to the property steward that he had given his jumper to his dad.

Playing in the Seconds, he found the older players 'struggling to hold their position and keep the extra bit of depression day money coming in' wouldn't give him a kick. Yet soon he was an established star with a regular job in the police.

Most clubs were soon in financial difficulty. Hawthorn finished the 1930 season with a debit of £378, and over the next few years was often unable to pay its players. Stan Spinks, one of its few stars, made a few bob by kicking balls over the northern fence of narrow Glenferrie Oval into Linda Crescent where his customers waited to collect them. 'You just had to be hungry for a quid in those days,' he explained.

Collingwood, one of the strongest clubs, faced a threatened strike by its players in 1932 when it cut match payments to 50 shillings. The club had also lost one of its famous players, Albert 'Leeter' Collier at the end of the 1930 season when he went coaching in Tasmania for £9 a week. Collier returned after two years, but others were lured from the VFL by similar sums.

Then as now there were clubs that managed to find a way round the limits set by the Coulter Law on player payments and signing-on fees.

Beginning with an overdraft of £780, South Melbourne embarked on an effective fund-raising campaign to assemble a team of stars from as far afield as Tasmania and Western Australia, the famous 'Foreign Legion' who took off the 1933 premiership before a record grand final crowd of 76,000. South's membership increased from 1900 to 4500 and there were four games in a season where the gate was over £1000.

That was one face of depression football. The other was seen out at Broadmeadows where a camp for unemployed single men appealed to the VFL to give them boots and a ball.

In 1932 Collingwood, Footscray and North Melbourne began admitting the unemployed free to their home matches. The practice became general in 1933, and by 1934 the demand was so great that Collingwood restricted free admission to locals. Most clubs assisted their suburban unemployed teams, and raised money for the workless.

The forms of compassion and generosity in the depression tended to be local in nature. People who were prepared to look after their own gave a cold shoulder to outsiders.

Football expressed a tribal loyalty that intensified in this time of hardship, just as the game itself was played with a new ferocity. The Premierships of Richmond in 1932 and 1934, and Collingwood in 1935 and 1936 lightened up the lives of the dispossessed.

There was the grace of a Hayden Brunton with his brilliantined hair and Brownlow Medals in 1931, 1932 and 1935; he drew in the crowds to the Smith Street shop where he worked until he became a theatre manager.

There was the lairising brilliance of Laurie Nash, the gun recruit of South's Foreign Legion who would ask opponents which foot he should use to drop-kick a goal from the half-forward line. And there was the rough-as-guts Jack Dyer, already cultivating his reputation as 'Captain Blood'.

'Captain Blood?', the Collingwood players retorted; 'more like Captain Bullshit'. They put their money on the indestructible 'Leeter' Collier. So the Myths of Melbournians' chief passion and chief solace accumulated.

Stuart Macintyre.

1933

The football business begins again, the joy of the winter

April 29. The season opened like a well-maintained motor car, on the first turn of the crank handle, in bright sunshine.

The closeness of the games, with three results of less than a kick and the first draw since 1929, with North Melbourne and Fitzroy scoring 11.13 (89) each, showed promise of a splendid season.

Large crowds indicated that the League's forecast that attendances will exceed last season's near two million total may prove correct.

Aside from the footballers themselves, a small army of trainers, boot studders, knitting mill hands, leather workers, printers, laundry men, masseurs, door keepers, doctors, and railway men have combined to bring off the opening round.

Among these paid workers are the umpires, who have attended a school in the summer, at which they receive instruction from an umpire's tutor, and sit for examinations. They then umpire practice matches, with their work assessed, before graduating to umpire junior matches.

Umpires cost the League about £2500 in the metropolitan area.

Umpire Ellingsen might require further instruction. During Carlton's 12.15 (87) win over South Melbourne 11.17 (83) he gave a free kick to a Carlton player, and took the number of the South player who felled him – but failed to make a report after the match.

The thrill of the contest, as Carlton and South play an opening thriller.

Oculist examines umpires' eyes

May 12. Football enthusiasts certain that many umpires are either 'one-eyed' or 'blind' may have some support for their view from none other than the Victorian Football League itself. Last night, 14 field umpires on the list were subjected to eye tests at Harrison House.

The oculist who made the examination will report the results to the League. It can be safely assumed that his findings will be kept strictly confidential!

The sporting public may now care to suggest a number of other tests they would like to have conducted, such as checks for deafness perhaps, and for secret membership of the opposition's football club!

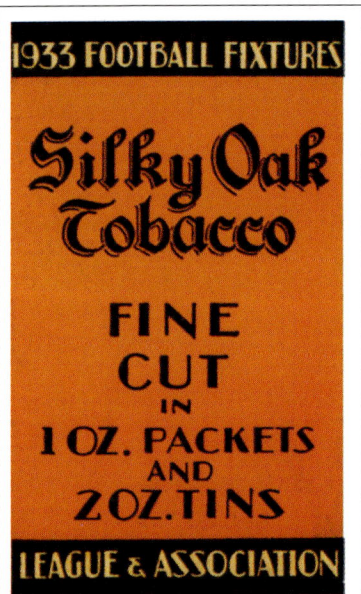

Fixtures put the League and the VFA in a rare combination.

Boxing champ signs up with Footscray

May 6. Not even the presence of Australian middle-weight boxing champion Ambrose Palmer in the Footscray defence could stop South Melbourne overrunning them in the last quarter. After trailing all day South got into gear to kick 7.5 to Footscray's two points, and win 18.17 (125) to 14.15 (99).

Although his team lost, Palmer was among Footscray's best players in his League debut as he battled gamely to hold out the South Melbourne forwards. Palmer, playing on a half back flank, displayed the strength that would be expected of a champion pugilist. Palmer was recruited from the Footscray District League (→ 22/8/35).

Saints earn a badge of courage

St Kilda's badge of honour.

June 30. The St Kilda committee has ordered a 'badge of courage' for the players who took part in the 'battle' with North Melbourne on May 27, which the Saints won 13.19 (87) to 11,17 (83).

The President, Mr F. Arlington Burke, described the match, which St Kilda won with only 15 men on the field, as the greatest moral victory in the club's history.

St Kilda gained an early lead, but the game erupted in the second quarter as the Northerners tackled unsparingly. St Kilda captain Clarrie Hindson fell with a broken ankle, and soon after forward Bill Mohr sustained two broken ribs. Even then St Kilda led at half time.

The rooms at the break resembled a casualty station, with five men receiving treatment. St Kilda went out

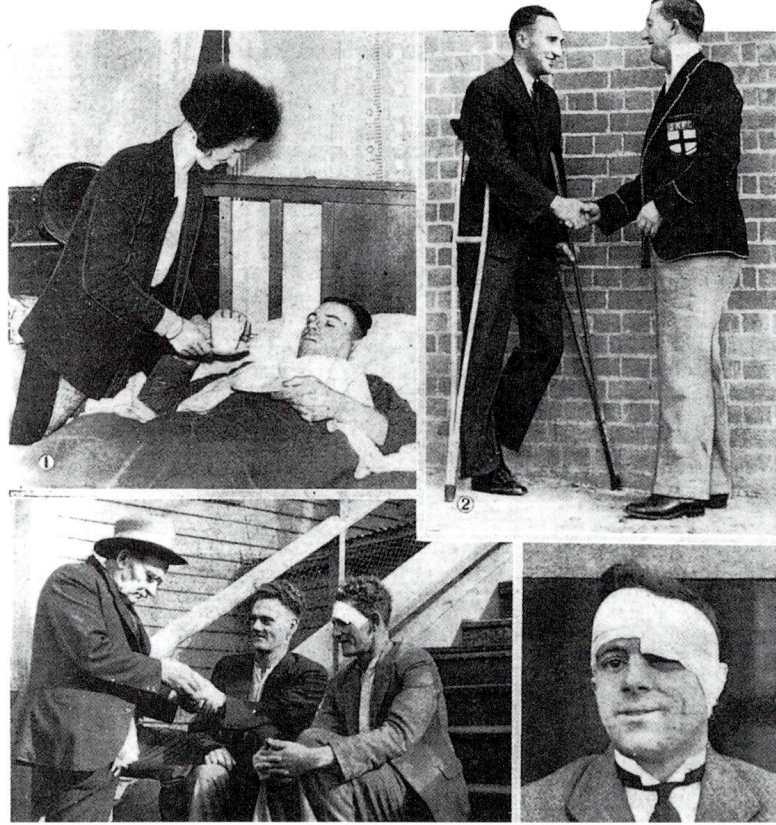

Saint heroes (clockwise) Mohr, Hindson, Bence, Matt Cave and Bill Downie.

a ruckman and a forward short, and had a number of other players hurt. Then Jack Anderson was knocked unconscious, Bill Roberts was felled twice and Roy Bence was KO'd and carried off.

At one stage the game was stopped after a wild melee in the centre.

But the remaining St Kilda players still ran rings around their disorganised opponents.

One sporting action from North saved their day. Their tough ruckman John Lewis sent his team-mate out of the centre, leaving each team with only one follower (→ 7/8/37).

The Mayblooms' mustard pot jumper: yellow with brown.

VFL wins hearts and minds in Riverina

Aug. 18. The recent visit by the Melbourne team to play representative teams of the Riverina District in NSW has paid off handsomely.

The Riverina's geographical situation has made it a cross-over point between the rival codes of rugby and Australian Rules, and there has been almost a war as the officials on both sides seek to promote their game.

While the Australian Football Carnival has been in Sydney, leaving a yawning gap in Melbourne's Saturday, the Fuchsias have played before big crowds at Leeton and Narrandera (→ 20/11/37).

Rules and rugby merger not on

Aug. 14. The NSW Rugby League has abandoned its idea, presented to the Australian National Football Council, that the two codes should be merged and a 'national game' created. The apparent confusion at a 'secret' trial match played in Sydney three days ago may have settled the matter.

The rugby position, put by its Secretary, Mr Harold Miller, was that the new game should be fast and a succession of thrills. The grounds in Sydney and Melbourne could not hold the crowds that would flock to the spectacle, he thought. But the trial match suggests otherwise.

Is Haydn Bunton paid too much?

Bunton: slapped on wrist.

May 24. Fitzroy's Haydn Bunton, regarded as the greatest footballer playing, will not be lost to the game. He has been merely 'reprimanded' by the VFL Permit Committee for having broken the Coulter Law regarding player payments.

The matter goes back to 1930 when the young champion from Albury, now the winner of two Brownlow Medals, was being wooed by four clubs, including Richmond, Carlton and Essendon.

It transpired, on the information of former Fitzroy club Secretary Tom Coles, that Bunton was paid £3/10/- a week, even though he was still playing in the country. The Coulter Law stipulates that players should receive £3 a week, only for VFL matches played (→ 13/9/35).

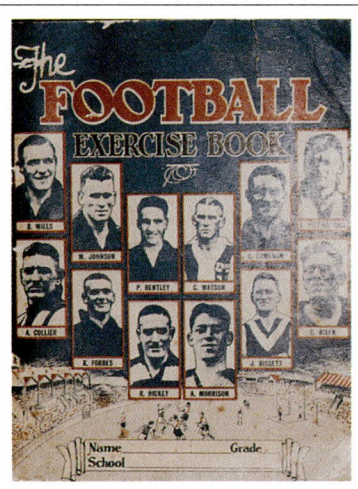

If the mind wanders from reading, writing and arithmetic, you can dream about the footy and watching the stars on Saturday 'arvo'.

Pratt local hero in South's Foreign Legion flag

South Melbourne captain-coach Jack Bissett and Secretary Dick Mullaly welcome an incoming brigade of the Foreign Legion.

Pratt finds alternative target.

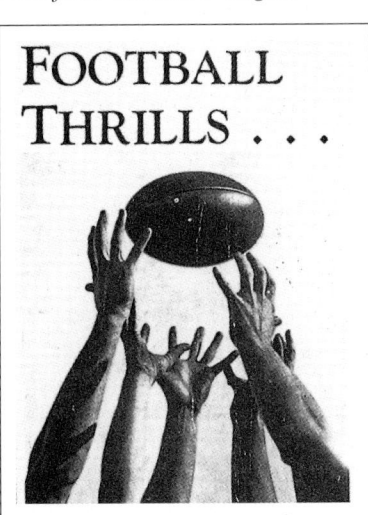

FOOTBALL THRILLS . . .

Book early for a seat on the special Carnival train to Sydney.

Sept. 30. South Melbourne repaid chain-store king Archie Crofts' investment in the South Foreign Legion by winning the 1933 Flag in front of a record 75,754 fans.

Scores were South Melbourne 9.17 (71) to Richmond 4.5 (29).

It was the first Premiership for South Melbourne since 1918, won under the astute eye of ruckman and captain-coach Jack Bissett.

Bissett is Victorian, as is fellow ruckman Peter Reville and goalkicking legend Bob Pratt. Pratt had already kicked 100 goals before the Grand Final, and added a modest three today.

South's team boasted Tasmanian Laurie Nash, South Australians Jack Wade and Ossie Bertram, and the Western Australians Brighton Diggins, Bill Faul, 'Brum' O'Meara,

and 19th man 'Blue' Beard.

Not all champions, but welded into a champion team.

Critics of South Melbourne, like Brownlow Medallist Ivor Warne-Smith writing in the *Argus*, call it 'fair weather play'.

Warne-Smith has been critical of the fixed backline with the rucks changing in the forward line, and the reliance on full-forward Pratt to score most of the team's goals.

He said South Melbourne play 'a most spectacular game, with terrific speed, accurate passing, and leading out into position.

'If the ground happens to be wet the pace must slacken to that of an ordinary team. If gusty, accurate passing is practically impossible.'

These reservations did not affect South on the day – there was a slight

breeze to kick against but they were the more desperate team, from the opening bounce.

The spirit of South's eight-goal last quarter in the great Second Semi win over Richmond seemed to carry over into the Grand Final.

Celebrations after the match began with the players travelling by charabanc to the South Melbourne ground where thousands of fans awaited them, followed by a reception at the Town Hall, and presentation on stage at the Tivoli Theatre.

Chicken Smallhorn a popular winner

Sept. 30. Fitzroy winger Wilfred Smallhorn was presented with his Brownlow Medal at the MCG – the first time the Brownlow has been presented this way.

Smallhorn was cheered by the record Grand Final crowd but would rather have been playing.

Fitzroy missed their first Finals since 1919 by two points.

Small, courageous and quick, 'Chicken' Smallhorn won by a vote from Essendon halfback Bill Lowenthal.

Lowenthal was unlucky because he injured an ankle in the Carnival, and missed the last three rounds.

Proud 'Chicken' Smallhorn.

1933 Statistics

Leading Goalkicker:
R. Pratt (S. Melb) 109
Brownlow Medallist:
W. Smallhorn (Fitz)
Finals: First Semi-final Carl 10.11 (71) Geel 12.12 (84); **Second Semi-final** Rich 11.1 (77) S. Melb 14.11 (95); **Preliminary Final** Rich 13.5 (83) Geel 10.14 (74); **Grand Final** S. Melb 9.17 (71) Rich 4.5 (29)

Ladder:	W	L	D	%	pts
Rich	15	3	-	141.1	60
S. Melb	13	5	-	127.5	52
Carl	13	5	-	114.4	52
Geel	12	6	-	130.4	48
Fitz	11	6	1	105.6	46
Coll	11	7	-	112.9	44
Foots	11	7	-	97.7	44
N. Melb	7	10	1	85.2	30
St K	6	12	-	80.9	24
Melb	3	15	-	82.0	12
Haw	3	15	-	73.3	12
Ess	2	16	-	77.1	8

Bumper crowds herald season's promise of excitement

A stirring start to the season as Collingwood and South players watch the Premiership Flag unfurled.

May 26. The football is keen this season, with the crowds loving the high-scoring efforts of the leading teams. Each glamour side has a high-flying full-forward and people are flocking to see Bob Pratt (South), Jack 'Skinny' Titus (Richmond), Harry 'Soapy' Vallence (Carlton), George Moloney (Geelong) and Gordon 'Nuts' Coventry (Collingwood).

The season opened with a record home-and-away attendance of 128,000, and 100,000 has been topped every week since.

An army of traders is profiting from this enthusiasm. Knowing that small boys like to chew coconut at the game a Victoria Market wholesaler has shipped in 25,000 coconuts from Fiji. He reckons this to be a month's supply.

The discerning barracker likes to soothe his throat with an orange and as many as 10,000 have been purchased at one match.

The Tramways Board is doing bumper trade on Saturdays, and one football manufacturer plans to make 20,000 footballs this season.

Players, umpires, gatekeepers, caterers and bar traders, peanut and sweet vendors and the *Record* boys are all beneficiaries of the booming season. The Great Depression is over, at least in the football world.

Police help end 20-player brawl

July 14. Police helped officials to break up a vicious brawl involving 20 players during the third quarter of a fiery clash between Carlton and Collingwood at Victoria Park.

Three Carlton players were reported after the brawl in which numerous blows were struck. Earlier, Collingwood's Syd Coventry was knocked out by a blow to the head and had to leave the ground with concussion. The game, won by Collingwood, 13.17 (95) to 10.5 (65), was the most spiteful in years.

The heavy cross-wind made play difficult, and many players resorted to rough-house tactics. Ten players were injured in a bruising encounter. Each side blamed the other for causing the brawl.

Fitzroy pots goal in-off small boy

June 30. The new Governor of Victoria, Baron Huntingfield, witnessing his first Australian Football contest, saw an incident unlikely ever to be repeated. Colin Benham, Fitzroy ruckman, marked the ball just as the final bell rang. He was in range of goal, but as his kick would have no effect on South Melbourne's win, other players ran for the pavilion while boys jumped the fence in their usual excited way. Benham's kick was destined to be a behind, but struck one running boy and was deflected between the goalposts. As the ball had not hit another player, the field umpire had no alternative but to award the goal. South Melbourne, 13.19 (97), defeated Fitzroy, 13.10 (88) (→28/8/36).

Pratt and Nash star in South Melbourne firmament

Pratt gets a visit at lemon time.

Pratt's goals keep piling up.

Laurie Nash often plays at centre-half-back, but he got his chance at full-forward for the State team against South Australia. His 18 goals showed that South have a ready-made replacement if ever Bob Pratt is unable to play.

Aug. 11. South Melbourne's goal-kicking wizard Bob Pratt passed the century in VFL goals with his tally of 11 goals against Carlton last week – after just 13 games this season.

He seems certain to smash Gordon Coventry's record of 124 goals if he can remain healthy for the rest of the season.

South won handsomely, 23.15 (151) to Carlton's 17.8 (110), a result which seemed unlikely at half time when Carlton led by ten points.

After the interval came what the *Australasian's* Jack Worrall has described as a 'wild delirium of goal-getting', brought about by 'transcendent football'. South kicked 13 goals two, and Pratt kicked eight goals two of the total in the third quarter.

Worrall went on about the dazzling, perfect and brilliant football they played. 'The handpassing, though some of it should have been disallowed, the foot-passing, the shepherding, the marking, the leading-out and anticipation, the pace and the certainty of it all left the Blues dumbfounded. It was executed with a coolness, a smoothness and a skill that proved invincible', Worrall wrote.

Pratt who came to South aged 18 from Mitcham in 1930, was: 'A freak footballer, and one apparently made of whale bone. He can twist in the air at all angles, frequently marking the ball when out of position, can cover enormous distances with punts, is as persistent as a terrier on the ground, and can kick either foot in any position, whether on the run or standing still.'

At South the captain Joe Scanlon said 'Now Bob, what we require of a full-forward is a couple of hundred goals a season, so hop in and do your best and if you have any luck see that the head does not swell'.

No chance of that with the modest champion. He says that there is nothing to it. 'It's easy. All you have to do is get the ball and put it through'.

Easier said than done, but Pratt is helped by his team-mates, such as Austin Robertson and Jack Bissett and by the excellent work of Laurie Nash at centre-halfback.

Nash could easily be a champion forward himself – as his feat of kicking 18 goals for Victoria against South Australia testifies (→ 2/5/36).

Every week Pratt takes marks like this over Richmond's Maurie Sheahan.

The rock of the South defence is the tough, strong-marking Laurie Nash.

Eras end for Hopkins and Syd Coventry

BOB. MIRAMS

Alan Hopkins: almost a medal.

Sept. 22. Two of the great names of football, Alan Hopkins of Footscray and Collingwood captain Syd Coventry, have announced that they are hanging up their boots.

Hopkins, Footscray born and bred, is the son of a former club stalwart Con Hopkins. He has been a tireless worker in the centre over 151 games and nine years.

Nicknamed 'Banana Legs', he has an awkward, close-to-the-ground gait that belies his speed and unsettles opponents. He has come close to the Brownlow Medal four times.

Coventry has played 227 games. The highlight of his career might be counted as the 1927 Brownlow Medal, but he would say that leading the Magpies to four successive Premierships gave him the most satisfaction.

North sit on bottom

Sept. 15. After promising much towards the end of last season, North Melbourne finished at the bottom of the ladder yet again, this time without winning even one game.

During the season coach Dick Taylor was replaced by Tom Fitzmaurice who failed to lift the club out of the doldrums. The time has come for North to bring in new blood rather than continue relying on players who have failed too often in the past.

Tigers prick South Melbourne bubble

Oct. 10. In weather made to order for the most important day of the football year, Richmond fielded its best team and outplayed South Melbourne to become easy winners of the Centenary Grand Final, 19.14 (128) to 12.17 (89).

The Tigers lived up to their sobriquet, and embarked on a spree of goalkicking. Only towards the first change did the Southerners look like matching the teamplay of Richmond. They were outplayed through the next two quarters.

South faced a 10-goal deficit then, and it did not help that Laurie Nash kicked his sixth point.

Then Nash went berserk to kick four quick goals and revive the spirit of '33. But it was too late and the last remaining interest was in seeing Bob Pratt kick his second goal to make his season's tally 150.

Jack Titus kicked six to be among Richmond's best players, along with Jack Baggot and Gordon Strang. The 'Three Musketeers', Kevin O'Neill, Maurie Sheahan and Martin Bolger, were superb in defence. Young ruckman Jack Dyer did not spare himself. His vigorous play in the packs made many openings which helped to bring about South's downfall.

1934 Statistics

Leading Goalkicker:
Bob Pratt (S. Melb) 150
Brownlow Medallist:
Dick Reynolds (Ess)
Finals: First Semi-final S. Melb 11.12 (78) Coll 9.21 (75); **Second Semi-final** Rich 19.20 (134) Geel 7.8 (50); **Preliminary Final** Geel 7.6 (48) S. Melb 15.18 (108); **Grand Final** Rich 19.14 (128) S. Melb 12.17 (89)

Ladder:	W	L	D	%	pts
Rich	15	3	-	121.3	60
Geel	14	3	1	135.4	58
S. Melb	14	4	-	140.2	56
Coll	13	4	1	121.9	54
Carl	12	6	-	116.3	48
Melb	9	9	-	97.2	36
St K	9	9	-	95.8	36
Fitz	7	11	-	95.7	28
Foots	6	12	-	85.0	24
Ess	5	13	-	83.5	20
Haw	3	15	-	67.8	12
N. Melb	0	18	-	66.4	0

A superb mark by Richmond defender Gordon Strang keeps South out.

Vote checkers from the VFL are hard at work scrutinising the field umpires votes at the Brownlow Medal count, held at Harrison House. They are, from left, E. McCutchan, J. Smith, Dr K. McCarthy, VFL Secretary L. H. McBrien and committee chairman S.W.Ramsay. The Medal went to Essendon rover Dick Reynolds, who beat the dual medallist Haydn Bunton of Fitzroy. Reynolds has just completed his second year with the Dons.

MCG Story – The hub of football

The regrettable truth is this, the Melbourne Cricket Ground should be called the Melbourne Football Ground. It is very nearly the most thoroughly footballed ground on earth.

In the season there are four football matches every week-end, two Victorian Football League firsts and two reserves. On cunning occasions like the Queen's Birthday, when a carefully selected Monday becomes a long week-end, there are six matches at the Melbourne Football Ground ... I beg your pardon ... Melbourne Cricket Ground.

Four teams call the MCG their home. Melbourne since 1861, Richmond since 1965, North Melbourne since 1986 and Essendon since 1993. Collingwood has a de facto status too, so the MCG is really home to five football teams plus the Australian Football League headquarters.

It was not always thus. Certainly not. There was a time when Australian Rules Football was a lesser activity, something to be despised and it was certainly not allowed to sully the sacred turf of the Melbourne Cricket Ground. There was a tradition for this. Back in England cricket and football, soccer, rugby or whatever, were always played on separate grounds. Indeed often the cricket and football grounds were side by side. How absurd to contemplate cricket after the turf had been churned by football.

In 1856 T.W. Wills, secretary of the Melbourne Cricket Club, wrote a letter to *Bell's Life*, a sporting journal, suggesting that the MCC should form a football club as a means of keeping cricketers in good condition during the winter months.

Football did actually begin in 1858, but matches were always played in the park outside the MCG In 1869 there was an application to the Governor-in-Council for permission to use the ground for athletic sports besides cricket. This was granted and there was a charity match between the Melbourne Football Club and the Police Force. However, the committee still refused to believe that football would not ruin the ground, and it was many years before football on the MCG became a regular thing.

The Melbourne Cricket Club built an ingenious grandstand for James Lillywhite's cricket tour of Australia in 1876-77. It held 2000 people and it was double-sided. At the end of the cricket season it would be re-constructed so that the seats faced the other way.

This meant that during the summer the spectators could watch the cricket in the MCG, then in the winter the football out in Richmond Park. Even in 1876 few believed that a football ground, a sea of mud in August, could be a beautiful cricket playing turf in September.

Yet during the winter of 1877 there was a football match between the Melbourne and Carlton clubs which added 95 pounds 12 shillings and eight pence to club funds, an enormous sum in those days. This had a profound effect on club thinking.

From here on football crept into the MCG. Then on August 31, 1884 the double-sided ground was destroyed by fire, some say from a cigar butt left smouldering in the skittle alley down below. It was a good burn, and the double-sided stand disappeared, its like was never built again, and football settled in at the MCG

And how it grew. The 1912 football Grand Final between Essendon and South Melbourne drew a record crowd of 52,000. The *Australasian* was ecstatic. It said: 'Surely if ever there was any doubt in anybody's mind as to which is the national game of the land, the attendances and the money taken at the finals of both League and Association on the last day of the season should be enough to dispel any illusions'.

And so it continued. The Great Southern Stand '1250 feet' long began construction in 1936. That produced a Grand Final crowd in 1938 between Carlton and Collingwood of 96,834.

Then there was that extraordinary Grand Final of 1956 between Melbourne and Collingwood. The splendid new Northern Stand had just been completed for the Olympic Games. Yes, there have been bigger crowds, like 121,696 between Carlton and Collingwood in 1970, but in 1956 the official figure was 115,902. Officials estimated 2000 more broke their way in and 25,000 were locked out. They were jammed in the aisles, they clambered on the roofs. Some climbed up into the girders and others sat precariously on the narrow parapet at the top of the new stand.

But it was very interesting. The hostility between cricket and

football continued. The Victorian Football League resented bitterly the fact that cricket owned or controlled nearly all the grounds. Collingwood's Victoria Park was an exception.

So the Victorian Football League, later to become the Australian Football league, decided to build its own ground and headquarters at Waverley, which it felt was the true population centre of Melbourne. Here was a ground designed purely for Australian Rules Football, never to be sullied by cricket. It opened on April 18 1970. Mr Jona MLA, a Liberal member told the House that club football might not be played any more on the MCG and possibly the finals would not be held there after 1971.

There was an uneasy truce for a decade. Two elimination finals and the preliminary final often were played at Waverley. The crisis came with a promise that the 1984 Grand Final would be at VFL Park. There were some deeply emotional stories before the 1983 Grand Final. Most papers treated the MCG as if it were in the intensive care ward and close to death. This was the last Grand Final ever at the old ground. Flowers and obsequies were appropriate.

But in the end there was peace. Some have described it as a get-together akin to peace in Northern Ireland. The Premier, John Cain, forced the issue, but agreement came about because there were some enlightened men who were prepared to see each other's point of view, Ross Oakley, and Alan Schwab, commissioners of the Australian Football League, Sir Bernard Callinan and Dr Donald Cordner both presidents of the Melbourne Cricket Club and Dr John Lill, the secretary.

The AFL and the MCG agreed to replace the old Southern Stand with the new Great Southern Stand as a joint venture. AFL would have its headquarters there plus seats for members.

What's more, the AFL gave a promise that the Grand Final and the Preliminary final would be staged at the MCG for the next 40 years.

So the stand was built, cost $140 million, and the MCG often called the Old Paddock, has been the holy shrine of Australian Rules Football ever since the new stand opened in 1992. Indeed it can go even further than that – to the deep shock of old Aussie Rules supporters, it has played host to State of Origin Rugby League matches.

In 1994 the Rugby League contest between New South Wales and Queensland attracted an astonishing 87,161 spectators, a record for Rugby League.

Oh yes, that was something they could never achieve in Sydney and a lovely tribute to the Old Paddock. **Keith Dunstan**

And the Big Men Fly – the pioneer full forwards

All League footballers were special then, in that bold era whose spartan span was pegged out by the Wall Street Crash and the outbreak of the Second World War. But the full-forwards! They had a glow of their own: they were the matinee idols, the matadors, the trapeze artists – all of that, and rather more. They were the ultimate tribal heroes, whose Saturday exploits demanded sometimes freakish talents.

And such a medley of legends: Bob Pratt, Gordon Coventry, Harry Vallence, Jack Titus, Bill Mohr, Ron Todd, George Moloney, Laurie Nash. From among them, between 1929 (Coventry) and 1940 (Titus), came 12 separate centuries of goals. A dozen heavy dents in history. Nobody had ever kicked 100 goals in a single season before, and nobody would again until John Coleman in 1949. Coleman did it three times; but he was the only one to do it between 1941 and 1967.

Of all that marvellous congestion of full-forwards of the thirties, just one has so far been accorded a place in the Sport Australia Hall of Fame: Bob Pratt. He topped the goal-kicking three times, in 1933, 1934 and 1935, and set a record of 150 that would be equalled once (in 1971, by Peter Hudson) but never beaten.

Some said that the facet of his game that separated him from the rest was his capacity to lift high off the turf, and do amazing things while he was up there. The phrase 'and the big men fly' was born during those Depression days; true, the champions did fly high, with outstretched palms hauling in grabs that seemed miraculous, but they weren't really so big ... not by today's standards. Few of them topped six feet. Pratt was just over five feet ten inches, which made him a good inch taller than Titus and Nash.

But the way Pratt flew! Sixty years later Dick Reynolds, the treble Brownlow winner, retained the vivid memory of Pratt's bootstops sailing above his head – not once, but often. Pratt launched himself early, with apparent disdain for the manner of his re-

turn to earth, and had a knack of screwing his body as he soared, so much that commentators christened his a 'whalebone' action.

One of them, the former champion footballer and Test cricketer John Worrall wrote of Pratt in *The Australasian*: 'He can twist in the air at all angles, frequently marking the ball when out of position, can cover enormous distances with punts, is as persistent as a terrier on the ground, and can kick either foot in any position ....'

In 1995 Pratt was the sole survivor of the Golden Age full-forwards, a man of nimble and general memory. Collingwood's Jack Regan was his emphatic choice as the best full-back he'd played against. 'It was an honour for me to beat him, and it was an honour for him to beat me – and believe me, it happened both ways'.

One day at three-quarter time, Regan was taken off Pratt. As they passed each other taking up their positions, Regan asked: 'How many goals've you kicked'? Pratt's response was, 'About nine'. Regan shook his head disgustedly: 'If you'd heard (coach Jock) McHale at the break, you'd 've thought it was 19'.

Laurie Nash, Pratt's Test-cricketing team-mate at South, seems an unlikely inclusion in that illustrious chorus line of full-forwards. He rarely played there, after all; Pratt had the job with that team. But one day in 1934, when Pratt was unavailable through injury and the chosen full-forward, St Kilda's Bill Mohr, broke a finger in the first quarter, Nash found himself playing as spearhead for Victoria against South Australia. He played with a flair that came close to genius, pulling down screamers, spinning both ways, booting home shots from impossible directions and distances, showing off shamelessly. The MCG belonged to him that afternoon.

He finished the day with a record 18 goals three behinds from 21 shots, 14.2 in the second half.

It was Nash who, when asked to name the finest player he had

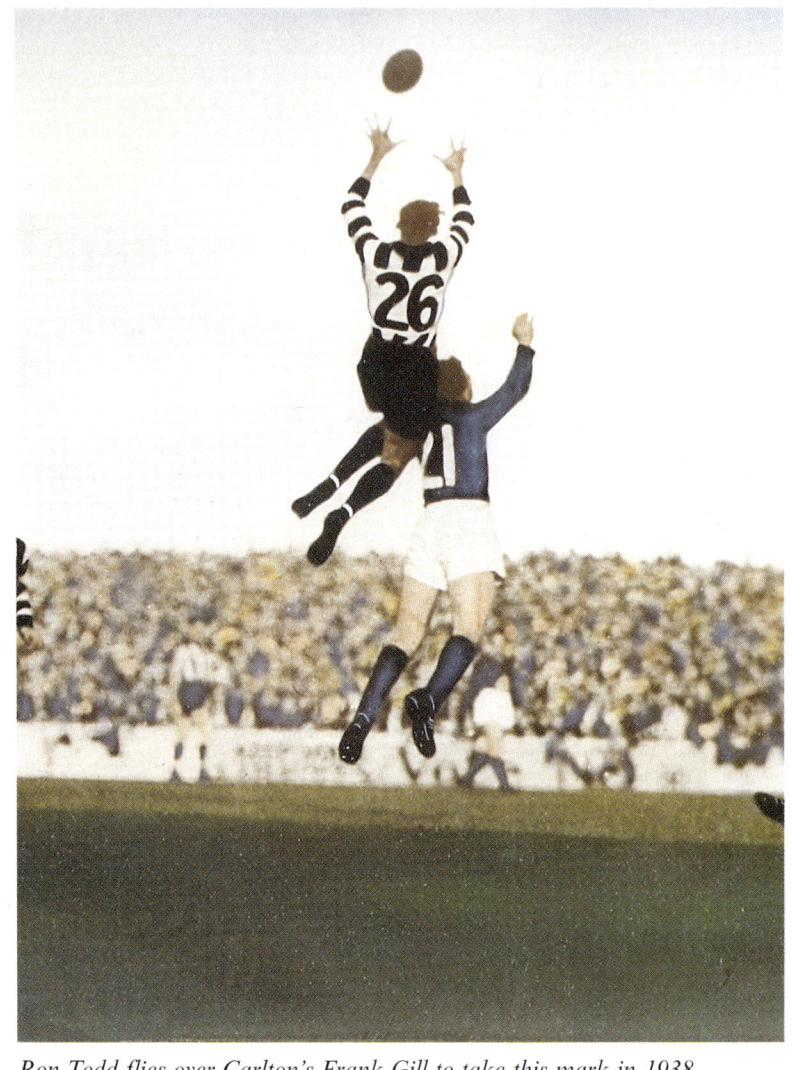

Ron Todd flies over Carlton's Frank Gill to take this mark in 1938.

ever seen, responded promptly: 'I look at him every morning, when I'm shaving'. That sort of cocky confidence caused problems when he was playing centre-half-forward to Pratt's full-forward. Too often the two players found themselves in competition, and South selectors finally solved the problem by moving Nash to centre half-back, where he remained formidable.

Pratt might be seen as the finest of the era. But no full-forward in League history had a greater impact on the record books than Gordon Coventry, who took over at Collingwood from the great Dick Lee in 1922, and topped that club's goalkicking every year from then until 1937. He was the first ever to kick 100 goals in a season (124 in

1929), the first to play 300 matches and the first to kick 1000 goals (he still holds the career record of 1299).

One day against Fitzroy in 1930, he kicked 17 goals, setting a record that stood for 17 years.

'Nuts' Coventry stood half an inch below six feet, and was respected as a tough but fair player. His record was unblemished for 17 years until a day in August 1936, when the Richmond full-back Joe Murdoch provoked him by hacking constantly at a crop of boils on his neck. Finally, he could take it no more. He lashed out, dropped Murdoch, and three nights later found himself fronting the League tribunal.

The Tribunal ruled that Coventry had been the agressor, took no account of his impeccable career,

146

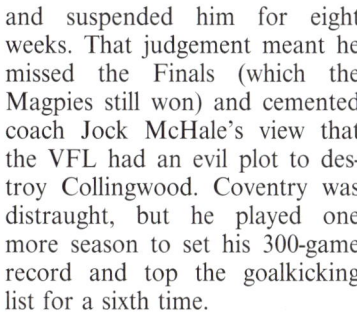

Bob Pratt flies over Richmond's Maurie Sheahan for another brilliant mark.

Bill Mohr, the St Kilda great needed no 'sit' to rise up and grab this mark.

and suspended him for eight weeks. That judgement meant he missed the Finals (which the Magpies still won) and cemented coach Jock McHale's view that the VFL had an evil plot to destroy Collingwood. Coventry was distraught, but he played one more season to set his 300-game record and top the goalkicking list for a sixth time.

Collingwood had a divine way with full-forwards. In the 32 years until that suspension there had been only two, Lee and Coventry, and between them they had kicked more than 2000 goals. With Coventry out, a new treasure was waiting, in the lanky form of Ron Todd. He landed four goals from 13 shots to help win the 1936 Grand Final, then took over the spearhead past when Coventry retired the following year.

Todd was a natural, genuinely tall (at 6 feet 1 and a half inches) with a tremendous spring and pace that had brought him success as a professional runner. He was also a character, who once nonchalantly commended an opponent whose shoulders had helped him to reach breathtaking altitudes as 'the best step-ladder a man could ever wish for'.

Camera gear wasn't sophisticated in those days, but the pictures which endure of Todd's more spectacular marks are some of the finest of the genre. In 1938, his first year as full-forward, he was unstoppable; he kicked 120 to head the goal-kickers, and in the Preliminary Final snared 11 goals. The next year he again topped the list, with another 120 and another 11-goal Preliminary Final tally. In three finals matches that season he kicked a total of 23 goals – which stood as a record until broken by Gary Ablett 50 years later (in four matches).

Todd by then was probably the greatest drawcard in the League.

In March 1940 he was persuaded (by bookmaker Bill Dooley and a down payment of £500) to join the Victorian Football Association club Williamstown. There he became an awesome force, kicking an Australian record 188 goals in 1945, with a single 20-goal bag against Oakleigh. Collingwood, a club which relished a good grudge, never forgave him.

Geelong's George Moloney (109 in 1932), St Kilda's Bill Mohr (101 in 1936) and Richmond's Jack 'Skinny' Titus (100 in 1940) qualify among the century scorers of the era, alongside Pratt (3) Coventry (4) and Todd (2). Each of them topped the goalkicking list. Carlton's Harry 'Soapy' Vallence never reached the ton, but he kicked 11 goals in four matches (two of them finals), and in 1931 he beat Moloney, Coventry and Mohr to win the goalkicking with 86. (In one game that year between Collingwood and St Kilda both Mohr and Coventry kicked 11).

Together that whole group represented a defining moment in football, a time when the traditional goalsneak approach (characterised by the nimble Moloney and the cheeky, taunting Titus) met and meshed with the new, high-flying game of Pratt and Todd. Football was more deliberate then, and for all their fascinating blend of styles, those forwards shared something: an uncanny capacity to win possession of the ball, high up or on the ground, and convert opportunities into goals.

Their exploits, in an age that belonged to the battler, made them pathfinders ... for a glorious procession that would contain the likes of Coleman and Hudson, Dunstall and Ablett.

Champion full-forwards were a distinctive breed then. Still are, really. **Harry Gordon**

1935

Footscray try to stir up their supporters with song

The new look Footscray cheer Alan Hopkins (now of Yarraville) at the Hopkins Testimonial match between the clubs.

Jan. 19. The Footscray Football Club wants more coordinated vocal enthusiasm from its supporters in the coming season. Already the committee has decided to conduct community singing at matches at the home ground. Gramophone records suitable for amplifying through loudspeakers will be bought. Also in the interests of more inspiring football, the search is on for club songs for supporters to sing to arouse their fellow Footscray followers and inspire the players, too.

The Committee is now considering the appointment of a 'cheer leader' so that the best results from the club's 'battle' songs can be obtained from the singing supporters.

If these initiatives produce the desired results, we will no doubt be treated to aural contests all over Melbourne on a Saturday, as opposing 'choirs' vie for attention.

Soon it could be that supporters have as much to contribute to their team's honour and pride as the players themselves! To do better than the other side's 'choir' will become a serious matter, requiring attendance for 'choir practice' on a Thursday night! (→ 12/7/38).

Saint will-o'-wisp resigns captaincy

April 30. St Kilda captain Colin Watson has shocked the Saints by resigning after the first round.

The St Kilda veteran, who only agreed to turn out for the Saints if he was made captain, has been cleared back to Warrnambool. Watson's poor form against Fitzroy in the opening round probably prompted him to hang up his boots and return to the family farm. He had earlier complained that he had to pay men to milk the cows while he was playing footy. The 1925 Brownlow Medallist quit at the end of last season but was persuaded to play on.

A veteran of many seasons, and countless close finishes, the time-keeper is one of many honorary workers who keep football clubs working smoothly.

League lends North £500 to survive

Feb. 4. The North Melbourne Football Club has been rescued from a grave peril by an interest-free loan of £500 from the Victorian Football League. North had been faced with its most dangerous foe to date – a huge debt of £1,200.

The North Committee, determined to find a way out of the club's jeopardy, applied to the League for aid. In granting the loan, the Victorian Football League has required North to raise a further £500 through its own efforts. Certain North Committeemen have guaranteed a bank overdraft to clear the rest of the debt (→ 14/6/36).

Big crowd sees game under lights

March 30. The practice game between Richmond and South Melbourne was the first between League teams played under electric light.

25,000 people turned out to watch the fun with a white ball at Olympic Park and went away impressed with the standard.

Neither team displayed much desperation, as they treated the match as an exhibition fundraiser. Richmond won, 14.8 (92) to 8.8 (56)

Some dark and dim spots were apparent on the ground, and players were occasionally dazzled by the lights in their eyes, but 'night football' is playable.

Rubber ball too bouncy for footy

April 10. Players and officials have given the rubber football the thumbs down. The rubber ball was used as part of an experiment during several pre-season practice matches.

St Kilda coach Dan Minogue said that the ball regularly tricked players. It was inclined to float in the wind, and was far too lively in ground play.

Hawthorn players said they were bewildered by the rubber ball. Players in the Richmond and Oakleigh game were unanimous that the ball was too tricky. They used a leather ball in the second half.

Hawthorn hat trick a first for club

Sept. 7. Playing at its home ground, Hawthorn Football Club today completed its first hat trick ever by winning against Fitzroy, 14.26 (110) to 15.6 (96). In the number of behinds booted by the Mayblooms can be seen an onslaught of shots in a dogged determination to get the ball through the posts, any posts, and prevent the invaders from stealing an important victory, their fifth win for the year.

This being round 18, Hawthorn's three-in-a-row ending has come too late to lift them above tenth place on the League ladder, but augurs well for next season. New playing coach and captain, Ivan McAlpine, who previously led Footscray, is doing well with a side seemingly resigned to the habit of defeat. In fact, they are a team so used to adversity that a certain strength of character has been taught, and is now being utilised as a potent weapon. We saw this indomitable spirit work to dramatic effect in last week's match against Geelong. Despite playing at Corio, where Hawthorn had never won before, the Mayblooms brought about a complete collapse of the home team. Assuming the lead all through, Hawthorn administered a sound drubbing to Geelong by kicking 13.9 (87) to 7.17. (59).

The game that started this end-of-

Three cheers for the gentlemen.

season rally for Hawthorn was fought against Essendon in round 16. Hawthorn may be developing a tendency for winning the hard way, for in that game, as today, a proliferation of behinds did the job, 8.26 (74) to 9.12 (66).

The side has been playing it 'the hard way' in another sense. Ironically, the team's hat trick has been won without the players being paid a penny. Currently troubled financially, Hawthorn have had nothing in their bank account to reward them. Humorists might see this as an argument for the non-payment of players. However, the truth remains that there are many out of work for whom £3 per game is their only income (→ 16/5/36).

Percy Bentley stops Jack Regan and lets Richmond's Skinny Titus in.

'Old Boy' retires after 46 years

July 5. R.W.E. (Reg) Wilmot, better known as 'Old Boy' of the *Argus*, was presented with a mahogany log-box by the VFL, upon his retirement from journalism.

Reg Wilmot played for Essendon in the great Premiership teams alongside Albert Thurgood from 1890 to 1893, kicking 23 goals.

He joined the *Argus* in 1889, and became a powerful advocate of Australian football and cricket.

Wilmot has been an active secretary of the Australian Amateur Boxing and Wrestling Association, and the Victorian Amateur Athletic Association.

Girls and boys are equal in VFL eyes

April 27. The League has discovered that schoolgirls, too, like to go to the football on Saturday afternoon. It has decided the concession tickets, known as 'Schoolboy Tickets' will now be renamed and stamped as 'School Tickets'.

The decision followed a proposal on behalf of the girls by the Collingwood delegate, Mr R.T. Rush. He said that, while the number of girls seeking the season ticket would probably be small, the girls should have the same claim.

The tickets cost 5/- for the season, and entitle the schoolchildren to admission at any ground.

Parachute invasion stops footy match

Sept. 7. Geelong were rallying spendidly in the third quarter of their match with Essendon when small boys swarmed on to the ground, as numerous as a flock of seagulls, and halted play. Irresistibly drawn by the sight of small parachutes and papers falling from a miniature balloon traversing the ground, the boys raced after treasure with no regard for the game in progress.

While the crowd roared with laughter, the police chased the small boys, who quickly made off with the prizes. Geelong's rally thwarted, they lost 11.13 (79) to 14.23 (107).

Brick truck hits Pratt; South hit brick wall

Oct. 12. Collingwood's road to victory in the Grand Final over South Melbourne last week was made smoother by the unfortunate accident to the legendary goalkicker Bob Pratt.

On Grand Final eve Pratt was travelling to Prahran by tram, when on alighting he was tackled by a brick truck. While not badly hurt, Pratt was taken to hospital and missed the Grand Final.

Obviously this was a severe blow to South, as Pratt had kicked 16 goals in the two earlier games, including six in the Southerners' Second Semi victory, 15.14 (104) to 11.17 (83). Jack Regan, 'Prince of Full Backs' had to be moved into the ruck for this game.

In the Grand Final Regan played at centre-halfback on Laurie Nash, and the recalled 216-game veteran Charlie Dibbs played fullback on South's stand-in Roy Moore. Neither Southerner kicked a goal.

The absence of Pratt was a hole that could not be filled – no one knew how to lead out or inspire the other forwards. The result was that South kicked just seven goals for the match, its lowest for the season.

At the other end Collingwood were positive and well organised.

Collingwood were a happy band with their trainers and supporters after their great Grand Final victory.

Their veteran Gordon Coventry, who once carried Pratt's mantle as the best full-forward in the game, still had the wiles and ability to kick four goals. The 19-year-old Phonse Kyne chimed in with two from centre-half-forward. Kyne was described in the *Australasian* as a 'superman' along with Regan, Harold Rumney and centreman Marcus Whelan. The Colliers were magnificent, and all in all it was 'a triumph of organisation and football sense'.

The *Australasian* said Collingwood had winners everywhere. 'Their defence was magnificent, their forwards inspirational, their team work and knowledge of a bet- ter brand than their opponents, while their marking was sublime'.

For South Austin Robertson was best, showing courage under a good deal of provocation in a game that was the best of the Final series, but also the nastiest. Final score: Collingwood 11.12 (78), South Melbourne 7.16 (58) (→ 3/10/36).

Modest Bunton wins third Brownlow

Sept. 11. Fitzroy champion Haydn Bunton has won his third Brownlow Medal, the first player to do so in the history of the League.

Bunton was a convincing winner, receiving 25 votes. His nearest opponent was Essendon captain Keith Forbes with 17 votes, while Carlton's Keith Shea finished in third place with 16 votes.

Bunton won his other two Brownlows in 1931 and 1932. He was bitterly disappointed not to make it three in a row when he polled poorly in 1933. He was runner-up in 1934 by just one vote to teammate 'Chicken' Smallhorn.

Part of the credit for Bunton's win this year must go to the Fitzroy coach Percy Rowe who used him as a utility player putting him closer to the action. At the presentation, Bunton said that the award of the Brownlow Medal was an honour that he shared with his team-mates.

Haydn Bunton: well ahead in the voting, he has made history in winning his third Brownlow Medal.

1935 Statistics

Leading Goalkicker:
R. Pratt (S. Melb) 103
Brownlow Medallist:
H. Bunton (Fitz)
Finals: First Semi-final: Rich 19.11 (125) Carl 14.20 (104); **Second Semi-final** S. Melb 15.14 (104) Coll 11.17 (83); **Preliminary Final** Coll 14.10 (94) Rich 9.12 (66); **Grand Final** S. Melb 7.16 (58) Coll 11.12 (78)

Ladder:	W	L	D	%	pts
S. Melb	16	2	-	137.6	64
Coll	14	2	2	121.4	60
Carl	14	3	1	141.6	58
Rich	12	6	-	117.4	48
St K	11	7	-	110.6	44
Melb	8	9	1	101.2	34
Fitz	8	9	1	90.2	34
Ess	7	11	-	89.6	28
Geel	6	11	1	96.3	26
Haw	5	13	-	80.9	20
Foots	2	14	2	73.5	12
N. Melb	1	17	-	65.1	4

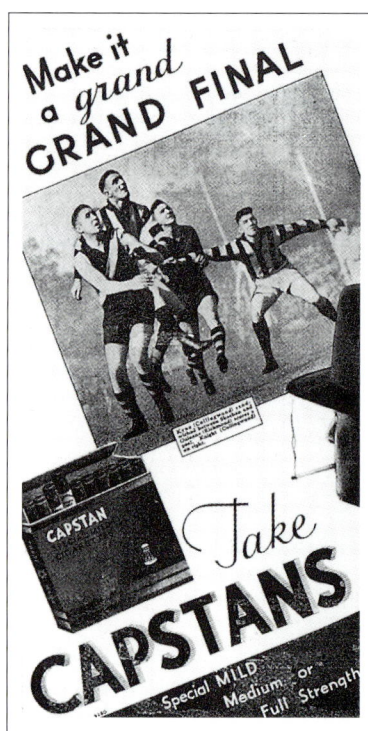

1936

April 30. Tom Leydin, the Carlton and Fitzroy rover of the 1880s has died.

May 2. Bob Pratt kicks his 500th goal in League football with his first for South in their win over Melbourne, 14.24 (108) to 13.9 (87).

May 30. Jack Worrall in the *Australasian* says that football teams are becoming 'standardised' as the weaker learn from the stronger. They don't play with the individual styles of earlier times.

June 6. A dispute over player transfers has strained relations between Geelong and Richmond. Geelong's printed invitations to Richmond officials for half-time refreshments are returned torn in half with insulting messages. Richmond win, 13.12 (90) to 6.14 (50) (→ 15/6).

June 13. Gordon Coventry kicks his 1200th goal for Collingwood in their win over Melbourne, 14.5 (89) to 9.13 (67). Coventry has played for the Magpies for 17 years.→

June 13. Wal Lee has completed 50 years service as trainer to Collingwood and its predecessor Britannia. Wal is the father of the legendary forward Dick Lee.

June 15. Geelong coach Charlie Dibbs, recruited from Collingwood, resigns after loss to Hawthorn, 12.19 (91) to 7.6 (48). Reg Hickey is made captain-coach (→ 22/8).

June 29. Twelve thousand watch King's Birthday holiday exhibition game at Princes Park. VFL 16.21 (117) defeat VFA, 10.10 (70).

July 25. Melbourne kick 10.5 in the last quarter to South Melbourne's one point to come from behind and win 22.16 (148) to 14.12 (96) (→ 30/9/39).

Aug. 8. Victoria just defeat South Australia, 13.27 (105) to 15.13 (103), in Adelaide.

Aug. 29. Geelong defeat Richmond, 12.9 (81) to 8.7 (55), putting Richmond out of the final Four for the first time in 10 years (→ 6/10).

Aug 29. Carlton score a behind on the bell to defeat Collingwood, 13.12 (90) to 13.11 (89), ensuring the Blues a place in the Finals (→ 24/9/38).

Sep. 5. Wooden spooner Fitzroy fail by a point to win last game. South win, 11.14 (80) to 11.13 (79) (→ 31/8/38).

Help to Mould the Brown and Gold

Ted Poole: Hawthorn stalwart.

May 16. Could it be that the 'improved' Hawthorn, as the advertisements put it, will rise to stardom? A membership drive, to 'help mould the brown and gold' is under way, and now Hawthorn has amazed all followers by running Carlton to a close finish at the Hawthorn Oval after beating Footscray last week.

Introducing systems and tactics that they had never played before, Hawthorn had victory within their grasp but were flattened when full-forward Jack Green sustained an injured knee. Hawthorn lost, 14.13 (97) to 16.11 (107) (→ 30/4/38).

Old father time

May 2. Geelong's timekeeper, Peter Burns, has begun his 54th year of involvement with football. In the past 30 years of clock-watching for Geelong, he has missed only seven matches. Before taking on this role after his retirement as a player at age 36, Burns had been captain of Geelong. But his greatest time as a player was his earlier years as a tireless ruckman for the Swans.

He was idolised by South Melbourne fans, and it is said that small boys of that city had a nightly prayer which went: 'God bless Mummy, God bless Daddy, and God bless Peter Burns.'

Gates crashed in Punt Road dispute

June 27. Organised gate-crashing is becoming a menace at the Richmond ground. Ugly incidents were avoided today through the clever tactics adopted by the ground management in dealing with concerted attempts to block some turnstiles and rush others. Assisted by the constabulary, staff aided the onrushing clusters of demonstrators, rather than attempting to block them. Some were physically hefted over the turnstiles into the ground, but then prevented from leaving again to rejoin their fellows in making further nuisance.

It is suspected that the deliberate campaign of harassment at the Richmond ground is intended to reduce the Club's income to such an extent that it will be forced to withdraw from the League competition.

The symbols of Saturday.

Jack McMurray whistles up 300th

Aug. 30. Jack McMurray, the League's most senior umpire, has officiated in his 300th League game.

This is a milestone for McMurray who has umpired more games at senior level – both in the Association and the League – than any other umpire in the history of the game. His distinguished career has seen him umpire more than 20 finals.

McMurray began his football career as a player with Port Melbourne (one of two clubs his father played for) before exchanging his boots for an umpire's whistle.

Shinboners score record comeback

June 13. Losing must get so boring, that you have got to win for a change. How else to explain North Melbourne's huge turn around against Footscray today.

The Shinboners had plodded along to 41 points down at the last change, when they erupted.

North stormed home, kicking 7.6 for the quarter to take their score to 12.19 (91). The bewildered Saints kicked only one point to go to 11.9 (75). This was a record 'comeback', and is only North's second win since 1934. (→ 29/7/44).

Gordon Coventry and Wal Lee, 50 years a Collingwood trainer.

Gay night for Tom the Turk

Oct. 1. Tommy 'The Turk' Lahiff doesn't mind a bit of rough stuff on Saturday afternoon as he gives his all for Essendon. His opponents would have been shocked to see him on Monday night, plastered with lipstick, rouge and mascara under a blonde wig, wearing 'falsies' and high heels.

But such is the life of a football club, where players mix in with supporters and the local community to raise funds and have a bit of a laugh. Out at Essendon, which is almost a world unto itself, the social life around the club has been in full swing lately.

Tommy's transformation came with the presentation by the Essendon Footballers' Dramatic Club of the comic play *Nothing But the Truth*, at the Town Hall. It was described as an hilarious suc-

cess by the *Essendon Gazette*.

Tommy joined captain-coach Jack Baggott to play Sabel and Mabel, the gold-digging sisters who complicate the lives of the Ralston family. Other cast members who were prepared to switch sexes and provoke barrages of laughter from the audience were Bruce Anderson, Keith Forbes and George 'Ginger' Bell. The players recieved many floral (and other) tributes at the end.

Last night another Essendon Football Club occasion swelled the coffers of the social club. The Show Eve Dance at the Paramount Hall, Ascot Vale, was described by the *Gazette* as a particularly gay night. Highlight of the evening was the Ugly Man competition, which was won by young rover Dick Reynolds.

Football goes on the country, in this instance at Percy Leason's town of Wiregrass. Sometimes old footballers, turned umpires, forget themselves.

'Nuts' boils over

The moment of Coventry's downfall, as he tangles with Joe Murdoch.

Aug. 4. Collingwood's goalkicking champion Gordon 'Nuts' Coventry was sentenced by the VFL Tribunal to eight weeks suspension.

Coventry will not be able to play again this season, and has said that he may not play again.

Great interest by football supporters generally, but Magpies in particular was exhibited. The result was flashed on the screens of Collingwood's picture theatres.

VFL President Dr. W. C. McClelland was in the chair at the Tribunal, assisted by Melbourne University Professor of Geology, E. W. Skeats, and Mr A. W. Moir

Coventry was involved in a fight in the third quarter with Richmond's feisty fullback Joe Murdoch, a game which Collingwood went on to win 14.12 (96) to 11.14 (80).

Murdoch received four weeks as the purported 'victim.'

Both players were charged by boundary umpire Chegwedden with having 'deliberately fought'.

Coventry's defence was that 'half way through the third quarter I went up for a mark and got a blow on the head. I do not remember what happened after that'.

Doctors after the game dressed a severe head wound.

For his part Murdoch said that Coventry was 'muttering to himself' in the third quarter and that if he had hit him it was in retaliation for being hit himself.

Coventry after the hearing maintained that Murdoch, before the blow that caused his concussion, had been bashing him on a very painful outbreak of boils on the back of his neck.

If Coventry had hit Murdoch it was in retaliation for the attacks on his boils. Coventry's 16 season unblemished record was of no account.

Dons' hill is windy

Aug. 15. Champions became ordinary mortals in the 50-mile-an-hour gale which made the ball like a badminton shuttle at most grounds today. Conditions were especially trying on Essendon's wind-swept hill. Magnificent though this ground is, its exposure led to some absurd moments in the game against Collingwood. The gale fairly roared across the ground and kept whipping kicks out of reach and out of bounds, despite the best efforts of both sides. This hurly-burly game was won by the visitors 14.16 (100) to 8.10 (58).

Rain stops play

July 4. The entire round of VFL matches was postponed today because of rain which fell constantly all day Friday, and all day today, with just a brief respite at midday.

With all grounds under water and further rain forecast the Adverse Weather Committee of the VFL had no other option.

The season will be shifted forward one week, with the Grand Final to be played on October 3.

Fortunately rain insurance of £1,600 was taken out by football clubs and caterers with Eagle, Star and British Dominion.

Another Brownlow born in Albury

Dinny Ryan: great defender.

Sept. 9. Following in the footsteps of Haydn Bunton, that other great Fitzroy footballer from Albury, Denis 'Dinny' Ryan has surprised the football world by winning this season's Brownlow Medal.

Ryan, Fitzroy's centre-halfback did not even win his club's best-and-fairest award; that honour went to Haydn Bunton. Ryan had to be content with the club trophy for 'most improved player'. Ryan's Brownlow win continues Fitzroy's remarkable run of successes in the League's best-and-fairest award. Fitzroy players have won the medal five times in the past six years. Last season it was won by Bunton for the third time.

It was not just the football world that was shocked by Ryan's win – so was Ryan, who said he was thunderstruck when informed of the news by Fitzroy Secretary, Mr H. Trevena. 'I do not know whether I am on my head or my heels,' he said.

Ryan polled 26 votes (21 first votes, 4 second and one third) to win from Geelong's Reg Hickey (21) and South Melbourne's Herbert Matthews (20). Ryan came to Fitzroy as a full-forward but wayward kicking saw him switch to centre-halfback where his high marking and direct play make him one of the League's outstanding defenders.

Magpies' Flag, South second again

Oct. 3. Collingwood made it two Premierships in a row on Saturday. It again beat South Melbourne, this time before a bumper crowd of 74,091 at the MCG.

Collingwood's success with five Flags in ten years since 1927 has been the despair and envy of all other clubs.

This one was achieved with what Jack Worrall in the *Australasian* said is 'the team of the year'.

'Men must be made of iron to stand the modern method in a Grand Final. The high marking was capital, the handling and cleverness of Collingwood's small men something out of the common, the team work excellent, and the knowledge and judgement supreme. The game was won by team work and brains, and every man pulled his weight. Not so the losing team.'

Alby Pannam was best for the winners, with five goals. He was as elusive and slippery as an eel, and ran in and out of packs with the smoothness and certainty of water.

The Collingwood machine with its business-like, common-sense methods on and off the field rolls onwards, its members enjoying with success an abiding confidence in the fitness of things.

Harry Collier and Jack Bissett with the Governor, Baron Huntingfield.

Saints' Bill gets 100 Mohr goals in year

Sept. 5. St Kilda's mercurial full-forward, Bill Mohr kicked his 100th goal for the season with an eight-goal tally in the Saints' thrilling one-point win against Carlton.

Mohr went into the game needing seven goals to reach his ton for the season. Mohr has been in brilliant form all year, unlike the Saints who have been most inconsistent, again missing out on the Finals.

Within minutes of the start of play against Carlton, Mohr had the St Kilda faithful on their feet when he steered home his first goal, closely followed by a second, then a third. His century came in grand style in the final quarter when he flung himself at the ball, grabbing it as it bounced, then eluding Carlton's fullback Park to send it through the posts for the 100th time. The crowd rose to applaud the modest Mohr.

Old Pivotonians' Jubilee reunion

Oct. 6. The Geelong Football Club staged a wonderfully successful Jubilee reunion of its 1886 VFA Premiership team.

Nine members of that team, which went through the season undefeated, were present for a day including a visit to the old Argyle football ground in Aberdeen Street where Geelong then played, and the reunion dinner at the Victoria Hotel. Speeches from the dinner were broadcast on 3GL.

Oldest player present was G.A. Rylah who played for Geelong in 1875 and 1876.

VFL Vice-President Dave Crone said that the spirit of football never died, as proved by the youthfulness of the men who were assembled.

The Mayor of Geelong led the singing of the 1886 verses of *Geelong Boys Are We* (→25/9/37).

1936 Statistics

Leading Goalkicker:
Bill Mohr (St K) 101
Brownlow Medallist:
Dinny Ryan (Fitz)
Finals: First Semi-final Carl 11.22 (88) Melb 14.13 (97); **Second Semi-final** S. Melb 10.17 (77) Coll 12.18 (90); **Preliminary Final** S. Melb 13.11 (89) Melb 8.15 (63); **Grand Final** Coll 11.23 (89) S. Melb 10.18 (78)

Ladder:	W	L	%	pts
S. Melb	16	2	118.5	64
Coll	15	3	135.6	60
Carl	12	6	124.8	48
Melb	12	6	118.8	48
Geel	11	7	125.8	44
Rich	10	8	107.9	40
St K	9	9	96.1	36
Ess	6	12	85.1	24
Haw	6	12	80.9	24
Foots	5	13	86.5	20
N. Melb	4	14	75.9	16
Fitz	2	16	68.9	8

1937

May 1. Most popular man with small boys in South Melbourne is Billy Windley, former player and now ball steward. He has old, used footballs in his gift, and disposed of 45 into eager young hands last season.

May 22. Fitzroy rover Percy Parratt paid tribute in the *Sporting Globe* to team-mate and great full-forward Jim Freake who died this week. Freake kicked 442 goals in 174 games for Fitzroy between 1912 and 1924.

July 10. Footscray, 22 points down at three-quarter time, hold Essendon scoreless and kick 5.2 themselves to win 11.11 (77) to 9.13 (67).

July 31. Ballarat League has suffered a decline since the days it played the VFL regularly, and suggests reducing teams to 15, and a reversion to old laws to restore their standing.

Aug. 14. Victoria retain the Australian Championship at the Ninth Australian Football Carnival in Perth, defeating WA 14.13 (97) to 13.11 (89) before a record Subiaco crowd of 40,000.

Sept. 25. Jack Worrall writes in tribute to the great play of Collingwood's veteran Collier brothers in their win over Melbourne in the Preliminary Final – by deliberately misquoting Shakespeare: 'age cannot wither them, nor custom stale their infinite variety.' Collingwood won 16.11 (107) to 7.10 (52).

Sept. 26. 1000 people witness the final act of the Geelong Flag when a mock 'magpie' is given a funeral service and buried in Corio Oval.

Oct. 30. Con Hickey, secretary of the Australian National Football Council, and former long-time Secretary and delegate from Fitzroy has died aged 73. He first suggested playing a game in Sydney for Premiership points in 1903.

Nov. 20. The VFA has revoked its permit agreement with the VFL, and has suggested new rules including teams of 16, three points for a poster, two-handed throws, kick off from the centre after goals, and one man from each team to fly for the ball (→ 16/4/38).

Debuts
Bob Chitty (Carl)
Des Fothergill (Coll)

Retirements
Gordon Coventry (Coll)
Doug Nicholls (Fitz)

Up and down start for Redlegs and South Melbourne

May 29. Oh! How have the mighty fallen! And the humble been raised up! After six rounds South Melbourne have struggled to record only one win, and that today against the lowly Hawthorn by three points, 15.11 (101) to 13.20 (98).

Meanwhile Melbourne look set for a superb year, having won all of their first six matches in dashing style. They have accounted for Richmond, Essendon, Carlton, Collingwood, St Kilda and Footscray.

South seem to be just a shadow of the great Foreign Legion side that won the Flag in 1933 and played in the last four Grand Finals.

The most obvious gap in the ranks is at full-forward – where the mighty Bob Pratt is out through injury. This lack of a focus has unsettled the whole side.

Melbourne, on the other hand, seem to have a steady combination and are working with great precision to get the ball into the hands of their forwards, Jack Mueller, Norman Smith and Ron Baggott. Centreman Alan La Fontaine and rover Percy Beames have been among the driving forces. Their toughest game was against St Kilda, when they scored three time-on goals to snatch the game, 12.23 (95) to 12.18 (90).

But the grittiest win in these early games was St Kilda's in round two, over the hapless Hawthorn. Hawthorn led 8.7 to 0.0 at the first change, but the Saints overhauled them in the last quarter to win 15.22 (112) to 14.15 (99).

WHEN YOUNG BERT PLAYED WITH WIREGRASS LAST YEAR, HE SEEMED ABLE TO DO WHAT HE LIKED WITH BALL AND OPPONENTS

The parable of the March champion, as seen by Percy Leason from Wiregrass.

Bunton restless

Jan. 27. Haydn Bunton, captain and coach of Fitzroy last year, is seeking the same job at South Melbourne.

A few days ago Bunton announced he would not seek reappointment at Fitzroy, and now the South Melbourne Committee has revealed his late application to join the Swans as player coach. There will be at least ten other applicants in the contest for the position. But Bunton, three times a Brownlow Medallist (1931,'32,'35), must be considered a very strong contender.

He is one of the finest players ever seen, a rover averaging 28 kicks a game. The only blot on his career was accepting a £222 persuader to join Fitzroy in 1930 (→ 24/1/38).

Saints wrestled out

Aug. 7. A stranger wandering into the Melbourne ground might have been excused for asking if the match between Melbourne and St Kilda was a practice game. You could hardly credit that these were two leading teams playing for the right to enter the Semi-finals.

The standard of play was far below that expected from the third and fourth teams in the competition, with little system, too much interference with the man and little of the clever evasion which is the spice of the game.

Melbourne were the better disciplined side and had the call in the air, running out winners 18.16 (124) to 11.18 (84) (→ 16/9/39).

Dons' dapper Dick does double

Classical Cats maul Magpies for Flag

Sept. 1. Dick Reynolds, the Essendon utility, was at a club dance at the Essendon football pavilion when telephoned with the news that he had won the Brownlow – again.

Essendon delegate Bill Brew who made the call said he was 'particularly pleased that 'Our Dick' has won the Brownlow Medal. He is an excellent example of all that is best in our game, for he makes the ball his object always.

'He is a district product, and is not only an excellent and fair player, but a great club man.'

Reynolds said 'It was nice to win the Brownlow Medal for the second time, but I think Herbie Matthews is a little unlucky'.

Matthews finished second with 23 votes to Reynolds' 27.

In the voting it was interesting to see that no fewer than 15 Hawthorn players polled votes, more than any other club, indicating both an even team and a lack of stars,

Collingwood's sensational 17-year-old Des Fothergill scored 13 votes in just 12 games.

Matthews polled in 11 games, with six first votes, two second votes and three third. The umpires gave Reynolds votes in 11 games, with five firsts and six seconds.

Celebrations, and a cartoon from Sam Wells, as Reg Hickey's Cats down the Magpies in the Grand Final.

Sept. 25. Geelong played brilliantly to win the 1937 Premiership, overpowering Collingwood in a game that was never in doubt after the Cats had settled down.

The leader at the end of the home-and-away round, they were so charged with energy when they took the field that Premiership jitters were evident until about midway in the second term. By then they were three goals behind. Then the players began playing the same tune, producing such a sparkling display of teamwork and individual skill that even the Magpies' most valiant efforts were of little avail.

Although beaten at every turn, the Collingwood side also played fine football, contributing to the feeling among spectators that they were witnessing one of the best Grand Finals in years.

A record football crowd of 88,540 got full value from the brilliant work of the two sides. Geelong forward-ruckman Jack Evans kicked six goals.

In the herculean struggle of the final term, Geelong's superior stamina resulted in their scoring 42 points to Collingwood's hard-won ten. Final scores: Geelong 18.14 (122) Collingwood 12.18 (90). This was the Cats' 14th successive win, and third Premiership.

No doubt the happiest man in Geelong tonight will be captain and coach Reg Hickey. He had the confidence of all his men from the first game of the season, and set a fine example today (→ 15/4/44).

1937 Statistics

Leading Goalkicker:
Gordon Coventry (Coll) 72
Brownlow Medallist:
Dick Reynolds (Ess)
Finals: First semi Coll 18.12 (120) Rich 10.9 (69); **Second semi** Geel 19.11 (125) Melb 16.17 (113); **Preliminary Final** Melb 7.10 (52) Coll 16.11 (107); **Grand Final** Geel 18.14 (122) Coll 12.18 (90)

Ladder:	W	L	D	%	pts
Geel	15	3	-	135.3	60
Melb	15	3	-	131.2	60
Coll	13	5	-	129.0	52
Rich	11	6	1	108.0	46
Carl	11	7	-	110.9	44
St K	10	8	-	101.3	40
Fitz	7	11	-	93.1	28
Haw	7	11	-	84.4	28
S. Melb	6	11	1	89.9	26
Ess	5	13	-	90.6	20
Foots	4	14	-	81.8	16
N. Melb	3	15	-	64.2	12

Reg Hickey and Gordon Coventry watch Les Hardiman go for the mark.

Saturday arvo at the footy final

Sept. 18. A Preliminary Final at the MCG calls on all the resourcefulness of the barracker.

Some might find that, however exciting the game, a cushion or two will ease the pain, especially for Melbourne supporters.

Some might feel like a hot dog, to re-fuel a hungry Magpie, peckish after a spot of encouragement for the boys in black and white.

Others like the bottle boys are more concerned with gathering the castoffs, and exchanging them for a bit of 'sugar'.

And it's not just the boys who barrack, ladies are on tiptoe with enthusiasm – for Collingwood, who won 16.11 (107) to 7.10 (52).

A cushion to ease the pain.

Football finery for the ladies.

A customer for the hot dog man in his corner behind the grandstands.

The bottle boy has work to do.

Coaching legend Jack Worrall dies, but his football writing lives on

Jack Worrall died on November 17, aged 74. He was a great footballer for Fitzroy and won three Flags for Carlton, and two for Essendon as coach. He was an excellent cricketer for Carlton, Victoria and Australia.

In addition he wrote about football and cricket for the weekly the *Australasian* for 25 years.

In almost his last piece, published on September 25, he wrote of Collingwood that 'other clubs come and go, but mostly go, enjoy their brief share of publicity and limelight, though Collingwood, like Tennyson's brook goes on forever'. So did Jack Worrall.

In this story he wrote of the

'football brain' that must direct the other physical qualities of as a player. This was just another example of Worrall's aptitude for felicitous coinages in the language of football we all use today.

'Many coaches consider they have nothing to learn, though they have much to forget' (1937).

In 1912 in his first season as a writer Worrall decided to name the finalists as 'the Four'. He wrote 'I am strongly in favour of the present system of deciding the Premiership ... the scheme which produces a Grand Finale'.

By 1913 there was 'what may be termed the Preliminary Final', won by St Kilda, making a

'Grand Final' necessary.

The other essential to the game is the 'free', a term first used by Worrall in 1915.

It was 'anybody's' game, eventually won by the 'best team on the day', at 'the Mecca of League football' possibly by Carlton, 'noted for their third term' (1912).

But 'however capable a coach may be, he can only deal with the material in his charge' (1915).

'Apparently the clubs are well manned but the track galloper is not always a great public performer' (1913).

'There is no reason why a man cannot be a footballer and a gentleman' (1913). 'It is no good

carrying a gun if you cannot shoot straight, and it is not much use being a footballer if you cannot kick accurately' (1914). 'Football is grand training for the more serious game of war' (1916).

'When people talk about what the League should do they forget that the League is only the mouthpiece of the different clubs and has no distinct entity' (1915).

'History proves that many football managements never learn anything from adversity' (1915).

'The less throwing means more kicking, and after all the game is foot ball' (1924).

Dogs are barking as Footscray start winning games

July 2. The rising fortunes of the Footscray Football Club have the dogs barking in Barkly Street and the shoulders squared in Droop Street. This may yet be the year of the Tricolours.

Footscray are in second position after today's great win over Richmond. Two weeks ago they beat the mighty Collingwood, 13.9 (87) to 10.5 (85). They are a game ahead of Collingwood, Richmond and Melbourne.

Today's game was played on one of those windy days beloved by Footscray, when the westerly sweeps down the ground. Footscray had 4.9 to 1.0 on the board at the first change and went on to win 13.20 (98) to 7.4 (46).

Behind the Footscray rise is a great spirit around the club, brought on by the return of old players to support the team, and supporters' social events (→ 17/5/41).

Alf Sampson of Footscray leads Collingwood's Ron Todd to the ball.

VFA breakaway puts game in danger

April 16. With the dramatic breakaway of the Association from the League, Australian Football is in a state of war. The League itself is partly responsible for the rebellion. The Association has decided to 'go it alone' out of sheer frustration, having had its aims for achieving equal status blocked by the League, and now intends to ignore the senior body altogether.

Football itself may suffer if cooperation between the bodies disappears. The Association has been the testing ground for innovations in the game, later adopted by the League. Among them were: the reduction from a 20-man side to 18 on the field with one man in reserve, the introduction of boundary umpires, the numbering of players, and the appointment of an independent tribunal to deal with complaints against players.

To its credit, the League has not been too proud to adopt such innovations for the good of the sport, but could remain aloof to any Association initiatives now. We may see the evolution of two sets of rules, and a division similar to the chasm between Rugby Union and Rugby League (→ 5/7/44).

Ron's on his Todd for spectacular marking

May 21. The crowds are flocking to watch the new forward sensation Ron Todd. He has such a remarkable leap, such concentration and such sure hands that defences are hard pressed to hold him. But all that concentration goes when he kicks for goal, and it is costing the Magpies matches.

His display against Richmond two weeks ago was described as invincible, and he kicked nine goals. The pundits say he should have got 17, and the scoreline of 11.26 (92) was not enough to overcome Richmond's 15.12 (102).

Today he kicked nine and could have had more, but Carlton swept the game away 19.16 (130) to 17.12 (114) (→ 23/9/39).

The sheer brilliance of Ron Todd is shown in this fine mark against Geelong.

Reynolds scores a Brownlow treble

Blues break drought after 23 years

Dickie Reynolds on the dash.

Brighton Diggins leads them out.

Jim Park of Carlton arrives too late to stop Albert Collier's kick.

Aug. 31. For the second successive year and for the third time Dick Reynolds, the Essendon rover, has won the Brownlow Medal, equalling Haydn Bunton's record.

Reynolds, who first won the medal in 1934, received 18 votes. Stan Spinks, the Hawthorn centreman, was runner-up with 17.

Four players were equal early, with Reynolds winning on the third round.

1938 Statistics

Leading Goalkicker:
Ron Todd (Coll) 120
Brownlow Medallist:
Dick Reynolds (Ess)
Finals: First Semi-final Foots 10.16 (76) Coll 18.9 (117); **Second Semi-final** Carl 16.17 (113) Geel 10.21 (81); **Preliminary Final** Geel 14.14 (98) Coll 21.9 (135); **Grand Final** Carl 15.10 (100) Coll 13.7 (85)

Ladder:	W	L	%	pts
Carl	14	4	116.1	56
Geel	13	5	129.2	52
Foots	13	5	124.3	52
Coll	12	6	117.6	48
Melb	11	7	106.0	44
Rich	10	8	111.8	40
Ess	9	9	102.3	36
St K	9	9	91.8	36
N. Melb	6	12	74.7	24
Fitz	5	13	88.6	20
Haw	4	14	82.4	16
S. Melb	2	16	71.8	8

Sept. 24. Carlton's appointment of South Melbourne 1933 Premiership centre-half-forward Brighton Diggins as captain-coach for 1938 brought them the Premiership Flag. They beat Collingwood 15.10 (100) to 13.7 (85).

The Blues, who had finished outside the Four in 1937 despite some brilliant players, have now become a polished, powerful and very fit unit.

Carlton finished the year a game clear on top, losing four matches, including one to Collingwood.

They sailed through the second Semi against Geelong, winning 16.17 (113) to 10.21 (81), Ken Baxter kicking eight of their goals.

Collingwood also disposed of Geelong in the Preliminary Final, 21.9 (135) to 14.14 (98), setting up a much anticipated contest.

A record crowd at an Australian sporting event, 96,834, witnessed a splendid Grand Final, with Carlton holding the edge in the first half.

Collingwood got to within nine points in the third term, before Diggins' defence steadied the Blues. The Magpies came on again in a thrilling last quarter and were only four points down with minutes to go. Goals to Jack Hale and Jack Wrout sewed it up for the Blues.

It wasn't a day for full-forwards, Jack Regan keeping Carlton's 'Soapy' Vallence to one goal, and Jim Park holding Ron Todd. Diggins was best on ground (→ 20/5/39).

Creepy round 13

July 23. Believers in the occult or those inclined to superstition were loud in their talk of the astonishing results of round 13, with four games being decided by a single point.

In another, the difference was a mere three points and one was settled by six.

North Melbourne nudged out South Melbourne 13.18 (96) to 14.11 (95), Essendon 17.17 (119) beat Collingwood 17.16 (118), Melbourne 9.16 (70) triumphed over Hawthorn 10.9 (69) and Geelong 14.20 (104) trumped St Kilda 15.13 (103).

Big Cats bag

June 4. A new League record was set by Geelong in their match with South Melbourne today, but it may not be one to raise grins of pride in the clubrooms. They kicked 32 behinds, beating the previous record of 31, also kicked by the Cats in 1934. By quarters the sequence of inaccuracy ran 7, 7, 8, 10. More to their credit were the 19 goals also scored in a match in which they more than doubled the Swans score.

The Cats were ahead by only eight points at half time, then peppered the posts and won the game 19.32 (146) to 10.10 (70).

Maroons marooned

Aug. 31. Fitzroy are failing sadly and appear to be heading for a disastrous season next year.

Fitzroy began this season with a loss to Collingwood, then to Footscray, Melbourne, Carlton, Geelong, Essendon and Richmond. They then managed to beat Hawthorn, South Melbourne and North, before starting another chain of losses. With no Flag since 1922, they were wooden spooner two years ago.

Even with Brownlow Medallists 'Chicken' Smallhorn and 'Dinny' Ryan still playing, the team seems to lack star material (→ 30/9/44).

How the teams got their names

CARLTON

Carlton has always been known as the Blues, or the Navy Blues and musically as the Old Dark Navy Blues. Some newspapers before the First World War referred to Carlton as the Brewers. An attempt to introduce the Cockatoo mascot after World War Two was not successful.

COLLINGWOOD

Large numbers of magpies frequented the banks of the Yarra River near the Victoria Park ground. The colours of the uniform match those of the majestic bird, and the club motto: 'Floreat Pica' can be translated as 'May the Magpie prosper'.

ESSENDON

Essendon became known as the 'Same Olds' to differentiate it from the Essendon VFA club, which existed between 1900 and 1921. The term ''Dons', an abbreviation of the club title, has been in popular use for most of this century. During the early 1940s, with the club's base being close to the war-time airport, the term 'Bombers' became popular.

FITZROY

The club was originally known as the Maroons. From before World War Two until 1957 the team was sometimes referred to as the Gorillas. That mascot ten-

ded to be a target for derision. In 1957 the Lions emblem was introduced by club officials and immediately became popular.

FOOTSCRAY

Originally the team was known as the Tricolors. In 1928 it was dubbed the Bulldogs, after a genuine bulldog accidentally led the players out against Collingwood.

GEELONG

The provincial team was often named the Pivotonians for the first quarter-century of VFL competition. The term referred to the hub of primary and secondary industry for the Western District of Victoria, formed by the city of Geelong. In 1923 the Cat emblem was introduced through a series of coincidences relating to the club's good luck during the season seemingly being provided by the presence of a black cat. Sam Wells, the *Herald* newspaper cartoonist of the time; Ken McIntyre, a young Geelong supporter later to develop a series of finals systems, and club captain Bert Rankin all contributed to the adoption of the feline symbol.

HAWTHORN

From 1932 Hawthorn teams were known as the Mayblooms, using the same colours as the flower of that name. From time to time the term 'Mustard Pots' was used. In 1942 Roy Cazaly decided that a more aggressive image was required so the Hawk became the new symbol.

MELBOURNE

Until 1933 the club was referred to as the Redlegs or the Fuchsias. When legendary coach Frank 'Checker' Hughes was appointed he introduced the fiercer Demons tag. Apparently, during a break in play when the team was playing poorly, Hughes told his players, 'You are playing like a lot of flowers! Lift up your heads and play like Demons!' Had he coached the team 50 years later he would have been proud of one champion 'Fuchsia', star wingman and captain, Robert Flower.

NORTH MELBOURNE

Originally the team was referred to as the 'Shinboners', resulting in a tough team image. The name possibly originated from a tendency for uncompromising Northerners to swing their boots in the vicinity of opponents' lower legs. To add credence to the name several local butchers decorated their display windows with beef leg-bones in blue and white colours. In 1954 the Kangaroo motif was used for the first time after the club committee decided that the team needed a more suitable identity.

RICHMOND

The unlikely term 'Yellow and Black Angels' was often used to describe teams until 1920. Newspaper writers sometimes referred to them as 'Wasps'. The following year the Tiger first gained acceptance as the club mascot. A Mr Miles, one of the club's keenest supporters, often perched himself in a tree just outside the Punt Road Oval to watch matches because he could not afford the cost of admission. He associated the club colours with a tiger and with his booming voice would encourage the players with the call, 'Eat 'em alive, Tigers!' He was a cult figure, and his catchcry became the Richmond symbol.

ST KILDA

In early times the Seagull was associated with the club. An attempt was made to name it the Panthers, but the concept was never popular. The logical term, Saints has always had credence and has become universal in the past 40 years.

SOUTH MELBOURNE

Originally, the team was referred to as the 'Southerners' or 'Bloods' or 'Blood Stained Angels'. In 1933, because of the influx of Western Australian recruits, the club was dubbed the Swans. The vicinity of Albert Park Lake to the club's home ground of that era may also have contributed to the adoption of the Swan as the club emblem.

UNIVERSITY

During the seven seasons in which University participated in the competition (1908-14) its uniform consisted of a black guernsey with a blue 'V' and thin waist band, and black socks with blue tops. Its players were affectionately known as the 'Students' or the 'Professors'. 'Uni's' supporters were renowned for their studious barracking at their first home ground, the East Melbourne Cricket Ground.

Col Hutchinson,
Official AFL Historian

May 20. Prime Minister Robert Menzies, a Carlton supporter, visits the rooms of the opposition team for the second time this year – and Carlton lose again. Hawthorn score a memorable win, 13.8 (86) to 11.17 (83) (→ 31/7/43).

June 24. Timekeepers add an astounding 28 minutes 11 seconds of 'time-on' in the Essendon and Hawthorn game, won by Essendon 19.11 (125) to 16.19 (115).

July 1. Victoria defeat South Australia 21.13 (139) to 15.19 (109) in Adelaide. Jack Dyer and Jack Regan receive two guineas each as best players for Victoria.

July 29. VFL sides play in Tasmania, NSW, Ballarat, Bendigo and Melbourne, while the Victoria side was beating South Australia at the MCG, 27.18 (180) to 15.19 (109). All players receive 30 shillings.

Aug. 11. Football legislators from other States are amazed at the rapidity with which the VFL has paid off its £21,200 debt on Harrison House. Just £7000 is now owed after ten years. VFL balance sheet discloses a surplus, including equity in the building, of £18,197.14.3.

Aug. 14. Canadian journalist Paul Malone says in the *Argus* that 'Australian football makes American football look like a ladies game. Furthermore, the Australian game makes even English Rugby, which looks like murder to Americans, appear softer than somewhat as Damon Runyon would say'.

Aug. 19. Seemingly organised fights break out at Essendon, culminating in a fierce brawl at the end of the game. 1000 watch as a gang of North Melbourne youths attack a small number of Dons. Police arrest five. Essendon win, 14.17 (101) to 9.7 (61)

Aug. 26. All VFL matches are abandoned today as League grounds are under water.

Sept. 23. Collingwood's sharpshooter Ron Todd pots 11 goals in Collingwood's hard-fought Preliminary Final win over St Kilda, 20.14 (134) to 15.15 (105).

Oct. 4. Hawthorn's Bert Mills has won the *Argus* newspaper's 'popular footballer contest' with 150,000 coupons lodged out of a total of 750,000.

Retirements
Dinny Ryan (Fitz)
Ron Todd (Coll)

Awful collision puts Ambrose Palmer down for the count

April. 22. Footscray ruck-rover, and former national boxing champion, Ambrose Palmer was seriously injured in today's opening round clash against Essendon.

Palmer, who was sandwiched between two opponents during the last quarter, sustained multiple jaw, cheekbone and skull fractures. He was carried from the field on a stretcher and treated in the dressing rooms by the Essendon club medico, Dr Hardy, before being rushed to the Alfred Hospital.

After the game, Dr Hardy said that when he first examined Palmer, he feared that the player's injuries could have been life-threatening.

Palmer is no stranger to serious injuries. He was forced to retire from the ring for some time after receiving a badly cut eye against the American boxer Young Stribling.

One of Australia's greatest professional pugilists, Palmer made his League football debut for Footscray in 1933.

Boxer turned footballer Ambrose Palmer on a pre-season training run.

Revised rules bring on scoring spree

May 1. The aggregate score of Saturday's round two games, 200 goals 177 behinds, is a League record.

In all games except reigning Premier Carlton's 11.13 (79) loss to Geelong 14.8 (92), and North Melbourne's 11.11 (77) loss to Hawthorn 17.13 (115), each team scored over 100 points.

Biggest aggregates of the day were Melbourne's one-kick win over Essendon, 21.15 (141) to 19.21 (135) and Collingwood, kicking the sweep, 21.20 (146) to South Melbourne 15.17 (107).

Observers, such as 'Forward' in *The Age*, put this scoring spree down to the rule changes introduced this season, which have had the effect of speeding up the game.

The abolition of the dropping-the-ball rule, which now forces players to kick or handpass when tackled, is one change. Players can drop or bounce the ball only if they are not held firmly by their opponent.

The other crucial change, said 'Forward' is the use of the 'scientific' flick pass, which just falls short of the VFA's 'galvanising throw-pass'.

Two new coaches stationed at Essendon

June 30. Essendon's loss to North Melbourne in round six so displeased the club's Committee that they ordered coach Jack Baggott to work the team harder. An incensed Baggott resigned on the spot with these words: 'I feel that the secretary and a small section of the committee have overstepped their authority by advising me to give the players more intensive training.'

Forced into a quick hunt for a replacement coach, dangerously far into the season, the Essendon Committee has decided to spread the risk and appoint joint coaches. Dick Reynolds, captain of the side, will share responsibility with Harry Hunter, who retired as a player ten years ago (→ 19/9/42).

Carlton's Ken Baxter can mark like Ron Todd, but he kicks like a mule.

Saints alive in the Final Four

The Saints' team run on to the MCG for their first Final in ten years.

Sept. 16. The sight of the most famous Saint of them all, Dave McNamara attending training wearing his jumper, and offering advice, has been one of the inspirations of the 1939 St Kilda side.

McNamara, elected President in the reform ticket that has taken over the club, was responsible for the stability and purpose that propelled St Kilda into the Finals for the first time since 1929.

Wisely ex-Carlton rover Ansell Clark was retained as captain-coach.

For a time St Kilda were on top of the ladder, winning eight games in a row for the first time since 1907, but three losses allowed Carlton to slip into the Four in Round 16.

St Kilda's hopes were not helped by the postponement of the final round because of constant rain.

However, a win over bottom team South Melbourne 11.13 (79) to 6.16 (52) was sufficient to keep the Blues at bay.

Richmond had been favoured to win the first Semi today, the first Saturday of the war.

But before the game, in addition to the ordinary massage, the Saints were given a 'scalp massage' – which had the desired effect of focusing their thoughts.

Veteran forward Bill Mohr, Anselm Clark, and rovers Clarrie Vontom and Alan Killigrew fed off the the ruckwork of Roy Fountain and Reg Garvin. These two put Tigers Jack Dyer and Percy Bentley out of business. St Kilda won 10.12 (72) to 6.6 (42) (→ 13/8/40).

Demons win Flag

The Demon with his trident is Melbourne's fearsome new symbol.

Sept. 30. The long-range planning of Melbourne's coach F.V. 'Checker" Hughes and Secretary Percy Page paid off today when the Demons swept Collingwood away in the Grand Final, scoring 21.22 (148) to 14.11 (95).

Hughes and Page have been recruiting steadily and the strong team that took to the field is the result.

The goal-to-goal line of Jack Mueller at fullback, tall and dashing Geoff Jones, Alan La Fontaine in the centre, and Ron Baggott and the shrewd Norm Smith up forward, provided a strong backbone. Wingman Ray Wartman and halfback Frank Roberts also played well.

Collingwood started well, with their usual pace and cleverness, but Melbourne's marking and ruck strength asserted itself and gradually wore the Magpies down. The last quarter was all Melbourne.

Collingwood were hampered by injuries to ruckmen Bervin Woods (elbow), Albert 'Leeter' Collier (leg) and Phonse Kyne (boil on neck).

The Demons celebrated with dinner at The Australia Hotel, a bus tour of the city and a dance back at the clubrooms (→ 28/9/40).

1939 Statistics

Leading Goalkicker:
Ron Todd (Coll) 120
Brownlow Medallist:
Marcus Whelan (Coll)
Finals: First Semi-final Rich 6.6 (42) St K 10.12 (72); **Second Semi-final** Melb 15.14 (104) Coll 12.18 (90); **Preliminary Final** Coll 20.14 (134) St K 15.15 (105);
Grand Final Melb 21.22 (148) Coll 14.11 (95)

Ladder:	W	L	D	%	pts
Melb	15	3	-	128.4	60
Coll	15	3	-	122.0	60
Rich	13	5	-	118.0	52
St K	13	5	-	116.5	52
Carl	12	6	-	123.1	48
Ess	8	10	-	97.0	32
Geel	7	11	-	92.4	28
Fitz	6	11	1	89.2	26
N. Melb	6	12	-	91.3	24
Haw	5	12	1	86.1	22
Foots	4	14	-	82.6	16
S. Melb	3	15	-	70.8	12

Richmond's powerful ruckman Jack Dyer has something to smile about, as the recipient of the Argus Trophy for the newspaper's best player of 1939. Dyer, who is known for his tough play, has been with the Tigers for nine years.

Magpie Marcus' bottler Brownlow

Sept. 6. Marcus Whelan has had a great year in the centre for Collingwood, and his performance has been recognised in the award of the Brownlow Medal for best and fairest in the League.

Whelan (23 votes) won by three votes from Footscray rover Harry Hickey and triple Brownlow Medallist Dick Reynolds of Essendon, who won last year.

Whelan was recruited from Darley, near Bacchus Marsh, and has been with the Woods since 1933. He went back to the country after three games, and had to be wooed back to the club in 1934.

He soon slotted into the centre position, vacated by the classy Jack Beveridge, and began to display the coolness and polish that has characterised his work. He is a fine high mark and kicks long and accurately.

There may be bigger names from the glamour teams, but Hawthorn's Bert Mills is the spectators' favourite, according to an 'Argus' readers' poll.

1940

March 8. Recently married Jack Dyer has been refused a clearance by Richmond to coach Yarraville and won't cross without one.

May 11. The feeble bell at Collingwood is not heard by Umpire Hawkins while the Magpies kick a behind. Fortunately, this does not alter the result, Collingwood defeating Carlton 18.19 (127) to 12.18 (90).

May 17. The VFL Finance Committee has decided to do everything possible to assist war funds. One penny per club membership ticket, and 5 % of the profits from each match has been voted. (→ 19/5)

May 19. ANFC President Robert Rush has announced that the Hobart Football Carnival will not proceed. He said: 'With the nation in a death grip with a powerful foe overseas, everyone realises that the time has arrived when all those linked with sport must throw aside the materials of the sporting fields in favor of uniform of Democracy.' (→ 30/5)

May 30. Collingwood footballers have asked their delegates on the Committee to request that their match pay be reduced from £3 to £1. Footscray has said that if the League reduces payments by £1 by decree, Footscray will add a £1 bonus (→ 6/6)

June 6. Carlton players hand over their Provident Fund of £1026 to the War Loan.

June 8. Melbourne, with record 34 behinds, defeat North, 12.34 (106) to 8.1 (49).

June 14. The VFL has decided to reduce player payments to 30/- per match, and to use the outer gate takings for patriotic purposes (→9/5/42).

July 17. Hec de Lacy in the *Sporting Globe* reveals that trainers, so essential to the well-being of injured players, receive between £1 and £1.10.0 per week for a head trainer and between 12/6 and £1 for others – for attendance on four days.

Debuts
Kevin Curran (Haw)
Fred Fanning (Melb)
Leo Merrett (Rich)
Keith Miller (St K)

Retirements
Percy Bentley (Rich)
Harry Collier (Coll)
Reg Hickey (Geel)
Wilfred 'Chicken' Smallhorn (Fitz)

Hawthorn top VFL Ladder for first time

Andy Angwin: Hawthorn wingman.

April 27. Perennial underdogs Hawthorn started the new season on a dominant note, thrashing North Melbourne by 72 points to top the ladder for the first time ever.

The final score, Hawthorn 25.11 (161) to North Melbourne 13.11 (89), was a club record. A bold move by the selectors to go for new blood paid off with Hawthorn leading all day. Hawthorn played fast and systematic football before an enthusiastic crowd of 12,000.

Hawthorn's brilliant rover Alec Albiston was chaired from the ground after kicking ten goals.

Reynolds delivers the goods for Dons

March 7. A weekday job for many an Essendon player involves fighting fires. This line of work can be traced to the club's President, Arthur Showers, being also President of the Melbourne Fire Brigade. But now the club is helping its most important player to prosper in a very different profession.

It has found a grocery and dairy produce round for brilliant captain and coach, Dick Reynolds, reasoning that helping Reynolds will make him want to stay with the club.

The Committee has sent members a letter designed to set him up with a ready-made clientele: '...should you be able to place a portion of your business with DICK, it will be greatly appreciated,' it says.

Pratt, Todd 'desertions' weaken League

April 20. The move of champion League players to the VFA, with or without a clearance, has reached a 'war footing' with the switch of Ron Todd to Williamstown.

A huge crowd is expected at the humble Yarraville ground to see the former Collingwood champion play. Todd has declared himself upset with 'the whole business'.

He has many former league colleagues to greet, as some 50 top notch VFL players have been lured with offers of big payments.

Bob Pratt is at Coburg, Laurie Nash at Camberwell, Bill Faul is at Prahran, George Ogden and Soapy Vallence at Williamstown, Roy McKay is at Brunswick, and Tommy Lahiff at Port Melbourne – to name just a few (→ 15/4/45).

Percy's Pucka throat

Aug. 9. Percy Beames, the Melbourne rover, having returned after missing several games with a leg injury will miss again tomorrow.

He has been struck down with that malady popularly known as 'Pucka throat'. It is a flu-like bug fond of footballers in training at the Army base at Puckapunyal.

These men might be better off if they could transfer and train at Caulfield under new instructor North's Bill 'Bomber' Wells.

The great Collingwood rover Harry Collier has retired after 253 club games over 15 years.

Ron Todd tries his new uniform.

Forbes' extra step flabbergasts Fitzroy

June 17. Fitzroy's veteran acquisition, rover Keith Forbes, took one step too many in time-on in the King's Birthday holiday match against Melbourne at the MCG.

Scores were level in time-on when Forbes received the ball on his own, ran towards goal, and kicked it through for a goal.

Alone among the more than 19,000 people present, the umpire thought Forbes had run too far, and gave Melbourne a free kick.

The Redlegs managed to rush two behinds in the remaining time and won the game 12.15 (87) to 12.13 (85).

After the game Fitzroy officials were flabbergasted at this unusually legalistic interpretation of the rule, and Melbourne officials said they considered it a lucky win.

Forbes has come to Fitzroy to kick goals, and to be denied one in this way was disappointing.

He played 152 games with Essendon between 1928 and 1937, kicking 415 goals. He kicked another 50 for North Melbourne in 31 games in 1938 and 1939.

As a rover, he has twice kicked eight goals in a game.

In this game Fitzroy centre-half-forward Claude Curtin, nephew of Federal Labor Party leader and former Brunswick footballer John Curtin, kicked 6.4.

Patriotic Premiership gives Saints first Flag

Aug. 13. St Kilda have won the League's first patriotic one-day carnival Premiership at the MCG.

Playing fast, bright and entertaining football, the Saints decisively beat a tiring Richmond by 24 points in the Final. It is the first Flag won by St Kilda, who have yet to win a League Premiership. The match, played before a crowd of 30,000, raised £3500 towards the war effort, despite a poor turn-out by MCC members.

In the last of 11 games played by 12 clubs, St Kilda were too strong for Richmond who badly missed the injured Dyer in the ruck. Final scores: St Kilda defeated Richmond 4.2 (26) to 0.2 (2).

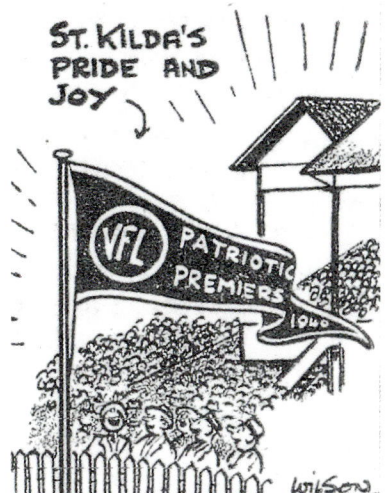

A Flag to warm the Saints.

Matthews ties up Brownlow with Fothergill

Herb Matthews: South's finest.

Sept. 5. A rare dilemma has arisen in the awarding of the Brownlow Medal. At last night's count it became impossible to separate Herb Matthews of South Melbourne from Des Fothergill of Collingwood.

Each had received 32 votes from the central umpires; the same number of first preferences (7); even the same number of seconds (5) and thirds (3). The only other means to break the tie – the number of games each had played – proved fruitless when it was confirmed that here, again, Matthews and Fothergill were twins.

Unfortunately, the rules of the Brownlow forbid the awarding of two medals; yet to give it to one would be impossible. There is talk of the only way out being to give each man a duplicate medal (→ 14/7/45).

Game plan wins Flag

The crowd singing the National Anthem before the Melbourne-Richmond semi-final. Club flags and colors were prominent.

The crowd caught up in the thrilling match between the Yarra Park neighbours.

Sept. 28. Richmond were favourite for the Premiership Flag today, but Melbourne produced a brilliant game plan and had a resounding win, 15.7 (107) to 10.8 (68).

The victory was a triumph for the Melbourne coach 'Checker' Hughes, who had taken the Tigers to the Flag in 1932.

Hughes identified six 'danger players' and set some of the lesser lights in the Melbourne team to bottle them up, leaving free rein to the Demons' more brilliant players.

Jack Dyer was deemed such a worry that Jack O'Keefe was told to shadow him, and all players were instructed to keep the ball away from him. Dyer had a frustrating match on the wet ground.

George Smeaton and Kevin O'Neill were to be wrong footed by close-playing forwards, while Frank Roberts was to use his strength to unsettle the Richmond full-forward 'Skinny' Titus.

The difference to the hard-fought Semi-final, which Richmond won by a goal, was immediately obvious. Melbourne were playing with purpose and confidence from the outset, with Fred Fanning and Jack Mueller giving drive in the ruck and Percy Beames and Alan La Fontaine controlling the centre packs.

So great was the Demon control that by half time they were 10.11 to Richmond's 4.2.

The Tigers attempted to break through in the third quarter and were still trying at the end, but Jack Mueller had become a rock in defence, taking some terrific marks. Norm Smith capped the Melbourne effort with seven goals.

Melbourne's celebration included a visit to the Stadium to watch the boxing (→ 27/9/41).

The 2/14th Infantry team ready to play in the Puckapunyal competition.

1940 Statistics

Leading Goalkicker:	Ladder:	W	L	%	pts
Jack Titus (Rich) 100	Melb	14	4	125.8	56
Brownlow Medallist:	Rich	12	6	120.0	48
Des Fothergill (Coll) &	Ess	12	6	108.2	48
H. Matthews (S. Melb)	Geel	11	7	102.9	44
Finals:	Carl	10	8	111.3	40
First Semi-final Ess 13.14 (92)	Foots	9	9	108.9	36
Geel 10.14 (74); **Second Semi-**	Fitz	9	9	92.3	36
final Melb 14.17 (101) Rich 16.11	Coll	8	10	100.6	32
(107); **Preliminary Final** Melb	Haw	7	11	88.0	28
12.18 (90) Ess 12.13 (85) **Grand**	S. Melb	7	11	87.3	28
Final Rich 10.8 (68) Melb 15.17	St K	5	13	86.8	20
(107)	N. Melb	4	14	75.1	16

1941

March 11. Geelong players refuse to attend first training session under honorary playing coach Les Metherell unless guaranteed a payment topped up by club to £3, not League basic payment of 30/- (→ 12/7).

May 3. Dave Brilliant, the Wimmera star centre-half-forward, has gone home despite making a bright impression at St Kilda.

May 3. Three planes fly over Essendon, 'bombing' the ground with a football, which will be autographed and auctioned for the Mayor's Aeroplane Fund.

May 10. Footscray are on top of the ladder with three wins from three games after defeating South Melbourne 16.4 (100) to 7.16 (58). Officials point out that 16 of 19 players are from the local area.

May 17. A Footscray councillor and his wife gain admittance to the Collingwood stand. Mrs Councillor can't help barracking, but is swiped by a Collingwood Amazon and told to get back to dirty Footscray. And the 'Scray lose 14.10 (94) to 14.11 (95) (→ 2/9/44).

May 24. Collingwood 3.2 (20) defeat Melbourne 3.1 (19) in the 'lightning Premiership' at the MCG before 19,572, adding £1526 to patriotic funds.

June 7. 'Checker' Hughes says after Melbourne's loss, 14.20 (104) to Footscray's 20.12 (132), 'Last week the players were on their toes, today they were on their heels'.

June 7. Jack 'Skinny' Titus plays his 250th game for Richmond and celebrates with ten goals in Richmond's 17.15 (117) win over Hawthorn 8.14 (62) (→ 21/5/42).

June 28. A fight during the match sees Saint 'Cracker' Knight and Magpie Albie Pannam challenge each other to 'meet at the Stadium'. Management 'will oblige'.

July 12. Geelong players who earlier went on strike over payment have unanimously agreed to a further cut to £1 for away and 30/- for home matches (→ 9/5/42).

Debuts
Don Cordner (Melb)
Ted Cordner (Melb)
Les Foote (N. Melb)
Lou Richards (Coll)

Retirements
Jack Hale (Carl)
Wilbur 'Bill' Mohr (St K)

Wartime football comes under fire

A big crowd turned out at the MCG for the fund-raising 'lightning Premiership.'

Aug. 16. A battle has been raging back and forth in the press over whether the football season should be continued in time of war.

Canon E.S. Hughes, President of the Victorian Cricket Association, fired the first shot when he supported a Government appeal for the discontinuance of organised sport during wartime. He ridiculed 'this fine winter game, with its bartering and buying of players'.

But Lieutenant-Colonel Gowand, of the Australian Comforts Fund, said the troops in the Middle East were 'football mad', and could not get enough footballs. A football was kicked into no-man's land from the trenches to signal the first A.I.F. attack in Libya.

League delegate Mr R. Bruce Hogg says that the criticism of players receiving £3 a week comes from the affluent classes. He has had a fair bit of hate mail since.

The *Footscray Advertiser* says the thrills of football for workers who have been glued to the grindstone for 60 or 70 hours may help them to face another working week.

Small Magpie encounters large Tiger

July 19. Collingwood defeated Richmond at a wet Punt Road Oval 13.14 (92) to 10.14 (74), with little Lou Richards in just his seventh game kicking a goal and providing some buzz around the packs.

Richards was able to rove to a Magpie ruck which was on top except for the third quarter, when Jack Dyer inspired a Tiger fightback.

Richards' uncle Alby Pannam also played well, and with Gordon Coventry kicked four goals.

There is something in the Pannam/Richards bloodline that produces champion footballers – beginning with grandfather Charlie Pannam who first played in 1897, followed by the second Charlie who started in 1917, and now Uncle Alby in 1933. Lou is the third generation.

Richards played in the 1940 Collingwood Reserves Premiership and since making his debut against Carlton has not looked back (→ 13/9/44).

Richards: Magpie dynasty.

Rabbits litter Cats' new playing arena

May 10. Melbourne had a pleasant day in the country when they visited the new home of the Geelong Football Club, Kardinia Park.

The old Corio Oval has been taken over by the Defence Department for wartime purposes, forcing the club to move.

The ground is surrounded by tall trees, giving it a pleasant rural aspect, and this is compounded by the fact that the occasional rabbit pops up and dashes around the oval. One was neatly captured by a boundary umpire, who handed it to some eager boys on the fence.

A sheepdog also decided to take the field at the start of the game and did a few laps. It was then content to watch the game, unless anyone approached it, when it took off again. It was finally cornered by two policemen during the half-time interval.

Despite all these rural distractions Melbourne's strength in the centre, their steadiness and their forward accuracy enabled them to win, 16.12 (108) to 13.9 (97).

Cricket team of footballers injured

May 3. Carlton's champion rover Jack Hale was among 11 players injured in the game against Richmond. Nine of the injured were from Carlton, now coached by former Tiger Percy Bentley.

This statistic helped the Tigers to a ten-point win, 13.12 (90) to 12.8 (80), in a tough game at Punt Road.

Hale is the worst with a broken right leg suffered in an entanglement with Tiger Bernie Waldron.

The injury will certainly prevent Hale from playing for the rest of this season, and could be more serious.

Hale is renowned for his fearlessness. In a game against Collingwood he overheard 'Leeter' Collier chastise a team-mate for not going in hard enough.

Hale said 'I wouldn't like you to talk to me like that'. Collier replied 'I wouldn't have to'.

Carlton fans remember Hale as the player who kicked the 'sealer' in the 1938 Grand Final. He first played for the Blues in 1933, and has scored 68 goals in 113 games.

Ron Barassi dies at Tobruk

The Melbourne players at attention as the Last Post sounds at the MCG.

Aug. 16. 31,549 Australians rose to their feet as the Last Post sounded before the Melbourne and Collingwood game at the MCG in honour of Ron Barassi, who was killed at Tobruk.

Players, trainers and officials of both sides stood on the ground with bowed heads, in a moving tribute to a courageous player and gallant soldier.

Barassi had played 55 games for Melbourne after his debut in 1936. He was 19th man in Melbourne's 1940 Premiership team.

Barassi leaves behind a son, Ron Jr, whom Melbourne have vowed to help in every way.

Melbourne quite rightly won, 17.8 (110) to 11.21 (87).

Norman Ware is top Dog in League

Sept. 15. Norman Ware of Footscray has become the first captain-coach to ever win the Brownlow Medal. His win also marks a first for the Footscray club. Four times previously the club has had a player in second position for football's highest award, but now at last they have a Brownlow Medallist for the honour board.

At age 30, Ware is the oldest player so far to have won the Brownlow. He came from Sale to join Footscray in 1932. Ware has also won his club's best and fairest this year although tieing for that honour with Arthur Olliver, the man who consistently helps him win many games for Footscray.

Ware is 6ft 4in, a height with obvious advantages in the ruck, but despite his size he moves fast and turns with great agility. Norm Ware has always been noted for his fairness on the field, and has polled consistently well in the Brownlow, often finishing among the first ten contenders. In the past decade, his second lowest score has been seven,

Ware: Bulldogs' first medallist.

achieved in his debut year.

He was vice-captain of Footscray's first Finals side, 1938, when they lost the first Semi to Collingwood. This is Ware's second year as captain, his first as coach.

Although a serving soldier, Norm Ware has to date been able to serve his club as well as his country, being stationed in Melbourne at Royal Park as a postal officer.

Demons hat trick

All eyes in the huge crowd are on a Melbourne defender as he clears.

Sept. 27. Melbourne are celebrating a hat trick of Premierships after their decisive win over Essendon today, 19.13 (127) to 13.20 (98). The score is flattering to Essendon, which made a complete mess of the first three quarters, and did all their best work when the game was lost.

The match was played before a crowd of 79,687, an increase of more than 10,000 on last year.

Melbourne's achievement is the more impressive because 12 of their senior list players were unavailable on Grand Final day, because of injury or military duties.

Essendon, with decisive wins in both the Semi-final and Preliminary Final, seemed overcome by a collective attack of nerves. Even allowing for the tricky wind their handling was atrocious, while Melbourne displayed assurance and skill.

By quarter time Essendon had dug themselves a big hole, having scored only 1.1 to Melbourne's 6.6. Gordon Abbott in the ruck and wingman Ern Coward were among the few Essendon players matching their opponents.

Melbourne, with sky-high confidence sky-high, outscored the Dons against the wind and virtually sewed up the game.

Best players up forward were rover Percy Beames, who scored six goals, full-forward Norm Smith, three and Jack Mueller, three.

Smith again played a brilliant decoy role, allowing Mueller to use his marking skills, and Beames to gather the ball unattended.

Other good players were backmen Wally Lock and Ted Cordner, centre Alan La Fontaine and ruckman 'Spud' Dullard. Dick Reynolds and backman Wally Buttsworth were Essendon's best.

1941 Statistics

Leading Goalkicker:
Norm Smith (Melb) 89
Brownlow Medallist:
Norman Ware (Foots)
Finals:
First Semi Rich 11.15 (81) Ess 21.9 (135); **Second Semi** Carl 11.16 (82) Melb 16.13 (109); **Prelim. Final** Carl 9.14 (68) Ess 13.15 (93); **Grand Final** Melb 19.13 (127) Ess 13.20 (98)

Ladder:	W	L	%	pts
Carl	14	4	120.3	56
Melb	14	4	117.2	56
Rich	14	4	116.7	56
Ess	13	5	130.3	52
Coll	12	6	110.9	48
Foots	10	8	110.5	40
Fitz	8	10	96.3	32
S. Melb	8	10	90.0	32
N. Melb	6	12	92.9	24
Geel	3	15	83.0	12
St K	3	15	81.9	12
Haw	3	15	68.2	12

Jan. 21. Collingwood's Jack Regan, 'the Prince of fullbacks' has announced that he intends to enter the religious life as a lay brother in the Salesian community in Sunbury.

March 18. The Prime Minister, John Curtin, says in Canberra 'I have no objection to men in the forces or those engaged in essential work engaging in football'.

April 13. Collingwood's trainer of 50 years Wal Lee has announced his retirement.

May 8. The VFL has discussed ground availability for the coming season, and agreed that grounds be allocated on a week-by-week basis.

May 9. The VFL season commences with play at a high standard because of the availability of players from suspended Geelong and the VFA. Servicemen are admitted half price (free last season). Players to receive 30/- per match, field umpires £3 (12/4/44).

May 27. Richmond officials claim that Jack Titus, with 265, has already passed Percy Bentley's record number of 263 games.

May 27. The sight of a sparkling performance from a well-built player in a Victorian jumper excites comment at Richmond training – but it is Melbourne's Jack Mueller, training 'away' by agreement.

May 27. St Kilda all-rounder Keith Miller has been transferred interstate by the RAAF, and is unlikely to play this season.

July 6. A 1940 Richmond member's ticket which has survived battle at Tobruk, Syria and Libya, with the signatures of 27 soldier supporters, has been returned to the club for safekeeping.

July 12. A combined services team, including Alan La Fontaine, Jack Mueller and Alby Pannam, just loses to Fitzroy/Richmond, 20.13 (133) to 19.11 (125) before a Sunday crowd of 25,000, raising £850 for Patriotic Funds.

Sept. 2. Letter writers to *The Age* regard Sunday football as a desecration.

Debuts
Jack 'Chooka' Howell (Carl)
Bill Hutchison (Ess)
Bill Morris (Rich)
Max Oppy (Rich)
Charlie Sutton (Foots)

Truscott flies in to hero's welcome

'Bluey' Truscott runs out with team-mates Percy Beames and Jack Mueller.

May 16. The solid build has filled out a little, and the final score was atrocious, but today's match against Richmond belonged to Melbourne's hero, Squadron Leader Keith 'Bluey' Truscott, D.F.C. and Bar.

The fighter pilot, home on leave from duties over the English Channel, was given the honour of leading the Melbourne team out, and received a thunderous welcome.

He did not have a good game, nor did the Melbourne team. Richmond romped home with a score of 30.16 (196) to 18.9 (117). The aggregate is a League record.

Both teams, as is usual these days, were weakened by having to find last minute replacements for players who are on military service in local areas, but could not get leave.

Truscott said later he enjoyed himself, and requested privacy for the rest of his leave (→ 21/9/43).

Marriage improves goal kicking of ex-Cat

Aug. 15. With Geelong in wartime recess, Lindsay White has been kicking goals for South Melbourne instead – on the understanding that he will return to Geelong when they are able to resume.

White, 20, was married today in Geelong, but honeymooned at the Lake Oval this afternoon.

Marriage has proved an inspiration for a return to form.

White celebrated by kicking a bag of 11 goals in South Melbourne's big win over North Melbourne, 22.13 (145) to 12.13 (87).

White's long drop-kicks are a joy to watch, as is his long, fast leading-out. His background as a professional sprinter stands him in good stead in this facet of the game.

Today's tally puts White at the head of the list for League goalkickers with 63, now two goals ahead of Richmond's 'Skinny' Titus.

Geelong, grounds out for duration of the war

May 9. Football continues to be affected by the war. The Richmond Secretary, Mr M. Fleming, says that 15 regular players of 1941 would not be available because of enlistment or work in essential services.

In the meantime, Geelong have been forced to withdraw from the competition because of rail and road transport restrictions, and a shortage of players due to enlistment.

The VFL has insisted that Geelong pay a £100 annual fee to ensure they remain eligible for the competition after the War.

The Army has taken over parts of the Collingwood ground, including the public bar, at Victoria Park to quarter 150 members of the Army Provost Corps. The ground itself will be available for the time being.

For this season at least Footscray will play home games at Yarraville Oval, St Kilda at Toorak Park, Melbourne at Punt Road, and South Melbourne at Princes Park.

The MCG was taken over on 7 April and became Camp Murphy. The United States Air Force moved into the grandstands, pitching tents on the ground.

Bay 18 in the Southern Stand is the picture theatre, the PX is in the members' tearoom and and a floor built over the road in the Southern Stand is known as 'Pneumonia Alley'. It is expected that the MCG will accommodate up to 14,000.

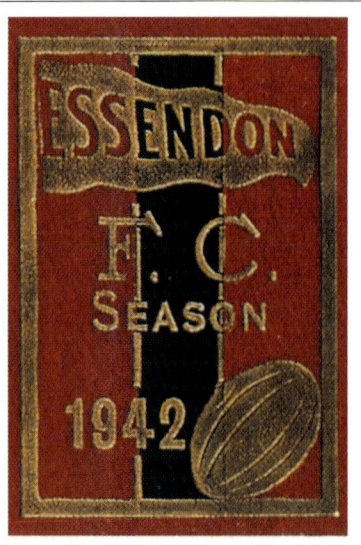

The Dons are still playing.

Essendon win austerity Grand Final

Sept. 19. Essendon, despite a shaky start, are the new League Premiers after thrashing Richmond by 53 points in front of 49,000 at the Carlton ground. It was the largest crowd of the season, and had the MCG been available there would have been thousands more there.

Both sides showed Finals nerves in a tough first quarter. Essendon squandered chances by kicking six points before their first goal.

Although Richmond took an early lead, the second quarter was all Essendon as they took complete control. The Dons were able to create the loose man, allowing Dick Reynolds to roam at will and dominate play. The Dons piled on the goals to be 34 points ahead at the half-time break.

Richmond tried to get back in after the break, but Bob Bawden, Jack Symonds and Brian Randall all missed easy shots.

Outplayed, Richmond then resorted to rough-house tactics, keeping the umpires busy. Six players – four Richmond and two Essendon – were reported.

But Essendon dominated, mainly through Reynolds, Laurie Dearle and Ern Coward. Final scores: Essendon 19.18 (132) defeated Richmond 11.13 (79) (→ 8/5/43).

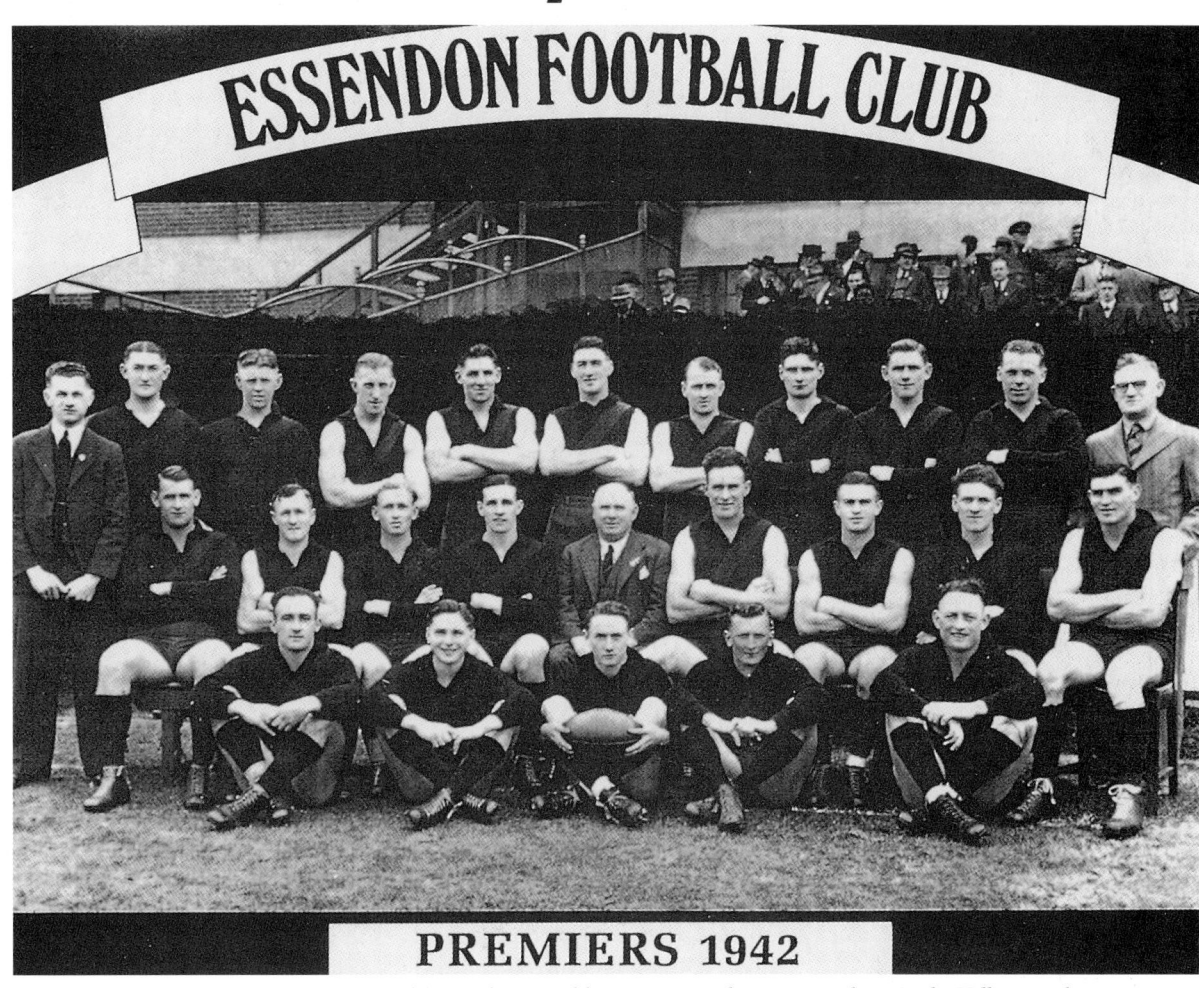

PREMIERS 1942

The victorious Essendon side, captained by Dick Reynolds, in a team photo out at the Windy Hill ground.

1942 Statistics

Leading Goalkicker:
L. White (Sth Melb)
Brownlow Medallist:
No Brownlow due to war.
Finals: First Semi-final S. Melb 13.13 (91) Foots 7.22 (64); **Second Semi-final** Ess 8.8 (56) Rich 11.12 (78); **Preliminary Final** Ess 19.10 (124) S. Melb 14.12 (96); **Grand Final** Rich 11.13 (79) Ess 19.18 (132) [Byes add 4 points]

Ladder:	W	L	Bye	%	pts
Ess	12	3	1	127.1	52
Rich	11	4	1	134.5	48
S. Melb	11	4	1	129.0	48
Foots	10	4	2	126.0	48
Carl	10	4	2	120.2	48
Fitz	8	7	1	104.9	36
St K	6	8	2	81.9	32
Melb	5	10	1	85.2	24
N. Melb	4	10	2	78.2	24
Coll	2	12	2	76.0	16
Haw	1	14	1	65.6	8

Dyer and Reynolds' half-time call

Sept. 19. There was a delay in resumption of play after half time in today's Grand Final, when the captains of the teams spoke to the crowd over the loudspeaker system.

Dick Reynolds of Essendon and Jack Dyer of Richmond made speeches in support of the wartime Austerity Loan.

The captains seemed at ease before the big crowd, and spoke of the need for sports lovers to do their bit for the war effort. Both men are in war-related occupations, Dyer as a policeman and Reynolds as a munitions worker. They received a good-natured and quiet hearing.

Patriotic Funds and War Loans have been part and parcel of life in Australia in this war and the last, as the nation channels its resources into survival (→ 14/6/44).

A Combined Services team before the game against a League side chosen by the Lord Mayor of Melbourne, Sir Frank Beaurepaire, held at Richmond. The Services team, which won 15.17 (107) to 14.18 (102), included League stars Alan La Fontaine, Jack Mueller, Alby Pannam and Norm Ware, while Norm Smith, Jack Dyer and Bob Chitty were in the League side.

1943

April 17. Melbourne champion Alan La Fontaine tells *Sporting Globe's* Hec de Lacy 'somewhere in Australia' that he intends to retire, aged 32.

May 20. Melbourne gain clearance for another Cordner in the shape of Don and Ted's 19-year-old brother Denis, at present in the Navy (→ 5/6).

May 20. Flight Sergeant and Richmond centre-halfback, Bill Cosgrove is at present flying a Beaufighter in New Guinea. He has named it 'Jack Dyer IV: Tigers, Eat 'em Alive'.

May 22. Hawthorn, renamed the Hawks from Mayblooms by new coach Roy Cazaly, show their talons in a splendid win over Melbourne, 17.15 (117) to 10.12 (72). →

June 5. The three Cordner brothers, Ted, Don and Denis play together for the first time in the game against Richmond. Denis has the first kick of the game, but Melbourne lose, 17.11 (113) to 21.15 (141).

June 12. Fitzroy captain-coach Fred Hughson plays the defensive game of his career, personally repulsing seven Richmond last quarter attacks as Fitzroy hang on to win 14.11 (95) to 12.17 (89).

June 16. Bill Busbridge has died. He debuted at 16 in 1904, played 103 games as one of Essendon's best big men before the first War.

July 31. Carlton give Collingwood a 104-point defeat and kick their highest score, 28.10 (178) to 11.8 (74). Jim Francis kicks eight and Jack Wrout seven for the winners (→ 1/9/45).

Sept. 18. The VFL has appointed a sub-committee to look at post-war football, including a two-tier competition including the VFA. VFA President J.J. Liston says the VFA's door is open for negotiation.

Sept. 19. Two teams of girls from the Department of Aircraft Production play a curtain raiser to the senior match between Air Port and Foundry at the Ascot Sports Ground. A collection is taken up for the Fags for Fighters Fund.

Debuts
Bill Brittingham (Ess)
Doug Heywood (Melb)

Retirements
Ambrose Palmer (Foots)
Jack Titus (Rich)

'Up there Cazaly' around the battlefields

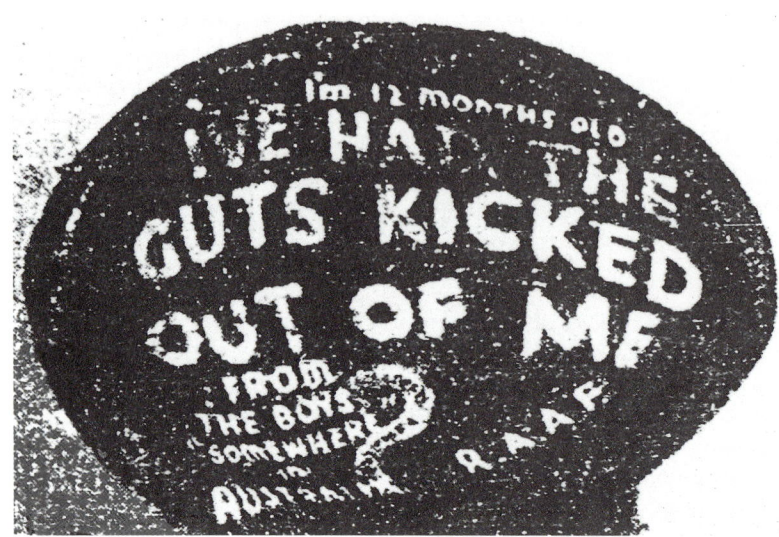

RAAF boys stationed in the bush have asked the League for a new ball.

April 28. Someone 'somewhere in Australia' came across two tall posts alongside two smaller posts.

A match was under way featuring well-known players Alan La Fontaine from Melbourne, Noel Price of Fitzroy and Les Foote from North Melbourne among the stars.

News too of other games around the battle fronts, where the cry 'Up there Cazaly' is often heard as the boys go into action.

'Somewhere in Egypt', actually the Alexandria Sporting Club, teams from the RAAF played in front of an amused but impressed international audience.

Premiers plaque: Stalag 333.

Thomas, Truscott among honoured dead

Sept. 21. Len Thomas who was captain-coach of North Melbourne in 1940 has been killed in action.

Thomas joins the increasingly long honour roll of Australian footballers killed in the war.

When asked why he didn't wait til the war caught up to his age group, Thomas replied 'Well a fellow just can't be out of a thing like this'.

Melbourne's intrepid airman Squadron Leader Keith 'Bluey' Truscott, D.F.C. and Bar, was also killed earlier this year flying Kittyhawks off northern Australia.

Harold Ball, who played in Melbourne's 1939 and 1940 Premierships, posted as missing after the fall of Singapore, was killed in battle.

John Atkins, Ron Barassi and Noel Ellis have also paid the supreme sacrifice.

Len Thomas while at South.

South and Don fans in 'pay-off brawl'

May 8. An all-out brawl in the last quarter marred Essendon's opening round defence of the their Premiership title against South Melbourne.

An Essendon player was knocked out behind play sparking off a free-for-all between about a dozen players from both teams. Police and trainers converged upon the scene. Some players tried to stop the fighting, while others sought revenge.

The game began with the unfurling of the 1942 Premiership Flag. The brawl capped off a fierce and sometimes spiteful contest which Essendon won by 25 points, 18.9 (117) to 13.4 (92).

US giant out throws our best kicks

July 4. American serviceman, and former football player for the Huntington Golden Bears, Bill Jost has regained his unofficial title as longest propellor of a football in the free world.

Fred Hughson of Fitzroy dropkicked an Australian football an amazing 83 yards 11 inches in May, to Jost's throw of an American football of close to 70 yards.

At the Independence Day carnival no one's form was quite as good. North Melbourne's Alf Hacker defeated other rivals in kicking our ball, but managed 'just' 62 yards to Jost's 63 yards one foot for the title.

Hawthorn lose tense race for Four

July 31. Hawthorn have lost their first chance for the final Four after going down to North by one point in an agonising finish.

Roy Cazaly has renamed the team the Hawks this season, and they have been fiercer on the ground. But, for their most vital game since joining the League, Hawthorn lacked a spearhead in Wally Culpitt, unable to obtain leave from the RAAF. Goal-less until half time, the Hawks attacked incessantly in the second term and rose towards a win or draw, until dropped by the bell on 7.16 (58) to North's 8.11 (59).

Gritty Chitty plays despite one digit loss

Aug. 21. Carlton's star utility player, Bob Chitty was among the Blues' best in their 66-point win against North Melbourne today, despite losing the top of a finger in a workplace accident during the week.

It was a typically courageous performance by Chitty who, playing in the centre, was instrumental in setting up many of Carlton's most effective attacking moves. The accident happened while he was working at a munitions factory.

It was at first thought that Chitty would have to miss the game, but doctors sewed up the wound and he was cleared to play.

Bob Chitty goes for the punch.

The players may not be household names, and the fortunes of the St Kilda club generally have not been something to crow over, but there is good news somewhere if you look hard enough. The Seconds celebrated their back-to-back Premierships with this handsome memento of the team.

Tigers over line

Sept. 25. In a hard-slogging Grand Final match against Essendon today, the Tigers played more consistently to become the 1943 Premiers by a tight five points, 12.14 (86) to 11.15 (81). This is the smallest margin in any Grand Final in 22 years.

Richmond led by ten points at the first change, and by eight at half time. But the crowd of 38,334 at the Carlton ground saw Essendon battle to a five-point lead at three-quarter time. Essendon's success in this quarter came from consistently sending the ball forward to a teammate, while the Tigers, feeling the pressure, began to fumble.

Their attacks were outmarked, and the smaller Essendon men were handling the ball better. The stage was set for a thrilling finale.

The crowd was at fever pitch when Richmond went to a two point lead – 9.10 to 8.14 – thanks to a goal from captain Jack Dyer. In several charges in response, the Dons could not break past Richmond's halfback line. The sides seemed evenly matched in a bone-crushing struggle to gain points. Young Max Oppy (18) roved outstandingly for the Tigers. So did Dick 'Hungry' Harris, who booted one of his magnificent dropkicks for his own sixth goal, putting Essendon in real trouble. Later, his seventh goal for the match made Harris leading goalkicker of the season.

In the final minutes, Tom Reynolds and Hugh Torney goaled for the Dons, putting them within one point of the Tigers.

Badly needing a goal, the Tigers' Jack Dyer, going for a throw-in, was pushed from behind and on his free kick seemed to hang the decision of

Jack Dyer leads the Tigers out.

the match. He goaled. But Tom Reynolds quickly replied.

A relentless struggle went back and forth, into the time-on period, with supporters on both sides feeling the agony as behinds brought the Dons within a goal's reach of evening the score. The final bell only moments away, the Dons had a breathtaking last chance, as Norman Betson poised for a shot at goal. But his kick fell short, to be fisted through by a Tiger for a behind.

It was one of the most thrilling matches in years, with never much between the hard-working sides.

1943 Statistics

Leading Goalkickers:	Ladder:	W	L	D	%	pts
Dick Harris (Rich) 63	Rich	10	5	-	123.1	44
Brownlow Medallist:	Ess	10	5	-	115.2	44
No Brownlow due to war	Fitz	10	5	-	109.0	44
Finals:	Carl	9	6	-	125.0	40
First Semi-final Fitz 13.16 (94)	Haw	9	6	-	103.9	40
Carl 5.13 (43);	Foots	7	8	-	93.6	32
Second Semi-final Rich 9.17 (71)	Melb	7	8	-	88.7	32
Ess 13.16 (94);**Preliminary Final**	S. Melb	6	9	-	105.8	28
Rich 12.14 (86) Fitz 8.13 (61);	N. Melb	5	9	1	77.0	26
Grand Final Ess 11.15 (81) Rich	Coll	5	10	-	89.6	24
12.14 (86)	St K	1	8	1	73.9	10

Captain Blood: If ya don't mind, umpire

Jack Dyer was given the name Captain Blood in 1935, in honour of the Tasmanian swashbuckler Errol Flynn who was running through extras in Hollywood at the time.

Dyer was running through opponents on the football field, with hard, but within the rules, tactics of the time – the shirt front, the hip and shoulder, together with a few toe-to-toe stoushes.

Football, like life, was tough in Melbourne in the depression years when Dyer made his name. There were few rules but some conventions about how a bloke might be hit (and who).

For example, kicking was rightly frowned upon, and football scores were evened up on the field not outside it. And young blokes might be given a measure of 'protection' in their first games, as Dyer was against North Melbourne in 1931.

The Shinboners were given the message 'Lay off the kid. Touch him and they'll carry you off in pieces'.

Although Dyer was a skinny and gangly 18-year-old in those early years, photographs reveal a man who looked old and experienced when he was young.

Curiously enough it took a great deal of cajoling to get Richmond interested in young Dyer.

Despite being a star for Richmond Hill Old Boys in the fearsome Metropolitan League, and for the Yellow Cabs team in the even more brutal Wednesday afternoon competition, young Dyer had to ask for a clearance to the hated Collingwood before Richmond had a look at him. Dyer says that he told his Dad that he was going to train with Richmond and, without looking up from his paper, his Dad observed, 'You'll be killed'.

And he almost was, being tested out in an early practice match by Joe Murdoch, a wily and experienced backman. Dyer didn't get a kick – but showed the legendary coach Checker Hughes enough determination and ability to be named on the bench in the first game of 1931.

Jack Dyer was born in 1913,

and spent his early years, until the age of seven, not in Tigerland, but in the bush at Yarra Junction.

There his house bordered on the Yarra Junction oval, and the team used a room in the house to change in. Young Jack grew up in a football dressing room.

He was a football fiend who played without boots until he was ten, toughening the 'foot' aspect of football. By 1925, at the age of 12, he showed sufficient promise to be given a football 'scholarship' to that nursery of great footballers, the Catholic secondary school system in Melbourne.

Dyer first attended St Ignatius, under the tutelage of Brother Peter. It seems that this man, a great influence on Dyer's life, was transferred to the more upmarket De La Salle, and arranged for a further scholarship for young Jack.

Living in Richmond with an aunt, Dyer says he had to walk the long way home to avoid the Richmond gangs who, according to Dyer, maintained that if you didn't have a prior record you were a social outcast. 'College boys' were especially juicy targets for these larrikins.

Playing 'take no prisoners' school football for Brother Peter, who hated to lose, Dyer learned a couple of useful body tactics. One was the 'don't argue' fending a player off with one hand while the ball was tucked under the other arm. The other was, when pursued hotly by an opponent, to stop suddenly while turning the shoulder in their direction – letting them shirt-front themselves.

Brother Peter said Dyer was the 'best schoolboy footballer in the world'.

Dywer played Saturday afternoon football from 1927 with the Richmond Hill Old Boys. The

Richmond Hill mob were initially coached by Brother Peter.

Dyer's first game was by courtesy of Jack Bissett, then playing for Richmond, who feigned a hand injury to 'help the kid out.'

Dyer played a blinder against North, helped by his team-mates, but did not do well in the next game against Footscray and was dropped. Bissett's generosity cost him £6 in match payments.

Dyer came back later that season when Perce Bentley was injured on the eve of the Finals. Dyer had been reported playing for Yellow Cabs in the Wednesday League, but luckily got off. He played in the losing 1931 Grand Final side.

He had become a fixture but, after 14 games in 1932, badly injured his knee, and missed playing in the 1932 Premiership side.

In 1933 he made a comeback, not getting more than two kicks in seven games before turning things round in a game against Geelong.

At the end of the season he injured his 'good' knee, which meant that he couldn't twist and turn on that one either. Dyer played in the 1934 Premiership.

Despite his fearsome reputation as a hard man of football, Dyer was reported only five times and suspended only once, despite innumerable incidents.

As a footballer he was fast, fearless, straight kicking and, despite his knees, durable.

He became a policeman in 1934, and coach of the Tigers in 1941. In a reserved occupation he could police and play, and was captain coach in the 1943 Flag side. He retired in 1949 after an epic 19 years and 312 official VFL games.

For Jack Dyer, the Captain Blood media legend after 1949 has obscured the superlative on field achievements of the younger Tiger footballer. But both the legend and the football achievements of the barefoot boy who started kicking a paper 'tootie' around Yarra Junction two lifetimes ago make Jack Dyer a football immortal.

April 12. The League decides to keep player payments at 30/-per match, allowing up to an additional £2 to be paid into player provident funds.

April 15. The *Sporting Globe's* Hec de Lacy says of player payments that 'Every man in Australia today is where the manpower officials want him. If manpower demands are satisfied, and a man finds it possible to play, why should any payment to him be questioned?'

May 3. Jim Bohan, Hawthorn's champion pivot, has been named captain (→ 27/8/45).

May 3. Jack Dyer, the Richmond coach, makes identical twins Keith and Fred Cook wear different coloured tags at training. 'They get me all up-ended. I said to one "Is it you or your brother who isn't here." '

May 13. The late arrival of the Melbourne train at Geelong delays the start until 3.32. Geelong lose their first game at home after re-entry to the League to South Melbourne, 11.18 (84) to 9.11 (65).

May 16. Richmond have been allowed by the Deputy Director of Rationing to appeal to supporters for 924 clothing coupons. 524 have arrived and the club can purchase 18 pairs of boots and 50 pairs of knickers immediately.

May 27. League players have determined to form a union so they might speak with a single voice on welfare matters, and have a club where they can fraternise together.

June 10. Thousands of spectators storm the lightly patronised Members' Reserve Grandstand at St Kilda when it begins to rain during the drawn game between St Kilda and Essendon, 9.17 (71) each. Officials do not stop them.

June 14. Percy Beames, the Melbourne captain, has told the *Sporting Globe* 'If I had a free will and all the players in the League to choose from I'd pick Jack Dyer before I considered any other player in the game.'

Aug. 7. Ray Brew, former Carlton captain, player and Secretary, has been elected first Secretary of the Victorian Footballers' Club at a meeting at the Savoy Theatre

Debut
Ern Henfry (Carl)

Retirement
Percy Beames (Melb)

Less footy leads to more bush delinquents

It was good physical activity like this that kept the bush kids off the streets.

May 31. There has been no organised sport for juveniles in country Victoria since the war began. The chairman of the Children's Court points to this as a major cause for rising rates of delinquency in all country districts.

'Good type club life and club discipline are badly needed at the moment,' says Mr L.R. Ripper. 'This applies particularly in the country, where there is an absence of men.' He has called upon municipal councils to 'give a bold lead' in reviving sporting clubs for country youth, before a generation of youngsters is raised without a sound knowledge of the self-sacrifice and self-discipline demanded by team spirit.

Commenting on this in *The Sporting Globe*, Hec de Lacy writes: 'It has become a national boast that the Australian's fighting spirit inherited from sturdy pioneers has been developed on our playing fields... There has been a tough code of behaviour and of personal expression demanded in Australian games.'

VFL and VFA talk merger again

July 5. Moves are again afoot to stage a conference between the League and the Association to discuss a possible merger between the two rival football organisations.

The issue of unifying the bodies controlling football in Victoria is likely to be the main item on the agenda. The first step is to organise a suitable conference. It is understood the Association has instructed its President, Mr H. Zwar, and its Secretary, Mr Snooke, to meet with their League counterparts, Dr W. McClelland and Mr L. McBrien to name a date and set an agenda.

Both sides are reluctant to discuss any details at this early stage until more details are known.

The main problem facing a possible merger is the thorny issue of promotion and relegation which is regarded as an anathema by many League clubs who fear the consequences of relegation. The Association's representatives believe any talks must be open and conducted in a spirit of give and take. They say the parties should lay their cards on the table without any preconditions.

Any merger would require framing a clear and uniform set of rules which at present vary between the two bodies. The proposal is now to be put to the ANFC for its official endorsement.

Loyal clubmen buy Cats back into VFL

April 15. After some tense manoeuvring and a cash payment Geelong have been readmitted to the VFL.

The Cats had to drop out of the competition in 1942, as they had been rendered uncompetitive by road and rail restrictions and a lack of players due to war service.

The club has remained operative in so far as it has kept a Committee and also found the £100 a year required by the League to retain affiliation during 1942 and 1943. Committeemen Basil Collins, Jack Jennings, Norm Drew, Jack Ross and Harry Pullen gave their time and money to keep the club going.

There were further obstacles, as the League claimed further debts owing of £1000. The Committeemen and supporters again stumped up the money.

Then, after a tense and not unanimous vote, the League delegates approved Geelong's re-entry. The home ground will be Kardinia Park, which is now regarded as a better venue than Corio Oval (→ 10/4/45).

Austus football, a sporting alliance

July 26. The international potential of Australian football has been in the news as Australians spread across the globe on war duties.

A newspaper in Canada quoted in the *Sporting Globe* said: 'If you want to get a first hand look at a bunch of guys rehearsing for something resembling mass suicide, come out and watch the Aussies engaged in what they delicately term "light football practice".'

Hec De Lacy, in the same paper, lamented the confusion of hard to understand rules that prevents Australian football taking off around the world, especially in the places where it has been demonstrated by our troops. They have taken footies with them wherever they have gone.

Perhaps the answer lies in the sport of 'Austus', invented by Ern Cowley who played for Carlton in 1911. This combination of the Australian and US games has been awarded the Helms Athletic Foundation Medal in New York as a noteworthy contribution to sport.

North storm home for bizarre win

July 29. The exception, the oldest rule in the football book, was proved at Arden Street.

Bad kicking is bad football, yet North Melbourne won a game kicking fewer goals than their opponent Richmond, who were the essence of sharpshooting.

Richmond had kicked 13.2 (80) at three-quarter time to North 7.8 (56).

But in a frenzied last quarter Richmond kicked just one more goal, while North booted four, and 13 behinds. The last behind, kicked on the bell, gave them a one-point win, with three goals less, 11.21 (87) to 14.2 (86) (→9/6/45).

Little Lou walks tall among the smalls

Sept. 13. Today the writers of the *Sporting Globe* voted Collingwood rover Lou Richards the outstanding small man for the 1944 season. H.A. De Lacy gave the following reasons: 'Richards has brought roving to a beaten ruck back to a football art ... Again and again Richards has battled on and beat the opponent rucks single-handed.'

A quick thinker, Richards snaps goals from anywhere. 'Perhaps if Richards has a fault it is that he tries to do too much ... Still, what can be expected when a fellow has to take all the risks in a side not nearly strong enough?'

Broadstock incident has Tigers roaring

Aug. 25. A lot of work has gone on this week to get Richmond to play Essendon in the Final. The players only agreed to turn out when the President, Mr H. Dyke, told them he would field the Seconds rather than forfeit the game.

The Tigers are incensed by the suspension of their centreman Jack Broadstock, who was rubbed out for eight weeks for having 'kicked or intended to kick' Noel Price in the semi-final against Fitzroy.

Mr Dyke also told the players he would assist them in seeking to establish a VFL Appeals Board.

Maroons' Final joy

The proud Premiers. The boys from Fitzroy get together for their team photo.

Sept. 30 The Grand Final between Fitzroy and Richmond was played in very hot conditions at the Junction Oval before a jam-packed crowd of 43,000.

The tram and bus strike did not prevent anyone getting to the ground. The Railways ran a four-minute service from the city to St Kilda Station, ferrying 1500 people at a time. A total of 32,000 went to the ground by train.

So crowded was the ground that spectators climbed nearby trees and the grandstand to get a view. At least a dozen people had to be taken away by ambulance officers.

Fitzroy had beaten Richmond twice before in the season, once in round 15, 16.10 (106) to 7.14 (56), and in the Second Semi, 11.15 (81) to 10.10 (70).

Yet it was Richmond's stars, led by Jack Dyer, who were fancied to defeat the tradesmen of Fitzroy.

However, Richmond did not count on the team spirit and will-to-win of Fitzroy, playing in their first Grand Final for 21 years.

Captain Fred Hughson said 'the spirit of the team was the whole thing. They would not accept defeat and any one of them would have bled for Fitzroy – they would have walked on broken glass. It was a beautiful feeling to go out on the field with them'.

Hughson pulled a tactical masterstroke by winning the toss and so kicking against the hard, hot and dusty 'brick-fielder' of a wind blo-

Fred Hughson: the mastermind.

wing from the north.

Hughson felt his team were so fired up they could contain the Tigers, and they did, holding them to just two goals, while kicking only one.

Dyer told Hughson after the game that he 'had all the players in the world to win the game but I didn't have one like your big ruckman Bert Clay. You got your two-goal lead and we just couldn't get over the top of big Bert. He just patted the ball down to Ruthven all around the ground ...'

Richmond needed two Jack Dyers, one in the ruck, in addition to one playing at full-forward.

Fitzroy won 9.12 (66) to 7.9 (51). The celebrations in the dressing room were so memorable that they were recorded by Norman Banks of 3KZ, and presented to the club.

Hickey's kick boots 'Scrays into Four

Sept. 2. Footscray today fought a desperate last quarter to snatch a one-point victory over Carlton. The win, from a kick taken after the bell, puts them in the Final Four.

With the scores level, the Footscray centreman Harry Hickey marked 55 yards out from goal just moments before the bell rang. Scores were tied at 88 points each. High drama reigned as the 35,000-strong crowd held its breath.

A solitary kick would decide which team would go on to fight out the Finals. For the Bulldogs, Hickey's kick was all-important because Carlton had the superior percentage which would put them into the Finals in the event of a draw.

As Hickey prepared for the kick of his life, his team-mate Miller ran over to steady him. Hickey swung into the kick, going all out for distance. The ball flew high and true, but so did Carlton defender, Bob Chitty who marked above the pack, only to have the goal-umpire rule he had caught the ball over the goal-line, awarding Footscray a point and passage into the finals. A delirious crowd spilled onto the oval. Final scores: Footscray defeated Carlton 12.17 (89) to 13.10 (88).

1945

April 10. Geelong appeals to supporters for clothing coupons as the club cannot take delivery of new guernseys without them.

April 21. Laurie Nash has returned as good as ever after seven years to centre half forward at South Melbourne.

April 21. Jim Miller, the Footscray wingman, is kicked unconscious at Richmond, and thinks he's swallowed some broken false teeth. The Doc tells him they'll show up – somewhere. His team beat the Tigers, 16.9 (105) to 14.11 (95).

May 2. Clyde Helmer who played 71 games for Geelong has tragically been reported killed in action.

May 5. Essendon create something of a record when they kick 22.18 (150) to beat Carlton 7.8 (50). This is the same score as the Dons round one win over Hawthorn, except that the Hawks managed 12.7 (79).

May 19. Carlton's new recruit Ken Hands, nursed by the Blues since he was 16, makes a stunning debut on the half-forward line in the Blues' win, 12.18 (90) to St Kilda 11.13 (79).

June 9. Fitzroy kick their highest score against Collingwood, winning 23.15 (153) to 8.10 (58).

July 8. South Australia outclass Victoria, 17.23 (125) to 10.13 (73), in Adelaide.

July 13. South Melbourne have suspended Captain Herb Matthews and Keith Smith for disciplinary reasons, after their refusal to play in the match against St Kilda in the positions directed to. South win 14.22 (106) to 6.14 (50).

July 21. South's Herb Matthews, Laurie Nash, Ted Whitfield and Vic Castles use so much hand ball in their win over Richmond, 14.11 (95) to 10.17 (77), that observers feel it isn't football.

Aug. 27. Hawthorn officials measure a drop-kick of Jim Bohan's which goals in the third quarter at 67 yards. The Hawks beat North Melbourne, 11.11 (77) to 10.10 (70).

Debuts
Ron Clegg (S. Melb)
Don 'Mopsy' Fraser (Rich)
Ken Hands (Carl)
Bill Twomey (Coll)

Retirements
Herbie Matthews (S. Melb)
Laurie Nash (S. Melb)

Morale up and crowds are back for the Victory season

South Melbourne's top ruckman, Jack Graham, is ready for a big new season.

April 25. With the war in Europe nearing its conclusion, the football public has had a boost to morale and attended the opening round in large numbers.

Experts in the *Sporting Globe* made predictions on the basis of form shown in round one.

Readers were invited to 'get on the Dons' band wagon now', think of Footscray as 'better than last year when the side finished fourth'.

Richmond have 'too many misfits in the side'; Collingwood have returned to 'zig-zag forward work which so often spreadeagled orthodox defence'; Carlton are 'undersized and fail in the air'; Hawthorn are 'a weak side with little foundation'.

St Kilda 'needs gingering up'; Melbourne 'will be a hard team for anyone to handle'; North offered 'a nervous bungling display that helped bring about their own defeat'; Geelong is 'not a Final Four proposition' and Fitzroy is 'as good as last year's Premiership side'.

All will be revealed over the new distance of 20 rounds.

North's slashing start to season

June 9. A resurgent North Melbourne continued upon their winning way by notching their sixth victory win in a row, easily downing Hawthorn by 38 points.

The win is a club record in the League, and further confirmed that North Melbourne can no longer be considered to be the League's easybeats. North are now in second position on the ladder, and well on the way to their first Finals appearance.

Since moving from the Association 20 years ago, where they were regular Finals performers, North have been languishing among the bottom four teams each season.

The change in their on-field fortunes can be traced to the last few games of 1944 when they first showed signs of their real potential. Under the astute coaching of Robert McCaskell the team have been playing a positive style of football that was much in evidence against Hawthorn today.

Safe high-marking and clever use of handball gave North a steady passage forward where Bill Findlay finished off the good work with seven goals allowing the royal blue

North champion Les Foote.

and whites to coast to an easy win. Another player in fine form is their captain, 'Dally' O'Brien who has been leading by example all season.

Those teams to feel the might of the new North Melbourne have been Geelong, Footscray, Fitzroy, South Melbourne, Melbourne and Hawthorn. Essendon awaits next week. Will they be the first to break North's winning streak?

Final scores: North Melbourne defeated Hawthorn 16.10 (106) to 10.8 (68).

Magpies fiddle while Todd fumes

April 15. Incensed and humiliated by the Collingwood Committee, Ron Todd has stormed back to VFA club Williamstown.

Todd, one of the great full-forwards, left Collingwood in the lurch when he departed for Williamstown in 1940. Now, after war service with the RAAF, he has tried to rejoin Collingwood. He told Committee members that he had the five happiest years of his life there.

Todd was invited to a Committee meeting to put his case, but found himself waiting outside the Committee room while arguments raged within about his return.

From the raised voices Todd realised that there were some who had not forgiven his 'betrayal' of the club. He left Victoria Park, and has now re-signed with Williamstown.

There are some at Collingwood who believe that Todd had only used Collingwood as a lever to jack up his deal with Williamstown. He has, rightly or wrongly, been expelled from the club and deprived of 'all the privileges of an ex-player'.

Blues keep winning to climb into Four

Sept. 1. When Carlton crashed to the worst defeat in their League history in round three, thrashed by Essendon 22.18 (150) to 7.8 (50), the Blues' fortunes were at a low ebb.

On the bottom of the ladder with no wins, and a percentage of 57, the Finals were not on the agenda.

By round 11, they had crawled into ninth place – defeating ladder leaders South Melbourne by a goal, 8.8 (56) to 7.8 (50), in a fifth win.

If Carlton won eight of the last nine games, they might just creep into the Four.

The next week against Melbourne, the Blues held on to win by a point, 12.9 (81) to 12.8 (80).

A three-point loss to Essendon, 11.9 (75) to 10.18 (78), two weeks later held up proceedings – Carlton would now have to win six in a row to make the Fnals.

This they did, finishing off with wins over Geelong, 23.23 (161) to 9.13 (67), and Footscray, 16.19 (115) to 8.14 (67), to finish a game clear in fourth place.

Carlton needed all of the 20 rounds of the extended season to make it – but they did, with a head of steam and the Finals to be played at 'home', Princes Park (→ 3/10).

1945 Statistics

Leading Goalkicker:
Fred Fanning (Melb) 67
Brownlow Medallist:
No award due to war
Finals: First Semi-final N. Melb 8.20 (68) Carl 14.10 (94); **Second Semi-final** S. Melb 13.10 (88) Coll 11.11 (77); **Preliminary Final** Coll 12.8 (80) Carl 13.12 (90); **Grand Final** S. Melb 10.15 (75) Carl 15.13 (103)

Ladder:	W	L	D	%	pts
S. Melb	16	4	-	131.8	64
Coll	15	5	-	128.8	60
N. Melb	13	7	-	111.1	52
Carl	13	7	-	106.9	52
Foot	12	8	-	108.9	48
Fitz	11	8	1	119.1	46
Rich	11	9	-	103.4	44
Ess	10	9	1	113.8	42
Melb	8	12	-	99.1	32
Haw	6	14	-	85.6	24
Geel	2	18	-	64.9	8
St K	2	18	-	62.2	8

'Bloodbath' marks war's end

The headlines say it all as the 'Truth' newspaper tells the story (with pictures) of the violence in the Grand Final.

Oct. 3. Carlton can take some credit for their win in the roughest Grand Final in VFL history. It brought the first Flag in League history from fourth place.

Another first was that the four finalists were different clubs from those who played in the 1944 Finals.

The Grand Final, won by the Blues 15.13 (103) to South Melbourne's 10.15 (75), has been described by some as a 'bloodbath' and by others as a 'miracle'.

The bloodbath saw nine players reported on 15 charges; the miracle saw Carlton win 13 of 14 games.

VFL Tribunal last night passed judgement on the rough play.

From South Melbourne Ed Whitfield was suspended until the end of 1946, Jack 'Basher' Williams received 12 matches, 'Gentleman' Jim Cleary and Don Grossman each eight matches. Herbie Matthews was severely reprimanded, and Keith Smith's charge was dismissed.

From Carlton Bob Chitty and Ron Savage received eight weeks suspension while the Ken Hands charge was not sustained.

Coincidentally Ron Savage was

Thoughts on how the players should dress for Grand Finals in the future.

awarded Carlton's best-and-fairest award for 1945. Ken Hands was named most promising player, and says he can't remember anything about the Grand Final, having played most of it in a daze.

The miracle aspect in the Finals began with Carlton easily beating North Melbourne, 14.10 (94) to 8.20 (68), after leading 13 goals to two at three-quarter time.

It continued with the comeback against Collingwood in the Preliminary Final, where all seemed lost again. The Blues were 28 points behind at three-quarter time and playing poorly, 6.9 (45) to 11.7 (73).

After Collingwood scored the first goal of the final quarter to lead by 34 points it definitely looked over – but a melee developed and this

caused something of a transformation in the game.

Jim Mooring belatedly went roving, and Carlton kicked seven goals without reply, four to Lance Collins, to win 13.12 (90) to 12.8 (80).

Then came the Grand Final, where a huge crowd of 62,986 somehow squashed into Princes Park. Demobbed soldiers were there in numbers, bottles were thrown on to the ground, and police had to help break up on-field fights.

During one brawl in the last quarter Carlton centreman Clinton Wines bombed away for a goal, which effectively ended the game.

This final stanza of the Carlton miracle was written by Wines, Vin Brown, Ken Baxter, Bert Deacon, Hands, Rod McLean and Chitty.

Jan. 21. Arthur Olliver is appointed Footscray playing-coach at a reportedly large but undisclosed salary (→ 15/6).

April 17. Hawthorn select brilliant centreman Jimmy Bohan as captain (→ 9/4/47).

April 27. Goal umpire at Carlton and Melbourne match is punched by spectator, but is rescued by woman who jumps the fence (→ 3/7/48).

May 11. Small boys run a rescue service for balls that go over the fence at Glenferrie Oval, particularly as Essendon kick 24.13 (157) to Hawthorn's 8.6 (54) (→ 15/6/50).

May 28. VFL Secretary Like McBrien says VFL plans to use training films to assist umpires and players to understand the rules (→ 28/4/58).

June 8. Fitzroy captain Fred Hughson makes remarkable run, taking ball from full-back to full-forward. Fitzroy 14.14 (98) defeat Hawthorn 9.10 (64).

June 8. North Melbourne fail to score in the first and third quarters of a windy match against Melbourne, but still win 9.2 (56) to 3.9 (27) (→ 10/5/47).

June 15. Dick Reynolds takes extraordinary mark stretched out on his back, as Essendon beat Collingwood, 16.22 (118) to 11.10 (76) (→ 26/4/75).

June 22. Bottom side Geelong thrash Essendon, 18.18 (126) to 12.15 (87) (→ 13/8/49).

June 26. Hawthorn's hundred gamer Alec Albiston is described by Percy Beames of *The Age* as 'the gentleman of football' (→ 2/7/49).

June 29. Victoria, 19.9 (123), draw with SA, 18.15 (123) at Princes Park (→ 6/8/47).

Aug. 31. Melbourne have won 10 of their last 11 games, to climb into the Four from ninth in mid-season (→ 8/8/53).

Aug. 31. Richmond, needing a win and a Melbourne loss to make the Four, kick 16 goals from 18 shots, but Essendon still win by a point, 16.18 (114) to 18.5 (113).

Debuts
Vic Chanter (Fitz)
Fred Flanagan (Geel)
Bob Rose (Coll)
Roy Wright (Rich)

Retirements
Jim Bohan (Haw)
Bob Chitty (Carl)
Ted Cordner (Melb)
Norm Ware (Foots)

Olliver's Bulldogs have bright start to season

June 15. Footscray, in the new postwar 'bright' royal blue, red and white jumpers stand at the head of the Premiership list after defeating Fitzroy at the Western Oval in a close match today.

New captain-coach Arthur Olliver is earning his large salary of £14 per week, judging by this success.

The win, 16.10 (106) to 15.9 (99), was Footscray's ninth in succession, a club record, and they are the only unbeaten side at this stage.

Veteran rover Jim Thoms, who is having a purple patch in his tenth season with the club, was Footscray's leading goal scorer with three goals. The Scrays shared the scoring duties among 11 players.

Thoms was probably the first '20th man' to influence a game when in the first match of the season his fresh legs helped Footscray to beat Essendon.

In the last few minutes Thoms lifted his team as he gave a goal away, kicked one himself and added a behind to seal Footscray's victory, 15.10 (100) to 14.14 (98). This has been Essendon's only loss this year.

In the Fitzroy game Evan Rees and George McLaren played well for Footscray, while Alan 'Baron' Ruthven (four goals), Claude Curtin (five) and Fred Hughson stood out for Fitzroy.

Arthur Olliver's awkward kicking style is disguised in this cover photograph.

Record crowds at split round opening

April 22. The 68,000 who attended the second half of the Easter split round opening to the season, when added to Saturday's 78,000, meant a record one round attendance of 146,000 was achieved.

In the first postwar season, it's king football again in Melbourne.

40,000 packed into the St Kilda ground to watch a bloodless but entertaining replay of last year's 'Bloodbath' Grand Final between South Melbourne and Carlton.

Both sides were missing their suspended players, but South had the great Bob Pratt back after his time in the VFA.

Unfortunately Pratt broke down with a serious leg injury after kicking two goals. Carlton's Ken Baxter kicked seven. Carlton won, again, 18.9 (117) to 16.13 (109).

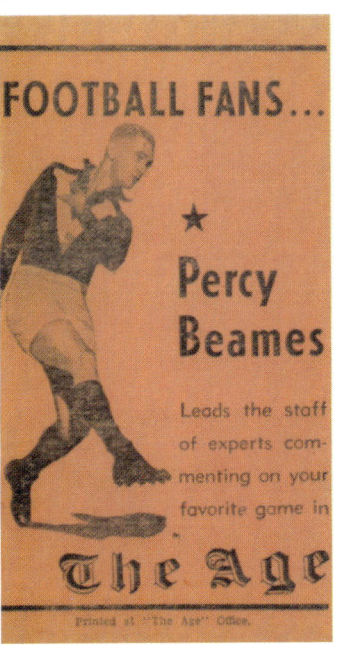

FOOTBALL FANS...

★

Percy Beames

Leads the staff of experts commenting on your favorite game in

The Age

Former Melbourne and Victorian rover and State cricketer Percy Beames takes up the pen.

Under-19 boys join 20th men in League

Feb. 19. An important development this season will be the introduction of the Under-19 Grade competition – the third 18. Meanwhile one new rule of the game has been adopted. Meeting in Adelaide today, the Australian National Football Council approved a motion from Victoria that a 20th player may be used on the same conditions as the present 19th man – to replace a player injured and forced to leave the ground.

Victoria put forward another motion, that a 120ft inner circle be created within which no players other than rucks and rovers are allowed during bounces, but this was defeated. So was a motion jointly put by NSW and Tasmania, that the field umpire be authorised to order off players he deemed guilty of foul play (→ 12/3/91).

Players race from ground for brawl

May 20. War broke out at Princes Park last Saturday at the game between Carlton and North Melbourne, but it was not the usual on-ground brawl. This time two North players went into the crowd to settle some imagined scores with heckling barrackers, and there were some dangerous moments before police restored order.

As far as the football went, Carlton won the game after a slow start, 11.15 (81) to North Melbourne's 9.11 (65). Carlton's acrobatic full-forward Ken Baxter kicked five goals and his efforts gave his side a distinct edge.

North put in a lacklustre effort and kicked just two goals to Carlton's six in the second half.

It was a niggly affair, brought about to some extent by the gusty wind, but it is hard to imagine what would cause players to jump from the race and attack spectators.

A reporter on the scene for *The Age* said the players 'came to halts with several spectators'. No players or spectators were reported or arrested by the police who curbed the potential melee (→ 18/8/51).

League requests same size grounds

The boundary line is too close for Jim Cleary against Fitzroy.

Aug 17. A proposal by the League to try to minimise the differences in the size of football grounds was acted upon at the Melbourne Cricket Ground today in the Melbourne and Hawthorn match. It was the first postwar game played on the MCG.

The out-of-bounds ring on the MCG was drawn 12 feet in from the fence, reducing the playing dimensions to 174 yards by 156 yards.

Hawthorn, coming from their pocket-handkerchief oval at Glenferrie, should have benefited but they were soundly beaten.

In the last quarter Melbourne came from behind to slam on seven goals seven behinds to Hawthorn's three points to win 18.15 (123) to 13.8 (86).

Jack Dyer kicks a ball burster

Aug. 3. Bubbles are burst, balloons are pricked! Deflation comes in many ways, and it made a visitation on the Richmond strongman Jack Dyer and his team today.

Richmond suddenly had a big chance to enter the Four after round 15 as they battled with Footscray at the Punt Road Oval.

But Footscray are having a good year, and have their own Finals aspirations, and led the Tigers 13.13 to a woeful 7.17 at three-quarter time.

Captain-coach Dyer called for an all-out effort, and he led the charge as the hard-hitting Tigers started to reel in the match.

It got to seven points down in time on, but the great man had the ball and was running into an open goal. He kicked the ball, but it burst with an audible report, and died off his boot to slew away for a behind. Even then the Tigers were not done, as 'Mopsy' Fraser grabbed the kick-out and scored a goal to level.

But the bubble really burst as Footscray's Bill Wood marked on the bell, and goaled, to make the result Footscray 14.15 (99) to Richmond 12.21 (93) (→ 7/8/48).

The life story of DES FOTHERGILL

Like Test players Laurie Nash and Keith Miller, Des has played football and cricket for Victoria.

Des was born in Northcote, Melb., on July 15, 1920, and played with North Preston School.

For Collingwood Technical School he played in curtain-raisers before crowds of 40,000.

After playing first-grade cricket for Northcote, Fothergill at 16 joined the famous Collingwood football team.

Fothergill caused a stir in 1941 by following goalkicker Ron Todd to Williamstown in the rival Association without clearance papers.

For his new team, Des played superbly and won the two highest awards, the Recorder Cup and the Victorian Football Assn. Medal.

Next year, 1942, he enlisted in the AIF. He served in the Army for the next three seasons.

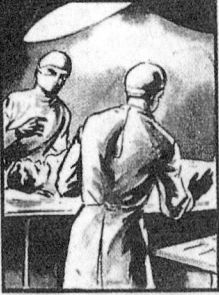

He was one of the star sportsmen of his unit. While playing in a football match in the Northern Territory he went down with leg injury.

Army doctors in Adelaide operated on Fothergill's right knee and removed two pieces of bone.

Back with Collingwood in 1945 he won a Melbourne newspaper's trophy—the Brownlow Medal's wartime equivalent.

Is it a bird? Is it a plane? No, it's Collingwood's Des Fothergill, the latest comic strip hero and bigger than Superman in a Melbourne winter.

Surprised Cordner wins the Brownlow

Cordner: still an amateur.

Sept. 4. Don Cordner, Melbourne's brilliant follower, expressed great surprise when he won the Brownlow Medal last night. His own pick for the award had been Alan Ruthven, but Cordner came in four votes ahead of the Fitzroy rover in the first count since its suspension in 1941 for the duration of the war.

Winning by one vote from Bill Morris (Richmond) and Jack 'Chooka' Howell (Carlton), equal second, Cordner is the first doctor and the first amateur player to win the Brownlow.

Writing about the famous Cordner family of footballers in *The Age* last week, Percy Beames said 'One of the most popular and respected players ever to wear a League guernsey, Don is also possessed of a great heart. No odds are ever too great for him'.

After the Medal went to Cordner, Beames commented today in *The Age*: 'He is an ornament to the code, and exemplifies everything that is fine and decent in the game, in addition to which he has all the attributes of a champion player'.

Joining Melbourne in 1941 with his brother, Edward, also a doctor, Don Cordner made his debut in a semi final game. The Cordner brothers are following the footsteps of their father, Dr Edward Cordner, and their uncle Dr Harry Cordner, who both played for University in the League. Harry had previously played 11 games for Melbourne.

Dons draw stalls Semi progress

Sept. 14. A point in the dying seconds of the game earned Essendon a desperate draw just as it looked as if Collingwood would win the second semi final at the Melbourne Cricket Ground in front of a record crowd of 77,370.

The unlucky Collingwood had led, in a tight game, since early in the second quarter. The Magpies played the better football, with greater teamwork on the day. They were faster to the ball, and only inaccurate kicking for goal cost them a handy lead during the hectic final quarter.

Essendon, on the other hand, were slower and failed to capitalise on their height advantage over Collingwood, employing spoiling in the aerial duels.

It was a solid defence, grim determination and superior fitness in the final stages that allowed the Dons to haul back the Magpies' lead at the final bell.

The draw is only the second ever in a second semi final, the other being that between Collingwood and Melbourne in 1928. Final score: Collingwood 13.22 (100) drew with Essendon 14.16 (100).

1946 Statistics

Leading Goalkicker:
Bill Brittingham (Ess) 66
Brownlow Medallist:
Don Cordner (Melb)
Finals: First semi final Foots 15.12 (102) Melb 17.18 (120);
Second semi final Ess 14.16 (100) Coll 13.22 (100); **Second semifinal Replay** Ess 10.16 (76) Coll 8.9 (57); **Preliminary Final** Coll 14.16 (100) Melb 16.17 (113); **Grand Final** Ess 22.18 (150) Melb 13.9 (87)

Ladder:	W	L	%	pts
Ess	15	4	140.7	60
Coll	13	6	125.2	52
Foots	13	6	117.8	52
Melb	13	6	104.8	52
Rich	11	8	115.8	44
Carl	11	8	102.1	44
S. Melb	10	9	106.5	40
Fitz	9	10	118.7	36
N. Melb	8	11	91.2	32
Geel	4	15	70.9	16
St K	4	15	70.0	16
Haw	3	16	70.5	12

Bombers' Flag

Oct. 5. After the adventures of the second semi final draw and replay, Essendon had the luxury of a week off. They watched an exhausted Collingwood go down to Melbourne in the Preliminary Final, 14.16 (100) to 16.17 (113), confident that playing at their very best they were a match for the Demons.

Essendon's captain-coach Dick Reynolds looked back at the round three clash with Melbourne when Essendon kicked ten goals in the first quarter. He said that the team played the finest football he had seen in his 14 years in the game.

Essendon won 21.15 (141) to 12.13 (85), but lost the second encounter 10.13 (73) to 9.24 (78).

In the Grand Final, Melbourne's 'home ground' advantage was doubtful, as they had played just four games there after football resumed at the MCG in Round 17.

73,743 turned up, perhaps expecting that Essendon would sparkle from the opening bounce.

But the Demons, coached by the redoubtable 'Checker' Hughes, had some tricks up their sleeves for the Grand Final. Fred Fanning lined up in the ruck, not at centre-half-forward, and began the game dominating the ruck, with Melbourne kicking five goals before Essendon scored one. Jack Mueller was in especially devastating form.

The Bombers fought their way back later in the quarter, especially through the work of Gordon Lane at centre half forward. Quarter-time scores were Melbourne 8.3 (51) to

Alby Rodda tackles Percy Bushby.

Essendon 7.2 (44).

The second quarter was a defensive battle that ended with Melbourne just three points up.

Nothing in the first half prepared Melbourne for what Essendon did in the third quarter.

In one of the most paralysing quarters played in a Grand Final, Essendon kicked 11.8 to 1.1. It was the most devastating eclipse of a team in living football memory. The Dons had the game at three-quarter time, 20.15 (135) to 11.5 (71).

The final quarter was a cakewalk. Gordon Lane kicked his seventh, and Bill Brittingham his fourth and 66th for the season. Bill Hutchison and Wally Buttsworth also played very well in Essendon's 22.18 (150) to 13.9 (87) triumph (→ 24/9/49).

Essendon's Premiership winning side in determined mood before the match.

1947

Lou a Collingwood Commo or something?

June 2. After Collingwood's one-point loss to Richmond, 10.13 (73) to 10.14 (74), the feeling that Collingwood was 'fading out' and losing the 'close ones' developed.

Lou Richards organised a players' meeting, with Jack Burns and Mac Holten, at the club to discuss the problem.

Coach Jock McHale, on hearing about this, waited for the Collingwood conspirators.

He told them 'We've never had a players' meeting since I've been here. What are you? Three Commos or something? Now buzz off!'

Needless to say, the meeting then did not take place (→ 19/4/50).

Lou Richards: offending Magpie.

Dogs have their days on the footy field

July 16. When radio man Mel Morris interrupts his commentary for 3DB with the words 'and there's a little dog on the field', the listeners know that they're in for a bit of fun. Morris usually abandons any interest in the game to describe attempts to trap the offending beast.

This year the capering canines have even come under official notice at the VFL.

At the exciting match between Essendon and St Kilda on May 3 – which the Dons won 21.10 (136) to 19.11 (125) – umpire Ian Cleland was forced to abandon play, as a small dog chased the ball, getting under the feet of the players. Eventually Dons' ruckman 'Bluey' McClure lunged and caught him.

But the Devonport Dog has captured official attention. The dog was capering up forward when – wham! – it was laid out by the ball. The ball then rolled on, and on through the goal. The goal umpire raised the digits – the dog had scored!

VFL Umpires Coach Bill Blackburn has now ruled that the decision was correct, and it has implications for all Melbourne clubs with holes in their fences (→ 12/8/61).

Fred Fanning kicks record 18 goals

Fanning: Melbourne marksman.

Aug 30. Melbourne full-forward Fred Fanning broke the League goalscoring record when he kicked 18 goals from 19 scoring shots in his side's rout of St Kilda.

Fanning kicked 12 goals straight in the first half. He scored seven goals in a scintillating second-quarter display of high marking and deadly accurate kicking.

St Kilda rallied in the third quarter and a tighter, spoiling defence kept the big Melbourne marksman down to a meagre three goals. Fanning, however, was too big and too strong on the day for his main opponent, Alan Stretton.

He received fine support from his team-mates as he bagged four more goals in the final quarter and Melbourne ran out 93-point winners, 27.9 (171) to 10.18 (78) (→ 22/4/78).

Bohan bolts for VFA, cops five from VFL

April 9. Former Hawthorn captain Jim Bohan has been suspended for five years by the League after transferring to Association club Camberwell without a clearance.

Bohan played 131 games for the Hawks and kicked 145 goals after joining them from Kew in 1938. He represented Victoria against South Australia last season and was among the best on the ground. He has been training with Camberwell since early in the season. Bohan said he thought Hawthorn had treated him harshly after giving them eight years' loyal service (→ 30/3/49).

Demons deny a bribery charge

June 4. Melbourne Football Club had nothing to do with an attempt to bribe two Footscray players into pulling out of last week's match. This assurance comes from the Secretary of the Footscray club, Mr Roy Russell, who said: 'As far as my club is concerned Melbourne club is blameless. They have the talent capable of beating us without condoning such underhand action.' He also said the man involved was 'known to us', and had approached Marty McDonnell and another Footscray player offering a sum of money to withdraw. Both flatly refused. The VFL may investigate.

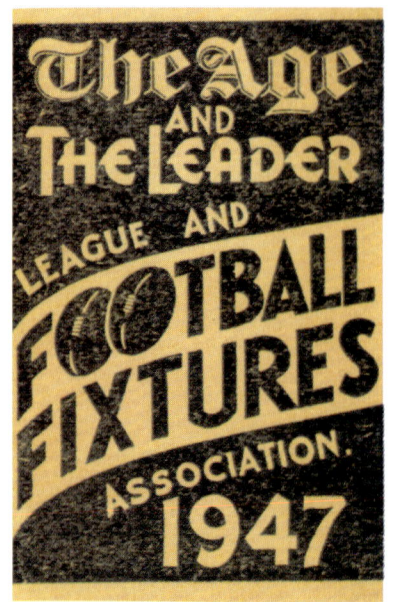

McDonald boxes back to fitness

McDonald: can run and box too.

Aug. 10. Norm McDonald, Essendon's first year Aboriginal half back flanker, is one of the fastest players ever to pull on a boot, or a glove.

McDonald, injured early this season, had a cartilage removed from his left knee.

As part of his rehabilitation he took up boxing, winning three out of four matches at the Stadium.

McDonald's quick recovery and slippery speed are crucial to Essendon's success.

Vics first carnival loss in 26 years

Aug. 6. Two champion players, making clumsy kicks rarely seen from either, cost Victoria a victory against Western Australia in the Carnival competition today. It was Victoria's first defeat at a carnival since 1921. The West displayed teamwork and skill to surprise the Victorians.

Victoria were five points down when Fred Fanning marked on the final bell, in easy distance of goal. Pandemonium broke out at the North Hobart oval when the top goalkicker of 1945 booted a behind.

But the match would not have been hanging over his head if Alan 'Baron' Ruthven had not missed goaling from only 15 yards out, three minutes earlier (→9).

Carlton win with a goal on the bell

Sept. 27. In retrospect the move that won Carlton the Flag was the appointment of Ern Henfry as captain. In the Grand Final he was as cool as the weather was warm, before a lockout crowd of 85,815, as Carlton stuck with Essendon in the first half by kicking straight.

At half time it was 8.0 to 8.11. The Bombers had burned a lot of fuel.

In a gruelling third quarter both teams kicked 2.4, and with ten minutes to go in the last Essendon were still 12 points in front.

Suddenly Carlton became energised, and Henfrey, 'Chooka' Howell and Ken Hands, finally overcoming the resistance of Essendon's gallant Wally Buttsworth, combined to set up a goal by Fred Davies and then a miss from 15 yards.

Ken Baxter replaced injured Bert Deacon and was swung into the ruck in the last nine minutes. With 44 seconds to go, five points the difference, Baxter charged into a boundary ruck contest in the forward pocket, and got the ball out to an unguarded Fred Stafford who snapped a left footer through.

The bell rang, and Carlton had won by a point, a delirious 13.8 (86) to Essendon's dumbfounded 11.19 (85) (→28/9/68).

The vital moment. Fred Stafford boots the winning goal for Carlton.

1947 Statistics

Leading Goalkicker:
Fred Fanning (Melb) 97
Brownlow Medallist:
Bert Deacon (Carl)
Finals: First semi final Fitz 16.7 (103) Rich 11.9 (75); **Second semi final** Carl 14.15 (99) Ess 11.17 (83); **Preliminary Final** Ess 16.13 (109) Fitz 14.12 (96); **Grand Final** Carl 13.8 (86) Ess 11.19 (85)

Ladder:	W	L	D	%	pts
Carl	15	4		134.0	60
Ess	14	5		122.8	56
Fitz	13	6		126.7	52
Rich	12	7		109.1	48
Coll	11	7	1	112.4	46
Melb	11	8		117.1	44
Geel	11	8		103.3	44
S. Melb	8	10	1	97.0	34
Foots	8	10	1	96.1	34
N. Melb	4	15		77.7	16
Haw	4	15		76.4	16
St K	1	17	1	58.7	6

Deacon wins Blues' first Brownlow

Sept. 3. Carlton's brilliant half back Bert Deacon has won the Blues' first Brownlow Medal.

Universally regarded as one of the fairest, as well as the best, players in the League, Deacon was, typically, visiting injured colleague Ron Hines in hospital while the count was taking place.

Deacon was recruited from Preston, and played a handful of games for Carlton while in the Army between 1942 and 1944.

In 1945 he was loaned back to Preston, but was recalled when Carlton made the Finals, playing in the winning Grand Final side.

It was in the 'Bloodbath' that his fair-mindedness became legend when he grabbed South's 17-year-old Ron 'Smokey' Clegg and told him to 'stay out of it, son'.

Deacon played a full season in 1946 and finished fourth in the Brownlow that year.

Carlton's Bert Deacon: brilliant, and one of the League's fairest.

1948

Big crowds and booze ban in season opening

May 29. While St Kilda has banned liquor, and bumper crowds have turned out at some matches, the talk of the season's opening has been the amazing slump of last year's Premiers, Carlton.

Carlton have not changed their personnel markedly this year, but seem to be suffering from a Premiership 'hangover'. Having unfurled their Premiership Flag they lost their second round match to Fitzroy, scraped home against Geelong, then lost by 2 points to Footscray, 2 points to Collingwood and 28 points to Essendon.

Today they dragged themselves off the MCG, having been thrashed by Melbourne 15.12 (102) to 7.9 (51), scoring only one goal in the second half.

The start of the season was marked by the biggest ever crowd to attend Victoria Park – 47,224 – to watch Collingwood play South Melbourne on Monday, April 26, the Labour Day holiday. Collingwood won 18.17 (125) to 10.12 (72).

Drunken brawls in the crowds at both St Kilda's Junction Oval and Princes Park have led the St Kilda Cricket Club (the ground controller) to ban liquor sales in the outer and grandstand.

The quick decision has been possible because the cricket club had never got round to licensing the liquor vendor, Mr P. Lennon. Mr Lennon will be told the good news tomorrow (→ 26/8/59).

Bombers sign 23-goal kid

Aug. 21. The 19-year-old John 'Deadshot' Coleman has kicked 23 goals for Hastings against Sorrento.

As Essendon experts such as Dick Reynolds consider Coleman to be 'another Jack Titus' it is perhaps surprising he is not already wearing the red and black.

Coleman had a rather unimpressive few practice games last year, and this year complained that no one would kick the ball to him.

Essendon's promise of a run in the Seconds next year has not reassured the young ex-University High School star, and he is entertaining nibbles from other clubs. Essendon have him 'signed.' (→ 16/4/49)

With the Flag flying behind him, Bert Deacon chases Fitzroy's Alan Ruthven.

Kick-off scores point on long, windy day

Aug. 14. The notorious northerly blew so powerfully at the Western Oval during the Footscray and Geelong game that a frustrated Cats' fullback, Bruce Morrison, had to watch in horror as the football flew back over his head and through the point posts after his kick-off. He had scored a behind for Footscray.

The wind was so bad that the ball was out of bounds for a lot of the time, skittering around in the sparsely populated outer as patrons attempted to catch it and return it to the field.

In fact the most noteworthy feature of the game was the time spent not playing football. In the first quarter it was 11 minutes and five seconds, in the second 13:46. In the third quarter 11 minutes 40 seconds compounded the general misery of the day, and 8 minutes 8 seconds were added to the last.

This added up to an amazing total of 44 minutes and 39 seconds, and a record extension of play in a game everybody – players, officials and spectators alike – wanted to see over and done with.

All afternoon the players had trouble kicking straight. They were either kicking into the face of the howling gale or sending huge torpedo punts flying with the wind behind them. Three footballs were lost during play. Footscray, specialists in playing the notorious local winds, defeated Geelong 11.25 (91) to 7.15 (57) (→ 7/5/60).

Gorillas fade from first to seventh

Sept. 4. Fitzroy lost their eighth game in a row today when downed by top team Essendon, 10.11 (71) to 7.11 (53). The outcome was no surprise, as the Dons have been undefeated in the last 11 games, but it confirms the 1948 Maroons side as having suffered the greatest fade-out in League history. From top spot they have plummeted disastrously to finish their year in seventh place.

Beginning the season brilliantly, with five straight wins, Fitzroy went all the way to round 11 with only two defeats. They were on top of the Ladder, a sure finalist.

Then the uncanny slide in their form began. A 16-point loss to Geelong was followed by a 29-point loss to Carlton in round 13, and a 36-point thrashing from Melbourne the following week.

No amount of effort by coach Charlie Cameron or captain Alan Ruthven could turn them around. Even the bottom team, St Kilda, beat them by eight points. The closest they came to a win was against the Hawks, with a three-point loss in round 16.

Charlie Cameron's resignation is expected.

1948 Statistics

Leading Goalkicker:
Lindsay White (Geel) 86
Brownlow Medallist:
Bill Morris (Rich)
Finals: First semi-final Coll 17.17 (119) Foots 12.12 (84); **Second semi-final** Ess 13.16 (94) Melb 8.10 (58); **Preliminary Final** Melb 25.16 (166) Coll 15.11 (101); **Grand Final** Ess 7.27 (69) Melb 10.9 (69); **Grand Final Replay** Ess 7.8 (50) Melb 13.11 (89)

Ladder:	W	L	D	%	pts
Ess	16	2	1	137.2	66
Melb	13	6		124.9	52
Coll	13	6		118.3	52
Foots	12	7		103.2	48
Rich	11	7	1	125.6	46
Carl	10	9		113.0	40
Fitz	9	10		112.8	36
N. Melb	8	11		83.6	32
Geel	7	12		89.7	28
S. Melb	7	12		82.8	28
Haw	5	14		75.7	20
St K	2	17		59.9	8

Demons do it for 'Checker'

Oct. 9. Melbourne swept Essendon aside today to emphatically win the Grand Final replay, 13.11 (89) to 7.8 (50). The effort was a remarkable reversal of form from the second semi final, which Essendon won by six goals, and from last week's drawn Grand Final, when Essendon kicked themselves out of a Flag by scoring 7.27 to 10.9.

The Demons have created a record by playing four hard Final games in a row to get the Flag.

Today Melbourne seemed much more positive, intent on providing a rich parting gift to the retiring coach, 'Checker' Hughes.

Really, Hughes seems to have arranged his own present as he had the perfect forward set-up, with Jack Mueller in outstanding form. Bringing Mueller out of retirement for the Finals was a master-stroke, as he has kicked 20 goals in three games.

He has combined perfectly with the canny full-forward Norm Smith, who has contributed in some way to nearly every goal, mostly with his accurate passing.

Melbourne also had winning key position players in Lance Arnold at centre half-forward and Denis Cordner at centre half-back. They neutralised Essendon's two potential dangers in attack, Ted Leehane and Dick Reynolds.

The game was virtually all over at quarter time, as a brilliant Melbourne burst had yielded 6.2 to three points (→ 17/9/55).

Don Cordner leads the Demons through the 'Good luck Checker' streamers.

Tigers' Bill Morris a quiet achiever

Sept. 6. Brilliant Richmond ruckman Bill Morris has won the 1948 Brownlow Medal. Morris polled 24 votes beating Carlton's Ollie Grieve by three votes with Essendon's Bill Hutchison (17) in third place.

Morris is only the second Richmond player to win the League's best-and-fairest award. 'I'm so excited I don't know whether to laugh or cry,' Morris said, 'Football is the best game in the world, and this is my greatest moment.'

The quietly spoken Riverina-born player almost didn't play football. His father is an avid rugby fan, who at one stage threatened to send his son to a school where Australian Rules wasn't played.

Morris: 'greatest moment'.

John Coleman kicks twelve in dream debut for the Dons

The exciting new face in the football world, recruit John Coleman.

April 16. A star is born. Essendon's John Coleman kicked 12 goals against Hawthorn in his first League game today. In a sensational start to the football season, the young recruit from Hastings had his first goal on the board within seconds of the opening bounce.

The much talked about player, who has scored phenomenally in the country, lived up to his pre-season promise with eight goals to his name just after half time. Coleman scored all his 12 goals from high punts and thrilled the 15,000-strong crowd with his fast leading and high-marking. Coleman, who was best on the ground, showed great skills in baulking, and used his comparatively light frame well in getting into position to mark. His kicking was out of the manual.

He also impressed by setting up two goals for his team-mate Ted Leehane. Coleman swung the game Essendon's way early on and was too good for Hawthorn first game fullback Fred Wain, who was replaced by Lionel Johnston in the second quarter. The Dons won by 63 points. Coleman was cheered from the ground. Final scores: Essendon defeated Hawthorn 18.12 (120) to 9.3 (57) (→ 12/8/50).

Today's footballers: are they any better?

April 9. Carlton coach Percy Bentley scoffs at the idea that today's players are inferior in their abilities to those of yesteryear.

Bentley said that the football champion of 20 years ago, matched against the present-day player, would be like a man who tries to catch a polo pony mounted on a Clydesdale. He was replying to charges by former Essendon champions Tom Fitzmaurice and Charlie Hardy that football had deteriorated into 'speed craziness', was less scientific and had suffered because of negative, spoiling tactics.

Bentley predicted that football is about to enter its golden era. This season and the next, he says, will see the game blossom into its greatest glory. 'The kids of today would leave champions of 20 years ago standing for pace, and bamboozle them with science.' (→ 28/4/51)

20,000 locked out in Punt Road crush

June 13. Fences collapsed and many people fainted in a wild crush at the Richmond and Carlton game today. The Richmond ground has a capacity of 43,000 but 50,000 people tried to force their way inside. The ground was full an hour before play began. Police reinforcements were powerless to stop those still pushing and jostling to get in. A boundary fence went down. Spectators were fainting. Worried health officials ordered all gates to be opened to ease the pressure. It was then that several hundred frightened people tried to get out, colliding with thousands straining to get in.

Police and ambulance officers rescued women and children, passing them overhead. Some of the crush was alleviated when hundreds jumped the rails to sit around the edge of the playing field. Remarkably, no one was seriously injured (→ 13/8).

'Win or hand in your guernsey': coach

July 2. A half-time ultimatum by Hawthorn coach Alec Albiston, urging his players to 'win or hand in your guernseys', helped turn a 39-point half-time deficit into an eight-point win against St Kilda.

'If you chaps don't want to play League football hand in your guernseys and let's give them to someone who does,' he said.

His efforts were aided by a telegram from injured Hawk ruckman, Kevin Curran in hospital with a broken jaw. 'I'll not hear of defeat. Go in and win', Curran cabled.

After reading out the telegram, Albiston added, 'I know you can play League football. Come onto that ground, and don't let us disappoint our team-mate in hospital'. Hawthorn kept a close check on the Saints' stars and rallied for their second win of the season, 14.13 (97) to the Saints 13.11 (89) (→ 19/4/50).

Ron 'Smokey' Clegg is popular winner

Ron Clegg: second to South.

Aug. 31. South Melbourne centre half-back Ron Clegg has won the Brownlow Medal on a count-back from Hawthorn half-back flanker Col Austen, after both players polled 23 votes. Clegg was awarded the Medal because he received six first votes to Austen's five.

Clegg was joint favourite with Geelong's Fred Flanagan who polled a disappointing 14 votes. St Kilda's Harold Bray was third with 20 votes, while Essendon's first-year sensation, full-forward John Coleman, was next with 15.

The South Melbourne champion is a popular winner and has also taken out two other major media awards in what has been an outstanding season. He is the second South Melbourne player to claim the Brownlow, the first being Herb Matthews in 1940 (→ 16/6/51).

Young Harry Debut

July 16. The youngest field umpire ever in the Victorian Football League is Harry Beitzel, who was only 21 when he umpired his first League game at the end of last season. Youth seems no handicap, as he handles seasoned players with the firmness of a veteran.

Beitzel had early training in the craft of the umpire from his father, Arnold Beitzel, a former League footballer with St Kilda and Fitzroy after the First World War.

He joined the VFL umpires' class in 1946, and after a solid grounding around the country was promoted to senior level (→ 16/7/57).

Coleman century in Bomber blitz

Sept. 24. The first of the 90,453 people who crammed into the MCG to watch Essendon's annihilation of Carlton in this year's Grand Final arrived at 5.15 a.m. 20,000 were queued up by the time gates opened.

The last were still there at 6 o'clock, waiting for the young hero of the day, John Coleman, outside the dressing room door.

Coleman, in his first season, kicked his 100th goal with the last goal of Essendon's rout. The goal was derived, appropriately enough, from a pass from captain-coach Dick Reynolds.

At the end of the game thousands of fans were already on the ground, having sat beside the boundary line for the match.

Some of them chaired Coleman from the ground, minus his jumper which he had swapped with opponent Carlton's Ollie Grieve.

But it wasn't a one-man show. 'Bluey' McClure dominated the ruck and the Essendon backline, led by Norm McDonald, kept Carlton to two goals by half time. Bill Hutchison wrought havoc with his roving and brilliant passing.

And there was Coleman.

Essendon won, 18.17 (125) to Carlton's 6.16 (52) (→ 23/9/50).

FREE WITH THE ARGUS

John Coleman kicks his sixth goal for the day and 100th for the season.

Jack Dyer turns out for his League record 307th game for Richmond.

1949 Statistics

Leading Goalkicker:
John Coleman (Ess) 100
Brownlow Medallist:
Ron Clegg (S. Melb)
Finals: First Semi-final Coll 8.6 (54) Ess 20.16 (136); **Second Semi-final** N. Melb 14.7 (91) Carl 15.13 (103); **Preliminary Final** N. Melb 9.7 (61) Ess 11.12 (78) **Grand Final** Carl 6.16 (52) Ess 18.17 (125)

Ladder:	W	L	%	pts
N. Melb	14	5	119.1	56
Carl	13	6	126.4	52
Coll	13	6	123.5	52
Ess	13	6	120.7	52
Melb	12	7	113.1	48
Rich	10	9	116.7	40
Fitz	10	9	97.8	40
Geel	9	10	111.8	36
Foots	7	12	83.9	28
S. Melb	6	13	80.5	24
St K	4	15	73.5	16
Haw	3	16	61.1	12

THE BIG LEAGUE

When the grounds were all around

A day at the footy in the 50's and 60's needed a bit of planning, with the consultation of maps and time-tables, movement orders, kit inspection and the mustering of supplies as part of the morning routine.

We were off, on the crowded trams and trains, on a journey into the unknown, passing little known lines of demarcation as we approached the enemy territory.

Each team had its heartland, with the MCG the geographical hub of the football world.

From there the lines radiated out, into the distant lands of Essendon and Footscray, and into the tough territories of Arden Street and Victoria Park, where opposing supporters stood small and said little.

The journeys to the Lake and Junction Ovals were a picnic outing, a day at the seaside, by comparison, just as Kardinia Park seemed a place of wholesome country values. Glenferrie Oval was as safe as a church, and sometimes as quiet.

Princes Park and Brunswick Street epitomised old fashioned football, and the ghosts of footballers past seemed to be hovering about. At Punt Road there was little spectator space, and always a throng pressing in on the tiny ground, with its strange, off-centre goal posts.

These grounds were muddy. The pampered, well drained turf of today can cope with all but the wettest conditions, but the 50's and 60's men often played in quagmires for weeks on end, with a ball acquiring the added weight of water and mud as the game progressed.

Strong marking men, with big hands to take the whack of the wet ball, were great players to have on wintry days. Ted Whitten and Denis Cordner come to mind. There were lots of smaller rovers then adapted to burrowing in the packs and getting down to the wet ball.

These grounds could be dangerous places for the spectator. It was fine in the nice old stands, and around the fence seats, where the worst fate might be a poke

An all too familiar sight of the 50's and 60's - The Demons on a roll.

with a knitting needle or umbrella, or a ringing in the head from the screaming.

It was in the shoulder to shoulder crush of the terraces that trouble could occur, on those slippery mud and blue metal slopes. Here the beer was consumed in unfettered quantities and the language was lewd, profane and scatalogical.

The merest thing could create a fight, and most seemed to come from a need to fight, rather than any deep insult. 'What are you lookin' at, you drongo', might be enough to start an all-in brawl.

But the warning signs were clear, and right minded people began to edge away from any imminent donnybrook.

'There's a blue on here', they would say and, sure enough, there would soon be a space around a couple of maddened figures, swinging with everything.

The police, the rapid reaction force of a more leisurely time, could be seen wading through the crowd, and it was even money that it would be all over when they arrived.

Some parts of the outer were obviously not places for women or small boys, but their presence brought out a chivalry unknown today. Miscreants were told to 'cut out the swearing' and 'watch the game.'

Down the back were the 'amenities', dark and evil structures which were positive sink holes of humanity on match days, when the distended bladders of the masses sought relief.

There were no polite 'in' and 'out' signs, but just a heaving crush of bodies around the doorways. There always seemed to be an overflow, in large and small currency.

But, these miseries apart, we were there to watch the game, to support our team and our players. Not many people seemed, as they do today, to go to the football just to see 'a good game.' There were six matches on Saturdays and you went where you team went, to watch them play.

Until the 60's there was no TV to allow the illusion of having seen the game. You were either there or had to make do with the imagining allowed through the newspapers and the radio.

Waiting for the *Sporting Globe* to arrive at the newsagents on Saturday was more of a pleasure if you had been at the game, and won. You could then pore over all the detail spelled out by Messrs Kerville, de Lacey and Bye, and live the glorious moments again.

As with every era of football there were great players, great characters and great teams. There were teams on the rise and teams in decline, in the endless cycle of youth, ambition, success, ageing, failure and renewal.

Melbourne supporters were riding high through the 10 years from '54 to '64. The Demons were always in the finals, and usually winning the Flag. Collingwood was the arch rival and Essendon was usually around, but the Demons' master coach Norm Smith seemed to create an intensity that enabled them to win the big ones – and often with ordinary players in the side.

For most people football became more interesting with the Demon's decline. It was exciting to see teams like Hawthorn, St Kilda, and Richmond in the spotlight after years in the wilderness.

Ron Barassi's move to captain-coach Carlton brought howls from the Melbourne supporters, and the mass destruction of no. 31 jumpers, but it was an emphatic full stop to an era. From now on club loyalty would no longer be the rock on which football was built.

A sense of place, of belonging to the local tribe, also broke down. There were mass meetings and threats, even down to the stoning of the President's house, when St Kilda opted to move to Moorabbin and seek more lucrative pastures on which to play. Suddenly other clubs began to look around. North was looking at Coburg, Fitzroy at Preston. Many clubs, and the league itself, saw the future in the ever expanding outer suburbs.

On the field the greatest drawcard, the superstar of the 50's was John Coleman, his every movement capable of unleashing a sea of newsprint. His injury was one of those moments in sporting history, like the death of Phar Lap or the Tied Test. His wedding was of Hollywood proportions.

He was handsome, pale and studious looking, and seemingly self-contained until he made that graceful run and tremendous leap.

It was timing and balance, it was spring and perfect judgement, and hands that held marks.

There were other great forwards around – Jock Spencer, Lindsay White, George Goninon

and Jack Collins, to name a few, but Coleman dominated. Jock Spencer matched him for glamour, but not on the scoreboard.

Neil Roberts beat everyone for glamour as he paraded in the goal square under the beseeching eyes of the teenage girls, but the position was perhaps too distracting and he found himself and his football as a tough leader of the backline.

The full backs, like Vic Chanter and Jack Hamilton, are remembered as hard men who were there to intimidate, with their bulk and bad manners, the slim heroes of the forward lines.

After Coleman the big name was Barassi, the tearaway star player of a champion side. You could see the whole side lifting when Barassi was having a big day in his newly minted ruck rover role.

Everyone, regardless of allegiance, admired Bob Skilton, the greatest kick winner of his time. His efforts were never enough to lift the undermanned South Melbourne out of the ordinary, and he played in only one final (in 1970) but he was South's best and fairest nine times, its leading goal kicker three times, and a permanent State player.

His three Brownlow Medals were earned with the most tremendous hard work and skill.

Some imports brought new dimensions to the game in Victoria. Western Australian ruckman Graham 'Polly' Farmer was the springboard of Geelong from 1963 to 1967, and showed the value of creative handball from the packs.

Darrel Baldock brought his stocky frame from Tasmania and demonstrated how to move a ball in and around packs until the time was right to break clear. He was a magnificent wet weather player.

Fellow Tasmanian Ian Stewart, winner of three Brownlows, combined superbly with Baldock and then went to Richmond to do the same with the great centre-half-forward, Royce Hart, yet another Tasmanian.

Another player in the genius class was Alex Jesaulenko, who arrived at Carlton from Canberra at the age of 22 and displayed phenomenal ball getting and handling skills and spectacular marking. Of all the great marks in two decades the best remembered is undoubtedly Jezza's leap over John Jenkins in the 1970 Grand Final.

The man dubbed 'Mr Football' is in the background of the photo of another well remembered mark, by Footscray rover Merv Hobbs in the 1961 Preliminary Final against Melbourne.

Whitten seemed to be all football, tough, enduring, a great mark and kick and the protector of his players.

He excelled at centre-half-back, where he could seem impassable, but he could play anywhere. He invented the flick-pass and had Footscray using it to advantage before it was outlawed.

His career ran right through the two decades of the 1950's and 60's, as player and playing coach, and his name was always in the football news that swirled through the years.

After the game the next real assignment was the *Sporting Globe*, mandatory if the team had won and only optional if it lost.

In defeat one sat in stoic silence on the public conveyance, ignoring the flushed excitement of winning supporters. In victory one could discuss the game with strangers.

But there was always the week ahead – the Sunday TV mayhem of World of Sport and the more earnest Tony Charlton Show, the Monday papers with their lode of after-match reflections.

Friday was Alf Brown's day as he spread himself across the Herald sports pages, analysing each game and each team, man on man. And so it was on again – tomorrow. **John Ross**

Feathers fly in football birds' nest squabbles

April 19. The turmoil over coaching and captaincy matters at Collingwood and Hawthorn has been resolved, if not to the satisfaction of all.

At Hawthorn the dispute involving Alec Albiston, former captain-coach, has resulted in Albiston and Col Austen being cleared.

Albiston was replaced as coach by Bob McCaskill but believed that he had been promised the captaincy. Instead McCaskill decided it should be given to a reputedly tougher player in Kevin Curran.

McCaskill has also changed the Hawthorn uniform to brown and gold stripes, but more will need to be done than change jumpers to make this club win games.

The divisions at Collingwood are worse. The Committee's decision on April 13, on the casting vote of President Harry Curtis, to appoint Bervyn Woods as the Magpies' coach over Phonse Kyne was greeted with anger and incredulity.

At Collingwood's final practice

Kevin Curran in the new jumper.

Bervyn Woods: short stint.

game Woods was jeered at and the Committee members who voted for him were in physical danger.

By contrast Phonse Kyne was carried around the ground on the shoulders of the crowd.

Kyne received a £200 cheque from John Wren, with a note that the decision was 'amazing and incomprehensible'.

Woods resigned the next day, and the 'old guard' of the Committee, Curtis, Frank Wraith and Bob Rush, were voted out by members at a mass meeting at the Collingwood Town Hall (→ 8/9/71).

46,973 see Saints give Blues hell

May 20. A crowd of 46,973, a record for a home-and-away game at the Junction Oval, saw St Kilda down Carlton by 19 points and establish themselves as a Finals contender after so many seasons as the League's perennial underdogs.

Trams and trains to the St Kilda Cricket Ground were overcrowded and queues of up to 300 yards formed outside the entrance gates.

St Kilda, as if overawed by the occasion, started nervously and kicked six behinds before scoring their first goal early in the second quarter. The crowd in the stands went wild and this seemed to spur on the Saints who soon took the lead when their full-forward Peter Bennett scored their second.

Once St Kilda got their noses in front their fast-running game had the more experienced Carlton line-up struggling to stay in the match.

In the final quarter, Carlton threw everything at the young Saints in an effort to overhaul them, but the St Kilda defence led by Bruce Phillips and Keith Drinan held firm.

St.Kilda defeated Carlton 10.14 (74) to 8.7 (55) (→ 7/6/52).

INSIDE
Key Men in the Big Game .. Page 3
Jewish New Year ...... Page 5
CORONATION STORY ... Pages 8-9

The idol of the Fitzroy supporters, Alan 'Baron' Ruthven, has a big year ahead as he tries to captain them back up the League ladder.

Bombers' crushing Grand Final win

Achilles tendon puts White out of game

July 1. Lindsay White, Geelong's captain and champion forward, snapped an achilles tendon during the game against South Melbourne today. The injury may bring his career to an end, leaving him with 542 goals in 144 games.

Lindsay White played for South Melbourne during the war years when Geelong was in recession, and in the 1942 Preliminary Final kicked nine goals, seven from drop-kicks. In 1944 he returned to his old club. His pro sprinting background made him hard to catch, and he often used mighty drop-kicks to goal from as far out as 60 yards.

'Peanut's' great stab-kicking debut

June 3. Only 16 years old, and peanut-sized, Collingwood recruit Thorold Merrett showed the poise and passing ability of a veteran as he helped Collingwood down Footscray in a brilliant debut.

He sent a stream of deadly accurate stab-passes to full-forward, Bill Twomey. The Cobden teenager, rejected by Richmond, was spotted by Collingwood Secretary Gordon Carlyon when he came to Victoria Park to play Country Week cricket. Merrett's coach, former Magpie Jack Murphy, confirmed his potential, and the Pies have a future champion (→ 11/6/60).

Call to investigate VFL ground squalor

June 7. The *Sporting Globe* has called for immediate action to be taken to rectify the squalid and unhygienic conditions at League grounds before an outbreak of sickness.

The League says the matter is in the control of the ground managers, who have failed to supervise toilet facilities – which are gruesome, and often in close proximity to bars and food vendors.

Not enough bar service is provided, and not enough glasses are washed properly. The six o'clock swill is nothing compared to getting a beer at the football (→ 2/5/51).

The crowd has spilled over the fence as 87,601 people await the first bounce in the Grand Final at the MCG.

Sept. 23. Grand Final queues began forming at 9.30 last night and were thousands of people long when the gates opened this morning.

It was North Melbourne's first Grand Final appearance in 25 years of trying in the VFL, and is said to be Essendon captain-coach Dick Reynolds' last game as a player.

Essendon defeated North in a tough Second Semi Final, 11.14 (80) to 11.11 (77), when John Coleman pounced on a ball after a boundary throw-in was palmed his way.

North then had to overcome Geelong in the Preliminary Final, which they managed to do after being blitzed, kicking against the wind, in the first quarter.

At quarter time Geelong led 7.3 to 1.0. By full time North Melbourne had won a Grand Final place, 14.16 (100) to 12.11 (83).

87,601 fans, a majority seeming to favour North, eventually packed the MCG for the Grand Final.

Reynolds to Coleman brought up the first of seven Essendon goals kicked with the wind in the first quarter, while North managed four.

With the breeze, North managed just one goal, and when rain fell in the third quarter they faced a difficult task 20 points behind.

It has to be said that in trying to win the game in the last quarter, North went the knuckle, cleaning up best on ground Dick Reynolds, Ron McEwin, Bert Harper and Ted Leehane. Coleman had received attention all day.

Essendon withstood this assault, going on to win, 13.14 (92) to North Melbourne 7.12 (54).

After Dick Reynolds in his 319th game, Essendon's best players were half-back Norm McDonald and ruckman Bluey McClure. But after 18 years at Essendon it was Dick Reynolds' Flag (→ 29/9/62).

His great moment — and Essendon's, too!

Dick Reynolds savours the victory.

1950 Statistics

Leading Goalkicker:
John Coleman (Ess) 120

Brownlow Medallist:
Alan Ruthven (Fitz)

Finals: First Semi-final Melb 6.8 (44) Geel 13.10 (88); **Second Semi-final** Ess 11.14 (80) N. Melb 11.11 (77); **Preliminary Final** N. Melb 14.16 (100) Geel 12.11 (83); **Grand Final** Ess 13.14 (92) N. Melb 7.12 (54)

Ladder:	W	L	D	%	pts
Ess	17	1		162.2	68
N. Melb	13	5		123.4	52
Melb	12	6		123.2	48
Geel	10	8		124.4	40
Fitz	10	8		110.5	40
Rich	10	8		102.0	40
Coll	9	9		110.4	36
Carl	8	9	1	93.3	34
St K	8	9	1	86.3	34
Foots	5	13		91.7	20
S. Melb	5	13		75.5	20
Haw	0	18		49.8	0

Coaching from Jack Worrall to Len Smith

The men who have coached our football teams have created many changes in their quest for victory. One hundred years ago the captain had the responsibility for training, selection and style. Paid coaches came to the fore in the early part of the century. And with payment came pressure. Perform or be replaced.

Champion former players were the first selected to coach teams. In fact to this day only a handful of men who never actually played VFL have been entrusted to oversee it. Reputation and profile has too often outweighed creative thinkers who were not good enough to have played at senior level. This has been the way of football. Maybe it is slowly changing. Former Fitzroy player John Worrall became secretary/coach at Carlton in 1902.

He coached Premiership teams in 1906, 1907 and 1908 to become a Blues legend. It is said that his organisational ability and hands on approach were the reasons for his success. Perhaps Worrall was the first truly professional coach.

The most durable of all coaches was Collingwood's 'Jock' McHale. He coached over 700 games in an uninterrupted span from 1913-1950. His passion for his beloved Pies was his greatest asset. Inconsolable after a loss, he bled and made his players bleed for the mighty Magpies. Not a great one-on-one teacher the distant Jock was called 'Sir' or Mr. McHale by his players.

He was adamant that players hold their positions and used match practice at training to reinforce his view. He refused to play wingmen who ran forward to shoot at goal. The enterprising 'Jock' even drew lines on the field to indicate the path the ball should take into the forward zone.

McHale's hatred of defeat set the standard at Collingwood. Victories were much celebrated. Losses were felt like a death in the family. But a great virtue of McHale's was positive thinking. By the Tuesday after a Saturday's defeat he would never mention

Norm Smith (right) greets a Flag.

the loss. Everything would be directed to the upcoming game and all the reasons put forward as to why they would win.

Throughout his coaching days McHale was adamant that he show his team spirit too. He would only accept the same payment as his players, no more. How things have changed. Today it is not uncommon for the best players to be paid twice as much as the coach. McHale coached Collingwood to 8 premierships.

In 1927 Richmond 'Checker' Hughes was appointed non-playing coach of the Tigers. It was the start of a coaching career that would affect future generations and many other VFL clubs.

'Checker' was a stickler for fitness. 'Fit players are harder to injure than fat players' was his cry. He trained footballers harder than ever before. And he was one of the first coaches to go outside his club to aggressively recruit. It is said that his knowledge of people and their temperaments made him a coaching psychologist. He knew who would respond to a scathing verbal blast.

And he knew which ones lifted by a pat on the back. Four times the Tigers were runners up. They

eventually won the flag in 1932 proving that 'Checker' didn't lack in perseverance either.

Hughes crossed to Melbourne in 1933. With only one flag in thirty years, Melbourne were regarded by many as a 'soft' club. He started the toughening up process by changing the teams' nickname from Fuchsias to Demons. And play like Demons they did, winning four Premierships under his reign. Hughes was the first coach to really study the strengths and weaknesses of the opposition, and to plan accordingly. He also worked closely with individuals trying to improve their weaknesses.

And with plenty of variety thrown in to make training interesting 'Checker' Hughes probably is the Godfather of modern coaching. His coaching career ended in 1948 but he was the mentor of the great Norm Smith, who in turn was the mentor to Ron Barassi.

The Smith brothers Norm and Len were coaching pioneers throughout the fifties. Len, according to Norm, was the ideas man. But because Len coached inferior teams, he didn't ever become a Premiership coach.

Norm, the more practical of the two coached the Demons to six Premierships between 1955-64. To Norm, a tough taskmaster on the track, the team came first, second and third.

A reflection of the man is shown by the fact that 51 players played in the Premiership teams he coached, but not one came anywhere near winning a Brownlow Medal. Norm was honest with his players, treated them all equally and liked his players to play with controlled aggression.

They would not receive any nonsense from the opposition and would 'fly the flag' for each other.

Norm Smith defied convention. He would often play shortish players in key positions. Particularly at full forward he would have a short decoy lead wide to open up space for a taller marking forward pocket to move into. Norm was not lavish with

praise as he expected good players to play well. But he would soon let you know if he thought you weren't pulling your weight. This trait was definitely passed on to Ron Barassi.

Len Smith coached Fitzroy and Richmond in the 50's and 60's. He was a quiet fatherly type who knew how to build a player's confidence. He was the first coach to document his coaching philosophies and was generous with his information.

Len Smith was one of the first, if not the first coach to see handball as an attacking weapon.

He urged players to move the ball on quickly, especially after a mark had been taken. For sixty years players had walked back slowly after marking the ball and then indicated where they would kick the ball. Len wanted to change all this but with inferior players his methods were open to criticism.

He was indeed a brave man to dare challenge the status quo. Len Smith was a deep thinker, listed are some of his ideas documented in the fifties. Some have come to fruition, some still may.

1. Captains toss the coin 15 minutes before the game so as coaches can give specific instructions in regard to wind/ground conditions.

2. Four boundary umpires to speed up play.

3. Allow coaches onto the ground during quarter break.

4. Draw a large circle in the middle of the ground and when the ball is bounced to start play allow in only four players from each team.

5. Pay a free kick for kicks out of bounds on the full.

6. Pad goal posts to 8 feet.

7. Standardise ground size to reduce home ground advantage.

8. Time clocks for all to see, controlled by official time keepers.

9. Regular coach and umpires meetings.

10. Allow 19th and 20th men to be inter-changeable.

He was obviously a man with a vision for the game.

Robert Walls

1951

Critic hails a 'new era of football'

At the pinnacle of the new football era, Essendon's full-forward John Coleman.

April 28. Football is in its cleverest, its greatest era, according to the senior football writer of the *Sporting Globe*, Hec de Lacy.

And he has plenty of modern and old-time footballers to back him up, including the recently retired triple Brownlow Medallist Dick Reynolds, and Carlton coach Percy Bentley.

De Lacy says that the game has never before reached such heights of excitement, or been so spectacular. The old game was slower, and more neatly regulated, while 'this is the day of the mobile opportunist'.

A reason for the change, says de Lacy, is the gradual adoption by the League of rules devised by the Asso-ciation to create more flowing play.

The one rule not adopted has been the throw pass, but the hand pass has evolved to be as near to throwing as possible, and the game has opened up accordingly.

This maintains perpetual action, and allows players to break into the open and use the accurate stab-kick or the punt pass to find a team-mate.

Dick Reynolds told de Lacy that there should be two field umpires now to keep up with the faster game, while Percy Bentley said that Laurie Nash and Haydn Bunton would have revelled in today's game, but Syd Coventry would have been too slow (→ 17/4/54).

Clegg takes 32 marks in draw

June 23. In what is regarded as one of the greatest marking displays since Carlton's Alec Duncan took 33 in a game in 1927, Ron 'Smokey' Clegg took 32 and saved South Melbourne in the drawn game against Fitzroy. Final score was 12.13 (85) each.

Clegg also saved the game by tackling Fitzroy's Don Hart who dropped the ball in the last seconds. After the free was given, Eddie Hart kicked a disallowed behind which would have won the game. It was 'Clegg's Match'.

Hawks' first since 1949 – Cash stars

May 5. Hawthorn delighted their fans today with their first win since 1949. In a rugged game the Hawks won 12.15 (87) to St Kilda's 9.10 (64), overhauling the Saints in a four goal second-term burst, in which new forward Pat Cash was prominent. Hawthorn then held on to the lead while St Kilda grew tired.

Enthusiastic supporters showed their appreciation to players after the game with plenty of £5 notes. Two small boys even added a 6d and a 3d, glad that coach Bob McCaskill now has a team to match the best.

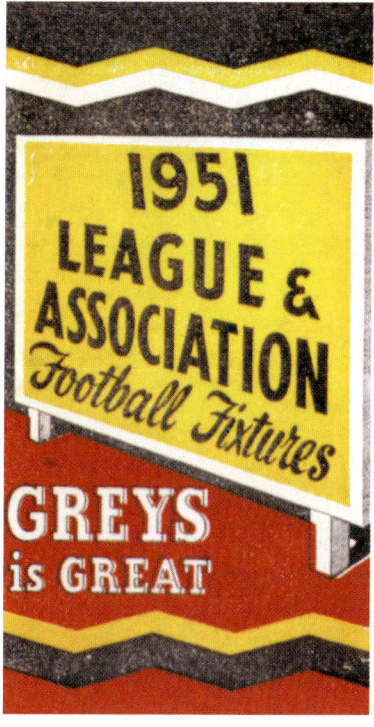

Football is 'run like a penny dip'

May 2. Football is a million-pound enterprise in Melbourne, but it is still being run like a penny dip, says the *Sporting Globe's* Hec de Lacy.

There isn't the slightest regard for the comfort of patrons, he says, no attempt to sell the game bigger and no flair for promotion.

De Lacy continues that winter's biggest show has Melbourne gripped as usual, but conditions at most League grounds are disgraceful.

'The treacherous sloping banks and primitive sanitary conditions are dangers to health and safety.

'It isn't possible to book a ticket, let alone a seat, to a League game.

'And the best games are being hidden from the public.

'The magnetism of the mighty MCG is demonstrated every time a big game is played there. 37,200 watched Melbourne, 7.15 (57), downed by Collingwood, 15.16 (106), yet next week Essendon will play Collingwood at the smaller ground of Windy Hill. This will draw up to 30,000, while at the MCG it would attract 60,000.

'The desires of the public are not being studied. They are hungry for football, and nobody but a fool or a management white-anted by club interests would think of playing top games except to a capacity house at the MCG. But the game is still back in 1896.' (→ 26/4/75)

Jack-in-a-box full-forward Keith Warburton, of Carlton, shows his sensational marking skills.

Coleman rubbed out on eve of Finals

Sept. 4. The Bombers' hopes of making it three Flags in a row took a nosedive with the suspension of John Coleman for four matches.

Without Coleman's average contribution of four goals a match in this relatively lean season the task of kicking a winning Finals score looks even more remote.

The attention Coleman has received this year from opposition backmen has reduced his output.

A crowd of several hundred fans waited outside Harrison House for the result, which they greeted with tears, groans and jeers.

After the Tribunal hearing Coleman was also distressed, and in the crush managed to nearly knock himself out on a lamppost.

He was driven away in a car, laid out on the back seat.

Carlton's Harry Caspar, who was also suspended for four matches, was regarded as the instigator of the clash in the ugly game.

Even the umpires who gave evidence said that Coleman was only defending himself. 'If I'd been in the same position I would probaby have done the same thing myself,' said goal umpire Allen.

Boundary umpire Kent said Coleman 'was under provocation. It was only after he had been struck a second time by the Carlton player'.

The Tribunal did not acknowledge provocation as a reason for striking out the charge.

The Essendon doctor said that at half time Coleman had a severe cut over his eye, and that he was not in complete possession of his senses or in control of his emotions.

For his part Caspar alluded to unspecified provocations and said that he had not thrown a closed fist punch whatever else he threw.

The incident resulted in both Coleman and Caspar being hooted by their opposition barrackers whenever they went near the ball.

In the third quarter a lemonade bottle whizzed past Coleman's head.

Coleman kicked seven goals in the game, which Essendon won 16.12 (108) to Carlton 9.10 (64)

Field umpire Barbour had to be escorted from the ground by police, through a mob of Carlton supporters. One policeman said 'Apparently the Blues can't take it' (→ 18/4/53).

The fateful moment: John Coleman faces up to Carlton's Harry Caspar.

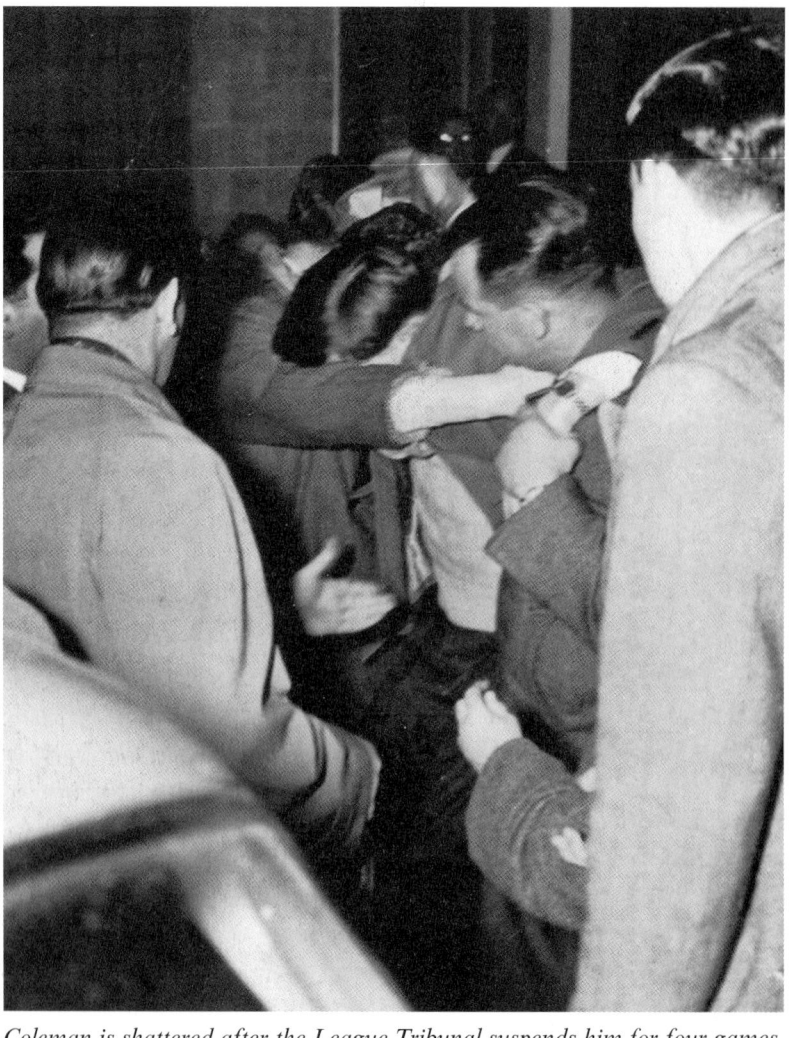

Coleman is shattered after the League Tribunal suspends him for four games.

Geelong Flag completes Cat quadruple

George Goninon kicks for goal.

THE RED CARPET ROLLED FROM THE M.C.G. TO MALOP ST GEELONG!

VFL PREMIERS 1951

CAPT. FLANAGAN · BERNIE SMITH · HYDE · "HUTCH" · 86 GOALS

Fred Flanagan and his teammates, Bernie Smith, John Hyde, Bill McMaster and George Goninon.

Sept. 29. Geelong was a ghost town today. All the black cats in town could have walked down Little Malop Street, without surprising a solitary human being.

If the humans weren't at the MCG they were glued to the house, listening on the radio to their team beating Essendon to win the Premiership, 11.15 (81) to 10.10 (70).

Tonight Geelong is a boom town, with the streets alive, car horns blaring and an estimated 15,000 outside the Town Hall to welcome home the victors.

What a year they have to celebrate – top of the Ladder at the end of the home-and-away games, Bernie Smith as Brownlow Medallist, George Goninon as top goalkicker, and Premiers.

Geelong won in a tense last quarter. They got to 39 points ahead, but Essendon rallied to come within nine points. Two goals were engineered by Dick Reynolds, who came out of retirement to the bench, and came on in the last quarter.

But Geelong rallied and held the ball up forward, where Fred Flanagan and Bob Davis had previously cut the Dons' defence to ribbons.

The MCG gates were shut at 12.30 p.m., and even then the crowd of 85,795 spilled over the fence and inside the boundary (→ 27/9/52).

Bernie Smith is amazed at news of Brownlow Medal win

Sept. 5. Bernie Smith, Geelong's dashing back pocket, won the Brownlow Medal with 23 votes, three clear of South Melbourne's Ron 'Smokey' Clegg on 20, with Essendon champion Bill Hutchison in third place on 16.

Smith received votes from the umpire in nine of 18 home-and-away games, being awarded six three pointers, two of two and one of one.

Smith, who came from West Adelaide in 1948, says he has achieved one of two football ambitions by winning the Brownlow.

The other is being part of a Geelong Premiership side, which may well happen in the next few weeks.

Curly-haired 23-year-old Smith paid tribute to coach and Geelong legend Reg Hickey: 'Anything I have achieved in football is due to Hickey. He is a great coach and a gentleman' (→ 21/4/85).

Great work for the camera by Geelong's Bernie Smith as he hears the news that he has won the Brownlow Medal. All he wants now is a Premiership.

1951 Statistics

Leading Goalkicker:
George Goninon (Geel) 86
Brownlow Medallist:
Bernie Smith (Geel)
Finals: First Semi-final Ess 8.13 (61) Foots 8.5 (53); **Second Semifinal** Geel 22.20 (152) Coll 10.10 (70); **Preliminary Final** Coll 10.8 (68) Ess 10.10 (70); **Grand Final** Geel 11.15 (81) Ess 10.10 (7)

Ladder:	W	L	D	%	pts
Geel	14	4		135.4	56
Coll	14	4		125.6	56
Ess	13	5		121.2	52
Foots	12	6		113.0	48
Fitz	10	6	2	105.2	44
Rich	10	8		116.9	40
Carl	8	9	1	107.0	34
S. Melb	8	9	1	93.0	34
N. Melb	7	11		85.4	28
St K	5	13		82.2	20
Haw	4	14		75.0	16
Melb	1	17		70.5	4

March 19. VFL decides on 19 rounds of home-and-away matches so that local public will not lose a round due to matches played at interstate and country venues (→ 30/4/70).

March 29. The VFL is reported to be considering a shareholding of £50,000 in the construction of the Olympic Stadium at Princes Park which would, after the Olympics, become a permanent home for football (→ 7/6).

March 29. VFL has scrubbed efforts to establish a Players' Appeal Board with jurisdiction over transfers (→ 15/4/55).

May 10. Geelong say that Bob Davis has no hope of getting a transfer. 'We want his football. No ifs or buts.' (→ 30/9/58).

May 31. Collingwood Secretary Gordon Carlyon is told to stop whingeing by other League Clubs when he repeats his complaint about playing Richmond in Sydney (→ 14/6).

June 7. Record home-and away crowd of 58,543 see Melbourne inflict Collingwood's first defeat for season, 12.10 (82) to 6.14 (50), at MCG (→ 16/6/58).

June 7. League Secretary L.H. McBrien says the possibility of Finals at a 125,000 capacity Olympic Stadium at Princes Park had not been discussed and 'as far as football is concerned the MCG will always be the MCG' (→ 17/3/54).

June 28. Collingwood 'midget' Bob Rose plays his 100th game, the last 80 without a break, in the Pies' 12.13 (85) to 9.10 (64) win over South.

July 5. A spectator jumps the fence and attacks Richmond defender Don 'Mopsy' Fraser from behind in Collingwood's fiery win, 10.19 (79) to 8.8 (56) (→ 27/7/57).

Aug. 30. John Marr of Hawthorn was kicking a goal when Tom Allsop of Hawthorn was infringed by a North Melbourne player. Umpire Jack McMurray gave Allsop a free – and he scored again. Hawthorn still lost 12.10 (82) to 8.11 (59) (→ 30/8/58).

Debuts
Allen Aylett (N. Melb)
Tony Ongarello (Fitz)
Neil Roberts (St K)

Retirements
Bill Brittingham (Ess)
Vic Chanter (Fitz)
Ern Henfry (Carl)
Fred Stafford (Carl)

Premiership points at stake in interstate and country games

June 14. Today was named 'National Day' by the League, and marks the first time VFL games have been played for Premiership points outside the Melbourne-Geelong area since 1904.

In a novel attempt to promote Australian football, the VFL dispatched Round 8 games to Victorian country districts and interstate.

Weather was a threat. In Brisbane heavy rain has postponed the Geelong and Essendon game until Monday night, to be played under lights. There was bad weather at all the other grounds, too, yet crowds were surprisingly good – even in the absence of some drawcard players kept at home to represent Victoria in the same-day game against Western Australia, at the MCG. Denis Cordner's State obligations cost the Demons dearly in Hobart, where a record crowd saw the Maroons down the Demons, 13.12 (90) to 10.10 (70). The Melbourne ruck was useless without him.

The Sydney game, played in constant drizzle, became one-sided when Collingwood overwhelmed Richmond in the second quarter and won, 10.12 (72) to 5.6 (36). In Albury the contest was a thriller, with North and South Melbourne trading goal for goal until the Swans got ahead in the final term, 18.10 (118) to 14.12 (96). Meanwhile, at Yallourn, St Kilda beat Footscray in the mud, 7.7 (49) to 5.4 (34). And Carlton's big men swamped the young Hawks at Euroa, 17.15 (117) to 11.14 (80) (→ 15/7/67).

Ten Tall Men

May 31. The ten tallest League players as measured by the management of the State Theatre will receive a footballer's kit-bag with the compliments of actor Burt Lancaster on the occasion of the premiere of his film *Ten Tall Men*.

The ten tallest in the VFL are Geoff Leek (Essendon) 6 feet 4 1/2 inches, followed by Kevin Easton (North), Denis Cordner and Tom McLean (Melbourne), Jack 'Chooka' Howell (Carlton), George Swarbrick and Bill McMaster (Geelong), John Gill (Essendon) and Brian Gilmore (Footscray), all 6 feet 4 inches, and Colin Thornton (North) who is 6 feet 3 1/2 inches.

VICTORIA'S FOOTRALL CHAMPIONS

Premiership Match

RICHMOND v COLLINGWOOD

"Red-Blooded Opponents"

1920 DICK LEE (Collingwood)

1930 JACK REGAN (Collingwood)

1940 RON TODD (Collingwood)

1950 JACK OROURKE (Richmond)

SYDNEY CRICKET GROUND

SAT. JUNE 14th.

NOT an Exhibition Game!

FOOTBALL *Fixtures* 1952

WITH COMPLIMENTS FROM *Pelaco*

£500 to field team

March 26. League clubs that budgeted about £12,000 last season to put a team on to the field, will have to find £15,000 this year – which amounts to about £500 a week for playing and training.

There are four main sources of income – club memberships, one-third of net gate receipts, a League Finals dividend of about £1000 and donations from patrons.

Some expenses of one club last season were players' wages £2700, provident fund £700, training staff £739, insurance £87, outfitting uniforms for Seconds and Thirds £700, materials for Firsts £1066, and medical supplies £547 (→ 31/5/73).

White balls used in seas of black mud

July 26. It has been a miserable season of football.

For week after dreary week games have begun with the umpires picking their way delicately through seas of mud and water. They throw the ball up and watch a slithering, sliding contest where a solid kick is an achievement, a chest mark a major feat, and an overhead mark a miracle. There were four inches of rain on one recent weekend.

All this is watched in comparative silence by muffled figures in the stands and the huddled figures under umbrellas in the outer.

At the Hawthorn and Geelong game on June 28, it was possible to count by sight all the patrons in the outer.

The MCG staff now have a mopping up roller, and this was used on July 5 to mop up the Fitzroy marsh, which has been reckoned by the *Sporting Globe* to be a menace to public health. The ankle-deep mud at Fitzroy has not been helped by the use of sawdust, which has given it the appearance and consistency of blackberry jam.

White balls have been introduced, and this has helped players to find the ball in the mud. They have been declared a success.

Keith Warburton lies gravely ill

Sept. 10. Keith Warburton, the Carlton centreman in the First Semi Final, is still seriously ill at Prince Henry's Hospital, though doctors say his excellent physical condition helped him through the main crisis.

Warburton suffered a knock in the Blues' one-point loss to Fitzroy, 8.20 (68) to 10.9 (69), but thought nothing of it at the time.

Near midnight at a club dance, he collapsed and was discovered to be suffering from a severed artery leading to the bowel. He underwent a three hour operation on Sunday, and has been given almost continuous transfusions of blood since.

Team-mates, friends and the football public have responded magnificently to appeals by the Blood Bank.

It is expected that Warburton will be off the danger list tomorrow.

Cats scratch Magpie hopes

Sept. 27. 49,000 delirious fans at Kardinia Park watched Geelong demolish Final Four side Carlton 10.17 (77) to a miserable 3.14 (32) in the last home-and-away game.

After that they might have been forgiven for thinking that the Grand Final was as good as won.

Nothing in the Second Semi would have changed their minds. Geelong doubled Collingwood's score, 14.16 (100) to 6.10 (46), with the Geelong following division of Bill McMaster, Russell Renfrey and Neil 'Nipper' Trezise dominating.

Collingwood were never in the hunt in the Grand Final, especially after Bob Davis drilled a drop-kick 65 yards if it was an inch, for the second to the Cats.

Many thought Geoff Williams, Geelong's first-year half back flanker was best on ground, from the most attacking back pocket in the game, Bernie Smith, Peter Pianto, and full-forward George Goninon.

Geelong's ability to attack from the full back line towards a quality forward line has made them the successful team of the season, and winners of the Grand Final.

82,890 were at the MCG, thousands more were listening in. A *Geelong Advertiser* reporter said that 'bounce off time in Melbourne was switch on time in Geelong'. Radios went into action as the crowds roared at the MCG. Ryrie Street at 3.30 p.m. was a remarkable sight. Tramlines seemed to stretch like a bush railway line into empty horizons. The reporter counted one car, one parked motor cycle, three Chinese seamen and a dog between the Post Office and the Geelong Theatre.

When the final siren blew, and the radios brought the result, the silent tension seemed to lift from the empty but victorious city.

Geelong, 13.8 (86), defeated Collingwood, 5.10 (40).

It's that man again! Fred Flanagan is chaired off the ground after the victory.

Richmond's gentle giant Roy Wright is interviewed by Alwyn Kurts of 3XY at a break in training after his Brownlow Medal win. Small boys from Tigerland are all ears as their hero discusses his footy fortunes.

1952 Statistics

Leading Goalkicker:
John Coleman (Ess) 103
Brownlow Medallist:
Roy Wright (Rich)
Finals: First Semi-final Fitz 10.9 (69) Carl 8.20 (68); **Second Semi-final** Geel 14.16 (100) Coll 6.10 (46); **Preliminary Final** Coll 11.15 (81) Fitz 9.8 (62); **Grand Final** Geel 13.8 (86) Coll 5.10 (40)

Ladder:	W	L	D	%	pts
Geel	16	2	1	134.7	66
Coll	14	5		144.4	56
Fitz	13	6		105.4	52
Carl	11	6	2	112.4	48
S. Melb	11	7	1	105.5	46
Melb	9	9	1	103.0	38
N. Melb	9	10		96.8	36
Ess	8	10	1	113.6	34
Rich	8	11		92.6	32
Foots	5	14		77.1	20
Haw	5	14		69.6	20
St K	2	17		68.1	8

1953

April 1. Rights to football radio broadcasts are in dispute. The VFL insists that stations which broadcast the full game be given preference over horse racing stations. Ground managers, who control rights, want the additional revenue from secondary broadcasts. Rights money is divided 50/50 between the ground manager and the home team (→ 17/7/54).

April 18. Big first round crowd of 136,000 see John Coleman kick ten in Essendon's 17.9 (111) win over Fitzroy 12.16 (88). Bill Twomey gets nine of Collingwood's 17.16 (118) to South's 11.11 (77) (→ 2/5).

April 24. The success of the night football exhbition match at the Showgrounds between Collingwood, 12.12 (84), and Fitzroy, 5.8 (38), is a challenge for the League. The *Sporting Globe* speculates on electric light soccer or VFA attracting the crowds (→ 19/8/93).

May 2. John Coleman kicks 11 of Essendon's 13.11 (89) but Dons lose to South Melbourne 13.21 (99) (→ 29/5/54).

May 16. Ron Barassi, son of the late wartime hero, debuts as 20th man for Melbourne in their 4.6 (30) loss to the 'Scray's 9.21 (75) (→ 30/4/55).

May 20. St Kilda's refusal to clear John Coffey to Morwell has caused the Victorian Country Football League to refuse any country clearances to St Kilda.

May 23. 'Historian' in the *Sporting Globe* says that only one of six players reported to the Tribunal has been suspended this year, because umpires are not represented, and their evidence is discounted (→ 16/5/62).

June 3. 'Checker' Hughes is critical of the VFL decision to ban trainers from taking messages from the coach to players (→ 11/4/64).

July 4. Hawthorn officials and coach Jack Hale object to *Sporting Globe* writer Hec de Lacy's suggestion that it merge or move. de Lacy cites financial difficulties and small ground and crowds.

Debuts
Ron Barassi (Melb)
Keith Bromage (Coll)
John James (Carl)
Hugh Mitchell (Ess)
Murray Weideman (Coll)
Don Williams (Melb)

Retirement
Pat Twomey (Coll)

Magpies and Dons end Cats' winning run

Peter Lucas helps kick Collingwood to a win over Geelong.

Aug. 8. The Geelong bubble has finally burst. After a record number of 23 wins in a row they finally succumbed to the former record-holder, Collingwood.

It seems that the strain of winning for so long had got to the Cats. With a draw included they had been 26 games without a loss. The press and radio men have been predicting the fall for week after week.

The Cats had to beat North Melbourne four weeks ago to break the record, established by Collingwood in 1928-29. The strain was nearly too much, and they trailed by seven points with three minutes to go. A rushed point, and a goal by Ron Hovey equalised and the winning point was put through by George Swarbrick in the last 30 seconds.

The League leaders – stacked with accomplished players like Bernie Smith, Bob Davis, Fred Flanagan, George Goninon, Peter Pianto and 'Nipper' Trezise – then struggled to shake off Hawthorn and Footscray.

Everything went wrong in the game against Collingwood at Kardi-nia Park last week. Playing brilliantly they should have led by six goals, but missed shots from close range by 'Dead-eye' Goninon, Flanagan, Davis and Pianto. Collingwood seemed dead on their feet at half time, as Geelong led 5.11 (41) to 4.5 (29).

But complacency must have set in with the Cats, and they began to let the Magpies back into the game. Bernie Smith, a peerless back pocket, played too loosely on Collingwood's champion Bobby Rose who started to cut holes in Geelong's defence.

Collingwood ran away from the tired Cats in the last quarter to win, 10.15 (75) to 7.13 (55).

Today it was Essendon's turn to bring the Cats back to the field and open up the fight for the Premiership. They won, 8.13 (61) to 7.8 (50), before a record crowd of 41,000 at Windy Hill.

The architect of the Essendon win was Jack Clarke, who beat three opponents in the centre and set up many attacks. Only poor kicking, especially by John Coleman, prevented a bigger win (→ 2/7/55).

Brownlow Bomber Bill Hutchison

Hutchison: stab-pass specialist.

Sept. 2. Essendon's captain and great rover Bill Hutchison has at last won a Brownlow Medal, aged 30.

Last season he lost on a count-back to Roy Wright, and he was third in 1948 and 1951.

Dick Reynolds says Hutchison is the greatest player he has ever seen, courageous, scrupulously fair, with magical ball skills.

Hutchison came to Essendon as an 18-year-old in 1942, playing in that year's Premiership.

He has played in nine Grand Finals, including the 1948 draw, for four Flags.

Every Essendon kid's dream on a Saturday morning is to get Dad to fill the family car with Bomber fuel at Hutchy's Golden Fleece service station in Keilor Road (→ 18/6/82).

A bright new face at Melbourne is **Ronald Dale Barassi,** the son of the former player who was killed at Tobruk during the war.

Collingwood are back on top again

Mick Twomey takes a big mark.

A glorious day for Collingwood, and a part of the big crowd takes to the oval to celebrate a great victory.

Sept. 26. Collingwood repeated their surprise Second Semi Final win over Geelong with another surprise in the Grand Final. The game was in front of a jam-packed crowd of 89,060 who paid an all-time record of £11,248.6.9.

510 spectators more than the Health Department's safety limit had gained entrance, and many hundreds more demanded their money back as they could not see.

One said: 'This is a scandal.

They've taken our money knowing we wouldn't be able to see.'

Others had jumped fences or slept outside the ground.

First arrivals to queue for tickets were two young women who took up station yesterday afternoon, one missing a dental appointment. 'I'd rather have a toothache than miss the Grand Final,' she said.

The crowd spilled on to the arena at 12.40 pm, ten minutes after the gates were closed.

Among the spectators who could see were Collingwood fullback Jack Hamilton, out with a broken hand, and Geelong halfback Russ Middlemiss who injured his knee in the Second Semi.

The game was a typical pressure-packed Grand Final where, after an even first quarter, Collingwood, with Des Healey, Bob Rose and Thorold Merrett playing well, fought to a nine-point lead.

Then, in the third quarter, with a

freshening breeze, the Magpies kicked five goals two, with Lou Richards, Des Healey, Bob Rose and full-forward Keith Batchelor seeing Collingwood in front by 29 points.

Although Geelong fought back in the last quarter, and were on top of a tiring Collingwood by the end, the score at the siren was Collingwood 11.11 (77) to Geelong 8.17 (65).

Des Healey was best on ground and Bernie Smith best for Geelong (→ 20/9/58).

15-year-old catches selectors' eye

Aug. 22. At 15 years and 287 days old, Collingwood's Keith Bromage became the youngest person to play in a senior League game.

He kicked two goals, first from the half-forward flank, and then at full-forward in Collingwood's well-deserved win over Richmond.

There were only 17 fit Magpies on the field in the last quarter when they booted four goals to one in a come-from-behind win, 13.17 (95) to 12.9 (81).

Bromage attracted selectors when they saw him in an end of game kick-to-kick. Today he didn't set Punt Road on fire, but he contributed and finished the game out well.

Bromage was 28 days younger than Wels Eicke the St Kilda champion who made his debut in 1909 at 15 years and 315 days.

Plenty of rain and a burst drain turned the Western Oval into a swimming pool on May 23, and had players slithering around in search of the ball. Footscray kicked 10.6 (66) and had Fitzroy scoreless until the last minutes, when captain Alan 'Baron' Ruthven swiped at the ball for a desperate goal.

1953 Statistics

Leading Goalkicker:
John Coleman (Ess) 97
Brownlow Medallist:
Bill Hutchison (Ess)
Finals: First Semi-final Foots 6.13 (49) Ess 5.11 (41); **Second Semi-final** Geel 8.12 (60) Coll 13.12 (90); **Preliminary Final** Geel 8.15 (63) Foots 5.7 (37); **Grand Final** Coll 11.11 (77) Geel 8.17 (65)

Ladder:	W	L	D	%	pts
Geel	15	3		143.3	60
Coll	14	4		123.5	56
Foots	13	5		136.5	52
Ess	13	5		129.9	52
Carl	10	8		107.6	40
Fitz	10	8		85.0	40
N. Melb	9	9		107.8	36
S. Melb	9	9		104.7	36
St K	5	13		68.2	20
Rich	3	14	1	81.3	14
Melb	3	14	1	80.1	14
Haw	3	15		68.5	12

1954

April 10. Carlton's speedster Laurie Kerr has done pre-season training in four states while covering the Royal Tour as a journalist for the *Argus*.

April 17. St Kilda, led by new coach Les Foote in the centre, surprise Footscray with a 9.10 (64) to 7.11 (53) win.

May 8. Hawthorn's John Kennedy plays a great rucking game, but the Hawks lose to North 10.13 (73) to 11.10 (76). He attributes his form to his teacher transfer from the country (→ 27/4/60).

May 15. Hawthorn defeat Geelong for the first time since 1948, 14.13 (97) to 13.14 (92). 'Candles' Thompson is best on ground for the Hawks, 'Troubles' Flanagan kicks seven for Geelong.

May 29. John Coleman kicks 14 of Essendon's 22.13 (145) against Fitzroy 7.12 (54) (→ 5/6).

June 12. The former North Melbourne Shinboners are now dubbed Kangaroos, and they hop all over Collingwood, 13.13 (91) to 10.12 (72).

June 16. *Sporting Globe* says that country champs Ballarat should be admitted to VFL.

June 19. 43,313 see Victoria massacre South Australia at the MCG, 26.16 (172) to 6.9 (45) Roy Wright is named best on ground, while Jack Collins kicks ten goals (→ 23/6/56).

July 17. ANFC member Jack Mulrooney warns of the threat of television to football. He recommends charging a substantial fee and limiting live coverage to preserve crowds at the grounds (→ 1/4/57).

July 17. Indian Chief of the General Staff, Cariappa, has recommended Australian football as a recreation for the Indian Army (→ 15/4/95).

Sept. 7. After Melbourne's win in semi-final over North, 16.14 (110) to 11.14 (80), North players Percy Johnson and Laurie Icke, and Melbourne's Bob McKenzie have all been suspended for four weeks.

Debuts
Brian Dixon (Melb)
Bob Johnson Jr. (Melb)
Laurie Mithen (Melb)
John Peck (Haw)
Ian Ridley (Melb)

Retirements
John Coleman (Ess)
Jack 'Chooka' Howell (Carl)
Max Oppy (Rich)
Alan 'Baron' Ruthven (Fitz)

'Candles' gives Hawks high profile

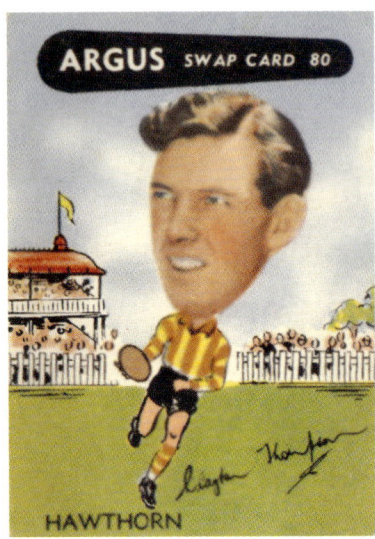

Thompson: a lot to learn.

May 1. The long-awaited clash between the Hawks' Clayton 'Candles' Thompson and Melbourne's Denis Cordner arrived today, after the Demons had tried to block Thompson's transfer from Sturt. They need not have been so fearful of 'Candlepower'. Denis Cordner outmatched Thompson, making Hawthorn's huge recruit look lost and lacking in a knowledge of foot disposal. None the less, it proved to be the Hawks' day. They won in most positions, were faster and better organised, and fought off a last-quarter bid by the Demons to come home 11.9 (75) to 9.10 (64) (→ 15).

"Firm Favourites!"
FOUR SQUARE
CIGARETTES
MADE IN AUSTRALIA
by GEORGE DOBIE & SON, AUSTRALIA LTD.
FOOTBALL FIXTURES, 1954
League and Association

Knee threatens Coleman's flying days

June 5. A silence descended over Windy Hill today as Essendon's great full-forward John Coleman lay on the ground, obviously in agony. He had flown for a mark in the forward pocket and crumpled to the ground as he landed awkwardly.

The excitement of the close game between Essendon and North Melbourne was forgotten, and club allegiances temporarily abandoned, as 20,000 people watched Coleman carried from the ground.

He was taken to Sacred Heart Hospital, Moreland, and the immediate news is that his knee has been severely dislocated.

Essendon, five points down at three-quarter time, were staging a spirited comeback when the injury occurred. As the two reserves were already on the ground they were left with 17 men, but they still finished all over North to win 14.14 (98) to 10.15 (75).

Coleman had kicked five goals by the time of his injury. He has been in his usual sensational form this year, and kicked 14 goals last week against Fitzroy, his personal best tally and an Essendon club record. In the six matches he's played this year he has kicked 42 goals to easily lead the goalkicking.

Coleman has topped the goalkicking in all but one year since his sensational first year in 1949. In that year he scored 100 goals and in the following year 120. In 1951, the year

J. COLEMAN

Coleman: landed awkwardly.

of his suspension for striking Harry Caspar of Carlton, he came second to George Goninon (86) with 75 goals, and he has scored 103 and 97 in his last two seasons.

Coleman has been a great drawcard, as even people without club allegiances have turned out to watch his thrilling play, and the state of his knee will have a direct effect on Essendon's finances (→ 9/5/55).

Jack Hamilton not in Magpie territory

Aug. 14. It has been revealed that Collingwood's strong and relentless back Jack Hamilton has been playing for the wrong team since he joined the League seven years ago.

Carlton had tried to recruit him from the Ivanhoe Amateurs, only to be thwarted by Hamilton's home address being 20 yards inside Collingwood's recruitment territory.

Now none other than Jack Hamilton himself has discovered that in fact he lived 20 yards *outside* the Magpies' nest, in unallotted territory. So Carlton could have had him after all. Jack sorted this out while working as a clerk at League headquarters, but he's a Collingwood loyalist now (→ 21/11/84).

Jack Collins trains one of his 'cuties' for a charity match.

Maroons land two Gorillas in big bet

July 24. You could have got 10/1 against bottom of the Ladder Fitzroy beating top team Collingwood – and plenty of the Fitzroy 'Gorillas' did just that before today's match.

Fitzroy players and supporters won around £2000, or two gorillas in betting parlance, in side wagers. There is little betting on football, so this was an interesting occurrence.

Strong man Norm Johnstone had £100 to £20 and few, knowing that, would have got between him and the goals as he began one of his characteristic charges. His team-mates seemed equally determined.

Fitzroy won 12.9 (81) to 6.13 (49) and, in the words of Secretary Jack Buckley, 'Our team can produce football equal to the best ... this is a good team. Now we're confident, look out' (→ 1/8/59).

Johnstone: a heavy bet.

Time to 'throw out the knucklemen'

April 17. Writing in the *Sporting Globe*, H.A. de Lacy said today: 'Star League players are being victimised by muscle men and crash merchants waging an incessant vendetta against the matchwinners.' He has called upon the League to discipline not only the bullying players, but the clubs and club officials who 'send them out to "quieten" the good player on the other side'.

Mr de Lacy goes on: 'The game is attractively robust, but when virility turns to violence it is time to step in'. He cites the increasing incidence of a promising younger player being ruthlessly 'run through and flattened' after taking a kick, obviously to intimidate him before he becomes too good (→ 28/3/66).

'Think big. Act big': Chairman Luke

March 17. Mr Ken Luke, Vice-President of the VFL, says Australian football needs a ground of its own. But, he says, no one seems to bother so long as thousands clamour for admission to the Finals at the Melbourne Cricket Ground.

In a searching look at the future of football Mr Luke said the VFL had to 'Think big and act big!'

He said that he recognised the MCG as a national asset, but the revenue split from games there meant that the VFL was not receiving money that could be spent on developing the game. If the League owned a ground capable of holding a crowd of 125,000 people, there would be more money to benefit the clubs and the game in Victoria.

He also criticised the control of football grounds by cricket clubs, who held them 'because of some ancient Crown grant'.

'With millions attending football and a handful attending cricket it isn't democratic that the minority should fleece the majority.'

Mr Luke said that Victoria needed a football organisation that would think and act for the State rather than for the club.

'I would begin by putting control of the VFL in the hands of an executive. This would mean no more rule by delegates. The game should be

K.G. Luke: vision splendid.

beyond the temptations of club interests. It certainly isn't at present.'

Mr Luke also called for: abolition of the Coulter Law limiting payment to players of £5 a week; and abolition of District Football under which clubs control players from specific districts.

He said that there was nothing dishonourable about paying a player what he is worth, and that 'a lad should be able to play with the club he likes' (→ 12/9/62).

Gentle Giant Roy Wright picks up Brownlow Medal

Sept. 1. Roy Wright, like a barrel of Victorian claret, took a long time to mature as a footballer, but when he did the vintage has been superb – resulting in his second Brownlow Medal in three years.

His 1952 Brownlow was won with 21 votes after a count-back from Bill Hutchison, but his dominance was such that there was hardly a need to count at all this year.

Wright scored an astonishing 29 votes to win from Collingwood's Neil Mann with 19. He has won every award on offer this season, overcoming illness and injury that kept him out of some games.

While kept out of the side by players such as Bill Morris and Jack Dyer, Wright looked and learned. The man known as 'the gentle giant' now has a big leap for a big 16-stone man, a huge hand to palm the ball, and a 76-inch wingspan.

Roy Wright in the ruck for Victoria this year against South Australia.

Dogs demolish Demons

Footscray's Ted Whitten gets a kick away ahead of Demons' Stuart Spencer.

Sept. 25. Geelong finished on top of the Ladder for the fourth year in a row, in an even season where just six points separated Footscray, second, from Collingwood, seventh.

But the Bulldogs snarled at the right end of the season, defeating the Cats 11.19 (85) to 8.14 (62) in the Second Semi, and earning a rest.

In the Preliminary Final, Melbourne completed the disappointment of 1954 for Geelong by disposing of them 10.7 (67) to 7.8 (50).

Captain-coach Charlie Sutton, who missed the Second Semi through injury, was back refreshed and resolute for the Grand Final.

But he nearly didn't make it to the ground – the steering column of his Holden broke on the way, owing to the potholes in the roads in Altona, he said.

The MCG provided a much smoother road to success for Sutton and the Bulldogs.

80,897 had camped and tramped their way to the ground, 80 % of them supporting the Bulldogs who were determined to become the first of the teams admitted in 1925 to win a VFL Flag.

They went wild when the siren sounded, reserving special cheers for Sutton, and for centre-halfback Ted Whitten.

Rover John Kerr, with 24 accurate kicks, was best on the ground, along with full-forward Jack Collins whose seven goals equalled the best in a Grand Final.

Footscray won, 15.12 (102) to Melbourne 7.9 (51).→

WEG on the Bulldog's win.

Charlie Sutton is the pride of Footscray

Sept. 25. Charlie Sutton is Footscray. His big heart pulses for the club and he backs it up with plenty of muscle and inspiration for his players. He cranked up the Footscray team which took the Premiership from an ordinarily talented side into an almost fanatical unit which would not allow itself to be beaten.

Captain-coach Sutton's efforts today were typical of the man. He told his players to concentrate on the ball and declared: 'I'll look after the rough stuff.'

He gave a few Melbourne players the benefit of the weight of his 'pocket tank' tackles to let them know that the Footscray boys meant business. And, despite the fact that he has been sidelined with injury for the last few weeks, he played with the skill that has earned him a State jumper 18 times.

'Resting' in the forward pocket, instead of playing his usual back pocket position, he booted three invaluable goals.

No matter that laconic full-forward Jack Collins kicked 7.3, that rover John Kerr played the game of his life or that Ted Whitten was a rock at centre half-back. It was Charlie's game.

He has always played it hard, but when he crossed over from his local team at Spotswood in 1942 (two hours before his zone was handed over to South Melbourne) he didn't have the meat on his frame to cause much trouble. He took a few years to establish his place in the side, but once he had seized the back pocket he made it his own with his hard bumping style and his fearless dashes down the ground.

A genuine local boy, he has always been a club man, mixing his loyalties only with his growing contract business and his family. He describes his wife, Chubby, as 'one out of the box' and has three girls and a boy – 'a young Bulldog'.

When he was given the coaching job three years ago he put the club to the fore, and instilled the same loyalty in his players – the loyalty that brought the Grand Final win.

He hates fair weather supporters, and recently welcomed those who came to the rooms after a loss against Collingwood.

'Glad to see you here', Sutton told the gathering, 'particularly as we were beaten today.'

'As I keep saying to the boys. "Stick to the club. The club will never let you down." '

Charlie's coaching addresses are straightforward – like the man. He talks from the heart, and he hits home. His main pre-game advice is: 'Forget names and reputations. Have confidence in yourself. You can do it.' He has been a good tactician, but he doesn't like moving young players when they are not doing well. 'It upsets their confidence', he says (→31/7/57).

A toast to the Bulldog hero, Charlie Sutton .

1955

April 15. Tom McNeill who played eight games with St Kilda in 1951-52 has returned from England after studying conditions and contracts of professional footballers in Europe determined to form a footballers' union (→ 28/10).

April 16. Doug Beasy, Carlton half-forward says that as a forward he likes the new 15-yard penalty rule against players delaying proceedings because it speeds up play.

April 25. South Melbourne create a mascot record when 15 kids in uniform lead team out after half time against Fitzroy. It works; they win: 16.11 (107) to 9.15 (69) (→ 11/5/79).

April 30. Ron Barassi tells the *Sporting Globe* that at age six he told his Mum his ambitions were to play for Melbourne, and retire at 45 (→ 5/4/60).

May 7. Hawthorn score a rare victory over Collingwood at Glenferrie coming from 14 points behind at three-quarter time - winning 12.12 (84) to 12.3 (75) (→ 23/4/62).

May 9. Doctors operating on John Coleman's knee have decided to remove the cartilage as well as floating pieces of bone. They say it won't affect his play if and when he is able to return (→ 11/4/56).

May 21. At North Melbourne Second 18s (instead of Thirds) tried as 'curtain raiser' to main game for first time (→ 23/3/81).

June 1. Hawthorn say they will pay junior clubs £10 for each player who transfers and plays a senior game.

July 14. Laurie Icke and Mick Grambeau have been reinstated and resume training at North Melbourne after farcical suspension by Committee. The players were alleged not to have tried hard enough in North's recent defeat, 10.8 (68) to 8.13 (61), by bottom side St Kilda.

Oct. 28. VFL decides to object to Australian Football Players' Union registration (→ 29/11).

Nov. 29. VFL has briefed QC to oppose registration of AFPU (→ 21/6/63).

Debuts
John Dugdale (N. Melb)
Ray Gabelich (Coll)
Allan Jeans (St K)
Kevin Murray (Fitz)

Retirements
Les Foote (St K)
Des Healey (Coll)
Lou Richards (Coll)
Bob Rose (Coll)

15-yard penalty to stop interference

March 21. The VFL has brought in a rule designed to prevent time wasting on the field and interference with players who have taken a mark or been awarded a free kick. From now on umpires will have the power to award a 15-yard penalty against the offending player.

The rule has been brought in mainly to stop players holding the man who has marked the ball to allow time for their team-mates to pick up their men. Another time-wasting tactic is to play on for a few seconds, or to relay the ball back via a few team-mates (→ 16/4).

Tony Ongarello lines up a place kick

May 7. After an epidemic of bad kicking in the Fitzroy and Geelong game, with 11 behinds in a row scored in the first quarter, Fitzroy's wayward full-forward Tony Ongarello resorted to a couple of place kicks. To hoots of derision from the Fitzroy supporters the first one wobbled through for a goal.

Fewer hoots greeted the second effort, which was a perfectly executed 'placer' worthy of Albert Thurgood. Despite these heroics Fitzroy still lost, 10.13 (73) to Geelong's 11.17 (83).

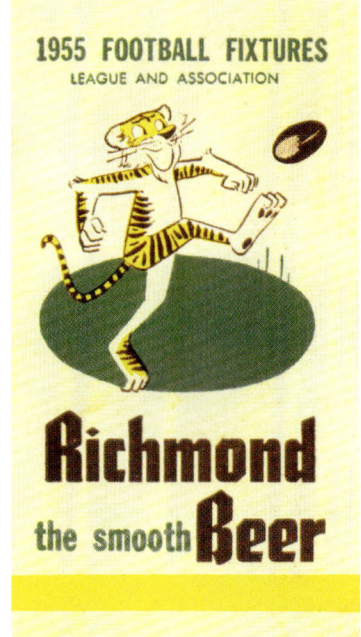

Magpies stop Demons in 'match of year'

Demons' brew: Barassi, Williams, McMahen, Smith, McGivern and Marquis.

July 2. Just when it seemed that no team would be able to beat Melbourne, Collingwood managed to be in front when the siren went.

After ten successive wins Melbourne have lost their first match.

In round seven South Melbourne were 29 points up with less than ten minutes to go, but could only watch while the Demons kicked five goals to win, 11.6 (72) to 10.11 (71).

Two weeks ago Melbourne were 25 points behind at three-quarter time against Richmond but kicked 7.6 to win, 13.16 (94) to 11.12 (78).

But in a pressure game before 33,000 at Victoria Park it was the Magpies who came from behind to beat an inaccurate Melbourne 7.6 (48) to 5.15 (45).

The *Sporting Globe* reported that the last quarter was 'the cream of football. The kicking was beautiful, the marking almost perfect on both sides and when the ball hit the ground the vigorous tackling was real he-man stuff'.

Defenders Lerrel Sharp and Ron Kingston, wingman Des Healey, and forwards Murray Weideman, Bob Rose and Lou Richards starred for the Magpies. For Melbourne, defenders Don Williams and John Beckwith, and rucks Denis Cordner and Ron Barassi took the honours (→ 21/7/56).

Lou Richards and Les Foote are kings of the kids at State school.

'Dark horse' wins Brownlow Medal

Fred Goldsmith: pipped the favourite.

Aug. 31. South Melbourne's full-back Fred Goldsmith won the Brownlow Medal by one vote from frequent bridesmaid, and 1954 winner, Essendon's Bill Hutchison.

Journalists, who had lined up interviews with the favourites, were caught on the hop.

Luckily the Victorian full back was on duty at the Eastern Hill fire station, and could indicate that, having come third in his club's best and fairest, and in the *Sporting Globe* awards, he should have been rated more highly.

Dogs miss Finals by less than a whisker

Aug. 20. Footscray have missed out on a place in the Final Four by an agonising 0.6 of a per cent. It's by that tiny margin that Essendon are in there instead. Each team has had 12 wins and six losses, finishing the home-and-away series on 48 points.

Towards the end of the season every point scored for and against became crucial. It was here that Essendon edged up the closest advantage in the history of the fourth place tussle. Going into Round 18, Footscray, trailing Essendon by 3.1 per cent, met North and Essendon played Hawthorn. Both contenders won well, but the arithmetic of margins put the Dons that tiny fraction ahead of the Dogs.

Dashing Demons grasp Flag

Sept. 17. Melbourne gave a display of disciplined power football to outlast a tenacious Collingwood in a torrid Grand Final. The Demons were seven points up at the last change and went on to win, 8.16 (64) to 5.6 (36).

The game finally swung the Demons' way after the horrendous crash between Collingwood wingman Des Healey and Melbourne's young 19th man Frank 'Bluey' Adams late in the final quarter.

Healey was in full flight with the ball down the outer wing when Adams ran on to the ground as a replacement and crashed into him.

Both players were pole-axed and had to be stretchered from the ground, leaving umpire Harry Beitzel to sort out an ugly melee between the Demons and the aggrieved Collingwood players.

While the injured were being taken off, Ian Ridley booted Melbourne's seventh goal, and shortly afterwards Noel Clarke kicked the sealer. Collingwood were down to 17 players.

Best for Melbourne in the bruising encounter were Denis Cordner, Ron Barassi, Peter Marquis and Ian McLean, while Collingwood's were Jack Hamilton, Bobby Rose, Des Healey and Neil Mann (→ 15/9/56).

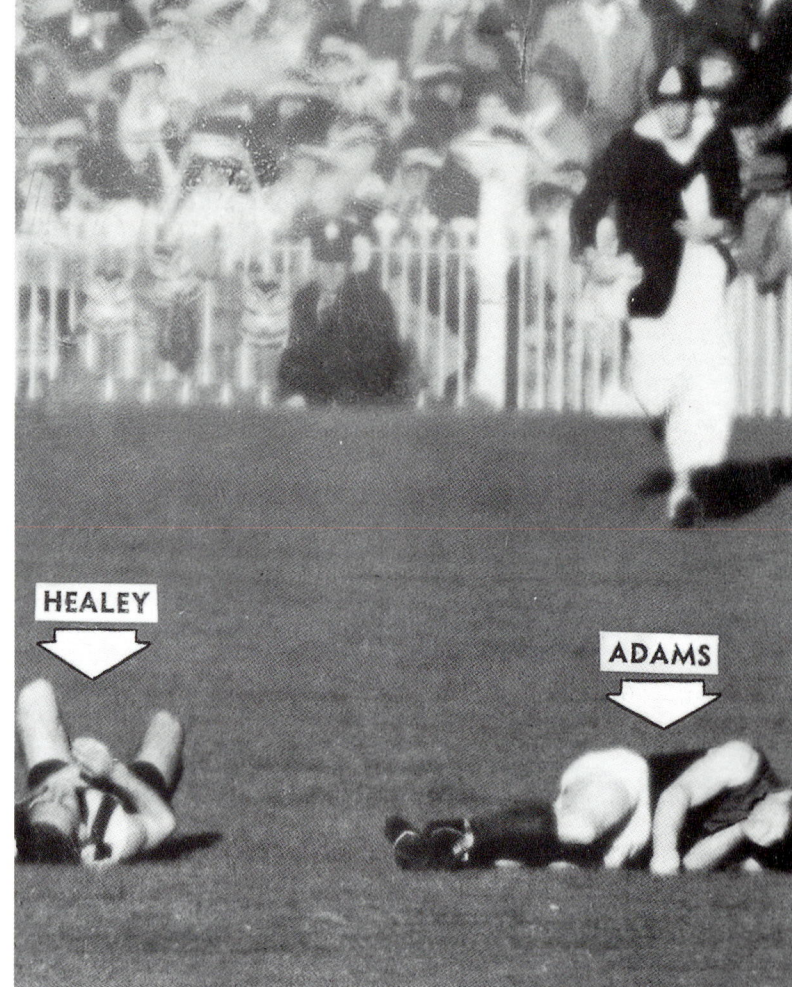

After their horrendous last-term collision, Des Healey of Collingwood and Melbourne 19th man Frank 'Bluey' Adams lie unconscious on the ground.

1955 Statistics

Leading Goalkicker:
Noel Rayson (Geel) 80
Brownlow Medallist:
Fred Goldsmith (S. Melb)
Finals: First Semi-final Geel 9.7 (61) Ess 7.11 (53); **Second Semi-final** Melb 8.8 (56) Coll 6.9 (45); **Preliminary Final** Coll 14.12 (96) Geel 13.6 (84); **Grand Final** Melb 8.16 (64) Coll 5.6 (36)

Ladder:	W	L	%	pts
Melb	15	3	150.5	60
Coll	14	4	127.5	56
Geel	14	4	122.8	56
Ess	12	6	130.6	48
Foots	12	6	130.0	48
Rich	9	9	106.1	36
Carl	9	9	98.6	36
Haw	8	10	94.0	32
Fitz	6	12	88.5	24
S. Melb	5	13	87.8	20
N. Melb	3	15	76.3	12
St K	1	17	45.4	4

The coaches, Phonse Kyne of Collingwood and Norm Smith of Melbourne have been opponents on and off the ground. They are in good spirits as they wish each other luck.

Despite a desperate attempt by Ron Barassi to block the kick, Collingwood defender Neville Waller gets the ball forward in the Grand Final at the Melbourne Cricket Ground.

1956

The football passion of Saint Killigrew revives the faithful

May 26. Allan Killigrew, football's hot-gospeller, has revived passions at St Kilda in a way that could well lift the club off the bottom of the ladder and turn the wooden spooners into a force in the League.

If the man himself is any example, the Saints' new coach has all the right ingredients to inspire his team on to greater heights. Killigrew was a rover in the St Kilda side that last made the Finals in 1939. He was a courageous player who, after the war, won a battle with tuberculosis of the spine.

It is this fighting spirit, coupled with a great love for the club, that Killigrew brings to St Kilda. But there is more than sentiment to this emotional man. He displayed a necessary ruthlessness by slashing the club's player list, retaining only 16 players from last year and adding 29 new names.

'Nobody is going to laugh at St Kilda,' he declared. Since the drastic culling, player morale at the club has risen noticeably, as have their performances on the field. Killigrew has also embarked upon a shrewd recruiting campaign that is already starting to show benefits. His inspirational match addresses and ability to communicate with players make Killigrew the right man for football's toughest job (→ 11/5/63).

Alan Killigrew exhorts the St Kilda faithful to cheer the Saints on to victory.

Coleman retires, has lost 'spring'

April 11. John Coleman has announced his retirement from League football. The greatest full-forward since the war has lost his necessary spring. Despite strenuous efforts at recovery, he has decided that the knee injured in 1954 will not even now stand up to the rigors of playing in the League.

Coleman played 98 games, and kicked 537 goals – an average of over five goals a match. He played in the 1949 and 1950 Premierships and no player has been more sorely missed by all football supporters.

Coleman, who trained as recently as last night, said: 'the knee has given me some trouble, and I could not stretch out with confidence. I realise now that I would be foolish to risk permanent injury by trying to play' (→ 6/4/61).

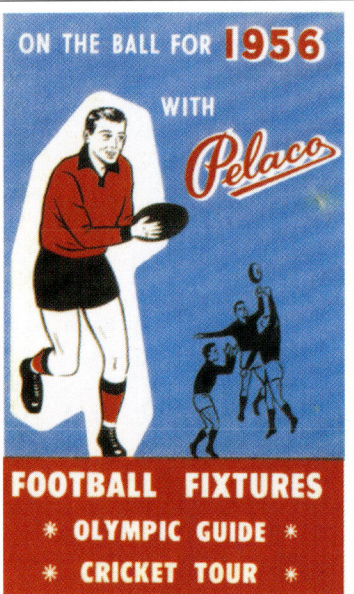

ON THE BALL FOR **1956** WITH *Pelaco*

FOOTBALL FIXTURES
* OLYMPIC GUIDE *
* CRICKET TOUR *

A sporting bonanza is coming in this Olympic Year, and the footy fixtures are augmented with a guide to the Olympics and the Test cricket tour to England.

Johnson blinded in football accident

June 9. A *Sporting Globe* appeal fund for young North Melbourne fullback Brian Johnson has reached the sum of £10,000.

Johnson is blind in the right eye after an accident in the opening match at Arden Street. He has blurred vision in the left eye, but it is expected that this will improve.

Accidents have been in the news lately. Last week Geelong rover Peter Pianto went down in a head clash with team-mate Bob Davis, and Fitzroy captain Bill Stephen was so concerned that he stayed with Pianto and tended to him until he was in the trainer's hands.

Today young Hawthorn ruckman John Kennedy requested that he go back on the field after half time. The request was denied. Kennedy had a broken arm (→ 27/4/57).

Dogs and Blues scrap over Four

Aug. 18. A huge crowd of 45,000 came to see which side would make it into fourth place this season – Carlton or Footscray. The Dogs had had a gruelling struggle to earn this chance to bump the Blues off the rung. When the Dogs took the lead in the second term they held on with a classic defensive display for the rest of the game, with Ted Whitten repulsing the Blues' attacks from centre-halfback. Footscray dislodged the Blues from the 1956 Finals, 8.14 (62) to 6.9 (45) (→ 28/4/58).

Bad temper on show under bad lights

Sept. 17. South won the League's inaugural night Premiership tonight, defeating Carlton 13.16 (94) to 13.10 (88). The night series has been described as a 'loser's championship highlighted by beer and brawls' as it comprises the eight teams outside the Four, but that did not prevent a night record of 32,450 roaring their support.

They were better lit up than the oval – taking advantage of legal beer outside the six o'clock swill. Uneven lighting and brawls were also featured (→ 27/9/60).

Ray Gabelich models the Olympic exhibition match uniform.

Demons a thrashing machine

Denis Cordner v Laurie Rymer.

Sept. 15. A Melbourne and Collingwood Grand Final is football's 'top-of-the-bill' offering and it drew an amazing crowd of 115,802 people to the MCG today.

The anticipation was high, but the event was a boilover. Only Demons' supporters could leave the ground fulfilled, after watching a great team overwhelm a dazed opposition, weakened by a tough series of Finals. The result was a 73-point win, 17.19 (121) to 6.12 (48).

Collingwood had no answer to Melbourne's strong following division, with Denis Cordner and Bob Johnson too tall for Neil Mann and Ray Gabelich, and with Ron Barassi repeatedly ripping the ball out of the centre. Stuart Spencer roved well, and was devastating in the forward pocket, kicking five goals.

Melbourne's 'decoy' full-forward Athol Webb kicked five goals himself and created diversions to assist Spencer and Bob Johnson, who kicked three goals while 'resting'.

Melbourne's centre line of Brian Dixon, Ken Melville and 'Bluey' Adams was supreme. The defence seemed too strong and mobile for the Collingwood forwards, although Murray Weideman at centre-half-forward and flanker Bill Serong fought hard.

Collingwood's stars of the Preliminary Final win over Footscray – Bill and Mick Twomey, fullback Harry Sullivan, wingman Thorold Merrett and full-forward Ken Smale – were all well down (→ 21/9/57).

The huge crowd of 115,802 has nowhere to go but over the boundary.

1956 Statistics

Leading Goalkicker:
Bill Young (St K) 56
Brownlow Medallist:
Peter Box (Foots)
Finals: First Semi-final Geel 6.5 (41) Foots 5.13 (43); **Second Semi-final** Melb 11.14 (80) Coll 8.16 (64); **Preliminary Final** Coll 15.6 (96) Foots 7.15 (57); **Grand Final** Melb 17.19 (121) Coll 6.12 (48)

Ladder:	W	L	D	%	pts
Melb	16	2		146.0	64
Coll	13	5		125.9	52
Geel	13	5		121.9	52
Foots	11	7		114.2	44
Carl	10	7	1	113.7	42
Ess	10	8		95.8	40
Haw	7	10	1	88.9	30
Fitz	7	11		89.3	28
S. Melb	6	11	1	88.1	26
Rich	6	12		86.8	24
St K	4	13	1	88.0	18
N. Melb	3	15		69.6	12

A Brownlow out of the Dog Box

Aug. 22. With 22 votes to his credit, Footscray's champion centreman Peter Box has won the Brownlow Medal by a clear margin of six, from Geelong rover Peter Pianto on 16 and South Melbourne defender Jim Dorgan, 15.

Box was at home with his wife, and unaware of his victory until an excited neighbour knocked on the door, having heard the results on the radio.

Peter Box, 24, will have the unique honour of receiving his Brownlow Medal at a presentation on the MCG arena before the start of the First Semi-final against Geelong on Saturday. Winning the medal crowns a determined struggle by Box to get back into League football after suffering severe cuts to one leg in 1952, when he was knocked from his motorbike by a car.

The Cordner football dynasty

The two great players in the first years of the short-lived League club, University, were the brothers Cordner, Harry and Edward.

They were both medical students who owed allegiance to the University, although Harry had his first season at Melbourne, while a schoolboy at Melbourne Grammar. He would play school football on Wednesday and then League Football on Saturday.

A strong marking forward, he kicked seven goals in a match against Geelong. He played 29 games as a centre and forward, before medical duties in Western Australia claimed him.

Edward Cordner was the pillar of the defence for the University team, playing 60 games between 1908 and 1912. He ended his football career as his medical work demanded more of his time.

They were both strong and handsome men, fair haired, square jawed and resolute in the way they played the game and conducted themselves.

It is too difficult at the distance to judge their relative worth as players, but Edward was the one who left a legacy to Australian Football in the shape of four sons who played for the Melbourne Football Club.

The Cordner boys were in the mould of their father, students at Melbourne Grammar, good looking, fair haired, tall and strong. In their school football they came under the guidance of E.C.H. 'Bully' Taylor, regarded as the doyen of school coaches, and a committeeman of the Melbourne Football Club (also author of the club's centenary history).

There was never a doubt that the Cordners were destined to play for Melbourne.

The first to appear at the Melbourne Cricket Ground were Ted and Don, who were both medical students and playing amateur football for the University.

Ted was a dashing defender and made an immediate impact, but his career was cut short as he entered naval service as a doctor in 1943. He was a very strong mark and an excellent kick, the

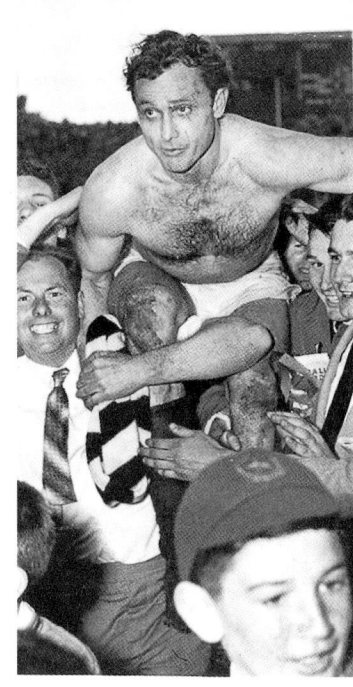

Denis Cordner: 1955 Finals star.

best of the Cordner brothers.

Ted had such a good season in 1943 that, had a Brownlow Medal been awarded, many judges believe he would have won it. He played 51 games for Melbourne before finishing his football with Old Melburnians in the strong amateur competition.

Don made his debut in the 1941 semi-final and at that stage had only played football in the under-19 amateur competition. The Demons were casting around for someone to match the high marking in the Carlton side and the young Cordner had shown out in practice against the brilliant centre half-forward Ron Baggott.

He continued with Melbourne and his medical studies, graduating as a doctor in 1945. By that time he was one of the outstanding followers in the League.

When he won the Brownlow Medal in 1946 Percy Beames wrote in *The Age*: 'As a mark, taking height and safety into consideration, I would say he has never been surpassed. He has a magnificent leap, rare judgment and steel-like fingers.'

He added, in a statement that might sum up feelings on all the

The Cordners at home: father Edward with sons Denis, Don, Ted and John.

Cordners: 'He is an ornament to the code and exemplifies everything that is fine and decent in the game.'

But there was still more to come. Denis Cordner had been blooded in 1943, most notably by being 'collected' by Richmond's Jack Dyer in his first game. After navy service and three years in the amateurs he re-appeared in 1948 – in a Grand Final. A weekend before he had stood on a beer keg as captain-coach of University Blacks and told his team that unless they won they wouldn't get a drop of it.

They won.

He was snatched to play centre-half-back in the drawn 1948 Grand Final, and the replay in which Melbourne were easy winners. He played well, but never played the position again, becoming an icon in the following division and finishing his career in 1956 after 152 games.

Cordner was cool and laconic on the field, noted for stopping to a walk as soon as he left the players race. But he was always where he should be, and was a fine mark, a good tap ruckman and an outstanding team player.

He was rated a great wet wea-

ther player, and his marking technique in the wet, in which he funnelled the ball down his fingers and arms to his chest has never been successfully emulated.

Although Don won the Brownlow, Denis was held by many at Melbourne to be an even better player. He was a regular State representative, Melbourne's best and fairest in 1950 and 1954 and captain from 1951 to 1953, until he relinquished the post.

The fourth brother John played six games in 1951 and could have gone on, but science studies and a post in nuclear science in England took priority.

A stir ran through the Melbourne club and its supporters in the early 1980's when another Cordner appeared on the scene.

David was the son of Ted, recruited from Old Melburnians. He was in the mould – tall, fair haired and with a tremendous spring.

He kicked 119 goals in the under 19's in his first season, but he was dogged by injuries and was never able to live up to his early promise.

He played 53 games for Melbourne between 1983 and 1987, and then six for Sydney.

The incredible lightness of being Coleman

For a generation of small boys and big barrackers, John Coleman epitomised what Australian football was all about. In just 98 games of League football he did something improbable in each one - and something impossible in most of them. Seeing the impossible on a regular basis gave followers of all club persuasions a reason to go to the footy. Coleman drew crowds between 1949 and 1954 like no other player.

That is why those few lucky enough to witness his debut performance of 12 goals against Hawthorn in 1949 took away an indelible 'I was there' memory of a legend starting work.

Around Essendon in the 1950s fathers would drive slowly past the shrine in which Coleman had an interest, saying to their wide-eyed sons - 'That's Coleman's pub.'

Looking at the Coleman cult makes it all the more remarkable that there was such a lack of interest shown by Essendon in the young goal kicker. Perhaps it had something to do with being a late bloomer in the scoring department.

Coleman couldn't even make the primary school team at Port Fairy, where he was born in 1928. He lived there on the west coast until moving to Ascot Vale and the Essendon catchment area at the age of 12.

As a schoolboy he played for St Thomas's in the Footscray District League and for University High School.

Pale and skinny but tall and intense, Coleman played all over the ground developing his marking, if not kicking skills.

At 16 his parents moved to Hastings where he began a Bradman-like orgy of scoring - kicking 136 in 1947, and 160 in 1948, including one bag of 23 goals.

The 'Dons had him by then on a Form Four, but in the few practice games that he played in those years his erstwhile teammates wouldn't pass to him, and he didn't show any scoring form.

Coleman was nearly 20 and felt that if he couldn't get a go with the Bombers he would stand out for a year and play for Richmond.

In the first practice match in 1949 he was again starved of opportunities. *Herald* football writer Alf Brown blasted the selfish Essendon players, with good effect because in the next game they made a point of kicking to him.

He kicked a bag, forcing the selectors to give him a chance. Coleman was picked in the first game of 1949.

Early in his career he had a solitary attack of vertigo.

The story is told that he raced in behind a pack and sprang early, and found himself hovering at the back of the flying footballers. He propelled himself still further into the air off the hips and backs of the players ahead of him. He soared to meet the ball, grasping it firmly - and looked about.

Coleman discovered that he was at a terrifying height, his feet 10 feet from the ground, his head a good 16 feet, and that it was a long and dangerous drop. He let go the ball in fear and crashed to the ground.

After that event, in all his sky-scraping marks, he obeyed the cardinal rule of sky climbers and never looked down.

Reports of Coleman's flying ability rivalled those of Smithy. Secretary of the WAFL Bill Orr said in 1949 'Man or ghost he is the best forward I have ever seen. Yet he isn't seen, he isn't even remembered by the players, but suddenly like a flash of light he illuminates the whole scene. He hurls himself into the air with incredible precision.'

Coleman's lack of weight (just over 12 stone) seemed to be a kind of weightlessness, and seemed to have something to do with his ability to fly so high.

Opposition players often remarked on his flying feats. Tough North Melbourne back pocket Pat Kelly said in 1950 that on one occasion he 'looked up for the ball and I was flabbergasted to see the stop-studded soles of Coleman's boots. He had jumped clean over my head.'

Although he could fly Coleman was no angel. For someone who had nerveless physical skills, he

John Coleman flies high again.

had a very short emotional fuse.

This was undoubtedly primed by the 'treatment' he received from some of the toughest full back ever to play the game - hard men such as Mopsy Fraser, Ollie Grieve, and Norm Johnstone.

They thought he was susceptible to the 'needle' - which he sometimes was. But the 'needle' rarely stopped him kicking a bag of goals.

In one game in 1951 Coleman was reported by two boundary umpires, after Geelong players had dealt with him in a scrimmage and nothing was done. Coleman told one to 'shut up' and the other one to 'pull your head in'. He was reported for misconduct in that he disputed a decision.

The ingenious defence was that Coleman could not dispute a decision because boundary umpires do not make decisions. The field umpire said Coleman had not disputed any of *his* decisions and so he was reprieved.

But not without a parting shot from the Chairman of the Tribunal, Dr William McLelland, that his conduct was 'reprehensible'.

This feeling about the great man might have had some bearing on the sentence when Coleman re-appeared a few weeks later, reported for retaliating to some treatment from Carlton's

Harry Caspar. Both players received four weeks which was of no account to Carlton and Caspar, but which almost certainly cost Essendon the Flag.

Once in 1950 Coleman was having trouble with Tiger Mopsy Fraser, and coach Reynolds perhaps for the only time actually moved him away before half time.

At the interval Coleman confronted Reynolds and said, 'Do you think I'm a blasted squib? You put me back on Mopsy and I'll get the damned goals'. Which he did - five in the third quarter set up an Essendon win.

In 1954 he injured his knee playing against North Melbourne, the week after he kicked his career best tally of 14.5 against Fitzroy.

At first the injury was thought to be just a bad strain, and after a cartilage operation, and 1955 off, he began training again in 1956.

But he could not put pressure on the knee, and feeling he had lost his legendary leap Coleman retired on 11 April 1956, to concentrate on business.

In 1961 he reluctantly became coach of Essendon after some back room work.

Coleman was a fitness fanatic, a strict disciplinarian, a hard worker of the players, and an imaginative and shrewd tactician.

Essendon won the 1962 Premiership in Coleman's second year, and did it again in 1965.

The mid-sixties are regarded by some as an era of 'foot brawl' but it was also the era where Coleman built a skilful and direct team.

Coleman retired as coach at the end of the 1967 season. Illness and trouble with the knee had kept him from his best as coach in 1966 and 1967.

John Coleman died of a heart attack at the tragically early age of 45, on April 5, 1973.

He won two Flags with his boot, another two with his brain, and lost one with his temper. He was one of the all-time greats.

Coleman is alive as the image of Australian football that comes to mind, even in people who never saw him play.

April 22. Opening round shocks as Fitzroy beat reigning Premiers Melbourne 7.11 (53) to 6.14 (50); Hawthorn beat Carlton 15.12 (102) to 10.6 (66) and Essendon defeat Collingwood 13.15 (93) to 8.10 (58).

April 27. Hawthorn disappointed by news that outstanding recruit, ruckman John Winneke, won't play, as he has law lectures on training nights (→ 14/4/60).

April 27. Collingwood rover Lloyd Williams breaks leg at MCG and lies in agony while 12-minute search is made for stretchers, locked away since Olympics. He is carried off on a table top (→ 24/4/65).

May 11. Fitzroy have 51 shots at goal in losing to Richmond, 16.10 (106) to 10.31 (91) (→ 27/4/68).

June 1. Hawthorn a Flag hope after defeating Footscray, 11.11 (77) to 7.8 (50), and going to top of Ladder.

June 8. Essendon full-forward Fred Gallagher kicks 12 goals in win over Geelong, 21.12 (138) to 15.12 (102).

July 13. Melbourne escape with draw against Collingwood, 6.13 (49) to 7.7 (49), after Ian Ridley snaps goal on siren.

July 13. Ted Whitten rejects £2000 offer to coach Swan Districts - said to be the richest ever bid for a Victorian footballer.

July 16. Umpire Harry Beitzel speaks in defence of Noel Teasdale, a player he reported. Teasdale of North is out for two weeks instead of four.

July 20. Lou Richards calls for an end to 'empty Saturdays' by scheduling 'unwanted' interstate games at the end of the season (→ 20/6/59).

July 27. Umpire Frank Schwab is pelted with bottles and rubbish by Essendon supporters after a controversial free kick gives the winning goal to Melbourne, 11.7 (73) to 9.18 (72) (→ 27/5/59).

Debuts
Neville Crowe (Rich)
Alan Morrow (St K)
John Nicholls (Carl)

Retirements
Peter Box (Foots)
Jack Hamilton (Coll)
Ken Hands (Carl)
Bill Hutchison (Ess)
Peter Pianto (Geel)
Jock Spencer (N.Melb)
Bill Stephen (Fitz)

Television brings footy home out of the cold

April 1. The League has decided to allow television stations ABV2, HSV7 and GTV9 to broadcast the last quarters of three matches each Saturday afternoon this season.

Each League ground with the will be visited at some stage during the season.

The Manager of HSV7, Keith Cairns, said that three cameras with different lenses for close-ups and wide shots would telecast each game from a special stand, with a director in a van outside selecting the best picture at any moment.

Tony Charlton has been appointed the first commentator for HSV7, Ian Johnson for GTV9 and Ken Dakin for ABV2.

Cairns said that HSV7 had gained valuable experience with the outdoor 'telecast' of the demonstration game at the Olympics, and rehearsed with 'closed circuit' telecasts of three finals last year.

These telecasts removed all fears that Australian football is too fast for effective viewing (→ 20/3/61).

Football is back, and this winter it's on the box in the corner.

Gorillas to Lions

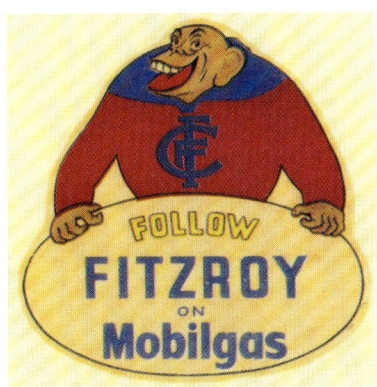

No longer in style at Fitzroy.

May 30. Fitzroy have a new name. They will now officially be known as the Lions, a name the club believes fits in with their traditional never-say-die spirit.

The club symbol has long been a subject of contention at Fitzroy. Previously the club had adopted the Gorillas as a name to supplement the Maroons and the Roys, which were not thought to be stirring enough. Fitzroy dropped the Gorilla tag in 1952 after rival supporters kept referring to Fitzroy as 'Apes'.

The club has redesigned the lion emblem for its official products.

Sutton sacked in Footscray furore

July 31. Charlie Sutton, peremptorily dismissed as Footscray coach on July 9, shook hands with new coach Ted Whitten before the away game at St Kilda on July 13.

But Sutton was humiliated by Footscray, being refused admittance to the rooms on the pretext that he might upset the new coach.

He was not permitted by officials to to congratulate Wally Donald on his 200th game during half time in the game against Carlton, which they lost 11.13 (79) to 7.10 (52).

Charlie Sutton's wife, Chubby, says that the club's treatment of a faithful servant is disgraceful. She says Sutton has given his all to the team, at great cost to herself and the children, and now he has been discarded like an old pair of footy socks.

New Blues are Denis Strauch, Leo Brereton and John Nicholls.

Demons take hat trick with 61-point win

Bob Johnson and Geoff Leek.

Sept. 21. Outplaying Essendon all over the ground, a magnificent Melbourne won their third Premiership in a row today by a massive 61 points.

The crowd of 100,324 people saw an unequal game in which the Demons were not only stronger physically, but backing up much better as a team. They beat the Bombers in the air and used their dynamic half-back line to frustrate Essendon's attempts to reach goal.

A key player for Melbourne was ruck-rover Ron Barassi. Unsettling the Dons with his vigour, he kicked four goals in the first half. Meanwhile, the dominance of Melbourne's young defenders, John Lord and Dick Fenton-Smith, was leaving the Essendon full-forward flat-footed.

Another Demon of note was John Beckwith, who allayed fears concerning a leg injury by playing a magnificent captain's game. He stood supreme in defence. The second half saw explosive pace and beautiful long kicking by half-forward flanker Geoff Tunbridge, the Ballarat school teacher who still insists on playing for no pay except 8d per mile to drive his Volkswagen from his home and back.

Essendon seemed unable to combine as a team. Clever work by Jack Clarke and others in the centre was nullified when only three Bomber forwards contested with five Demon defenders. Often panicked by the bustling Demons, the Essendon forwards were frequently out of position, or were wasting effort by vying with each other for possession.

In an attempt to break the spell of Melbourne's superiority, Essendon put two rovers on the ball – but all to no avail. Right on the final siren Barassi, who had scored the Demons' first goal of the day, marked and kicked the last.

Melbourne won 17.14 (116) to 7.13 (55) (→ 26/9/59).

Bob Suter can't stop Barassi.

Hawks' first Finals

Aug. 31. In their first ever appearance in a Finals game, Hawthorn today defeated Carlton to win the first Semi-final by 23 points.

The Hawks have enhanced their Premiership chances, showing they have the skill and judgement to use the big MCG. They made clever use of the wind in the first quarter to open up an advantage that was never lost. Several Carlton attacks broke down through over-eagerness and the greasy conditions that followed a severe hailstorm. Hawthorn won easily, 10.11 (71) to 6.12 (48).

That's the ticket

Aug. 9. For the first time football fans will be able to reserve tickets for all League Finals.

Following negotiations between the League and the Melbourne Cricket Ground trustees, 89,915 seats for each Final will be available at Allans and six sub-agents in the city from 22 August. Written applications for tickets can be made now. Country people can book combined travel and admittance tickets. The new arrangements are expected to end the traditional overnight queues outside the MCG (→ 28/6/61).

1957 Statistics

Leading Goalkicker:
Jack Collins (Foots) 74

Brownlow Medallist:
Brian Gleeson (St K)

Finals: First Semi-final Haw 10.11 (71) Carl 6.12 (48); **Second Semi-final** Melb 8.19 (67) Ess 12.11 (83) **Preliminary Final** Melb 22.12 (144) Haw 11.10 (76); **Grand Final** Ess 7.13 (55) Melb 17.14 (116)

Ladder:	W	L	D	%	pts
Melb	12	5	1	138.8	50
Ess	11	7		118.3	44
Haw	11	7		116.7	44
Carl	11	7		99.5	44
Coll	9	8	1	101.8	38
Foots	9	8	1	99.1	38
Rich	9	9		93.9	36
N. Melb	8	10		95.1	32
St K	8	10		94.5	32
S. Melb	7	11		88.8	28
Fitz	6	12		84.1	24
Geel	5	12	1	88.2	22

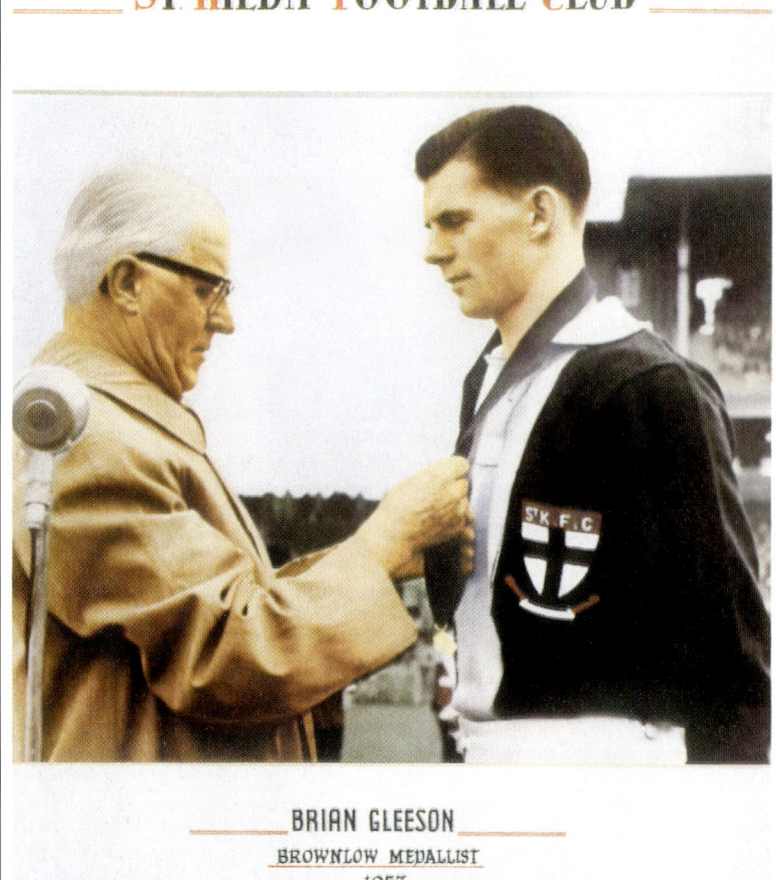

ST KILDA FOOTBALL CLUB

BRIAN GLEESON
BROWNLOW MEDALLIST
1957

Brian Gleeson of St Kilda receives the Brownlow Medal from K.G. Luke.

1958

100 years of football celebrated – 'greatest winter game'

Aug. 7. The Prime Minister, Mr Menzies, opened the Centenary Carnival of the 'greatest winter game' at the Melbourne Cricket Ground in July.

But the truest centenary occurred today, when teams from Melbourne Grammar School and Scotch College re-enacted what is regarded as the first game of Australian football, between the two schools on August 7, 1858. That match was declared a draw after three afternoons of play.

Dressed in cricket flannels and caps, approximating the football garb of last century, the teams put on an unruly but spirited display before a small crowd at the MCG.

Victoria won the major section of the Carnival, contested by the 'football States' and the VFA. The minor section was won by a combined amateur side, over Canberra, Queensland and NSW.

Old Scotch and Melbourne Grammar students in the re-enactment game.

Head count called for as Essendon suspects a 19th. man

Aug. 16. Essendon captain Jack Clarke demanded a last-quarter count of North Melbourne players. If they had more than 18 on the field North would have forfeited their score. Jeers from North supporters greeted the result: the numbers were right and North's victory assured.

The Essendon mistake came when John Waddington raced on immediately Brian Martyn was felled in the centre, but Waddington was replacing Albert Mantello, who had already left. North won, 11.14 (80) to Essendon's 8.14 (62).

The players line up, and the numbers add up, in the head count at Windy Hill.

Geelong Flyer leaves on a high note

Sept. 30. Bob Davis has ended his playing career as a senior citizen of football – captain of Victoria and Geelong and nominated captain of the hypothetical All-Australian side.

It has been a heady climb for a man with phenomenal football talent, but with a knockabout sense of humour that could convulse the Cats' dressing room. His distinctive, wholehearted laugh has echoed around the place for 10 years.

Adoring Cats supporters call him 'Whoofer' or 'The Geelong Flyer'. Like the train of the same name he works up a powerful head of steam, and has the size to crash through most obstacles. He has strong legs and a streamlined physique that seems to fill out the horizontally striped Cats' jumper.

He can mark, but he is not a high flyer. His special technique is in gathering or receiving the ball anywhere between the centre and the goal and winding up a withering run that ends with a shot at goal.

The other strong motor he had is around the mouth area, and he would have plenty to say on the field. Off-field he has always been a great ambassador for Geelong, smartly attired and with a friendly word for everyone.

Davis was a South fan as a boy in Clunes, but the Swans rejected him, and this was Geelong's gain.

He is an irrepressible character, and the young Davis had a lot of fun with his mates at Geelong – often at the expense of coach Reg Hickey.

One of Bob's particular skills was to judge the ball as it was kicked to him at training, do a forward somersault and then come up to his feet and mark the ball.

But he was all business on the field, and never looked like playing in the Seconds. He starred in both the 1951 and '52 Premiership sides, and has been a regular in Victorian teams over the years (→ 10/3/60).

The Geelong Flyer, Bob 'Woofa' Davis, gets into stride during training.

Roberts turns pro and wins Brownlow

Aug. 27. High-marking, good-looking Saint Neil Roberts has won the Brownlow Medal by two votes from Brendan Edwards (Hawthorn) and Bob Skilton (South).

This follows his win in the *Sporting Globe's* Haydn Bunton Memorial Medal last week.

Unlike the Brownlow, the Bunton came with a £100 prize which caused Roberts to turn professional.

Early in his career Roberts seemed an unlikely champion, but a switch from his glamour role on the forward line to centre hal-back in 1955 was the making of him.

Roberts has played over 100 games for the Saints. He is a surfer, skier and 1955 Victorian Pillow Fight champion (→ 18/5/66).

Roberts: The Saints' pin-up boy.

North cling on

Aug. 30. With just a minute or so to go in the First Semi, Fitzroy were in front. North rover Allen Aylett flattened Lion wingman Vin Williams. He groggily took the free and passed to 'Butch' Gale but umpire Bill Barbour made him take the kick again, this time over the mark.

Possession was gained by North, and the ball went down field to Noel Teasdale, who kicked the ball 60 yards for a goal. The siren went as the ball was bounced back in the centre – joy for North, fury for Fitzroy. North won, 10.10 (70) to Fitzroy 9.12 (66) (→ 30/6/62).

Lemon time goal

Aug. 9. South Melbourne wingman Ian Tampion kicked the goal of the season, an 80-yard drop-kick, at St Kilda – during the three-quarter-time huddle. Tampion had been given a free just before the siren went, and thought it too far out to score.

South captain-coach Ron Clegg said, as the huddle formed, that he might as well have a go, so Tampion retrieved the ball from umpire Bill Barbour and drop-kicked a beauty over the heads of the startled St Kilda defenders who hadn't dropped back far enough. South won, 15.9 (99) to 9.23 (77) (→ 22/8/64).

RICHMOND – "The Tigers"

CARLTON – "The Blues"

Magpies stop Demons' run for fourth Flag

It's Phonse Kyne's turn to cheer.

Sept. 20. Changing the players' numbers in the Grand Final, after they were listed in a newspaper without permission, did not stop 97,956 fans recognising which players were responsible for a great Collingwood win.

This 13th Premiership prevented Melbourne winning four in a row.

Magpie coach Phonse Kyne said: 'I feel perhaps the Melbourne players had a little more pressure on them ... we had nothing to lose.'

It was a tough affair compared the pure football of the 'preview' on June 16 when Melbourne, 12.12 (84), beat Collingwood, 10.13 (73), before an record crowd of 99,346.

That game was won through Melbourne's dominance of the air, through big Bob Johnson, Ron Barassi and Don Williams.

Today, it was the Magpies' hard-

No room to spare in, or on, the Southern Stand as the ruckmen do battle in the centre of the MCG.

hitting, play-on style which eventually unsettled the Demons, as well as 'Hooker' Harrison and Murray Weideman 'minding' Ron Barassi.

After a good opening, Melbourne were sucked in and began to overplay the man. They were outscored in the final three quarters to be beaten, 12.10 (82) to 9.10 (64).

Despite many 'incidents', Umpire Nash only made two reports from last-quarter clashes – Barassi for striking Weideman, and Harrison for charging Barassi (→ 6/10/90).

1958 Statistics

Leading Goalkicker:	Ladder:	W	L	%	pts
Ian Brewer (Coll) 73	Melb	15	3	123.7	60
	Coll	12	6	123.7	48
Brownlow Medallist:	Fitz	12	6	120.9	48
Neil Roberts (St K)	N.Melb	11	7	92.7	44
	Ess	10	8	111.3	40
Finals: First Semi-final Fitz 9.12	Haw	9	9	109.3	36
(66) N.Melb. 10.10 (70) **Second**	Carl	8	10	91.9	32
Semi-final Melb 11.12 (78) Coll	St K	7	11	92.2	28
4.9 (33) **Preliminary Final** Coll	S.Melb	7	11	88.7	28
14.12 (96) N.Melb 10.16 (76)	Rich	7	11	88.5	28
Grand Final Melb 9.10 (64) Coll	Foot	6	12	97.3	24
12.10 (82).	Geel	4	14	73.8	16

Ron Barassi (2) waits for Magpie Graeme Fellowes to knock the ball out.

The thinking men of football

In the 1950's Len Smith produced his coaching document, which he entitled 'The Golden Rules'. They were a distillation of decades of playing football, thinking about football and coaching football. They embodied his own successful approach to coaching and that of his more famous brother, the 'Master Coach' Norm Smith.

Rule 1: Get the ball through the goals in the quickest possible manner, but remember that kicking the ball into an opponent is a football sin. (Attacks should be started from the half-back line, and the quickest route to goal employed.)

Rule 2: Two men together at all times.

Rule 3: No packs or crushes.

Rule 4: Crumbs, crumbs, crumbs. (Three out of four possessions are gained by the ball spilling from a pack.)

Rule 5: Play close to an opponent (backmen).

Rule 6: Team spirit, intelligent talking. (Call specific instructions to your team-mates.)

Rule 7: Mind your opponent.

Rule 8: Stand on the mark.

Rule 9: Stop your opponent from playing on.

Rule 10: Tackle opponents in possession of the ball. (Legitimate

The Smith brothers – good footballers, good thinkers, and good mates.

tackling is the only way to take the ball from your opponents.

Len Smith brought along an ordinary Fitzroy team with commonsense rules like this to guide him. His teams became noted for their spirited finishes as he coupled the dictum of Rule 6 with his fine tactical work and a dash of inspiration.

His move to Richmond and the recruiting of fast, skilled six-footers laid the groundwork for

that team's rise to be a force in the 60's.

Norm Smith, more peppery and flamboyant than older brother Len, became famous as the paramount coach of the 50's and early 60's. He took the Demons to 13 successive finals appearances and six Flags and is credited with creating the great tidal waves of attack that started, as often as not, in the back line and swept the ball up field with both

aggression and teamwork.

Norm Smith was an original thinker and a strong, austere coach who demanded total loyalty to the team and could lift his players to great heights.

Len, as befitted his less flamboyant character, was a solid backman. He played 18 games for Melbourne, was discarded, and then 75 games with Fitzroy, with two years out for war service.

The younger Norm did not get the call up to Melbourne Seconds until 1934, and played his first senior games the following year. By 1937 he was full-forward and had stamped his class on the game, eventually playing 210 games with 546 goals for Melbourne, and 17 games for Fitzroy in 1949-50.

The *Argus* said of him: 'He neither bumps, nor executes fancy turns, but strolls about the field in a quiet sort of way, and one doesn't notice him particularly. The ball comes near him, and he picks it up, handballs to somebody nearby, or stab kicks neatly.

'The nonchalant manner covers a good deal of cleverness, a quick thinking football brain and a very cool head.'

Both Len and Norm Smith were the leading architects of modern football.

Les Foote – North Melbourne legend had all the football skills

In 1971 the North Melbourne Football Club Social Club took a postal poll of its members to see who they regarded as the club's 10 best League players.

The result was tied between Allen Aylett, who had been retired seven years, and Les Foote, who had left 20 years before.

Foote was one of the most accomplished players of all time – vying with such champions as Haydn Bunton, Ted Whitten and Dick Reynolds in the discussions of old timers.

Les Foote was a local boy who was nurtured through the strong North Melbourne Colts teams, virtually an under age extension of the club.

He became noted for his baul-

king and evasion skills, and revealed that he practiced them by walking through the crowded city footpaths, dodging and weaving through the oncoming people.

He could kick equally well with either foot and was a brilliant ball player, able to get low to the ground and control the ball in the packs.

Foote played in the vein much the same way as a later ball handling genius, Darrel Baldock.

As well as all this he was strong mark and sometimes a high flying aerialist.

Foote played his first game in 1941 at the age of 16, but the disruption of war gave him a comparitively short career of 135 games for North Melbourne, and 33

games as captain-coach of St Kilda in 1954-55.

When football resumed Foote began to stand out, both in his play and in his on-field leadership, and he was appointed captain of North in 1948, aged 23.

Foote was the star of the strong North teams which got yo the Grand Finals in 1949 and 1950, only to fall at the last hurdle.

Perhaps his greatest game was in the 1950 Preliminary Final against Geelong, when he almost single handedly dragged his side back from a seven goal deficit to win the game by 17 points.

Foote left to coach in Berrigan, NSW, when he was 27, but was lured back to the League in 1954 to coach struggling St Kilda.

Les Foote: good with either boot.

1959

See the barrackers a-shouting …

Rain, hail or shine, the barrackers will be there all through the season.

May 8. Bears might hibernate in the winter, but in Victoria barrackers hibernate in the summer, with the only activity a bit of maintenance on the winter's equipment.

Collecting masses of torn up paper, attaching coloured streamers to poles called 'floggers', attending to the mothballing of the beanie – that's the summer.

But a whiff of the eucalyptus in the autumn wakes them up.

Barrackers belong to a dozen different tribes, of course, but they have at least one thing in common: a belief that if you don't barrack for *someone*, you must have something wrong with you, or come from Mars, or Sydney.

Other common characteristics required by the barracker have been described by Jack Sheppard in the *Sun* as 'the stamina of the pole sitter, the patience of the bill collector, the lungs of a mule, the temper of a wounded buffalo, the audacity of a lion tamer, the enthusiasm of a car salesman and the confidence of a tight-rope walker'.

A football supporter likes one team, dry Saturdays, pies, high marks, training news, season tickets, shouting abuse, football gossip, next year's prospects, a funny comment, brawls in the Outer and the sound of the siren when his team is winning.

A barracker doesn't like the other team, strong winds, tall spectators, women with umbrellas. Or umpires (→ 19/8/64).

Race crash ruling

July 4. Carlton began the day virtually one man short when Bob Crowe stumbled while running down the race and injured his knee before reaching the playing field. He did not recover, limping with obvious pain whenever the ball came his way during the game, and failing to keep up with play. Carlton appealed to the umpire, and were allowed to substitute one of their reserves halfway through the first term, although technically Crowe's mishap had taken place off the field. But Carlton still lost to Fitzroy, 10.13 (73) to 21.13 (139).

Vics thrash WA

June 20. Victoria's 28-goal thrashing of Western Australia at the MCG renewed calls for an end to interstate football.

Spectators cried 'murder' as Victoria routed a pitifully weak opposition. The winning margin surprised many as Victoria fielded several out-of-form players.

Victoria began strongly as Wright let go a mighty punch, finding Arthur whose kick went to Skilton who goaled. For WA only Farmer, Sorrell, Langdon and Mumme showed League potential. Victoria won, 31.21 (207) to 3.11 (29) (→ 2/7/60).

What the umpire said to the player

May 27. Umpires have been doing a bit of talking lately.

In the Carlton and Melbourne game last Saturday, a Blues victory, 10.13 (73) to 9.7 (61), goal umpire Jack Lee was the kookaburra.

Carlton's Bruce Comben was knocked over by Melbourne's Ian Ridley after Comben had kicked. Umpire Alan Nash paid a free down field, and the two players exchanged words.

Then Umpire Lee ran out and had words with them – but after the game there were no reports.

It seems that Umpire Lee works for a cash register company and one had just been installed at Comben's Laverton shop. Comben said that Lee wanted to know how he liked it – a likely story.

Two weeks before, when Carlton beat Collingwood 14.10 (94) to 9.8 (62), an irate Magpie fan jumped the fence and had threatening words with umpire Bob Nunn.

A policeman rushed to the ump's aid, saying 'Hit him and I'll knock your block off.' Then an umpire's trainer chipped in, 'and I'll be in it too'. This was Al Basten, former Australian middleweight champ. The barracker fled (→ 18/5/68).

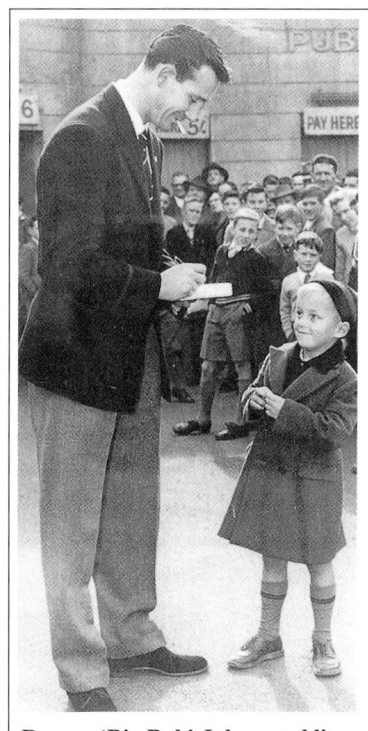

Demon 'Big Bob' Johnson obliges a young fan with his autograph.

Skilton's Brownlow after count-back

Skilton: fulfilled father's dream.

Sep. 2. South Melbourne rover Bobby Skilton has won the Brownlow Medal on a count-back after tying with St Kilda fullback Verdun Howell. Each scored 20 points.

It was a young man's night as Skilton is 20 and Howell 21. Skilton won because he had five first placings to Howell's three.

The win fulfilled a 12-year-old prediction by Skilton's father, a former Port Melbourne player who later turned to umpiring. 'When Bobby was eight, he could kick with either foot, and I predicted then that he would win a Brownlow Medal,' he said.

A delighted Skilton said his next ambition was to win a Premiership with South Melbourne (→11/9/63).

Bombers cool down hot Pies

Sept. 5. Essendon were just one point up on Collingwood at half time in the First Semi-final today, when the scores stood 4.8 to 4.9. But in the second half the Bombers delivered a rude shock to the reigning Premiers who had come to the game with ten victories in a row. They drew ahead by five clear goals in the third term, and by the end of the day had tipped the Magpies out of their Finals nest by a very convincing 38 points: Collingwood 8.14 (62), Essendon 14.16 (100).

The Dons' top goalkicker, Ron Evans, got his five goals from only six kicks.

Demons and Barassi supreme

Sept. 26. Melbourne's last-quarter dominance over Essendon today gave the Demons their fourth Premiership in six successive Grand Finals. It's not only their fans who are calling this team one of the greatest in the history of Australian football.

Essendon fought well, and the first three quarters produced some of the best football seen in a Grand Final. At the third change Melbourne were ahead by only one goal. But in the final term the Demons came out to overwhelm the young Dons with more strength, more experience, and more footballing brilliance to run out the victors by 37 points. 'Any side would have wilted under the relentless, killer football that this Melbourne side turned on', comments Bill Twomey in the *Sporting Globe*.

This year, for the first time, the Finalists were playing for the Premiership Cup. A crowd of 103,506 saw Essendon start strongly, going to a 13-point lead, largely due to magnificent roving by Jack Clarke and John Birt.

The Dons were looking superior into the second quarter. This fast young side, average age 22, were performing passages of spectacular football. Then they lost their big ruckman, Brian Sampson with an injured shoulder, and the balance shifted to the Demons, thanks largely to the dynamic performance of ruck-rover Ron Barassi.

Star of the Melbourne team, this amazing player is a veteran of 114 games, although only 23 years old. It was he who snatched the lead for the Demons, booting three goals just before half time to put them three points ahead.

With the teams so evenly matched, players on both sides were finding extra personal skills in the third term. Ken Fraser sent the crowd into raptures when he eluded three backmen to launch a long drop-kick for the Dons' ninth goal. But Bob Johnson saved the Demons with two quick replies.

Exactly one goal up at the start of the final term, the Demons ruthlessly piled on six more goals to Essendon's two. They had 14 shots for goal, compared to only three, and the game was lost for the Bombers well before the final siren: 17.13 (115) to 11.12 (78) (→24/9/60).

Orange time: Norm Smith addresses the troops.

1959 Statistics

Leading Goalkicker:
Ron Evans (Ess) 78

Brownlow Medallist:
Bob Skilton (S. Melb)

Finals:
First Semi-final Coll 8.14 (62) Ess 14.16 (100); **Second Semi-Final** Melb 11.15 (81) Carl 4.13 (37); **Preliminary Final** Carl 7.8 (50) Ess 8.9 (57); **Grand Final** Melb 17.13 (115) Ess 11.12 (78)

Ladder:	W	L	D	%	pts
Melb	13	4	1	142.7	54
Carl	13	5		109.3	52
Coll	12	6		121.6	48
Ess	11	7		112.4	44
Fitz	10	7	1	113.5	42
N. Melb	10	8		89.3	40
Haw	9	9		112.7	36
St K	9	9		94.3	36
S. Melb	8	10		103.4	32
Geel	5	13		78.5	20
Rich	4	14		73.9	16
Foots	3	15		73.3	12

1960

Bolte anger over postponed games

April 25. The Premier, Mr Henry Bolte, has criticised the League for not switching Saturday's four postponed games to today.

Mr Bolte described the League's decision as 'a proper mess'. The four matches that were postponed because of the wet conditions could have been played along with the two matches scheduled as part of today's Anzac Day programme.

Mr Bolte said the League should have taken the opportunity to play today and made suitable adjustments to the patriotic fund. 'All it has done is to make a mockery of the whole thing,' he said.

Instead, the season will be extended by one week. St Kilda v Melbourne and Fitzroy v Carlton will be played today (→ 31/8).

Five-quarter game

May 7. Footscray beat Hawthorn 6.17 (53) to 6.9 (45) in a game at Glenferrie Oval that finished at 5 p.m. after 32 minutes and 33 seconds of extra time was played – the equivalent of a fifth quarter.

Footscray timekeeper Norm Hector said the first quarter went 10 minutes, 46 seconds 'over time'.

Winds and negative play by Hawthorn backs caused the extended time. A man over the road had more kicks retrieving the ball in the first term than the Hawthorn forwards.

Four thrillers

July 23. It was a day of thrills with Melbourne, Hawthorn, Footscray and South Melbourne all winning their games by less than a goal.

Hawthorn won for the first time at Victoria Park, beating Collingwood 7.16 (58) to 7.15 (57). League leaders Melbourne had a fright against fifth-placed St Kilda, winning 6.13 (49) to 6.9 (45).

South Melbourne snatched a one-point win against a fast-finishing Geelong, 10.20 (80) to 11.13 (79). After trailing all day, Footscray got up by two points against North Melbourne, 9.10 (64) to 9.8 (62). Despite the close results, the Four remains unchanged – Melbourne, Essendon, Fitzroy, Collingwood.

Kennedy gets tough with Hawks

Super-fit Brendan Edwards leads the ragged chrous line of Hawks.

April 27. Hawthorn's new coach, John Kennedy, is determined to make his team the fittest in League history. When all Saturday's games were postponed due to incessant rain, he took his team on a gruelling 15-mile run.

Gary Young and John Peck, who failed to turn up, had to spend last night on a 90-lap barefoot run around Glenferrie Oval. Kennedy went with them, leading the exhausted truants to the end.

In addition to long runs, the Hawks are experimenting with circuit training, which centreman Brendan Edwards pioneered for the sake of his own fitness, making such improvements in strength and stamina that Kennedy has adopted his methods for the entire team.

He has also introduced a session of hard circuit training immediately before each Saturday game.

Kennedy has now committed Hawthorn to a 'run on' style of play, in which marking and kicking matter less than keeping the ball constantly on the move. The idea is to leave the opposition no time to catch their breath.

In this way Kennedy sees his team's growing fitness translating into match wins (→ 29/6/61).

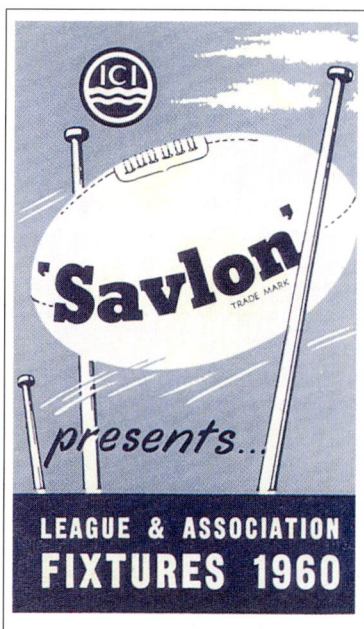

Big Bad Ruckmen

Aug. 20. There was fire enough to dry the mud during the Collingwood and South Melbourne clash today. A fierce brawl broke out in the second quarter after Collingwood ruckman Barry Harrison was felled and had to be taken off on a stretcher. A melee involving up to 24 men was followed by a running vendetta throughout the quarter, with individuals being dropped in the mud. Another major brawl occurred in the third term. Commenting in the *Sporting Globe*, Bill Twomey attributes the fiery inspiration for it all to Harrison and South Melbourne ruckman Ken Boyd being 'wrapped up in their own "bad man" publicity' (→ 31/8/61).

Francis outburst: Jeans bursts in

Oct. 11. St Kilda coach Jim Francis has attacked club President Graham Huggins, saying he is about to be sacked as coach.

Mr Huggins confirmed that St Kilda would be advertising for a new coach for 1961, but added that Francis was welcome to apply for the job. Francis says that he has been told by Huggins that he has no chance of being reappointed.

Early favourite for the Saints' coaching job is former player Allan Jeans, 27, who has been in charge of the reserves.

Francis was appointed coach at the start of the 1959 season following the resignation of Allan Killigrew and lifted the team up to sixth position. He has been widely regarded as a stabilising influence at the club, although his coaching style has been criticised as too conservative.

In an uncharacteristic outburst, Francis said that soon after joining as coach, he was compelled to 'get rid of certain players because they preferred to drink beer rather than train'. Francis also said that his coaching methods had the support of the players.

'Supporters who have phoned me say the job is all sewn up for Jeans,' he said (→ 26/8/61).

1960 Statistics

Leading Goalkicker:
Ron Evans (Ess) 67
Brownlow Medallist:
John Schultz (Foot)
Finals: First Semi-final Ess 7.15 (57) Coll 9.12 (66); **Second Semi-Final** Melb 14.18 (102) Fitz 4.16 (40); **Preliminary Final** Fitz 8.12 (60) Coll 9.11 (65); **Grand Final** Melb 8.14 (62) Coll 2.2 (14)

Ladder:	W	L	D	%	pts
Melb	14	4		143.1	56
Fitz	14	4		112.5	56
Ess	13	5		125.1	52
Coll	11	7		114.3	44
Haw	11	7		104.9	44
St K	9	9		101.7	36
Carl	8	9	1	99.0	34
S.Melb	7	11		92.3	28
Geel	6	11	1	95.5	26
Foots	6	12		90.4	24
N.Melb	5	13		80.3	20
Rich	2	14	2	66.7	12

It's five out of seven for Demons

Sept. 24. Melbourne have trounced Collingwood in the Grand Final, to win their fifth Flag in seven years. Only Collingwood's four in a row between 1927 and 1930 can be claimed as a feat of higher standing.

It was a disappointing and low-scoring Grand Final, played on a heavy ground, and the game was virtually over by quarter time, when the Demons had scored 4.3 to nothing. They went on to win 8.14 (62) to 2.2 (14), the lowest Grand Final score since 1931.

Again the burden of reaching the Final from fourth place has told – this time against Collingwood. After winning the First Semi in a hard-fought match against Essendon, and then scraping in by five points against Fitzroy, they soon showed the depth of their exhaustion.

They bounced out, expecting the wet ground to be in their favour, as in 1958. But Melbourne were fresher, fitter and faster, and they combined well from the start, sweeping the ball forward from every line in their characteristic fashion, inculcated by coach Norm Smith.

This pressure produced tidal waves of attack which broke on the Collingwood defence, and it is to the credit of defenders Mick Twomey, Ron Reeves and Kevin Rose that they held out so well.

The Demons' backbone was strong, with centre-halfback John Lord, full-back 'Tassie' Johnson and centre Laurie Mithen the best players. But it was a devastating team effort that brought the win (→ 19/9/64).

Thorold Merrett leaves the scene.

The Demons reign supreme after their seventh successive Grand Final.

Blond beanpole wins Brownlow

Aug. 31. Footscray's 'gentle giant', John Schultz, has won the Brownlow Medal. Regarded by other ruckmen as the League's most difficult opponent, Schultz is, none the less, scrupulously fair, which his Brownlow win now honours.

Only 21 years old, Schultz already has an enviable football reputation, having won the *Sporting Globe's* Haydn Bunton Medal for best League player this year. He had the rare distinction of being chosen for Victoria in his first season, and after only three years is vice-captain of the Bulldogs.

John Schultz: many honors at 21.

1961

Hawks on top after day of drama

July 29. From being two games clear on top of the ladder after round 11, the reigning Premiers Melbourne have lost top spot to Hawthorn, just three games later.

The rot set in when they drew with Fitzroy in shocking conditions in round 12. With conditions still heavy they then lost a low-scoring affair to Hawthorn in round 13, the Hawks scoring 8.10 (58) to the Demons' 5.10 (40).

Then today, while Hawthorn was winning a titanic struggle with Fitzroy, 13.16 (94) to 12.15 (87), Melbourne was going down to Essendon, 10.18 (78) to 13.9 (87).

If this uncharacteristic lapse in Melbourne's effectiveness continues, this season could end with another side heading the Ladder for the first time since 1954.

Hawthorn finished last year with six wins, but failed to make the Four. They have been improved by coach John Kennedy's controversial 'running game' and each man has now picked up the new style of play. The result is some dynamic and fast-moving team-work.

Kennedy has stuck to his law that no Hawk shall pause to steady himself while in possession of the ball, but should look to pass the ball quickly. At first there were too many wasteful disposals, but now the Hawks are bewildering some other teams with their speed (→ 15/4/67).

Boyd has no regrets over Nicholls incident

Ken Boyd leaves the Tribunal.

Aug. 31. Tough South Melbourne ruckman Ken Boyd has been suspended by the VFL for 12 matches, following the incident earlier in the month involving Carlton big man John Nicholls.

In that clash, which Carlton won 17.9 (111) to 7.10 (52), Boyd is alleged to have laid out Nicholls.

The incident was not reported by the umpires, but next day Nicholls said that Boyd was responsible.

Boyd gave an interview to Peter Bye and Ian McDonald of the *Sporting Globe* published on August 9, in which he said: 'I'm not ashamed I hit John Nicholls. I've a clear conscience on the whole matter. I was kicked in the stomach and the groin [at a centre bounce and] I was in terrific pain. I recovered, went back, turned Nicholls around and dropped him' (→ 4/9/63).

Bedlam and booze in the Outer

June 12. A journalist fresh from the polite playing fields of Europe and the United States says that he has not encountered elsewhere in the world 'such shocking and consistently bad crowd behaviour' as he has at the football in Melbourne.

John Fitzgerald in the *Herald* describes scenes in the Outer at various games as if from Bedlam, mostly brought about by booze.

Apart from the physically sickening conditions of buying beer, and using toilet facilities, Fitzgerald finds that many patrons are simply at the footy in order to drink.

Fitzgerald reports: 'Several women were subject to an afternoon of obvious discomfort and revulsion as a group of beer-drinking men became rowdier with every goal and every glass.'

'It seems Australian football, unique and spectacular, is getting a shabby deal from some of its "supporters",' he says (→ 1/4/79).

John James gets medal in pocket

John James: niche in defence.

Aug. 30. Carlton's versatile John James has won the Brownlow Medal with 21 votes from North Melbourne's Laurie Dwyer's 18.

James, in his ninth season for the Blues, has played just about everywhere, but credits this win to the selectors who shifted him from the halfback flank to the back pocket for the last four games.

James kicked a bizarre total of eight goals 43 behinds in his first season on the half-forward flank. One of the most popular winners of the Brownlow in recent years, James has found his niche: as a champ.

Saints in Four by five points

Aug. 26. St Kilda have won their way into the finals for the first time in 22 years and will meet Footscray in the first semi-final.

The Saints did it the hard way in the last round downing Wooden Spooners, North Melbourne by five points after trailing by 13 points at three-quarter time. A loss to the Kangaroos would have seen the Saints miss the finals yet again.

The season has been a triumph for St. Kilda's 27 year-old coach, Allan Jeans, and captain Neil Roberts. St. Kilda's hero was stalwart ruckman, Alan Morrow, who lifted the team in the final quarter. The Saints kicked 4.2 in the last quarter to snatch victory 10.12 (72) to North Melbourne 9.13 (67). Jubilant St. Kilda supporters carried the players from the ground (→ 10/8/76).

Kennedy's Commandos storm to Flag

Sept. 23. The Hawks trounced a tired and bewildered Footscray today, to win their first ever Premiership. Emotional scenes followed their great win, 13.16 (94) to 7.9 (51). A tight police cordon had to prevent ecstatic Hawthorn fans from invading the field to chair their heroes off.

Captain Graham Arthur added to the joy of the fans when he led his men in singing the club song through the loudspeaker system.

Footscray had led the scoring at each change to half time. They were eight points up at the start of the second half. Footscray started the day dominating the packs, but when rover Mervyn Hobbs' style was hampered after a heavy knock, and Keith Beamish was taken off at half time, Hawthorn began to win most possessions from around the packs.

Then the record crowd of 107,935 packing the MCG went wild with excitement, watching the Hawks pile on ten goals to the Bulldogs' two. It was a devastating display of power football as the Hawks took control of a hard-bumping game and swept the younger team aside.

Brendan Edwards was a match winner for the Hawks in the centre. Footscray swung Graeme Ion on to him, but to little effect. Edwards continued to get the ball away, and it was bouncing fast on a ground ideal for football. Goaling twice in the first three minutes of the third quarter, the Hawks soon became an inspired team.

Giant John Schultz, Footscray's best player for the day, found himself in so much trouble at one point that he was forced to boot a behind for the Hawks to avoid his eager opponents getting another goal.

In defence, in the air, and in attack the Hawks were doing everything right. Seldom were the Bulldogs given a chance to attack during the Hawks' rampaging third quarter. Another quick run of goals made it six for the term, and the Hawks looked every bit the Premiership side.

When Ted Whitten, the Bulldog captain, missed a goal it seemed as if the Bulldogs were cursed with the fumbles. In the final term they looked worn down, while Hawthorn's vigour created four goals to one, and secured the victory (→ 25/9/71).

Jubilation as Hawthorn skipper Graham Arthur is chaired from the field.

Footscray's captain-coach Ted Whitten is a sad witness to Hawthorn's joy.

1961 Statistics

Leading Goalkicker:
Tom Carroll (Carl) 54

Brownlow Medallist:
John James (Carl)

Finals:
First Semi-final St K 8.12 (60) Foots 9.15 (69); **Second Semi-final** Haw 12.8 (80) Melb 11.7 (73); **Preliminary Final** Melb 8.10 (58) Foots 13.7 (85); **Grand Final** Haw 13.16 (94) Foots 7.9 (51)

Ladder:	W	L	D	%	pts
Haw	14	4		125.1	56
Melb	12	5	1	131.2	50
St K	11	7		117.1	44
Foots	11	7		109.7	44
Fitz	10	7	1	116.8	42
Geel	10	7	1	100.4	42
Ess	9	8	1	109.5	38
Carl	9	9		96.5	36
Coll	5	12	1	84.8	22
Rich	5	13		78.9	20
S. Melb	5	13		72.2	20
N. Melb	4	13	1	79.1	18

Ron Barassi: super player, super coach

There is often a single image of the greatest players in characteristic flight, one that sums up who they were and how they played. There are many such pictures of Ron Barassi the player and they all bear the same mask of fierce, almost angry, determination.

'Barass' is getting his kick, right leg coming through like a log on a pendulum. His mouth is open in a grimace of effort, eyes staring at where the ball is going.

His left arm might be held by some spindly opponent, or it might be following through across his chest; his right arm arcs high to balance the drive off his left leg, and to give a swing of triumph.

In these pictures he's always getting his kick. He's in a Melbourne jumper, and so he's almost always winning a premiership.

The deeds of Barassi the coach, and Barassi the booster of the national and international aspects of Australian football, have tended to obscure the memory of Barassi the player, but it was as a player that he first became a legend, and it was for his deeds in helping Melbourne win six Premierships that he will always be remembered.

He played his first senior game for Melbourne in 1953, having born into the Melbourne tradition. His father, also Ron Barassi, played 55 games for the Redlegs between 1936 and 1940, and was instrumental in the 1940 Melbourne Flag. He was killed at Tobruk when his son was four.

Barassi played his first senior game in 1953, having trained with the Thirds in 1951, and played for them in 1952. He was just 17.

Barassi started in three games in 1953 and played another three from the bench. In 1954 he began in the Seconds, but after a few games partnered Denis Cordner in the ruck as a kind of big rover, or a small ruckman - the game's first official ruck rover. He was never dropped again.

Playing this new position not only got Barassi into the action, it also generated greater drive for Melbourne. The Demons finished

Ron Barassi shows the strength and tenacity that made him a super star.

11th in 1953, but rose to be second in 1954, in Norm Smith's third year as coach. That was the first of seven straight Grand Final appearances for the team, for five Flags.

Barassi played a key role in each of these premierships, as that player most necessary in Grand Final winning teams, the one who will do anything, chase everyone, and run through the proverbial brick wall to win.

Jack Dyer, another ferocious footballer, said in 1966 that 'it's hard to believe this star of the big man game is only 5 feet 10 and a half inches ... pound for pound and inch for inch he's the greatest'.

'Barassi's stamina will go beyond exhaustion, he has the ability to roll with any bump and, above all, has incredible accuracy kicking for goal. Few people realise that Barassi is a glorious kick. He's one of the best the game has produced. And he is the team man to end all team men'.

Dyer compares him to the greats he had seen and played with, Harry Collier, Ivor Warne Smith, Dick Reynolds and rates him with them, as a player.

Frank 'Bluey' Adams recalled one example of the great player's work in the 1959 Grand Final against Essendon, in Barassi and Peter McFarline's book *Barassi The Life Behind the Legend*.

Just before half time with Melbourne a couple of goals down, Barassi turned in 'the greatest five minutes of football ever by an individual in a Grand Final.'

'In that time he kicked three goals when the chances of doing so in each case were about 30 per cent. The first was a tremendously gutsy snap when he burst out of a pack with the ball and managed to kick truly with defenders draped all over him.

'The next two came from the strongest marks I have ever seen. One of them I have good reason to remember because I was roving at the base of the pack when it split apart as if it had been cut with a knife. You could hear the slap as Barassi's hands came around the ball. As he landed, his face was only a couple of inches from mine. He told me in no uncertain terms to get out of the way. He kicked the goals from about 30 metres out, just as he had a minute or so earlier.'

The exceptional year in Barassi's dominance of Grand Finals was 1958, when Collingwood invented the 'tag' to prevent Barassi dominating.

Barassi for once became so concerned with protecting life and limb from the attentions of Collingwood's 'Hooker' Harrison that Melbourne missed the chance to equal the Magpies' four in a row.

Later in the surprise one-kick win over Collingwood in 1964 he was perhaps not among the best players, but was cerainly the best on-field leader.

It was Barassi who whipped from man to man in a desperate last quarter, driving them on. he surged through the packs, talking and encouraging. The ball wouldn't run his way, but the playcrs could see the superhuman effort he was making.

It was a fanatical Barassi-lead Melbourne that fought on an on. They were hopelessly out of touch, but sheer fighting spirit kept them striving, and it was typical of that strange desperate side that back pocket Neil Crompton kicked the incredible winning goal.

The next year, he shocked the football universe by moving from Melbourne to Carlton, for money, career and opportunity. This £5000 purchase in a sense ushered in the modern era of the football business, which to a great extent has been the Barassi era.

For Melbourne he played 204 games and kicked 295 goals. Barassi then played 49 games for Carlton between 1965 and 1969, and was coach of the 1968 Premiership side, Carlton's first in 23 years. He then famously defeated Collingwood with coaching inspiration to win the 1970 Flag.

As coach of North Melbourne he took them to their first ever Flag in 1975, and then backed it up in 1977 after the draw.

Back at Mebourne as coach between 1981 and 1985 he did not have the players to work with, but did show his imagination by being part of the Irish experiment, recruiting and nurturing Jim Stynes, the 1991 Brownlow medallist.

And then, continuing his passion for the national game he took on the Sydney coaching job in 1993, retiring with a win over Collingwood at the end of 1995 that saw Brisbane sneak into the Finals for the first time.

Barassi finished after 512 games as coach with a win ratio of 53 % and ten Flags as player and coach. A living legend.

When showbiz came to football

In the dawning autumn of 1956 the sports department of the *Sun* newspaper was facing up to a truly awful prospect.

Captain Blood was leaving us. Jack Dyer was resolved to visit England, for the Derby, the Tests and Wimbledon. Jack, always capable of mangling the language with endearing aplomb, insisted that he would take in the French Riverina. In Paris he wanted to see the Latin Quarter Mile and the Folies Bergerac.

I was then in charge of the *Sun's* sports pages. The first replacement name I wrote down was that of Lou Richards, who was stumbling into radio commentary at the time on 3KZ.

I phoned and arranged a meeting with my editor Frank Daly. Lou brought along his wife Edna, who wore a Cup Day kind of black outfit and a pillbox hat. When they emerged from a lengthy discussion in the editor's office, Lou was on the *Sun* team; his side of the bargain was a payment of 10 pounds a week (four more than Dyer had been getting) and a promise that if he did the job well, he'd keep the job after Dyer's return.

For Lou just then the promise of a newspaper future, on what seemed like a healthy income, was significant. He had grown up in the back streets of Collingwood, played 250 games with the Magpies, captained the team to a premiership in 1953, and learned late in 1955 that in that club even skippers were expendable.

Whenever Lou gives me one of his books (and there have been several) he always inscribes it: 'To Harry, the name that made me a multi-media star.' Grammar was never his strong point. Modesty either. The truth is, that while I helped with some early navigation, Lou was a natural. And the guidance that gave his career extra dimension, way beyond the columns of the newspapers, came from the broadcasters Ron Casey and Doug Elliott of HSV-7.

Lou's *Sun* career did not take off instantly. It is not generally realised that ghost writing involves great skill, as well as a certain chemistry with the subject. After some false starts I arranged for Mike Courtney, ultimately an editor of distinction, to take over the ghosting. The effect was magical.

Lou became as cheeky in print as he'd ever been on the football field . . . Louie the Lip, purveyor of football selections that were often so off the mark that they became known collectively as the Kiss of Death. He would back his judgement with mildly insane wagers. Thus, after Footscray upset Melbourne in the 1961 preliminary final, he found himself cutting Ted Whitten's front lawn with a pair of nail scissors.

This event of course became news itself. Three thousand people packed Whitten's street that day, and the Sun had a great front-page picture. After that the promises, and the stunts, lost all sense of discipline. There was Lou on the tower of the T and G building, painting the flag-pole with a nail polish brush; sweeping Collins Street with a feather duster; rowing Bill Goggin across the Barwon in a bathtub; taking a bath in a horse trough in Flinders St. So corny. So awful. So many newspapers sold.

Another of Lou's great talents was the bestowal of nicknames. It was he who christened Leigh Matthews 'Lethal'. The well nourished Mick Nolan, of North Melbourne, became the Galloping Gasometer. Bruce Doull, who had a hair problem, became the Flying Doormat. Kevin Bartlett, who'd rather kick the ball than handball it, was Hungry.

It was natural, after the arrival of television, that show business began to mesh with sport.

At that time Michael Williamson was pushing the boundaries of variety with a caravan of Kia Ora sports parades that played to packed houses in assorted town halls. Ruckmen in tutus were much in demand. At the Melbourne Town Hall, Brian Dixon marched onstage ahead of a coffin, in which Frank 'Bluey' Adams sat up to sing *A Sick Stockrider Lay Dying*. At Hawthorn John Kennedy played a

guitar, and Roy Simmonds a banjo. At Footscray an unidentified fan upstaged Joffa Ellen with 52 separate bird calls. All proceedings were broadcast by 3AW.

Williamson migrated to Channel 7 late in 1959 to take over the Kevin Dennis Football Show on Friday nights and Football Inquest on Saturday nights. Reg Hickey, Jack Edwards, Butch Gale, Bluey Adams and Ted Whitten were all prominent.

The public appetite for footy on the box was insatiable. On Seven Ron Casey fronted *World of Sport*, a magnificently unstructured production, in company with Lou and Doug 'Leather-lungs' Elliott. Nine fought back with shows headed by Tony Charlton, a more urbane veteran of the Kia Ora circuit. On Thursday nights Richards was there again for *League Teams*.

This show, featuring also Jack Dyer and Bob Davis, was *supposed* to be devoted to roll calls of newly selected teams, with relevant comment. It evolved into such a pastiche of argument, bad jokes, Dyerisms and the swapping of favorite recipes that it attracted a cult following.

Inevitably, the rivalry between Seven and Nine was fierce. Ambushes were common, and out-of-town celebrities once in a while found themselves driven from the airport to the wrong studio, being interviewed by the wrong person.

Of all the shows in that lusty decade after the advent of television, one embedded itself firmly into the psyche of Melbourne. It was *World of Sport*, which in fact lasted 28 years. The American jockey Eddie Arcaro once described it as organised chaos; he was being generous. At times, amid the woodchoppers, the kicking and handballing, the sand shovelling, the giveaways of dog food, chocolates, hams and pies, the chaos was utterly disorganised.

To be inside WOS, behind the scenes, was like being at an alfresco picnic scattered with big cameras and 'on air' signs, of which nobody took much notice. It abounded with small children, many of them the offspring of the coaches, players and past players who seemed to fill the place.

Bruce Andrew, whose hair was parted so emphatically down the middle that it was claimed he used a theodolite, judged the kicking contests. The world champion cyclist Sid Patterson raced all-comers with a bike on rollers, the handballers aimed at a bullseye and the axemen chopped. One day a wayward axe flew across a set and split a cable in two. Nobody seemed upset.

And all the time Doug Elliott and Lou Richards dispensed Hutton's hams, Four-and-Twenty pies, Ballantyne's Entertain Mints and cans of food. These things mattered. It was said that Bob Pratt and Doug Elliott didn't speak for 20 years over a disputed claim for six cans of Kia Ora spaghetti. And one day Sir Robert Menzies, at Channel Seven early for a Meet the Press interview, was lured onto the show; he talked about cricket, and left with a Hutton's Gold Nugget Ham.

Appropriately, the pub Lou Richards bought in Flinders Street had great television potential. It could have been the subject of a great sit-com, funnier than *Cheers*, or *M*A*S*H* without the war. It was a journalists' pub, an annexe to the Sun and Herald, with a staircase from the street that was steep enough to be almost sheer. But that pub, the Phoenix, really is another story.

- Harry Gordon.

'Ideally suited to development as a ground for the League'

Sept. 12. The VFL has moved towards creating its own home of football by buying 197 acres of land in Melbourne's east in Waverley, not far from Sandown.

The Executive Committee of the VFL has decided that this land, currently used for dairying, is 'ideally suited for development as a ground for the League'.

A ground owned and operated by the VFL might in the future resolve some of the difficulties clubs and spectators experience in buying tickets for Finals at the MCG.

The VFL would also increase its revenue from big games, which at present is siphoned off by the MCC.

Last year 107,935 fans watched the Grand Final, but the VFL only received payment from 85,594. The other 22,341 were MCC members and guests (→19/4/63).

VFL officials inspect football's new 'paddock'.

Lord twins a puzzle in umpires report

The Lord twins a confusing duo.

May 16. Geelong's twins, Alistair and Stewart Lord, caused confusion at the AFL Tribunal last night when evidence showed the wrong one had been charged with having struck Richmond's Basil Maloney.

Alistair Lord was defended by Geelong President, Mr Jack Jennings, who was able to show that Alistair was nowhere near the alleged incident. The charge was dropped when Maloney declared he had no recollection of being hit by anyone. At the end of the hearing the chairman suggested that one of the twins should grow a moustache to aid in identification (→26/5/80).

Woods no longer have wood on Saints

April 23. St Kilda finally ended the longest hoodoo in League football, by defeating Collingwood at Victoria Park for the first time since 1919, 9.9 (63) to 5.8 (38). The Saints held Collingwood scoreless in the last quarter.

The biggest sensation of this Easter Monday game was the injury to boom 'recruit' Darrel Baldock.

Baldock, 23, is regarded as the best thing to come to Melbourne from Tasmania since John Batman.

Baldock over the past few years has signed more forms than a taxpayer, first for Melbourne and then South Melbourne, but it was St Kilda who got him to cross Bass Strait after the 1961 Carnival. Baldock captained Tasmania in those games.

After training with the Saints during the 1961 Finals, Baldock is expected to make a big impact on the team and the game this year.

Although somewhat small for a centre-half-forward he has uncanny ball skills and a desperation to get to the fall of the ball.

It was revealed that Baldock had cracked a bone in the arch of his foot at training, and has aggravated it in this game. He looks likely to miss four weeks, but showed enough courage and skill to suggest that he will be a real asset (→21/5/66).

Polly and Stevo's knees give way

Polly Farmer signing on for Cats.

June 23. Two of the big knees of football are up on cushions again. Polly Farmer left the ground clutching his suspect left knee in the second quarter at Essendon, while the Saints' star forward Bill Stephenson went off in the last quarter against Melbourne. Both their teams lost, with Essendon winning 15.17 (107) to 10.7 (67) and Melbourne winning 11.18 (84) to 11.6 (72).

The big knees will be up for discussion again, with both players hobbling in to 'World of Sport' on Channel 7, along with an orthopaedic surgeon, who will reveal all (→18/8).

Wade-Barry decision: courageous or wrong

Wade goes crook at Umpire Irving.

Sept. 22. With seconds to go in the replayed Preliminary Final between Geelong and Carlton today, it all came down to a marking duel between Cats' spearhead Doug Wade and his opponent Peter Barry.

Carlton's John James had just kicked what looked like the winning goal and the scores were Carlton 10.18 (78) to Geelong's 10.13 (73).

But Geelong made a last thrust and Fred Wooller sent the ball spinning towards Wade. He had the front position ... he had the mark, and a great roar rose from the crowd of 99,203 people.

But wait! Umpire Jack Irving ran in and ordered a free kick to Barry. No amount of ranting from Wade could change that. Barry cleared, and the game was over.

Irving said later that he had seen Wade reach back and tug Barry's shorts. He judged it 'holding the man'. Umpires adviser Allan Nash called it 'the most courageous decision I have ever seen' (→ 25/5/63).

Lord receives highest praise from umpires

Aug. 29. Alistair Lord was chaired down Ryrie Street, Geelong, before a cheering throng last night when the news came through that he had won the Brownlow Medal.

The 22-year-old Geelong centreman, from a Port Campbell farming family, has had a great year. He is noted for the way he dashes from the centre and sends beautiful dropkicks into the forward line.

He was well fancied for the Brownlow by Geelong supporters, but best on ground votes had him six behind Essendon's Ken Fraser and Kevin Murray of Fitzroy.

But, when votes were counted for the second best on ground, Lord scored 18 votes, to take him to 27. He finished with 28. He received votes in 13 of the 17 games in which votes were cast.

Fraser, Murray and Richmond captain Ron Branton were tied for second place, on 19 votes.

Lord, and twin brother Stewart, had a run-in with the Tribunal in May, but a mix-up over their identities left him in the clear and eligible for the Brownlow (→ 22/5/65).

Bombers fly high

Essendon captain Jack Clarke receives the Cup from Sir Kenneth Luke.

Sept. 29. Before the Grand Final, Essendon had played one game in a month, and that was a romp over Geelong in the Second Semi-final, 14.21 (105) to 7.17 (59).

In contrast Carlton had played three tough Finals games for a draw and two wins of less than a kick.

On top of that, the John Coleman coached Bombers had lost just two games during the season and were clearly the best team for the year.

So it proved in the Grand Final. Essendon kicked 6.5 to 1.1 in the first quarter and coasted home to win 13.12 (90) to 8.10 (58).

Geoff Leek, though carrying an ankle, contained John Nicholls, and the roving division of Jack Clarke, best on ground, John Birt and Hugh Mitchell had a birthday.

The Blues fought back in the second quarter, with Sergio Silvagni outstanding, but never looked like winning. Most of the 98,385 fans enjoyed a spirited match, where the best team of the season won on the day (→ 29/9/84).

1962 Statistics

Leading Goalkicker:
Doug Wade (Geel) 68
Brownlow Medallist:
Alistair Lord (Geel)

Finals: First Semi Final Melb 11.10 (76) Carl 11.12 (78); **Second Semi** Ess 14.21 (105) Geel 7.17 (59); **Preliminary Final** Geel 13.7 (85) Carl 12.13 (85); **Preliminary Final Replay** Geel 10.13 (73) Carl 10.18 (78); **Grand Final** Ess 13.12 (90) Carl 8.10 (58)

Ladder:	W	L	%	pts
Ess	16	2	130.4	64
Geel	14	4	139.3	56
Melb	14	4	125.8	56
Carl	13	5	112.9	52
Foots	11	7	108.5	44
St K	9	9	108.8	36
Coll	9	9	98.5	36
Rich	5	13	90.5	20
Haw	5	13	86.6	20
Fitz	5	13	79.9	20
N. Melb	4	14	73.1	16
S. Melb	3	15	74.4	12

The moment of delight, when the siren sounds to confirm the Dons' big win.

1963

April 19. The VFL considers names for the future ground at Waverley. Rejected were VFL Stadium, VFL Sports Coliseum – and Luke Park. 'VFL Park' is eventually chosen (→18/4/70).

May 11. Neil Roberts says that Allan Killigrew, who coached him at St Kilda, has mellowed coaching North Melbourne, although the fiery orator of old delivers the same message, 'loyalty, teamwork and fanaticism.'

May 25. Panic action by an umpire in the Wimmera League has the entire Stawell and Rupanyup teams reported. The teams report the umpire (→26).

May 26. Kevin Murray, the Fitzroy coach, has complained that 'when your team is down, they give you inexperienced umpires. It should be the other way around'. In the *Sporting Globe* umpire's awards, Don Blew was given 4/10 for his bewildering display.

June 10. Umpire Frank Schwab collapses with a brain haemorrhage at home. He won the '62 *Globe* Umpires' Award (→29/6).

June 15. S.A. 12.8 (80) beat Victoria 10.13 (73) for the first time in Melbourne for 37 years before 59,260 (→20/6/64).

June 19. Melbourne Secretary Jim Cardwell says that his club plays in the country to 'pay' for players. Country clubs keep the 'gate', Melbourne get a clearance, and the Coulter Law is circumvented (→11/6/64).

June 21. VFL has decided players in the Finals will get an increase of £2 to £17 for each game. Clubs pay £10 a week, plus provident fund, for home-and-away games (→11/4/70).

June 29. VFL Umpires have launched an appeal for Frank Schwab, who is recovering slowly in hospital.

Sept. 4. The VFL Tribunal has given four-week season-ending suspensions to Ron Barassi (Melb) and Des Dickson (Haw) plus two weeks for John Peck (Haw) (→27/6/64).

Oct. 3. Footscray win the Night Premiership 10.9 (69) to Richmond 9.9 (63).

Debuts
Carl Ditterich (St K)
John Northey (Rich)
John Rantall (S. Melb)
Ian Stewart (St K)

Retirements
John James (Carl)
Murray Weideman (Coll)

Blond bombshell's debut creates havoc for Demons

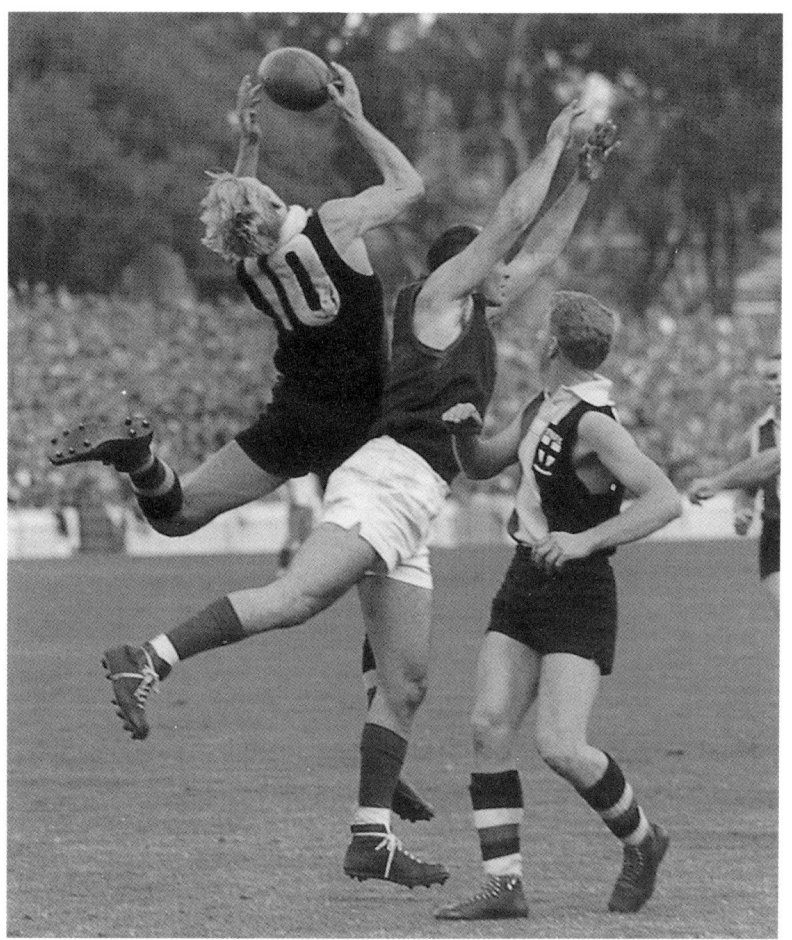

Carl Ditterich shows his athleticism as he marks in his first League game.

April 20. St. Kilda's 17-year-old Carl Ditterich was the star performer of the opening round. St Kilda have discovered a potential champion in the young ruckman who dominated in the Saints' 18-point win over Melbourne.

With his blond locks flowing, Ditterich took control in the ruck and turned the game into a nightmare for Melbourne's captain, Ron Barassi. Ditterich gave strong support to veteran ruckman, Alan Morrow who had 22 marks for the day. Together, the brilliant up-and-comer and the lion-hearted veteran should make a lethal following division for the Saints this season.

Ditterich, recruited from East Brighton, has been given former captain Neil Roberts' number 10 jumper. He has a huge leap, safe hands and bounds on to the field like a young stallion. With the Saints trailing by four points at the final break, it was Ditterich whose opening knock-out got the ball to Ian Stewart, whose pass found Bob Murray, who then goaled to put St Kilda in the lead.

Ditterich lit up the Saints' supporters in the 30,000-strong crowd. St Kilda defeated Melbourne, 13.5 (83) to 9.11 (65) (→25/3/66).

Polly Farmer is the handball master

June 12. Graham 'Polly' Farmer, Geelong's great ruckman, is one of the very few League players to have added a technique of his own to the game. He has perfected the spearing 30-yard handpass, and its use is spreading through the game. 'The feature has been infectious and almost the whole League is using it', says Neil Roberts of the *Sporting Globe*. Roberts believes it is being overdone. He comments: 'Used in attack, particularly from the centre bounce, it is devastating and very modern, but to see it used indiscriminately in defence is ridiculous, particularly when there is time to have a kick.' Roberts recounts seeing a Polly Farmer handball go disastrously wrong when it sped straight to the clutches of the opposition in the form of Bryan Kenneally who promptly made a goal of it for Melbourne (→2/6/65).

'I ask you. Is that fair?' Umpire B.K. Feld stands over unconscious South Australian player Brian Sawley during the interstate match in Adelaide on July 6. Victorian John Peck has been suspended for two weeks.

223

One bright day for the Lion in winter

Murray: riding high this week.

July 6. Fitzroy supporters are in a state of shock. The Lions, who have not won a game all season, came out and trounced the highly rated Geelong side, 9.13 (67) to 3.13 (31).

And they did it without their captain-coach Kevin Murray, who is with the Victorian team in Adelaide.

Murray has been a target of some club officials over Fitzroy's poor form. He has complained on HSV7's 'World of Sport' recently that 'weak sides get the inexperienced umpires', and that Fitzroy have suffered from their decisions.

But the Lions shocked the Cats today with their marking, teamwork and tenacious defence (→ 6/4/74).

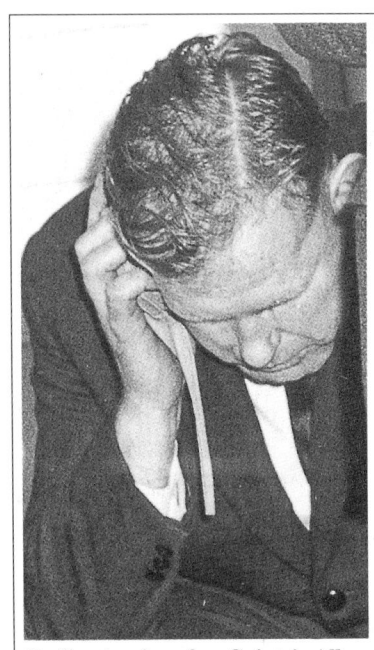

Radio tension for Saints' Allan Jeans as Essendon win but St Kilda get in Four on percentage.

Farmer shoots down Hawks

Billy Goggin eludes David Parkin.

'The Swede', Paul Vinar, breaks away to put Geelong back on the attack.

Oct. 7. Graham 'Polly' Farmer inspired Geelong's brilliant win over Hawthorn on Saturday, which brought the Cats their sixth Premiership. Farmer was the key man in the 15.19 (109) to 8.12 (60) triumph, and justified coach Bob Davis' prediction that the Western Australian champion would bring Geelong a Premiership.

Thanks largely to Farmer's work in the rucks, Geelong changed from a defensive team to an attacking force in the second quarter. They took 22 marks to Hawthorn's five; they kicked 70 times to the Hawks' 41. But wastage by their forwards allowed Hawthorn to stay in the game, only ten points behind at half time.

The Hawks took to the ground in the third term with enough vigour to control the action for about 20 minutes, getting to within a point before Colin Rice goaled for the Cats.

Then Hawthorn revealed the strain put on a team that loses the Second Semi Final. They played the final term drained of stamina after the tremendous effort they had put into the third. The Cats opened up play and found their normal, brilliant game, quickly adding four goals.

Hawthorn kept up the fight but the crowd knew Geelong were the 1963 Premiers. Commenting in *The Age* today Percy Beames said: 'Once they scented victory they swamped Hawthorn with a purpose that was almost cruelly heartbreaking' (→ 13/9/75).

John Devine and Ian Law tangle.

Skilton again

Sept. 11. Polling in ten games, South Melbourne's champion rover Bob Skilton has won his second Brownlow Medal.

Skilton scored 20 votes including four best-on-grounds to win by three from Saint Darrel Baldock and big Cat Polly Farmer.

On hearing of his win at the home of South Melbourne coach Noel McMahen, Skilton rated this season as better than 1959, but would trade both medals for a South Melbourne Premiership (→ 30/8/66).

1963 Statistics

Leading Goalkicker:
John Peck (Haw) 75

Brownlow Medallist:
Bob Skilton (S. Melb)

Finals:
First Semi-final Melb 9.17 (71) St K 8.16 (64); **Second Semi-final** Haw 11.16 (82) Geel 14.17 (101); **Prelim. Final** Haw 11.11 (77) Melb 10.8 (68); **Grand Final** Geel 15.19 (109) Haw 8.12 (60)

Ladder:	W	L	D	%	pts
Haw	13	4	1	130.6	54
Geel	13	4	1	128.2	54
Melb	13	5		147.9	52
St K	13	5		140.1	52
Ess	13	5		137.5	52
Carl	10	8		103.3	40
N. Melb	8	10		85.1	32
Coll	7	11		95.7	28
Foots	7	11		87.8	28
Rich	5	13		75.8	20
S. Melb	4	14		69.8	16
Fitz	1	17		57.5	4

Polly and Big Nick: giants of the ruck

For six years in the 60's two masters of their football trade would meet to do battle. Carlton against Geelong meant Nicholls and Farmer in the ruck, and extra takings at the gate to see the clash of the colossi.

They both had great physical attributes. They were both 191cm. (6ft. 3in.), but Farmer at 94kg had to concede from 6 to 8kg in weight to the immensely solid Nicholls.

Their styles were different. Nicholls could rely on holding his position, with his bulky frame, against taller but more lightly built ruckmen. Farmer flew for the ball, often taking off early, to get a ride on his opponents and get to the ball fast. He would be just as likely to take the ball from the ruck, land like a cat and spear a handpass to a team-mate as to try for a conventional palm out.

Nicholls was usually a 'palm' ruckman, but he admitted that he changed his methods to counter-act Farmer.

'I probably didn't jump as early as Farmer, but when I played him I did... With Polly I never gave him any advantage because I'd do the same things as he did.... We'd both jump early for position, particularly at centre-bounces, and quite often the ball would come down and neither of us would get it.

'Probably I used to regard him as a better player than I was, and probably more skilled than I was, so I really had to dish it up to him all the time in ruckwork. If I didn't attack him on an aggressive basis every time he would beat me.'

Nicholls feels that, for all the hype, they often tended to nullify each other. But that took nothing away from the spectacle ... it just meant that each had met their match.

'We used to play it hard, and because we used to jump early, we quite often had blood noses and things .....'

Both men came from greatly different routes to get to the centre of things in football.

Farmer, of part Aboriginal parentage, had a family background

John Nicholls and Polly Farmer. Two masters of ruck play in conflict.

from around the wheatbelt town of Katanning, where his grandfather was a surveyor.

He grew up at Sister Kate's Cottage Homes for Children, first in the Perth suburb of Cottesloe, and then at the country town of Greenbushes. He learned his football early, and attributes this to the fact that he limped, with the right leg slightly longer than the other. He always wore a shoe on his left foot, so that he could kick a football.

He came through high school and gained his certificate as a motor mechanic, but this was always a background to the great thing in his life – football.

After he had made the grade Farmer revealed his boyhood ambitions: 'I always had secret

ambitions long before I went to play League football, when I was playing out at Kenwick and Maddington. Those ambitions were I wanted to play with East Perth, I wanted to play in a Premiership side, I wanted to play for the State, and I wanted to play in Victoria. And I wanted to play in a premiership side in Victoria, and also for the State ... I always thought they were going to come true. It was just a matter of how long it took.'

Farmer played 10 years in Western Australia before coming to Geelong in 1962, at the age of 27. In that time he had played 176 games with East Perth, won the WA best and fairest medal, the Sandover Medal, twice and his club's best and fairest seven times

in nine seasons.

He had developed his brilliant, attacking handball, his spring for marks and hit-outs and his balanced cat-like landings. He was strong and he was an accurate kick. He was ready.

Nicholls career path was simpler, but no less illustrious. He and older brother Don were signed by Carlton at the same time, with centreman Don being the main quarry. But soon the big kid that came with the deal was starring with the Maryborough Seniors, playing his first matches at the age of 14.

By the time he played his first game at Carlton at the age of 17 the formidable shape was developing – the tree trunk legs, the massive torso, the heavily muscled arms. Nicholls could run, he could spring to take a mark, his hands were good and his football brain alert.

And he could ruck all day.

He also had a frightening persona, an inner reserve that forbade familiarity, and a cool blue stare that could wither an opponent, 'Big Nick', as he became known, always got respect.

Nicholls went straight into the side on Easter Monday, 1957, in the old-fashioned back-pocket-ruck position. He never played in the reserves and played 17 seasons with Carlton, his strength and his skill growing to a point that he was at the pinnacle of his craft – sharing the peak with Farmer. In their time there were so many good ruckmen – Neville Crowe, John Schultz, Gary Dempsey, Len Thompson and Carl Ditterich, to name a few, but these were the acknowledged champions.

Farmer played just 101 games with Geelong from 1962 to 1967, but had a huge impact on the club and on the game. So did Nicholls in his 328 games for Carlton between 1957 and 1974.

Both men went on to coach their clubs over the same period. Farmer coaching Geelong in 1973 - 75, with a best place of 6th in 1974. Nicholls coached Carlton from 1972 to 1975 – for a Premiership in 1972.

1964

March 14. The VFL decides to allow coaches on the ground at quarter time to address players.

March 21. Phonse Tobin, VFL Treasurer, says in his private view the VFL may have to bring in new teams from the outer suburbs near VFL Park to cope with changes in Melbourne's population (→ 18/6/81).

March 28. St Kilda's move to the Moorabbin ground next season has given itchy feet to other clubs – particularly Richmond, Fitzroy and North Melbourne (→ 4/4).

April 4. The St Kilda move stirs a hornet's nest among Saint and Moorabbin supporters, after Moorabbin was suspended by the VFA (→ 10/5).

April 11. St Kilda coach Allan Jeans will use a walkie-talkie radio to communicate with the club's official runner – on the ground (→ 18/6/71).

June 20. Victoria thrashes WA at the MCG today, winning 24.21 (165) to 7.11 (53), with Ted Whitten brilliant. Full-forward Doug Wade injures his knee (→ 19/6/65).

July 20. League hears 20 witnesses before deciding not to charge Geelong's Geoff Rosenow over the 'Killigrew incident' on June 27 (→ 29/8).

Aug. 1. Essendon 5.13 (43) and Geelong 6.7 (43) fight a sensational draw. 33 minutes into the last quarter Essendon's Ken Fraser scores a behind and is knocked over. He declines the offer of another kick, and the siren sounds (→ 25/5/95).

Aug. 8. Geelong, 8.9 (57), easily account for South Melbourne, 1.9 (15). The goal that saves South from goalless ignominy is kicked by first gamer Ian Randle (→ 20/7/89).

Aug. 19. Bill Twomey says that the South Melbourne ground is perfect except for a quiet spot in front of the Press Box where no barrackers shout, just the coaches (→ 17/6/72).

Aug. 22. Carlton wallops Fitzroy, 19.20 (134) to 7.12 (54) but finish tenth, their worst position in history. Fitzroy do worse, not winning a game for the season (→ 27/6/93).

Debuts
Denis Marshall (Geel)
John 'Sam' Newman (Geel)

Retirements
Allen Aylett (N. Melb)
Stewart Lord (Geel)
Fred Wooller (Geel)

'Killa' king hit in Geelong race

June 27. North Melbourne coach Allan Killigrew was felled by a Geelong player in the players' race at Kardinia Park today. A brief brawl resulted between players and officials and Killigrew emerged with his face covered in blood. As a result, North Melbourne players and officials did not go to the Geelong rooms as is customary after the match, and the visitors left the ground without communicating with the home team.

It had been a match filled with fire and incident, narrowly won by the Cats, 11.8 (74) to 10.12 (72). At half time three policemen told North Melbourne back pocket Ken Dean that they intended to charge him for a clash with Denis Marshall in the second quarter, when Marshall was knocked sprawling over the boundary. Other observers say it was a fair bump, not an attempt to put Marshall out of the game.

A Geelong fan is composing 'An Ode to Footbrawl' to mark an unsavoury day (→ 20/7).

Saints wriggle on Moorabbin hook

May 10. St Kilda members have been up in arms over the recently announced move to play at Moorabbin next year, and the plan for a name change to Moorabbin.

But, after a lot of heat and angry meetings, the members have voted for the move, following an announcement from the club that the Moorabbin Council's requirement for a name change has been withdrawn.

The original plan was that the Club would be called St Kilda-Moorabbin. After ten years it would be Moorabbin. But the loss of name, and with it the club's history, has upset supporters most.

The move is believed to have been brought about by the expected financial benefits to club and council, after stalemate talks with the St Kilda Cricket Club. It has the blessing of the the League.

But the cricket club has threatened legal action, and a mob of angry supporters have even stormed the Moorabbin home of Saints' President, Graham Huggins (→ 19/4/65).

Mick Aylett leaves the battlefield

July 18. Allen 'Mick' Aylett broke his left arm in North Melbourne's debacle against Melbourne in the first quarter. By the end the score was 18.15 (123) to 6.15 (51).

After the game he said, 'While the doctors were setting it I looked up and saw my wife and mother. There was no point in telling them my arm was broken, all I could think about was the most reluctant break I've ever had to make in my life.

'I said "You've just seen me play my last quarter".'

One of the game's finest rovers, Aylett played 220 games and kicked 313 goals for North Melbourne after his debut in 1952 from University High School. He won the 1958 Tassie Medal, and also played Sheffield Shield cricket for Victoria.

Allen Aylett: career at an end.

Geelong go to brink for Marshall

Denis Marshall: a lot of red tape before he kicks a football.

June 11. The Coulter Law has come under sustained criticism over the Denis Marshall affair.

South Melbourne great Laurie Nash says every club breaks it, and Bendigo League President Noel Murphy says the Coulter Law is 'a joke'. Given the way it is ignored, its days are surely numbered.

In the VFL no payments directly or indirectly are permitted to induce a transfer.

It's alleged that Geelong or someone close paid £4000 for Marshall's transfer from Claremont.

If found guilty Marshall could have been suspended and Geelong expelled from the VFL for up to 12 months. Close VFL observers noted this was unlikely to happen and the case would be swept under a carpet of legalisms.

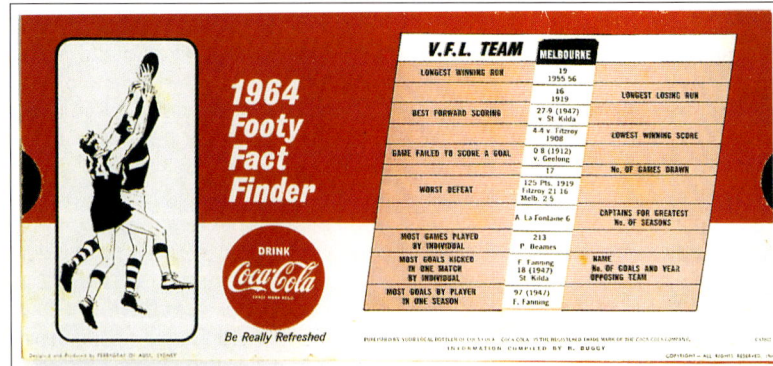

For the statistically minded the Coca-Cola fact finder tells you a lot of what you need to know about your team's record in 68 years of League football.

Let's talk about how big men fly, in between a meaty pie, woof

July 30. The football battle on TV and radio is nearly as fierce as it is on the paddock this year.

Three TV stations, and all radio stations bar two, are competing for the ears and eyes of football fanatics providing something about footy to listen to or watch every day.

Most popular programme, since it commenced in the 1962 season, is the 'replay' of highlights from two matches at six o'clock on Saturday nights on HSV7 and GTV9.

After the replay it's time for 'Football Inquest' on HSV7 hosted from the bench, or pulpit, by Michael Williamson. Since 1957 this show, a postmortem dissecting the afternoon's results, and interrogating star players in a friendly manner, has been compulsory viewing.

Sundays is 'World of Sport' day, also on HSV7. Hosted (or refereed) by Ron Casey, with the lugubrious Doug Elliott in charge of the pie warmer, and featuring an authoritative larrikin panel of ex-players, 'World of Sport' sprawls into the early afternoon.

This year's panel includes 'Captain Blood' Jack Dyer, Lou 'Lou Lou' Richards, the Professor 'Skeeter' Coghlan, the Brilliantined Bruce Andrew, Alan 'Baron' Ruthven and 'Gentleman' Jim Francis.

GTV9's Sunday contender, Tony Charlton's 'Football Show', has not quite managed to recreate the popular mayhem of 'World of Sport'.

The ABC shows this year include Roy Wright's 'Sports Cavalcade' on Tuesday evenings (→ 9/4/65).

Football gurus: Dyer, Andrew, Ruthven, Francis, Coghlan and Richards.

More great men under the eye of Mike Williamson for 'Football Inquest'.

Hassa's miracle kick saves Demons

Aug. 22. 'Hassa' Mann's miracle goal against Hawthorn last Saturday has become even more important in Melbourne's season after today's loss to Footscray.

The Bulldogs beat the inaccurate Demons 12.6 (78) to 4.14 (38) at the Western Oval.

Melbourne have finished the season on top of the Ladder, but only four points, and one game, ahead of Hawthorn in fifth place.

Had the result last week been reversed, and other results remained the same, it would have been Hawthorn on top, and Melbourne fifth.

Hawthorn had not been beaten at Glenferrie during the season, but

lost this one 10.9 (69) to Melbourne's 10.13 (73).

Hawthorn's playing coach Graham Arthur, on the field and in the fray, was not able to keep up with Norm Smith's last quarter, season-saving moves.

With Melbourne 16 points down at the last change, Smith shifted the quiet Brian Dixon to the opposite wing, where he soon kicked a goal, had a hand in two others, and in a couple of behinds as well. Then, in time-on Hassa Mann swooped on the ball in the impossible pocket at an impossible angle and threaded the freak goal that won the game, and top spot (→ 28/6/69).

Collis the best

Aug. 25. Carlton's centre half-back Gordon Collis won the Brownlow Medal with a healthy 27 votes, including seven best on ground, and votes in another four of the 17 games he played.

Ken Fraser (Essendon) and Phil Hay (Hawthorn) polled 19 votes each to be equal second.

Collis thanked his optician for the win. He didn't score last year when he couldn't sight the ball quickly.

He used to wait under the pack and 'the other chaps would be coming down as I started to go up'.

This season, with contact lenses, he says he's able to see the ball, instead of playing 'blind'.

Coleman and Vinar go toe to toe

Aug. 29. In a Semi Final full of angry incidents, even the coaches of Geelong and Essendon had to be restrained from joining a brawl in the third quarter. It involved Graham Beissel and Russell Blew of Essendon and Geelong's John Devine and Paul Vinar. John Coleman, the Essendon coach, charged on to the arena and tangled with Vinar. The Dons' doctor and a boundary umpire grabbed Coleman from behind and pulled him away, but not before Bob Davis, Geelong's coach, had rushed on to make his own feelings felt. He had selectors Tom Morrow and John Hyde with him. Umpire Ron Brophy had his work cut out to cool everyone down.

Bill Twomey of the *Sporting Globe* joked that John and Bob had better watch out or iron bars might be placed over the benches next year.

The atmosphere was electric and gave the match the feeling of a Grand Final. Once the Cats' smooth teamwork overcame the tension, they went on to win, 12.12 (84) to 10.5 (65), and looked like a Premiership side (→ 19/5/65).

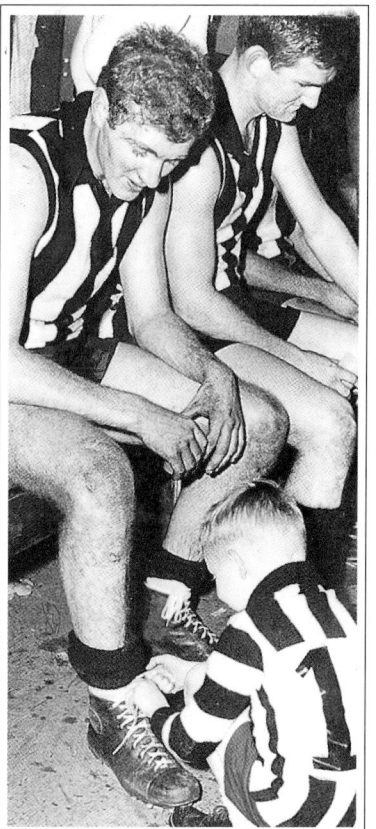

Worship at the feet of the master.

Crompton's kick foils Gabbo's gallop

The end of Ray Gabelich's gallop and a mighty goal for Collingwood.

Norm Smith and 'Checker' Hughes salute the Melbourne victory.

Captain Ron Barassi proudly shows the Premiership Cup to the crowd.

Sept. 19. What a last quarter! What a victory, snatched from the jaws of defeat, for Melbourne, courtesy of back pocket Neil Crompton, who was 100 yards out of position and had not scored a goal all season.

What a sad ending for a gallant Collingwood, whose skipper Ray Gabelich seemed to have sealed the result with his amazing run in the dying minutes of the quarter.

The epic last quarter of the Grand Final was played to the accompaniment of a constant roar from the crowd of 102,469.

After the game, which Melbourne won 8.16 (64) to 8.12 (60), it took a long time for the excitement to die down around the MCG.

In the rooms, the Melbourne players were stunned, seeming to hardly believe they had won the match. Gabelich and his side had given everything and had lost, but the captain was full of sportsmanship, saying that they had done their best and that Melbourne had proved to be the better team on the day.

It was a low-scoring, tough game, so different from the Second Semi when the Demons roared away to beat the Magpies by 89 points.

In the first three quarters of the Grand Final the defences were on top and the scores were always close. Collingwood had a two-point advantage at half time, but Melbourne scored the only two goals of the third quarter to be 11 points up.

Goals to Des Tuddenham and Gabelich, with Melbourne only able to manage behinds, left Collingwood three points down with 21 minutes of the quarter played.

Then came the supreme moment of the match. Tuddenham saw open space on the members' side and sent the ball out there, to be collected by Gabelich who, in the heat of the battle, had been left unattended.

Gabelich, 17 stone and not equipped with either great pace or ball skills, set off for the goal square from the half-forward flank. With Demon defenders streaking from everywhere to cut him off, he bounced the ball three times as he lumbered on, and each time nearly lost it.

But the Demons could not get to him and he slammed the ball through from five yards out.

Surely that effort was enough, in this low-scoring game, for Colling-

'The Age' cartoonist Sam Wells had no shortage of Grand Final material.

wood to win through. But the Demons came on again, and Hassa Mann marked right in front, but managed only a behind as Melbourne fans groaned in frustration.

Crompton's effort seemed so simple, almost an anticlimax. Brian Dixon drove the ball forward, and the ball fell from the hands of a huge back. Crompton calmly gathered it, ran a few paces and put it through.

Melbourne stacked the defence as Collingwood attacked repeatedly. Full-forward Ian Graham had a shot, but kicked out of bounds.

Collingwood were in attack, and there were only three players outside their forward line when the siren sounded to end the drama.

Melbourne's centre line had done much to keep it in the game, and among the best players were Mann, Dixon, and Frank 'Bluey' Adams in his last game. Collingwood's best were Laurie Hill in defence, ruck-rover Kevin Rose, ruckman Trevor Steer and rover Mickey Bone.

1964 Statistics

Leading Goalkicker:
John Peck (Haw) 69
Brownlow Medallist:
Gordon Collis (Carl)
Finals: First Semi Ess 10.5 (65) Geel 12.12 (84); **Second Semi** Melb 19.20 (134) Coll 6.9 (45); **Preliminary Final** Coll 7.6 (48) Geel 5.14 (44); **Grand Final** Melb 8.16 (64) Coll 8.12 (60)

Ladder:	W	L	D	%	pts
Melb	14	4		138.1	56
Coll	13	4	1	133.2	54
Ess	13	4	1	130.2	54
Geel	13	4	1	127.4	54
Haw	13	5		121.0	52
St K	10	8		118.4	40
Foots	9	9		88.1	36
N. Melb	8	10		87.2	32
Rich	6	12		84.9	24
Carl	5	12	1	90.3	22
S. Melb	2	16		68.0	8
Fitz	0	18		59.7	0

1965

April 9. *The Age* football writer Percy Beames joins ABV2's 'Focus on Football', with Roy Wright, Jack Dyer, Thorold Merrett, Harry Beitzel, Tony Ongarello and Ron Barassi (→ 21/4/66).

April 17. Ron Barassi in his first game for Carlton inspires big win over Hawthorn, 12.19 (91) to 8.6 (54) (→ 15/8/68).

April 24. Garry Young undergoes surgery for a perforated bowel after playing on despite injury in Hawthorn's loss 6.8 (44) to Essendon's 20.18 (138). Captain Graham Arthur told him 'Get up you weak bastard' (→ 12/4/75).

May 15. Essendon stop St Kilda's winning run of four games in a fiery clash at Moorabbin, winning 14.9 (93) to 7.14 (56) (→ 14/6).

May 19. Essendon coach John Coleman is the subject of a complaint by field umpire Barry Gaudion following the Shelton/Baldock melee on Saturday. A boundary umpire spoke to him at the time, but he was not involved (→ 15/4/66).

May 22. Alistair Lord makes a sensational appearance for Geelong in their 11.21 (87) to 8.8 (56) win over Fitzroy. Lord decided to play just half an hour before the game after earlier standing out of League football, in an attempt to gain a clearance to Burnie.

May 22. Essendon's Geoff Pryor introduces a sensible new idea to League football by wearing a mouthguard.

June 5. Norm Smith is the master coach when Melbourne account for former pupil Ron Barassi's inaccurate Blues 13.17 (95) to 6.22 (58) (→ 27/7).

June 14. Saints give Demons first defeat for the season, 18.14 (122) to 9.7 (61) (→ 12/6/67).

June 19. Bill Barrot dominates centre as Vics crush SA 19.17 (131) to 9.18 (72) (→ 10/7).

July 10. Injury hit and tired from two games in Western Australia, Victoria are thumped by South Australia 12.11 (83) to 3.1 (19) (→ 18/6/66).

Debuts
Stan Alves (Melb)
Kevin Bartlett (Rich)
Barry Breen (St K)
Bob Keddie (Haw)
Peter McKenna (Coll)
Kevin 'Cowboy' Neale (St K)
Barry Richardson (Rich)

Retirement
Mervyn Hobbs (Foots)

Saints go south for winter, Tigers prowl MCG

April 19. Three teams had mixed success in their first games at new 'home' grounds during the split opening round.

Coburg Oval was in shocking condition for its debut as a VFL ground. North paid the price, slithering to a loss to South Melbourne, 4.12 (36) to 6.10 (46).

36,283 supporters turned out at the MCG for Richmond's game at its new home, and saw the Tigers unluckily go down by just a kick to Melbourne, 6.5 (41) to 7.5 (47). Richmond's form suggests the move across the park may be beneficial.

St Kilda drew an extraordinary attendance of 51,370 to Moorabbin, and showed that they mean business down south with a hard-fought win over Collingwood 8.12 (60) to 8.6 (54).

The Moorabbin move, the subject of much bitterness, has been vindicated, not only from the playing point of view, but also by showing the huge potential support for football south of the Yarra (→ 27/4/82).

Farewell to the Junction as Darrel Baldock leads the Saints out.

Barassi defection stuns football world

Jan. 31. Melbourne captain Ron Barassi, the player who more than anyone embodied the Melbourne tradition of loyalty to the team, has finally succumbed to the persistent wooing of new Carlton President, George Harris.

Barassi will take his number, 31, to Carlton as playing coach.

The new Carlton regime had formulated the plan to acquire Barassi last season when the Blues fell to their lowest position ever, tenth, under coach Ken Hands and captain Sergio Silvagni. The Harris group felt a dramatic gesture and change in style was needed, and went after Barassi even before they had gained control of Carlton.

Initial negotiations before Christmas saw Barassi offered £18,000 with side benefits over three years.

Melbourne countered by appointing him assistant coach, and when the pot was further sweetened by Carlton Norm Smith offered to step down in Barassi's favour.

Barassi still wanted to leave, saying he had repaid any debts of loyalty to the club. The wrangling in both clubs continued in December, with 1963 Carlton captain John Ni-

Ron Barassi under foreign flag.

cholls almost taking a NSW offer.

Eventually Melbourne recognised Barassi's determination and right to secure his financial future by becoming the highest paid footballer of any Australian code.

Barassi's first comment after his clearance was: 'I'm aiming to mould the perfect team. No one has achieved this yet, but if you aim high enough, I think you have a better chance of success' (→ 17/4).

Star Busse

May 15. Neil Busse hasn't had too many fans at Tigerland recently, and the tall and skinny forward has been in danger of demotion.

But his efforts in defence against Hawthorn today had them roaring in adulation. Busse took mark after brilliant mark to repel the Hawks, who were trying to bounce back after Richmond had a 35-point lead at half time. The Tigers won 14.21 (105) to 8.12 (60). Jack Dyer's old adage, 'Ratbags to the backline', seems to have worked again.

Flick pass outed

June 2. The famous Footscray 'flick pass' has finally been given the flick by the lawmakers at the Australian National Football Council.

A legitimate hand-ball is where the ball is held on one hand, and hit with the clenched fist of the other hand. Backhanded or fore-handed swipes and pushes of the ball, such as practised with great success by Ted Whitten's Footscray teams over the past six years, are now deemed to be throws, and will be penalised (→ 2/5/92).

Somerville 'faints', but Bombers supreme

Ken Fraser accepts the cup.

Trainers and ambulance men remove the unconscious John Somerville, as Collingwood's Duncan Wright looks on.

Sept. 25. John Somerville was not in the Essendon line-up which swamped St Kilda to take the Premiership Flag today.

He was still resting with concussion after having 'fainted' in last week's Preliminary Final.

Duncan Wright of Collingwood was standing over him, but nobody in the 95,386 crowd has come forward as a witness, and questions by VFL and police have brought no charges.

The incident seemed to spur Essendon on last week and they went on to score a 55-point win.

But things were expected to be harder today, as the Saints, who finished on top of the Ladder, had had a week's rest after the Second Semi, won against Collingwood by a point.

Essendon have had to battle up from fourth place, but had easy wins over Geelong in the First Semi and then Collingwood.

After a tight first half they jumped St Kilda in the third quarter, kicking 5.8 to 1.3. The Saints got to within two points, as Essendon booted seven points in a row, but then Ted Fordham (2), Brian Sampson, John Birt and Hughie Mitchell all scored goals in a a brilliant burst of football. The Dons held the Saints out in the last quarter to win, 14.21 (105) to 9.16 (70).

Fordham was the difference, with his seven goals at full-forward, and he was well supported down the ground, particularly by forwards Ken Fraser and Geoff Gosper, and an outstanding following division of Don McKenzie, Sampson, Mitchell and Birt.

St Kilda had stars in Ian Stewart, Darrel Baldock and Ian Cooper, but they lacked the overall team strength of the Dons.

Norm Smith sacked for four days

July 27. Norm Smith has made a comeback as coach of Melbourne, after just four days in the football wilderness.

The direct cause of Smith's sacking was his view that there was a lack of support from the Melbourne Committee in the libel case brought against him by umpire Don Blew.

'Checker' Hughes had been appointed as replacement coach.

Smith, on the Tony Charlton Football Show, asked Melbourne supporters to make a public protest. He said of the Committee: 'Get rid of these blokes – that is the only way the club will progress.'

With the loss to North, 11.15 (81) to 9.6 (60), and threatened resignations of staff and players, the Committee had little choice but to reappoint their most successful coach.

Ian Stewart's surprise Brownlow win

Aug. 31. St. Kilda centreman Ian Stewart shocked the public and the pundits by winning the Brownlow Medal in a count-back from North Melbourne's Noel Teasdale after they had tied on 20 votes.

Stewart had six 'three votes' and Teasdale five. The remarkable Darrel Baldock, who won the *Sporting Globe's* Bunton Medal, was third with 18 votes, making it a great year for the Saints.

Stewart was astounded that he had won, saying 'I just can't believe it. I thought that 'Doc' Baldock or Noel Teasdale would win'.

Some consolation for Teasdale is his choice of prizes in winning the GTV9 award – a car, a South Sea Island cruise with £150 spending money or a runabout boat. He has already won two cars as 'World of Sport' and 'Football Inquest' awards on HSV7 (→ 30/8/71).

St Kilda centreman Ian Stewart gets the Medal, on a count-back after tying with North's Noel Teasdale.

1965 Statistics

Leading Goalkicker:
John Peck (Haw) 56
Brownlow Medallist:
Ian Stewart (St K)
Finals: First Semi Geel 7.9 (51) Ess 14.19 (103); **Second Semi** St K 13.24 (102) Coll 14.17 (101); **Preliminary Final** Coll 6.6 (42) Ess 14.13 (97); **Grand Final** St K 9.16 (70) Ess 14.21 (105)

Ladder:	W	L	%	pts
St K	14	4	136.3	56
Coll	13	5	130.2	52
Geel	13	5	121.2	52
Ess	12	6	132.9	48
Rich	10	8	125.0	40
Carl	10	8	110.7	40
Melb	10	8	96.2	40
S. Melb	9	9	89.4	36
N. Melb	5	13	80.8	20
Foots	4	14	77.1	16
Fitz	4	14	70.5	16
Haw	4	14	68.9	16

Bob Skilton the heart and soul of South

Bob Skilton was 17 when he first ran onto the ground for the South Melbourne senior team, as a stand-in rover against Footscray.

His Reserves coach, Peewee Condon, had told the selectors he wasn't ready for senior football. But they needed a rover, and that thickset body looked as though it could last the distance.

A few hours later everyone knew that Skilton would never play Reserves football again.

He had a sublime opening, receiving a perfect palm from the ruck and sending a skimming pass into the forward line. His confidence grew and he began to get kicks around the ground, to the point that the Footscray warhorse Charlie Sutton lined him up to try and knock the stuffing out of him.

Skilton skipped sideways at the fateful moment, leaving Sutton's shoulder to cleave the air. There were many awful crashes later in his career, notably with Eric Guy of St Kilda and John Nicholls of Carlton, but he was saved on that first day and allowed some injury free games to get used to playing at the top level.

He did have an engine in that strong body that could keep him going all day, and he backed it with agility and courage in the packs. He could mark, and at 17 he had kicked so often with either foot that he didn't know if he was left or right footed.

There were illustrious years to come – the captaincy, almost permanent State selection, three Brownlows, and nine club best and fairests. But the one thing he wanted was denied, a Premiership for his beloved South.

As a boy growing up in Port Melbourne Bobby Skilton hated South Melbourne. All his allegiance was with the rival suburb and the VFA club Port Melbourne, where his father, Bob snr., had been captain and coach.

Like all the kids around Bob was football mad, and his father saw to it that he was well prepa-

BOB SKILTON
SOUTH MELBOURNE

red in the skills of a game. He would kick a football with either foot against a factory wall for hour after hour.

He started playing at the age of 10 in an under 16 Port Melbourne YMCA team, a little kid brought in as a spare part, but who soon was getting a kick.

He continued to stand out in junior ranks, and his father thought then that young Bobby might one day win a Brownlow Medal. An upturning in his football life came with the arrival of Tommy 'The Turk' Lahiff as captain-coach of Port, and the unofficial coach of all the kids in Port. Lahiff had Bobby playing so well that he earned an invitation to train with South.

Bobby, at 14, wanted nothing to do with the hated South, but the club knew his potential and wouldn't clear him to Port or his fancied League club, Melbourne (a team he later coached).

His father insisted he should start with a League club, and he eventually ran out with the Fourths. Once he had the colours on a change came over him and he became the most fiercely loyal South man – rejecting countless lucrative offers to move to other clubs when he was the best rover in Victoria.

Bob Rose – the man in the middle of the Magpie machine

R. ROSE
COLLINGWOOD

Just as Bob Skilton was lacing up his football boots for his first senior season, the one man who could rival him for toughness and skill around the packs, Bob Rose, had prematurely retired from Collingwood and was heading for a coaching berth in the country.

Rose was not quite as consistent a ball winner or goal scorer as Skilton, but he was not far behind. And he was the toughest player for his size in the competition, hurting his opponents with his confrontational style of play.

Bob Rose came from Nyah West, on the Murray, the eldest of seven children in a fanatical Collingwood family, related to the football manufacturing Sherrin family. He captained both the football and cricket teams at Swan Hill High School, but he first came to Melbourne as a boxer, winning junior bouts.

While in Melbourne he turned out for Collingwood, a diminutive figure in a ragged jumper and holey socks. Once he started moving and displaying his ball skills he was soon signed up.

Rose started in the reserves in 1946, and played so well that he was second in the reserves best and fairest, despite playing the last six games in the seniors.

His baptism of fire in his first reserves match was orchestrated by a former Collingwood star Alby Pannam, who was then coaching the Richmond seconds. 'Alby hung on to me, stood on my toes, kneed me in the belly – gave me a physical thrashing. After that I realised what League football was all about.'

Bob Rose was soon making his own presence felt, hurling his own 5ft. 9in. and 79kg frame into the packs. His ball handling, his handball, his long kicking and pinpoint footpasses topped off his ability to win the ball in the packs, and he was soon winning regular acclaim as best-on-ground in Collingwood teams that were always near the top.

He won the club's best and fairest, the Copeland Trophy, in 1949, and three years running in 1951, 1952 and 1953, and in 1953 was second to Bill Hutchison of Essendon in the Brownlow. He played 15 state games.

In the last of his 152 games, the 1955 Grand Final against Melbourne, he was flattened by Demons' tough guy Noel MacMahen. He had been carrying injuries for years and, at age 27, decided to take a well paid coaching job at Wangaratta.

The second chapter of Bob Rose's association with the Magpies began in 1964 when he returned as coach. He had Collingwood in the finals every year but one between 1964 and 1970.

He turned out pacy, skilful teams, and had the total respect of his players. He had them in the Grand Final in 1964, 1966 and 1970, losing two by a kick and the third after being 44 points ahead of Carlton at half time. The famous 'Colliwobbles' became associated with Rose and he left Collingwood at the end of 1971 to coach Footscray.

He returned in 1985-1986 but the club was 'off the boil'. He is now on the Board of Directors and a life-member of the Magpies, and is still a driving force of the club.

The springtime of E.J. Whitten

Just 22,500 people crammed into the old Punt Road ground, Richmond, on Saturday 21 April 1951, when E. J. Whitten played his first game of League football.

E.J. wasn't EJ then. He wasn't Ted either. He was Teddy, a vulnerable 17 year old with a big reputation. He'd done all the pre-season the times demanded. Two months before the first game the Melbourne Sun had reported that 'Footscray will start training on Saturday 2 March, and on Sunday the footballers will play Geelong in a social cricket match at Werribee.' In the intra-club practice matches of the day Teddy 'shone' on 31 March and was 'outstanding' on 7 April.

He was selected at centre-half-forward for the opening match. He symbolised the new Footscray. The old guard had gone. Teddy, Peter Box (Brownlow medallist in 1955), Don Ross, Herb Henderson, Arthur Edwards, Jim Gallagher and Doug Reynolds all played their first games with Footscray in 1951. All seven were to appear for the Dogs in their first premiership in 1954.

Footscray's average age was 22 and the side was the youngest since the club's admission to the VFL in 1925. Saturday 21 April, 1951 was the beginning of a dynasty, certainly as measured by the history of a club which had played in only five finals in 26 years and won none of them.

It was heady stuff. All these talented kids led by the ultimate father figure and protector, the pocket battleship built like a footballer, Charlie Sutton.

Folklore has it that, after Teddy goaled with his first kick in VFL football, his opponent Mopsy Fraser said to him, 'You shouldn't have done that, son', and Whitten had been dispatched, unconscious, before half-time by the notorious knuckleman. Not so. Teddy was replaced in the last quarter with a sprained ankle.

But legend still makes its point. Teddy was as open as today's trading hours. He was a shade over twelve stone and just on 6'1''. Weights didn't exist and the

Teddy Whitten in the prime of his football life out at the Western Oval.

boy had nothing to protect him except his talent.

Jack Dyer, who coached Richmond against Footscray in his first game as a non-playing coach said, three weeks later, 'Whitten is the type who needs plenty of room'. But Footscray moved Teddy to full-forward where there was precious little room in the mud of a 1951 Melbourne winter.

Teddy recalled years later: 'After playing against Chanter you'd have thought I had taken up shaving my legs. He pulled all the hair from one of my legs as we jostled for position.'

But the flair was there from the beginning. The characteristic mark with elbows bent and the ball taken back behind his head; with the pose held just long enough for the crowd to pay its respects. Lair, but also native cunning in providing a milli-second for his next move, which was always to give the ball off to the team-mate in the best position.

To the fans of the 'Scray Teddy could do no wrong and did no wrong. His boyishness, spirit and obvious love for the game would have endeared him to anyone.

Whitten was a superbly proportioned athlete, although the enduring memory of his debut

season is legs - long legs, fast legs, leaping legs.

There were plenty of hiccups along the way for Footscray and for EJ. Mid-season in 1951 he was accidentally knocked unconscious twice - once in a match and once at training - and spent a combined 27 hours in hospital in coma.

Footscray finished the home and away season in fourth place. Drawn to play Essendon in the first semi-final. But Teddy was in doubt. As a National Service Trainee he was denied leave by the Army until Prime Minister Bob Menzies intervened. Footscray lost and Teddy was ordinary. When he returned to the Puckapunyal camp there was a telegram waiting for him from Menzies: 'It was a complete waste of time getting you leave for the final'.

In 1953 Sutton structured the power goal-to-goal line that was to drive Footscray to the flag the following season. Whitten became the new centre-half-back and made the position his own. His talents fitted this key defensive post perfectly. His pace, marking and run at the ball, together with his raking drop kicks and booming torps turned the old notion of defence on its head.

The Bulldogs won their first ever semi-final with an eight points victory over Essendon. Box and Whitten were Footscray's best. 'Scray went down to Geelong in the preliminary final, but when Ted and the team carried off Sutton shoulder high the mood was strangely celebratory. There was a premiership in the air.

Ted won the first of his five club championships in the Premiership year 1954 when Footscray cruised to a 51 point win over Melbourne in their first ever appearance on the last Saturday in September.

Ted starred, but in my mind the definitive best game he played in his entire club career was against Collingwood at Victoria Park in the opening match of 1955. Noted *Argus* football writer Hugh Buggy summed up: 'Footscray, playing with a power and quick-thinking resource kindled by the fire of youth, tore the Magpie 'machine' apart and rampaged through to an overwhelming 56-points victory. Boyish Ted Whitten, who had now advanced to champion stature, broke the hearts of the Magpies. Always a couple of thoughts ahead of three different opponents thrown against him, Whitten consistently cut off Magpie thrusts. He held 17 marks in man-to-man duels or in thrashing packs. Magpie attackers said later it seemed Whitten had taken 70 marks instead of 17. Amiable Ted became the main architect of Footscray's victory.'

'Amiable' was an unexpected word in the context of a football writer's post mortem. But Buggy got it right. The dictionary defines 'amiable' as 'feeling and inspiring friendliness; lovable'. This was the personality trait in Ted that was to flower and endear him to the football world and many outside it.

In the winter of his life came a long battle against cancer. EJ's summer, autumn and winter made an unforgettable impact on all those who knew him and those who knew of him. But there'll not be another springtime like it.

Noel Delbridge.

1966

Magpie mop top bags round one dozen

April 23. Peter McKenna, Collingwood's 19-year-old full-forward with the pop-star looks, became the first player to kick 12 goals in an opening round game since the great John Coleman did it in 1949. Coleman's feat was on debut.

McKenna's debut season, 1965, was not stunning. He played 12 games and was criticised for playing from behind, but this may have been because he was not played regularly at full-forward.

McKenna has worked hard over the summer to improve his speed and fitness, and with some better delivery from up the ground might be a success as a spearhead.

Collingwood defeated Hawthorn, 17.13 (115) to 9.8 (62) (→ 8/8/70).

Rising star McKenna is congratulated by Max Urquhart and Ian Graham.

Clay wakes up to sign with Tigers

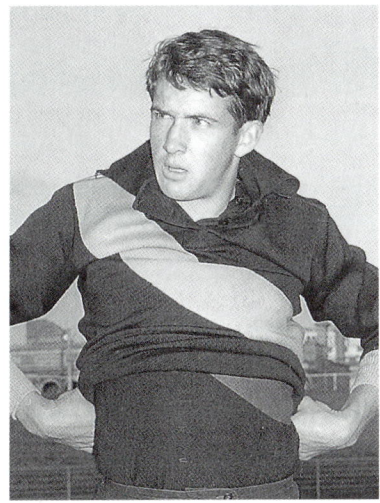

Dick Clay tries on the jumper.

April 23. 'I was tired and wanted to go to bed.' So said 21-year-old star full-forward Dick Clay, explaining why he originally signed with North Melbourne. North's agreement with Clay expired at midnight and today he signed to begin his League career with Richmond.

Clay, from Kyabram, kicked 120 goals in 1964. He said he was 'only a kid' when he signed with North, after having arrived home at midnight one night to find an official waiting. By 2 a.m. Clay signed so that he could get some sleep. He said his latest move came because of his admiration for Richmond's new coach, Tom Hafey.

Siren troubles cause early and late games

April 25. A groundsman at Princes Park caused football mayhem today when he threw a master switch that cut power from the siren.

The result was that Carlton and Richmond played an extra five and a half minutes.

The emergency bell was missing, from the timekeepers' box. It was found later in a wheelbarrow under the scoreboard.

The timekeepers tried to signal, the crowd jumped the fence and a mounted policeman galloped across the ground to tell the umpire, who couldn't be convinced.

At the correct time Richmond led by eight points, and eventually won 16.10 (106) to 14.16 (100).

There was siren trouble of a different kind at the Melbourne and St Kilda game. A phantom siren sounded early, making coaches and spectators think that the game had finished. St Kilda won, 17.7 (109) to 4.9 (33) (→ 13/5/67).

Wall-to-wall football on television

A perfect weekend's television.

Leo O'Brien tipped from Cat basket

April 26. Mr Leo O'Brien, Secretary of the Geelong Football Club, claims he has been sacked. 'Mr Jack Jennings, the President, insists that I have not been dismissed; he says I have been replaced. I have not had time to consult a dictionary to discover the difference,' said Mr O'Brien. His replacement, Mr C.M. Elliott, has the title 'general secretary-manager'. He comes from Sydney, which has prompted Mr O'Brien to wonder where his successor managed to acquire a knowledge of Australian Rules football superior to his own.

April 21. If you don't like football, don't watch television between six and seven on Saturday nights.

Following protracted negotiations between the VFL and the TV stations over replay rights it has been announced that every station will show portions of two matches at the same times.

This weekend's split round means that the dose will be repeated on Monday at 6 p.m. as well.

In addition, HSV7 screens the 'Football Show' on Friday night, and 'Football Inquest' on Saturday after the replay, as well as 'World of Sport' on Sunday including the 'Football Show' and panel.

ABV2 believes it has an advantage because its replays are screened without commercials (→ 7/4/67).

Rectangle stops the traffic in centre

July 30. Carlton coach Ron Barassi thinks the centre rectangle idea used experimentally today will be tested next in the Night Premiership series. The rectangle is an attempt to ease the crush of players around the centre bounce. Barassi thought it worked quite well at Carlton, and definitely eased congestion.

Former Collingwood star Bill Twomey, commenting in the *Sporting Globe*, was inclined to agree: 'It showed there's a good reason to start streamlining Aussie Rules.' The new rule had little effect on the game as a spectacle (→ 21/3/73).

Roberts' big mouth upsets the Saints

May 18. Neil Roberts, the 1958 Brownlow Medallist and former St Kilda captain, is now an ex-Committeeman, having suddenly ended 15 years service with the club. He was dismissed because of his comments on Channel 7 and in the *Sporting Globe*. The club blamed his criticism of the VFL and of an umpire, and a suggestion that Verdun Howell return to the backline.

In relation to the umpire, Roberts said the club apparently feared it might suffer if this umpire controlled a Saints' game.

Star forward rises over Apple Isle

Peter Hudson flies high for Tasmania, in a Carnival match against the VFA.

June 9. Tasmanians starred – for both sides – in the one-sided game between Victoria and Tasmania at the ANFC Carnival in Hobart. The VFL won 26.24 (180) to 11.13 (79). For Victoria, ex-Tasmanian Darrel Baldock kicked five and was best 'football wizard' on the ground.

But the eyes of football scouts looking for new talent were on Tasmania's best player, Peter Hudson from New Norfolk.

Hudson booted six goals and gave away two more in showing that he is a ready-made VFL player.

Unfortunately for the other 11 clubs, he has already signed a Form Four with Hawthorn.

Competition for Hudson's services has been hot for a number of years, since he made his debut in senior football in 1963.

He began his career playing for his school, New Norfolk High, in the morning, and for the local side, Upper Derwent, in the afternoon.

Upper Derwent were coached by his dad, Bob Hudson, at the time and they were the youngest and oldest on the field.

VFL clubs have been waving around cheque books with sign-on fees of $1000 or $2000, and aeroplane tickets to Melbourne to watch the Finals, like confetti.

Hudson has kicked 100 goals a season or more each year.

The main obstacle to running out for Hawthorn is the demand of New Norfolk for a $10,000 transfer fee, and Hudson's vacillation.

Hudson said of the transfer demand: 'It's crazy. No footballer's worth that much. Anyway I'm not a slave or a piece of livestock to be bought and sold' (→ 22/4/67).

Skilton plays on but retires as coach

Aug. 30. Bob Skilton's decision to quit as coach but play on for South Melbourne again raises the question of the future of playing coaches. Last year there were four, but Graham Arthur lost his post at Hawthorn at the end of the season, Ted Whitten's playing days at Footscray may be drawing to a close, so only Carlton's Ron Barassi looks safe.

Skilton, a double Brownlow Medallist, disagrees with Whitten and Barassi, who say they can help most by being on the ground. Skilton said 100 per cent concentration was needed. 'You can't do that as a captain-coach' (→ 5/9/70).

Abusive coaches given a warning

Aug. 20. The Victorian Football League is likely to crack down on Essendon coach John Coleman, reported by a boundary umpire for yelling obscene and abusive remarks at him during the game against Hawthorn today. Back in July, VFL spokesman Terry Young warned that coaches who criticise umpires risk disqualification. This was in response to verbal outbursts by Ron Barassi and several other coaches. Now, with Coleman to face the VFL's Investigation Committee, Mr Young's warning could be made reality (→ 11/6/73).

Bill Ryan's big hands can hold 38 eggs, or one football, easily. No wonder he's such a great mark.

'Stewart to Baldock' sends the Saints up to heaven

Brownlow Medallist Ian Stewart runs with his captain Darrel Baldock in the pre-Grand Final captains' parade.

In 1960, when 27-year-old Allan Jeans, recently retired Saints player, answered an advertisement for his club's coach, he did not give himself a great chance.

'I wasn't the best coach, just the cheapest,' he joked after his appointment late in 1960. He became the Saints' greatest coach in its most successful era.

In 1961 he soon had the scalp of 1960 Premiers Melbourne and later, for the first time in 40 years, a VFL team was held goalless when Richmond managed only eight behinds to St Kilda's 12.19 (91). The Saints made the Finals for the first time since 1939, but went out by nine points to Footscray in the First Semi.

Help was at hand, for brilliant 22-year-old Tasmanian Darrel Baldock, the game's most sought-after player, signed on in 1962.

In gruelling, muddy conditions at Glenferrie Oval next season he dazzled, drawing applause from the home grandstand, in a match-winning performance. Then, against North, he kicked five goals and gave another five away.

Jeans was later to say that the Saints never lost a game when Baldock played well.

In the opening round of 1963, with Baldock now captain, new stars shone. A 17-year-old ruckman, Carl Ditterich, began to bound around the ground, taking marks and applying some vigour. Another debutant was baby-faced Ian Stewart, so shy at 18 that he bought his own training guernsey.

In the centre he built one of football's memorable partnerships with Baldock, and they seemed to have a hand in all 14 goals against Richmond.

With Ditterich thumping the ball in a style that was to put him among the League's most feared ruckmen, the Saints piled on 17.14 (116) to North's 4.8 (32) to get into the Finals for the second time in three years, again finishing fourth.

After a frustrating and patchy 1964, with strife over the move to Moorabbin, the Saints had Verdun Howell in control at full-forward. In 1965 kicked nine goals in a record 24.12 (156) win

over Hawthorn 11.9 (75), while Stewart won his first Brownlow that year. His flawless left foot passes to Baldock had built St Kilda's charge.

Baldock's bravery, his perfect balance and extraordinary skill at easing from a pack to pass perfectly to position, were hallmarks.

He could do almost anything in the wet, took ferocious punishment and would even train alone, controlling two footballs at once.

When he injured his knee he was told to keep it in plaster for six weeks. Two weeks later he slipped into Moorabbin. No one suspected his selection on the bench in the season's last game.

Under immense pressure against Hawthorn and with barrackers bellowing for Baldock, Jeans sent him on in the third term. He soon goaled, inspirationally. Hawk David Parkin cited this as one of the most dramatic moments of his playing days.

The Saints won that game 14.9 (93) to 13.5 (83) – and then the Flag – via Baldock and a final, fateful kick by Barry Breen.

When the Saints came wobbling in to victory

Desperate Magpies try to prevent the kick that made St Kilda history.

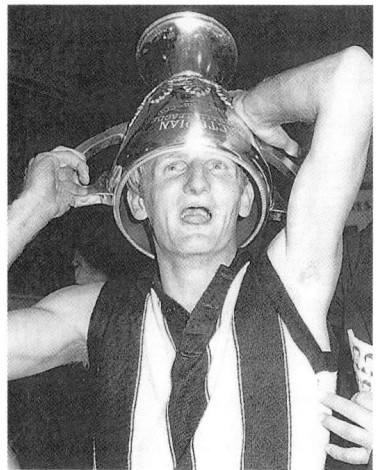

Ian Cooper tries the cup for size.

Coach Jeans greets captain Baldock.

Sept. 24. It took 69 years and a wobbly kick for a behind, in time-on, for St Kilda to win its first VFL Premiership, defeating Collingwood by a solitary point.

The Saints' long-suffering supporters were deliriously happy. The last Saturday in September finally belonged to them.

A strongly pro-St Kilda crowd of 101,655 at the MCG went mad when 18-year-old Barry Breen had the most important kick in the club's history to break the deadlock. Breen has not been noted for his kicking from centre-half-forward, but the target was big enough, even for him.

At the start, Darrel Baldock won the toss and the Saints kicked with the wind. St Kilda scored the first two goals before Collingwood captain Des Tuddenham posted a major for the Magpies. Ian Stewart was starring in the centre for the Saints.

Although St Kilda led by four points at the first change, it was already apparent that this would be a game of defences. Both coaches, St Kilda's Allan Jeans and Collingwood's Bob Rose, stationed ruckmen in the back pocket to thwart attacks with strong marking. Players threw themselves into the game and each time the Saints looked like breaking clear Collingwood rallied.

St Kilda were only four points up at the last change.

The Saints could have wrapped the game up early in the last quarter but kicked a string of points. Then Jeff Moran goaled on the run to put them ten points ahead. As the Saints squandered chances, the Magpies reduced the deficit to a point, only to see Neale mark and kick his fifth.

GRAND FINAL 1966

OFFICIAL ORGAN OF THE VICTORIAN FOOTBALL LEAGUE

COLLINGWOOD v ST. KILDA
SATURDAY, 24th SEPTEMBER

20c

SOUVENIR FOOTBALL RECORD · MELBOURNE CRICKET GROUND

Cover of the 'Football Record'.

Collingwood were finishing the stronger and Tuddenham's point levelled the scores at the 23 and a half minute mark.

St Kilda's determination to make history kept them going as Baldock went on the ball.

With precious seconds passing, Breen intercepted a Collingwood handpass and snapped for goal. The ball wobbled and then dribbled through for a point. Collingwood launched one last attack, but Saints' fullback Bob Murray marked and kicked as the siren sounded. Stewart, Brian Sierakowski, Ian Cooper and Neale starred for St Kilda while Terry Waters, Wayne Richardson, Len Thompson and Tuddenham stood out for Colling-wood.

St Kilda defeated Collingwood, 10.14 (74) to 10.13 (73).

Saints in Magpie clothing thrill to the applause of the Grand Final crowd.

1966 Statistics

Leading Goalkicker:
Ted Fordham (Ess) 76
Brownlow Medallist:
Ian Stewart (St K)
Finals:
First Semi Final Ess 15.6 (96) Geel 12.14 (86);
Second Semi-final Coll 15.9 (99) St K 13.11 (89);
Preliminary Final St K 15.4 (94) Ess 7.10 (52);
Grand Final Coll 10.13 (73) St K 10.14 (74)

Ladder:	W	L	D	%	pts
Coll	15	3		157.2	60
St K	14	4		142.8	56
Geel	14	4		137.6	56
Ess	14	4		121.0	56
Rich	13	4	1	123.2	54
Carl	10	8		107.9	40
N. Melb	7	10	1	93.7	30
S. Melb	7	11		98.7	28
Haw	5	13		74.2	20
Foots	4	14		68.9	16
Melb	3	15		78.2	12
Fitz	1	17		53.8	4

1967

Kennedy's Commandos fit to kill

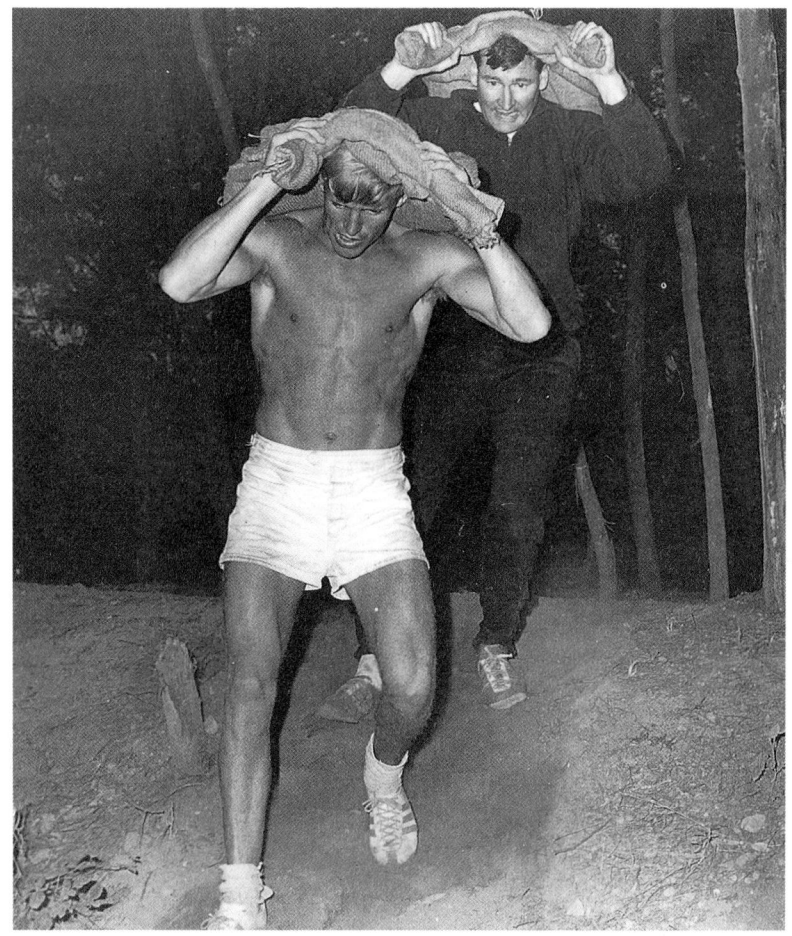

Hawthorn stars Peter Crimmins and Graham Arthur on the sandbag run.

April 15. The Hawks are training as never before this year. Work began in January when most other footballers are at the beach. It has now become clear that Hawthorn coach John Kennedy has instituted a gruelling training programme, designed to increase each player's fitness by at least 20 per cent.

In addition, Kennedy wants to improve the skills of marking, kicking, handball, palming, baulking, pivoting and blind turning.

To develop the most effective exercises he has again sought the advice of former Hawk player and fitness expert, Brendan Edwards. Edwards pioneered a system of circuit training for Hawthorn in 1960 while still a centreman for the club.

Edwards has delivered a 'blueprint' which involves a twice-weekly session at a training farm in Bulleen. The setting is idyllic, right on the Yarra, but the experience of the players is like a couple of hours spent in hell.

Here an obstacle course has been laid out whose tortures include swinging cables over the Yarra, 'dodgem' runs through the trees while carrying 50-lb sandbags, a 250-yard gravel track for building ankle and knee strength, a circuit of exercises to be done with a brick in each hand, crawls through pipes, hurdling fences, and a stockade climb.

Already this has been likened to commando training in the Army, and a nickname has been coined for the players, who are now 'Kennedy's Commandos'.

The training farm routine is in addition to normal football training at Glenferrie Oval, and is not the only fitness conditioning.

On two other days the players do weight training, and an intensive series of tests at Edwards' physical education centre at the Golden Bowl, Camberwell. Here the aim is to improve flexibility, agility, strength and endurance. If all this were not enough, John Kennedy starts the year's training with a rugged one-week stay at Percy Cerutty's camp among the sandhills of Portsea (→ 19/9/89).

Blues out of blocks with eight straight

June 12. Carlton lost their first match of the season with the last kick of the day, in the game against Richmond at Princes Park.

A crowd of 37,364 packed the ground to watch a thriller played in a Finals' atmosphere on the Queen's Birthday holiday.

Carlton seemed to have the game won when Ian Robertson goaled in time on. Then a desperate kick from Richmond's young centre-half-forward Royce Hart went 60 yards, the last half bouncing along the ground, to give the Tigers a 13.15 (93) to 14.7 (91) win (→ 14/5/95).

Ron Cook surprises Hudson at home

April 22. Schoolboy star at New Norfolk in Tasmania, senior player at 15, Peter Hudson was sought by at least four Melbourne clubs. Hawthorn Secretary Ron Cook kept flying to Hobart but became so frustrated by Hudson's indecision he had given up.

Then Hudson phoned him on holidays at Rosebud to say he wanted to be left in peace and would not be signing. The next he knew Cook was again at his door. 'He's going to drive me mad,' said Hudson. 'The only way I'll get him off my back is to go. So I went' (→ 27/4/68).

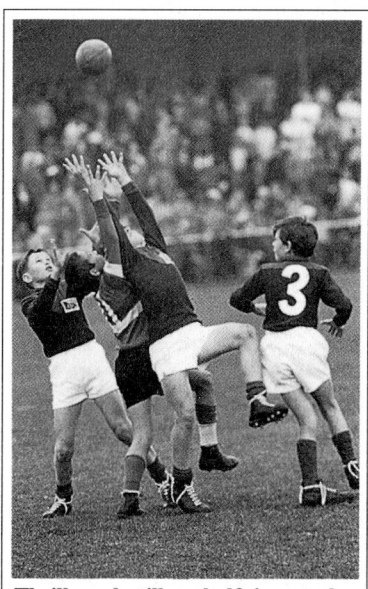

Thrills and spills at half time as the Little League takes to the field.

Lions migrate to new game park

April 15. Fitzroy's move to Princes Park this season has not kicked off as well as the Lions hoped.

In the last game at Brunswick Street last year they were walloped by eventual Premiers St Kilda, 17.22 (124) to 5.10 (40), and only won a single game all season.

St Kilda's move to Moorabbin in 1965 has had some bearing on the Saints' success. Fitzroy hopes for the same - but sharing a ground does not seem as advantageous as having one all of your own.

In their first game at Princes Park nothing much had changed, when Carlton cruised to an easy win, 18.22 (130) to 5.6 (36).

It is too early to judge Carlton's true form, but Fitzroy plainly need more than a change of scenery and a change of jumper to win games.

Their new guernsey with a lion on the breast and a royal blue top half looks smart, but the players do not appear comfortable at the Carlton home ground. The home and traditions of a founding VFL club are hard to shake off.

Fitzroy moved here because they were unable to come to terms with the Fitzroy Council over the length of lease and the cost of necessary renovations to Brunswick Street.

The club wanted a 40-year lease and $400,000 development loan; the council had offered a 21-year lease (→4/4/70).

Bobby Skilton is a Galah as he sets off on Harry Beitzel's tour of Ireland to promote our game and play Gaelic Football matches.

Did Neville Crowe clock Big Nick – and how hard?

John Nicholls may be acting a little after contact with Neville Crowe.

Reliable Ross Smith bags Brownlow

Aug. 30. 'Get out and do something: you've been an ordinary player for too long.' Those words from coach Allan Jeans inspired Ross Smith, the St Kilda rover, to complete a hat trick of Brownlows for his club. Centreman Ian Stewart won in the two previous years.

But it was Smith, 24, a physical training teacher, who scored 24 votes, to win by seven from North's Laurie Dwyer. Carlton's Alex Jesaulenko was third, with 15 votes in his first year as half-forward.

For Smith, the turning point in his career came just before the 1966 Finals. The Saints were light on for rovers, Smith was second stringer and Jeans threw him in to rove all day and to earn the No. 1 spot. 'He's a wonderful club man,' said Jeans, 'and this season has done everything I asked of him.'

For Smith, it was a case of paying a tribute to Jeans who, he said, had told him after the previous year's Grand Final: 'It's time you did a bit more about your game. That made me think during the summer, because until then I'd been just a player who went on to the ground

**ROSS SMITH
ST. KILDA**

Ross Smith: won by seven votes.

each week feeling lucky to get a game. I applied more concentration and, with the help of my ruckman, who looked for me more, I was able to develop plenty of confidence.'

A summer fitness campaign helped, especially as he had to rove for up to 80 per cent of a game alongside rovers such as Jack Clarke and Bob Skilton.

Sept. 14. Neville Crowe of Richmond has been suspended for striking John Nicholls of Carlton in the Second Semi-final last Saturday. The match was won by Richmond, 20.21 (141) to Carlton's 14.17 (101), so the Tribunal's decision means Crowe will miss playing with the Tigers in the Grand Final.

It is Crowe's first suspension, and he has never been reported in 151 games and 11 seasons with Richmond. It may be a case of bad luck rather than bad behaviour, as some observers of the incident said they saw John Nicholls' reaction but not Crowe's action in causing it.

In the *Sporting Globe* yesterday, Ian McDonald commented in his 'Sport Inside Out' column on the possibility of the findings going against Neville Crowe: 'Not only would it rob a player who has given a lot of service to the game from playing in the Grand Final and a possible Premiership side – it would be poor justice for an incident which was very much over-exaggerated and over-acted' (→8/7/72).

'$2 smarties' get something extra

July 29. Some ticket-hungry fans thought they were adding to their chances of success with Finals tickets applications by pinning a $2 note to the form as a 'sweetener'. Instead, they have lost out altogether, with the bribe being returned and their form stamped 'Invalid'.

They are not the only ones disappointed, but at least they have themselves to blame.

They form part of just over 30,000 applications to be returned. Only 3000 or so have been successful. Allans booking agency received over 34,000 in 24 hours after mail bookings opened.

Country fans were at a disadvantage, with little chance of having applications received by Allans in time to join the 'VFL Finals Raffle'. Applications closed the day after the coupon appeared in the *Herald*. Concerning the fairness of this, the VFL's Administrative Officer Mr Eric McCutchan said he believed that 'the regular football fan who goes each week is entitled to a preference' (→23/4/76).

Tigers hang on to beat Cats for Premiership

Joy for the Tigers as captain Roger Dean (fourth from right) leads them on a victory lap of the Melbourne Cricket Ground.

Sept. 23. Richmond today grabbed a nine-point lead over Geelong in the time-on period of a furious final quarter, and desperately hung on to it to win the Grand Final for the first time in 24 years.

It was a match of the highest standard from start to finish, full of many good players and brilliant bursts of team play.

Geelong, who were often slow starters this season, surprised Richmond with a fast and confident start. The Tigers were scoreless for 11 minutes, seemingly unable to break through, until Royce Hart booted their first goal.

But the confident Cats soon raced the ball down the ground with great skill, Bill Goggin exploding out of a pack to goal on the run.

The Cats were dictating play and held a well-deserved 15-point lead. Then Bill Barrot started to come alive in the centre for the Tigers, unleashing spectacular long drop-kicks, one with such drive that the ball went all the way, but was touched on its bounce through the goals, to register a behind.

By quarter time the Tigers were in front by six points.

In the second quarter, Barrot's long kicking from the centre was becoming a definite danger for Geelong. So were big Paddy Guinane playing full-forward and Royce Hart at centre-half-forward. Despite intelligent and inspiring captaincy from Polly Farmer, Geelong were being outscored. By half time the Tigers' lead increased to 16 points.

Geelong badly needed the same big burst of recovery that won them the Preliminary Final, and to the delight of their fans they raced into the third term with four goals in six minutes. This sudden change in the game bewildered the Tigers. They were left flat-footed by the Cats' superb play and return to full confidence. But they pulled themselves together and forced the ball down to Hart, who marked and got them a badly needed goal.

The crowd roared when Ken Newland, one of the Cats' best, flew over the top of a huge pack to take the day's most spectacular mark.

Into time-on in this hectic quarter, the Tigers had come back to just one point behind. Then Barrot got a behind from an enormously long kick to level the scores. And just before the siren the Tigers had managed another two behinds.

The final term was loaded with heart-stopping thrills. Win-at-all-costs commitment by both sides saw the scores being levelled four times. The crowd was literally in a frenzy.

It was anybody's game right into the time-on period. Ian McDonald of the *Sporting Globe* commented: 'The Tigers' tremendous will to win, spurred on by match winners Bill Barrot and Royce Hart, won the Flag for them in a fantastic finish.' The Tigers won, 16.18 (114) to 15.15 (105) (→ 20/4/68).

1967 Statistics

Leading Goalkicker:
Doug Wade (Geel) 96
Brownlow Medallist:
Ross Smith (St K)
Finals:
First Semi-final Geel 16.12 (108)
Coll 11.12 (78);
Second Semi-inal Rich 20.21 (141) Carl 14.17 (101);
Preliminary Final Carl 11.13 (79)
Geel 17.6 (108)
Grand Final Rich 16.18 (114)
Geel 15.15 (105)

Ladder:	W	L	D	%	pts
Rich	15	3		145.9	60
Carl	14	3	1	125.8	58
Geel	13	5		122.8	52
Coll	12	6		132.2	48
St K	11	7		122.7	44
Ess	8	9	1	106.0	34
Melb	8	10		88.8	32
N. Melb	7	10	1	94.2	30
S. Melb	5	12	1	82.0	22
Haw	5	13		70.3	20
Fitz	4	14		72.1	16
Foots	4	14		71.6	16

April 20. Richmond unfurl their 1967 Flag and then their firepower to overwhelm Carlton, 17.16 (118) to 10.12 (72), at the MCG (→ 27/9/69).

April 27. Peter Hudson kicks his 26th goal in three games. He boots eight of Hawthorn's 16.9 (105) in the win over Footscray 14.10 (94) (→ 20/7).

April 27. Collingwood kick a woeful 2.19 (31) to lose to St Kilda 10.7 (67). Carlton were even worse on Anzac Day, with 1.11 (17) to Essendon's 7.8 (50) (→ 9/5/77).

May 8. Sam Kekovich, the big bull from Myrtleford, says he will play with North Melbourne – if they 'satisfy' him with a satisfactory offer (→ 19/4/69).

May 18. Collingwood returns to form with a win over Essendon, 13.14 (92) to 9.12 (66). In last quarter a spectator jumps the fence to punch Umpire Sleeth (→ 5/6/71).

June 1. Melbourne player Brian Dixon is also a State MP on the move. His interstate training appearances are scheduled with the skill of a theatrical booking agent (→ 30/7).

June 1. St Kilda thrash Carlton in Sydney exhibition, 21.12 (138) to 11.14 (80), as do Australian football's 22,472 fans to Rugby League's 14,302 (→ 10/6/79).

June 1. 43,689 see Victoria defeat South Aust. 14.9 (93) to 5.10 (40) at MCG (→ 14/6/69).

June 5. Syd Jackson says he can't wait to win his court case against the WAFL so he can play for Carlton 'seriously'.

July 20. Peter Hudson kicks 12 goals against Footscray after two earlier bags of ten this season. Hawthorn win, 24.8 (152) to 10.10 (70) (→ 3/8).

Oct. 3. Hawthorn win their first Night Flag, 16.15 (111) to North Melb. 6.14 (50) (→ 1/7/86).

Oct. 7. Carlton defeat Sturt in Adelaide, 13.15 (93) to 6.20 (56), winning an easy $7000.

Debuts
Peter Bedford (S. Melb)
Gary Colling (St K)
Brent Crosswell (Carl)
John Greening (Coll)

Retirements
Graham Arthur (Haw)
Darrel Baldock (St K)
Brian Dixon (Melb)
Ken Fraser (Ess)
Denis Marshall (Geel)

Tassie Tiger Crosswell gives Blues bite

April 16. Carlton's promising recruit, the Tasmanian 'Tiger' Brent Crosswell, played well without starring in his first game against Geelong. The Blues won, 13.22 (100) to 7.12 (54), with Crosswell playing in the centre.

Crosswell was recruited as a schoolboy from Scotch College and Campbelltown in 1967, after former Carlton winger Berkeley Cox tipped off the club.

Coach Barassi made a trip to Tasmania to sign him up, later flying Crosswell and family over for a look around Melbourne.

He trained with Carlton at the end of the season, and came over early this year to start in earnest.

'Tiger' is completing his education at University High School while playing for Carlton. He's six feet one inches tall with a big spring and plenty of athletic ability, and ball skills and talent to burn. The coach seems to like his style (→ 8/5/75).

Carlton coach Ron Barassi gives new recruit Brent Crosswell the low-down.

VFL says new zones, more rounds

April 4. This year's season has been extended from 18 rounds to 20. While this should be more equitable, another major change is bound to cause discontent. The VFL has implemented its system of 'zoning' for the recruitment of players. Victoria and the Riverina are now divided into recruiting areas allocated to the League clubs, who cannot look outside their own zones for new talent emerging in 'the bush'.

The scheme was approved by the VFL Committee last September, despite strong opposition from the country leagues, and is now in force for the next three years.

The allocation was a matter of pot luck, literally. Club names were placed in the Premiership Cup, and the 12 zones in its lid, and a draw conducted. St Kilda, Carlton, Footscray and North Melbourne seem to have fared best.

The zones theoretically the 'weakest' have gone to Geelong, South Melbourne, Hawthorn and Richmond (→ 22/5/71).

Sundown quarter

May 25. Darkness descended as Essendon fought back in the last quarter. As rain poured down, the Dons snatched a two-point win over Richmond at Windy Hill, 11.14 (80) to 10.18 (78). In a match full of drama, Essendon's Bob Greenwood hit the post in the last term but was awarded a goal. By then it was hard to see players on either side of the ground.

Moves will now be made by the St Kilda, Carlton and Richmond clubs for matches to start at 2 p.m. instead of 2.20 p.m. (→ 30/5/87).

SOUTH MELBOURNE
MAX PAPLEY (34)
CENTRE

NORTH MELBOURNE
NOEL TEASDALE (43)
RUCK

MELBOURNE
HASSA MANN (31)
ROVER

13 Hawks given chop at barbecue

April 8. Hawthorn selectors have startled the team by dropping 13 of last year's seniors from the training list. Most of the victims heard the bad news first while mingling with supporters during a barbecue at a car rally organised by the club.

Among those dropped are ruckman Neil Ferguson (43 games), key defender John Dunshea (36 games), half-forward Mike Porter (23 games), and ruckman Norm Gordes (20 games).

The selectors believe it is time for a big refreshment of talent at Hawthorn. They have picked 13 recruits, and restored half-back flanker Ross Growcott to the senior list.

Norm Smith: 'You can't buy pride'

Aug. 17. Fiery ex-Demon coach Norm Smith, discussing present-day recruiting, warns the football world: 'You can't buy team pride with a cheque book.' Smith, now a TV commentator, had in mind the dollar value reputedly placed on the services of Peter Hudson when the Hawks eventually secured him from New Norfolk last season.

The haggling and bartering between New Norfolk and Hawthorn had gone on for months, with the Tasmanian club believed to have put a price of $10,000 on their star, which was beaten down to $8,000. Said the man himself: 'No footballer is worth that much' (→ 3/5/69).

Barassi, Dixon, Arthur are recruits for 250 club

Barassi: created a position.

Arthur: lured by chocolates.

Dixon: big possession man.

July 30. Carlton captain and coach Ron Barassi, Melbourne wingman Brian Dixon and Hawthorn half-forward flanker Graham Arthur have joined the elite band of players with 250 senior games.

Barassi is credited with being the game's first true ruck-rover, having carved out this role in the champion Melbourne team of the 1950s. Captain of Melbourne at the age of 24, Barassi made No. 31 famous for Melbourne until his astonishing defection to Carlton in 1964, when some Demon youngsters tore it from their guernseys. A number of Carlton tyros sewed it straight onto their navy blue jumpers.

Graham Arthur is the half-forward flanker who led Hawthorn to their first Flag in 1961. While his early ambition at Marist Brothers College, Bendigo, had been to follow his father to Essendon, it transpired that an official who took a box of chocolates for Arthur's mother won Graham for the Hawks.

Only the second player to win best and fairest in his first year at the club, Arthur was known for his brilliant teamwork and flashing hand-passes. He has been captain since 1960 and was coach in 1964-65.

Arthur is unusual for a half-forward flanker in that he is neither very fast, nor an outstanding mark. But he reads the play superbly and is tough and unflinching in the packs.

Brian Dixon's 250th game celebrates the skill of one of the great wingmen of postwar times. His ability to gain possession has been almost phenomenal.

Having come to Melbourne from Melbourne High, he steadily improved to star from 1954 onwards, winning the Demons' best and fairest in 1960 and the Tassie Medal for best and fairest in the Australian National Football Council interstate Carnival in 1961. He has been a Commerce lecturer at Melbourne University, and is now a member of the Parliament of Victoria.

Dixon has played in five Melbourne Premiership teams, and is capable of crushing even the best opponents. He is a brilliant high mark, but his kicking is sometimes ill directed. He has the habit of grabbing the ball and kicking it in the same motion, leaving the forwards to do the best they can.

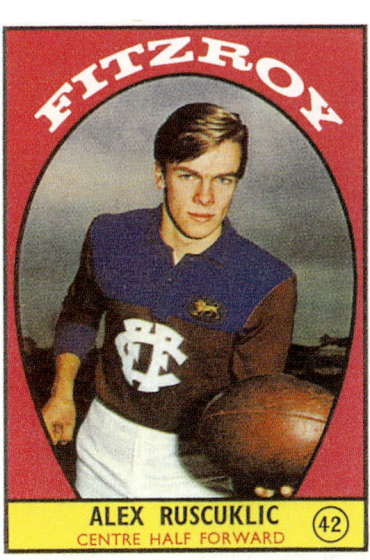

Hudson breaks drought of centuries

Aug. 3. 'I was out of breath, my ears were popping, and I felt the relief from my boots up,' said 'Mr Magic Boots', Peter Hudson, about kicking his 100th goal for the season today. It's been 16 years since any VFL full-forward has been able to feel the same way. The 22-year-old from Tasmania is the first to reach the century since 1952, when the legendary John Coleman of Essendon booted 103.

Hudson's 100th came up when he kicked his fourth goal in a sensational first quarter against Collingwood. Hawthorn went on to win 15.11 (101) to 10.16 (76).

John Kennedy said: 'He will get stronger, the best of Peter Hudson is yet to come.' Comparing him to Coleman, Kennedy said: 'Coleman was a freak mark. Peter is a better snapshot.' Another analyst calls him 'the best reader of other players' mistakes we've ever seen' (→ 17).

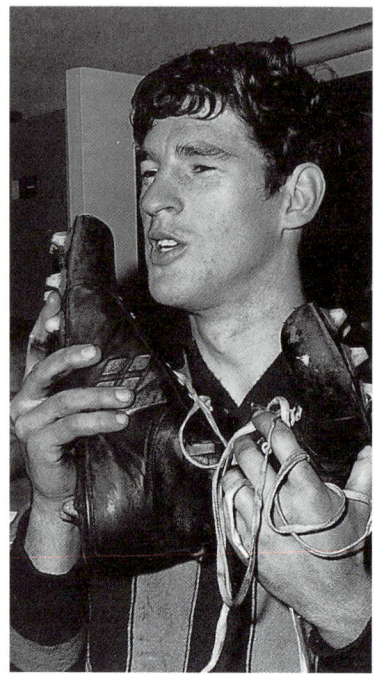

Peter Hudson and magic boots.

The kick that broke the 100-goal drought heads towards the target.

Sage defends Barassi from oracles

Aug. 15. After three consecutive losses, which followed ten wins in a row, Blue tongues were wagging and the Blue knives were out for Carlton captain-coach Ron Barassi.

The slump happened to coincide with his return to the playing arena after injury.

The critics say that he should stay off the field and concentrate on coaching, or even retire altogether.

But Hugh Buggy, writing in the *Advocate* makes a sterling defence of Barassi, player and coach.

He quotes Barassi as saying that his friends could understand that he didn't want to miss the thrill of playing, but could not understand why he was prepared to run the gauntlet of insults and criticism.

Barassi said: 'The truth is that after all these years my hide has been thickened far too much for any barbs to sting me.'

Buggy says Barassi got the Blues off their worst position ever in 1965, and a mid-season slump does not mean that they cannot win the Flag this year – the first in 21 years (→ 30/9/72).

Hungry Bartlett gets the money

Oct 1. Richmond rover Kevin Bartlett has scooped the money pool in VFL awards for the season.

Of the $61,785 available in prizes this season, Bartlett collected $6075, beating John Nicholls' $5850 and Peter Hudson's $3700.

His prizes included a Holden from Dustings of Burwood as winner of the HSV7 World of Sport award valued at $2512, a trip for two to Japan from Malaysia-Singapore Airlines, worth $2613, as runner-up in the Football Inquest award, awards from the *Sporting Globe* Bunton Medal and $200, *The Age*, Smiths Crisps and Marchants.

Nicholls won most cash in one award – the $5000 World of Sport Foodland Footballer of the Year.

Hudson won $1000 as British Paints leading goalkicker, $1250 as *Footy Week* best player, a gift of $500 from Hawthorn for kicking 100 goals, and the ABC Footballer of the Year trophy valued at $100.

North's Tom Allison won a car from Bob Jane worth $3420 in a GTV 9 goal kicking competition (→ 18/5/92).

Bobby Skilton is in good company as he receives his third Brownlow Medal at the First Semi Final at the MCG. St Kilda and Footscray captains Darrel Baldock and Ted Whitten were on hand to congratulate him, as well as the leading goalkicker for the season, Peter Hudson of Hawthorn.

Ken Fraser bows out gracefully

Sept. 28. Essendon captain Ken Fraser was unavailable for today's Grand Final against Carlton.

It should have been his last game in a great career, but the much-admired Fraser was replaced by the 17-year-old schoolboy Geoff Blethyn, who captured the imagination of the huge crowd by kicking the Dons' first two goals with his first two kicks.

Fraser missed the game due to a leg injury. He watched his side go down to Carlton by three points despite a desperate last quarter bid.

Ken Fraser led Essendon to the Flag in 1965 in his first year as captain. He was second in the Brownlow Medal in 1962, won his club's best and fairest in 1963, and again came second in the Brownlow in 1964.

A natural centre-half-forward, he was one of the fastest big men of his era, noted for his rare skill in being able to break away and lead to the flanks. He was in the Premiership team of 1962, beating Carlton that time, and in the 1959 side that lost to Melbourne. He was a regular state representative.

A quiet, religious man, his retirement today drew this accolade from Neil Roberts in the *Sporting Globe*: 'Congratulations Ken on a perfect football career. You were a fine example to any youngster on the football field and in the pulpit.'

Who's that up there? Why it's Geelong's Billy Ryan, on the shoulders of Saint Ian Synman.

Barassi flies his first Blue Flag

The siren sounds and Blues Adrian Gallagher, Brent Crosswell, Kevin Hall and John Nicholls start to celebrate.

Sept. 28. Carlton kicked a goal less than Essendon but still won by three points. The Blues were led by captain and coach Ron Barassi but he was not on the ground. That was where John Nicholls held sway.

President George Harris said that he now knew what his dental patients felt, having 'waited, waited and waited' through the second half where Carlton scored just one goal six to Essendon's three goals four.

Former Prime Minister, but still number one ticket holder, Sir Robert Menzies sent a telegram: 'From my hospital bed I give three cheers for the boys today.'

Luckily for the Blues they had a 6.8 to 5.1 buffer at half time – and could endure the last quarter where a kick from Brent Crosswell bounced in the goal square and took a hop like a Bill O'Reilly leg break to score yet another behind.

Aside from Nicholls' power in the ruck the mainstays of Carlton's win were speedy Gary Crane's 30 effective touches on the wing, Brian Kekovich's determined four goals four behinds and Sergio Silvagni's tireless work as a ruck rover.

A new record attendance for a Grand Final of 116,828 saw an uncompromisingly tough, tense game in which the marginally more skilful but inaccurate team were in front when the siren sounded.

Carlton won, 7.14 (56) to Essendon 8.5 (53) (→26/9/70).

Coach Ron Barassi urges the Blues on in his three-quarter-time address.

1968 Statistics

Leading Goalkicker:	Ladder:	W	L	D	%	pts
Peter Hudson (Haw) 125	Ess	16	3	1	130.3	66
Brownlow Medallist:	Carl	15	5		130.4	60
Bob Skilton (S.Melb)	Geel	15	5		106.8	60
Finals:	St K	14	5	1	136.0	58
First Semi-final Geel 19.13 (127)	Rich	14	6		123.0	56
St K 11.17 (83);	Haw	9	10	1	103.5	38
Second Semi-final Ess 8.11 (59)	Coll	9	11		94.5	36
Carl 13.17 (95);	Melb	8	12		83.9	32
Preliminary Final Ess 11.25 (91)	S. Melb	6	13	1	83.9	26
Geel 9.13 (67);	Foots	5	15		82.6	20
Grand Final Carl 7.14 (56) Ess	Fitz	4	16		80.7	16
8.5 (53)	N. Melb	3	17		74.3	12

1969

Mr Football plays 300th game

April 7. Footscray gave their captain-coach Ted Whitten a party for his 300th game when they walloped Fitzroy at Princes Park, 23.21 (159) to 15.13 (103).

Mr Football now has his eye on former Essendon great Dick Reynolds' record of 320 games played.

Footscray only won five games last year to finish tenth, and that was only a game more than 1967 when the Bulldogs 'won' the wooden spoon under Charlie Sutton.

Since the glory days of the 1961 Grand Final, it has been an uphill battle whether Whitten has been captain-coach, as he is again and was 1957-1966, or just captain.

But in this game at least, 'Wee' Georgie Bisset proved a real bulldog in temperament as well as size, kicking six goals. Ricky Spargo also chimed in with five from the forward pocket.

Mr Football played at centre-half-forward and roosted a goal for every hundred games he's played (→ 26/7).

'Do it for me then,' says Teddy.

Out-on-full rule is working well

July 2. Carlton and All-Australian captain John Nicholls has told the *Sporting Globe* that this season's new 'kicking out of bounds on the full' rule 'has done more to improve football than any other rule in operation in the 13 years I've been playing League football.'

He said that with the 15-yard penalty for not throwing the ball back to a player on the full it has made the game faster and more direct, and is the reason for this season's high scoring.

Today's ruckmen must be more complete players, able to run, handball, kick and mark around the ground because there are fewer ball-ups and boundary throw-ins.

Ruckmen cannot rely solely on their ruck work to be contributors to their team's success.

The new style of football is ideally suited to getting the ball direct to a leading full-forward (→ 7/6/71).

Collingwood stun Blues and umpires, too

April 29. Coming after a loss to the deadeye Hawks, Collingwood's annihilation of 1968 Premiers Carlton at Princes Park last Saturday was the thrust they need for the season.

The 64-point win in a game studded with brawls and spite was all the more remarkable since Collingwood were down five points at half-time but led by 70 points a quarter later.

To begin one of the most remarkable onslaughts in football history, Des Tuddenham shot from a pack to snap a goal, putting Collingwood in front in the sixth lead change.

Flamboyant ruck-rover John Greening then raced down the outer flank, tapping across to Tuddenham who handballed back for Greening's fifth of seven goals. In 15 minutes the Magpies rammed on 7.3. The overworked Carlton runner had to be restrained by umpire Ray Sleeth.

The Magpies were running wild, when Tuddenham booted their 18th goal. The final scores were 23.15 (153) to 13.11 (89).

Umpire Sleeth and the Carlton delegate clashed during the writing of match reports. All players were cleared: the umpires took too long to inform officials of the charges (→ 16/4/88).

The umpire remonstrates with John Nicholls of Carlton during the match.

The Super Forwards are back

Aug. 23. Contrary to Shakespeare, it has been a winter of content, especially for full-forwards in August.

The shootout between centurians Doug Wade and Peter Hudson attracted 30,000 fans to Kardinia Park and ended in victory for Wade and the Cats.

Wade kicked eight goals of Geelong's 16.14 (110), while Hudson booted six of Hawthorn's losing score 14.11 (95). Geelong kicked three goals in time on to snatch a remarkable win just when Hawthorn were looking forward to the trip back to Melbourne.

Wade's goal in the last minute, the result of a perefect lead to a Bill Goggin daisy cutter, and then a long torpedo punt was widely regarded as a miracle by Cat fans. It won the game and has seemingly ended Hawthorn's Finals hopes.

Quite an effective piece of play.

Wade was well served by his teammates up the ground, especially the quicksilver Bill Goggin who skimmed pass after pass at his chest.

Wily Peter Hudson was not so well looked after by his rovers Leigh Matthews and Peter Crimmins.

Aficionados of full-forward play who remained in Melbourne watched Collingwood's lightning leading spearhead Peter McKenna kick 16.4 in a reminder that he, too, is now in the top drawer of present-day full-forwards. The Magpies beat the Swans, 19.15 (129) to 6.22 (58), to gain a perch on top of the Ladder.

McKenna might well have beaten Fred Fanning's 1947 record of 18 VFL goals but for a lapse in the last quarter where he kicked four 'easy' behinds. In shots he has more than emulated Peter Hudson's effort of 16 goals one behind against Melbourne on May 3.

McKenna has 83 goals and, with one game and the Finals to go, may well be the third player in a season to kick 100 goals – which would be a League first. Wade has now kicked 120 and Hudson 112 goals.

It seems that high scoring this season is due to the 'kicking out of bounds on the full' rule speeding up play, and making it more direct.

But some credit must also be given to the remarkable assembly of talented full-forwards – all of quite different physical types and styles of play (→ 25/9/71).

Doug Wade goes into orbit at Kardinia Park during his eight-goal match.

**PETER McKENNA
COLLINGWOOD**

**PETER HUDSON
HAWTHORN**

Long day's journey on training Knights

May 31. Peter Knights, a 17-year-old Leaving student at Drouin High School, will play his first VFL senior game with Hawthorn today.

His biggest fan is local taxi service proprietor Mrs M. Plew, who has been his 'shadow' in his rise to VFL. Each Tuesday she collects Knights from school, drives him to training with the Hawks, watches him, then ferries him home.

On Thursdays he trains with the local club at Longwarry, where the coach is Bill Serong, formerly of Collingwood and North Melbourne. Knights said his shock selection meant a sleepless night (→ 1/1/87).

Spectacled Blethyn a muddy marvel

May 31. Geoff Blethyn showed remarkable courage for Essendon against Carlton, despite a loss of 6.9 (45) to 16.13 (103). The bespectacled Blethyn, who has his glasses strapped to his head with adhesive tape, was hurled face first into the mud in the third quarter. He just had time to tug a handkerchief from his shorts and wipe the dirt-spattered lenses, then he was back into the thick of it.

A lightly-built forward, Blethyn was rushed into the 1968 Grand Final team for only his third game, in which he kicked four of the Dons' eight goals.

Tigers give Cats kittens by 118

Sept. 6. Before a First Semi-final record crowd of 101,233 fans, Richmond turned the MCG into a slaughteryard, destroying Geelong by 118 points. The win, by 18 goals 10 behinds, was a record.

Richmond's 25.17 (167) to 7.7 (49) was the highest Semi-final score since the present Final Four system began. Best for Richmond were Mike Green, Kevin Sheedy, Francis Bourke, Roger Dean, Dick Clay, Bill Barrot, Colin Beard, Geoff Strang, John Northey and Eric Moore. At the end, only the magnitude of the score mattered.

Hafey's Tigers ride high

Umpires rush in to hear what Bill Barrot is saying to Kevin Hall.

Roger Dean leads the underdog Tigers out to vie for the 1969 Premiership.

Sept. 27. Having just scraped into the Final Four, Richmond took the Flag today with a 25-point win over Carlton.

Three hard games in a row were thought to have taken a toll on the Tigers. Carlton had performed professionally all season, and won the double chance and an easy road into the Grand Final. With Ron Barassi as coach and John Nicholls as captain, Carlton looked like winners.

But coach Tom Hafey was unconcerned about his team, despite criticism about over-training. It was Richmond's Eric Moore who goaled within seconds of the first bounce, followed by Royce Hart. Roger Dean was an inspirational captain, moving Brownlow Medallist Neil Roberts to observe later in the *Sporting Globe* that Dean was the toughest footballer he had seen.

At the first change 119,165 fans saw Richmond clinging to a four-point lead. Mike Green met the might of Nicholls and Peter Jones in a brilliant performance as sole Tiger ruckman.

In the second quarter both teams blocked, tackled and chased with desperation until Carlton cracked, leaving Richmond 22 points up.

In the third quarter Carlton battled to a four-point lead.

Furious in attack, running hard, talking to each other, the Tigers transformed themselves in the last quarter. Billy Barrot took a fantastic mark and then kicked an astonishing goal to lift the team.

The Tigers scored 4.7 to two points, winning their seventh Flag, 12.13 (85) to 8.12 (60) (→ 29/9/73).

1969 Statistics

Leading Goalkicker:	Ladder:	W	L	D	%	pts
Doug Wade (Geel) 127	Coll	15	5		129.0	60
Brownlow Medallist:	Carl	15	5		120.5	60
Kevin Murray (Fitz)	Geel	13	6	1	119.9	54
Finals:	Rich	13	7		124.6	52
First Semi-final Geel 7.7 (49)	Haw	13	7		98.8	52
Rich 25.17 (167);	Ess	10	9	1	102.5	42
Second Semi-final Coll 10.11 (71)	St K	9	11		103.2	36
Carl 16.11 (107);	N. Melb	8	12		87.5	32
Preliminary Final Coll 12.9 (81)	S. Melb	7	13		82.5	28
Rich 15.17 (107);	Fitz	7	13		82.4	28
Grand Final Carl 8.12 (60) Rich	Foots	6	14		85.5	24
12.13 (85)	Melb	3	17		83.1	12

Dean holds the Premiership Cup aloft for the faithful Tiger supporters.

Hafey lets champagne football flow

Tommy Hafey with his team.

One of the game's wizards, Royce Hart was in the Richmond Under-19s when he met Tom Hafey in 1966. 'He first struck me as being a man with very little to say,' Hart recalled. 'He was more intent on listening, especially about football.'

Tall and rawboned, Hart had arrived aged 17 from Tasmania, recruited by an outstanding talent-spotter, Tigers' Secretary Graeme Richmond.

Hart was in awe of Hafey, noting that it was said he had never been brought off for an injury, even with an eye half hanging out when he was captain-coach of Shepparton.

That, and Hafey's fitness fanaticism, impressed Hart. In pre-season cross-country runs players did not see much of Hafey, he was usually too far in front.

Hafey ran up to six miles a day, then swam. His fierce will to win and his loyalty were inspiring.

With this attitude, a play-on game that swept away the stop-and-start style of the past, scrupulous planning and new players such as Rex Hunt, Eric Moore and Dick Clay, Hafey began to build a Premiership team.

In his first year, the Tigers only just missed the Finals, Fred Swift kicking five goals in a last-round, 14-goal to four second half demolition of Fitzroy.

Swift took over as captain next season as Richmond signed Francis Bourke, Kevin Shinners and a future great, Kevin Sheedy.

Hart turned out for the first game, proving a sure-fingered mark. Long-kicking, quick-thinking and courageous, he had it all at full-forward.

Kevin Bartlett had settled into roving, Bill Barrot was the great centre man of the era and, with Bourke on the wing and Graham Burgin and Geoff Strang attacking from the halfback flanks, there was flexibility galore.

In a memorable Premiership win over Geelong, a 60-yard time-on kick by John Ronaldson, aimed at the goal square, goaled.

Barrot was man of the match, but the Tigers had great contributors in 'Bull' Richardson, Mike Perry, Hart, Billy Brown, Barry Richardson, Strang and Barrot.

Hafey's joy, celebrated as ever with tea while others had champagne, was followed next season by disappointment as the Tigers had a string of one-kick losses.

By 1969 the pressure on Hafey was enormous. But even a superb performance against Footscray by Dick Clay, backed by Rex Hunt's four goals in a low-scoring game, couldn't secure a win.

Against Carlton Barrot was pitched to full-forward by Hafey and ran wild with eight goals, while John Northey kicked five.

Breezing home against Geelong in the First Semi, Richmond had Clay, Bourke and Strang firing and Bartlett taking charge.

In the Grand Final, Eric Moore goaled, then Hart before Carlton got one. Crucially, Mike Green matched the big man power of Nicholls and Jones.

At the third-quarter siren Barrot took a great mark and goaled. Tiger ferocity swept them through the last quarter and, on top of this Premiership, they thrashed Sturt to become Australian champions.

Hafey had found the winning way for Richmond.

Kevin Murray, Fitzroy marvel

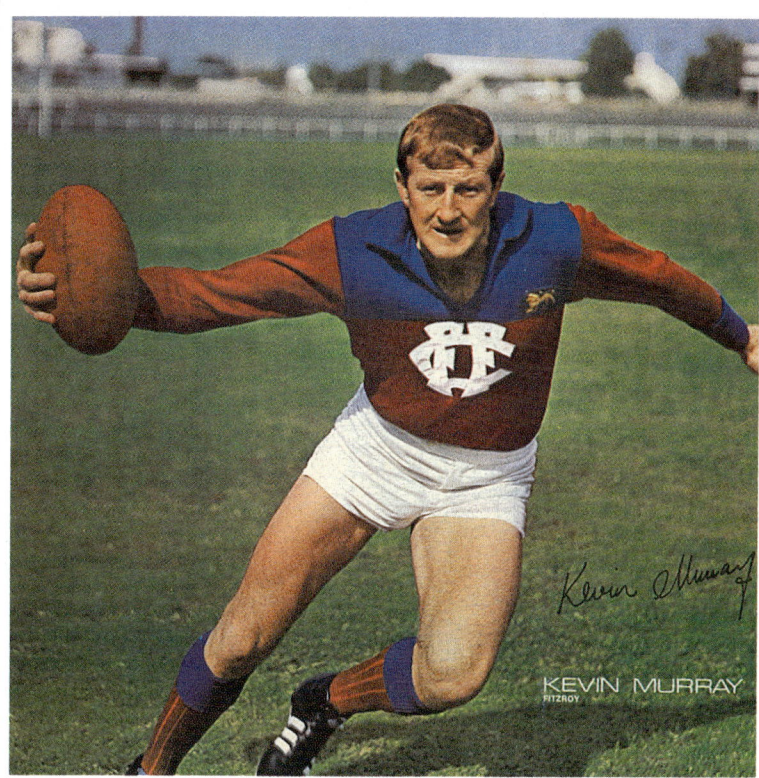

Kevin Murray – all honours to Fitzroy Brownlow Medal champion.

Sept. 1. After what seems a lifetime of playing and trying, Fitzroy's Kevin Murray has won the Brownlow Medal – at 31 becoming the oldest player to do so.

Kevin Murray made his debut for Fitzroy aged just 16 in 1955 on the half-back flank.

Kevin's father Dan Murray, also a half-back, played 66 games in three stints for Fitzroy between 1933 and 1945, and was 19th man in the 1944 Premiership side.

When young Kevin began trying to get a game with the Fitzroy Under-19s as a 13-year-old he did not expect to make the grade. He said: 'I never dreamed that I would be a League player. I went down to try to get a game but I was too young and skinny, although they let me train there.'

For two years he would go home and tell his Dad that he hadn't even been named as an emergency, and his Dad would tell him to keep trying.

Of course he did, and was good enough to climb into the Firsts in round four 1955 as the Lions' youngest ever player, playing 15 games for the season.

A brilliant future was predicted, Murray winning the best first-year player in 1955, and the first of his nine best and fairests in 1956. The ninth was this year.

Murray's determination to play despite injury – he has played in a back brace for many years – is legendary, as is the inspiration he provides a team not very successful in his time.

One of the few games he has missed was the 1958 First Semi-final loss to North Melbourne.

That was the last one, except when playing some of his 24 games for Victoria, or during 1965-66 when he coached East Perth to the Grand Final.

While in Perth he captain-coached the WA team in the 1966 Carnival, and was named an All-Australian – the first to achieve that distinction for two states.

Many judges believed that Murray might have won the 1960 Brownlow when he was second to John Schultz by one vote, and the 1962 medal when third to Alistair Lord, or last year when was third again.

Murray has played 307 senior games in the VFL and WA, and doesn't look like stopping, despite saying the Brownlow 'tops my career right off' (→ 16/6/73).

THE MODERN ERA

Living in the seventies

If you blinked, you missed it. Maybe it took place amid the car horns, the whistles and screams of delight when the New Year was ushered in at midnight, 1 January, 1970.

Or maybe it took place shortly after 3.30pm on the final Saturday in September of that year, deep beneath a grandstand at the Melbourne Cricket Ground.

There, in the sombre dressing rooms of the Carlton team, coach Ron Barassi clenched his teeth, wondered how on earth his team could retrieve an apparently hopeless situation, and uttered three legendary words: "Handball, handball, handball."

This wasn't just evolution. This was revolution. And at some point as 1970 dawned on the Victorian Football League, the game began experiencing the most dramatic changes in its history.

This was no slow metamorphosis, either. In the blink of an eye football seemed to become faster. The players seemed to be getting bigger and stronger. Speed was the new catch-cry. But most of all, the decade would be remembered as one of the game's most colourful and entertaining eras.

It was the decade of the 'Speccy', that one, unique trait of Australian football where one man uses the shoulders of many to reach for the sky.

The Speccy was an art and it had no better practitioner than Alex Jesaulenko. Here was a man who also showed how the game had changed; an Australian with an odd European type of name. So he became Jezza and throughout the '70s he would guide Carlton through one of its most successful periods, along the way establishing himself as one of the greatest to have graced the game.

The '70s. Here was a decade that produced some of the game's best theatre.

There was Phil Carman, the erratic genius, with his white boots, showmanship and talent to match. Had any other period of the game ever produced such an array of skilled and potent goalkickers?

Peter Hudson opened the decade with 146 goals, and followed up a year later with 150, equalling Bob Pratt's record, the one they always said would never be beaten.

Hawthorn had Hudson, Collingwood had Peter McKenna, North Melbourne made its charge for its first flag with Geelong's spearhead Doug Wade...all of them exciting players whose names alone could draw a crowd.

It was as though everyone realised that just around the corner lay the drab, some even said dour, 1980s, when coaches would demand more discipline from their players. They would be expected to be competent in more than one position. They would not be allowed the excesses and flair of their predecessors.

The 1970s crammed two decade's worth of individuals into one 10-year stretch. But it was off the field where the real revolution was staged. By the middle of the decade the Victorian Football League finally began to embrace the idea that it, too, was just another business out there in the corporate world, a world where only the fittest and the sharpest survived.

Sir Maurice Nathan, who had been appointed president of the VFL in 1971 after the 15-year reign of Sir Kenneth Luke, had been one of the first to recognise that unless football established itself along sound business lines it would pay a hefty price.

Certainly, footy was a unique game. And certainly, you couldn't regard the game just as a business. It was, after all, still a sport and one that few others in the world could match when it came to capturing the imagination and passion of the general public.

But by the middle of the 1970s Australian Rules could sense the hot breath of its competitors as they strove to catch up with a sport that had dominated Victorian life for most of the century. From their vantage point in Jolimont, VFL administrators watched with growing concern the increasing popularity of soccer.

In 1974, the Australian soccer team made its way into the finals of the World Cup. For a short time the country became obsessed with the round-ball code. Dire warnings were issued from within the League. Soccer was a sport that provided great ammunition for critics of Australian Rules. It didn't have the rough and tumble of VFL footy. Little Johnny could play it at school with precious chance of having his teeth knocked out or his uniform torn. And it was an international sport, too. You could travel the world and represent your country.

The reality was that soccer in Australia had not yet made it as a mainstream sport into the middle class. But the alarm bells sounded loud enough for action to be taken.

At the same time, football was beginning to feel the pinch from another opponent. The dollar. Now here was something everyone in football needed desperately. It had always been a factor, despite the nostalgic tears old-timers would shed over the good-old days. If you believed everything they said, the game had

been a marvellously amateur sport for years where the corruptive scent of a dollar bill might as well have emanated from a skunk. Money? Never heard of it. In truth it had always been an issue, right from the turn of the century when the game was periodically wracked by controversies over payments to players.

Even before World War I, when a young man could earn five shillings a week when he began work, a wage of 30 shillings a week could be made slugging it out on the fields around Melbourne. VFA clubs lured VFL players away with promises of greater cash and other under-the-table deals. And vice-versa. But by the middle of the 1970s the pressures were greater.

Clubs, with the establishment of social club venues, had discovered new sources of revenue. And at the start of the decade, two clubs in particular had decided to point the way to the future.

Richmond and North Melbourne both began courting the corporate world. The Tigers secured sponsorship deals with a beer company and began entertaining their benefactors with good food and wine before a match. At North, under the presidency of Allen Aylett, who had become the League's youngest club president, the Kangaroos had begun a campaign to lift themselves out of the VFL's basement, where they had dwelt for most of the time since

joining the competition in 1925. They needed money to do it.

In effect, the North Melbourne story would become the tale of football in the 1970s. To make it in this new era you needed more guile and cunning than ever before.

The 1973 season opened with a new rule: players with 10 years of service with one club were free to transfer to another club without the usual costly clearance fee. North had seen this rule coming and moved swiftly to secure many of the game's best, among them Doug Wade, Barry Davis and John Rantall. The 'Roos also opened the 1973 season with another new recruit: Ronald Dale Barassi.

Barassi always seemed to be lurking in the vicinity whenever a revolution was being staged. In 1965 he had signalled the start of a far more blatant professional era when he broke the hearts of Melbourne supporters by trading in his famous number 31 guernsey for a Carlton jumper. Five years later he would be accorded a permanent place in the game's lore with his impassioned plea for his Carlton team to "handball, handball, handball" in the second half of that year's Grand Final.

Trailing Collingwood by seven goals at half-time, Barassi's players followed his instructions to the letter. They came back to win one of the most famous premiership victories ever staged at

the MCG and, in doing so, set the scene for a new phase in the game where handball would become a lethal instrument, capable of dismantling an opponent's defence in seconds. Barassi arrived at North Melbourne just as Aylett's revolution began forcing its way through the palace gates. A fundraising drive had provided the club with more money than it had ever seen and with it came more influence and power, both on the field and off it.

By 1975 Barassi had delivered the goods by providing the club with its first VFL flag. Fittingly, it took place in a year of significant change. Colour television had been introduced into Australia that year and for the first time viewers at home, many of them in other states and rural areas who had never been to a League match before, finally got to see the teams in their true colours.

The League, anticipating some of the vast potential the colour medium could provide the game, had dispensed with the tradition of black shorts for the home side and white shorts for the "away" team in favor of coloured shorts. Within a year, the VFL logo would also be emblazoned on those shorts as the game moved into the marketing and advertising world.

Sir Maurice Nathan, spurred on by a young man called Jim McKay who worked at the League's advertising agency,

J.Walter Thompson, had set up the VFL's Properties Division. It was modelled along similar lines to the highly successful marketing arm of the National Football League in the United States, a country where Australian sporting administrators were looking increasingly for ideas and inspiration.

In 1977 the revolution sweeping the game off the field was capped off by the appointment of Aylett as the VFL's eighth president. A new general manager was also appointed: the former Collingwood fullback of the 1950s, Jack Hamilton. Under their aegis, the rest of the decade would lay the groundwork for the radical expansion of the game that followed.

But that year was also memorable for the drawn Grand Final between North Melbourne and Collingwood. Locked on 76 points each, the two foes met again the following week where North ran out comfortable winners by 27 points in a high-scoring match.

By then, a comfortable, almost predictable, reign of power had settled over the game. Between 1970 and 1989, only five teams would win the flag. Such a balance of power showed more than ever how important a well-funded and well-run club could be.

The modern professional era had truly arrived.

Garry Linnell

Feb. 11. Three Melbourne TV stations, HSV7, GTV9 and ABV2 agree to pay $1 million for replay rights to three VFL matches per round for the next four years. Clubs to get at least $11,000 a year (→ 3/4).

April 3. TV directors extend use of video-disc replay and 'creepy-peepy' back cameras in replays broadcast at Seven (→ 2/6).

April 5. Fitzroy play Richmond at the MCG in the first Sunday game, before the Queen and Royal party, winning 16.20 (116) to 14.12 (96) (→ 7/5).

April 5. At the presentation of the Royal party at half time, Princess Anne says to Tiger Bill Barrot, 'I understand there were a couple of punch ups before we got here. Do you think there will be any more?'

May 7. Melbourne City Council is opposed to Sunday football at venues it controls such as the MCG (→ 28/4/76).

May 9. Alex Jesaulenko kicks ten goals in Carlton's win over Fitzroy, 23.9 (147) to 15.20 (110) (→ 22/7/72).

May 23. Peter Hudson kicks 13 goals in Hawthorn's 21.20 (146) to 12.12 (84) win over South Melbourne.

June 2. GTV9 announces it is dropping all football panel shows, and will switch replays from Saturdays to Sundays at 5 p.m. (→ 21/6/72).

June 20. Essendon half-back flanker Doug Tassell has been killed in a car accident with two former Ararat team-mates. He played 20 games (→ 20/6/70).

Aug. 8. Peter McKenna kicks nine goals to reach century in Magpies' defeat of Blues, 13.23 (101) to 2.12 (24) (→ 24/4/71).

Aug. 22. South are in the Finals for the first time in 25 years after a 14.15 (99) to 10.20 (80) win over Fitzroy.

Aug. 29. Umpires, not invited to the Brownlow dinner, will hold their own social at Carlton Bowling Club (→ 31/8/70).

Sept. 17. Collingwood's Lee Adamson denies making racist remark to Carlton's Aboriginal player Syd Jackson, who was reprimanded for 'accidentally' striking him (→ 2/5/93).

Debut
Barry Cable (N. Melb)

Retirements
John Dugdale (N. Melb)
Laurie Dwyer (N. Melb)
Ted Whitten (Foots)

VFL Park is football's new home

There is plenty of parking space and lots of room inside for the footy patrons at the League's new stadium, VFL Park.

April 18. After 40 years of dreams and plans, Australian Football has its own home at the new VFL Park at Waverley. The early venues for football were roped enclosures dotted with potholes and patches of gravel. The playing area dwindled as spectators pressed forward.

Later, League grounds were designed for cricket, not football, so their sizes differed and players had to contend with the old Punt Road ground, the pocket-handkerchief oval in Brunswick Street, Fitzroy, and the constricted, almost wingless, Glenferrie Oval at Hawthorn.

Now the first stadium specifically designed for the game in the 122 years since Australian Football was first played, is open. With room for 70,000 people, the ground will bring money to the League that would otherwise have gone elsewhere. Reportedly, the VFL will get more money out of 50,000 people at Waverley than from 100,000 fans at the rented MCG. The $3 million cost of VFL Park has been raised by sales of the *Football Record*, match receipts and bank loans (→ 17/4/71).

Lions loose again

April 4. The peeling brown stands of Fitzroy's original home at Brunswick Street have given way to the dazzling white of the Junction Oval as the Lions head for their new den.

Next Saturday they use the ground for the first time in a match against St Kilda, the team that moved from the Junction to Moorabbin and to possibly more worries.

About $60,000 has been spent at the Junction, with repainting and repairing throughout, and the same amount on club rooms.

Fitzroy have had three unhappy years as tenants to a powerful landlord, Carlton (→ 9/5/85).

BERNIE BRIQUETTE'S

V.F.L. FIXTURE 1970

Now it's 22 rounds

April 30. Many football fans will applaud the latest innovation – this season every team will play each other twice. The introduction of the 22 rounds of home-and-away matches means a longer season, but is the fairest draw since the nine-club competition in 1924.

In 1969 the season began in the first week of April, but split rounds twice covered weekends.

There will be no split rounds this year, although the opening round Richmond - Fitzroy game was postponed to Sunday, 5 April, to enable members of the Royal Family to be present at the game (→ 31/3/79).

Bomber and Magpie players strike out

Geoff Pryor: one of the Dons' rebels.

Tuddenham: stripped of captaincy.

Len Thompson: compromise agreed.

April 11. Conflict over payments to players has boiled over at Essendon. Last week five senior players, Geoff Pryor, Barry Davis, Don McKenzie, Geoff Gosper and Daryl Gerlach, went on strike, and did not play in a scheduled practice game against South Adelaide.

They were not chosen for Essendon's first game of the season against Carlton, which resulted in the Dons being thumped, 21.19 (145) to 14.12 (96).

The players' demand was for $3 for each training session and a basic $40 per match for the first 50 games, with increments for each 25 games thereafter.

The rebel five turned up to training on the Thursday, but were not invited to the players' dinner. A new acting captain was named, and Chairman of Selectors Harry Hunter, when asked his reaction, said 'You may need an Obituary Column, it may be the end of them'.

The pay demand was refused by Essendon, who said that while they agreed that players should be paid more they awaited the outcome of a League decision in the matter.

The League announced that the minimum player payments could be increased to $35 a match. Essendon decided to set up a testimonial fund for retiring players in addition to the players' provident fund.

The players have agreed to this compromise, and played against Footscray in the round two match which Essendon also lost, 14.22 (106) to 10.14 (74).

Similar goings on at Collingwood saw Des Tuddenham and Len Thompson on 'strike' and not training with the team for three weeks over a demand for better pay. Both players eventually agreed to the compromise involved in the League offer, but Tuddenham was stripped of the captaincy (→ 10/7/92).

Magpies come back from 10 goals down

June 13. Collingwood, which gave new meaning to League football when they won four consecutive Premierships 40 years ago, achieved spectacular success with their recovery against St Kilda. Overcoming a ten-goal deficit in 50 minutes of play, Collingwood came back to win after lagging 1.8 to 11.8 just before half time. The final score was 14.23 (107) to 15.10 (100).

The early display of St Kilda was outstanding. However, the rebound by the Magpies stands as their greatest in 70 years.

Three players kick a ton of goals

Aug. 29. Today Alex Jesaulenko kicked five goals for Carlton against Melbourne, bringing up his century for the season. He also made VFL history, this being the first year three players have ever kicked 100 goals or more in one season.

In a field day for these three top forwards, Jesaulenko joined Magpie Peter McKenna, who booted nine goals today against the Swans to reach 128, and Hawk Peter Hudson, whose 11 goals against the Lions brought him to the amazing tally of 146.

Peter Bedford gets the Brownlow 'Live'

Aug. 31. The hot favourite for the Brownlow, South Melbourne's Peter Bedford duly took out the award with 25 votes to Gary Dempsey's 21, and Alex Jesaulenko's 20 in a 'live' count on HSV7, broadcast from the Dallas Brooks Hall. This is the first time the Brownlow has been telecast live.

Some viewers regarded the way the count was conducted more like a lottery than a suspenseful evening, and suggested that the games, and the votes from them, be indicated.

Bedford polled in 11 of 22 games, with five best on grounds. He will have to wait until the week after South's appearance in the First Semi-final to receive the medal.

Bedford came to South from Port Melbourne in 1968, and is also a Victorian cricketer (→ 25/8/77).

Royalty comes to the football, and Fitzroy's President, Mr Ern Joseph, introduces the Queen to defender Bob Hodgkin at the Sunday match against Richmond on April 5. The Sunday game was a novelty in Melbourne and attracted a big, good-natured crowd to see the Royals and the football.

Rowley's vision of Peter Bedford.

Whitten breaks games record and retires

Ted Whitten says goodbye to the Footscray faithful as his last game ends.

May 2. Ted Whitten, the VFL's number one player since the war, took to the field for Footscray for the final time today after setting a League record of 321 games.

Essendon great Dick Reynolds was in the players' room before the match to personally hand over his 320 record to Ted. Out on the ground, the crowd felt the emotion as the great 'EJ' tossed the coin for the last time.

There was no sentiment in the game itself, however, until the end. It was desperate football all the way, with the Bulldogs under tremendous pressure from the tough Hawthorn side.

In wet conditions Footscray thrilled the crowd with fast, play-on football. Whitten, although not winning many kicks, inspired his team with hard tackling.

When the final siren sounded, Teddy Whitten's Bulldogs had won by three points, 11.13 (79) to 11.10 (76). His passionate three-quarter-time address and a determination to 'win it for Teddy' had got the Bulldogs home.

Then came scenes never seen on a football ground before, as thousands swept on to the field to chair Whitten to the front of the stands where presentations were made by the Hawthorn Club as well as his beloved Footscray.

Then the field umpire, Maurie Marks, gave him with a mounted gold-plated whistle – a humorous salute to Ted's persistent 'umpiring' on the field (→ 10/5/80).

Barassi's masterstroke

Sept. 26. It was fitting that a record 121,696 of football's faithful crammed the MCG to watch Carlton and Collingwood play off for the 1970 Premiership, because it was a record-breaking game all round.

Carlton came back from a record 44 points down at half time to win, and they did it with what must have been a record number of backline hand passes in the second half.

Many of the Carlton section of the huge gathering felt like leaving the scene at half time, such was Collingwood's belligerent dominance. The scoreboard told one side of it, but it was the ease with which Des Tuddenham, Barry Price and the Richardson brothers drove the ball forward to Peter McKenna – who had five goals before half time - that had demoralised Carlton fans and, no doubt, players.

In the latter part of the second quarter Carlton were getting more of the ball, and Alex Jesaulenko took one of the most inspirational marks ever seen at the MCG, but Collingwood still outscored the Blues six goals to four.

Barassi at half time was less interested in those statistics than in one other – how many handballs.

He asked the players directly and their replies were much too optimistic. The figure was a miserable 16.

Barassi had something in mind. He recalled for the players the game in round 21, when they had been 27 points behind Hawthorn at quarter time, and had handballed, especially on the backline, around the man on the mark, and created attacking, running possession. They had won that game, kicking nine goals straight in the second quarter.

This is what Barassi wanted in the Grand Final, something different, something the Carlton players could believe in and could achieve.

Those who had left or were five minutes late getting back to their seat after half time, would have missed the football equivalent of a sudden cool change.

Ted Hopkins kicked two goals, Syd Jackson and Brent Crosswell kicked two more – making four in eight minutes and then it was seven in 12. The weather had changed.

By three-quarter time the deficit was still 17 points. Barassi, instead of berating the players, told them that, win lose or draw, he was proud of them. A groan came from the players, who would not hear of the word 'lose'.

Time on in the last quarter, and the best man on the ground, Brent Crosswell, roosted the goal that put Carlton in front, and Jesaulenko sealed it with another.

There had been 44 Carlton handballs in the second half. Carlton, 17.9 (111), defeated a stricken Collingwood, 14.17 (101).→

Skilton plays in first Final

Sept. 5. It was Bobby Skilton's day at the MCG as South's champion rover made his first Finals appearance after 15 years and 217 record-breaking games of football.

The vast majority of the record crowd of 104,239 were on the side of the triple Brownlow Medallist. The St Kilda football team, however, had other ideas and spoiled Bobby's big day by winning the First Semi-final by 53 points.

South's loss was not Skilton's doing. The veteran rover was among his team's best and his tussle with St Kilda's Brownlow Medallist Ross Smith was a highlight. After leading at half time, South had no answer to St Kilda's big men who dominated after the break to win, 22.11 (143) to 13.12 (90) (→ 18/4/77).

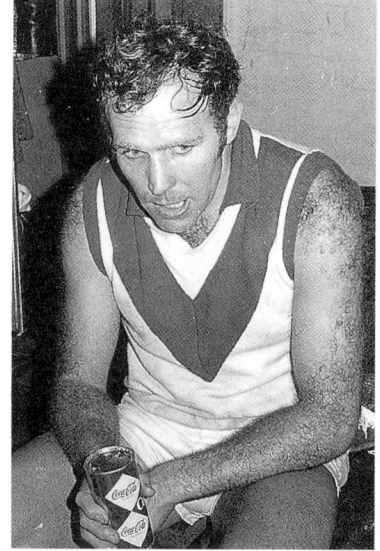

Bob Skilton savours defeat.

Carlton snatch the Miracle Grand Final

Magnificent mark of the match, by Alex Jesaulenko over Graeme 'Jerker' Jenkin.

Collingwood coach Bob Rose's face reveals the empty despair of defeat.

Exit Peter Eakins, pursued by flying Alex Jesaulenko.

1970 Statistics

Leading Goalkicker:
Peter Hudson (Haw) 146
Brownlow Medallist:
Peter Bedford (S. Melb)
Finals:
First Semi-final St K 22.11 (143)
S. Melb 13.12 (90);
Second Semi-final Coll 17.16 (118) Carl 17.6 (108);
Preliminary Final Carl 17.21 (123) St K 7.19 (61);
Grand Final Coll 14.17 (101) Carl 17.9 (111)

Ladder:	W	L	%	pts
Coll	18	4	136.5	72
Carl	16	6	112.3	64
St K	14	8	125.7	56
S. Melb	14	8	104.7	56
Geel	12	10	102.4	48
Rich	12	10	101.6	48
Foots	11	11	91.2	44
Haw	10	12	114.0	40
Fitz	9	13	82.3	36
Melb	6	16	83.5	24
Ess	6	16	81.5	24
N. Melb	4	18	79.1	16

Get ready Teddy, you're in

Sept. 26. Among other things, it had been agreed by Carlton coach Ron Barassi and selectors at the half-time break of the Grand Final, that forward pocket Bert Thornley would be given five minutes to lift his game, before replacement by blond waterskier and 'permanent' 19th man, Ted Hopkins. This was his 12th time on the bench this season.

Barassi had a growing feeling that the team did not have time to spare. As the team was about to file out Barassi roared at Hopkins, 'Get ready Teddy, you're in!'

And he was, kicking two goals in the opening Blues' blitz, four in all, and gathering 11 kicks.

Hopkins, lithe as lightning, pounced on fame, and became a legend in just five minutes (→ 7/10/72).

Ted Hopkins: sparked the revival.

Barrot and Stewart on merry-go-round

Bustling Billy Barrot: on the outer at St Kilda after his career change.

Ian Stewart: settling in well.

April 17. The long-awaited clash of the 'swapped' centremen failed to eventuate when St Kilda dropped former Richmond centreman Bill Barrot for the game against the Tigers at VFL Park.

While Barrot languished on the sidelines, the former St Kilda centreman and Brownlow Medallist Ian Stewart starred for Richmond as they downed the Saints by 19 points, 10.8 (68) to 6.13 (49). Stewart and Barrot switched clubs at the start of the season, instigated by Barrot's turbulence at Richmond.

Stewart figured in some brilliant play for his new club with strong marking and long kicking.

Barrot's short career with the Saints is at the crossroads, with coach Allan Jeans unhappy with his recruit's reluctance to take on defensive duties. Barrot will discuss his future with the club on Monday.

VFL President K.G. Luke dies

June 13. Sir Kenneth Luke, President of the VFL from 1956, has died at the age of 72. Happily, he lived to see his dream of a permanent home for Victorian Football realised with the opening of VFL Park at Waverley.

Sir Kenneth was knighted in 1962, and was chairman and managing director of K.G. Luke Group Industries.

His service to football began with his appointment as VFL delegate by Carlton in 1935. He was elected President of Carlton at the end of 1937. Sir Kenneth presided over the enterprising recruitment of Brighton Diggins in 1938, a Premiership year. One more Flag was won during his Presidency, in 1945, in a Grand Final staged at his beloved Princes Park.

From 1946 to 1955 he was Vice-President, and became the sixth President of the VFL in 1956.

His major achievement was VFL Park. In 1966 he turned the first sod on the land bought by the League in 1962. On April 18, 1970 the Governor of Victoria, Sir Rohan Delacombe unveiled a plaque to honour him as founder of the ground.

But this was not his only passion. Before the 1956 Olympics, Sir Kenneth had seen Princes Park as a 100,000 seat stadium for the Games, and for the VFL.

He was eventually thwarted in this dream, but told the 1953 Carlton AGM: 'I always thought that Carlton would be the people's ground. It is unfortunate that the premier Mr Cain should say "The MCG or nothing", and not listen to our claims. But we can still make our ground bigger and better.'

Luke: sowed the seeds of Waverley.

VFL on move

July 14. The VFL is moving headquarters, and Harrison House has been sold for $950,000, not far off the asking price. The new site for League administration will be at 84 Jolimont St, a short stroll from the sacred site of the MCG. The land cost $95,000, and the new offices should be built for around $300,000. Clubs are asking what will become of the surplus $600,000, fearing it will all be sunk in VFL Park when they need funds as urgently.

1971 VFL Football Fixtures

CARLTON DRAUGHT

FOSTER'S LAGER

VICTORIA BITTER VB

Talent scouts say zoning not working

May 22. Zoning continues to be the most controversial subject in football. So many clubs, city and country, have become disenchanted with the way zoning is working that the VFL may consent to a drastic revision of the whole scheme.

Country zoning was created in 1968 as a way to cut out the recruiting 'rat race', but several clubs have felt aggrieved ever since, believing themselves to be severely disadvantaged by being stuck with an 'arid' recruiting area.

Favoured by these clubs is a new scheme based on the American practice of 'drafting' (→ 30/8/72).

50-yard square opens up game

June 7. The Australian National Football Council rejects the idea of a 50-yard centre square as a way of easing congestion at centre bounces.

The enlarged square was tried out at the Carlton and Fitzroy game at Princes Park and succeeded in opening up the game considerably. Under the proposed change only rucks, rovers and centremen are permitted at centre bounces. Others must stand back behind painted lines.

VFL Administrative Director Eric McCutchan said that, although the League was disappointed with the decision, it would not go it alone in changing the rules (→ 22/4/75).

Percy Jones and the great fog game

Aug. 21. A thick and gloomy fog descended on the Junction Oval and on Carlton fans during the game between Fitzroy and Carlton. Carlton needed to win to ensure a place in the Finals, but lost in visibility that was near zero, 15.15 (105) to 11.16 (82).

At least one of the 22,413 fans thought he heard Carlton's Percy Jones call out 'I've got it!' when a hidden Lion asked if anyone knew where the footy was. The Fitzroy player snaffled the ball and kicked a goal. Fitzroy have their 11th win in a much improved season.

Peter Crimmins plays fantastic 100th game

May 15. Playing his 100th League game, Hawthorn rover Peter Crimmins had a feast against the Tigers today. The Hawks brought real football pressure to bear, and the Tigers were daunted.

It was one of those days where the confidence of one team puts the other side out of kilter in the first quarter and dictates the play for the rest of the game. The confident Hawks had winners all over the ground, whereas Richmond had few players worth noticing.

Peter Crimmins dominated around the packs, and his passing helped full forward Peter Hudson to a ten-goal tally.

The stunned Richmond team were held scoreless in the first quarter, and by half time were trailing by 58 points, a tribute to the Hawks' relentless attack and their good kicking for goal. The score at that stage was 15.7 to 6.3.

In the second half, the Hawks kept peppering the goal and, had they been more accurate, would have had an even bigger margin than the final score of 21.19 (145) to the Tigers' 12.6 (78) (→ 19/5/75).

Hawthorn's pocket Hercules Peter Crimmins shows the dash that wins games.

Fitzroy's high flyer is half-forward Laurie Richards, a noted aerialist from Perth in the WA League.

Big upheaval at Victoria Park

Sept. 8. Collingwood's disastrous fade-out, losing five of the last six games, has set the cat among the Magpie administration.

Collingwood lost the First Semi-final to Richmond 18.13 (121) to 11.11 (77) last Saturday, and even managed a bad case of deja vu in the last game of the season to Carlton – losing after being 42 points up at half time, 16.10 (106) to 13.9 (87).

Coach Bob Rose will coach Footscray next year, after eight seasons but no Premierships at Collingwood. The Magpies have played in seven Finals series, winning only three of the 13 games played.

President Tom Sherrin is believed to be under threat from a group led by Frank Galbally.

This reform group is unhappy at the lack of Finals success, and would prefer to see Des Tuddenham forgiven and made on-field leader, as well as coach.

The Annual General Meeting will decide in December (→ 9).

Carlton's Robert Walls takes a big mark and skittles the pack.

Barassi and Bob Rose quit coaching

Bobby Rose hard at work.

Barassi and heir John Nicholls.

Sept. 9. Coaches of Grand Final sides last year, gone today. That's the astonishing story of Collingwood's Bob Rose and Carlton's Ron Barassi.

For the Magpies, the loss in last year's Grand Final can doubtless be put down to injury to their three best first half players – Peter McKenna, Des Tuddenham and Wayne Richardson. But lose they did and a price had to be paid.

The story has a political twist involving squabbling over the club captaincy. Then Collingwood squandered a seven-goal half-time lead over Carlton, losing by 19 points only to be flicked from the Finals after one game.

Sacked skipper Terry Waters spoke out, saying the club needed a new coach and Committee, some new players and fresh thinking. Bob Rose then quit, citing strain.

The 1970 Grand Final was a match in which Barassi had amazing influence, and he was hailed as a master after the come-back win. Barassi declared he would again coach Carlton next year, but the Committee had other ideas and his contract was not to be renewed. Carlton missed this year's Finals, which did not help Barassi's cause (→ 11/6/76).

Ian Stewart wins third Brownlow

Stewart: has the Brownlow habit.

Aug. 30. Ian Stewart has become only the fourth player in football history to win three Brownlow Medals. The Saint turned Tiger won on the last vote in one of the most dramatic counts in history.

At the last vote Stewart was level with Peter Hudson of Hawthorn, Essendon's Barry Davis and John McIntosh of St Kilda. As the tension mounted, the Administrative Director of the VFL, Mr Eric McCutchan, called the last vote. Ian Stewart had been a late starter and initially appeared to be overshadowed by team-mate Royce Hart. But the 26-year-old former St Kilda captain, who won in 1965 and 1966 and has played 147 games in nine seasons, won in what he said was the greatest thrill of his life.

Hudson battles to goal of 150

Sept. 25. Peter Hudson was held to three goals in the Grand Final – but that was enough to equal South Melbourne full-forward Bob Pratt's 1934 record of 150 goals in a League season.

Pratt kicked just two goals to reach 150 in the South Melbourne losing Grand Final side. It was just his 21st game of the season.

Hudson kicked three, but had the consolation of playing in a winning Grand Final team. He played 24 games.

Pratt scored his 150 this way: 8, 10, 15, 6, 7, 4, 6, 5, 8, 7, 9, 8, 11, 11, 12, 3, 3, 5, 4, 6, 2. Hudson's came like this: 5, 4, 1, 7, 5, 3, 10, 7, 5, 5, 5, 6, 9, 7, 12, 6, 9, 6, 6, 3, 9, 10, 7, 3.

That averages out at about 7.2 goals per game for Pratt, and 6.2 for Hudson – both remarkable averages.

Hudson in fact had several opportunities to break the record.

First he accepted a hand-pass from Bob Keddie, who had marked, and kicked the ball through but this was disallowed because the umpire had blown time on.

Next he kicked one of his characteristic flat punts straight into the burly figure of St Kilda's Barry Lawrence.

And then he ran into an open goal, and managed to kick the footy out of bounds.

Perhaps this record, like Bradman requiring four runs in his last Test innings to average 100, is just destined never to be broken.

Instead of a record Hudson received a gashed right ear that required seven stitches (→ 1/4/72).

Peter Hudson marks over St Kilda's Bob Murray on his march to 150.

Hawks come back to crush the Saints

Sept. 25 Hawthorn's tenacious last-quarter effort wrested the Grand Final from St Kilda by seven points before 118,192 fans today. The Hawks won 12.10 (82) to St Kilda 11.9 (75).

Hawk star Peter Hudson's battle for one goal to break Bob Pratt's record 150 became a sideshow as the teams struggled hard in the last minutes of the game.

The match was fought in wet conditions, not conducive to high scoring, and was a man-to-man struggle with players throwing their weight into the packs.

St Kilda lost their fullback Bob Murray early, but Barry Lawrence was moved on to Peter Hudson and kept him well in check.

The Saints were two points up at half time and then went into attack for goals by John Bonney, Barry Breen and Ross Smith. They had a 20 point margin at the last change.

The Hawks were transformed when Bob Keddie was moved to full-forward, with Hudson taking the centre-half-forward post. Keddie was a match-winner, pouncing on the ball in thick packs, winning seven kicks and boosting the score by 4.2 in 16 minutes. The Hawks scored 6.3 for the quarter (→ 25/9/76).

One that got away for Peter Hudson and Hawthorn as the umpire ruled that he had signalled time-on before the kick.

1971 Statistics

Leading Goalkicker:
Peter Hudson (Haw) 150
Brownlow Medallist:
Ian Stewart (Rich)
Finals: First Semi Rich 18.13 (121) Coll 11.11 (77); **Second Semi** Haw 12.18 (90) St K 12.16 (88); **Preliminary Final** St K 16.12 (108); Rich 12.6 (78); **Grand Final** Haw 12.10 (82) St K 11.9 (75)

Ladder:	W	L	D	%	pts
Haw	19	3		153.7	76
St K	16	6		140.0	64
Rich	16	6		122.6	64
Coll	14	7	1	126.7	58
Carl	14	8		104.4	56
Fitz	12	10		106.9	48
Melb	11	10	1	109.5	46
Foots	11	11		88.7	44
N. Melb	5	16	1	66.8	22
Geel	5	17		82.1	20
Ess	4	17	1	75.7	18
S. Melb	3	19		69.9	12

No goal! Hudson gets the news.

John Kennedy discards the mask.

Hudson's shot for a record breaking goal ricochets off Barry Lawrence.

1972

April 1. Peter Hudson kicks eight goals for Hawthorn before breaking down with a knee injury. The Hawks defeat the Demons 15.14 (104) to 10.15 (75) (→ 27/5).

April 29. Peter McKenna, ordered to bed early by coach Neil Mann, responds by kicking 11 goals of Collingwood's 22.8 (140) win over North Melbourne 8.14 (62) (→ 12/6).

May 13. Footscray defeat Geelong at Kardinia Park for the first time since 1945, 16.15 (111) to 15.18 (108) (→ 20).

May 20. Footscray's run of away win 'firsts' continues with their first win at Victoria Park since 1961, 11.14 (80) to Collingwood 7.14 (56) (→ 29/7).

June 3. The VFL appoints former Carlton wingman Laurie Kerr's PR firm IPR to improve its image at a cost of $10,000 (→ 27/4/76).

June 3. The field umpire, not a team captain, will now toss the coin at start of games to avoid suspicion of gamesmanship.

June 10. Voters for the Tassie Medal at the ANFC Carnival in Perth will include two others in addition to the field umpire, after controversy in 1969, when Graham Molloy (SA) and Peter Eakins (WA) jointly won, but John Nicholls received only two votes (→ 12/5/73).

June 12. Peter McKenna kicks 13 goals in nightmare return of former Magpie Des Tuddenham as 'Dons coach to Victoria Park. Essendon lose to Collingwood 13.15 (93) to 23.10 (148) (→ 4/4/77).

June 17. Collingwood's cheer squad is on strike over VFL's ban on 'floggers' and showers of torn paper (→ 16/4/81).

June 21. Channel 7 Perth makes first test colour telecast of football at ANFC Carnival, showing Victoria 17.9 (111) defeating South Australia 8.9 (57). Some VFL guernseys are too dull (→ 30/4/74).

July 29. North Melbourne win their first game of the season, beating South Melbourne 12.15 (87) to 11.12 (78) (→ 7/7/73).

Aug. 26. Blue Greg Kennedy kicks 12 goals in 24.12 (156) win over Hawthorn 11.22 (88).

Debuts
Michael Malthouse (St.K)
Michael Tuck (Haw)

Retirement
Bob Keddie (Haw)

The Four becomes a Final Five

Feb. 2 The Final Four has become Five. The introduction of this new system means that the fourth and fifth teams meet in an Elimination Final. Second and third teams play a Qualifying Final.

On the second Saturday, the winner of the Qualifying Final meets the top team in the Second Semi Final while the loser of the Qualifying Final plays the winner of the winner of the First Semi Final. The winner of the First Semi Final then plays the Second Semi Final loser in the Preliminary Final. The winner of that game plays the Second Semi Final victor in the Grand Final (→ 1/3/91).

Free transfers after ten years service

Aug. 12. The decision by the League to grant players a free transfer, from the end of the season, after ten years service has angered officials who fear they may lose valuable players in a transfer free-for-all.

While legal advisers are examining the implications of the decision, some officials have suggested that it could open the way for bottom clubs to 'buy' a Premiership team. Clubs are also worried about likely rises in player payments.

Twenty-six top players are eligible this season, among them Carl Ditterich, Doug Wade, Barry Davis and Adrian Gallagher (→ 17/4/75).

New zone ideas anger the clubs

Aug. 30. Draft changes to country recruiting zones released by the VFL have some clubs 'hopping mad' although they are mostly minor alterations.

Major country league alignments, such as Footscray with the Latrobe Valley League and Carlton with the Bendigo League remain the same.

Clubs which have not had prime recruiting zones were hoping to improve their positions, but have not. And Richmond have gained nothing in addition to the poor Sunraysia League and would lose the Mallee to Essendon (→ 6/5/76).

Hudson to surgery, Tuck to full-forward

Peter Hudson: time off with family.

May 27. Michael Tuck, 18, has been thrown into one of the most important roles in football. In just his second senior game he is going to be Hawthorn's full-forward.

The news that Peter Hudson needs surgery on his injured right knee puts the spotlight on Tuck, a long-haired, 6ft 1in, 11 and a half stone plumbing apprentice and former Collingwood fan from Berwick.

'I have to admit I'm pretty nervous,' said Tuck. 'I never really thought I'd be filling in for Peter. It's a bit early to say I'm going to be his successor because I have to prove myself by kicking goals.'

Hudson, meanwhile, is resigned to not playing. 'I can have the operation at least knowing what's ahead of me,' he said. 'Before this, I didn't' (→ 25/8/73).

Hawthorn halfback Peter Knights grabs another against Collingwood.

Greening felled in tragic clash

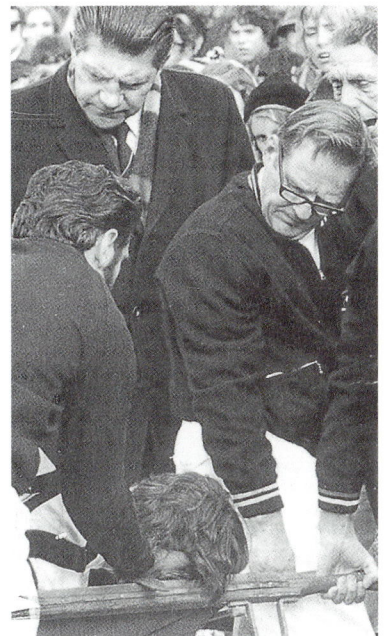

Concerned eyes over John Greening.

July 8. Two minutes after the start of the Collingwood and St Kilda game, the outstanding Magpie half-forward John Greening was carried unconscious from the Moorabbin ground. He went down 70 yards behind play and was later admitted, in a grave condition, to the Alfred Hospital.

The extent of Greening's injury was such that it brought a hush to the crowd, and caused coach Neil Mann to be among the Collingwood officials to rush to his side.

Feeling showed later in an all-in fight between the players, and then a long series of fights and fiery scrimmages. Saints' half-back Jim O'Dea was one of those on the receiving end. Collingwood won the match 9.13 (67) to St Kilda's 4.13 (37). However, St Kilda remain second on the ladder, with Collingwood in fifth place (→ 20/4/74).

North lure Barassi over breakfast

Sept. 30. Ultimately, the deal was done over breakfast. Ron Barassi had left Carlton announcing that he was finished as a coach, but before long he was commentating on TV, radio and in the newspapers.

At North Melbourne, the hunger for the superstar was strong. The method of recruitment was scarcely subtle: club chief Albert Mantello turned up at Barassi's office one morning and, as soon as he started talking to Barassi, he began kicking the leg of a desk. Barassi asked him to stop. Sure, said Mantello, as soon as Barassi agreed to coach North Melbourne.

Over breakfast with Mantello and the other forces at North, Allen Aylett and Ron Joseph, Barassi agreed to coach from next year, receiving a $50,000 interest-free loan and $35,000 a year.

Many felt that, in spite of Barassi's 1968 and 1970 Premierships at Carlton, his time had been running out, and a players' rebellion was in the air (→ 16/6/73).

On Thursday night you will get no better entertainment than 'League Teams' on 7. Who knows what Jack, Bob and Lou will say next? They don't.

Jezza's eleven minutes of magic

July 22. In just 11 minutes in the second quarter, Carlton wizard Alex Jesaulenko kicked six goals in a show-stopping demonstration of football magic.

Few, if any, more devastating bursts of play have been seen in the long history of football at Princes Park.

Essendon players literally seemed to be mesmerised by Jesaulenko, as he flew, wriggled, jinked, dodged, escaped and wove his way through packs of parked Bombers, as if he was Houdini himself.

'Jezza' gave away another couple of goals to David McKay and Brent Crosswell, in the Blues' total of 12 straight for the quarter.

A 49-point lead at half time put the game beyond doubt, but Essendon recovered from the Jesaulenko spell to fight back strongly in the second half, kicking ten goals to four by the awestruck Blues.

Carlton retained top spot with the 20.13 (133) to 17.15 (117) win, and the thought that their centreman mightn't be a bad full-forward.

Jezza: balance and brilliance.

Umpire attacked in Second Semi draw

Sept. 16. Umpire Ian Coates was attacked and left very groggy after the angry crowd swarmed on to the ground after the drawn Second Semi at VFL Park. Police arrested a 'long-haired male' of uncertain football heritage.

Carlton had slightly the better of a dour first half, steaming to a 17-point lead at half time – without their usual chief engineer John Nicholls having much of a role.

The Tigers, led by the high-marking exploits of big men Royce Hart, Rex Hunt and Neil Balme and the zippy play around the packs of Kevin Bartlett, kicked seven goals to three in the second half to be a goal in front in time on. It was a defensive, low-scoring game.

The Blues did not give up, even in time on and Alex Jesaulenko somehow managed to get the ball to Barry Armstrong in the last seconds of the game for a goal, and a draw.

Except for the ground invaders, the 54,338 fans were stunned when the siren sounded, with the score at 8.13 (61) each (→ 28/4/73).

Here's a first – a bespectacled full-forward who has kicked 100 goals for the season. Geoff Blethyn is the only Dons' player to have emulated John Coleman's feat. A police horse protecting him after his 100th rendered him sightless when it slobbered on his glasses.

Giant Magpie clinches Brownlow

Nicholls' game plan scores Blues' Flag

Thommo: big and brilliant.

Sept. 5. Giant Collingwood ruckman Len Thompson last night won the 1972 Brownlow Medal, edging out Melbourne's Greg Wells on the last vote of the night.

Thompson, the medal favourite, was tied with Wells on 22 points with only one round of votes still to be counted. Wells failed to win another vote and was left stranded on 22. The cheers went up from Collingwood supporters as it was announced that Thompson had polled three votes in a best-on-ground performance, giving him 25 votes and the medal for the best and fairest footballer in the League.

The 25-year-old Thompson was visibly nervous as the count neared its dramatic conclusion. He was sweating profusely and held his head in his hands, almost unable to watch.

It has been a fine season for Thompson after a disappointing year in 1971. He was determined to lift his game this year and embarked upon an exhaustive pre-season fitness programme under the supervision of leading running coach John Toleman. The big ruckman had set himself three goals for the season – to regain his spot as Collingwood's top ruckman, gain Carnival selection and win his third Copeland Trophy.

Thompson not only achieved all three, but has now added a fourth – the Brownlow Medal.

Oct. 7. Carlton captain-coach John Nicholls beat Richmond in his head before he beat them on the ground in the Grand Final.

Carlton and Richmond played three times in the Final series for a draw, a thrashing and, in the Grand Final, a glut of goals.

After the apparent devastation of the Second Semi loss, 9.15 (69) to 15.20 (110), Nicholls told the Carlton players that he believed they could win the Grand Final. He didn't mention the Preliminary Final that still had to be won, instead he spoke of his confidence in winning the Flag.

Carlton did beat, but failed to thrash, St Kilda 16.13 (109) to 13.15 (93). Confidence might be thought to have declined, but to Nicholls that game was just a stepping stone.

Nicholls' view was that the only way to beat the Tigers was to score more goals, a lot more goals, than they could.

To this end he decided to park himself in the forward pocket as a big target. He felt that he could beat Richmond back pocket Ray Boyanich.

Nicholls also thought that Robert Walls at centre-half-forward could run Rex Hunt off his feet and feed the other forwards. And he thought that Alex Jesaulenko was capable of anything, and everything, at full-forward.

And, finally, he thought that 'Percy' Jones was at last 'big' enough to play number one ruckman.

Nicholls said: 'Our whole game was built on attack, and it was one of those days where all the well-laid plans came off.'

The first quarter was perhaps the most evenly contested, yet Carlton kicked 8.4 to 5.4 with an ominous collection of goalkickers: Nicholls two, Jesaulenko two, Walls one.

In the second quarter those players kicked another six of the ten Carlton goals, resulting in a high scoreline of 18.6 to 10.9.

By the end Richmond had kicked the highest losing total in Grand Final history, but Carlton had kicked an even higher one.

Carlton won, 28.9 (177) to 22.18 (150). Jesaulenko kicked seven, Nicholls six and Walls another six. Walls was best on the ground, and Nicholls not far behind (→ 29/9/79).

David Mackay takes a big mark.　　*Robert Walls soccers a goal.*

How sweet it is! Robert Walls and Bruce Doull take the cup into the bath.

1972 Statistics

Leading Goalkicker:	Ladder:	W	L	D	%	pts
Peter McKenna (Coll) 130						
Brownlow Medallist:						
Len Thompson (Coll)	Carl	18	3	1	134.3	74
Finals: Elimination Final St K	Rich	18	4		117.7	72
18.16 (124) Ess 10.11 (71); **Qualifying Final** Rich 25.14 (164) Coll	Coll	14	7	1	133.8	58
	St K	14	8		115.6	56
18.12 (120); **First Semi** Coll 8.17	Ess	14	8		108.3	56
(65) St K 11.17 (83) **Second Semi**	Haw	13	9		111.1	52
Carl 8.13 (61) Rich 8.13 (61); **Second Semi Replay** Carl 9.15 (69)	Foots	11	11		94.7	44
	Melb	10	12		105.9	40
Rich 15.20 (110); **Preliminary Final** Carl 16.13 (109) St K 13.15	Fitz	9	13		96.8	36
	Geel	7	15		84.2	28
(93); **Grand Final** Rich 22.18	S. Melb	2	20		65.1	8
(150) Carl 28.9 (177)	N. Melb	1	21		62.9	4

1973

The Great Bomber John Coleman dies at the age of 44

April 5. The greatest full-forward of his time, Essendon's John Coleman, died today at his hotel in Dromana, at the age of 44. Football followers, no matter which team they support, were shocked and saddened.

Coleman played just 98 games, but kicked 537 goals between his debut in 1949 and the tragic knee injury in 1954.

Coleman kicked ten or more goals on 12 occasions; his biggest bag was 14.5 against Fitzroy in 1954. Coleman coached Essendon to two Flags, 1962 and 1965.

He had two hotels, in Brunswick and Dromana, and lived in Essendon. He was idolised in both districts, and took a keen interest in football in the Hastings area where he grew up.

Essendon and Richmond players will observe a minute's silence on Saturday. All of football mourns the loss of a champion.

A huge crowd at St Thomas', Moonee Ponds, to pay tribute to John Coleman.

Lethal boots eleven

The unstoppable Leigh Matthews.

April 23. At quarter time, Leigh Matthews had only one goal, and the Hawks a lead of only seven points over Essendon. These statistics gave little warning of the incredible 11 goals 'Lethal' Leigh would kick by game's end; a record for a rover in the Hawks' record win: 27.8 (170) to the Bombers' 15.12 (102).

Not so fortunate was Leigh's brother Kelvin who, while following his victorious brother into the players' race, forgot to duck and knocked himself unconscious on the race's concrete roof (→ 28/4/84).

Barassi has Roos jumping

June 16. The new look North Melbourne under supercoach Ron Barassi are still in the Five, but only just, at the halfway mark of the season despite the narrow loss to Melbourne. The Demons kicked on in the last quarter to win, 13.12 (90) to 12.9 (81).

With six wins, four losses and a draw with Footscray three weeks ago, the Kangaroo recruiting raid provided by the window of opportunity of the 'ten year' rule is already a success. Last year saw only one North win and the wooden spoon, so the addition of experienced players such as Doug Wade, Barry Davis and John Rantall has added great strength to the side.

But the form and disparate shapes of stalwart ruckmen Barry Goodingham and big rookie Mick Nolan are also proving important.

The win which really served notice that North Melbourne had come of age was against Richmond in round four, where they won with a spirited last quarter, 14.20 (104) to Richmond's 11.18 (84).

President Allen Aylett said after that match that he would have been 'satisfied with two wins at this stage, but to have three, with one over Richmond, is great. It has justified all the planning and work put in be-

Barry Davis a new Roo.

fore the season began'.

Ron Barassi says his players were 'magnificent ... It was a great day, a great win and I'm proud of the players. They did not let themselves down, the club, or me. In the second half they were magnificent. They gave their best, worked together and did everything I wanted.

'We can play better and will. Each week we have learned something which has helped.'

There has clearly been a great bound forward by the Kangaroos (→ 28/6/76).

Tuddy says diamond is not forever

March 21. The VFL is introducing the new diamond-shaped centre zone this season, but it won't work, according to Essendon captain-coach, Des Tuddenham. He says that in practice games half-forwards and wingmen were able to get to the centre by the time the ball was controlled by a ruckman.

Tuddenham said that to remove congestion in the centre a proper square should be set up, so than every player on the line is an equal distance from the centre. 'Under the diamond plan players are not able to break away without being put under extreme pressure,' he said.

Jeans reported for abusive language

June 11. St Kilda coach Allan Jeans has been reprimanded by the VFL Tribunal for abusive and insulting language towards three umpires.

They said that during quarter time Jeans had said: 'Coates, you bloody mongrel, give us a go.' Field umpire Ian Coates and boundary umpires Barry Woods and Bob Gulliver said this statement, or part of it, was repeated three times.

The four-minute hearing was only the second for Jeans. In 1967 Umpire Woods said Jeans had used abusive language to a field umpire, but the Tribunal did not hear the charge (→9/4/74).

Jezza gets the Yoo Hoo feeling.

Muddy tales of the Western Oval

Round and McKenzie struggle.

July 21. The Western Oval was more like a wet day on the Western Front in World War One than a football ground for the game between Footscray and Hawthorn.

Hawthorn rover Leigh Matthews said the conditions were appalling. The umpire couldn't run because of the mud, and if a player stood in the centre of the ground he had to scrape the mud off his boots before he could raise a trot.

There was an amazing number of 117 free kicks paid. But more amazing was that Hawthorn played the conditions better than Footscray, kicking the ball further.

Gary Dempsey stood out for the Bulldogs, being so tall, but Hawk rovers Leigh Matthews and Peter Crimmins reaped the soggy crumbs. Hawthorn won, 9.11 (65) to Footscray's 6.9 (45) (→27/7/89).

Keith Greig strolls to Brownlow win

Slightly built, but Keith Greig rules the wing for North Melbourne.

Sept. 3. North Melbourne claimed its first ever Brownlow today, as a surprised Keith Greig, 21, took the podium to the applause of an appreciative audience. A plumber by trade, Greig polled 27 votes in only his second season for North Melbourne.

Finishing two votes clear of Essendon's Graham Moss and four ahead of Hawthorn rover Leigh Matthews, Greig was still critical of his performance: 'I didn't think I played enough good games to have a chance of winning.'

In fact, the elegant Victorian winger had bet his father 20 cents that he would not win: 'I didn't think I had a chance, so I put some money on it. I don't bet very much, but this is one I won't mind paying up.'

Greig now looks to the future: 'If I can win North's first Brownlow this year, there's no way in the world we won't win North's first Premiership next year' (→7/9/74).

Hudson pays Hawks a flying visit

Hudson: kicking boot back.

Aug. 25. A crowd of 48,000 people went out to VFL Park to see Peter Hudson's much-heralded return to football. After barely a minute of play, the same people might have been wondering whether the journey was worth it; a jarring fall seemed to mark the return of the knee injury that had kept the great full-forward out of the game for almost two years. They should not have been worried.

Ninety-five minutes, four different opponents and eight goals later, and Hudson's triumphant return had been sealed.

Unfortunately for Hawk supporters, not even Hudson could stop Hawthorn from losing, 13.10 (88) to Collingwood's 16.10 (106). This defeat sees them out of the Finals race, and Hudson back on the plane to Tasmania (→17/6/75).

Boundary balls up

June 4. In one of the more freakish incidents in football, boundary umpire Greg McQueen 'helped' North Melbourne to a goal just before half time at Geelong.

The ball had been heading out of bounds when it accidentally ricocheted off McQueen's boot into the arms of Wayne Schimmelbusch.

Then it was in the hands of Doug Wade and through the goal. North won by a flattering margin of 31 points, 18.13 (121) to 14.6 (90).

Tough Tigers KO the Blues

Sept. 29. Revenge for Richmond's comprehensive loss to Carlton in the 1972 Grand Final was wrought in more ways than one with an equally comprehensive win this year in front of 116,956 fans on a hot blustery day at the MCG.

Coach Tom Hafey said the Tigers won because 'we were desperate to play tough football for the whole game' – perhaps a reference to the fact that Richmond played only half a game in the fantastic comeback against Collingwood in the Preliminary Final from, of course, 45 points behind. Richmond won that game, 15.15 (105) to 14.14 (98).

But perhaps tough football referred to the flattening of Carlton captain-coach John Nicholls three minutes into the first quarter, and the KO of fullback Geoff Southby in the second quarter.

Nicholls conceded that being a semi-comatose captain-coach with double vision had some effect on his ability to make the moves that Carlton needed.

Carlton half-forward David McKay said that the felling of Southby was 'one of the worst things' he'd seen in football but also said that Carlton had been 'beaten on the day by a better side'. Others were less charitable, labelling the Blues a 'flop' and unworthy of their claim to be the 'professionals'.

The expected domination of Percy Jones in the ruck did not eventuate – instead Michael Green and Brian 'Whale' Roberts gave Kevin Bartlett an armchair ride. Bartlett had 27 kicks to be best afield.

The other Tiger match winner was Kevin Sheedy who, in the words of Francis Bourke 'was magnificent. He really set us on the road to victory in the first quarter with creative handball, shepherding, plain hard slogging work and, of course, those invaluable three goals'.

Both sides had injury and illness worries before the game. For the Tigers Royce Hart and Francis Bourke had made quick recoveries, but for Carlton Trevor Keogh and Barry Armstrong were out, and Alex Jesaulenko and Neil Chandler were not 100 %. Carlton named Vin Catoggio for his first full game and he was overawed by the occasion.

Richmond won, 16.20 (116) to Carlton's 12.14 (86) (→ 28/9/74).

Royce Hart takes a big Tiger mark.

Geoff Southby tries to revive.

Roberts, Nicholls and Hunt contest.

Richmond ruckman Michael Green tries to break away from Alex Jesaulenko.

The camera catches Richmond's Laurie Fowler crashing into John Nicholls.

1973 Statistics

Leading Goalkicker: Peter McKenna (Coll) 84
Brownlow Medallist: Keith Greig (N. Melb)
Finals: Elimination Final Ess 13.13 (91) St K 24.14 (158); **Qualifying Final** Rich 10.11 (71) Carl 13.13 (91); **First Semi-final** Rich 15.18 (108) St K 9.14 (68); **Second Semi-final** Coll 12.15 (87) Carl 15.17 (107); **Preliminary Final** Coll 14.14 (98) Rich 15.15 (105); **Grand Final** Carl 12.14 (86) Rich 16.20 (116)

Ladder:	W	L	D	%	pts
Coll	19	3		125.5	76
Rich	17	5		117.6	68
Carl	15	7		126.6	60
Ess	13	9		104.4	52
St K	12	10		105.3	48
N. Melb	11	10	1	97.6	46
Haw	11	11		109.6	44
Fitz	9	13		90.7	36
Foots	7	14	1	88.2	30
Melb	7	15		91.8	28
Geel	6	16		78.4	24
S. Melb	4	18		79.0	16

April 6. Hawthorn beat 'hungover' Premiers Richmond, 15.14 (104) to 12.16 (88) (→ 28/3/81).

April 9. North coach Ron Barassi is severely reprimanded after a charge of misconduct, abusing a boundary umpire in North's loss to South 11.14 (80) to 15.10 (100) (→ 3/5/76).

April 13. Collingwood spoil Hawthorn's house warming party in their first home game at Princes Park, winning 10.11 (71) to 6.12 (48).

April 20. Tiger stars Francis Bourke (kicking), Royce Hart (striking) and Blue Robert Walls (striking) are reported after spiteful clash, which Richmond won, 18.11 (119) to Carlton 11.15 (81) (→ 22).

April 20. Michael Moncrieff, Hawthorn's 'stand-in' for Peter Hudson at full-forward, kicks ten against South Melbourne in the win 20.15 (135) to 8.18 (66).

April 20. Kelvin Templeton, a 17-year-old from Traralgon, kicks 6.3 in his Footscray debut. Collingwood win 16.16 (112) to 14.15 (99) (→ 12/8/78).

April 22. Richmond plan to use videotape in evidence in the Bourke/Hart Tribunal cases – for just the second time in VFL history (→ 16/6/89).

April 22. The VFL Tribunal has cleared Francis Bourke, reprimanded Robert Walls and outed Royce Hart for two weeks (→ 18/5).

April 27. Footscray pick 17-year-old Ted Whitten Jr for his first game.

June 3. Results of the Windy Hill brawl on May 18. Essendon runner Laurie Ashley, trainer Jim Bradley, and Ron Andrews, all six matches; Richmond's Steve Parsons, four weeks and Mal Brown, one week (→ 5/4/75).

Aug. 24. Kevin Murray plays 332nd game, and is believed to break the VFL record, in the Lions' loss, 14.16 (100) to Melbourne 20.13 (133).

Debuts
Malcolm Blight (N. Melb)
Simon Madden (Ess)
Peter Moore (Coll)
Bill Picken (Coll)
Ray Shaw (Coll)
Kelvin Templeton (Foots)

Retirements
Kevin Murray (Fitz)
John Nicholls (Carl)
David Parkin (Haw)
Barry Richardson (Rich)

Seven are charged after the Battle of Windy Hill

The horror scene at Windy Hill as players, spectators, police and officials join in the fight.

May 18. Windy Hill at Essendon, the scene of many rugged football duels, today became the venue for one of the most bizarre events in recent football history.

It began when, moments before the half-time siren, Richmond's Mal Brown tangled with Essendon's Graeme Jenkin. After the players had separated and begun making their way toward the players' race, the Essendon runner confronted Brown. Brown responded by dropping the runner.

Essendon's John Cassin headed to the runner's aid, while others lined up behind Brown. Soon police, spectators, players and officials were involved in a vicious brawl that lasted most of the half-time break.

After the mob had finally been quelled, one spectator and an Essendon trainer were left unconscious, while Richmond's Brian Roberts departed the field clutching a broken nose. Four players have been charged and charges against officials may follow.

The brawl obscured what was an exciting and tight thriller – Richmond eventually running out winners by 10 points, 16.19 (115) to 15.15 (105) (→ 3/6).

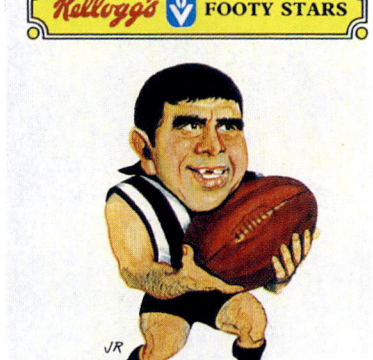

Seven is one-eyed about footy

April 30. Melbourne's winter TV madness, a wall-to-wall carpet of football shows and replays, shows a slight decline this year.

GTV9, which departed the competitive football preview and panel scene in 1970, has now taken itself from the field of football replays.

This leaves HSV7 well and truly on top of the football ladder, with only the ABC for competition.

ATV0 is only telecasting the VFA on Sunday afternoons.

ABV2's football panel show is at six on Saturdays, followed by match highlights. 'Focus on Football' is on Thursday nights, the panel including Harry Beitzel, Doug Heywood and Thorold Merrett.

HSV7 kick off with 'League Teams' on Thursdays, with Jack Dyer, Bob Davis and Lou Richards. Saturday has Michael Williamson's 'Football Inquest' at 6.30 with Jack Edwards, Bluey Adams, John Dugdale and Kevin Hall on the panel. Then there's *The Replay*. Sundays we'll watch 'World of Sport Replay' followed by 'World of Sport' and the 'Footy Panel' (→ 3/5/77).

Picken, Templeton pick of new crop

Aug. 17. Eighteen-year-old Bill Picken is the stand-out player in this year's crop of VFL newcomers. Picken, a matriculation student at Melbourne High, was snatched up by Collingwood ahead of other notable debutants such as Malcolm Blight, Mark Maclure and Simon Madden.

With a high jump best of 5ft 6in, Picken's giant leap and excellent high mark should assure him a long and prosperous future in football.

Picken, who has never seen a VFL Grand Final and only a few Finals, is an avid St Kilda supporter, and admits he is at Collingwood only because he was zoned to them. But with the welcome he's received from Collingwood supporters, we're sure he's feeling right at home.

Equally popular among the new recruits is Kelvin Templeton, whose ability as a long-kicking forward has made him an instant success among Bulldog fans. Recruited by Footscray this year from Traralgon, Templeton has more than lived up to expectations.

Indeed this year sees a flock of new recruits – if we include interstate players, 94 in all, possibly the best influx of talent in many years.

A welcome sight. John Greening of Collingwood in his first seniors game since he was felled in 1972. He starred against Richmond.

John Nicholls' long playing days are over after 18 seasons

The big engine of Carlton, John Nicholls, is applauded by team-mates and opponents at Victoria Park, Collingwood.

Aug. 3. John Nicholls has retired as a player, after a League record believed to be 328 VFL games. He will be 35 in ten days and did not play in the loss to Hawthorn today, 14.12 (96) to 18.12 (120), because of injury.

Big Nick first played for Carlton in 1957, and like a big blue gum has grown with the club, starting from a lowly position to winning three Flags, and being a consistent Finals performer.

He's called Big Nick but he isn't really very tall. He is wide, strong and has that indefinable something that enables him to command the field of play.

Such was this presence that when he was flattened in the 1973 Grand Final it demoralised the entire Carlton team for a time because they had never seen him down for the count.

Nicholls has one of the shrewdest football brains in the business, as was shown by the way he engineered Carlton's high-scoring win in the 1972 Grand Final.

Big Nick's battles with the Big Cat Polly Farmer will go down in the football annals as treasures of single combat.

He had an instinct for palming the ball to where his rover would be before the rover knew. His understanding with Adrian Gallagher has verged on the psychic (→ 31/3/76).

Kekovich in and out of hot water

April 3. Sam Kekovich is back at North Melbourne. After parting company with the club over summer, Kekovich trained again at Arden Street.

Kekovich, 24, said two weeks ago: 'I won't be at North this year.' He held talks with West Adelaide, but negotiations broke down and so Big Sam was back where he began.

He then phoned the club and was invited to a city restaurant to talk with North Melbourne President, Allen Aylett, Secretary Ron Joseph and Vice-President Albert Mantello. 'He was told he would not be cleared, and that his future was here, and, as a consequence, he has resumed training,' Joseph said. The enigmatic Kekovich has declined to comment.

Slamming Sam back in harness.

Greig again the umpires' favourite

Sept. 7. It was Keith Greig's second Brownlow Medal, but Hawthorn champion Leigh Matthews reckons it does not mean much any more. Not to detract from Greig's performance, but even he must wonder whether his form was consistent enough to poll so well.

Year after year many fine players hardly rate a mention, said Matthews. But when a player wins a Brownlow and only comes third or fourth in his club's best and fairest, something must be wrong.

He said it was impossible for an umpire to handle 36 players at the pace the game is played and pick best on the ground, let alone second and third.

Doug Wade gets 100 and thousandth

Sept. 28. One consolation prize from North Melbourne's Grand Final loss was that veteran forward Doug Wade added his 100th goal for the season.

Wade finished with a season total of 103 and so became the first North Melbourne player to kick 100 goals. Even the great Jock Spencer in North's previous Grand Final year managed 'only' 86.

Wade's goalkicking prowess is one of the primary reasons why North made it all the way to the Grand Final. The burly forward still has the knack of nudging full backs out of marking contests, and also leading into space.

During North's game against Hawthorn in the last round, Wade apparently brought up his 1000th goal in League football.

Mounted policemen turned back a large crowd intent on congratulating him. This was a miscalculation, as Wade really had wait until the Qualifying Final,the next week, to score number 1000.

Mr Richmond is beg-your-pardoned

Dec. 17. The VFL Board of Directors has finally dropped the $2000 fine it imposed against Richmond team manager Graeme Richmond over the Windy Hill Riot on May 18 this year.

While the Tribunal suspended the players involved on June 3, the VFL announced then that team manager Graeme Richmond was to be fined and suspended until December 31.

On June 21 State Cabinet met and discussed the issue. Following a police investigation Graeme Richmond and player Steve Parsons were charged.

Graeme Richmond and Parsons were cleared of the police charges on September 11, but a week later the VFL ordered Graeme Richmond to pay the fine or face indefinite suspension.

On the eve of the Grand Final he took out a Supreme Court writ seeking to prevent the VFL implementing their penalties.

Today's VFL decision brings the sorry saga to an end (→ 17/7/91).

Tiger, Tiger burning bright

Barry Cable gets his kick.

Michael Green savours the win.

Neil Balme breaks through.

Sept. 28. Richmond showed their class today, beating North Melbourne 18.20 (128) to 13.9 (87) to take back-to-back Flags.

Tempers frayed early in the Grand Final as 113,839 people saw North's Robbie Peterson go down behind play.

North's Sam Kekovich kicked the first goal after eight minutes, but Wayne Walsh replied, followed by teammate David Cloke. Barry Richardson goaled from an angle for the Tigers, then Doug Wade kicked his 100th for the season. Barry Cable cut North's deficit to just six points with an after-siren goal.

Tigers' coach Tom Hafey had told his players after a second fierce clash with Essendon during the season: 'It's Richmond against the world,' and he repeated this today as the game became spiteful.

Sam Kekovich clashed with Kevin Sheedy, while Peterson crashed Kevin Bartlett into the turf. Four others scuffled behind the play.

It was the time when a great team rose to the occasion. First Kevin Sheedy began getting possessions in the centre, then Gareth Andrews, Kevin Morris, Francis Bourke, Robert McGhie and Dick Clay were superb across the backline.

Pouring on a seven-goal second term barrage, Richmond pulled away from the desperate North.

Only North's accuracy kept them in the game. Tigers' captain Royce Hart was dominant at centre-half-forward, where he took some brilliant marks. Two more time-on goals sent North into the half time break 20 points down.

North's captain Barry Davis was unable to reappear and the Kangaroos began wasting chances by playing around the flanks in an attempt to work their way into the forward line. Again fighting broke out, but Richmond clung to a 19-point lead at the final change.

Richmond then unleashed a real burst, with goals by Barry Richardson, Sheedy, and Daryl Cumming. When Richardson kicked his fourth for the term, the Tigers were content to play out time.

When North's John Burns goaled on the siren, Richmond became the first side since Melbourne in 1959 and 1960 to win successive Flags.

Congratulating Richmond, Ron Barassi said he would have to teach his team to hate defeat as much as Richmond (→ 27/9/80).

1974 Statistics

Leading Goalkicker:
Doug Wade (N.Melb) 103
Brownlow Medallist:
Keith Greig (N. Melb)
Finals: Elimination Final Coll 19.10 (124) Foots 6.19 (55); **Qualifying Final** N. Melb 15.13 (103) Haw 8.17 (65); **First Semi-final** Haw 21.12 (138) Coll 13.10 (88); **Second Semi-final** Rich 10.13 (73) N. Melb 6.16 (52); **Preliminary Final** N. Melb 8.8 (56) Haw 7.9 (51); **Grand Final** Rich 18.20 (128) N. Melb 13.9 (87)

Ladder:	W	L	D	%	pts
Rich	17	5		129.3	68
N. Melb	16	6		138.8	64
Haw	15	7		125.4	60
Coll	15	7		104.6	60
Foots	13	8	1	108.8	54
Geel	11	11		93.4	44
Carl	10	11	1	105.8	42
Ess	10	12		97.6	40
S. Melb	9	12	1	83.7	38
St K	7	15		88.7	28
Fitz	4	17	1	71.3	18
Melb	3	19		77.1	12

Francis Bourke and Kevin Sheedy.

Neil Sachse crippled in awful football accident

April 12. In just his second game, Footscray's highly credentialled South Australian recruit Neil Sachse has been tragically injured in an accidental clash with Fitzroy's Kevin O'Keeffe.

The accident cast a pall on the game, which Footscray won 17.14 (116) to Fitzroy 11.17 (83).

Sachse looks certain to be left a quadriplegic after the incident at the Western Oval.

He was one of three highly regarded players recruited by Footscray for this season at a reputed cost of $100,000. The others are Peter Featherby from Subiaco in WA and Ian Low from Manuka in Canberra.

Footscray negotiated with Sachse's club, North Adelaide, for three months, before gaining his clearance for a little less than $50,000.

He is 190.5cm tall, 83 kilograms, and plays on the half-forward flank, kicking a goal in his first game. Footscray lost that one to Melbourne, 15.10 (100) to 17.9 (111).

Low also kicked a couple of goals, and looks like developing into a useful forward.

Featherby from Subiaco played in the centre and is a useful 185cm tall, speedy and a prolific kick getter. He has represented WA.

The infusion of this new blood has pushed Footscray champion Bernie Quinlan out of the side to 20th man.

With Phil Carman, Bruce Monteath, Mike Fitzpatrick, and Andrew Ireland, this will be an exciting year for new players.

Neil Sachse's tragedy shows that Australian Football is a real body contact sport, with all the attendant risks (→21/6).

Neil Sachse seconds from disaster as he crashes awkwardly into a pack.

Players realise the seriousness of the injury and rush towards Sachse.

Blues buy WA star

April 4. Carlton have secured a clearance from Subiaco in WA for ruckman Mike Fitzpatrick. He will line up in the ruck against Geelong.

After four months of negotiations, Peter McLean, Carlton's chairman of selectors, got the signatures in Perth, in exchange for utility player Peter Hall – and $30,000.

Fitzpatrick said he was very relieved – and surprised that the deal had been done. He is 22, 190.5cm and a Rhodes Scholar. He will take two years off – but not yet.

Violence marks season's opening

April 9. In order to curb violence on the field, the League has ordered umpires to crack down on rough play. The order comes in response to a violent opening game between Hawthorn and North Melbourne, in which all bar two players were involved in a brawl halfway through the final quarter.

Although there were surprisingly no reports in this game, across the entire round a total of seven players were reported.

This unacceptable level of rough play has meant that even tighter policing by umpires may not be enough. The Minister for Youth, Sport and Recreation, Mr Brian Dixon has gone so far as to argue for an 'order off' rule, whereby players could be sent to the sidelines for unduly rough play.

VFL Umpires Adviser Alan Nash said that was not necessary: 'Give players a decent penalty – that's the remedy. Our game has been going on for 100 years and it's too late to bring it in now' (→8/7).

Tuddy sacked with two years to go

Sept. 24. Des Tuddenham has been sacked as captain-coach of Essendon with two years of his contract to run. But he said the birth of his new son was more important than this.

Tuddenham, coach since 1972, was blamed for the Bombers finishing eighth with 10 wins, after they were unbeaten after the first four rounds.

He has been criticised for his emphasis on vigour with players who are renowned for their skill, and some clubmen resented what they saw as his lack of communication with players and officials.

Polly Farmer to go back west

Sept. 13. Graham 'Polly' Farmer will not coach Geelong next year.

He is believed to have decided to quit after flying to Launceston for a sportsman's night. Farmer has been coach of the Cats for three years but his position became doubtful recently when the club decided to defer for a month the appointment of a coach for next season.

Geelong finished 11th in 1973, and reached sixth last season, but again slipped to 11th this year. Farmer's former team-mate Billy Goggin is favoured as replacement coach.

Fabulous Phil – Toast of the Magpies

Aug. 16. Collingwood's 'Fabulous Phil' Carman stole the show at Moorabbin today with one of the best individual performances seen since the war. Carman kicked 11 goals, and gave away several others, to propel the Pies to a remarkable 19-point victory. Collingwood won 24.12 (156) to 20.17 (137).

At the 22-minute mark of the final quarter, the Magpies trailed St Kilda by 20 points. But then they piled on six goals, including five in a frantic four-minute burst, to escape with their Finals hopes intact.

That they did so is almost entirely due to Carman. Again wearing the white boots he displayed for the first time in his return from injury last week, he played as close to the perfect game as you will see.

Carman, a controversial and colourful character in South Australia, has starred in his first season in the VFL, showing why Collingwood and Norwood fought such a long and bitter clearance battle over his services. He is one of the most talented and exciting players to hit the VFL in years. Carman was brilliant in the first half of the season, playing in the centre, on the ball or in either of the key forward posts. But he broke his foot while playing for Victoria against Western Australia, and missed eight matches.

That injury could well cost Carman a Brownlow Medal in his first season.

Phil Carman looks a winner as he flies to mark over Barry Lawrence.

Second Battle of Windy Hill a disgrace

July 8. The casualty list of the violent game at Essendon on Saturday has been announced. Eight players were reported, and more could have been, in the worst violence on the field since the infamous Bloodbath Grand Final of 1945.

Carlton's Rod Ashman and Rod Austin were given four weeks each, and Phillip Pinnell two weeks. David McKay was found guilty and severely reprimanded.

Essendon's Robin Close received two weeks, Laurie Moloney two and Ron Andrews and Neville Fields were judged not guilty.

While some club officials called the whole episode 'press hysteria' it was a shameful episode in football history whatever the provocation.

Geoffrey Barker, writing in *The Age*, compared the game to bear baiting. He observed Essendon's Dean Hartigan dragged unconscious from the ground, Carlton's Craig Davis with blackened eyes and blood pouring from his broken nose after it.

The brawl broke out at the end of the second quarter after Carlton had been on a 14-goal spree. It appears that violence erupted when Craig Davis was flattened – but what ensued was quite unjustifiable.

As for the game, David McKay kicked eight goals in a best on ground performance, and Carlton kicked 12 goals to six in the second half, winning 27.13 (175) to Essendon's 15.5 (95) (→ 27/7/76).

John Pitura is now with Richmond, swapped for Roberts, Jackson and Teasdale by the Swans. He played 99 games with South Melbourne and kicked 71 goals.

Sam: 'bloody idiot'

July 24. Geelong captain John 'Sam' Newman was suspended on July 3 for two matches, after being found guilty of calling goal umpire Ralph Wigg a 'stupid !*!* idiot'.

A complaint by Newman and Geelong was rejected after the Umpires' Association spoke to Wigg and accepted his explanation.

The Secretary of the VFL, Mr Eric McCutchan, said that Geelong's complaint had been noted but that under the articles of the League, once the Tribunal made a decision it was final.

Geelong and Newman are consulting their solicitors concerning further action, while Newman maintains Wigg told him to 'get [expletive deleted]' (→ 13/9/80).

Plans for national league next year

Aug. 21. The National Football League will invite the top four or five VFL teams to participate in a national competition next season, also involving clubs from South Australia and Western Australia.

The games would be played during the regular VFL season with a large amount of prizemoney for the eventual winners.

NFL Secretary Keith Webb said that next year's matches were only an interim measure. In future seasons, starting in 1977, the NFL wants a national competition involving 34 teams – all VFL, WAFL and SANFL teams plus state sides from Tasmania, NSW, Queensland and Canberra (→ 16/5/76).

Bushfire victim Dempsey comes back to win Brownlow

Sept. 1. Having been burnt out in bushfires became just a memory for Footscray ruckman Gary Dempsey today when he snatched the Brownlow Medal from Melbourne captain Stan Alves.

In a mass finish, 26-year-old Dempsey polled 20 votes, just one more than Alves. Eight players were in the running with one three-vote to come, and they included the winner for the past two years, Keith Greig of North Melbourne

The last-vote win is becoming familiar, Ian Stewart having done it in 1971, Len Thompson in 1972 and Greig in 1973, although last year Greig received both of the final three votes.

With just two votes to go today, Alves led with 19, followed by Es-sendon's Graham Moss, Carlton captain Alex Jesaulenko, and Hawthorn's John Hendrie on 18, Phil Carman of Collingwood, Dempsey and Brian 'The Whale' Roberts of South Melbourne on 17, and Greig on 16.

Dempsey and Alves polled in eight of the 21 games in which votes were cast. Dempsey had been runner-up to Peter Bedford of South Melbourne in 1970.

But his 20 votes made the lowest winning total since Kevin Murray of Fitzroy won with 19 in 1969. Dempsey is the first Footscray player to win the award since 1960, when it went to another ruckman, John Schultz, also with 20 votes.

For Dempsey, his win was solace for missing the Finals.

Dempsey high above the pack.

Faces of the 70s. The League captains display the colours as they line up for the photographer at the Melbourne Cricket Ground.

North Melbourne are Premiers – at long last

The Year

Sept. 28. Having lost the 1974 Grand Final and then six of the first nine games, North Melbourne President Allen Aylett and supercoach Ron Barassi must have wondered whether the estimated $1 million and the buckets of blood sweat and tears expended had been worth it.

High-priced recruits such as Doug Wade seemed not to be fulfilling their promise. Dissension bubbled to the surface after Wade kicked three behinds, was dragged, and left the ground in round nine.

But North never gave up on Barassi's vision. Old sparring partner Brent Crosswell arrived from Carlton for the Collingwood game, and although North lost, 'Tiger' was best on ground. Wins accumulated as Barry Cable, Barry Davis, John Rantall, Keith Greig and David Dench melded better with the fiery athleticism of Crosswell and Arnold Briedis, and North climbed to third, a position from which no one had ever won a Flag in modern times ... (→ 24/9/77).

1975 Statistics

Leading Goalkicker:
Leigh Matthews (Haw) 68
Brownlow Medallist:
Gary Dempsey (Foots)
Finals: Elimination Final Rich 11.11 (77) Coll 10.13 (73); **Qualifying Final** Carl 12.4 (76) N. Melb 14.12 (96); **First Semi-final** Carl 9.8 (62) Rich 9.17 (71); **Second Semi-final** Haw 12.10 (82) N. Melb 10.11 (71); **Preliminary Final** N. Melb 10.16 (76) Rich 8.11 (59); **Grand Final** Haw 9.13 (67) N. Melb 19.8 (122)

Ladder:	W	L	%	pts
Haw	17	5	137.3	68
Carl	16	6	129.2	64
N. Melb	14	8	115.1	56
Rich	13	9	113.5	52
Coll	13	9	93.9	52
St K	11	11	101.4	44
Foots	11	11	94.8	44
Ess	10	12	90.7	40
Fitz	9	13	97.1	36
Melb	9	13	93.6	36
Geel	7	15	78.2	28
S. Melb	2	20	75.0	8

North's handy South Australian recruit Malcolm Blight takes a fine mark.

Solidarity at last, as the North huddle indicates 'this is our year'. North Melbourne have done it the hard way, and there is just one quarter to go.

The Game

Sept. 27. North Melbourne's planning to win their first Flag began with the recruiting of their galaxy of stars three years ago, but the planning to win the 1975 Grand Final began with a suggestion by Chairman of Selectors Max Ritchie on Thursday to select veteran Barry 'Lurch' Goodingham on the ground. This was designed to induce Hawthorn into playing gangling Bernie Jones.

It worked a treat. Goodingham trotted on the field and then off to sit on the bench. Jones played and had only a few more possessions than Lurch in the last quarter.

Doug Wade said that the game passed like a fantastic 120-minute dream, but when it was all over he pinched himself, kissed the ball, and then knew it was real.

North were on top from the beginning of the game, accumulating a deadly nine goals two before half time while Hawthorn struggled to five goals six, and then watched as the Kangaroos went up another notch. The winning margin of 55 points was the biggest since 1957.

Peter Knights stood out for Hawthorn, but every North player was part of the great day – Brent Crosswell, John Rantall, Keith Greig, John Burns, David Dench, Mick Nolan, Sam Kekovich and Doug Wade especially. North won, 19.8 (122) to 9.13 (67) (→ 28).

Peter Knights was Hawks' best.

Club will not fall apart says Collingwood President

The Committee stands on its record.

June 11. Declaring that all factions now ceased to exist at Collingwood, the club tonight elected airlines executive John Hickey to the Presidency as a damaging split was avoided.

Hickey, Vice-president and with only 12 months on the Senior Committee, was the only candidate to succeed Ern Clarke, who resigned almost three weeks ago. Former General Secretary Gordon Carlyon backed down from being a candidate for President and accepted a new Vice-presidency role.

Mr Carlyon, Collingwood's Secretary from 1950 to 1969, helped avoid an election because it would 'widen the split in the club'.

The deal came after a half-hour-long meeting last night between Mr Hickey, Mr Carlyon and representatives of Collingwood's two most famous families. David Galbally, son of Magpie stalwart Frank, called the meeting at which David, his father, his father's brother Jack and Vice-

Before his fall, ex-President Ern Clarke and Murray Weideman made up.

president Jock McHale Jr warned of the danger of division.

Later, David Galbally said that Collingwood could not afford an election at this stage. Dogged by division for five years, the club had been saved from turmoil by Mr Carlyon's compromise.

Behind the change was some sordid bickering. There was jealousy over special privileges for 'Fabulous' Phil Carman, players accusing each other of not cooperating on the field, and the greatest level of dissension in 70 years.

When the Richardson brothers were dropped for the first time after two losses, Wayne Richardson spoke out and was suspended for four weeks as the club foundered in acrimony with egos and personalities displacing unity and discipline.

Ern Clarke promised, however, that the row did not mean that the club would fall apart and now the promise is co-operation (→ 3/6/82).

Big Nick quits

March 31. John Nicholls has rocked the football world by resigning as coach of Carlton just before Saturday's opening round game against Collingwood.

Ian Thorogood has been appointed stand-in and there are moves to draft Alex Jesaulenko to coach.

Nicholls, who played for the Blues from 1957 to 1974, is regarded as one of the game's outstanding ruckmen. Of his 31 games for Victoria, five were as captain. Nicholls captain-coached Carlton to their 1972 Premiership, and the 1973 Grand Final where a KO in the first quarter demonstrated the problems of having a coach on the field of battle.

Blight's big bomb

June 5. Having been told by coach Ron Barassi that he was playing 'like a goose' Malcolm Blight proceeded to beat Carlton on his own.

Carlton were 27 points up at half time, and 13 points ahead in time on. Blight kicked four of North's five goals in the last quarter including the last two 'specials'.

One was Blight's first banana kick in competition to put North a point behind, and then an after-the-siren torpedo that was 'still going up' after 60 metres, to win the game.

Carlton fans smugly saying 'too late' to the Northerners all day were in a state of disbelieving shock at the result: North Melbourne 11.15 (81), Carlton 11.10 (76) (→ 25/9/78).

Hawks fly by night

Aug. 18. Hawthorn emerged from a six-week slump last night for a magnificent 48-point win over North Melbourne in the NFL Wills Cup Grand Final in Adelaide.

With North coach Ron Barassi in Geelong Hospital after a car crash and without Barry Cable, Brent Crosswell and Wayne Schimmelbusch, it was 18 minutes before Mal Blight kicked North's first goal. The ruthless Hawks were then 3.6 and overpowered North to partly avenge last year's humiliating Grand Final loss.

Frayed Jeans

Aug. 10. St Kilda coach Allan Jeans has had enough and is to quit at the end of the season. Jeans, 43, is the longest-serving coach in the VFL, having been with the Saints since 1961.

Football had been getting him down, said Jeans, who is a police sergeant at Russell Street headquarters.

'A coach gets tired of it,' he said. 'It is very demanding.'

If the Saints had made the Five last year he probably would have retired then (→ 26/6/82).

Not soccer, but Brent Crosswell suffers a hug from Gary Cowton.

League support averts umpires' strike over Tiger criticism

Field umpires Bill Deller and Tony Bryant are escorted from the field by police, before a hostile crowd.

June 17. VFL Directors probably halted an umpires' strike last night when they backed them in a dispute with the clubs.

The Directors expressed full support of the umpires after receiving a letter from their association. A strike was called for Saturday, 26 June, after Richmond criticised umpire Bill Deller over a report against their coach, Tom Hafey. Hafey was fined $150 by the Tribunal after Deller reported he had abused him.

After the Tribunal verdict, Richmond said they would complain about Deller's part in the incident and his umpiring. Tigers' President Ian Wilson said he was perturbed by Hafey's admission to the Tribunal that it was only by 'a freak of nature' that he was not facing a more serious charge.

The VFL Directors have also promised a tough new attitude towards the criticism of umpires.

The Directors acknowledged that the Umpires' Appointment Board is the sole judge of ability and performance of umpires and agreed that the Board had the right to appoint umpires as it saw fit.

Although no coach has ever been suspended for abusing an umpire, two other coaches have appeared before the Directors this year to explain criticism of umpires. They are Ian Stewart of South Melbourne and David Parkin of Hawthorn.

Stewart was fined $200. No action was taken against Parkin.

The League has decided not to take any action over a report by umpire Kevin Smith against St Kilda captain Carl Ditterich, who unintentionally broke the rules last Saturday by approaching Smith to ask for an interpretation during the interval (→ 8/8/81).

Wild West scenes at Windy Hill

July 6. Three players reported during Saturday's wild scenes were last night given suspensions ranging from two to four weeks.

South Melbourne centre half-forward Stewart Gull was given two weeks for striking his Essendon opponent Ron Andrews, while Don centreman Neville Fields earned four weeks for striking South rover Norman Goss, who was himself given two weeks for striking Fields. Gull said he had been king-hit and had retaliated.

Six players were reported after the matches at Essendon and the MCG, with all but two of the Dons and South sides involved in an all-in brawl during the second quarter.

Andrews was knocked out twice before half time. Gull, Goss and Fields were treated for concussion. In recent years Windy Hill has become notorious for thuggery.

Ron Barassi, car crash victim, taking charge of training at North, in his Ansett electric cart, only five hours after being discharged from hospital.

VFL sells logos in Properties Division

April 27. The VFL has moved into the travel business, with plans for an agency next year as part of the profitable Properties Division.

Already the Properties Division has become a profit-earner and there are hopes that travel will turn into a big money-spinner.

The St Kilda club, which has a successful sporting goods business at Moorabbin, will be the first club to open a travel service when it starts in June.

The VFL has held discussions with three leading travel agencies. The arrival this year of Dr Allen Aylett as League President has heralded a drive by the VFL into more entrepreneurial areas.

Graham Moss gathers Brownlow Medal for Bombers

Moss, poised as ever, shoots a hand pass past Carlton's David Dickson.

Aug. 31 Graham Moss, captain of Essendon and hot Brownlow Medal favourite, snatched victory on the second last vote last night.

Moss, 26, just pipped Hawthorn centre half-back Peter Knights, with Francis Bourke, the Richmond captain and champion defender, third.

Accepting the medal, Moss paid tribute to two coaches he had played under at Essendon, Des Tuddenham and Bill Stephen. 'Without these two I could have achieved nothing,' he said.

Knights' effort was all the more remarkable because he broke his collarbone two months ago, missing six games and only played again 10 days ago against Richmond. He was also out for last Saturday's game against Geelong.

Wrong race Ron in riot at Geelong

July 27. Collingwood assistant coach Ron Richards has been reprimanded for abusing the umpires in a half-time brawl at Geelong.

Collingwood's Ron Wearmouth was chased up the Geelong race by Geelong's Michael Turner. Collingwood Secretary Jack Regan told the VFL Tribunal: 'I thought to myself, he's caught the wrong tram, this bloke.' In a bad night for the Ronnies, Essendon's Ron Andrews got four weeks for striking Richmond's Graeme Bond (→ 12/9/77).

An even season but despondent Demons dogged by draw

Aug. 28. The 1976 season has gone right to the wire, with the Final Five places being decided on the outcome of several matches in a dramatic last round.

In a most even season, first and fifth spot were up for grabs right until the final sirens of round 22. Hawthorn trailed Carlton by 19 per cent and needed to beat Finals aspirant Geelong. As well, Footscray had to down Carlton for the Hawks to finish on top of the Ladder.

Melbourne, meanwhile, were making a late bid for fifth spot. This depended on Geelong dropping out of the Five by losing to Hawthorn, or Footscray losing to Carlton, whom they had not beaten at Princes Park for 12 years.

Another possibility for the Demons was if the size of a combined Geelong loss to Hawthorn and a Melbourne win against Collingwood was around 100 points.

Realistically, the Demons' best hope for a Finals berth was to replace Footscray on percentage.

The conclusion more than lived up to expectations, with Footscray playing possibly their best game of the season to lead Carlton for three quarters before the Blues pegged them back with a five-goal last quarter. Carlton bombarded the goals in the final minutes scoring three behinds – the last shot being touched just as a goal seemed certain. The game ended in a draw, giving the Blues top spot and the Bulldogs a place in the Final Five, but depriving the despondent Demons – who ran out 15-point winners against Collingwood – of their first Finals appearance for 12 years.

As for Hawthorn, they missed their chance for top spot, going down to Geelong by 25 points.

DEMONS 40 of 132
PETER KEENAN
FOLLOWER
HAVE FUN WITH SCANLENS GUM

SAINTS 65 of 132
RUSSELL GREENE
WING
HAVE FUN WITH SCANLENS GUM

LIONS 2 of 132
JOHN MURPHY
UTILITY
HAVE FUN WITH SCANLENS GUM

BLUES 23 of 132
BARRY ARMSTRONG
ROVER
HAVE FUN WITH SCANLENS GUM

Hawks do it for the little fella

Sept. 25. Hawthorn's 30-point win over North Melbourne in the Grand Final kept a promise to their cancer-striken captain, Peter Crimmins.

Every Hawthorn player went out on to the MCG with the extra determination to win the Flag for the 'little fella'. In an emotional finish to his pre-match address, Hawthorn coach John Kennedy told his team: 'There are lots of reasons why you have to win today. Most of all, though, win it for the little fella.'

Crimmins was too sick to attend the game, despite an offer by Deputy Premier Lindsay Thompson to provide him with a chauffeur-driven limousine. Instead, Crimmins, 28, sent a telegram, which Kennedy read out before the players took the field. 'Good luck to you and all the boys. It will be a long, hard 100 minutes but I am sure you will be there at the end. Regards. Peter Crimmins.'

Hawthorn avenged their defeat in the 1975 Grand Final with an outstanding display that blended creative football with uncompromising physical tackling. The Hawks took the initiative from the start and could have had the game sewn up by half time but for wayward kicking.

North Melbourne's negative tactics proved counterproductive. Not only did they fail to stop Hawthorn's key players, the Roos deprived themselves of attacking options by using Blight in defence and Greig tagging Matthews.

Hendrie cut the North defence to shreds, while Knights was near impassable in the Hawk backline. His soaring marks in the final term stymied any possibility of a North Melbourne revival. Hawthorn had winning players everywhere, while North relied on the efforts of a few, namely Dench, Blight and Cable.

As Hawthorn beat North Melbourne, 13.22 (100) to 10.10 (70), their critically ill skipper listened to every minute on the radio 'happy as a little kid' (→ 30/9/78).

Another big mark by Peter Knights, the mainstay of the Hawthorn defence.

Peter Crimmins fought cancer to the end, with the courage that made him a favourite son of Hawthorn and took him to the captaincy. He is pictured with wife Gwen and sons Ben (top) and Sam. He died on September 28.

1976 Statistics

Leading Goalkicker:
Larry Donohue (Geel) 105
Brownlow Medallist:
Graham Moss (Ess)
Finals: Elimination Final Geel 14.18 (102) Foots 14.11 (95); **Qualifying Final** Haw 14.19 (103) N. Melb 12.11 (83); **First Semi-final** N. Melb 14.9 (93) Geel 8.12 (60); **Second Semi-final** Carl 9.16 (70) Haw 12.15 (87); **Preliminary Final** Carl 9.12 (66) N. Melb 10.7 (67); **Grand Final** Haw 13.22 (100) N. Melb 10.10 (70)

Ladder:	W	L	D	%	pts
Carl	16	5	1	132.8	66
Haw	16	6		114.2	64
N. Melb	15	7		116.8	60
Geel	12	10		103.9	48
Foots	11	10	1	96.8	46
Melb	11	11		99.4	44
Rich	10	12		98.6	40
S. Melb	9	13		94.0	36
St K	9	13		90.1	36
Ess	9	13		88.2	36
Fitz	7	15		92.8	28
Coll	6	16		86.4	24

Graham Melrose feels the pain.

Debuts
Mickey Conlan (Fitz)
Jim Edmond (Foots)
Wayne Harmes (Carl)
Merv Neagle (Ess)
Michael Roach (Rich)
Ken Sheldon (Carl)
Paul Van Der Haar (Ess)
Tim Watson (Ess)

Retirements
Barry Cable (N. Melb)
Royce Hart (Rich)
Kevin 'Cowboy' Neale (St K)
Des Tuddenham (Ess)

The lights go out at VFL Park nightmare opening

A policeman guards the darkened field as the big VFL Park blackout reduces the Fitzroy and North night match to farce.

May 18. Football stars were dimmed last night by a power failure during the first evening match at VFL Park, Waverley.

The tussle between Fitzroy and North Melbourne began 55 minutes late after the State Electricity Commission's supply to the $1 million lighting system failed at 7.20, 10 minutes before the game was due to start.

Both teams were on the ground for the match in the $200,000 night series, then left, returned and went off again to spend the time kicking into nets in the dressing rooms.

A fuse is thought to have blown in the SEC feeder pole line in nearby Wellington Rd, Waverley. All power to the ground had to be turned off for 18 minutes from 8.05 while it was repaired.

The blown fuse was reflected in the reaction of an angry VFL General Manager Mr Jack Hamilton, who stood, hands on hips, and said: 'It's a pity things beyond our control prevented a great opening.'

Some of the 8468 crowd jeered and began slow hand-clapping after five minutes in the dark. There was a public appeal for patience.

'Blame the SEC not us,' said Mr Hamilton. A representative of the company that installed the lights said they had worked satisfactorily during 30 hours of tests on Saturday, Sunday and Monday.

Fitzroy, second bottom on the VFL Ladder, produced the night's second surprise and won, 16.12 (108) to 11.8 (74) (→ 9/7/80).

McKenna turns Blue

A recycled footballer moves on.

April 4. Peter McKenna, the champion full-forward who walked out of Collingwood over money last Thursday, today joined Carlton. North Melbourne and Fitzroy dropped out of the race for McKenna because of financial demands.

Carlton General Manager Keith McKenzie said: 'Peter is just the guy we want at full-forward.'

A big day for St Kilda's Rex Hunt, as he bagged eight goals against Fitzroy. Hunt marked everything and the Saints won 19.20 (134) to 14.14 (98).

Big mouth Balme

The bad news for big Neil Balme.

Aug. 23. Richmond ruckman Neil Balme, the third player this season to be reported for spitting, has been given two weeks suspension. He will not be in the Richmond line-up for the Elimination Final.

Big Balme hoisted field umpire Kevin Smith off his feet as Smith told him of the report for allegedly spitting at Carlton's Rod Ashman.

Balme told the Tribunal it must have been an accident. 'I don't recall spitting once, twice or 40 times. It is not a part of my game.'

The report soured Richmond's win by just three points, 15.13 (103) to 14.16 (100), which put them into the Five (→ 30/5/80).

Play lifts the lid on The Club

May 29. David Williamson's new play, *The Club*, is a triumph.

The club – any club – is an institution that is both friend and tyrant, providing camaraderie and security but exacting unremitting loyalty. Williamson's witty, intelligent play shows these loyalties under profound stress. The club has been in a slump for years and the new president, Ted, a meat manufacturer who never played the game, is determined there will be change.

But a $90,000 star recruit turns out to be a pot-smoking non-trier. There are recriminations, leading to a verbal free-for-all in a play not to be missed (→ 29/4/81).

Assumption nursery

Aug. 13. Assumption College, Kilmore – the famous recruiting ground of so many League champions – will celebrate its 1000th schools' football match tomorrow.

Assumption takes on Sacred Heart College, Adelaide, in the 21st annual game between the two schools.

Since being admitted to the Associated Grammar Schools' football competiton in 1959, Assumption has lost only seven games, five by less than a goal.

The ranks of former Assumption players in the VFL are enormous and include Pat Kennedy who led the college in 1921 and later represented Carlton and Victoria.

Since the end of the Second World War there have been at least 28 Assumption graduates who have gone on to play in the VFL. They are (their original clubs in brackets): Mike Green, Francis Bourke (Richmond); Frank Palmer, Mike Pavone (South Melbourne); Alex Gardiner, Jim Gallagher, Bill Goodridge (Footscray); Phil Ryan, Peter McCormack (Collingwood); Brendan Edwards, Peter Crimmins, Kevin Heath (Hawthorn); Denis Munari, Ray Garby (Carlton); Fred le Deux, Daryl Herrod, Peter Doyle (Geelong); Brian McCarthy (St Kilda); John Brady, Bernie McCarthy, Phil Ryan (North Melbourne); John Bahen, Brian Wicks, Renato and Laurie Serafini (Fitzroy); Peter Keenan, Ted Lees (Melbourne).

Brownlow in brown velvet

Aug. 29. South Melbourne's Graham Teasdale dressed to kill for tonight's Brownlow Medal count, donning a brown velvet dinner suit, and then slaughtered the opposition with 59 votes, 14 more than his nearest rival, Richmond rover Kevin Bartlett.

The win was, however, no surprise, as 'the word' was out and he was an unbackable favourite.

The former Richmond player was a tremendous pick-up for South in a swap two years ago for John Pitura. He was unhappy with his form at full-forward early in the season, but then dominated when switched to the ruck by coach Ian Stewart, winning the best-on-ground vote in nine matches (→ 12/4/79).

Carman out for Magpie day of destiny

The umpires separate Phil Carman and Don Scott after Carman was reported.

Sept. 12. Phil Carman, Collingwood centre half-forward and the highest-paid player in the VFL, is out of this year's Grand Final.

He was tonight suspended for two matches on a striking charge from last Saturday's Second Semi-Final against Hawthorn at the MCG.

The suspension came after a two-and-a-half-hour hearing at VFL House. Carman, 27, who kicked four goals on Saturday, had hoped to escape suspension to play in the Grand Final on Saturday week.

The Magpies went straight into the Grand Final to play the winner of Saturday's North Melbourne and Hawthorn Preliminary Final.

Carman was reported by boundary umpire Kevin Mitchell on a charge of deliberately striking Hawthorn ruck rover Michael Tuck with a clenched fist to the head in the first quarter. Carman denied to the Tribunal that he hit Tuck with a clenched fist (→ 23/5/78).

A Hudson hundred and Lethal firing

Sept. 3. Hawthorn's Peter Hudson returned to the Finals today after six years, and kicked six goals to top 100 for the season. Rover-forward Leigh Matthews has kicked 88 for the season so far.

This was a record fifth time Hudson has kicked a century and it helped Hawthorn to an easy 38-point win over North Melbourne in the Qualifying Final at the MCG, 19.11 (125) to 12.15 (87).

With Hudson pre-eminent and the dominance of his 1971 Premiership team-mates, Don Scott, Leigh Matthews, Leon Rice and Kelvin Moore, and a tough defence, the Hawks seem hard to stop.

Teasdale's sartorial splendour.

Magpies drawn, then quartered by Roos

Oct 1. North finally prevailed to take the Premiership in a hard-fought replayed Grand Final, after the heart-stopping draw against Collingwood last week. North were in front throughout, and had opened up a six-goal lead before a 10-minute Collingwood onslaught reduced their half-time lead to 11 points.

North took a firm grip on the game in the third quarter, and held off Collingwood's valiant efforts, which included an amazing solo run and goal by Phil Manassa. The final margin was 27 points, 21.25 (151) to 19.10 (124) and Collingwood have now lost all five of their Grand Final games since their 1958 win.

What a contrast to last week's thriller. In that game Collingwood led by 27 points at the last change, only to lose the lead in time on and then goal to even the scores on the siren. It was the first Grand Final draw since Melbourne and Essendon in 1948.

Amazingly, the Kangaroos did not kick a goal in the second and third quarters. And, equally bizarre, the Magpies' Phil Manassa hand-passed to David Dench's arms, leading to a goal that seemed to sew it up for North.

Collingwood did everything but inscribe their name on the Premiership cup in the third quarter, adding 5.4, while North had kicked 13 successive behinds since the 24-minute mark of the first quarter, with Arnold Briedis the worst offender.

The Magpies went in hard in the last quarter, and North coach Ron Barassi switched Daryl Sutton to full-forward after three sound quarters at full-back. Sutton marked and goaled. Phil Baker got one a minute later, and then came the Manassa disaster in the goal square.

Briedis marked in front, had to wait three minutes while Doug Gott was stretchered off with an injured knee ... then kicked a behind. Baker levelled the scores at 23 minutes, then goaled again.

Peter Moore managed a point for the Magpies after another seven desperate minutes. Two and half minutes later 'Twiggy' Dunne stood, oak-like in a pack of at least six players, to mark and convert with 40 seconds left.

Barassi said later: 'We should have won the game. I know that is a brave statement, but we did have five more scoring shots than Collingwood.'

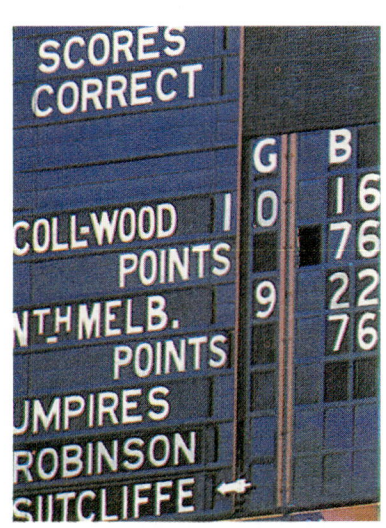
So it's on again next week.

Malcolm Blight has front spot against Billy Picken in this marking contest.

1977 Statistics

Leading Goalkicker: Peter Hudson (Haw) 110 **Brownlow Medallist:** Graham Teasdale (S. Melb)
Finals: Elimination Final Rich 13.10 (88) S. Melb 7.12 (54); **Qualifying Final** Haw 19.11 (125) N. Melb 12.15 (87); **First Semifinal** N. Melb 16.14 (110) Rich 9.9 (63); **Second Semi-final** Coll 17.10 (112) Haw 16.14 (110); **Preliminary Final** Haw 5.15 (45) N. Melb 16.16 (112); **Grand Final** Coll 10.16 (76) N. Melb 9.22 (76) **Grand Final Replay** Coll 19.10 (124) N. Melb 21.25 (151)

Ladder:	W	L	D	%	pts
Coll	18	4		130.7	72
Haw	17	5		133.6	68
N. Melb	15	7		117.8	60
Rich	14	7	1	113.7	58
S. Melb	13	8	1	110.6	54
Carl	13	9		111.9	52
Foots	10	11	1	101.4	42
Geel	8	14		82.7	32
Ess	7	14	1	82.8	30
Fitz	6	16		83.8	24
Melb	5	17		85.0	20
St K	3	17	2	73.5	16

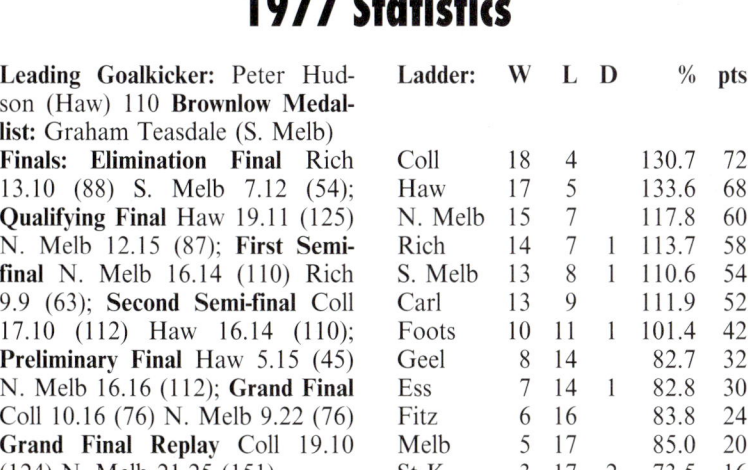

Collingwood defender Phil Manassa eludes North's John Cassin and gathers momentum on his run from half-back to goal in the replayed Grand Final.

Three cheers for the cheer squads

The Hawks are not the biggest club, but the brown and gold waves proudly.

North Melbourne followers get into the spirit of the big Grand Final day.

They call them the Collingwood Army: it's the biggest club with the biggest supporter base and its fanatical cheer squad likes to make its presence felt.

Coaching: from Smith to Parkin

In the 60s the game evolved again. Hawthorn, the cellar dwellers of football for so long, won their first ever Premiership to begin a chain of success. John Kennedy's coaching techniques would change the style of the game. Kennedy with his commando training drills turned footballers into muscular gung ho warriors. Pre-season training would never be the same again. For years summer training was a leisurely affair. Kennedy changed all that. For months in advance of the first game Kennedy had his men up early to run, swim, lift and wrestle. They became super confident athletes who wanted to play hard-hitting aggressive football. They intimidated the opposition and Kennedy, a rough tough academic, took no notice of traditional playing positions. The more crowded it was the better he liked it.

He moved his half-forwards to the midfield and the midfield to the backline. He congested the opposition forward line and opened up his own. Space was given to star forwards like Peter Hudson. John Kennedy played the game on his terms not the textbooks'.

Tom Hafey, with a liberal dose of Len Smith's philosophies, followed Kennedy's lead at Richmond. A super fit, aggressive team that kicked long and direct netted four flags between 1967 and 1974. It was a simple plan but with the great Royce Hart at centre half-forward and Kevin Bartlett crumbing cleverly at ground level, it worked.

It was Ron Barassi's turn to change the game. Barassi was the ultimate professional. 'Practice doesn't make perfect, perfect practice makes perfect' he exhorted. Barassi had learnt the value of team work and knowledge of the opposition from Norm Smith.

As the new Blues leader he immediately outlawed the drop kick. He said it wasn't a percentage kick, there was too much margin for error so it had to go.

He was the first coach to use video sessions to teach and prepare his charges. And, in the 1970

Grand Final he changed the course of football when he instructed his sinking Blues to handball and play on at all costs.

Until then handball was basically used as a defensive tactic where teams only had around 20 handballs a game. Not now, it was to be the start of the modern running receive game, where teams like Hawthorn through the 80s clocked up close to 200 handballs a game.

It was risky attacking football. Too many players paid scant regard to their opponents as they 'freewheeled' all over the ground looking for an easy kick. This led to some extremely high scoring games in the 70s and 80s.

Coaches were given more ammunition in the 70s. The old 19th and 20th men were replaced by the interchange bench.

Now any two players could be rested on the bench and thrown into the fray whenever the coach wanted. This gave coaches flexibility never seen before. Players could be rested through a game and specialist or impact players could be used at the coach's discretion.

It was the late 70s when coaches started to be employed

full time. Part-time and later full-time assistants were hired to help.

Organising the coaching staff to get the best out of the team's talents became the Senior Coach's responsibility.

David Parkin, four times Premiership coach, '78, '81, '82 and '95 is considered the best at this. It was in the 80s that strategies began to emerge. Most strategies are based on TIME and SPACE.

These strategies occur when the ball is dead, i.e. at a ruck contest, a kick-in, or when a player has stopped or slowed down play after a mark or free kick. This is when a team has the TIME to create the SPACES on the field that it requires.

To do this successfully, thinking, unselfish team-oriented players are required. It goes against the notion of keeping the ball flowing, but the idea is to give your team a better than 50 % chance of maintaining possession.

Fitzroy in the early 80s had much success with their kick in from fullback strategy.

Players would huddle together at centre half-back before breaking on the lead into space for the receive.

Essendon under coach Kevin Sheedy create a huge hole in their forward line for players to lead into. And Carlton under David Parkin have mastered the set plays at the all-important centre bounces.

In the last 20 years the trend at training sessions has gone from skill and match practice to simulated game situations. Players rehearse plays in their groups (backs, midfield, forwards) more than ever before.

Specific training for the role you are likely to play is commonplace in the 90s.

The 90s also saw the introduction of three interchange players. Now coaches can swing their teams around more than ever.

If a player is struggling for a quarter, he can expect to be shifted to another position or given a stint on the bench. Essendon coach Kevin Sheedy has become the master of player rotation.

One hundred years on perhaps the wheel has turned full circle.

West Coast Eagles coach Mick Malthouse has coached his team to Premierships in 1992 and 1994. Malthouse has led the change to a more conservative one-on-one contest game. It is a disciplined, team-oriented, dour style that eliminates the freewheelers. Scores are usually lower, but Malthouse has two Premiership medallions that prove its worth.

Today's well-paid full-time coaches with their numerous assistants and resources are a long way removed from the old Jock McHale and Checker Hughes. One hundred years ago it was a simple, much slower game. No doubt some of the basics remain - 'work for front position', 'keep your eye on the ball', 'protect your team-mate' – they all still hold up. But what would Jock think today when they talk of outriders, sweepers in the corridor, pack jumpers in the back half and blockers in attack. Enterprising coaches in their search for the winning edge have changed the game markedly. Have no fear, the changes will continue as coaches further their pursuit of excellence.

Robert Walls

Alex the Great – the Carlton Conquerer

Alex Jesaulenko was born to Russian and Ukrainian parents in Salzburg, Austria in 1945. He is the greatest artist to come from that city since Mozart.

The family migrated to Australia when Alex was four, and spent six months in what was euphemistically known as a 'migrant hostel' which, legend has it, was the one in the Exhibition Gardens, in the suburb of Carlton.

Having that early introduction to the spirit, if not the fact of football, the Jesaulenkos moved to Canberra, Alex aged four.

In the national capital, not far from where the inventor of Australian football, Thomas Wentworth Wills, was born in 1835, young Alex grew up – yet did not touch a real footy until he was 14. He honed his ball skills with soccer and his body work with rugby league.

When introduced to Australian football, Alex had found his true vocation. He quickly made a name for himself as a footballer for Manuka-Eastlake, and attracted the attention of 'scouts' from Melbourne.

After a flirtation with North Melbourne he signed with Carlton, under the guidance of Manuka-Eastlake Football Club President Jack Dorman.

Alex was a Commonwealth public servant at the time and Sir Robert Menzies was Carlton's Number One ticket holder (and Prime Minister).

Alex Jesaulenko found himself transferred to Melbourne, and playing for Carlton in Round One 1967, against Fitzroy. He was 22, old for a recruit, and he kicked a couple of goals in a 94-point romp over Fitzroy.

It was an auspicious beginning. Despite not having grown up with a footy for a pillow, he showed that he was one of the game's naturals, a prodigy.

'Jezza' played in the Ron Barassi-led side that lost the 1967 Preliminary Final to Geelong and played well in the tight victory over Essendon in 1968 that brought Carlton's first Flag in 21 years. He became used to success.

Carlton lost in 1969, and looked down and out in the second quarter in the 1970 Grand Final.

But then Jesaulenko took the mark over Graeme Jenkin which was the epitome of the 'screamer'. It was such a confident grab that it gave coach Barassi and Jezza's team-mates a sniff of a chance. And after goals by Ted Hopkins and 'Tiger' Crosswell Jezza kicked the sealer in that historic game.

This was his 115th goal for the season, making him the first (and only) Carlton player to kick a hundred in a season.

In the goal-scoring spree of the 1972 Grand Final, Jezza kicked seven of the 28.

Through this time he was not only a brilliant high mark, but was also a fearless and slippery player on the ground. One TV commentator dubbed Jezza the 'worm' for his ability to wriggle in and out of, and sometimes under, the packs. He won Carlton's best and fairest award in 1975 playing on the backline.

In 1978 Carlton turned to Jezza to win not just a game but to save the club. He was appointed captain-coach in Round Seven after Carlton had had more coaches than wins.

History records a stirring win over the Magpies in that game, and the next year in the Grand Final again over Collingwood.

Jezza's disappearance after that great win, in support of outgoing President George Harris, was a tragedy. His recall in 1989, after Robert Walls' sacking was a measure of the high esteem in which he will always be held by Carlton people, of all ranks.

Thompson, Dempsey, Moore, Moss and Round – medallists all

They were big, they were strong and they were rich in talent and grit that took them to the top. But they were also different from what had gone before.

Five ruckmen of the 70s, all Brownlow Medallists, have a special place: Gary Dempsey, Peter Moore, Graham Moss, Barry Round and Len Thompson.

Dempsey, who was suitably tall and well developed, had enormous ability to give his smaller men first ball use. And he was a towering mark, particularly in defence.

His early career at Footscray was sadly curtailed when he was badly burnt in bushfires near his home at Truganina, west of Melbourne. He had shocking scars on his body, but he came back to win his Brownlow in 1975.

His 207 games at Footscray between 1967 and 1978 produced 105 goals. He then switched to

North Melbourne in pursuit of the Premiership that eluded him, playing until 1984.

At about 199cm and 101kg, Magpie Len Thompson was known for his rover-like skills.

Brownlow Medallist in 1972,

he was a strong mark, but it was his all-round ability that marked him as a modern star.

Moore was just a centimetre below Thompson's height but about 4kg heavier. He was in Thommo's tradition of great height, speed, strength and skill and, after having spent two years as a forward, took over from Thompson in the ruck in 1979, winning the Brownlow Medal that season.

Moore crossed to Melbourne after some internal wranglings at Collingwood, and gave that side great service, winning his second Brownlow in 1984.

Round had too many ruckmen ahead of him at Footscray, where he played for seven years from 1969. Released to South Melbourne the following year, he soon became their star ruckman, adding his sensational marking to his round-the-ground skills.

He opted for Sydney when the Swans moved in 1982, having tied with Bernie Quinlan for the Brownlow the previous year. The fearless Round was the Swans' captain for five years and Sydney's first football hero.

One of the wonderful ruckmen from the West, Graham Moss was another fine high mark.

Seldom beaten in the ruck, he used his body excellently, creating opportunities for his rovers with his handball.

He captained Essendon in 1976, the year he won his Brownlow in spite of an early-season knee injury, and then returned as captain-coach of his old Western Australian side, Claremont.

Moss was generally easy going, but had a reputation for straight-speaking: when Richmond beat the Bombers he accused his team-mates of letting themselves down by treating football like a game.

The trials and more trials of Carl Ditterich

There is no mistaking Carl Ditterich's intentions as he lets go at Simon Madden. Terry Cahill is downed at left.

June 5. St Kilda's Carl Ditterich was today reported for the third time in 10 games this season.

As the Saints were being tipped out of the Five with a 34-point loss to Collingwood before 72,000 spectators at VFL Park, Ditterich was being reported for a third-quarter incident with Shane Bond. Field umpire Kevin Smith reported Ditterich and Bond for striking each other in the head.

Ditterich had been found guilty of striking Richmond's Jim Jess in the third game this season. He was reprimanded.

He was then found guilty of striking Essendon's Simon Madden in round seven on May 13. Again he was not suspended.

Essendon also laid a complaint against Ditterich, alleging that he had struck rover Terry Cahill, but this was later withdrawn.

Angered at having his name taken today, Ditterich prowled around as his team listened to coach Mike Patterson and even ventured in the direction of the umpires before turning back.

In just three weeks the Saints have slipped from third to sixth place.

Ditterich was suspended when St Kilda won the Grand Final in 1966, and joined Melbourne in 1973 under the now-abandoned 10-year rule. There he won a best and fairest award, before returning to St Kilda as captain in 1976 and 1977 (→ 6).

Carlton's third coach in seven games

May 11. Alex Jesaulenko went to Carlton this morning determined not to be the new coach. But within an hour the club Committee had changed his mind and he will take over from stand-in coach Sergio Silvagni, who succeeded Ian Stewart after he quit because of ill health three weeks ago. John Kennedy, Neil Roberts and Silvagni were offered the job before Jesaulenko, but declined.

Appealing to Jesaulenko's loyalty and spirit, President George Harris, said he was doing an enormous favour in a difficult situation.

'This is the worst situation any club could be in, to appoint a coach with seven games gone,' he said.

Robert Walls resigned as Carlton captain last week and has not returned to the club. Jesaulenko said he would try to get him back – and to restore hard work and discipline.

Jezza ponders the new situation.

At 32, Jesaulenko has been with Carlton since 1967 and now he is player-coach, a position he said he would never take. He will play for two or three weeks, but if his form slips he will give up playing.

At training tonight he penalised almost every player, ordering 20 push-ups for mistakes (→ 27).

Pair of Lions chew up Swans

April 22. As storm clouds rolled over the Junction Oval today, Fitzroy looked finished. Then Bob Beecroft and Garry Wilson turned around a 32-point deficit to South Melbourne at three-quarter time.

The pair kicked 17 of their side's 21 goals, including 12 of the last 14, to win, 21.17 (143) to 18.16 (124).

Six goals down halfway through the third term, the Lions took the lead just before time-on, adding four goals before the siren.

Emotional supporters wildly acclaimed every effort of full-forward Beecroft and rover Wilson as they led the charge for the Lions' first win of the season.

Beecroft was keen to give credit to coach Graham Campbell for keeping him in one position throughout the game (→ 15/8/82).

283

Big football name killed after game

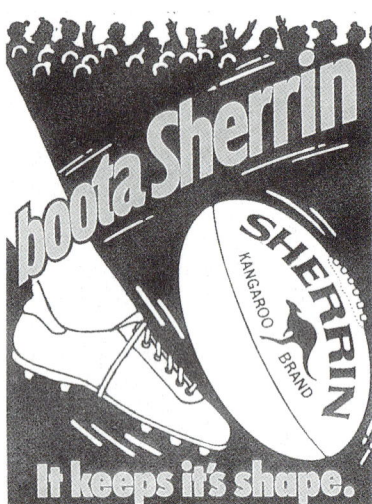

The big name in footballs.

April 2. Tributes have been pouring in for the former Collingwood President Tom Sherrin, who was killed in a car accident last night while returning from the match against Geelong at Kardinia Park.

A Collingwood Committeeman from 1952 to 1974, he was made a life member in 1953 and was President from 1963 to 1974.

Aged 60, Mr Sherrin was today described as an elder statesman of the club. Collingwood President John Hickey said his background, knowledge and experience were invaluable. 'The whole football community will miss him.'

Richmond President Ian Wilson recalled his own first meeting of League Directors when Mr Sherrin rose to declare: 'What is good for Collingwood is good for football.' 'He was the most charming person I have met in football' (→ 24/3/87).

Tom Sherrin: a Collingwood life.

Ton for Templeton, new Western wonder

Aug. 12. Footscray's Kelvin Templeton today became his club's first player to kick 100 goals in a season.

His name goes into the records with greats such as Gordon Coventry, Ron Todd and Peter McKenna of Collingwood, South's Bob Pratt, Richmond's Jack Titus, John Coleman of Essendon, Geelong's Doug Wade and Larry Donohue and Peter Hudson of Hawthorn, all of whom topped a goal century in a season.

Templeton, 21, who was recruited from Traralgon in the Latrobe Valley, eclipsed Footscray's previous best, Jack Collins' 84 goals.

Sadly for Templeton, however, the Bulldogs went down to Collingwood, 11.16 (82) to 10.6 (66).

Playing in shocking, muddy conditions at Victoria Park Templeton had kicked one goal and two behinds from five shots including one out of bounds and another into the man on his mark from about 15 metres out.

Hundreds of spectators jumped the fence to congratulate him when the champion full-forward landed his 'ton' in the third quarter with a shot from the forward pocket.

He then brought his total to 101 goals for the season and three for the match.

But the Magpies, one point up at the last change, were not to be denied. Billy Picken was moved from defence to attack, replacing Phil Carman who did not reappear after half time, and he goaled to lead the Magpies last charge. Amazingly the Magpies had 11 different goal kickers for their 11 goals, an unparalleled feat in League football (→ 22/9/80).

Adoring Footscray fans swamp Kelvin Templeton after his 100th goal.

Players now warm the 'interchange' bench

March 30. After being tested in night matches, the use of 19th and 20th men in interchanges begins in all three grades on Saturday.

The use of reserves or emergencies was introduced by the VFL in May 1930, when a 19th player was allowed to replace an injured man. This was extended to a 20th man in 1946.

The idea of interchanging the 19th and 20th men began as a trial during night matches last year and has now been accepted by the VFL.

The new rule gives coaches and strategists far greater flexibility in planning sides, with replacements being made during the game to rest or discipline those who have not been performing up to standard.

It also ends the risk of a side being depleted when non-injury changes have been made to desperately strengthen a team.

Baby Bomber is teacher's pet

Little Timmy in grown up game.

June 27. Tim Watson, Essendon's schoolboy half-forward, has one particularly favourite lesson.

At the start of each week he is in the gymnasium where his physical education teacher is Mr Ken Fletcher, who is also Essendon's captain.

Known as 'Fletch' to his pupil, the 30-year-old teacher at Essendon High keeps a close eye on Watson, 16, who is in his second year with the Bombers.

'I try not to talk about school when I'm at the club,' said Watson. 'All the blokes give me a ribbing from time to time when they know I've got homework after training.'

Fifty-goal game at South Melbourne

Aug. 19. In a goal-scoring bonanza at the Lake Oval today South Melbourne and Geelong kicked a total of 50 goals. In a game played at a sizzling pace, Geelong won by 12 points, 26.11 (167) to 24.11 (155). Full-forwards Stewart Gull (South) and Larry Donohue each kicked eight goals.

From the start, both teams used attacking football. Little pressure was applied, with players giving their opponents lots of latitude. The game finished 10 minutes after other matches because of the time it took to get the ball back after each goal.

Barassi's Big Vs flunk homework

May 28. Victoria's best footballers have gone back to the classroom under 'schoolmaster' Ron Barassi.

The North Melbourne and Victoria coach told the State squad of 27 players to turn up at training today with an essay of about 300 words. But Hawthorn's Michael Tuck and Kelvin Moore did not have their essays ready this morning. Six other players missing from yesterday's special training session at North Melbourne, because of injury or for other reasons, also did not do their essays.

Barassi appeared to have stern words with Tuck as preparations began for the game against Western Australia at VFL Park on June 10.

Earlier, Barassi said 'I want the players to tell me how important they think the game is, and what their attitudes will be.

'I want to get them thinking about the game so that they are more involved.'

Today, he said that he was disappointed that word had leaked out about his essay demands. 'I could not give a hoot what people think about me asking the players for essays,' he said.

'I think it's a good idea and that's all I need for me to do something. I'm not saying any more about it.'

But a State squad player said 'Since when has a Victorian team been picked on anything else but football ability and form' (→ 3/6).

Blight's Brownlow is football's worst kept secret

Marks that win Brownlows. Malcolm Blight takes one of his screamers.

Sept. 25. North Melbourne champion Malcolm Blight won the Brownlow Medal tonight – and then the League appeared certain to conduct an inquiry.

The investigation will be into an alleged leak of voting details. Blight's win had been confidently predicted for more than a week.

Blight, 26, won by one vote from Hawthorn's Peter Knights, with early favourite Garry Wilson of Fitzroy third. Knights led for most of the night, with Blight winning on the third-last vote in counting that lasted 80 minutes.

This was particularly hard on the brilliant Hawthorn centre half-back, who missed the 1976 Brownlow by only three votes to Essendon's Graham Moss.

Rumours of widespread disclosure of votes were strongly denied by the League General Manager, Mr Jack Hamilton. 'It's disturbing, I must say,' he commented.

Mr Hamilton said rumours that Blight would win easily had been disproven, as had rumours that Garry Wilson would not poll well.

Now Blight, North's blond aerial star, has a chance to become the first player since 1966 to win the Brownlow Medal and play in a Premiership side in the same year.

'I thought I had a most consistent year, but I really didn't think it would go this far,' said Blight. 'I'd like to think someone had an educated punt on me and that caused all the publicity' (→ 11/9/82).

World of Sport 1000

Sept. 30. It's in the *Guinness Book of Records* and now it's had a surprise presentation. At North Melbourne's Grand Final breakfast today HSV7's *World of Sport* won North's Personality of the Year award as it topped 1000 programmes.

The nation's top sporting celebrities turned out at the breakfast in tribute to the show.

The wag of the programme, Lou Richards, and HSV7 General Manager Ron Casey, introduced stars of the show, such as axeman Jack O'Toole, boxer Johnny Famechon, swimmer Dawn Fraser, athlete Herb Elliott, cricketer Max Walker and yachtsman Jock Sturrock (→ 9/4/80).

There's a Grand Final coming up and North fans muster at the Arden Street ground to watch the boys at training.

Hawks grind out another Premiership

Sept. 30. Hawthorn today took out Flag No. 4, their second in three years, proving themselves a super side of the 70s.

The Hawks had sweet revenge for their humiliating 67-point loss to North Melbourne in last year's Preliminary Final, winning by 18 points in front of 101,704 people.

It was a typical grinding Hawthorn victory, although North had the Hawks on the run late in the second quarter, going into half time with a four-point advantage.

In the next 20 minutes Hawthorn closed North down, with the only exciting work for North coming from their high-flying forward Phil Baker, who had four goals by half time and finished with six.

At the last change Hawthorn were 22 points in front and they kept up the power, skill and teamwork to maintain their break and win 18.13 (121) to 15.13 (103).

Yet again the team finishing on top of the Ladder have lost the Flag. Since the present Finals system began in 1972, only Carlton (1972) and Richmond (1974) have won Premierships from that position.

David Parkin has joined John Kennedy as the second Hawthorn coach to bring home the Premiership. Parkin captained Hawthorn's Premiership side in 1971 under coach John Kennedy, who also planned the triumphs of 1961 and 1976.

Today a turning point came six minutes into the third quarter when Alan Martello snapped over his shoulder into the scoreboard-end goal. In the next 12 minutes Haw-

Ron Barassi and North officials sit glumly in the coaches' box, while David Parkin and his cohorts whoop it up.

thorn kicked 6.3 to North's one behind.

Leigh Matthews, Kelvin Moore, Peter Knights, Michael Tuck, Michael Moncrieff and company won new appreciation for the men of brown and gold, while youngsters Robert DiPierdomenico and Terry Wallace showed a fierce ability to win the ball.

'Dipper' did a superb job at half-back on Arnold Briedis, while Wallace kept pushing the ball forward from the centre.

The Roos suffered heavily from the loss of suspended ruckman Peter Keenan and injured Steven Icke and Brent Crosswell. Brownlow Medallist Malcom Blight was virtually out with a torn groin muscle after just five minutes, and Stan Alves also limped off in the second quarter (→ 24/9/83).

1978 Statistics

Leading Goalkicker:
Kelvin Templeton (Foots) 118
Brownlow Medallist:
Malcolm Blight (N. Melb)
Finals: Elimination Final Carl 15.15 (105) Geel 9.18 (72); **Qualifying Final** Haw 23.16 (154) Coll 14.14 (98); **First Semi-final** Coll 15.18 (108) Carl 13.15 (93); **Second Semi-final** N. Melb 10.13 (73) Haw 12.15 (87); **Preliminary Final** N. Melb 14.12 (96) Coll 12.12 (84); **Grand Final** Haw 18.13 (121) N. Melb 15.13 (103)

Ladder:	W	L	D	%	pts
N. Melb	16	6		120.9	64
Haw	16	6		117.7	64
Coll	15	7		113.3	60
Carl	14	8		116.8	56
Geel	12	10		102.3	48
St K	11	10	1	93.1	46
Rich	10	11	1	102.9	42
S. Melb	9	13		100.3	36
Fitz	8	14		96.5	32
Ess	8	14		94.3	32
Foots	7	15		90.6	28
Melb	5	17		69.1	20

Riding high! Fabulous Phil Baker of North takes one of his many gigantic leaps in the Grand Final to mark over Hawthorn full-back Kelvin Moore.

Carlton's financial woes brought into the spotlight

July 27. *The Age* has published a series of *Insight* reports on the financial arrangements of the Carlton Football Club Ltd under President George Harris.

Headlined as a 'financial mess' and the 'George Harris capers', the articles disclose that several of the non-football business ventures of the company which took over operations of the football club have lost substantial amounts of money in the past financial year.

These operations include Carlton Marketing Services which controls the Carlton Bluebirds, the 'cheerleader' troupe which has lost $29,918. The Bluebirds cost $2000 for a spot.

Other loss-making marketing activities include hinged chopsticks called 'chowsticks', 'kiss of life' oxygen masks, SF35 odour-inducing chemical and plastic irons.

The Carlton Football Club's sports medicine centre in Royal Parade opposite Princes Park is said to have lost $106,133 in the last financial year. The company owning the property has made a small profit.

A land and housing development company with interests in Bundoora lost $14,062. Total losses last month are put at $53,282, with the associated companies losing $145,113 in the last financial year.

Harris sought a Supreme Court injunction last week to stop publication but this was rejected by Mr Justice Anderson who, however, said that the headline was 'inflammatory.'

Carlton members and supporters are anxious about the financial state of the club, how relevant such businesses are to football, and how the disclosures will affect the team.

Deflation for George Harris.

Big Carl gives Demons a bit of devil

A wonderful sight. Carl Ditterich, now a Demon, greets the umpire.

April 21. New Melbourne captain-coach, Carl Ditterich has fired up last year's wooden spooners in his first season at the helm.

Ditterich's first move on his return to Melbourne from St Kilda was to dump 18 players from the Demons' final training list, and today he showed that he will be leading by example with a best-on-ground display in the seven-point loss against South Melbourne.

Swans' coach and former St Kilda team-mate, Ian Stewart, was so impressed that he sprinted through the rain to congratulate the 32-year-old Ditterich. 'It was the best game I have ever seen Carl play. He should have been another Nicholls or Farmer,' Stewart said.

The third round match was close until three-quarter time, with Melbourne four points ahead at the first change, trailing 0.5 at half time, and by 2.1 at the last change.

South kicked 5.2 in the hard-fought last quarter to Melbourne's 6.2, taking the Demons' tantalisingly close to a second win from three games this season (→19/7/80).

Drought in Outer

March 31. Footy fans gave the VFL's designated dry zones a lukewarm reception as the season got going at Waverley, Carlton beating Essendon by 21 points, 14.17 (101) to 11.14 (80).

Most footy fans supported a dry area at the ground, but rejected moves for a total ban on alcohol. They were more critical of the high price charged for a beer.

A police report released last week, said alcohol caused most 'unruly and violent behaviour' at football matches. It called for increased dry areas and a ban on taking liquor into football grounds (→5/5/82).

True and false boots

May 19. The Junction Oval became a circus ring today as Hawthorn kicked 16 behinds before goaling.

The Hawks' losing score of 11.24 (90) to Fitzroy's 14.18 (102) came in a game in which Hawthorn did not goal until seven minutes into the third quarter. Coach David Parkin had hoped to win without injured Leigh Matthews and Peter Knights. But his team only got as near as they did because of Fitzroy's fancy stuff.

Trailing 0.14 to 8.13 at half time, the Hawks kicked 7.1 in 22 minutes, but then again began missing (→3/4/93).

Trucking magnate takes over Saints

Sept 7. St Kilda's new Chairman, trucking-magnate Lindsay Fox, has wasted no time slashing into the Saints' $1 million debt by raising $250,000 in only 48 hours.

Fox, a former Saints ruckman, called in to rescue the debt-ridden wooden spooners, has embarked on a ruthless shake-up of the administration, sacking club manager Garry Murphy and calling for the resignation of the Committee. The future of coach Mike Patterson is still undecided.

Fox said he would need five years without an election to achieve his aims. He was also keen to entice successful former players and administrators back to the club.

So far, Fox's fund-raising has been encouraging, with two sponsors, International Harvester and JC Hutton P/L, promising $100,000 over five years. The Saints are looking for three other backers to raise sponsorship to half a million dollars.

While the financial news impressed the players, they were told by their new supremo that tough discipline would be imposed.

Fox has had members of the 1966 Premiership team address the players so they could get used to feeling like winners. One of the motivators was Premiership coach Allan Jeans, who years ago told Fox that he 'was not good enough' as a player (→ 26/6/84).

Keith Greig, in Sydney for North Melbourne, gets his foot stuck in the Sydney Cricket Ground fence.

Goals galore by Fitzroy in season of enormous scores

	G	B	P
FITZROY	36	22	238
MELBOURNE	6	12	48

Fitzroy's great scoreline as they have the biggest win in VFL history.

Barassi 'wowed' by $5000 VFL fine

Aug. 8. North Melbourne were today fined $5000, the highest penalty in VFL history.

The fine followed coach Ron Barassi's outburst against umpires on July 7. Today Barassi said: 'That's a big fine, wow.'

'No,' he added, 'I didn't speak in haste and I don't amend my views.'

Barassi said he conferred with club President Lloyd Holyoak before calling for the sacking of umpires' adviser Allan Nash, who has since announced he will resign, while saying this was not connected with Barassi's outburst (→ 5/4/87).

'Up There Cazaly' on everyone's lips

Sept. 13 Singer-writer Mike Brady today demanded a fee from the VFL to sing his hit 'Up There Cazaly' at the Grand Final on September 29.

'My manager and I believe that I shouldn't do it for nothing,' he said.

But the General Manager of the League, Mr Jack Hamilton, said: 'Barry Crocker, Keith Michell and Johnny Farnham have regarded the invitation as an honour. They haven't sought payment and no payment has been made.'

Mr Hamilton said negotiations are continuing with Brady's manager. Brady said: 'The last thing I want to see is a squabble with the VFL.'

July 28. Fitzroy got into the record books today with a huge win over Melbourne, scoring 36.22 (238) to a miserable 6.12 (48). It has been a season of very big scores, with the greatest victims being St Kilda and Melbourne.

In round five, Geelong set a record with 15 straight goals against St Kilda, to better the previous record of 13, achieved several times.

They shot from 5.8 (38) to 20.8 (128) in an amazing burst of accuracy, and won 22.10 (142) to 17.10 (112). The barrage could hardly have been worse for the Saints, coming a week after their record 178-point loss to Collingwood.

A quiet Saturday and Richmond are getting done by Hawthorn, but Michael Roach brings the crowd alive with a screaming chest mark.

Moore beats Bloggs for Brownlow

Harmes' way wins it for Blues

Sept. 29. Wayne Harmes won the inaugural Norm Smith Medal for best on ground in the Grand Final. With one piece of inspiration, perspiration and desperation he also won the game.

Eighteen minutes into the last quarter, Carlton had their noses in front by four points. Collingwood had kicked the two previous goals and had the momentum. Alex Jesaulenko injured his ankle and his leadership left the ground with him on a stretcher.

This, then, is how it happens: Harmes has the ball on the members' wing, heading towards the scoreboard goal. No one's at home so he lets fly with a kick in the general direction of the goals.

It's dribbling, trickling, it's nearly out of bounds, in the forward pocket.

But out of the blue, here's Harmes! He's chased his own kick. He dives, he thumps it across to the goal square – and there's Ken Sheldon who gathers the ball and goals.

It was one of Sheldon's four kicks in the last quarter and it was the the hysterical, historic sealer.

Carlton saw out the next minutes to win by less than a kick – 11.16 (82) to Collingwood 11.11 (77).

They had been put to a stern test of character by the never-say-die Magpies. It took some big performances from the new Blues – especially by first-year desperado Wayne Johnston – to win. Bill Picken was best for Collingwood. He had 14 kicks – and received 7 free kicks.

But the game was won in Harmes' own way (→ 26/9/81).

Moore's spectacular style.

Sept. 24. Collingwood ruckman Peter Moore had settled for a quiet evening in front of TV tonight before being told to get to the Southern Cross Hotel.

Once there, he found himself the surprise winner of the Brownlow Medal. Moore, 22, beat Fitzroy rover Garry Wilson and Melbourne centreman Robert Flower, polling 22 votes, followed by Wilson's 21 and Flower's 19.

With six three-votes to go, he said: 'I've got no chance. How could they possibly pick me?' A wild card in the voting was 'B. Bloggs of St Kilda', read out three times by VFL General Manager Jack Hamilton before he realised he was the victim of a practical joke.

Wayne Harmes shows the Blues spirit to snatch victory in the last seconds.

It's tough in the slush at the MCG, and mud slides are part of the fun.

1979 Statistics

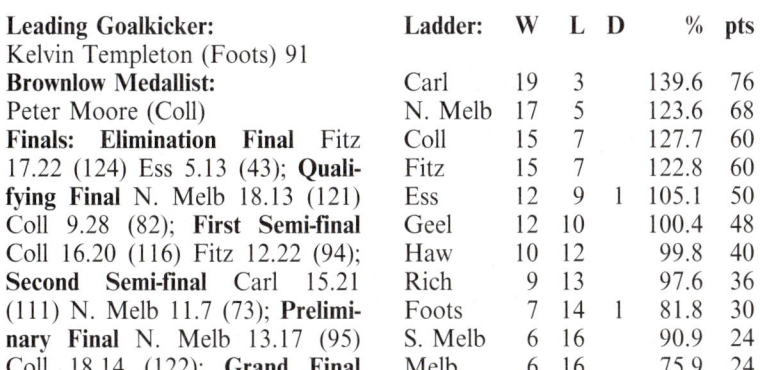

	W	L	D	%	pts
Carl	19	3		139.6	76
N. Melb	17	5		123.6	68
Coll	15	7		127.7	60
Fitz	15	7		122.8	60
Ess	12	9	1	105.1	50
Geel	12	10		100.4	48
Haw	10	12		99.8	40
Rich	9	13		97.6	36
Foots	7	14	1	81.8	30
S. Melb	6	16		90.9	24
Melb	6	16		75.9	24
St K	3	19		65.0	12

Leading Goalkicker:
Kelvin Templeton (Foots) 91
Brownlow Medallist:
Peter Moore (Coll)
Finals: Elimination Final Fitz 17.22 (124) Ess 5.13 (43); **Qualifying Final** N. Melb 18.13 (121) Coll 9.28 (82); **First Semi-final** Coll 16.20 (116) Fitz 12.22 (94); **Second Semi-final** Carl 15.21 (111) N. Melb 11.7 (73); **Preliminary Final** N. Melb 13.17 (95) Coll 18.14 (122); **Grand Final** Carl 11.16 (82) Coll 11.11 (77)

Five points separate the joy of Carlton (right) and Magpie dejection (left).

1980

April 9. US cable TV network ESPN has paid VFL $100,000 for rights to broadcast the match of the day (→ 14/4/85).

April 27. North Melbourne beat Footscray in Sydney before small crowd of 13,476, 26.21 (177) to 8.7 (55) (→ 10/9/86).

May 10. John Rantall becomes League record holder with 334 day games, for South Melbourne, North Melbourne and Fitzroy (→ 6/8/83).

May 24. A rumpus springs up between Footscray City Council and the VFL over a plan to play Sunday soccer at the Western Oval (→ 2/8/81).

June 28. North coach Ron Barassi says 'It wasn't the worst display by a North side. It was the worst performance by any side, anywhere, any time' after Geelong's win 13.6 (84) to 4.3 (27) (→ 12/12).

July 5. Victorian teams defeat WA, 18.15 (123) to 15.12 (102), and Queensland, 28.18 (186) to 16.10 (106), but manage to lose to a fanatical ACT, 11.16 (82) to 13.17 (95) (→ 16/5/83).

July 8. Fitzroy coach Bill Stephen, who announces he will retire at the end of the season, is aged 52 but says he feels 150.

July 10. The VFL Trainers' Association has lodged a claim for a pay rise to $35 a week for the first five years service.

July 19. Richmond kick 34.18 (222), their highest score, to defeat St Kilda 11.4 (70) Michael Roach kicks 10 (→ 12/4/82).

July 19. Melbourne coach Carl Ditterich says he will finish at the end of the season and that Melbourne is duty bound to go after Ron Barassi.

July 26. Reserves umpires John Russo and Geoff Morrow test 'beepers' that sound when the siren does (→ 27/3/82).

Aug. 19. Lou Richards rows Billy Goggin across the Barwon in a bathtub after predicting that Geelong could not beat Collingwood.

Debuts
Justin Madden (Ess)
Chris Mew (Haw)
David Rhys-Jones (S. Melb)
Brian Taylor (Rich)

Retirements
Carl Ditterich (Melb)
John 'Sam' Newman (Geel)
John Rantall (Fitz)
Max Richardson (Fitz)
Len Thompson (Fitz)
Robert Walls (Fitz)

Carman loses head over Carbery and Sidebottom

Calm down Carman, says team-mate Simon Madden as trouble brews.

... too late, the deed is done.

May 26. The operation of VFL Tribunals as both judge and jury was criticised by Mr Justice Starke in the Supreme Court today.

He was hearing an application by Essendon's Phil Carman to discharge or quash a VFL decision against him made on April 21.

Judge Starke noted that the Tribunal, having convicted players, then had to sentence them.

He said it was unsatisfactory for players' advocates to appear before the Tribunal.

This represented a 'half-way house' attitude, he said. 'Players should have the right to their own legal representation, or none at all.'

Carman had been suspended for four weeks for striking St Kilda captain Garry Sidebottom and for 16 weeks for head-butting boundary umpire Graham Carbery.

Mr A.G. Uren, for Carman, said the player was denied natural justice when his advocate, Mr Brian O'Shaughnessy, was not given an opportunity to plead.

Carman, a professional footballer, had no opportunity to put forward a submission on his character and likely loss of income if he were disqualified.

Mr Justice Starke said Carman's nine appearances before the Tribunal did not leave much in the way of character. Tribunals such as this should, he said, be left to hammer out their own affairs (→ 4/4/88).

Bruce Doull wrestles with mind games

April 14. Carlton's Bruce Doull and Footscray's Shane Loveless were today suspended for two matches by the VFL Tribunal.

They had been reported after a wrestling match in the third quarter last Saturday at the Western Oval.

Doull was reluctant to be photographed, entered through a side door, then waited for five minutes after the decision and fled VFL House by a rear exit. Carlton General Manager Jim Allison said Doull wanted his privacy and had asked VFL officials to help him avoid photographers.

The hearing was told that Doull had also missed hearing renowned motivator Dr Norman Vincent Peale talk on positive thinking tonight at nearby Dallas Brooks Hall.

The great survivor John Rantall runs out for his League record 334th game, with his third club, Fitzroy. The great half-back flanker played 260 games with South, with a stint at North for 70 games and a Flag.

Dyer 'ere, there and everywhere

Jack Dyer was talked into radio in 1952 and hasn't stopped talking since – on the wireless, and with television pictures, on *World of Sport* beginning in 1959 and and *League Teams* in 1964.

Since then he has been to Australian football language what Dr Spooner and Mrs Malaprop were to conventional English.

They gave us spoonerisms and malapropisms. But they never played 312 games for Richmond. Jack Dyer has given the Australian language a wonderful range of Dyerisms

Dyerisms have a singular distinction, in that they are funny, but you know exactly what he meant to say.

When describing Carlton's Peter Bosustow as 'a good ordinary player' you knew exactly what he meant. Or Gary Dempsey as a 'tarantulope' because 'you can't catch him and you can't mark over him.'

A certain kind of player 'goes where the ball ain't'. He is a 'fringe area player' or 'fruitfly'.

A transcript of a radio call is a joyful rendition of you know what he meant about everything, except the score.

Here is a passage of play from the 1978 Grand Final: 'On the kickout it's out towards the wing position, the pack fly again, over the top of the pack and a good mark has been taken here. It looks like ... it is ... Cowton with the ball. He immediately handballs it in the air, away they go as Henshaw comes down the ground.

'He's going for the short pass. It's not a good one at all. It's punched away by Martella. Another punch up in the air. In goes Demper ... de pier ... ear ... domenica ... in after it again.'

Robert DiPierdomenico is in good company – along with everyone with a long name from another country.

Speaking of which, Jack Dyer was once asked about his opinion on the topic of euthanasia.

He replied thoughtfully. 'They're just as good as what we've got 'ere, aren't they?'

Sam Newman hangs up white boots after 300 games

Sept. 13. John 'Sam' Newman, Geelong champion, retired today after a 300-game career during which he kicked 110 goals and played eight games for Victoria.

Coming to the Cats from Geelong Grammar, Newman was a renowned mark and excellent team player, and had a sizeable leap coupled with much natural ability.

Seriously hurt in a 1967 Semi-Final, he had to have part of his kidney removed. Returning strongly, he was awarded club best and fairest the following year.

Somewhat flamboyant in his white boots, Newman encountered many injury problems, needing three ankle operations, but still starred at centre-half-forward.

A request to be cleared to Richmond in 1976 cost him the captaincy he had held for two seasons.

The big Cat Sam Newman, tireless champion of VFL football, gets to 300.

Banished Jezza becomes a Saint

April 8. Alex Jesaulenko, captain-coach of Premiers Carlton last season, will become playing coach of St Kilda, replacing Mike Patterson two games into the season.

Jesaulenko left Carlton last December, putting loyalty to former Carlton President George Harris above everything else in the ructions at Princes Park.

Harris was deposed at the AGM in December, a decision reconfirmed at an extraordinary meeting in February. Concern had been expressed over the finances of the club under his administration.

Jesaulenko went to St Kilda as a player and takes over as coach at the behest of Lindsay Fox, who is the new St Kilda President.

Carlton confirmed Peter Jones as coach, and Ian Rice as President.

Night games not the same says critic

July 9. Football at night in the Escort Championship played at VFL Park lacks the excitement of daylight games at the MCG, according to a columnist for *The Age* newspaper, Garrie Hutchinson.

Lighting football seems to diffuse concentration, he says. 'It's because it's difficult to see; the ball is often lost in the air or the empty seats.'

The result is a strange brand of football where everyone tries to play close to the ground.

'The truth is that Australian football is designed for daytime, with the old-fashioned wind, rain and sunshine, using a leather ball on odd-shaped grounds.

'It's specific to its environment: transplanted it dies.'

Rules bisect circle

March 30. The VFL has acted on the amount of physical interference at the centre bounce.

A line across the centre circle will separate ruckmen, who must stand on the defensive side of the line.

The aim is to eliminate excessive wrestling, such as that between Collingwood's Peter Moore and North Melbourne's Gary Dempsey in last year's Preliminary Final.

Someone in the crowd has thrown a full can at Garry Sidebottom.

Demon avenger Carl Ditterich fights for justice and victim Tony Elshaug against 'villains' Andrew Ireland and Stan Magro.

Late siren gives North night Cup

Schimma brandishes the trophy.

July 15. North Melbourne won a sensational Escort Cup Grand Final tonight with a goal against Collingwood kicked after the last siren.

A stunned record night crowd of 50,478 saw Kerry Good awarded the mark by umpire Ian Robinson, clearly taken after the siren. Celebrating Magpie fans had streamed on to the ground.

But Good goaled from 30 metres out for North to take the cup and $64,000.

There were loud boos and jeers as VFL President, Dr Allen Aylett, presented the cup to North captain Wayne Schimmelbusch.

The siren could be heard from the Press box, just a few metres from the timekeepers. This lapse renews the case for umpires to be fitted with 'electronic beepers' connected to the timekeepers' button (→ 26).

Robbie Muir in trouble over Shaw

May 30. Robbie Muir's clash with Collingwood's Ray Shaw has ended in three weeks' suspension at the VFL Tribunal.

The St Kilda half-forward flattened Shaw. 'He spat in my face,' Muir explained. 'The umpire said he saw spittle flying in the air, but wasn't sure where it had come from.

'It obviously didn't come from me, because I was the one who reacted.'

Tribunal Chairman John Schultz said he would walk away in such a situation.

Templeton most votes, Roach most goals

Sept. 22. League history was made today when Footscray's Kelvin Templeton became the first key forward to win the Brownlow Medal.

Templeton, who turns 24 next week, won in the last few minutes from an outsider, Essendon centreman Mervyn Neagle.

Templeton, one of the League's top full-forwards, was switched to centre half-forward by new coach Royce Hart. Templeton trained two and three times a day over summer to add weight and build strength for the position.

Templeton's win deflated the big leak that Richmond centreman Geoff Raines was a certainty. Third and fourth were last Saturday's opposing ruckmen, Rod Blake of Geelong and Collingwood's Peter Moore.

The tension mounts for Tempo.

North and Melbourne play for nothing

Aug. 2. North Melbourne and Melbourne played for no money at Arden Street today.

The crowd of 7500, which paid $6267, meant that it cost each club between $15,000 and $20,000 to field the teams. North won 12.15 (87) to 7.15 (57).

The cost of the game, including police, ambulance, ground staff, cleaning, insurance, armed escort, staff meals, payroll tax, hire of uniform coats, umpires, observers' fees, footballs, admission tickets and ground improvement fund, added up to $6767.50.

Had the ground manager not kicked in by cutting expenses, the costs would have been greater. (→ 16/6/84).

Parkin leaves nest, Barassi goes home

Dec. 12. Ron Barassi, whose contract as coach of North Melbourne expires at the end of 1980, will make his long-anticipated second coming at Melbourne, where he first played in 1953.

David Wilson, in *The Age*, has revealed that back in 1977 a company associated with Melbourne Executive Director Dick Seddon bought an option on the contractual rights to Ron Barassi's services after his time at North Melbourne.

It was further revealed that Barassi will cost around $240,000 over the next three years. Melbourne have not appeared in the Finals since 1964, and it appears that Barassi will have his work cut out for him.

In other coaching moves, David Parkin of Hawthorn resigned on September 12 after 20 years as a Hawk.

He has been linked with Carlton, after the Blues' disappointing Finals series under 'Percy' Jones. Jones says he would like to coach again.

Former Tiger Kevin Sheedy has been appointed coach of Essendon, beating challenges from Don Scott, Allan Jeans and John Nicholls. North Melbourne are expected to name Malcolm Blight playing coach (→ 21/4/81).

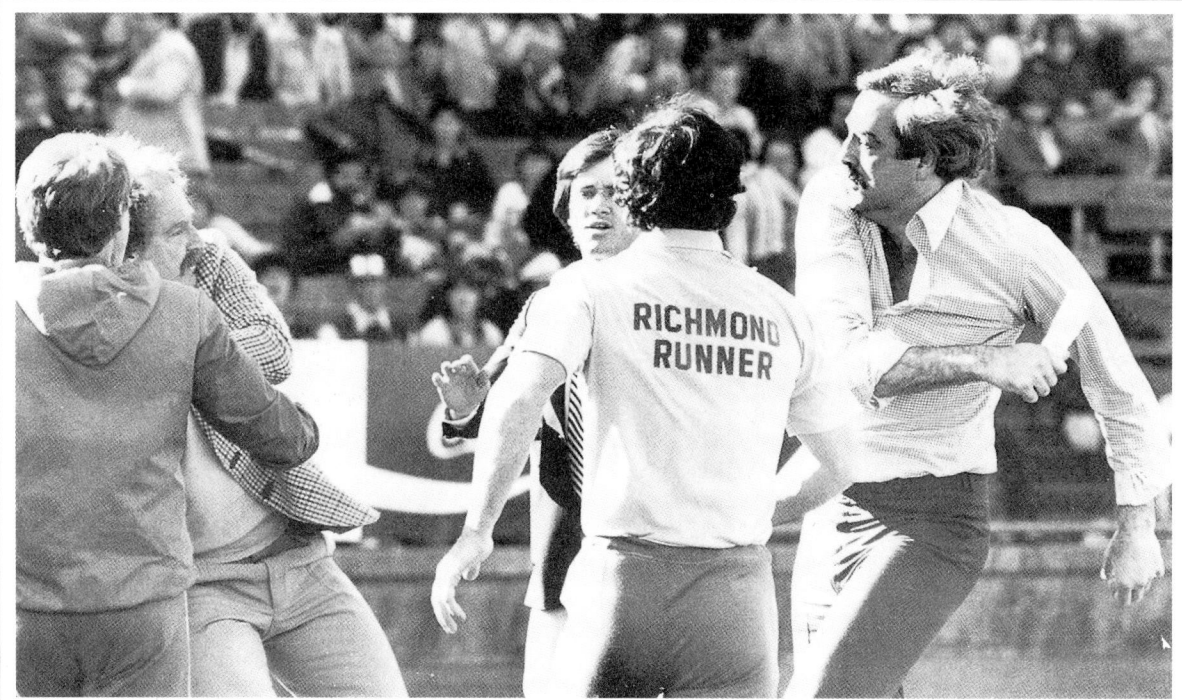

Tempers flare at Waverley and coaches Tony Jewell of Richmond and 'Percy' Jones find something to chew over.

Kevin Bartlett has glorious Finals series

Sept. 27. Kevin Bartlett, the player who felt 'unwanted' at Richmond just a year ago, played his 339th game in the Grand Final, and was instrumental in the Tigers' emphatic thumping of the Magpies.

Bartlett kicked his last and seventh goal at the 26th minute of the last quarter to the unrestrained jubilation of team-mates.

Bartlett scooted around the boundary line, potting goals from close-in, two skinny arms raised above that familiar balding head like a demented clockwork toy.

No Magpie could get near him to stop the mayhem – just as no one could in the other two Finals games the Tigers played.

Bartlett kicked a total of 21 goals

Peter Daicos takes a marvellous mark in the Preliminary Final.

for the Finals series, equalling the record for a series.

'Hungry' won the Norm Smith Medal as best on ground. He was certainly the spirit of the Tiger win. However, he was aided and abetted by players such as Mark Lee and the centre bounce gang who got the ball in his direction.

Geoff Raines, Bryan Wood, Robert Wiley, Mervyn Keane and Dale Weightman cleared the centre square at will with a hand pass and a long kick in the direction of David Cloke and Michael Roach and that pesky 'crumber' KB.

Cloke's six-goal haul from centre-half-forward was a reminder of the palmiest days of Royce Hart. Not as graceful perhaps, but as effective.

For all but the most ardent Richmond fan, the game was disappointingly over by half time when the lead was 11.11 (77) to 4.10 (34)

Tony Jewell, the unsung hero of Richmond's season, said after the game: 'Coaches are nothing. They are the most overrated breed in the world. Without great players there would be no supercoaches. I coach because I still want to be as close as I can to the playing side. I'm nothing more than a frustrated player who wishes like hell he could be out there.'

That might have been echoed by Collingwood coach Tom Hafey – there was certainly not a lot he could do from the sidelines as Collingwood lost another Grand Final, the seventh since 1958.

Richmond defeated Collingwood, 23.21 (159) to 9.24 (78) – a record winning margin in a Grand Final.

Kevin Bartlett shows the determination that has made him the Finals star.

1980 Statistics

Leading Goalkicker:
Michael Roach (Rich) 112
Brownlow Medallist:
Kelvin Templeton (Foots)
Finals: Elimination Final N. Melb 14.12 (96) Coll 14.20 (104); **Qualifying Final** Carl 10.14 (74) Rich 18.8 (116); **First Semi-final** Carl 15.12 (102) Coll 22.20 (152); **Second Semi-final** Geel 11.5 (71) Rich 14.11 (95); **Preliminary Final** Geel 13.11 (89) Coll 13.15 (93); **Grand Final** Rich 23.21 (159) Coll 9.24 (78)

Ladder:	W	L	D	%	pts
Geel	17	5		125.1	68
Carl	17	5		121.0	68
Rich	16	5	1	134.4	66
N. Melb	14	7	1	123.8	58
Coll	14	7	1	114.4	58
S. Melb	13	9		101.7	52
Ess	10	12		105.4	40
Haw	10	12		94.4	40
Melb	5	17		79.0	20
Foots	5	17		75.1	20
St K	4	16	2	69.2	20
Fitz	4	17	1	86.0	18

Mickey Malthouse and Jim Jess are jubilant over the victory.

1981

Barassi a 'messiah' among coaches

April 21. Ron Barassi, the Premiership captain and best and fairest for Melbourne in 1964, has now returned to coach them and is being hailed as the 'Messiah', who will lead the Demons from the wilderness of 16 bleak years.

He comes from coaching Carlton and North Melbourne to two Premierships each, but Melbourne supporters see him as back in his rightful place, the place where he made his reputation over 204 games in 12 glorious years.

Garrie Hutchinson of *The Age* writes: Because Barassi was always successful, it's difficult to comprehend just how phenomenal he has been. In the 28 years he has been in football, including a year just watching, he has missed out on only five Finals series. Now he might remake the stuff of legends' (→ 11/4/83).

Doug Cox permit saga ends in KO

Doug Cox heads for the exit.

May 23. Doug Cox, the player at the centre of a clearance row between St Kilda and Richmond, was knocked out during play when the two teams met at VFL Park today.

St Kilda were given permission by the Supreme Court yesterday to field Cox. The Saints also obtained an order that the Master of the Supreme Court will review a decision by VFL Directors to forfeit St Kilda's eight Premiership points, fine the club $4000 and revoke Cox's permit to play with St Kilda.

Cox replaced the injured Fidler on the Saints' line-up, but had little influence on play and was concussed trying to break a tackle in the last quarter. Despite a last-quarter comeback by St Kilda, Richmond led all day to win by 31 points, 20.16 (136) to 15.15 (105).

Richmond claim St Kilda are playing Cox without a valid permit (→ 28/5).

Featherby gathers 43 kicks in game

July 18. Geelong centreman Peter Featherby displayed prolific statistical brilliance in his team's win over Melbourne at the MCG today.

Featherby, 29, had 43 kicks, eight handpasses and 13 marks, which was probably the best ever performance by a Geelong player. It was among the greatest performances in the VFL since Bob Skilton was at his Brownlow-winning best at South Melbourne in the 60s.

The Cats won with 22.35 (167) to 12.7 (79) (→ 11/4/92).

Fehring's big roost travels 90 yards

April 11. St Kilda ruckman Jeff Fehring stunned the big crowd at Moorabbin when he booted a sensational 85-metre torpedo punt – or 90 yards, one foot and seven inches – to score a valuable goal in the last quarter for the struggling Saints.

Unfortunately, the booming punt was kicked in anger by Fehring minutes after being reported for striking Collingwood ruck-rover, Mike Taylor. But Collingwood won 23.19 (157) to 19.21 (135).

Fitzroy runner Ray Keane remonstrates with South's Graham Teasdale, after Teasdale and Fitzroy rover Garry Wilson had tangled.

32 umpires get one week for striking: juniors take over

Aug. 8. Sixteen junior umpires were drafted to officiate at today's League games after 32 senior field umpires resigned at midnight over a dispute with the VFL.

The ages of the replacement umpires range from 18 to 22 and none has umpired a Senior or Reserve grade match. They normally umpire under-19, country, metropolitan and junior games.

Despite their youth and inexperience, the stand-in umpires officiated without incident and there were no reports. Players were asked to be tolerant of errors. One of the young umpires officiating at the South Melbourne and Carlton game was 19-year-old Brad Beitzel, the son of umpires' director Harry Beitzel.

'There is no doubt that this was the biggest thrill of my life,' he said. Brad Beitzel said he would be available next week if needed.

A new face with an old name. Brad Beitzel shows that he's in charge.

Swans to fly north to Sydney

July 29. The VFL Board of Directors today gave South Melbourne permission to play 11 games in Sydney next year.

The matches will be on the Sydney Cricket Ground on Sunday afternoons and shown live on Melbourne TV.

League General Manager Mr Jack Hamilton said a substantial majority of clubs voted for the move.

Among the reasons for the decision was the primary aim of the VFL to become established as a fully national game.

Long-term trends in the economics of sport were also considered as was the unanimous desire of the South Melbourne Board for Sydney games. The stimulus to the game in New South Wales through a substantial injection of extra money for promotion and development was also a factor.

It is proposed that South Melbourne should keep the Lake Oval for training and administration. But legal action by the 'Keep South at South' group is likely. Already there is a petition calling for an extraordinary meeting of South members, at which an attempt to sack the Board is likely (→12/5/84).

Up they go again! This time Carlton's Peter Bosustow defies gravity.

Pleasant Sunday afternoons begin

Aug. 2. Sunday football came to Melbourne today and the atmosphere resembled September.

The day was acclaimed a success by everyone except Collingwood who lost to Essendon, 12.16 (88) to 9.15 (69), and were bumped from the top of the VFL Ladder.

The match was the first Sunday game in Melbourne since a first round match played before the Queen at the MCG 11 years ago.

The 64,149 supporters delighted officials. Crowds queued from 9 a.m. to be admitted at noon for a two-hour wait for action. Alcohol was banned (→8/9/84).

Time and Daniher find Carlton out

Aug. 17. Amazing scenes at Princes Park when Carlton captain Mike Fitzpatrick, trying to slow the game down in time-on, was penalised by umpire Ian Robinson for time wasting. Carlton led by 13 points, and Fitzpatrick held the ball for 60 or 70 seconds while umpire Robinson waved his arms.

This would have been funny if it hadn't been for Essendon's Neale Daniher kicking three goals in time-on to snatch a win for the Dons reminiscent of Malcolm Blight's deeds for North in 1976.

Essendon won by a point, 14.15 (99) to 15.8 (98) (→25/3/85).

Footy professor illuminates game

April 29. *Up Where Cazaly?* is the first book to take an academic look at the social and business history of Australian football.

It was written by the late Professor Ian Turner and completed by Leonie Sandercock.

Ian Turner was well known as the 'footy professor', delivering the famed and funny Ron Barassi Memorial Lectures from 1965 to 1978.

In one he reported the billboard outside a church 'What would you do if Jesus came to Hawthorn?' and the graffiti – 'Move Peter Hudson to centre half-forward'.

Sidebottom misses the Finals bus

Sidebottom's fatal bus stop.

Sept. 19. Intense security at Geelong for today's Preliminary Final cost the expensive, controversial forward Garry Sidebottom a place in the side when he missed the bus to VFL Park.

The security was such that a communication breakdown with the club's interchange players only hours before today's loss to Collingwood meant Sidebottom stayed at home at Lara.

The former St Kilda captain had expected to be told about his place in the team, but the message did not get through and he assumed that he wasn't playing.

Coach Bill Goggin quickly summoned forward Peter Johnston, who fortunately had his gear in his car at the ground.

19 possibilities in last round

Aug. 29. In perhaps the most momentous final round in League history, seven teams fought for five places today.

In heavy going at Victoria Park, League leaders Collingwood managed just one point against an inspired Fitzroy's first quarter of 4.4.

A half-time Magpie total of 0.2 grew to 4.9 to the Roys' 8.11 at the final siren. Collingwood now meet Geelong in the Qualifying Final.

At Carlton David Parkin has the Flag within reach in his first season as coach after today's win over Richmond gives his side the break.

Essendon, who today lost to Geelong, meet Fitzroy in the Elimination Final (→ 29/8/92).

Carlton's spirited win

Sept. 26. In the Carlton dressing room before the Grand Final, coach David Parkin had chalked on the blackboard 'Twenty players together working to capacity will win!'

In the Collingwood rooms is a picture of the 1979 Grand Final loss, torn in two. One half is defeated Magpies, the other jubilant Blues. A sign: 'This could be you.'

The tension was immense. Geoff Slattery wrote that it was like a 'tug of war between two computers, each programmed to resist. And resist'.

Coach Parkin said: 'Both sides were putting so much defensive pressure on each other, somebody was going to have to take a risk if the game was to be won.' Defenders Bruce Doull and Bill Picken were impregnable at either end.

Parkin made some moves, but in the third quarter it was Collingwood who made a decisive break, kicking five goals straight. The Magpies were 21 points in front.

But Carlton crept back a little way with two goals, Collingwood nine points up. Parkin at three-quarter time decided not to tear strips off the team. Instead he said Collingwood were tiring and that Carlton were fresher – and would win.

Mike Fitzpatrick, universally regarded as the player of the Finals, began to believe they could win.

And they did, by an unbelievable 20 points, 12.20 (92) to 10.12 (72).

At the end of the game Collingwood looked like the wrong half of the picture, and Peter Moore threw away his runner-up medal.

Carlton, however, were just delirious (→ 25/9/82).

Reliable Carlton halfback Peter McConville makes sure of the mark.

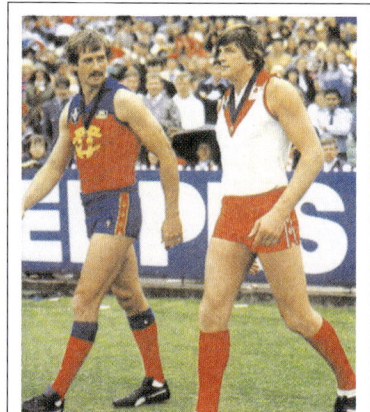

Joint Brownlow winners Bernie Quinlan and Barry Round.

1981 Statistics

Leading Goalkicker:
Michael Roach (Rich) 86
Brownlow Medallist:
Bernie Quinlan (Fitz), Barry Round (Syd).
Finals: Elimination Final Ess 13.16 (94) Fitz 16.13 (109); **Qualifying Final** Coll 13.20 (98) Geel 16.16 (112); **First Semi** Coll 19.19 (133) Fitz 19.18 (132); **Second Semi** Carl 16.17 (113) Geel 11.7 (73); **Preliminary Final** Geel 11.9 (75) Coll 12.10 (82) **Grand Final** Carl 12.20 (92) Coll 10.12 (72)

Ladder:	W	L	%	pts
Carl	17	5	130.3	68
Coll	17	5	122.6	68
Geel	16	6	129.8	64
Ess	16	6	127.6	64
Fitz	14	8	112.1	56
Haw	13	9	109.4	52
Rich	13	9	105.3	52
N. Melb	10	12	104.1	40
S. Melb	8	14	85.8	32
St K	5	17	85.2	20
Foots	2	20	65.8	8
Melb	1	21	63.5	4

All the Presidents' men

It was 1970 when Len Thompson had his first real brush with power in football. He was a young man then, already building a handsome reputation in the Victorian Football League as a strong ruckman with an outstanding career still in front of him. He was entitled to think, too, that he knew how to handle the rough stuff the game was capable of dishing out.

Football was, after all, hard on men like Thompson. They had to earn their keep. Opponents knew that if you could take a big man out of a game, the match was half won. In a physical war of attrition, the ruckman was always on the front line, taking the shots.

Thompson thought he knew a little about where the real power in football lay. That was, at least, just before the start of the 1970 season. He and his skipper at Collingwood, Des Tuddenham, became embroiled in a pay dispute with the club administration that saw the pair walk out, demanding a more generous return for the hours of toil and service they were putting in.

One day Thompson was pulled aside by the Collingwood President, Tom Sherrin.

'You know,' said Sherrin. 'We really don't have to negotiate with you at all.' 'Why's that?' asked Thompson.

'Because we own you Len,' replied Sherrin. 'We own you.'

Football has two histories. The first and most well known has been enacted on the many playing fields across the country. Out there, in the mud and cold of a winter afternoon, tales of triumph and despair occur each week.

The game's other history, however, is far more secretive. It has been played out in the boardrooms hovering over those very same playing fields since the game first began. And its participants, the Presidents who run the clubs and are ultimately responsible for their success or failure, compete with just as much vigour and tenacity as their players.

They are the men who have been the real power behind the game for much of this century. Like Tom Sherrin, most of them

have boasted strong views to match their personalities. And along the way they shaped and changed the game into what it is today.

One of the most outstanding of them, a man who set the benchmark for many of those who followed, was Sir Kenneth Luke. He had left school at the age of 14, shortly before the start of World War I, to become an engraver. By 1938 he had become President of Carlton. Here was a self-made man who knew what he wanted and was a firm believer in football's right to its own destiny.

In the early 1950s he saw a chance for Carlton to establish their home ground at Princes Park as the premier sporting venue in Victoria. Impatient with State Government inaction over preparations for the 1956 Olympic Games, he put together a plan that would see Princes Park become the major Olympics venue.

Only after it became clear that Luke was serious about his bid did the State Government move to upgrade the Melbourne Cricket Ground and make sure the Olympics were staged at the biggest arena in the State.

The experience set the scene for one of the biggest developments ever undertaken in the game's history: the establishment of VFL Park in Waverley. Luke became the VFL President in 1956 and was the driving force behind the League's decision to purchase 212 acres of prime market garden land out in the far-eastern suburbs of Melbourne. Tired of the interminable squabbles with the Melbourne Cricket Club over revenue from football matches played at the MCG, Luke decided football had a right to determine its own future.

But the mould for many of the modern-day businessmen and Presidents had been cast. There would be many incarnations, but one of them was George Harris. Many of Harris's critics found it fitting that he, too, hailed from Carlton, a club quick to establish close links with the business community. Harris would leave a vast

imprint on the game over three decades. In 1965 he was one of the driving forces behind Carlton's successful attempt to lure Ron Barassi from Melbourne to Princes Park. The Barassi coup was, for many, the true beginning of the modern era, where money became the prime mover in the football market.

Harris was a feisty combatant who demanded success. When the Blues lost the 1973 Grand Final to Richmond, a lot of sweet talking had to be done to dissuade him from lambasting the players in front of Sir Robert Menzies and his wife, Dame Pattie, at a hotel function after the game.

To the man in the outer, weren't Harris and others like him indicative of the changes sweeping the game into uncharted territory? If his name wasn't appearing on the front and back pages of newspapers for his views on football, he was there as a man caught up in a furore over attempts to secure overseas loan funds for the Australian Government. When he stood down in 1979 as President for the second time, just months after a memorable Premiership victory over Collingwood, it was with the usual flair, splitting the club and creating headlines.

But if Harris was gone, a whole tribe of similar men had replaced him. There were few shrinking violets heading VFL clubs by the time the 1980s began. At North

Melbourne, Bob Ansett had assumed the helm, desperate for the club to regain the influence and success set up by Allen Aylett.

At St Kilda there was Lindsay Fox, a former club ruckman who had made his fortune in the rough and tumble of the trucking industry. By 1983 Fox would have an enormous impact on the game as the driving force behind the Silvio Foschini court case that would see the VFL's player rules declared invalid.

The names would change down the years. John Elliott (Carlton), Geoffrey Edelsten (Sydney Swans) and Ranald Macdonald (Collingwood) were just a handful of many who swept into the game from the business world.

Elliott planned in the mid-1980s to form a breakaway competition because he was unhappy with the VFL. Macdonald swept to power at Collingwood with an American presidential-style campaign, but fell short of his ambition to capture a Premiership. Geoffrey Edelsten became the first private owner of a League club.

But why were these men attracted to the game, apart from the usual passion for the sport they shared with millions of other Australians? Certainly, the presence at a club of a man with high standing in the corporate world would inevitably help attract more sponsorship dollars.

But what was in it for the men themselves? The game couldn't offer them money. It could, however, offer them more prestige and a permanent place in football's history. You could be the managing director of one of the country's largest companies. You could control products and be responsible for the incomes of thousands of Australian families. But nothing like that could afford you the sort of status that went with winning a Premiership Flag.

Football in the modern era had been forced to confront the raw truth that it was now an industry. A new style of administration was required. The Presidents became the men who took care of business.

Garry Linnell

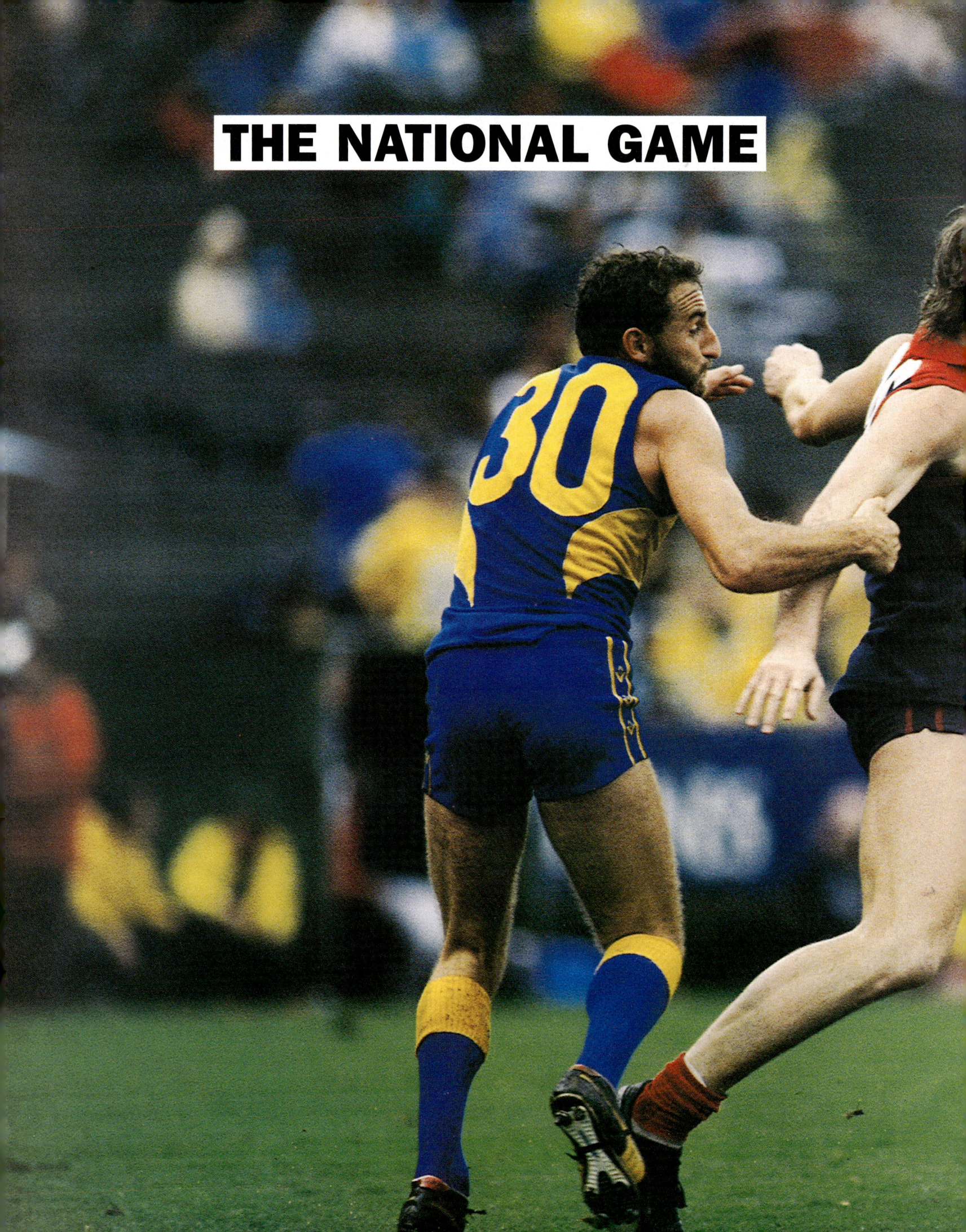

THE NATIONAL GAME

The national game goes nationwide

A snapshot of football at the beginning of the 1980s might begin with the end of the 1970s.

One picture is Alex Jesaulenko, muddy, ankle injured, being carried off the MCG in the 1979 Grand Final. Pesky Collingwood have been disposed of in traditional fashion by Carlton.

There were 12 clubs in the Victorian Football League then, and there were six games played in Melbourne and Geelong on Saturday afternoons. There was a Final Five, but that had been introduced in 1972, so it was already a 'tradition', giving the opportunity for an outbreak of 'eliminitis' for the fifth-finishing team.

By the end of the 1980s there were 14 teams with three from interstate, a VFL Commission, games played at night and on Sundays. In 1988 the West Coast Eagles made the Finals for the first time.

This was the national game with a vengeance. In 1979 the VFL was run as it had always been by men who had graduated from the ranks such as the dry-witted Collingwood full-back Jack Hamilton. The President was North's champion rover, and dentist, Allen Aylett, who had something of an evangelist's vision of where the game might go.

But the creative tension in administration was, following the tradition, between the League administration and the clubs – the Directors of the League, usually the Presidents, and the men on the ground, the Secretaries. Graeme Richmond may not have been Secretary at Richmond by the end of the 70s but his spirit and methods surely lived on.

At Carlton George Harris, the quintessential 70s President, was back in the saddle, but the new brand of 80s President was waiting at the gate – Ian Rice.

Cut to a scene at Princes Park, in February 1980. A crowd has assembled in front of the Carlton Social Club to listen to Carlton stalwarts and players explain to members why President George Harris had departed.

Financial losses by non-football business enterprises, they

said. And worse, why captain-coach and legend Alex Jesaulenko had followed him. Misguided mateship, they said.

Explanations were thin on the Princes Park turf, but one thing was clear and that was that the 70s were over, and something new was beginning. It was football in the 80s.

Perhaps the 70s had another year to run. Over at Richmond, they forgot to tell the players and coach Tony Jewell. The 1980 Richmond side played as if it was 1973, and from the footy point of view it looked as if they somehow represented what was to come on the field.

Scribes talked of new eras, not a decade-long Premiership hangover. They exulted in the football style of a bygone age, and in the unlikely form of Kevin Bartlett, who turned from old chook to spring chicken with a 21-goal Finals series.

The team had a full-forward in Michael Roach, a centre-half-forward in David Cloke, a big mobile ruckman in Mark Lee and zippy small men to bang the ball forward – Geoff Raines, Bryan Wood, Dale Weightman, Mervyn Keane – and of course old Hungry himself, Kevin Bartlett. It even had the dourest back pocket since Kevin Sheedy and Michael Malthouse.

This was the 1973-74 Tigers with new legs. But the next year it wasn't Richmond who continued the football era – but Carlton, under the first mini-entrepreneur President Ian Rice, and ex-Hawk David Parkin as coach, who won back-to-back Flags in 1981 and 1982 playing what proved to be 80s football.

That might be characterised as pressure, possession and power. The characteristic players in the Carlton Premierships of these years were Wayne Johnston, Mike Fitzpatrick, Bruce Doull, Peter Bosustow and Ken Hunter. Professional big occasion players with a touch of the desperado.

By the end of 1983 a new kind of President was sworn in at Carlton. This was a genuine man of the 80s, the beer baron, and

corporate takeover king, John Elliott. One of the maxi-entrepreneurs, used to success and quick decision-making.

That meant that by the end of 1985 the passionate Parkin was out, destined for a mellowing period at Fitzroy, and Robert Walls, the thinking man's coach, was in, and Carlton went on another buying spree intended to buy another Premiership.

In came champion Croweaters Stephen Kernahan, Craig Bradley and Peter Motley (tragically injured in a car accident in 1987) to start playing in 1986. Parkin perhaps had worn out his message with the players, but fifth place in 1985 was, in any event, not good enough.

At Richmond the new broom swept in the biggest entrepreneur of all. Alan Bond became President in 1986, having reached the height of his sporting fame as winner of the America's Cup. But this did nothing to alleviate the on-field gloom of the Tigers, and 'Bondy' soon found that he didn't have the time as doomsday, the Crash of '87, approached. He was gone having never really arrived, as were the Tigers for the rest of the decade.

Football itself was on something of an ebb tide as the seasons passed. Total attendances at home-and-away matches were below three million in 1983-1987, years which coincide with the rise to dominance of the Hawthorn

machine and the efficient, even great, but colourless Essendon sides of 1984 and 1985.

But there were plenty of flamboyant Hawthorn players in those incredibly successful years – love them or be bored by them. As one blonde star faded with Peter Knights, another rose in Dermott Brereton. John Platten arrived from SA in 1986 , Robert DiPierdomenico provided a memory of Kennedy's Commandos of old, the backline, typically with Kelvin Moore or Chris Langford at full-back, Gary Ayres the dual Norm Smith Medal winner, had a commanding strength. And the consummate full-forward Jason Dunstall was there to finish off most attacks.

It was this team and style of play that endured through the 80s, and further, and which, despite the occasional interpolation of Essendon and Carlton, dominated the decade. Seven Grand Finals in a row, 1983-1989 is a record which speaks for itself.

At Essendon, Kevin Sheedy was appointed coach in 1981, and lasted the decade, becoming the dean of coaches, an imaginative and influential thinker about the game, but only two Flags, with, pound for pound, probably the two best sides of the era – the 1984 and 1985 teams with Simon Madden, Tim Watson, Mark Harvey, Terry Daniher and the under-sung Leon Baker.

And what of Collingwood? The decade began with two (more) Grand Final losses, and the sacking of Tom Hafey as coach in 1982. After that the on-field affairs of the club got worse, with a 12th place in 1987. A bizarre new broom had swept through the administration of the club, in the form of Ranald McDonald and the New Magpies – but this just proved that Collingwood was among the many things not improved by the principles of the 80s entrepreneurs and the view that Collingwood just had a 'marketing problem'. It had a football problem.

Leigh Matthews, taking over as coach after the new broom had swept on, had a quick effect – the

Magpies back in the Finals in 1988 and 1989 – and of course creating new legends in 1990.

Matthews himself was a cause and an effect of the game's problems in the mid-80s, by being central to Hawthorn's success, and then in an aberrant moment in 1985 swinging an arm at Neville Bruns. The conviction, deregistration and appeal were part of the intrusion of the law on to the football field.

As were the moments of idiocy from Mark Jackson, and flashes of despair from Robert Muir.

Fortunately the game passed on from this kind of play, but the other legal issues involved in player transfers, restraint of trade and related issues did not – at least until the institution of the national draft, contracts and the salary cap in the mid 80s.

This took a lot of heat out of the legal issues while not eliminating them entirely. It was curious to see the great free enterprise Presidents grudgingly buckling under to 'football socialism'.

While the football was played season after season, the larger game was changing. It was felt by VFL management that the game should become truly national, and that there should be fewer teams in Melbourne.

The beginning of the national push was shifting South Melbourne home games to Sydney in 1982 where they promptly became the Sydney Swans, seeking a new supporter base. South Melbourne had lost a lot of their support in the local area, had not played in a Grand Final since 1945 and, despite developing great champions such as Bob Skilton, were not competitive.

Given what happened with Footscray and Fitzroy at the end of the decade, South Melbourne went quietly. In Sydney they were bought by the medical entrepreneur Dr Geoffrey Edelsten and became the first privately owned VFL club. With Tom Hafey as coach, and a few sensational players on the SCG such as Greg Williams and Warwick Capper they made the Finals in 1986 and 1987.

The financial position of Sydney, however, was precarious beyond decade's end and, despite

every injection of VFL cash, player concessions and administrators, the harbour city has proved to be intractable.

The question of what to do about South Melbourne (and the other less successful clubs) was one thing, but whether football should have been expanded to Sydney first was another.

The VFL became the VFL Commission in 1984 with powers to plan and administer the game except for some reserved functions such as admission of new clubs. Here a substantial majority of clubs have to agree. West Coast and Brisbane were admitted in 1986, and played their first games in 1987.

While taking some time to find their feet, West Coast proved that there is something in the water in Perth by winning 11 games, and threatening the stability of the competition by promising to be too good. West Coast, after local boys Ron Alexander and John Todd had been less than successful, finally got tough and appointed Michael Malthouse as coach – but that wasn't until 1990.

There was no question that we now had a national competition, but we still wondered how many teams could be competitive and financially viable in Melbourne.

After a VFL Seminar in 1989 about the future of the game, the question of merging Melbourne clubs became a matter of concern.

At the end of the year it seemed as if there was going to be a forced, or encouraged, merger bet-

ween Footscray and Fitzroy.

But it has to be said that, as the national game played by teams representing a number of different local football communities, the 80s gave no help to those who want to end that relationship.

Local football communities where there is a relationship still in existence will do almost anything to keep their team in their own colours. Just as the wider community would do almost anything to keep the game at the shrine of football, the MCG.

This was the lesson of the Footscray contretemps. It had ramifications for the VFL as it headed into its tenth decade as the most important social and political institution in Melbourne. While the goal posts had in fact shifted in favour of a strong national competition, that is, one that eventually would have at least one competitive team in each mainland capital city, there was also a view that Melbourne had such a local tradition and commitment to football that no more teams would be forced out of the competition.

The VFL might well raise the bar for teams to qualify to stay in, but that would be a way of proving that these clubs had the commitment.

That was how matters stood at the end of the 80s. The VFL had re-established its place, despite groans from the Outer, as the biggest sports entertainment business in the country, at the same time as we witnessed a flowering of the game of football itself towards the end of the decade.

Going to the footy had changed from the Saturday afternoon tradition to one that involved nights and TV, and Sundays and Fridays – there was simply more of it.

Tactics had become more sophisticated, whether that meant using the interchange Sheedy style so he had a total team of 20 on and off the bench, to Robert Walls' development of 'dead ball' situations – the 'huddle' and its consequence, the 'flood' at kick offs.

Rules altered to cope with other tactics – the Peter Moore/Gary Dempsey wrestling matches of 1979 saw the centre

line across the centre circle making ruckmen jump at each other. Sheedy's sophisticated time-wasting tactics, scragging and not giving the ball back, giving his players time to 'man up' were met with the 50-metre penalty.

The great players of the decade were remarkable not so much because they had endured, but because they were footballers whose exquisite skills with body and ball were coupled with a passionate commitment and a physicality that would be outstanding in any era.

The Carlton players Bruce Doull, Wayne Johnston, Mike Fitzpatrick, Ken Hunter, Hawthorn's Leigh Matthews, John Platten, Michael Tuck, Chris Langford, Gary Ayres and Jason Dunstall, Essendon's Simon Madden, Tim Watson, Mark Harvey, Terry Daniher, – plus Fitzroy's Bernie Quinlan, Melbourne's Robert Flower and Sydney's Greg Williams – some footballers, in any decade.

Plus one other, Gary Ablett. Fittingly Ablett reached his first peak as one of the game's immortals in the 1989 Finals series, particularly in the Grand Final. His nine- goal effort nearly stole the unpinchable game from Hawthorn.

Geelong finished just a kick short, and anyone who was at the game knows that if it had gone one minute longer Ablett would have at least kicked a goal to level the scores. Two minutes and he would have used his unparalleled skills and unrivalled willpower to change the course of football.

That he didn't is a kind of tragedy for Geelong fans but, as they say in the classics, it was extraordinarily good for football.

Jezza left the ground in 1979 and soon became a Saint. Ablett left the ground in 1989 as something even more wonderful, masquerading as a mere footballer.

As the barrackers looked into the footy future after that great day at the sacred turf, they knew that no matter what else happened in Australia in the fag end of the twentieth century, they were part of the greatest show on earth, again. The Australian national game.

Garrie Hutchinson

March 25. New $4 million colour scoreboard at the MCG.

March 27. The umpires fail to hear the siren, and an unearned point gives Carlton a draw against Fitzroy, 16.17 (113) to 17.11 (113).

April 7. VFL appoints Alan Schwab as Assistant General Manager to Jack Hamilton. He will gradually 'fade' from Sydney (→ 18/6/93).

April 12. Richmond kick their highest score against Essendon, 25.22 (172) to 16.14 (110). Coach Francis Bourke says he was tearing his hair out at the Tigers' mistakes (→ 18/6/83).

April 14. Footscray President Dr Tony Capes denies that coach Royce Hart's job is on the line, but calls a crisis meeting of players.

April 27. A study considers St Kilda sharing the SCG and Moorabbin with South Melbourne, as dual home grounds.

May 18. Kevin Bartlett faces his first striking charge at the VFL Tribunal in 369 games. He is cleared.

June 3. Essendon's Neale Daniher, who has not played a game this season and is not expected to play for 12 months, resigns as captain.

June 11. Footscray appoint Ian 'Bluey' Hampshire as coach.

June 18. Essendon great, Bill Hutchison dies after a short illness.

June 20. The Sydney Swans kick their highest score against St Kilda, 30.19 (199) to 15.13 (103), at the SCG (→ 16/5/93).

June 26. After Hawthorn's defeat of Carlton, 17.14 (116) to 12.10 (82), coach Allan Jeans says: 'You win in most positions, you make the least number of mistakes, and you win the game. That's football' (→ 10/6/85).

July 20. The Swans win the Night Flag, defeating North 13.12 (90) to 8.10 (58).

Debuts
Gary Ablett (Haw)
Dermott Brereton (Haw)
Jim Krakouer (N. Melb)
Phil Krakouer (N. Melb)
Richard Osborne (Fitz)
Gary Pert (Fitz)
Maurice Rioli (Rich)
Paul Roos (Fitz)

Retirements
Malcolm Blight (N. Melb)
Barry Breen (St K)

It's a garden party for Swans in Sydney

Happy Swans Barry Round and Max Kruse enjoy their win.

The Swans players are launched in style at the Sydney Opera House.

March 28. A host of happy football fans turned out at the wet Sydney Cricket Ground to watch the Swans play their first game at their new home, and to thrill to their win over Melbourne, 20.17 (137) to 16.12 (108). South President Bill Collins, best known as a racing broadcaster, said he would have been happy with a 'half a point win'.

Tens of thousands watched the telecast in Melbourne, the first of six $10,000 winner-take-all affairs, also for Premiership points, sponsored by Channel Seven.

After all the hoopla of the Swans move north and their Opera House introduction to Sydney, a win was a great relief to the League and the new administration. There must have been some bitter-sweet satisfaction to the old South supporters, left behind in Melbourne.

Their team retain the name South Melbourne for now, but will be the Sydney Swans within months.

Swans administrator Alan Schwab said: 'South could be a great club in this city if everything is done the right way from now on.'

Bob Hawke was presented with his No. 1 ticket at No. 1 guernsey wearer Lady Fairfax's harbourside mansion 'Fairview', where she gave a garden party.

Swans captain Barry Round eyed the tables groaning with oysters and declared: 'It sure beats pies and sauce in the South rooms.'

Next week it's back to the grindstone with a game against North – at Arden Street (→ 1/7/84).

Another Ablett drops in on the Hawks from Drouin

Geoff Ablett wins footballers' sprint.

April 3. Gary Ablett, priority recruit for Hawthorn, made a fine start to his VFL career in a win over Geelong today, 13.19 (97) to 11.12 (78). Gary Ablett joined his brother Geoff in the Hawks' line-up.

Coming off the interchange bench in the second round on a wet afternoon at Princes Park, Ablett kicked 1.1, took two good marks and executed five kicks and one handball.

Running out beside Leigh Matthews, Ablett was later to say: 'It took some time for me to really believe that I was good enough to play football alongside that man.'

Ablett had been recruited from Drouin, but stood out last year with a back injury. This year he only agreed to move a week before the season began (→ 1/3/83).

Gary Ablett: new face at Hawthorn.

Krakouer brothers show footy magic

April 3. The Swans flew back from last week's Sydney excitement, and faced a team of hungry Kangaroos in the Arden Street paddock. It was not a happy day for the visitors. They were beaten by 40 points, 24.13 (157) to 16.21 (117), and by two Krakouer brothers who cut holes in the Swans' defence.

Phil and Jim Krakouer, the two young Aboriginal footballers from WA, kicked seven goals between them, and had a hand or a foot in about 13 others.

In two games the Krakouers have had a remarkable impact. They have their own unique style of play, and seem to have a kind of location-finding device, which guides passes between them and also to team-mates.

Older brother Jim is the slighter of the two, and has a mindspinning array of pirouettes and blind turns, as well as a lot of that striding, long-kicking WA style. He said: 'Yeah, we played all right together.'

Phil, a chubbier, more languid exponent of the left-foot game, kicks bullet passes, somehow off his wrong foot, that go exactly where he wants them.

Malcolm Blight, himself no shrinking violet when it comes to doing the impossible, kicked six goals, but had to dip his lid to the new boys from the West.

The magical Krakouer boys.

Wacko Jacko proves a handful for two Ronnies

Jacko does a balancing act.

He gets a serve from Ron Barassi.

May 24. Melbourne full-forward Mark Jackson was today suspended for two matches after the VFL Tribunal was told he had been struck in the testicles during a game against Essendon on Saturday.

Jackson, 22, said that when standing in the goal square he felt a whack on the head and a blow to his left testicle.

'It hurt quite a bit and I was bitterly upset,' he said.

Jackson, who was recently suspended for two matches for striking, said he was not guilty of striking

Essendon acting captain Ron Andrews with a clenched fist.

Thumping the Tribunal table, Jackson said: 'If you are going to hit someone, you don't muck around ... I'm telling you my way (what happened).

'I thought it degrading. I took a swipe and missed ... after a second's delay, he (Andrews) fell on the ground. I stood over him, waiting for him to get up.'

Andrews told an 80-minute hearing that there had been a lot of jostling, shoving and pushing but

And 'hits' a smiling Andrews.

Jackson had not hit him in the face. He also denied hitting Jackson, in either the face or the groin area.

Jackson, who was an obvious victim of verbal abuse from his coach Ron Barassi during the game, said he had acted under extreme provocation.

He said his nose had been broken in three places at the five-minute mark of the first quarter. (Essendon officials stated after the game on Saturday that another of their players had accidentally collided with Jackson.)

Two-can limit a sobering law

May 5. The VFL has taken a strong measure to ensure greater sobriety at matches by introducing a two-can limit on fans and banning them from bringing in alcohol.

A supporter, Robert Dickson, 27, died a month after being hit on the head while protecting his six-year-old son during a fight at the Carlton and Fitzroy game at Princes Park.

There has since been a public outcry over drunken violence at football.

The two-can rule can be traced to military tradition and is still in force with the Australian Navy at sea and the Army.

Advertisements have warned fans that containers will be searched at grounds and the limit is two small opened cans per purchase.

Easter Monday a bumper football day

April 12. On a brilliant Easter Monday 90,564 people packed the MCG to see Richmond kick their highest ever score against Essendon, 25.22 (172), to 16.14 (110) for a 62-point win. This was only the fourth time in home-and-away history that such a crowd had been attracted. They saw a quality performance, as the Tigers' final quarter was devastating.

The split round crowd total of 213,199 was the third highest recorded and today's 143-point win by Hawthorn over Footscray was their highest margin since beating Geelong by 118 points seven years ago.

Geelong, meanwhile, had their best win over Melbourne, 21.12 (138) to 5.16 (46) a 92-point victory, eclipsing by 4 points the 1930 margin (→ 10/6/89).

New members for Sacked Coaches Club

June 3. Footscray coach Royce Hart today joined last week's new member of the Sacked Coaches Club, Tom Hafey.

Hart was 'demoted' to Under 19's coach after just eight wins from 54 games, thus saving the club an estimated $90,000 payout.

Coach since 1980, Hart played 187 games for Richmond, kicking 366 goals and representing Victoria 11 times. Under him, the Bulldogs have had only eight wins in 53 games.

Tom Hafey was sacked last week after Collingwood had won just one game and lost nine this season. He also took the Magpies to losses in four of the past five Grand Finals. He was replaced for this season by assistant Mick Erwin (→ 16/9).

Mickey Conlan an amazing dasher

July 24. Not once, but five times, Mick Conlan showed his explosive qualities today when he burst through powerfully for Fitzroy, his solo efforts helping to demoralise Hawthorn at VFL Park.

Barrel-chested Conlan's strength was shown in the second quarter when he seized the ball near the half-back line and began an amazing charge, shrugging off tackles, weaving and bouncing the ball until he passed accurately to the injured Matthew Rendell who goaled.

Fitzroy kicked 27.8 (170) to 18.15 (123) (→4/4/94).

Blight tops season with ton of goals

Sept. 11. Champion North Melbourne forward Malcolm Blight became North's second leading VFL goalkicker after finishing the season with 103 goals today.

For 32-year-old Blight the milestone was at least some consolation for North Melbourne's 52-point loss to Hawthorn in the First Semi-final at the MCG.

The former North Melbourne captain-coach, and Brownlow Medallist, joins South Melbourne's Bob Pratt (1935), and Essendon's John Coleman (1952) and North's Doug Wade (1974) in bagging 103 goals in a season.

Blight: more football honours.

Silvertail 'New Magpies' take over

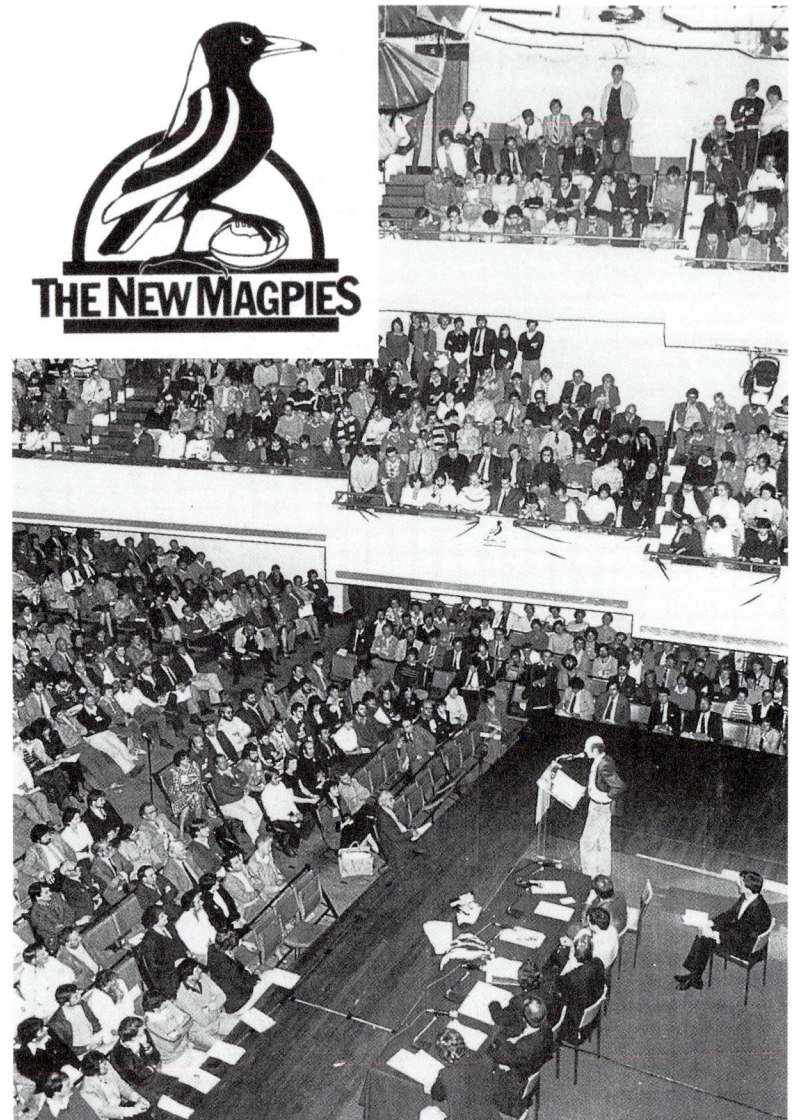

The new Magpie President, Ranald Macdonald, about to address the faithful.

Sept. 16. Media chief Ranald Macdonald today swept into power at Collingwood, following the sacking of coach Tom Hafey and months of dissension.

Macdonald urged supporters not to expect too much too soon. His New Magpies ticket consists of four Woodsmen business types and three ex-footballers: Allan McAlister, Bill Weston, Ian McPherson, Len Thompson, Terry Waters and Brian McKenzie.

McKenzie had been absent for much of the campaign, however, and was criticised for resigning from the Reserves Committee to join the ticket, while Waters had been involved in a row over the captaincy in 1971.

Thompson was described by immediate past President John Hickey as someone who 'has had several opportunities to win a Premiership for Collingwood, but didn't.'

Macdonald, publisher of *The Age* newspaper and an adopted descendant of its founder, David Syme, was seen as having style, fame and media access. His background of Geelong Grammar and Cambridge University, hence his well-rounded vowels, was thought to be of some appeal to Collingwood's more affluent members.

At a rally at Dallas Brooks Hall last month, lawyer David Galbally castigated the old Committee for lack of planning, tightfistedness, lack of recruiting, coddling players and sacking Hafey.

Now the whole committee is gone in the first populist election for 20 years (→14/4/86).

Young Dermott in promising debut

Sept. 11. First game player Dermott Brereton was a hero of today's First Semi-final win by Hawthorn over North Melbourne at the MCG, 24.22 (166) to 18.6 (114).

Before the game, Hawks star Leigh Matthews told 18-year-old Brereton: 'Sometimes young players do not like to get in other players' way. So I told Dermott, "If you see the ball, go and get it".'

Coach Allan Jeans refused to allow Brereton to be interviewed, saying an interview ban during the Finals was also in force at Richmond. (→16/9/89).

Young Brian's life enhanced by win

Sept. 20. Melbourne centreman Brian Wilson today became the third Footscray reject in two years to win the Brownlow Medal. And he did so at his third VFL club in four years.

Former Bulldogs Bernie Quinlan, now of Fitzroy, and Barry Round of the Swans, shared the medal last year.

Wilson, 20, polled 23 votes to beat former North team-mate Ross Glendinning, 18 votes, with Hawks Leigh Matthews and Terry Wallace on 17. Wilson is the first Melbourne player to win the Brownlow since Don Cordner in 1946.

Brian Wilson: third club lucky.

Johnston dominates Blues Grand Final win

Wayne Johnston savours the victory.

1982 Statistics

Leading Goalkicker:
Malcolm Blight (N. Melb) 103
Brownlow Medallist:
Brian Wilson (Melb)
Finals: Elimination Final Ess
16.19 (115) N. Melb 19.14 (128)
Qualifying Final Haw 16.9 (105)
Carl 25.13 (163); **First Semi-final**
Haw 24.22 (166) N. Melb 18.6
(114); **Second Semi-final** Rich
16.17 (113) Carl 13.12 (90); **Preli-
minary Final** Carl 13.16 (94) Haw
8.15 (63); **Grand Final** Rich 12.13
(85) Carl 14.19 (103)

Ladder:	W	L	D	%	pts
Rich	18	4		126.2	72
Haw	17	5		131.6	68
Carl	16	5	1	127.5	66
Ess	16	6		125.2	64
N. Melb	14	8		109.6	56
Fitz	12	9	1	102.5	50
Syd	12	10		103.3	48
Melb	8	14		90.4	32
Geel	7	15		90.4	28
Coll	4	18		85.5	16
St K	4	18		71.7	16
Foots	3	19		68.1	12

Sept. 25. With hindsight, and after all the adventures of this spectacular Grand Final, Wayne Johnston had won the game in the first 90 seconds.

That was where ferocious aggression at the ball showed Richmond which team had their mind on the job, and that it was some other Carlton which had been eaten alive in the Second Semi.

Johnston kicked a goal and nearly knocked over the goal post after a handball from Mark Maclure. He tackled Alan Martello in the goal square so hard that the ball popped out to Wayne Harmes for a goal.

Then he caused a bit of mayhem in the centre square, Fitzpatrick kicking off the ground to Ashman in the goal square ... and Carlton were 18 points up after five minutes.

A lot more went on. The elegant and courageous Ken Hunter was knocked out cold by Jim Jess, a fair bump. Kevin Bartlett threatened a bit of his 1980 magic. The wonderful Maurice Rioli strode the turf like a champion racehorse. And in time-on Richmond were in front. Then Ross Ditchburn was ko'ed – and guess-who took the kick. Johnston's second goal put the Blues four points up at quarter time.

Towards the end of the second quarter Richmond were 18 points ahead after three Cloke goals, but no one felt they had the match won.

As it came to pass, Carlton kicked five goals to none in the third. A plump streaker tried to molest that heroic stoic Bruce Doull. Mike Fitzpatrick kicked two goals, proving to be the decisive big man in yet another Grand Final. Peter Bosustow did one or two things with body and ball that no one else has ever done. Carlton 17 points up.

There were more twists in the Tigers' tale. Bartlett and Jess goaled, and then Jess had a potential handball to a certain goal levitated away from him by the magician Doull. Then a Johnston tackle started a sparkling exchange of passes down the ground and Bosustow goaled. And that was more or less it.

Johnston was the dominator, Fitzpatrick the perpetrator for the winners and Maurice Rioli the cool operator for the losers. He also won the Norm Smith Medal. Final score: Carlton 14.19 (103) to Richmond 12.13 (85) (→ 26/9/87).

The ever-reliable fist of Carlton's Bruce Doull upsets David Cloke's mark.

The essence of the game is conveyed by Leunig on Grand Final morning.

Ablett and Moore are on the move

April 1. Stars Gary Ablett and Peter Moore are on the move.

Ablett has had difficulty adapting to life in Melbourne, and with Hawthorn. When he failed to attend pre-season training he was fined $500 and the Board sought an indefinite suspension.

Now he has gone to play in the Ovens and Murray League.

Meanwhile, Collingwood rejected Moore's application to transfer to Melbourne because Moore is only 25, Magpie captain and a Brownlow Medallist. But Moore has gone to the Supreme Court claiming restraint of trade (→9/5/86).

Ross Oakley goes to Board of VFL

Aug. 12. Ross Oakley, former St Kilda wingman and rover, will succeed Ron Cook as Hawthorn's representative on the VFL Board.

Oakley played 62 games for the Saints between 1962 and 1966, kicking 38 goals. In 1965 he missed the Grand Final and in 1966 he missed both the Preliminary Final and Grand Final, due to knee injuries. Knee problems forced him out of the game in 1967 at the age of 24.

He is now managing director of the insurance firm AAMI Ltd.

Oakley coached Old Collegians and joined the Hawthorn Committee two years ago.

Brewery owner new Blues President

Sept. 30. Gung ho businessman John Dorman Elliott has been elected President of Carlton. And he has started in typical blunt style.

'Fighting for what would have been our third successive Premiership, we gave way to a malaise of complacency,' he said in the club's annual report. 'We failed to remember how hard it is to stay at the top.'

Elliott is best known for having taken over a small Tasmanian jam maker, Henry Jones IXL, and using it to power his way into control of the massive pastoral and brewing company, Elders IXL.

Foschini runs out on day of clearance drama

Man in the middle of a clearance row, Silvio Foschini, leaves the Court.

April 24. Swans coach Ricky Quade today consulted a barrister before launching into a speech following his team's defeat of St Kilda at the Sydney Cricket Ground.

'We won on the ground and all their lawyers can't take the four points from us,' Quade said. 'It's a shame football has come to this.'

Quade was referring to the defection of Paul Morwood and Silvio Foschini to St Kilda.

He said today's win had been anticipated since St Kilda's raid on Swans players in November.

Last week Morwood played for the Saints although, according to the League, still a Swan. St Kilda President Lindsay Fox and Foschini last month won a Supreme Court ruling declaring League clearance rules invalid and a restraint of trade.

Fox and other Saints officials were snubbed today, being served pies while Swans guests dined on rack of lamb and wine.

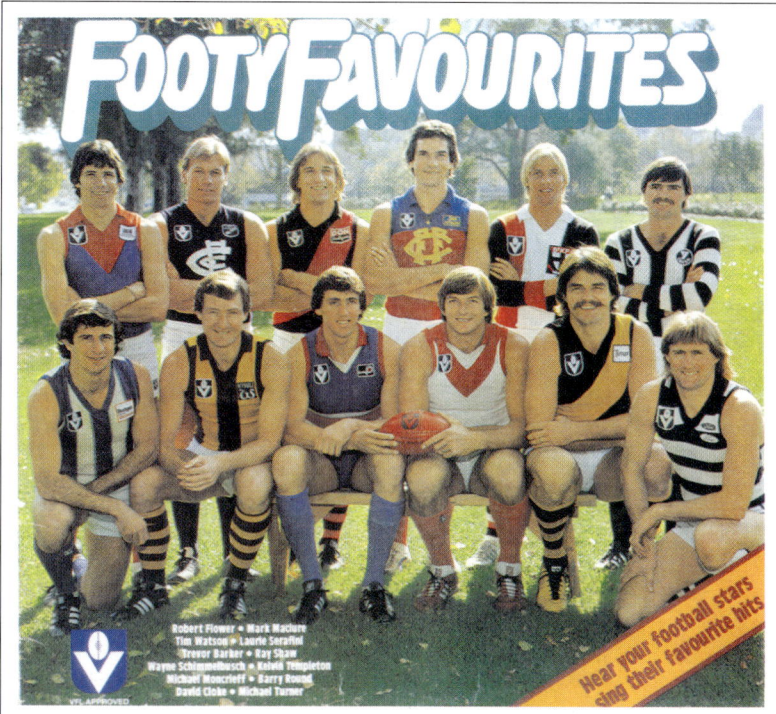

The song stranglers. Men to admire sing songs to hate forever.

Bartlett still hungry after 400 games

Aug. 6. Little has been left for Richmond to celebrate this season except today's 400th game by the great Kevin Bartlett.

Bartlett, 36, has been the subject of great fanfare and 81,966 were at the MCG today to see him turn out against Collingwood.

Like the rest of the season this, too, was a disappointment for the Tigers, who lost 13.11 (89) to 11.13 (79).

Tonight there was a party for Bartlett at his Glen Waverley home and tomorrow there'll be a Bartlett open day at the Punt Road Oval, where fans may have their photos taken with their hero, for $2 a pop.

Over a total of 19 injury-free seasons, beginning in 1965, Bartlett showed that he was a natural rover, with a lot of courage, skills and pace, married to a remarkable ability to read the play, and to stay out of trouble.

His nickname of 'Hungry' arose because, it was said, he would rather shoot at goal from 50 metres than pass to a team-mate.

Every VFL honour has come his way, except winning the Brownlow Medal. Richmond's best and fairest five times, leading goalkicker three times and captain of the 1979 Tigers, he captained Victoria in 1980 and represented the State 20 times.

Playing in five Premiership sides, he kicked seven goals in the 1980 Grand Final win over Collingwood, winning the Norm Smith Medal (→1/9/90).

Bartlett: still going strong.

Robert Flower blooms for Demons

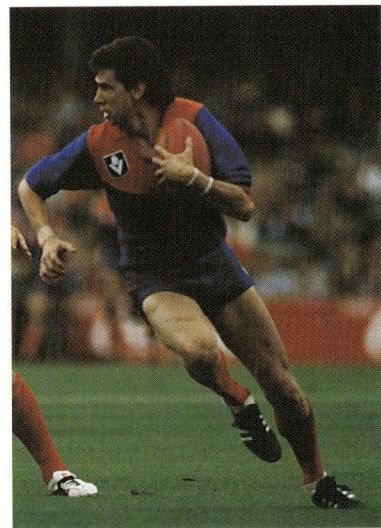

Robbie Flower: 53 disposals.

June 18. Robert Flower showed how the game should be played when he captained Melbourne to their 14-point win over Richmond at the MCG today.

Although on the wing, he roamed widely from the halfback line to half-forward and the centre, picking up marks, kicks and handballs.

He had 22 kicks, 15 marks, 16 handballs, two goals and two behinds, showing that even after a decade with the Demons he is, pound for pound, probably the finest footballer of the last 10 years.

Coach Ron Barassi said of Flower's match: 'A fantastic game, close to the best I've seen him play, including the games I've coached against him.'

Warming the sets

Aug. 5. In the first VFL game for Premiership points to be played under lights since Geelong met Essendon in Brisbane in 1952, Sydney succumbed to Geelong at the SCG.

Reduced to just 15 able-bodied players, the Swans kicked 5.10 in the last three quarters against 16.16. Five Swans were badly hurt.

In a match that had many spiteful moments, the Swans could not withstand Geelong's pressure, conceding seven goals in the last 11 minutes, to lose 10.15 (75) to 20.21 (141). Geelong's unlikely hero was teenage ruckman Damian Bourke who starred against Barry Round.

Superboot hotter than briquette

Aug. 20. Fitzroy's Bernie Quinlan booted his 100th goal for the season today.

But he took the whole match to do it at the Junction Oval, where Collingwood could not afford to lose a vital round but did. Fitzroy bolted away with a nine-goal final term to win 19.13 (127) to 7.21 (63).

Quinlan started the day on 98 goals and showed what a superb player he is, even at 32.

In his 177 games at Footscray between 1969 and 1977 he kicked 239 goals as star centre-half-forward, topping the goalkicking scores with 48 in 1971.

But his inconsistency caused concern and when money woes beset the club he was put on the market. Although Collingwood seemed likely to get him, once again they botched the deal and Fitzroy secured his signature.

Quinlan could have made all the difference to the Magpies' drive for a Flag and the ineptitude shown was among the circumstances that led to the sacking of coach Tom Hafey and then the whole administration.

At Fitzroy he reached superstar status, sharing the Brownlow with his mate Barry Round in 1981. He was also runner-up for his club's best and fairest that year, a position he won in three successive years.

Moved to full-forward after problems with both his Achilles tendon and his knee, he has become the greatest goalkicker in the League (→3/9/84).

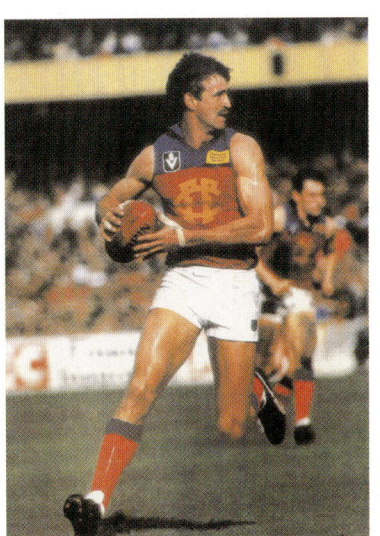

Quinlan: fired up at Fitzroy.

Ross Glendinning a cool champion

Glendinning: always in command.

Sept. 19. North Melbourne champion Ross Glendinning polled 24 votes to win the Brownlow Medal.

This put him one ahead of Richmond's Maurice Rioli, with Essendon ruckman Simon Madden third on 22.

Glendinning, a former Western Australian in his sixth year with the Roos, turned 27 on Saturday.

The win 'helped ease the pain' and disappointment of last Saturday's Preliminary Final loss to Essendon.

Glendinning is the third North player in 10 years to win the medal, but only the second Western Australian. He recalled tonight how David Robb, when North General Manager, flew to Perth in November, 1976, stepped off the plane and helped Glendinning drive his car across the Nullarbor.

Season of scores

June 18. Fitzroy replaced North Melbourne on top of the Ladder today with a massive win, 34.16 (220) to 10.10 (70).

North were reduced to a hapless, hopeless state as Fitzroy ran riot at the Junction Oval, restricting North to 2.7 in the last two quarters, while themselves banging on 21.8.

Ruckman Matt Rendell beat Gary Dempsey and kicked eight straight goals, while Laurie Serafini, Gary Pert and Graeme Hinchen played with style beyond their years. Richard Osborne, just turned 19, blotted out captain Wayne Schimmelbusch (→26/7/87).

Walls furious over a Bomber elbow

Bill Duckworth, Walls on boil.

Sept.10. Fitzroy coach Robert Walls was among the action today.

He remonstrated with a pack of Essendon players and officials about an incident involving his rover, Leon Harris, at the MCG.

The flare-up came just as players walked from the ground at half time. Walls said later that he would have let down his side if he had not done something.

His protest came, he said, after Harris was hit with an elbow in the face. 'I felt that for such a courageous and small player to be felled that way was not right' (→ 5/6/89).

1983 Statistics

Leading Goalkicker:
Bernie Quinlan (Fitz) 116
Brownlow Medallist:
Ross Glendinning (N. Melb)
Finals: Elimination Final Ess 17.12 (114) Carl 12.9 (81); **Qualifying Final** Haw 19.13 (127) Fitz 19.9 (123); **First Semi-final** Fitz 12.14 (86) Ess 16.13 (109); **Second Semi-final** N. Melb 6.12 (48) Haw 13.10 (88); **Preliminary Final** N. Melb 12.6 (78) Ess 25.14 (164); **Grand Final** Haw 20.20 (140) Ess 8.9 (57)

Ladder:	W	L	%	pts
N. Melb	16	6	127.8	64
Haw	15	7	128.7	60
Fitz	15	7	126.7	60
Ess	15	7	120.3	60
Carl	13	9	105.2	52
Coll	12	10	103.0	48
Foots	10	12	86.6	40
Melb	9	13	86.8	36
Geel	8	14	87.9	32
Rich	7	15	88.8	28
Syd	7	15	77.5	28
St K	5	17	78.6	20

Hawks' record win crashes Bombers

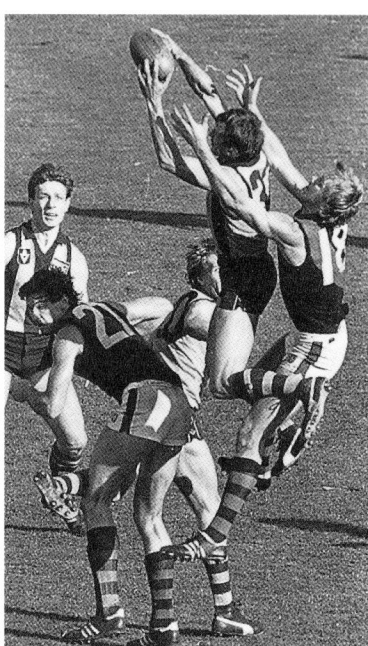

Colin Robertson takes a grab.

Robert 'Dipper' DiPierdomenico upended after grabbing a diving mark.

Sept. 24. In typically humble style coach Allan Jeans saluted his Hawthorn players after they sank Essendon by a VFL Grand Final record margin of 83 points today. The score was 20.20 (140) to 8.9 (57).

'You have played well,' he said, 'enjoy yourself, but above all, be modest. There are losers in the other room.'

Jeans, who felt the pain of Grand Finals losses against Essendon in 1965 and against Hawthorn in 1971, said he knew how Essendon coach Kevin Sheedy felt. 'I've been the lucky one today,' he said.

Earlier, Jeans wept and embraced his players in front of the members' stand at the last siren.

He later paid tribute to the character of players such as Leigh Matthews, Kelvin Moore and Peter Knights for making his job easier.

Matthews, the captain, was even able to joke about the result: 'In the last quarter we had so little to do we wrote a speech. There wasn't much tension and at the three-quarter time team huddle I saw we were 14.3 in front and I've never heard of a side kicking 15 goals in the last quarter.

'It was then I decided to compose a Premiership speech.'

The Hawks were supreme, never allowing Essendon into the game.

The previous worst Grand Final loss was Collingwood to Richmond by 81 points in 1980 (→ 27/9/86).

Hawthorn's brilliant forward Dermott Brereton marks in the goal square.

It's a funny game, football

The explosion of football during the mad 80s from an essentially suburban game into a national phenomenon dragged the subcultures of the game from the pubs and clubs through the back pages, to prime time television, and multiplied radio's long-time love affair with the game.

Stars of the field became stars of page, screen, and microphone. It had always been a natural for former players to become experts. But suddenly they were recruited not for their experience and knowledge about leather and liniment, but a capacity to drop a one-liner in the midst of serious footy conversation.

Didn't matter whether the line reached the heights of great comedy, it was the sheer incongruity that made football's huge audience laugh.

The rawness of the dressing room and the so-called sportsman's night came to prime time with Sam Newman and *The Footy Show* on Nine.

The loudness of a late night bar, a bar full of winners, came to radio with Rex Hunt.

But it wasn't all raw and crude and rude, and boys own stuff. *The Coodabeen Champions* took bar talk, and humour, and football values, and suburban traditions and that wonderful 'born in the outer' sense of the absurd, to the airwaves, and created much more than a cult following.

They worshipped the game through sharp humour, they did not feed off it as so many of the others did.

Seven, no doubt wary after providing 30 years of anything-goes zaniness with *World Of Sport*, and not a little arrogant (it, after all, had exclusive rights to televise the game itself), was late on the scene.

The Footy Show (Mark I) stole Sunday noon from Seven in 1993, and then stole prime time to boot the following season. *Four Quarters*, Seven's 1995 prime time response, was a year late on the scene, but quickly created its own brand of wholesome, caring, chat and panto.

The strangest thing about all

this new age humour was that such a passionate, committed, deadly serious game had become as much an arena for gags as for superlative sporting feats.

Maybe not so strange after all. It's a natural development of a great product that the more powerful and pervasive it becomes, the more people want to read about it, hear about it, and see it, and the more advertisers are prepared to underwrite the growth in its exposure, wherever that exposure might be.

There was good taste, and bad taste, and so much in between. John 'Sam' Newman, a devotee of Woody Allen, learnt his one-liners from the best of them. The Newman humour was always biting, cutting. Newman would search for a weakness in a quarry and, once that frailty was discovered, he would exploit it to the limit. He played the one-liners like he played the game itself.

He was a natural on the sportsman's night circuit, that vile excuse for grown men (rarely women) to gather in boozy groups, and listen to former champion sporting heroes recounting gross exaggerations about their careers and their foes.

The language was of the gutter. Anything went. Smart-arses in the audience were sought after, and belittled. Newman was a master of the circuit. No wonder.

Newman might be the star of *The Footy Show* but the format is one that is a natural for males, and a titillation for women. It is a camera in a dressing room. The humour of the closed culture of the club, of the team, of the Saturday body-cruncher is exposed. The excuse is football.

Did it work? Of course it did. *The Footy Show* was a ratings sensation. You could bet on 600,000 plus viewers on any Thursday night in Melbourne. Nothing on Football's sub-culture rates better.

Certainly not the Seven Network's late starter *Four Quarters*. Seven allowed *The Footy Show* a year's start before deciding that sport was more than live action.

Four Quarters, hosted by Sandy

Roberts and former Essendon star Tim Watson, was a combination of talk show, comic strip, gossip, and pantomime. If you left *The Footy Show* feeling seedy, *Four Quarters* made for an ideal relaxant at the end of the week.

While Newman was the on-field champion (300 games with the Cats) who continued his exploits on the very different field of television, *The Coodabeen Champions* made it big by making bar talk respectable, on alternative radio RRR, then the ABC, and then on commercial radio, 3AW.

The bar was built for post mortems. A meeting place, given strength by its spirituous liquors, and packed houses. Football was the lead item on the agenda in the hilarious pre-game warm-up, with callers like Peter from Peterborough and Ivan from Ivanhoe.

The conversation was intense, but leavened by the knowledge that it was just talk. Sex and violence were for the off-season.

The Coodabeens (Jeff Richardson, Simon Whelan, Ian Cover, Tony Leonard, and Greg Champion) never did, and never would, play the game like Newman, but they could put a generation of pub talk into a huge vat, tip it about, whirl it around, and give it new life on radio.

They were the first to put another slant on football. They took conversation about the game to new levels, made possible by their true passion for the game and its

players. Their characterisations were unerringly true. Their songs (performed, and written by Greg Champion) were a dutiful mix between raising heroes to deities, and making them very human at the same time. This was indeed the stuff of champion performers.

Raucous Rex Hunt was no Sam Newman on the field. He was successful at three clubs, Richmond, Geelong and St Kilda, taking a Premierships with the Tigers in 1969 and 1973.

Hunt entertained on the field with high-marking and long-kicking. Off the field, he made his mark in the media first as a fishing expert, and occasional around-the-grounds man for several radio stations.

He finally got his chance at the big time on 3AW, and he took his break with both hands, and a fast-moving, fast-talking mouth, linked to a mind that was, shall we say, different.

Hunt created a new form of calling the game, combining detail, noise, fantasy, fun, and folly. It might have seemed like mayhem, but it was carefully considered theatre.

The style, and the stylist had their haters. More often than not 3AW's rival for ratings, the ABC, won the hours before and after the football.

But when the ball was bounced or, as Hunt might say, 'The air conveyance makes its journey into the ether', the crowd switched to AW, and its comic strip of the air. Theatre had won.

There's an irony to all this. In the late 70s, when VFL President Dr Allen Aylett described a future in which football would be a product, creating all sorts of marketing opportunities that few had to that time thought of, he was loudly derided.

In some of those preview/review shows of the time, his view of the future became something of a joke. Some joke. A decade later the same shows, given new legs, life and focus were making jokes of many different colours, off the back of a great product.

Football.

Geoff Slattery

1984

March 31. Bad boy recruits Mark Jackson and Gary Ablett star in Fitzroy thrashing – and are reported. Geelong 23.10 (148), Fitzroy 15.9 (99) (→).

April 14. 22 goals in three games to Dons big fish, 206cm Paul Salmon, eight against Collingwood, beaten 26.13 (169) to 16.10 (106) (→23/6).

April 18. Swans and Fitzroy night game is postponed after TAA plane from Sydney is delayed three hours.

April 28. North Melbourne play the first of four 'home' games at the MCG and win 16.17 (113) to Melbourne 14.14 (98).

April 28. Hawthorn's Leigh Matthews plays his 300th game, against Footscray. The Hawks win 22.9 (141) to 13.16 (94).

May 12. Some VFL clubs are not cooperating with the Task Force set up last year by the VFL. They say the report may lead to fewer clubs (→ 19/5/85).

May 12. Kardinia Park gatekeeper says to Peter Daicos: 'I don't care who you are, no one gets past without a ticket.' So he borrows David Cloke's 200-game medallion to get in, play, and win. Collingwood 19.14 (128), Geelong 11.17 (83) (→13/5/85).

May 15. Victoria withstand SA attack to win 16.12 (108) to 16.8 (104). Stephen Kernahan kicks ten for SA (→ 16/7/85).

May 16. Officials of Carlton, Collingwood and Richmond discuss forming of a breakaway 'superleague' (→9/4/95).

June 4. Footscray deserve the win over Collingwood, says first year coach Michael Malthouse. 15.10 (100) to 13.17 (95).

July 24. Essendon win second Night Flag in four years, defeating Sydney Swans 13.11 (89) to 5.8 (38) (→17/3/90).

Aug. 7. St Kilda, last on ladder, sack coach Tony Jewell (→28/8/87).

Sept. 3. Bernie Quinlan kicks his 100th goal in Fitzroy's 24.20 (164) to 15.17 (107) win over St Kilda (→1/4/95).

Debuts
Darren Millane (Coll)
Greg Williams (Geel)
Danny Frawley (St K)

Retirements
Gary Dempsey (N. Melb)
David Dench (N. Melb)
Geoff Southby (Carl)
Garry Wilson (Fitz)

Saints saved by 22 cents in the dollar

Saints: still in the big League.

June 26. The future of St Kilda brightened today with an announcement that a significant number of creditors accepted a payment plan.

Seven former players and coaches said they were willing to accept 22.5 cents in the dollar from the administrators of a scheme of arrangement.

But the money owed to football creditors is only a small percentage of the $1.45 million total debt.

Hawthorn coach Allan Jeans, who had 22 years at St Kilda, said the seven had reluctantly agreed because an alternative was the destruction of the club. General creditors must now accept 7.5 cents in the dollar (→ 26/6/95).

Gary Ablett at home in the country

March 31. Stunning was the only word to describe Gary Ablett's return to VFL for Geelong at Kardinia Park today.

One of five new Cats players in the opening match against Fitzroy, Ablett was on a wing and beside him was another first-timer, Greg Williams, and club captain Mick Turner.

They were devastating, with 90 disposals between them, including Ablett's 21 kicks and two handballs.

Geelong won by 49 points, Ablett kicking three but being reported by three umpires for striking rover Garry Wilson with a forearm to the head. Geelong kicked 11 goals in the third quarter (→ 27/5/89).

Sensational Salmon landed by knee

June 23. Paul Salmon, Australia's hottest football property, may be out for a year after hurting his right knee today.

The 19-year-old Essendon full-forward-ruckman had to be stretchered off late in the third quarter of the match against Collingwood at Victoria Park.

Leading goalscorer with 63 goals in 13 games, Salmon had been called to the ruck where he inspired the Bombers' comeback for a 34-point win which took them to the top of the Premiership Ladder.

Salmon said he had grabbed the ball out of the ruck at the centre bounce and was about to kick. 'I knew it was going to happen a split second before I kicked. I saw the player coming through and something clicked at the back of my knee and I went down.

'It was very sore, very weak and very numb and I couldn't move it after that ... I've always dreaded having a knee injury' (→ 29/6/85).

The big fish at full stretch.

League sails on stormy financial seas

League Chief Commissioner Jack Hamilton doing a financial balancing act.

June 16. The VFL's financial crisis is much worse than has been publicly disclosed, with the League and the 12 clubs losing $1.9 million last season.

A confidential report by the VFL Finance Director, Michael Tilley, presented to club Presidents and Directors, shows that operating expenses exceeded revenue last year by $1.9 million and that six clubs were technically bankrupt at the end of the season.

These clubs are Fitzroy, Footscray, Collingwood, St Kilda, Sydney Swans and Geelong.

The report shows that the gap between what clubs spent and their earnings increased almost nine-fold, by $1.7 million, in just 12 months. In 1982 club expenses were only $200,000 ahead of revenue.

Although League officials now believe the splurge is under control, there are some financial experts who say that its consequences will be felt for many years.

At the end of last season all clubs' debts were $7 million ahead of realisable assets.

Rickety Ricky to resign as coach

Swan stand-in coach Bob Hammond.

July 8. Sydney Swans coach Ricky Quade resigned as coach last week, following the sacking of captain Barry Round. His departure left the Swans without the two team leaders chiefly responsible for establishing the club in Sydney two years ago.

Quade went to hospital with a stomach ulcer, the same ailment that put him into hospital for two weeks in September last year.

He was unable to coach the Swans in their 31-point loss to Collingwood, 19.17 (131) to 14.16 (100), but today caretaker coach Bob Hammond, from South Australia, got the team up to a win over Fitzroy, 14.12 (96) to 9.14 (68).

Club officials said Quade's return depended on his health.

The sacking of Round last Friday was believed to have followed friction between the former captain and Quade (→ 16/3/85).

Cheer squad strike

May 26. The Carlton cheer squad have gone on strike, allegedly over access to a social club room.

This revolutionary act today produced an astonishing piece of radical defiance: cheer squad members with poles but no prose.

No painstakingly penned messages of hope or scorn greeted the Blues when they ran out at Windy Hill today.

The big men, who brace themselves to burst dramatically through the crepe, were bemused by the surrealistic sight (→ 26/5/91).

Jack Hamilton first full-time Commissioner

Nov. 21. Jack Hamilton has been appointed as the first full-time Commissioner of the VFL.

This follows a report critical of the League's decision-making processes, describing them as deficient and the League secretive and insensitive to the needs of supporters.

A League task force recommended that a five-member commission independently run the game, leaving the clubs to get on with the business of competing.

Hamilton, who has been described as an ultimate football politician, has been under enormous strain, with plans by Carlton President John Elliott for a breakaway competition and *The Age* newspaper publishing a detailed series laying bare the VFL's ineptitude.

One report claimed a high level of dissatisfaction with the VFL administration over the style of manage-ment by Hamilton, the VFL General manager, and the League President Dr Allen Aylett.

Early this month the clubs appointed a sub-committee to investigate the task force's recommendations. Hamilton's appointment flows from this, but it now seems that Dr Aylett will not have a role.

During many of these negotiations Dr Aylett has been in Ireland in his role as President of the National Football League for a schoolboys' tour and again when a series of 'Tests' were played against Ireland under composite rules.

As a tough fullback for Collingwood and a key VFL administrator Hamilton has been a strong man. But as this season limped to a close with finals crowds down, and lack lustre Premiliary and Grand Finals, there is a lot of work ahead for him (→ 4/6/86).

Collingwood forward Denis Banks is having a fine season generally, and is taking some spectacular marks. This looks like the mark of the year.

Robbie Muir goes out with a bang

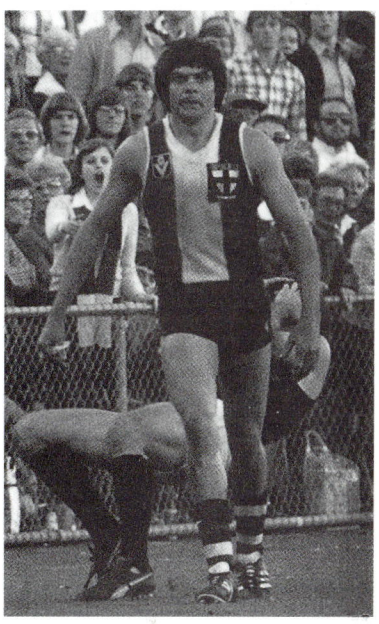

Robbie Muir has that look again.

May 8. St Kilda's volatile Robert Muir may have ended his playing career in the VFL today.

He was suspended for 12 weeks by the Tribunal after a dramatic third-quarter display on Saturday.

As an umpire advanced to report him, Muir took out his mouthguard and shouted abuse before hurling his mouthguard to the turf. He was reported for abusing a goal umpire, threatening a field umpire, headbutting Carlton's Bruce Doull and striking former team-mate Val Perovic.

Muir said the umpire made it worse by following him, while the umpire said he had been 'scared'. Over 68 games with the Saints, Muir has kicked 23 goals (→ 6/5/85).

Great Sunday Final

Sept. 9. A Sunday Elimination Final drew 74,000 followers to the MCG today to see Collingwood dispatch Fitzroy by 46 points.

A State Government Minister praised the day as a success and there was optimism about a similar Final next year.

At the end of the day the Lions were making noises about keeping Robert Walls on as coach next year, while Collingwood were complaining at having to play a cut-throat Semi-final against Carlton on Saturday after just six days of rest.

Peter Moore wins his second medal

Sept. 24. Hot favourite Peter Moore, the Melbourne ruckman who switched from Collingwood last year, today won his second Brownlow Medal.

Moore, 27, is only the second player to achieve this at different clubs. Ian Stewart won two at St Kilda in 1965 and 1966 and his third at Richmond in 1971.

For most of the count Moore and his captain Robert Flower had it between them, until Collingwood ruckman David Cloke split them with three votes in the last round to finish second.

A back injury which put Flower in hospital for the latter part of the season made it clear that Moore would end ahead of him.

Moore, a former Collingwood captain, cost the Demons $160,000 when he made his move. Tonight he thanked the club for its faith.

Sydney Swans ruckman Steve Taubert polled surprisingly well to finish fourth on 15, a vote ahead of Hawthorn's Michael Tuck, Essendon's Simon Madden and Footscray's Doug Hawkins.

1984 Statistics

Leading Goalkicker:
Bernie Quinlan (Fitz) 105
Brownlow Medallist:
Peter Moore (Melb)
Finals: Elimination Final Coll 23.15 (153) Fitz 15.17 (107); **Qualifying Final** Haw 18.14 (122) Carl 13.14 (92); **First Semi-final** Carl 14.9 (93) Coll 17.16 (118); **Second Semi-final** Ess 15.15 (105) Haw 16.17 (113); **Preliminary Final** Ess 28.6 (174) Coll 5.11 (41); **Grand Final** Haw 12.9 (81) Ess 14.21 (105)

Ladder:	W	L	%	pts
Ess	18	4	128.2	72
Haw	17	5	131.7	68
Carl	13	9	115.8	52
Coll	13	9	109.1	52
Fitz	11	11	102.6	44
Geel	11	11	94.3	44
Foot	11	11	93.8	44
Rich	10	12	90.9	40
Melb	9	13	104.3	36
Syd	9	13	88.1	36
N. Melb	5	17	81.7	20
St K	5	17	75.5	20

Bomber blitz buries Hawks

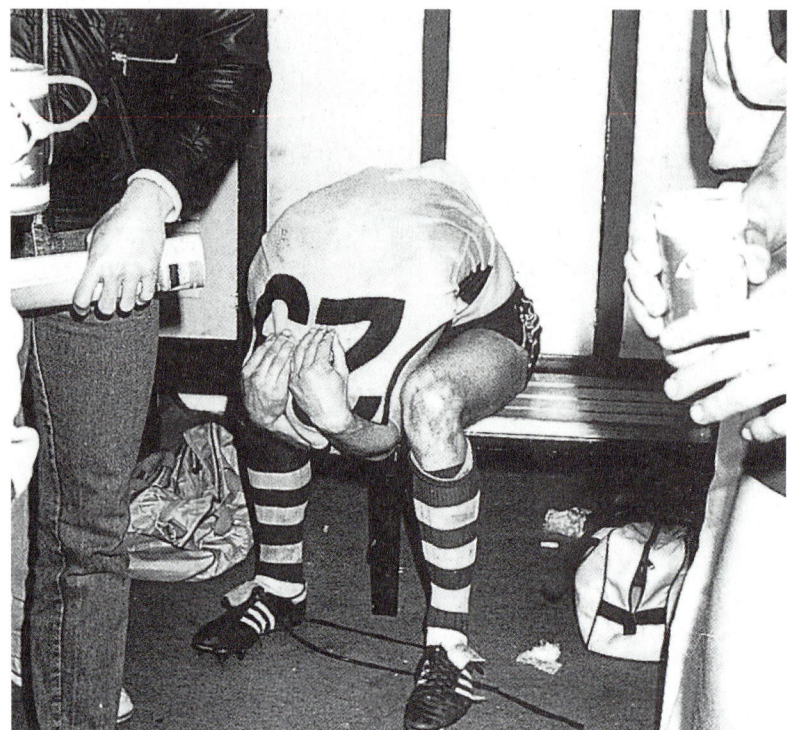

The Hawks have lost, and Dermott Brereton communes with his feelings.

Timmy Watson, one of Dons' best.

Sept. 29. Kevin Sheedy's coaching magic and the fierce spirit he has bred into his players in four years paid off with an Essendon Grand Final win today.

In a stirring last quarter that reinforced their role as a power in the 80s, Essendon won by 24 points. And it ended a 17-year monopoly on the flag by Richmond, Carlton, Hawthorn and North Melbourne.

Having also won the national Night Premiership, the Bombers are easily the best club in Australia.

Playing Shane Heard on Robert DiPierdomenico was a Sheedy masterstroke, because for once the big Hawthorn dynamo was held to ordinariness.

The attendance was the smallest at an MCG Grand Final for 29 years, with only 92,685 showing up.

The VFL has been forced to keep the Grand Final at the MCG and this contributed to the comparatively modest gate. Space for 44,000 MCC and VFL Park members was taken by only 31,000.

Some had thought Hawthorn would take back-to-back Premierships, but Sheedy switched Paul Weston from defence to centre half-forward, captain Terry Daniher to centre half-back and recalled Simon Madden from the bench, where he

had spent the third quarter. Another defender, Peter Bradbury, went to half-forward.

The Dons kicked 9.6 in the final quarter, breaking free of the Hawks' attempts to choke their free-running game.

Tim Watson got the ball moving quickly and Essendon were firing. Two quick goals by Leon Baker and Bradbury shut the Hawks down.

In the last quarter, too, there was a sensational collision involving Di-Pierdomenico which resulted in Kevin Walsh being knocked senseless.

The final scores were Essendon 14.21 (105) to Hawthorn 12.9 (81). Winning goalkickers were Leon Baker (4), Bill Duckworth (2), Tim Watson (2) and singles to Terry Daniher, Peter Bradbury, Mark Thompson, Paul Weston, Roger Merrett and Merv Neagle.

Burly Bill Duckworth won the Norm Smith Medal for best on the ground (→ 28/9/85).

The siren sounds and the Dons come from everywhere to celebrate the win.

1985

Last President retires, power to Commission

To the life! VFL President Allen Aylett's portrait is unveiled at VFL House.

Feb. 6. With today's formal adoption of the VFL Commission, the VFL Board is no more.

As well, Dr Allen Aylett, a former North Melbourne champion and VFL President for eight years, retired today, having expressed 'regret, sadness and frustration' at what he saw as leaving a task unfinished.

As President of North Melbourne and then the VFL he oversaw a 300 per cent rise in income from $6.5 million in 1976 to almost $24 million this year, South Melbourne's move to Sydney, a new market in TV audiences and national development.

He was disappointed that the Tribunal has not been brought up to date. 'Consideration should be given to fixing guidelines for set penalties,' he said.'Under the present system there are too many grey areas.'

He also said that the Sydney Swans' results had been disappointing: 'But the League must take its share of the blame ... the whole exercise was insufficiently funded from the word go' (→19/8/89).

HSV7 pulls plug nine minutes early

April 14. With nine minutes to go in the match between the Sydney Swans and Fitzroy at the Sydney Cricket Ground tonight, Channel Seven pulled the plug.

The match was all but over, with Fitzroy cruising to a win 26.15 (171) to 18.12 (120), and the Swans' magnificent season start was history.

But Seven had had enough by about 5 p.m., and for Fitzroy fans at home that was it. *Age* football writer Garry Linnell phoned Seven three times without getting a reply.

A replay of a documentary, as it happens by Swans supporter Mike Willesee, replaced the football.

Channel Seven's decision is even more puzzling in light of its demand for exclusive rights for the football this season, ending the ABC's Saturday night replays (→27/3/87).

Gary Ablett stars at Geelong.

Barassi and Moore in public feud

May 4. Melbourne coach and dual Brownlow Medallist Peter Moore had a remarkable clash at the MCG on Saturday.

During the third quarter of the match against North Melbourne the Demons began to flag after a brilliant start.

North slipped in several goals late in the quarter, one from an easy mark dropped by Moore. But this was not his first mistake, for the 208-game veteran looked tentative in his first game after a neck injury.

Barassi sent a runner to bring Moore off. Moore sent the messenger away. Barassi sent another message. Roaring into the phone, he said: 'Tell Moore that if he doesn't come off he's suspended ... '

Again the runner went and returned alone. By now Barassi was incandescent with rage and screamed into the phone: 'Tell him to act his age and get off. He's a team man for Christ's sake and tell him to get off now.'

A reluctant Moore trudged off. Approaching the boundary he raised a single finger in the direction of his coach. But this must have gone unnoticed, for Barassi spoke to him at three-quarter time and Moore went back on (→31/8).

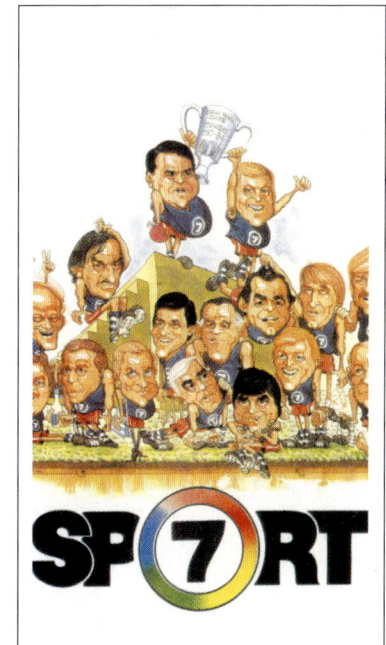

Pick the champions in Seven's team of football experts and commentators.

Life in Little League revealed

Magistrate finds Matthews guilty of on-field assault

No ball in sight as Hawthorn and Geelong players and officials sort themselves out after the last-quarter brawl.

Alex Hutchinson takes the field.

June 26. In 1967 when the State Savings Bank first sponsored games by the Mini League at half time, newspapers reported that Princes Park pie sales at half time fell by 50 %.

Since then the Mini League has become the Little League, and thousands of primary schools and boys and girls have had a taste of the big time at half time.

The thrill of the kids having a big ground to themselves for 20 minutes is outweighed only by the pride of mums and dads who watch.

The current arrangement where schools in VFL clubs' areas play perhaps one game every three seasons can lead to mismatches.

In a recent game Carlton were represented by kids mostly in grade three wearing jumpers that hung to the turf and floppy shorts.

St Kilda on the other hand had a smooth combination of whopper kids from grade six.

One of the Carlton boys interviewed after the match was nine-year-old Alex Hutchinson in his first ever game of football. He said: 'There was nothing good that happened with our team.' He had one kick, and St Kilda won 6.11 to nothing.

When taunted by a Saint that the Blues were on the bottom of the Little League, he retorted that the Saints were on the bottom of the Big League. He was happy – and Carlton won 20.19 (139) to 16.11 (107) in the Big League.

Mark Jackson attacks Gary Ayres.

Aug. 13. Hawthorn champion Leigh Matthews will appeal against a decision by Magistrate Brian Clothier finding him guilty of assaulting Geelong's Neville Bruns.

Matthews was fined $1000 for the offence which occurred in the Hawthorn and Geelong game of June 15.

The proceedings in the Magistrates' Court are the penultimate chapter in this sorry affair for football.

The conviction and fine might be seen as Matthews's third punishment – first a broken nose in the game, second a four-week suspension by the VFL and now the conviction.

The Matthews/Bruns incident, or its aftermath, went unseen by umpire Ian Robinson. Matthews was not reported, but five other players were for other incidents, on a total of 17 charges.

These players included Geelong's Mark Jackson, who was the instiga-

Neville Bruns with broken jaw.

tor of much subsequent aggravation in this spiteful game.

Jackson was found guilty of striking Gary Ayres, Chris Mew, and Chris Langford twice, and was suspended for eight matches.

Geelong's Bernard Toohey got one week and Gary Ablett one week for time wasting. Gary Ayres was cleared.

It is not easy to judge what effect Jackson's bizarre behaviour had on Matthews, but later in the game he swung a wild arm at Neville Bruns, and broke his jaw. After this he was crashed by Steve Hocking, suffering a badly broken nose.

For his part, in July Matthews was investigated by the VFL and deregistered for four weeks by the VFL Commission for conduct unbecoming a VFL player. A police investigation was also launched.

But somehow the Matthews incident, not the Jackson ones, generated an immense amount of publicity.

Leigh Matthews after the Court case.

'Wacko' Jacko escaped because he was reported and is known as a volatile showman. Matthews is a hard uncompromising player and the incident was not taken up straight away by the football system.

Whatever the reason, the investigation has ended the polite fiction that football assaults are somehow legal, and that police and the law are prevented from invading the field of play.

A football field is no more isolated from the law than any public place. The rules of the game allowing assaults – known in football as tackles – do not supersede the law.

Matthews perhaps made a strategic as well as tactical mistake in pleading guilty to the offence in court, rather than arguing that on-field deeds should be dealt with by football regulations and Tribunals. A guilty plea might be seen in the future as a precedent for other interventions by the police (→ 19/4/88).

Unfashionable Dogs scoop awards

Sept. 23. Footscray's Brad Hardie tonight became only the second VFL player to win a Brownlow Medal in his first League season. This has not been achieved since Haydn Bunton's medal for Fitzroy in 1931.

Hardie, 23 next month, won with two votes in the last round when Carlton's Justin Madden scored a single vote. The red-haired Bulldog, piled on a strong finish, polling 22 votes to Madden's 21, with Fitzroy defender Paul Roos third on 16.

Hardie was voted best and fairest on the ground five times, second-best three times and third best once.

With his hair colour and distinctive long-sleeved guernsey, Hardie stands out. He said he had felt under undue pressure from Bulldog fans and the media in his first year from South Fremantle.

'As well as personal pride, the fear of failure is a big motivation for me,' he said. 'Early in the year I had an injury – I couldn't pull the pin and not play – yet some people were saying I was just not good enough for VFL football.'

Last year Hardie captained South Fremantle and won the Tassie Medal for best player in the interstate series. On Saturday he was voted best on ground against Hawthorn, although Footscray lost.

The victory cheer for Hardie was almost drowned out by cheers for a three-vote award to Collingwood's Tony Shaw.

$6.5 million for Sydney Swans

Leanne: the good doctor's wife.

A cheque from Dr Geoffrey Edelsten and a handshake for Jack Hamilton.

July 31. High-flying Sydney doctor Geoffrey Edelsten tonight became the first private owner of a VFL club. The VFL Board of Directors voted unanimously to allow him to take over the ailing Sydney swans, who have only won five matches out of 17 this season.

In less than two hours the Board took the historic decision to accept a $6.5 million offer from Dr Edelsten ahead of businessman Basil Sellers.

The 11 other VFL clubs each get $263,000 from the deal. Their fear now is based on which players Sydney will try to poach.

As champagne corks popped tonight, Dr Edelsten said: 'I believe it is a great investment and history will prove me right.'

He has an agreement with the VFL that there will be no quick sackings and no immediate changes in the Sydney coaching and administrative staff.

VFL Chief Commissioner Jack Hamilton said the deal was 'one-off'. 'They [the Swans] are in a unique position and it should not be regarded as a precedent for Melbourne.'

Other clubs will also share in five per cent of the Swans' yearly profit.

He said Dr Edelsten would have the exclusive right to a VFL club in Sydney or New South Wales for the next five years.

'It has been very long and very difficult,' Hamilton said. 'We have had, since 1858, clubs being managed in a certain way and what we contemplated here was a change that rested very heavily on whoever's responsibility it was for making that decision.'

The deal safeguarded the interests of all VFL clubs, he said, and offered a continuing compatibility with the other 11 clubs (→ 6/4/86).

Hardie: Hercules in pocket.

Barassi and Walls in coaching swan songs

Aug. 31. Two coaches bowed out of VFL football today – Ron Barassi and Robert Walls.

Barassi has given it away, temporarily at least, after Melbourne finished second bottom, losing 16 games and winning just six.

In spite of this he was today cheered each time he moved from the coach's box.

After the match he said he was leaving with mixed feelings, but was looking forward to watching the Finals and going to a game every week next season.

He was not disconsolate, telling reporters: 'Cheer up. It's not as though there's a death in the family. There is life after footy, you know.'

In the Fitzroy changing rooms Robert Walls told his players the that he had decided last Monday night to resign.

Three weeks earlier the players had asked him to stay and he had agreed. Later events, however, caused a change of heart.

As club chief executive Keith Wiegard said the coaching position would be decided within a week, Walls was spending his last official moments with the young Fitzroy, who had finished ninth.

The Lions have made the finals three times in Walls five seasons as coach, as tribute to his ability to get the best for a teams without great players. (→ 5/5/93).

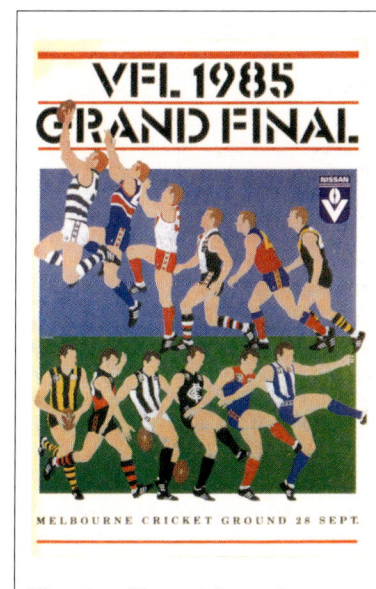
There's a big match coming.

The Bombers fly up to another Flag

A farewell to the Hawthorn skipper Leigh Matthews after 332 games over 16 years. The Hawks' cheer squad put art where their heart is on the Grand Final run through.

The Hawthorn and Essendon players have their minds off the game as they get into a melee on the wing.

Sept. 28. Essendon are today being hailed as among the mightiest teams in VFL history after their crushing Grand Final win over Hawthorn.

Two Premierships in a row means that coach Kevin Sheedy will stay at Windy Hill to try to equal Collingwood's record run of four Flags from 1927.

The match was memorable for Hawthorn only because it was Leigh Matthews' last and Dermott Brereton kicked a record eight goals and was reported three times.

More than 100,000 fans saw Essendon 1.3 up at the end of the first quarter, edge ahead by 2.6 at half time, 4.6 at three-quarter time, then power on 11 goals to win by 26.14 (170) to 14.8 (92).

Essendon's three teams had been in overpowering form in the last round, kicking 90 goals against the Swans, including 25 by Under-19 star Laurence Schache.

Hawthorn had gone down to Essendon by 40 points in the Second Semi-final and barely pipped Footscray in the Preliminary Final.

After the game Sheedy told his players: 'It took you five years to play four quarters of football, but I'm patient. It was a wonderful effort of football, the way football should be played.'

Simon Madden, who won the Norm Smith Medal, was outstanding in the ruck and helped destroy Hawthorn within 20 minutes of the first bounce (→ 25/9/93).

1985 Statistics

Leading Goalkicker:
Simon Beasley (Foots) 105
Brownlow Medallist:
Brad Hardie (Foots)
Finals: Elimination Final Carl 16.11 (107) N. Melb 20.6 (126)
Qualifying Final Foots 8.14 (62) Haw 22.23 (155); **First Semi-final** Foots 19.23 (137) N. Melb 16.11 (107); **Second Semi-final** Ess 14.18 (102) Haw 9.8 (62); **Preliminary Final** Haw 16.13 (109) Foots 15.9 (99); **Grand Final** Ess 26.14 (170) Haw 14.8 (92)

Ladder:	W	L	D	%	pts
Ess	19	3		138.4	76
Foots	16	6		120.9	64
Haw	15	6	1	130.8	62
Carl	15	7		115.5	60
N. Melb	13	8	1	97.9	54
Geel	12	10		100.6	48
Coll	10	12		100.8	40
Rich	9	13		91.2	36
Fitz	7	15		93.8	28
Syd	6	16		94.5	24
Melb	6	16		77.8	24
St K	3	19		64.7	12

The Dons' ruckman-forward Simon Madden rises for a brilliant mark.

Handballing to a new Blue generation

In 1985 and 1986 the players who took Carlton to two Grand Finals arrived at Princes Park.

Some were bought from over the border, such as Stephen Kernahan and Craig Bradley from SA, and David Rhys-Jones from Sydney, but others such as Stephen Silvagni, Mil Hanna and Peter Dean were home grown.

Kernahan took over from Mike Fitzpatrick as the leader who was to take the next generation or two at Carlton through the 1986 and 1987 Grand Finals, and into the 90s.

Some of the players from Fitzpatrick's time, such as Wayne Johnston, the 'Dominator', and Ken Hunter, the first player to be known as 'God', played through the decade but others were beginning to handball to the next generation.

Fitzpatrick in the ruck and at centre half-forward was a key player, perhaps *the* key player in the 1979, 1981 and 1982 Premierships. He played the last of his

150 games in 1983. The Rhodes Scholar was allegedly told at one stage by coach David Parkin that he was too intelligent to be a great footballer. Fitzpatrick showed on the big occasions that his football brain was no obstacle to success, and a big heart and real skills as a ruckman were added advantages.

Many of the players in 1981 and 1982 were young enough to

carry on through the 80s.

Ken Hunter was widely regarded as the most courageous player to pull on a Navy Blue jumper, because he looked so fragile. Some of his marks were so recklessly brave that watchers feared for his existence. His co-operation with Bruce Doull was psychic.

Wayne Johnston saved many

of his most fearsome performances for Grand Finals, but the Dominator was a force over 209 games through the 80s. He got more hard balls than just about anyone else.

Peter McConville and David Glascott are in many ways the quiet heroes of those teams.

Wayne Harmes was the winner of the 1979 Grand Final with that tap to Ken Sheldon. Jim Buckley, though smaller, was almost his equal in pack crashing and doing deeds on the burst.

Sheldon's frequent partner in the 'crime' of goal sneaking, was often the great Rod Ashman, whose 236-game career ended in 1986. His occasional but enormous torpedo punts are the stuff of Carlton legend.

Peter Bosustow only played 65 games in three seasons, 1981 to 1983, but he kicked 146 crucial goals in them. His rocket-like career matched his leaping ability. His party trick was an ability to drop-kick 40 metres – backwards.

The Life and times of Hawthorn's 'Lethal' Leigh Matthews

Leigh Matthews looked indestructible on the football field, and he played that way. He was probably one of the most fearsome sights for opponents of his era as he steamed into a contest intent on getting the ball and knocking anything out of his path.

He was essentially a ball player, possessing wonderful skills in handling, marking, handpassing and kicking. He could baulk and weave like the best rovers, making space to set up a pass or a goal. But the image remains – of a solid frame, the strong arms and legs, and the look of complete concentration.

It is that image that caused Lou Richards to dub him 'Lethal Leigh', (a name change from 'Barney', after Barney Rubble of *The Flintstones*) and set the seal on his reputation.

And players did go down. Matthews admits he played the game to the hilt, but in pursuit of the ball. He became Public Enemy No. 1 in Western Australia in

1971, when he crashed into rover Barry Cable, who had to be helped from the field.

He was shattered by the 1985 incident with Geelong's Neville Bruns which caused him to be deregistered for four weeks and convicted for assault (successfully appealed).

These incidents apart, he will be remembered for a lot of hard

football, over 332 club games, for winning Hawthorn's best and fairest eight times over 17 seasons, for kicking 915 goals, a record for a rover, for captaining the Hawks for five years, for representing Victoria 14 times, for being involved with distinction in four Premierships.

Leigh came to Hawthorn from Chelsea at the age of 16, having

already played a senior season in suburban football. He was part of a footballing family, and his brother Kelvin (built on similar lines) played 155 games at Hawthorn and Geelong and made the State team.

In the early years Matthews shared the roving with the dashing Peter Crimmins, and he was given long spells in the forward pocket to employ his particular goal sneaking skills.

With Crimmins gone he took over the roving role and remained a dominant player, but as other rovers came along he went back to spending long periods up forward, sometimes at full-forward.

He had the strength and ability to outmark far taller men. He headed the goalkicking in 1975 with 68 goals, and had a season best of 91 in 1977.

After his retirement he was immediately sought as a coach and took over at Collingwood in 1986. In 1990 he gave them their long-awaited Flag.

1986

'Mad Farmer' has Demons on the run

Jan. 31. John Northey has sent his Melbourne charges on a country run that turned out to be bang on.

Northey had them running through the bush on an 11-kilometre time trial, with top results.

The speed of the run was enhanced by the fact that, as each group of players came around a particular bend, a farmer suddenly appeared, yelling at the players and firing a shotgun over their heads.

The 'irate farmer' turned out to be a motivational mate of coach Northey.

Sewer men fear Grand Final flush

Sept. 27. Grand Final day is a peak time for sewers. Half time, says the Board of Works, can mean the biggest flush of all.

'We can't really enlarge the sewers for one day,' a spokesman explained. 'They cope, that's all.'

This is one of the oddities of a day that Essendon fan Sir Frank Little, Catholic Archbishop of Melbourne, compares to his church's rites. 'It's a secular equivalent,' he said. 'Every deeply felt loyalty and conviction has its signs and symbols.'

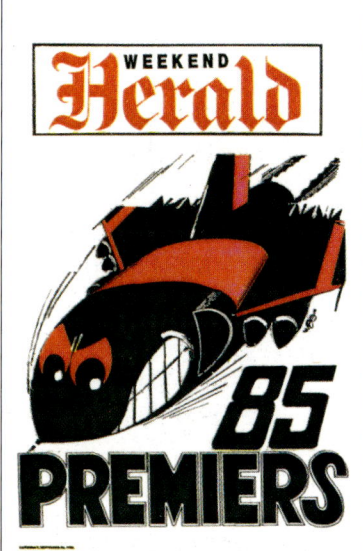

A much a part of Grand Final day as the match itself; the WEG winning team poster from the Herald, on sale straight after the game.

Ranald leaves footy to Bondy and Bob

April 14. Ranald Macdonald resigned today as President of Collingwood after coach Bob Rose quit following Saturday's humiliating 43-point loss to North Melbourne.

The departure of the former newspaper publisher was accompanied by the sacking of the General Manager, Peter Bahen, who bitterly attacked the club Board for destroying his business reputation.

Senior Vice-president Allan McAlister is interim President and assistant coach Leigh Matthews assumes Rose's job.

Macdonald swept into office as head of the New Magpies in 1982 promising greater efficiency on and off the field. Last week players had to take a 20 per cent pay cut.

The club lost their three opening games this year. Centreman Geoff Raines refused to accept the pay cut and appears likely to join Ladder leaders Essendon next week.

Bahen lamented Macdonald's departure, saying: 'Unfortunately, with everyone screaming for blood, there had to be a few bodies.'

Macdonald said he took full responsibility for the situation at the club, which has debts of $2.9 million. Attendances this season have dropped by 20 per cent.

With the promised land still a long way off, Ranald Macdonald departs.

Swans let Rioli return to Tiger den

May 9. Brilliant Maurice Rioli has been released from his Sydney Swans contract and now returns to Richmond.

Rioli has been a controversial figure since signing with Sydney just two months ago. Several Swans players took a pay cut to fit him into the club's salary cap.

Then the VFL refused to allow Rioli a permit because of the salary cap and called on the Swans to make further pay cuts if they wanted him to play.

The Swans were thought to be $70,000 above the limit.

Rioli then won a Federal Court order forcing the VFL to give him a permit to play, but a possible $10,000 fine and loss of Premiership points changed that.

Melbourne: world's knee surgery capital

July 8. Melbourne, whose place at the forefront of scientific, medical and cultural advances has been little celebrated, has become known as the cruciate ligament capital of the world.

Indeed, Melbourne is to knee surgery what Mecca is to Islam. Former Richmond star and physiotherapist Barry Richardson estimates that one in five VFL players will suffer serious knee injury. About four per cent of all VFL players will need need knee reconstruction surgery.

As well, as many as 10 per cent of the state senior and under-21 netball squads may need knee reconstruction. About 200,000 women play netball in Victoria, so the level of injury seems frightening (→3/6/95).

Hamilton to retire after 38 seasons

Jack Hamilton: ready for a rest.

June 4. Jack Hamilton, a tough player who joined Collingwood in 1948 and rose to be VFL Commissioner, is to retire.

A year after he joined the Magpies he began as a junior clerk with the VFL, was promoted to General Manager in 1977 and first Commissioner in November last year.

'It's a job any three people can do,' he said. Asked would he join the Magpie Board, he said 'I've just got off Devil's Island, I'm not going to live on Alcatraz' (→ 30/5/90).

Ross Oakley takes over a VFL committed to change and growth

Aug 15. The VFL have announced that former St Kilda player Ross Oakley, an insurance executive, will become Chairman of the VFL Commission when the present Chairman, Jack Hamilton, leaves the post on October 10.

Oakley, 43, has had an outstanding business career, and has also been a strong member of the Board of the Hawthorn Football Club.

He was approached to apply for the VFL post and has beaten Alan Schwab to the the position, but Schwab will stay on in the No. 2 post, as Executive Director.

Oakley played 62 games for St Kilda before his career ended with a knee injury on the eve of the Saints' Premiership win in 1966.

Oakley will take over an organisation committed to a far-reaching expansion. Earlier this year the VFL outlined plans for a 14-team competition of the 12 current sides plus new teams from Queensland and Western Australia.

A possible change of recruiting zones for each VFL club will be made by independent commissioners before October 8.

The draft system would apply to

New VFL chief Ross Oakley (right) with Alan Schwab and Jack Hamilton.

players living outside recruiting zones, with each club able to draft a maximum of 10 players.

The club that finished last on the Ladder would have first choice in the draft, and the top side last pick. October 22 will be draft day.

In the expanded competition

clubs must nominate 50 players by the second Wednesday in October, and after the draft, when 10 more players would be added. The list would be again cut, this time to 50, by March 18 of the following year.

The present salary cap restrictions will continue to apply.

Lions fight to survive, but they put a roar into the Finals

Sept. 20. Debt-ridden, downtrodden and fighting for their very survival as a club, Fitzroy went under to Hawthorn in the Preliminary Final today.

For a club that had peered into the abyss of extinction, it was a brave effort. As coach David Parkin said: 'We have been fighting a rearguard action since the fourth-last home-and-away game.'

Leon Harris, the Lions' only small man capable of curbing John Platten and Richard Loveridge, was knocked out by Robert DiPierdomenico about two seconds after running on to the ground.

Full-back Gary Pert could scarcely walk with an ankle injury. Captain Matt Rendell hobbled with a torn hamstring until removed.

For a team that struggled midseason to attract 10,000, the Lions drew 50,000 and more to the Finals, 80 % of them cheering Fitzroy.

At the end it was but a gallant attempt, with Hawthorn winning 16.14 (110) to 7.12 (54) (→ 14/4/91).

A week earlier and a triumphant moment as the Lions win the First Semi. Bernie Quinlan and Leon Harris celebrate.

Diesel and Dipper bag the Brownlow

Diesel, Dipper double dipping.

Sept. 22. Hawthorn's raging bull Robert DiPierdomenico, and quiet Sydney centreman Greg Williams have shared the 1986 Brownlow Medal.

'It is unusual for me to be speechless,' the Big Dipper said tonight as Williams stared into the crowd, silent in disbelief.

Williams, who once left Carlton because he was homesick and couldn't get a kick, thought he was lucky to beat Fitzroy's Paul Roos, the favourite. Williams led voting from the first round (→ 26/9/94).

1986 Statistics

Leading Goalkicker:
Brian Taylor (Coll) 100
Brownlow Medallists:
Robert DiPierdomenico (Haw)
Greg Williams (Syd)
Finals: Elimination Final Fitz 8.10 (58) Ess 8.9 (57); **Qualifying Final** Syd 15.14 (104) Carl 18.12 (120); **First Semi-final** Syd 13.11 (89) Fitz 13.16 (94); **Second Semi-final** Haw 13.6 (84) Carl 16.16 (112); **Preliminary Final** Haw 16.14 (110) Fitz 7.12 (54); **Grand Final** Carl 9.14 (68) Haw 16.14 (110)

Ladder:	W	L	%	pts
Haw	18	4	141.6	72
Syd	16	6	118.4	64
Carl	15	7	141.9	60
Fitz	13	9	100.2	52
Ess	12	10	120.3	48
Coll	12	10	109.2	48
N. Melb	12	10	98.6	48
Foots	11	11	97.7	44
Geel	7	15	82.1	28
Rich	7	15	78.4	28
Melb	7	15	74.9	28
St K	2	20	71.9	8

Hawks fly higher than the Blues

Hawk Gary Buckenara takes the mark of the match, probably the year.

The Hawks' Roman gladiator, Robert DiPierdomenico, goes after the ball.

Sept. 27. Carlton spent about $1 million on players, but Hawthorn had the stars and the relentless pressure to gallop away with the Grand Final today by 42 points.

The Hawks had a far better side for this year's Finals than in the previous two seasons. John Platten took the roving pressure off Richard Loveridge, Michael Tuck eased into the captaincy by playing better than he had for years, while Gary Buckenara was also back to his best.

With Greg Dear providing ruck potency, Allan Jeans had a team that was tackling harder than ever, running in numbers, moving the ball smoothly, with handballs at twice the rate of other sides.

Before a crowd of 101,861 at the MCG Jeans set out to counter Carlton's man-to-man style and prevent them from unsettling his Hawks. 'We went for a flexible side and aimed to have an open forward line where our forwards would have plenty of room to lead out,' he said.

Gary Ayres was given the job of taming David Rhys-Jones on the wing. Rhys-Jones had been a match-winner against Hawthorn a fortnight ago but Ayres, in his first wingman's role in five years, showed great strength and skill, subduing his opponent and setting up forward thrusts with such authority that he won the Norm Smith Medal.

Rodney Eade blocked Craig Bradley, limiting him to six kicks while getting 20 himself. Peter Schwab tagged Wayne Johnston all over the ground, even into centre bounces, breaking down Blues' attacks.

Jason Dunstall gave Bruce Doull a sorry career finale in his 356th game, Dunstall showing great composure and skill for six goals.

Buckenara was too brilliant and physical at full-forward for Peter Motley and Peter Dean, while Dermott Brereton could not be contained by Jon Dorotich.

Again, Stephen Kernahan was made impotent by Chris Langford and then Paul Abbott.

A seven-goal burst in the third act sealed it as Carlton captain Mark Maclure was taken off. Wayne Johnston limped to the bench, followed by his shadow Schwab.

Hawthorn won by 16.14 (110) to 9.14 (68) (→ 24/9/88).

Doull makes the football do the talking

Bruce Doull was not capable of playing a bad game. In fact, if there was to be a measurement for football reliability it should be called a 'Doull'.

So rarely was he beaten during his illustrious 356 games for Carlton that the two occasions are remembered.

Once was in in the opening round of 1985, when Doull broke John Nicholls' record of 328 games. That day Footscray forward Simon Beasley kicked nine.

The other game was Doull's last, the 1986 Grand Final, which from an overall Carlton point of view is best forgotten.

There remain the 354 games where Doull created a legend, where he sits at the top table of Carlton immortals, with Nicholls and Alex Jesaulenko.

In these games he developed such a fierce concentration on the football that he seemed to be able to influence it in its flight.

In one game, a night Semi-final against Footscray in 1986, Doull is running with the flight of the ball as it heads towards a Footscray chest in the goal square.

Without turning his head, he punches both arms into the air, connects with the ball, and sends it away from the waiting arms. He

Bruce Doull: a game built around skill, balance and concentration.

skips around the confused Bulldog. How could he see the ball? He couldn't. It just behaved as it was willed.

On other occasions when an opponent fluked a mark near goal and was taking a shot, Doull would concentrate on the ball, and the player's mind and foot,

causing the footy to veer away from goal as if hypnotised.

When he first played for Carlton in 1969 Doull was more flamboyantly hirsute than the grey-bearded, head-banded and brooding champion of later years. He seemed to be taller, faster and skinnier but with the weight of

years he developed an economy of movement and an uncanny knowledge of how the ball is going to behave.

Doull's defensive tactics were really offensive skills in the Carlton teams of the 70s and early 80s. His attacking handball out of the backline, his punching the ball to a team-mate as well as precision kicking changed the way the backlines worked.

Doull was the general in a unit which featured Geoff Southby and later Ken Hunter – a tradition that he handed directly to Peter Dean and Stephen Silvagni.

Memorable backline moments include Ken Hunter running through half back to find the ball coming over his shoulder from Doull, taking the mark, not breaking stride and delivering to Mike Fitzpatrick in the goal square. 'Your goal Doullie!' was the cry.

One of the rare occasions Doull spoke was at his Testimonial Dinner in 1983. He told a story about his first coach Ron Barassi, who improved his footy by sending him to the City Gym, to a judo instructor, and then to a psychologist. 'He'd got it into his mind that I was a quiet person.'

Doull didn't need to speak. He let his football do the talking.

Still Hungry after all these years

Bartlett: appetite for goals.

Kevin Bartlett is one of three towering figures in Australian sport whose skill forced a change in the rules. The others are Don Bradman and Walter Lindrum.

Just as those geniuses had to be curbed, so rival coaches set out to tighten the laws that he exploited with such brilliance.

Probably no other player had ever been able to drop a ball so quickly when tackled, earning him a generous number of 'frees'.

So the coaches carped and complained, taking their rage to the umpires' advisers. Slow motion videos were studied and eventually the rule was changed. Now players must handpass or kick when tackled.

Bartlett was untroubled, for he had 20 years at Richmond, where

in 403 League games he kicked 778 goals.

He was a skinny local kid when he walked into the club in 1962, on the lookout for a game and, as he was to show, even then his timing was impeccable. The club was about to undertake a massive recruiting drive.

His skills were apparent but he had trouble being cleared from a youth club team. Not to be denied, he found a role at Richmond ... as a boundary umpire, then was best in the Under-17s.

Once in the Seniors he was to win just about every honour in football, except a Brownlow Medal. Richmond's best and fairest five times, thrice its leading goalkicker, captain in 1979, he played in five Premiership sides (1967,

1969, 1973, 1974 and 1980).

Always worth watching, Bartlett's victory salute, with two arms raised in glee after erupting into goal, portrayed his passion. Although his nickname showed his boundless appetite for goals, a team-mate, the triple Brownlow Medallist Ian Stewart, noted that Bartlett's goals in critical times were uniquely consistent.

A sports psychologist, Dr Noel Blundell, was unable to ever forget the sight of Bartlett salivating at three-quarter time at Windy Hill in 1983 as Richmond headed for a record 74-point, 13-goal zapping of Essendon.

Kevin Bartlett had a crack at coaching Richmond for four hard years from 1988, then returned to the commentary box.

1987

Jan. 1. Coaching moves at new clubs. Peter Knights is coach of Brisbane, Ron Alexander coach of West Coast (→ 20/7/89).

March 1. Anthony Daniher follows brothers Neale, Terry and Chris to Essendon (→ 22/5/90).

March 28. Darrel Baldock returns to St Kilda as coach, but Saints lose 15.11 (101) to Cats 14.18 (102) (→ 8/8).

April 12. Ticket muck-up: umpires Ian Robinson and Peter Cameron pay own way to second VFL match in Perth. Sydney defeat Eagles 18.16 (124) to 14.13 (97) (→ 11/5/91).

April 18. 300th game for North's Wayne Schimmelbusch in 19.22 (136) win over Geelong 18.19 (127) (→ 3/3/93).

April 20. Magic Maurice Rioli plays his 100th game for the Tigers in the loss, 15.10 (100), to the Magpies, 16.14 (110).

April 29. Melbourne win their first Premiership for 16 years: the Night Flag, 8.10 (58) to Essendon's 8.6 (54).

May 27. Victoria fight back but lose to South Australia, 11.15 (81) to 12.13 (85) (→ 5/7/88).

May 30. VFL has fined 12 of 14 clubs a total of $19,000 for late starts this season (→ 8/2/94).

June 14. Jason Dunstall kicks 11 goals in Hawks' 24.21 (165) to Bears' 11.4 (70) (→ 6/8/88).

July 26. Sydney kick 36.20 (236) to demolish Essendon at the SCG 11.7 (73) (→ 3/5/92).

Aug. 28. Tony Jewell quits as coach of Richmond, to be replaced by Kevin Bartlett.

Aug. 29. Carlton captain Stephen Kernahan kicks a goal after the siren to beat North and secure top spot – 20.9 (129) to 19.11 (125) (→ 12/4/93).

Debuts
Simon Atkins (Foots)
Gavin Brown (Coll)
Nathan Burke (St K)
Paul Dear (Haw)
Garry Hocking (Geel)
Chris Lewis (W. Coast)
Chris Mainwaring (W. Coast)
Mick McGuane (Coll)
Earl Spalding (Melb)
Jim Stynes (Melb)
'Nicky' Winmar (St K)
John Worsfold (W. Coast)

Retirements
Mark Browning (Syd)
Robert Flower (Melb)
Maurice Rioli (Rich)
Wayne Schimmelbusch (N. Melb)

West Coast and Brisbane Bears open their VFL accounts

The colours of the Bears bring a northern dimension to the League.

All change on TV footy merry-go-round

March 27. Just hours before the national competiton was due to be launched at the MCG tonight the VFL announced a major sponsor.

Sportsplay Television Systems, a fledgling satellite station will become a joint corporate sponsor of the competition. Sportsplay will bring League football to hotels and clubs throughout Australia this season.

The deal, believed to be worth $1 million for a year, includes displaying the company's name on umpires' shirts, a move always before resisted by the VFL, which has cast aspersions on the advertising on the backs of Sydney rugby league players' jumpers.

Only small logos on players' guernseys and umpires' shirts have been permitted, but such discretion has clearly become too expensive.

The Sportsplay name will appear on ground arena signs, goal posts and in the *Football Record*.

Scores of sponsors have rejected VFL submissions to take over as major sponsor since CUB withdrew last November (→ 28/5/88).

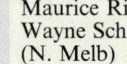

Two of the happy faces of HSV7's 'World of Sport', 'Doutta' Doug Elliot and Lou Richards, can still smile as the show fades out after 28 years and 1355 episodes.

Bond has no time for the Tigers

March 24. Perth millionaire businessman Alan Bond today quit as Richmond's President, just three days before the season starts.

Although the announcement will surprise fans, it comes as no shock to the Tigers' Board because of Bond's immense business interests.

Richmond Director Andrew Fairley said Bond is massively involved in his media group and Hong Kong business. His company sponsorship of Richmond stays.

Bond said it was 'a most difficult and trying time' for the club, which needed a President who could devote most of his time to making it successful (→ 18/8/90).

March 29. Three interstate sides, West Coast, Brisbane and Sydney, have had wins over Richmond, North Melbourne and Collingwood.

They demonstrated a new atmosphere in Australian football and one that threatens to overpower traditional teams such as the Magpies.

Although without several key senior players, Collingwood were demolished at Victoria Park by a side playing textbook football. Sydney scored 25.15 (165) to 11.8 (74).

The Eagles earned their first VFL win today against Richmond, turning a 33-point deficit at three-quarter time into victory, 20.13 (133) to 16.23 (119). Brisbane made an unexpectedly fine start, scoring 19.23 (137) to down North, 15.14 (104) (→ 2/9/95).

Butch Gale among friends at the end

Butch Gale: Fitzroy strong man.

March 24. Former Fitzroy captain Alan 'Butch' Gale died suddenly tonight while addressing players.

Gale, 56, had been invited by Fitzroy coach David Parkin to speak at a players' dinner.

Gale was only 17 when he began his 14 years with Fitzroy in 1948. He represented Victoria for five years, captaining the state in 1959.

One yarn has it that his legs were so badly cut in a 1950s game that he collapsed, and awoke to see a funeral director standing over him – Phonse Tobin, North's President.

BRISBANE BEARS

The modern day football fan is well aware of Australian Football's quest to gain a foothold in Queensland. It comes as a surprise, therefore, to find that the game once flourished in Queensland late last century. A Queensland Football Association was formed in 1879 and it was an active and progressive organisation. A thriving competition grew up around Brisbane and football prospered in other parts of the state. For example, there were also three clubs in Ipswich at this time. Queensland sent representatives to the 1883 Intercolonial Football Conference in Melbourne.

By 1884 it was estimated that there were 339 football clubs and 212 schools playing Aussie Rules compared to 22 rugby clubs. Football was played in the major secondary schools and rugby was pushed into the background. Even as late as 1886 few boys at Brisbane Grammar School were aware of the rules of rugby. 1884 marked the first intercolonial clash between Queensland and New South Wales and, although the Queenslanders lost, there was still optimism about the game's future in the northern state.

The Queenslanders took part in the first Australasian Football Carnival in Melbourne in 1908 and the Queenslanders were considered so worthy of patronage that they were nominated to host the 1914 titles.

The 1950 carnival was also played there, but by that stage Australian Football was very much second fiddle to rugby. Down through the years there were a number of exhibition games played in Queensland between League teams.

As part of the VFL's promotional round in 1952 Essendon and Geelong played for Premiership points at the Brisbane Exhibition Oval. When the League decided in 1986 to go national there was plenty of interest from the northern state. Three different consortiums expressed their enthusiasm to secure the licence for a Queensland team. At one stage feelers had been extended to Fitzroy to relocate to Brisbane, but that idea had faltered.

In the end it came down to a choice between one syndicate headed by Paul Cronin and the Queensland Australian Football League, opposed to another group led by former Australian Tennis Open promoter John Brown.

The AFL Commission favoured Brown's syndicate, but the financially strapped Melbourne clubs believed the QAFL-Cronin syndicate could produce more 'up-front' money.

After the QAFL-Cronin syndicate won the licence late in 1986 it ran into trouble raising the $4 million licence fee, and in November 1986 Christopher Skase stepped in to assist with finance. (Three years later it would be revealed that the original $4 million licence fee remained owed to the bank that had loaned it to Skase.)

Another strange decision was to play home games at the Carrara ground, on the Gold Coast, rather than in the Brisbane metropolitan area. At first it was supposed to be a temporary move, but Skase was determined that Carrara remain the club's permanent home. He threatened to withdraw financial support and that would have crippled the club.

The Brisbane Bears began life with a collection of largely cast-off players. For their support they looked mainly to expatriate Victorians on the Gold Coast.

Australian Football may have been Number One in Queensland in the 1880s, but it did not at first attract much attention among the rugby mad locals.

Russell Holmesby

WEST COAST EAGLES

Australian Football in Western Australia was almost displaced as Number One winter sport after just a year.

The 'Victorian' system, as it was known, was first played in WA in 1880. Rugby took over after one year, but Aussie Rules was kick-started again thanks to the lead given by Willy Bateman and Harry Herbert, two young men who had just finished their schooling in Adelaide and had returned to Fremantle.

The decision between codes must have been a fine balance as the Fremantle Rugby Club was convinced to change codes!

Fremantle was a pivotal location in the game's Western Australian origins. In 1884 the West Australian Football Association was formed and the first senior club was called 'The Fremantle', a name that was used until 1898. First club in Perth was 'The Rovers', but it was the team from the port which dominated, winning six consecutive Flags from 1891 to 1896.

Willy and Lou Bateman, Paddy Knox, Leo Waters and Harry Fry were the big names in WA football at that stage. Gold strikes in 1892 changed the entire complexion of life in Western Australia and there was a direct impact on football. Some of Victoria's finest footballers crossed the Nullarbor to try their luck on the fields around Coolgardie and Kalgoorlie.

Within a couple of years Coolgardie had a population of 15,000 people and it was a magnet for fit young men in their 20s. Footballers like 'Jigger' Morehouse, Jack Lorraine, 'Dolly' Christie, and Barney Grecian headed the rush and then came the biggest of them all – Albert 'The Great' Thurgood.

Western Australia soon established itself as the second most powerful footballing state. The point was not lost on Victorian clubs, and in the early 1930s South Melbourne decided to use Western Australians as part of the campaign for a Premiership.

By the late 1930s the tables were turned and Victorians were aghast to see top men like Haydn Bunton and Keith Shea packing their bags and heading west.

The WA clubs may have hated losing players on the one hand, but by the 1980s they were financially dependent on the pirates from the East.

In 1983 seven of the eight WAFL clubs were insolvent. When a National League was mooted in 1986 the Western Australians knew that they had to pursue one of the National League licences on offer.

But knowing the football capacity of the state there was apprehension among Victorian clubs that they might be about to create a monster when they granted the licence in 1986. The new club had to find a way of funding its beginning and, apart from finding $4 million for its licence, it also had to consider operating costs. Indian Pacific Limited was the company formed to operate the West Coast Eagles. It was floated on the stock exchange, but the public response wasn't as great as anticipated.

The club wasn't about to be stopped and back in Melbourne ex-Sandgropers were urged to come home and play for their home state's team. Ross Glendinning, later to be made captain, was one of the prime movers.

An attempt to win back Hawthorn pair Gary Buckenara and Paul Harding ended up in court and the Eagles lost, but that was just a hiccup.

In years to come there would not be many times when the Eagles ended up on the losing end of anything, on or off the field.

Russell Holmesby

Ton up Tony Lockett does it for the Doc

Aug. 8. The Saints did it for 'the Doc' today, beating a tough Footscray side 15.14 (104) to 15.11 (101) in a thrilling game.

And Tony Lockett did it for his ailing coach, as well as for the 23,000 enthusiastic supporters at Moorabbin, kicking eight goals and bringing up his first hundred-goal season.

With five wins on the trot, the Saints are having their best season in a decade, due in no small part to the big full-forward Tony Lockett, and the influence of the legendary Darrel Baldock.

Baldock, however, who has been unwell for some weeks, was admitted to hospital on Thursday after what appeared to be a slight stroke.

His message from hospital was succinct. 'Don't stuff it up', he said.

The good news for the Saints is that 17-year-old Nathan Burke played a terrific game. He has great poise for a player too young to list his favourite nightclub in the Footy Record.

Dean Rice stood out, as did the immensely talented first year player Nicky Winmar. Some of the older brigade including Peter McConville, Trevor Barker and Danny Frawley, showed they have still got a lot to give to the Saints (→ 26/8/89).

Stephen Kernahan is swept up by his team-mates after scoring the winning goal for Carlton over North, to keep top spot.

Demons' Finals surge ends in Gaelic tragedy at Waverley

No press please, says John Northey, as the shattered Demons contemplate the game that got away.

Sept. 19. Melbourne's beloved captain Robbie Flower appeared set for his first Grand Final. The Demons had been Night Premiers but then struggled.

The parents of Demon Irishman Jim Stynes had flown out for this match. All that was needed today was a win over Hawthorn.

It had been a remarkable season, with a troubled start by Melbourne: one win and two losses before downing St Kilda, in spite of 12 goals from Tony Lockett. There came an embarrassing five-point defeat by the Bears, but when all teams had played each other the Demons were ninth, two games out of the Five.

Things improved until North's Alastair Clarkson from Kaniva, in his first game, marked and goaled in time-on for a two-point win.

After round 21, when Melbourne put down the Eagles, every place was up for grabs. Footscray led Melbourne for three quarters, but a 4.4 last quarter changed that.

With this win, Demon fans packed around transistor radios at the Western Oval, tensely awaiting the result of the Geelong and Hawthorn game where the Hawks had been behind all day. A Geelong win would eliminate Melbourne.

Red and blue beanies and scarves were flung into the air as Jason Dunstall kicked two and the Hawks

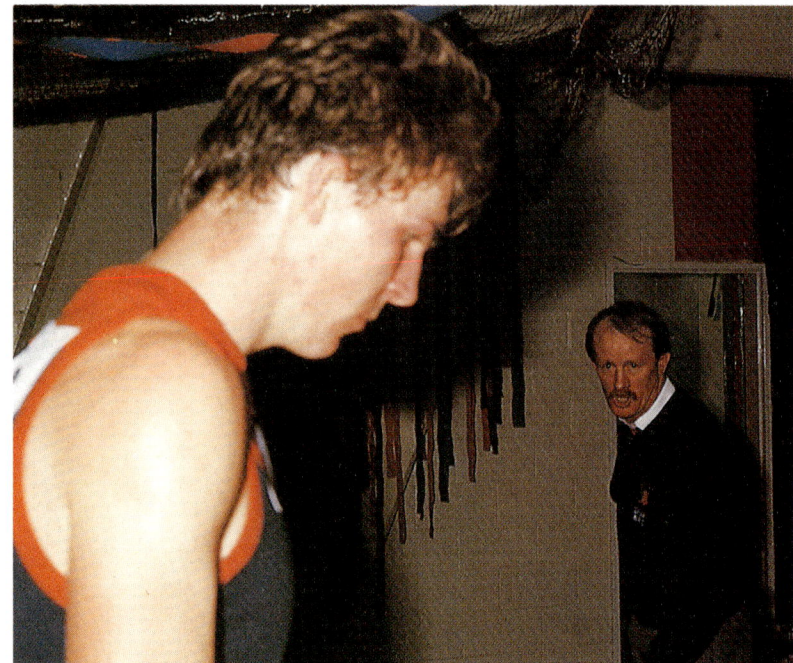

'Don't ever do that again', John Northey tells a crestfallen Jim Stynes.

stole the game by three points.

Melbourne surged on to win two Finals and face Hawthorn in the Preliminary Final.

This time it was the Demons who were in front in a remorseless struggle. Leading into the final quarter, Melbourne were kept goalless as the fiercely determined Hawks added three goals. Each side kicked six behinds, but still Melbourne held on to the lead.

Then the inconceivable happened. Hawthorn's Gary Buckenara was given a free kick. Jim Stynes ran between Buckenara and Demon Rodney Grinter, incurring a 15-metre penalty. Buckenara trotted up to within easy distance for a goal and a two-point win. And that was it, the Hawks by 11.14 (80) to 10.18 (78)(→ 23/9/91).

Year of the Rat, and Plugger too

Sept. 21. St Kilda's massive Tony Lockett and Hawthorn's little John Platten tonight tied for the Brownlow Medal.

As rumours of a leak swept the counting yet again, interstate bookmakers refused to take any bets on Lockett two and a half hours before the count began.

The first full-forward to win the medal, Lockett said: 'You read these stories and you don't think much about them. To win one of these is just unbelievable.'

With 20 votes, Lockett and Platten were five votes clear of Footscray's Tony McGuinness and Brian Royal and Carlton's Paul Meldrum.

Lockett kicked 117 goals this year (→·15/8/91).

The Brownlow boys, with medals, ready for the press barrage.

He might be flashy, with his white boots and golden hair, but this boy Warwick Capper can mark, this time with a beauty over Chris Langford.

Blues too hot for Hawks

Sept. 26. Just as he did five years before, the Dominator, Wayne Johnston, set up the 1987 Grand Final win for Carlton with a fierce opening.

At the opening Johnston cleaned up Hawthorn's strong man Robert DiPierdomenico and got himself reported. He kicked the first two goals, hurt his ankle – all in the first few minutes of the game.

The first quarter continued in a tough and unrelenting fashion, with the Hawks seeming to come off second best. However, Hawthorn crept to a quarter-time lead with four goals in time-on, but that had an unreal quality to it. Michael Tuck was out on his feet, and others were looking quite seedy.

The reality was that the Hawks, on a hot afternoon of over 30 degrees, battered after the physically and emotionally draining Preliminary Final win over Melbourne, and losing Jason Dunstall before the game, were not ready. The rested, collected, tougher and cooler Carlton believed they should win.

David Rhys-Jones won the Norm Smith Medal as best on ground for a complete blanketing of Dermott Brereton who had only six kicks and no goals for the game.

By the end of the afternoon the two were chatting away as if they were at a picnic in the park, acknowledging that the game was over.

The move of Rhys-Jones on to Brereton was an inspired move by coach Robert Walls. Rhys-Jones was unusually disciplined, supreme in the air, and played with great

Rhys-Jones fails to touch one.

poise and timing.

Other outstanding backline players for Carlton were Tom Alvin who attacked while not giving Gary Buckenara a smell, and Stephen Silvagni who performed acrobatically.

Up forward Stephen Kernahan was curbed by Chris Langford, yet kicked three important goals. Ken Hunter provided moments of inspiration and courage.

Craig Bradley gave the idea of an attacking centreman a new dimension with his three goals and David Glascott was very productive.

Hawthorn beat Carlton twice during the season, but the Blues turned the tables twice when it counted – in the finals. Carlton won the Grand Final 15.14 (104) to 9.17 (71) (→30/9/95).

1987 Statistics

Leading Goalkicker:
Tony Lockett (St K) 117
Brownlow Medallists:
Tony Lockett (St K)
John Platten (Haw)
Finals: Elimination Final N. Melb 5.10 (40) Melb 22.26 (158); **Qualifying Final** Haw 23.18 (156) Syd 8.9 (57); **First Semi-final** Syd 10.13 (73) Melb 21.23 (149); **Second Semi-final** Carl 11.14 (80) Haw 10.5 (65); **Preliminary Final** Haw 11.14 (80) Melb 10.18 (78); **Grand Final** Carl 15.14 (104) Haw 9.17 (71)

Ladder:	W	L	D	%	pts
Carl	18	4		138.0	72
Haw	17	5		147.1	68
Syd	15	7		129.5	60
N. Melb	13	8	1	99.4	54
Melb	12	10		108.0	48
Geel	11	10	1	100.3	46
Foots	11	10	1	95.7	46
W. Coast	11	11		97.9	44
Ess	9	12	1	89.5	38
St K	9	13		90.8	36
Fitz	8	14		91.5	32
Coll	7	15		76.4	28
Bris	6	16		79.3	24
Rich	5	17		82.5	20

Melbourne's Robbie Flower: the players' player

While Melbourne wallowed in the black pit of football failure in the 1970s and into the late 80s, there was always one player worth turning up to watch – the incomparable Robbie Flower.

Through a succession of coaches – John Beckwith, Ian Ridley, Bob Skilton, Dennis Jones, Carl Ditterich, Ron Barassi and John Northey – the Demons failed to make the Four, or Five, for 22 years.

Then, after 15 years of virtuoso performances and with his wiry body feeling the strain, the Demons marched Robbie Flower into the Finals in 1987.

The euphoria of the last round win over Footscray and the brilliant Semi-finals wins was largely generated by the possibility of getting a Flag for Robbie.

'Let's do it for Robbie', was the catchcry of the club and their supporters. That they failed is agonising history. That they tried so hard and went so far brought a climactic ending to a great career.

Flower might well be judged the most skilful footballer of his time. He controlled the ball as if his opponents didn't exist; he jinked, and waltzed and baulked his way through packs; he found space for himself and created it for his team-mates; he passed precisely by hand and foot; he set up plays on the back-line and completed them up forward; he outmarked bigger opponents with superb judgement as he floated into the packs.

Flower's favourite area of play was the member's wing at the MCG. If the roars of the faithful spurred him to greater heights as he put on his magic displays, he never showed it. He was always modest and contained in his demeanour. Leadership came not from loud noise, but from natural character and inspiring play.

And with Flower on the field, even in its lowest moments, there was always a chance for Melbourne, and a sense of pride among the supporters.

Flower looked an unlikely starter when he joined Melbourne from Murrumbeena Districts in 1973. At around 10 stone and six feet, the kid looked too frail for the big League. But it was 10 stone of muscle and sinew, with legs that pumped hard and long arms and fingers which controlled the football perfectly.

In all his playing days of 272 League games, he never rose above 12 stone, despite the weight training and gym work

Robbie Flower: made it look easy.

prescribed to beef him up.

It turned out that he didn't need to be any bigger to play better, but some padding might have helped to absorb the buffeting he regularly received from frustrated opponents.

His play took him into the senior team in his first year and he was in the champion class after two seasons. From 1976 he was in every State team chosen, unless prevented from playing through injury.

The wing was his natural home but, like other champions in weak sides, he was used around the ground to try to lift the team. Ron Barassi even put him on a half-back-flank, arousing the ire of supporters. But he dominated there, as well. In his last years he was stationed mostly on the half-forward flank, and he made that position his own with his brilliant anticipation and marking.

He played many spellbinding games, but one against Richmond in 1983 serves to illustrate his superiority. On that day he had 22 kicks, 15 marks and 16 handballs and kicked two goals.

Garrie Hutchinson wrote this of the performance: 'The game looks easy at this level. All you have to do is get by yourself a lot, escape predatory opponents, not be there for the tackle on you, appear invisible to opponents with the ball and grab them from nowhere, fly through the air, run rings and have all day to think about what to to with the ball.'

Robbie Flower was an inspiration right to the end, but he was not tempted to try again after 1987. His durable frame had taken too many hits and he was ready to look on from the selectors' bench.

The VFL's Flying Circus makes a long weekend for players

Australian football has often encountered the tyranny of travel.

A train strike in 1902 led to a match at Corio Oval being cancelled and, the following week, the visiting side having to embark at Port Melbourne by boat for the Port of Geelong.

Geelong always had to travel down the highway every second Saturday to meet the city enemy, not always bringing the whole side, but in 1987 everything changed. Now there were home grounds at Carrara on the Gold Coast for the Brisbane Bears and Subiaco Oval and the WACA in Perth for the West Coast Eagles, both clubs formed the previous year.

Twice this year North Melbourne had to cross the Nullar-bor, losing the first encounter by 74 points, but winning the second under lights by 11 points.

Club officials now had to decide whether to fly over several days before a game, or on the match eve. There were complications, too, when travel arrangements for umpires became unstuck and they were in danger of not making it to WA on time.

But if the travel was proving troublesome, the attendances interstate, especially in Perth, were demonstrating the worth of a truly national competition. A crowd of 38,274 turned up to see the Eagles clean up Collingwood in Perth by 57 points.

For years there had been the cry, 'And the big men fly'. Now they really did.

After the flight, the 'look at the ground', the warm up, the game, the after match, the airport, it's hard for the boys to stay awake – even after a win.

Grinter gets six for Terry Wallace 'tackle'

The moment of impact, as Rod Grinter's fist connects with Terry Wallace.

April 19. Melbourne defender Rodney Grinter was tonight suspended for six matches for striking Footscray centreman Terry Wallace.

Grinter was found guilty of bringing the game into disrepute when he hit Wallace in the face. The charge was laid after an inquiry by the VFL Investigations Officer, Max Croxford, who studied an incident 14 minutes into the first quarter of the game at the Western Oval which led to Wallace being borne from the ground by stretcher.

The Tribunal took just under five hours to make its decision, hearing evidence from 18 witnesses.

Grinter, his left arm still bandaged from the clash, told the three-man Tribunal he had been trying to punch the ball away from Wallace and only had eyes for the ball.

Wallace was travelling at full pace when hit on the face (→ 3/6).

The Channel 7 football commentary team and friends, ready for another big season. The team is (from left) Dennis Cometti, Peter Landy, Bernie Quilan, Don Scott, Ian Robertson, Malcolm Blight, Sandy Roberts and Drew Morphett.

50-metre penalty not waste of time

May 11. The VFL's new 50-metre penalty for time wasting will be raised at an umpires' meeting tonight.

The National Director of Umpiring, Bill Deller, said the umpires' interpretation of the rule had been excellent during practice matches, but there had been problems in the first couple of rounds.

'I think we have paid some that we shouldn't,' he said. Several coaches had raised the issue in recent weeks.

Melbourne scored two goals from 50-metre penalties on Saturday, but TV replays showed the second incident was just trivial.

Powerplay down $18m on Swans

May 12. The ill-fated Powerplay's association with the Sydney Swans seldom looked as decayed as the day the offices' phones were cut off, reports the *Sydney Morning Herald* in a special series.

For all the stories of tardy payments to players, the phalanxes of disgruntled creditors and the increasingly spartan head office, the failure to pay Telecom for half a week was damning.

Last week's final schism between Powerplay and the club it had owned sinced July 1985 was a salutary commentary on meshing private enterprise with sport (→ 19/5/90).

Few injuries from violence: report

June 3. Violence on the football field has been receiving a lot of attention. But, according to the VFL Medical Officers' Association, football is not the violent sport that many people have imagined it to be.

A three-year study by the association found that only 4.7 per cent of League injuries were the result of illegal acts.

The President of the association, Dr Shane Conway, said his members could not condone the distortion and 'excessive attention that some sections of the media have given to football violence' (→ 4/4/90).

Polly Farmer is fined for talking

April 5. The VFL has refused to be swayed on its decision to fine Polly Farmer $1500 for criticising umpires. This is despite an attempt by the Confederation of Australian Sport to have the fine revoked.

VFL Executive Commissioner Alan Schwab stressed that any public reference to the performance of umpires was banned.

In a speech at the Sport Australia Hall of Fame at the MCG, the former Geelong great said 'most umpires are wimps at their best'.

TV time rules the umpires OK

May 28. Fans at Princes Park today grew restive as they waited for the last quarter to start.

And little wonder. Timekeepers at all games have been given strict instructions that, because of television commitments, six minutes must elapse between the end of the third quarter and the start of the fourth.

Players were ready, the umpire was ready but all waited for six more long minutes. Even the coaches were speechless (→ 11/8/90).

Bulldogs stand up for home in the west

July 8. The VFL is against Footscray changing their name, VFL Commission Chairman Ross Oakley said today. Breaking the silence on talks with the Bulldogs, he said Footscray's grandstanding over their ground damaging the case for ground rationalisation.

Footscray say they cannot survive at the Western Oval by themselves, are not allowed to share it and claim they are being railroaded out of the VFL after being refused permission to switch home games to VFL Park.

Mr Oakley said: 'We want Footscray to remain as a football team representing the Western suburbs. Sixty-five percent of Footscray's support base is from the western suburbs, but they said they would be able to generate new support from Waverley if they played at VFL Park.'

Warwick Capper is now a Brisbane Bear

June 12. Warwick Capper looks like repaying some of the $400,000 plus transfer fee the Bears paid Sydney. On his 25th birthday today he kicked eight goals in the Bears' 48-point win over Richmond.

He booted three in each of the first two quarters at Carrara until Richmond coach Kevin Bartlett moved Stephen James to full back just before half time.

Capper's 8.3 and his endeavour were highlights for coach Peter Knights who still found room for improvement in his team, especially in the last quarter. 'A lot of players were lairising,' he said. 'We are not good enough to do that.'

Bartlett, on a high a week ago after a win over West Coast, could scarcely believe today's result.

Warwick takes new team to heart.

Carlton's Stephen Silvagni takes a huge mark against Collingwood.

David Parkin exits Lions coaching den

Aug. 21. David Parkin plans to resign as coach of Fitzroy after Friday's game and take his first break from football in 30 years.

The triple Premiership coach assembled his team after training at South Melbourne this morning and told them he would not seek the job next year. Later, 45-year-old Parkin said he could only think of four games this season when he was happy with the players' commitment.

'The difficulty is going to be coping with the loss of something that has filled 20 of the 24 hours a day for your whole life,' he said (→ 7/9/90).

Wrong score is a Footybet fiasco

Aug. 6. The TAB says it will 'most likely' pay dividends on the corrected 74-point margin in today's Hawthorn and Fitzroy match.

After a dispute over the winning margin, the TAB suspended payment on Footybet tickets. The 72-point margin to Hawthorn, sent to the TAB by an attendant who had not waited for the all-clear flag, was later amended.

Thomastown punter Vince Martella, 30, stands to win $67,000.

Only a small number of winners with 72-point tickets were paid before the mistake was found and payments frozen.

Rhys pioneers suspended sentence

May 2. David Rhys-Jones, Carlton's volatile utility player, tonight made history in his 20th appearance before the League Tribunal. He is the first player to be given a suspended sentence/good behaviour bond on a striking charge.

Rhys-Jones must serve three weeks suspension and then be ready for a further three-match penalty if he is found guilty of another on-field violation over the next two seasons.

A charge of striking Matt Ryan of Collingwood was sustained, but not that of striking Gavin Crosisca with a forearm to the head (→ 22/9/89).

Healy takes medal back to Sydney

Healy: a shattering year.

Sept. 19. Sydney may be looking for a new coach and a new owner, but tonight it gained a Brownlow Medallist in Gerard Healy.

Healy won by four votes in one of the widest fields for several years. He polled 20 votes to beat Essendon ruckman Simon Madden and Hawthorn full-forward Jason Dunstall.

For the 27-year-old ruck rover who played for most of the year with a groin injury and had to cope with the Swans' off-field traumas, it had been 'a shattering year'.

'Sometimes I wish my name was Greg Healy,' he said, referring to his brother, who captains Melbourne in the Grand Final on Saturday.

Temper! Dermott Brereton and Billy Duckworth laugh it off.

Hawks demoralise Demons

Sept. 24. In perhaps the most ruthless and conclusive triumph in Grand Final history, Hawthorn today stamped their greatness by drubbing Melbourne 22.20 (152) to 6.20 (56).

Melbourne came from fifth spot to be sentimental favourites. But the 93,754 crowd saw a goalkicking display by Hawks' forwards Jason Dunstall (7), Paul Abbott (6) and Dermott Brereton (5).

Partly propelled by memories of the defeat last year, the Hawks were able to show exemplary aggression and discipline.

Vice-captain Gary Ayres, 'Conan' to his team-mates, became the first player to win two Norm Smith Medals, despite sustaining a fractured cheekbone in the first quarter.

Beginning in the back pocket, he was put on Greg Healy when Chris Wittman was forced off 10 minutes in with a dislocated left elbow.

Ayres reduced Healy to harmlessness, while helping orchestrate Hawthorn's attack from defence.

Coach Alan Joyce, who replaced the stricken Allan Jeans for one year, said, 'I have never seen a more awesome, more inspiring passage of play than at the 15-minute mark of the second quarter. I saw about a dozen Hawthorn players in a wave going down the field.

'It was a human chain, crashing through a desperate opposition and forcing the ball forward.'

The Hawks broke an eight-game winning streak when they lost to Sydney in July, but finished the season on top with 19 wins (→ 30/9/89).

Hawthorn forward Dermott Brereton has the ball at his fingertips.

A wall mural salutes the VFL Grand Final and the Hawthorn win.

1988 Statistics

Leading Goalkicker:
Jason Dunstall (Haw) 132
Brownlow Medallist:
Gerard Healy (Syd)

Finals: Elimination Final W. Coast 10.11 (71) Melb 11.7 (73); **Qualifying Final** Coll 16.11 (107) Carl 22.13 (145); **First Semi-final** Coll 12.10 (82) Melb 13.17 (95); **Second Semi-final** Haw 9.12 (66) Carl 6.9 (45); **Preliminary Final** Carl 14.14 (98) Melb 19.6 (120); **Grand Final** Haw 22.20 (152) Melb 6.20 (56)

Ladder:	W	L	D	%	pts
Haw	19	3		142.3	76
Coll	15	6	1	112.7	62
Carl	15	7		119.4	60
W. Coast	13	9		111.9	52
Melb	13	9		102.1	52
Ess	12	10		108.4	48
Syd	12	10		99.7	48
Foots	11	11		104.3	44
Geel	10	12		104.9	40
Rich	8	14		85.1	32
N. Melb	7	14	1	89.5	30
Fitz	7	15		83.8	28
Bris	7	15		74.6	28
St K	4	18		82.1	16

Joy for Platten and Dunstall.

1989

May 16. Victoria beat WA in Perth 19.12 (126) to 10.12 (72). Jason Dunstall kicks nine (→ 22/5/90).

May 30. Tony Lockett described his backhanded movement as a 'shrug' to get rid of Eagle Guy McKenna, but the tribunal thought otherwise. Four weeks.

June 12. 87,653 fans pack the MCG to see Geelong beat Essendon 12.17 (89) to 4.11 (35) – despite Essendon receiving 20 frees to 6 in the first quarter (→ 1/7).

July 1. An amazing crowd of 91,960 at the MCG watch Victoria defeat SA in the State of Origin match 22.17 (149) to 9.9 (63) (→ 25/4/95).

July 22. Hawthorn's Jason Dunstall kicks 11.2, just short of Collingwood's total score, in the Hawks' win, 21.11 (137) to 11.11 (77) (→ 5/8).

Aug. 5. Jason Dunstall kicks his 100th goal for 1989, and the game winner with his fifth, at the 27-minute mark of the last quarter, 14.11 (95) to Carlton's 14.6 (90) (→ 21/3/92).

Aug. 9. North Melbourne President Bob Ansett says he is considering an offer from a Queensland entrepreneur to buy the privately owned football club and relocate to Brisbane (→ 6/8/90).

Aug. 19. Chairman of the VFL Commission Ross Oakley announces that the VFL will be known as the Australian Football League from the start of next season (→ 20/3/90).

Aug. 20. Brisbane have their finest moment in the VFL, defeating Hawthorn 12.5 (77) to 9.7 (61) at Carrara.

Aug. 26. St Kilda defeat Melbourne in Saints coach Darrel Baldock's final match at the MCG, 16.8 (104) to 10.12 (72). Nicky Winmar kicks nine.

Sept. 19. North coach John Kennedy announces he is quitting and that Wayne Schimmelbusch will take over.

Debuts
Wayne Carey (N. Melb)
Craig Kelly (Coll)
Derek Kickett (Ess)
Michael Long (Ess)

Retirements
Trevor Barker (St K)
Simon Beasley (Foots)
Ken Hunter (Carl)
Geoff Raines (Bris)
Michael Roach (Rich)
Ken Sheldon (St K)

Ablett becomes top Cat with 14 against Tigers

May 27. On a hazy autumn afternoon at the MCG today Gary Ablett's greatness shone. In 90 minutes he shredded Richmond's defence, establishing a 14-goal record.

Four in the first quarter, two in the second, three in the third, including a left-booter while off-balance, and five in the final 10 minutes ... the display was awesome.

Five players were put on him, all failing. His record surpasses by a goal Doug Wade's Geelong best.

Ablett's record was more impressive because he was not full time in the forward line, but would leave the forward pocket to swap places with Bruce Lindner on the wing. After running a while and garnering possessions from the centre bounce, Ablett went forward to catch his breath. Geelong won massively, 32.19 (211) to 10.17 (77) (→ 30/9).

Gary Ablett is all balance as he snaps one of his 14 goals against Richmond.

Magpies resist flight to Waverley

May 19. As the VFL forced Collingwood to move their round ten match with Geelong to the MCG, a petition is urging the Magpies to stay at Victoria Park.

The petition began circulating today. It wants the club to resist VFL attempts to move their home ground to VFL Park, and wants more home games at the Magpie nest.

Magpie President Allan McAlister wants the petition delayed until he meets its backers (→ 12/6/92).

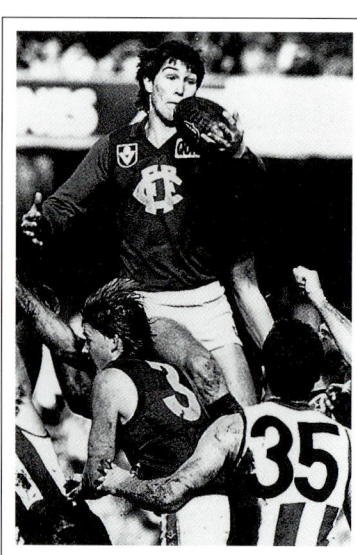

Fitzroy's Alastair Lynch on high.

Hawks' astounding 56-point comeback

May 6. In one the finest home-and-away games of the decade, Hawthorn today came back from 56 points down shortly before half time to defeat Geelong by eight points.

Again it was a Gary Ayres day. When he moved to the centre Hawthorn started to get their running game under way. Then Chris Langford was put on Gavin Exell who had four second-quarter goals.

Geelong had kicked seven second-quarter goals in a mere 12 minutes, but the Hawks kicked the first six goals in the third. Still four goals down in the last, Hawthorn, with Gary Ayres, Gary Buckenara, Dermott Brereton and James Morrissey rampant, won 26.15 (171) to 25.13 (163).

Sea of mud

July 27. The boggy MCG will be given 21 days rest before the VFL Finals in September.

After Saturday's Geelong and Collingwood game there, two round 19 games have been switched to VFL Park.

Talks with the Melbourne Cricket Club following VFL concern over the ground have involved soil experts who suggested the break.

Simon Madden is 321 and still going

Madden reaches a mighty milestone.

Aug. 19. From Baby Bombers to Blue Rinse Bombers. That step has been talked of lately as Terry Daniher passed 250 games, Tim Watson is not far off it and Garry Foulds should join the 300 club next week.

Today Simon Madden will pass Dick Reynolds' Essendon record of 320 games. Madden, 31, overcame disappointment at losing the captaincy in 1982 and time in the Reserves to become the game's best ruckman (→ 29/8/92).

Williams outed in trial by video

June 16. Last Friday Victorian captain and Brownlow Medallist Greg Williams finally lost patience with being knocked about and scragged by Carlton defender David Rhys-Jones.

The Sydney Swans centreman apparently saw his tormentor's head low in a pack and near the ball. His arm went in and Rhys-Jones went out, with a broken jaw.

But all seemed well in Sydney. 'No reports' said the umpires.

But the recent decision to allow for the the viewing of 'the video' and tehn making reports sank Williams. Later viewing of the match video exposed Williams' action and brought a five-week suspension at tonight's VFL Tribunal. Williams said his intention was to hit the ball.

Diesel: caught in the act.

Will Weagles ever win in Melbourne?

July 15. The West Coast Eagles had an odd experience today. They kicked a goal in Melbourne and raised a cheer from the crowd.

The fact that it was their only goal for the day and came in the second quarter of a miserable match might have had something to do with it.

The spectators' cheers were ironic, sympathetic or perhaps just to exercise lungs and vocal cords that were in danger of atrophy as Essendon raced to a devastating victory – 25.10 (160) to 1.12 (18).

The Eagles are not having a great year, having won only two matches in 15, and none in muddy Melbourne. Coach John Todd's future would now seem to be in the hands of others.

Lights out for Knights as coach of Bears

Flamboyant forward Warwick Capper seals fate of two coaches.

July 20. Just four days after the opening of a $4.9 million lighting system at the Brisbane Bears' home ground at Carrara on the Gold Coast, the lights went out for coach Peter Knights.

With a year of his contract still to run, and just seven games left to play this season, the private owners of the club summarily sacked him yesterday afternoon.

Board members Christopher Skase, Paul Cronin and Des Brooks have not released reasons for Knights' abrupt termination, but obviously the team's poor playing record has something to do with it.

The Bears have won just three games this season, despite having been, frustratingly, in winning positions half a dozen times.

The 12-goal loss to Geelong under the expensive brand new lights before a showbiz crowd on Saturday was particularly galling to the owners.

This match was preceded by a 90-minute light show that was supposed to be just like a movie premiere, fitting in with the Skase vision of Carrara becoming an outdoor entertainment venue on the Gold Coast.

However, to make this succeed an accomplished football team is required – and paradoxically that seems unlikely to happen while the Brisbane Bears are not playing where the football public live – in Brisbane.

Knights blames the lack of football experience by the entrepreneurial owners, saying former actor and Chairman Paul Cronin is 'somebody who doesn't understand the game,' and citing lack of communication with the management.

'Christopher Skase at times was there, although he hasn't been around very much this season,' Knights said.

Potential coach Robert Walls, who lost his job at Carlton because of a loss to Knights' Bears earlier in the season, ruled himself out.

'I reckon what they've done to Peter Knights is lousy. If they are interested in me, I wouldn't be interested in them. That lets them know how it stands,' Walls said.

Paul Feltham, specialist sports psychologist at Brisbane, is expected to be appointed today.

Knights asked: 'Can I go back to playing? It sure beats the hell out of coaching.'

He is unlikely to remain a member of the Sacked Coaches Club.

Walls knocked over, Jezza resurrected

June 5. Following Saturday's three-point loss to Brisbane, 17.13 (115) to 18.10 (118), with a goal kicked by Warwick Capper, Carlton coach Robert Walls has been sacked.

And once again 1979 Premiership coach, favourite son and legend Alex Jesaulenko has been recalled to halt a Carlton slide.

Under Walls, Carlton won the 1987 Premiership, but this season have just two wins from ten games and 13th place, in their worst start to a season since 1901.

Former Premiership captain Mike Fitzpatrick has also been appointed Chairman of Selectors in the Carlton reshuffle.

Carlton, who have never won the wooden spoon, will again have to find something extra for Jezza.

The fall of Robert Walls.

VFL seminar hints at club mergers

July 4. The VFL will be encouraging Victorian clubs to merge.

It will be offering financial incentives to struggling clubs to get together and so reduce the number of Victorian teams. This would open the door to other interstate teams, but VFL Commission Chairman Ross Oakley says there is no definite timetable for mergers.

These plans were revealed at a seminar in Hobart attended by 50 club delegates and VFL administrators. Clubs usually mentioned as merger candidates are North Melbourne, Footscray and Richmond.

Among other VFL priorities are to build up the competitive strength of interstate clubs and refuse private ownership of any more clubs.

Old stars come out for retro Brownlows

Harry Collier: reward at last.

Aug. 11. Eight retrospective Brownlow Medals dating back to 1930 were presented tonight.

They went to medallists who now qualify because of a rule change and who were beaten on countbacks, or who tied and got a replica.

The first to get the Brownlows were Harry Collier (Coll) and Allan Hopkins (Foots), who lost to Stan Judkins (Rich) in 1930.

Nell Hutchison, widow of Essendon rover Bill Hutchison, received the 1952 medal, shared with Richmond's Roy Wright. Des Fothergill (Coll) and Herbie Matthews (S. Melb) received 1940 medals. Col Austen (Haw) 1949, Verdun Howell (St K) 1959 and Noel Teasdale (N. Melb) 1965 also received medals.

Vander's reprieve

Sept. 22. The VFL Tribunal has decided to reopen the case involving Essendon's concussed and suspended forward Paul Van Der Haar.

He was not named in Essendon's team for the Preliminary Final against Geelong, but if cleared could play in the Grand Final.

He was suspended for three matches on Monday night. Van Der Haar was knocked out in a collision with Hawk Dermott Brereton in the second quarter. He returned in the third, only to be reported 90 seconds later for striking Greg Dear's head with a right forearm (→ 30/5/90).

The Bulldogs are too tough to die

Oct. 30. Internal bickering and social change brought Footscray to the edge of extinction. From such despair came a community surge of support which saved the club.

Like many such grassroots movements it had something of a starting point in an insult. In May 1989 Ron Barassi, a pre-eminent if often undiplomatic voice of football, blamed poor attendances at Footscray on the influx of Vietnamese people and drug addicts moving from St Kilda.

Footscray's crowds had been dropping, but Barassi had been insulting in his grouping. He was not, nor ever would be, a social commentator of any sensitivity.

This remark, and a VFL plan to band Footscray with Fitzroy brought people into the streets.

Given just 19 days to raise $1.5 million for the club debt, the volunteers rallied. The Footscray Cheer Squad paraded to the club song to have $20s and $50s thrust at them by Vietnamese stallholders at the Footscray Market. A $300,000 sponsorship came from chemical makers ICI. Supporters, especially older women, door-knocked.

The club that had only won a single Premiership, in 1954, and been runners-up once, in 1961, showed that it had a backing that would keep it alive.

Footscray had been around for 106 years and had won a hat trick of VFA Flags among its nine before joining the VFL in 1925. Its symbol, the bulldog, is among the most stubborn, never-say-die creatures. Just like the club.

The defiant Bulldog, symbolic of the pride of the western suburbs people.

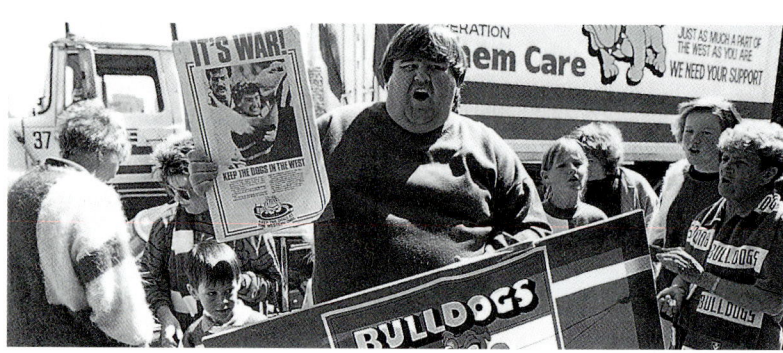

Where there's a will ... supporters rally for the money to save the club.

'Demolition' Dermie

Sept. 16. Dermott Brereton succeeded in destroying Kevin Sheedy's plans in a quarter of fired-up football today.

The Second Semi-final saw 'Demolition Dermie', beaten in the first half, exert a profound influence on the game. Brereton's third quarter completely changed the momentum of the game.

His shirt front of Paul Van Der Haar and tackle on Darren Williams forced them from the ground. Hawthorn kicked 5.6 to two goals in the third quarter to win, 16.16 (112) to 11.10 (76) (→ 19/8/93).

1989 Statistics

Leading Goalkicker:	Ladder:	W	L	D	%	pts
Jason Dunstall (Haw) 138	Haw	19	3		153.2	76
Brownlow Medallist:	Ess	17	5		131.4	68
Paul Couch (Geel)	Geel	16	6		146.8	64
	Melb	14	8		96.5	56
Finals: Elimination Final Melb	Coll	13	9		112.8	52
17.9 (111) Coll 13.10 (88); **Quali-**	Fitz	12	10		97.4	48
fying Final Ess 24.13 (157) Geel	Syd	11	11		100.1	44
11.15 (81); **First Semi-final** Geel	Carl	9	12	1	92.4	38
22.21 (153) Melb 12.18 (90); **Se-**	N. Melb	9	13		89.6	36
cond Semi-final Haw 16.16 (112)	Bris	8	14		78.8	32
Ess 11.10 (76); **Preliminary Final**	W. Coast	7	15		86.7	28
Ess 10.10 (70) Geel 24.20 (164);	St K	7	15		84.3	28
Grand Final Haw 21.18 (144)	Foots	6	15	1	87.0	26
Geel 21.12 (138)	Rich	5	17		70.9	20

Ablett, Brereton rock MCG in Grand Final thriller

Hawthorn withstood a ferocious physical assault by Geelong in the first quarter, and a marvellous football fightback in the last quarter to win the Hawks' first back-to-back Premierships.

In the end the score was Hawthorn 21.18 (144) to Geelong 21.12 (138). Few of the 94,796 present doubted that the result would have been different had the game lasted another minute. Ablett would surely have kicked one more.

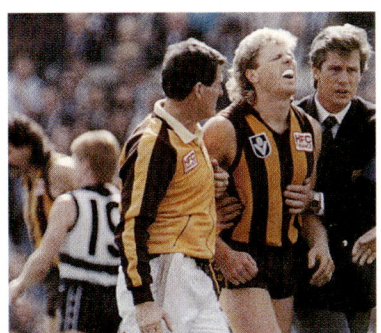

Dermie – down but not out.

Hawks' heart wins an amazing Final

Sept. 30. From the opening bounce when Geelong's Mark Yeates smashed through Hawthorn's Dermott Brereton, the Hawks knew their quest for back-to-back Flags was going to be hard fought.

Hawthorn's Anthony Condon said when he saw this 'Hell's bells, there are no rules today.'

Brereton, bruised kidneys, ribs and all, should have left the field but refused coach Allan Jeans' order. He took a mark and goaled instead.

Jeans sent another message to Brereton: 'Inspirational.'

John Platten, with severe concussion, and Robert DiPierdomenico, with a collapsed lung, were in hospital after the game.

Champion rover Platten was forced from the ground at quarter time, and said he could not remember receiving his winners' Medal.

'Dipper' played the whole game, unaware of the extent of his injury, but was choking by the end.

Other Hawks wounded in the fray included Gary Ayres (hamstring), Michael Tuck (split webbing on hand) Darrin Pritchard (cork thigh) and Peter Curran (ankle).

Curran said after the game that Jeans' half-time speech, asking Hawthorn players to 'pay any price' to win was the most inspirational he had ever heard.

The players had stood up to the onslaught in the first half, and did it again in the second half (→ 28/9/91).

Gary Ablett makes sure of a mark, despite close attention from Chris Langford.

A DISAPPOINTED GARY ABLETT WALKS BACK TO GEELONG....

Ablett takes the direct route home to Geelong after the Grand Final.

Ablett, no! Langford, yes!

Ablett inspires Cats' desperate revival

Sept. 30. Gary Ablett won the Norm Smith Medal as the best player on the ground in the Grand Final – but more than that, he won the hearts and imaginations of football followers of all persuasions.

Geelong fans knew he was capable of anything; now everyone knows he is a football divinity.

Ablett kicked 27 goals in the Final series, including 9.1 today, but it wasn't the quantity of goals so much as their inspirational quality.

Perhaps Ablett's feat in the second quarter where he went up in the ruck in front of Bay 15, grabbed the footy, landed, spun and kicked a freakish, but purposeful, goal was the most spectacular one.

The game was lost by Geelong in the first quarter, when they went the biff while Hawthorn played with the ball. The Cats had scored just two goals against the Hawks' 8.4.

The quietly spoken Ablett said after the match: 'We just let them get away far too early in the game and we just couldn't get back.'

'It's a team game and I think individualism is irrelevant,' he said.

But in the end it took an individual effort of perseverance and brilliance to get Geelong back to within a goal. Hawthorn coach Jeans, who refused to comment on the likely outcome of a hypothetical extra few minutes, said: 'We were in front when the siren went, and that's what counts' (→ 8/6/91).

The Hawthorn Way of old fashioned values

The Hawthorn way was born in the football wilderness, on a side of the Yarra where winning wasn't everything, when the Hawks were beaten week after week, and the wooden spoon was the big event of the year.

It was after the days when committees shuffled teams before a game of cards, after the years when the champions left early, when the great Jimmy Bohan packed his boots for the VFA and Col Austen walked away.

Somewhere in the 1950s and 1960s the Hawthorn way was found by men who understood people as much as football, men like club Presidents Dr Sandy Ferguson and Phil Ryan, and coaches Jack Hale and John Kennedy.

And 'We're a happy team at Hawthorn' became the theme at the 'family club' where the players sang songs after dinner with the coach and his wife.

But they also became a proud and tough and fit team at Hawthorn as Hale and Kennedy developed the play-on, bulldozing game that was pioneered by Hale's predecessor, Bob McCaskill, and taken to near-perfection in the 1980s by Allan Jeans.

Full-pace training drills shaped a team that ran almost automatically under pressure.

With nine Flags since 1961 and a record 13 successive Finals appearances, Hawthorn stands alone. The factors behind its success are not unique. Hawthorn just seemed to find the formula better than most.

The club recruited people with ability and character. Senior players were moulded as leaders to inspire the side at critical times. Many League coaches graduated from the Hawthorn school.

Hawthorn never bought Premierships. It nurtured the League's allocated zones and reaped a harvest that included Don Scott, Peter Crimmins, Michael Tuck, Peter Knights and many more. Most Hawthorn players came up the long way, by an apprenticeship in the Seconds, learning that the laurels in life are won by the sweat of the brow.

Persistence is the Hawthorn way. Peter Hudson once joked that he only came to Hawthorn to get a little guy called Ron Cook off his back!

Hawthorn's way is as unpretentious as the old brown overcoat John Kennedy wore as coach for 14 years. It is being humble in victory and taking de-

'Dipper' takes the heat.

feat on the chin, rarely squealing when the umpires or Tribunal make a bad decision. Problems are kept in-house. Old-fashioned values like decency, honesty, integrity, discipline, and good financial housekeeping really do matter and the club is pained when it fails to meet the standards it sets.

Playing for the guernsey did not disappear. Leigh Matthews and Jason Dunstall could have made fortunes at other clubs.

Colourful personalities like Dermott Brereton and Robert DiPierdomenico fitted in so well because everybody is accepted in the Hawthorn family.

The club is never too harsh in criticism or effusive in tributes. It was high praise when Allan Jeans called the magnificent Finals campaigner Gary Ayres 'a good driver in heavy traffic'.

Hawthorn's way is as efficient as the 1988 coaching handpass from Allan Jeans to Alan Joyce and back to Jeans, as smooth and stable as a long line of capable coaches, captains and Presidents.

To most clubs today, the Hawthorn way is as harsh and unyielding as the running wall of brown and gold that always seemed to be charging along the central corridor at Waverley or the MCG. But to the faithful who embraced long years of struggle it is as friendly and satisfying as a barbecued sausage from big Bob Yeoman on a winter training night.

Club historian Harry Gordon called Hawthorn's story *The Hard Way*. And the simple wisdom of Allan Jeans summed it up for the players: 'To know where you're going, you must remember where you've come from.'

Damien Cash

Diesel power fires up football's engine room

Diesel – skill before speed.

Greg 'Diesel' Williams is one of football's greatest, but also most physically unlikely, modern champions.

The 1986 Brownlow medallist was rejected by Carlton, twice, as being too slow in the legs before being given a chance at Geelong by coach Tom Hafey to show what he could do as part of an inspired centreline – Gary Ablett on one wing, Williams in the middle and Michael Turner on the other wing.

Williams had arrived at Geelong after three years playing in the Bendigo Football League's team in the country football championships. His coach was Dennis Higgins, and what he said to Diesel was important to his development as a footballer.

Higgins told Williams that most games are decided by the players in the two metres around the ball, when it is in dispute. He told him that the ball is on the ground 90 % of the time so you don't have to be able to jump very high.

And 'If you have good touch and a fast combination of eye and brain and can therefore make fast and accurate disposals, you don't have to be an expert at ducking and dodging'.

These ideas might have been tailor-made for a smaller less than speedy player such as Williams.

Add to this analysis of how games are won the fact that Higgins has been quoted as saying: 'Williams is the first player to use handball as the first option in the

heaviest traffic. He is the first player to have equal skills in each of four limbs.'

Add that to a superior football brain, excellent peripheral vision, courage and and a bit of aggro, and you've got a great and unusual footballer.

Williams left Geelong after two seasons and 34 games and went to Sydney with Tom Hafey, and a much bigger amount of cash than the $5000 extra, to $50,000, he had asked Geelong for.

The SCG might have been made especially for him. His handballs out of the centre are better than a kick, he can drift all over the ground knowing he will always be near the action, and he has had, until recently, a talented team of imports to play with.

1990

March 17. Essendon win pre-season Night Flag, defeating North Melbourne 17.10 (112) to 10.16 (76) (→ 20/3/93).

April 4. Collingwood's Tony Francis is suspended for six weeks over a kicking incident in his first game. West Coast defeat Collingwood 14.16 (100) to 8.6 (54) (→ 22/3/92).

May 5. Essendon defeat Collingwood 15.11 (101) to 10.15 (75) at the MCG before 63,318 – in the last game in front of the intact old Southern Stand. (→ 25/3/92).

May 22. NSW defeat Victoria in a State of Origin shock 13.8 (86) to 10.16 (76) at the SCG. Selector Ted Whitten says it is a shock to the system (→ 3/5/94).

June 3. The *Sunday Age* tips Tony Liberatore to win the Brownlow Medal.

July 7. John Longmire kicks 14.2 in North's 31.14 (200) win over Melbourne, 10.13 (73).

July 14. Treasurer Paul Keating is told by Collingwood President Allan McAlister 'If you want to become Prime Minister, this is the way to go about it,' when made ticket holder 6483. The Magpies defeat Carlton 17.11 (113) to 8.11 (59).

July 29. Hawk Gary Buckenara retires, after four Premierships and a chronic knee injury.

Aug. 3. Michael Tuck plays his 400th game in Hawthorn's tight win over North, 15.18 (108) to 14.14 (98) (→ 1/9).

Aug. 6. AFL defers decision on admitting Port Adelaide to the League after the SANFL makes a last-minute bid to enter its own team (→ 19/9/92).

Aug. 12. Essendon defeat Collingwood in the 'Grand Final preview' at Waverley, before a crowd of 65,000, 13.6 (84) to 11.12 (78), despite live telecast in Victoria (→ 22/3/92).

Aug. 26. 'Save Our Skins' rally nets $150,000 to help Richmond remain afloat.

Debuts
Ben Allan (Haw)
Tony Francis (Coll)
Chris Grant (Foots)
Brett Heady (W. Coast)
Paul Kelly (Syd)
Peter Matera (W. Coast)

Retirements
Rod Carter (Syd)
Gary Buckenara (Haw)
Gerard Healy (Syd)
Wayne Johnston (Carl)
Paul Van Der Haar (Ess)

Pelerman purchases Brisbane Bears

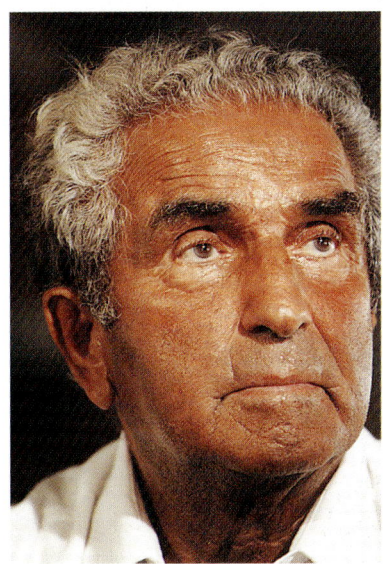

Pelerman: big birthday buy-up.

Feb. 15. Reuben Pelerman, a 76-year-old entrepreneur, bought the Brisbane Bears today in a belated Valentine's Day present for his wife. The 'gift' will cost $10 million over five years.

Coach Paul Feltham was less enthusiastic as he was immediately sacked despite having won five out of seven games after taking over from Peter Knights. Pelerman meets the players tomorrow. Unheralded Norm Dare will become the new Bears' coach (→ 25/3/91).

Straitened Swans tighten belts

May 19. Sydney Swans executive Geoff Slade admitted today that the contracts for his club's players are null and void now 20 per cent pay cuts have been enforced.

He said contracts would have to be renegotiated for next season.

The Swans continue to struggle for crowd support, with next week's State of Origin game regarded as an important indicator.

Crowds have declined to an average of about 10,000, compared to 26,000 in the heady days of 1986.

The difficulty in explaining to Sydney Cricket Ground crowds just what is happening has been demonstrated by the sight of two elderly women in red-and-white applauding a Geelong mark over a Swan.

Jack Hamilton dies in car accident

May 30. Jack Hamilton, the 61-year-old former VFL Commissioner was killed today in a one-car accident between Whittlesea and Kinglake.

His wife, Joan, 60, sustained minor injuries.

Police believe Hamilton's car overturned when he swerved into gravel on a corner of the Whittlesea-Yea road about 10 kilometres from Whittlesea on a stretch notorious for accidents.

The former Collingwood full-back played 154 games between 1948 and 1957, but missed the 1953 Grand Final win through injury.

Ron Barassi today told a favourite Hamilton story about the first meeting of the VFL Rules Review Committee. 'Before we were even convened, before anything was official, old Jack stood up and said, "I want to make it clear that Barassi's bid for two goal umpires at either end has got no chance". The meeting dissolved into laughter.'

Hamilton himself was known for his wit. 'It wasn't until my kids were 15,' he once said, 'that they found out my first name was Jack. They thought it was Bloody.'

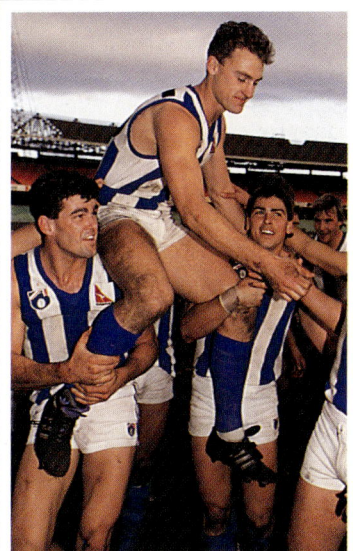

North's John Longmire broke a club record when he kicked 14 goals in the win over Melbourne, 31.14 (200) to 10.13 (73).

League's new name marks new era

A new League, a new Logo.

March 20. The Australian Football League is now the official name of the competition.

In the middle of last season the rights to the AFL title were handed over by John Adams, a Director of West Coast and former General Manager of North Melbourne, who had registered them. No money was involved. A 93-year tradition has ended with the passing of the blue and white logo, with its football and big V, which had symbolised the game (→ 15/3/92).

Football Record is a real lifesaver

April 7. A bundle of *Football Records* squeezed through a rubber seal allowed air into a lift trapping Carlton President John Elliott and most of the club's Committee.

A radio outside the door at VFL Park relayed the game to the trapped officials, who were freed by lift mechanics after an hour. An overloaded lift was blamed.

Angry Elliott, who had flown in from Tahiti to see the Blues play Collingwood, was riding with his father, AFL Commissioner Peter Nixon, and others to the VIP enclosure when the lift jammed.

Once freed, the Blues officials were even more unhappy, watching their team go down by 35 points, 13.9 (87) to the Magpies 19.8 (122).

Hawthorn's Michael Tuck tops record League total with 404 games

Just what you need when you have played 404 games and want a rest. A pesky rover threatens to kiss you.

Sept. 1. Michael Tuck took to the field for his 404th game today, every one of them played for Hawthorn. He broke Kevin Bartlett's long-standing 403-game record and, showing no signs of being near the end of his long career, could well move up to a 420-game tally if he completes a full season next year.

Tuck came to Hawthorn from Berwick as an 17-year-old in 1971, playing his first senior game the following year. He is now 37, but his stamina and running speed seem undiminished. The day after a game he's reputed to get around slowly, and painfully sometimes, but when playing the ball few can match his turn of speed, or his tenacity.

In today's game against the Demons, the Melbourne cheer squad banner read 'Congratulations Tucky, it's a pity we're going to spoil the party'. And they did.

Melbourne won by 12 points: 17.14 (116) to the Hawks' 15.14 (104). Tuck's own form was also not up to its usual standard.

Rhys' silver jubilee

May 30. David Rhys-Jones tonight escaped a lengthy suspension when cleared of charging by the Tribunal.

In his 25 appearances before the Tribunal the rugged Carlton utility player has been suspended nine times for a total of 22 matches during his senior career of 175 games.

Over his head now hangs a four-match suspended sentence. He said he was leading into open space when Fitzroy wingman Darren Kappler marked and jumped to try to spoil, but was late.

The Four Danihers

May 22. Four Daniher brothers helped to show the way in tonight's historic win by New South Wales over Victoria by 10 points at the Sydney Cricket Ground.

Anthony, Chris, Terry and Neale have never played together at Essendon, but tonight Anthony's booming punts from fullback kept clearing the centre.

Two of the brothers got a goal each and Anthony was among the best players. North Melbourne's John Longmire kicked eight goals.

Dunstall returns with added protection

July 7. Jason Dunstall was nervous before today's comeback. He had been out since May 26 when his skull was fractured at VFL Park in a game against Melbourne.

Today he kicked 3.4 in Hawthorn's big win over Geelong, 18.10 (118) to 7.8 (50).

When Dunstall fell with the ball and rolled on to his back, as he had done so many times, on that May afternoon Earl Spalding's knee hit his head. 'I remember the knee hitting me in the face,' said Dunstall of the freak accident.

'When I sat up my right eye closed immediately. I didn't have any pain, but I remember thinking, It's going to be hard to play.'

He had immediately left the ground.

'The pain started when I got to the rooms. It was like being hit repeatedly with a sledgehammer. When I wasn't thinking about the pain I was thinking about how long I was going to miss.'

He was injected with morphine for the pain and then vomited in the ambulance on the way to hospital.

Doctors inserted a titanium rod held in place by two screws. 'Origi-

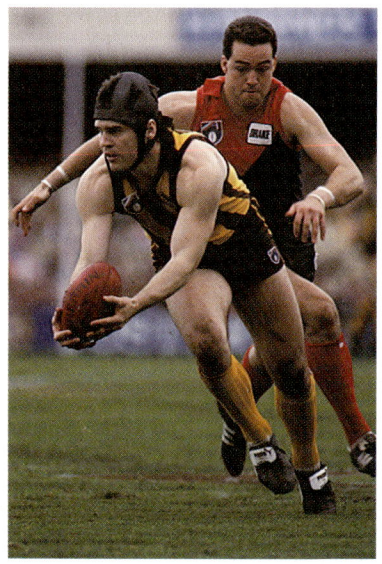

Dunstall on the point of collision.

nally they planned to take a bit of fat from the abdomen to support the damaged bone, but the break was in three nice-sized pieces and they were able to wire them together.'

Wearing his new helmet and with short hair for the first time in a decade, Dunstall was back at training on June 5. Today his main worry was a lack of kicking skill.

Tigers' $1m debt

Aug. 18. Richmond are struggling for survival. Facing interest payments of $500 a week, and a time and debt equation which works out at $13,330 a day between now and the end of October, the club are in desperate straits.

By then they must pay back $800,000 to the ANZ Bank as part of a debt of more than $1 million.

Today club President Neville Crowe called on supporters to emulate a seven-year-old's gift of $50.40 from his moneybox.

Blues dump hero

Sept. 7. Carlton have sacked coach Alex Jesaulenko, after a disappointing 34 games and two finishes in eighth place. He could not reproduce the inspiration as coach in his second stint that he did as playing coach in 1978-1979.

He will be replaced by 1981-82 Premiership coach David Parkin, who was also sacked in 1985.

Parkin said: 'I've missed it. I've missed the contact on the day, the player contact. Most of us have it in our blood. We're a bit silly.'

The Thoughts of Chairman Yabbie

Allan 'Yabbie' Jeans is one of the most successful coaches of the modern era. With an involvement in League football that has stretched over nearly 40 years, as player and coach, only a handful of coaches have more Premierships than Jeans.

As coach of St Kilda from 1961 to 1976, Jeans coached them in 332 games, won 193, lost 138 and drew one, for the famous 1966 Premiership.

At Hawthorn between 1981 and 1987 and 1989-90, Jeans coached 221 games, won 159, lost 61 for one draw and six Grand Finals, and the 1983, 1986 and 1989 Flags. Some would count 1988 as well when Hawthorn were coached by Alan Joyce while Jeans recuperated from a brain haemorrhage.

At Richmond in 1992 he coached 22 games, for 5 wins and 17 losses. Jeans' total of 575 games and 357 wins is outstanding.

Allan Jeans played 77 games for St Kilda, 1955-1959. He was injured in 1960, helped with the Reserves, and was appointed senior coach the next year – the youngest non-playing coach in VFL history.

Beyond the raw statistics of Jeans' commitment and success is a student of the game, and a philosopher of life.

As befits a man who was for most of his coaching career also a Senior Sergeant of Police, his coaching style emphasised discipline and self discipline . This is reflected in some of the 'homilies' he delivered before and after games. Like the best homespun philosophy there is more than a thread of truth in them.

Some sayings are possibly apocryphal and ascribed to philosopher Jeans – such as 'Football is a game played on an oval with an oval ball, so anything can happen'. That could well have come from the brain of a fevered physicist but it is also true. After winning the 1986 Grand Final, Jeans said: 'Success needs no explanation. Failure will not accept any alibis.'

In 1985, he gave Gary Buckenara advice he gave to many players who want to be part of the

Jeans: keeping it simple.

Hawthorn success machine: 'Get yourself fit and you will be part of the ride.' This fits in with his description of Gary Ayres as a 'good driver in heavy traffic'.

He told Harry Gordon in the Hawthorn history *The Hard Way* 'I like to tell them stories. I like to keep it simple. That's why I talk about football being like cooking sausages ... that you can fry them, curry them, put apple sauce with them. They're still sausages, all you're doing is dressing them up. The basics are still the basics.

'The message I told them for the [1989] Grand Final was about buying shoes, about having the choice between a really good pair that was dear and another pair that didn't fit as well. If you bought the cheap pair, you'd regret it, you'd say "I wish I paid the price". I kept asking them what they'd be saying next day. Whether they would be saying 'I wish I'd paid the price yesterday.'

On umpires: 'They make mistakes but they don't make as many as players make.'

On wet day football: 'The species that doesn't adapt to the conditions becomes distinct.'

On post-match interviews: 'I just say nothing so I can't say anything wrong.'

On the other team winning: 'They won in most positions and made the least amount of mistakes – so they won.'

On football: 'From the first bounce to the end of the game there are only three phases ... when the ball is in dispute, when we've got it, and when they've got it. And there are two teams out there, aren't there? And each player has got two arms and two legs.'

Sumich behind lets Magpies breathe again

Peter Sumich ponders what might have been, as the match heads for a replay.

Sept. 8. West Coast looked capable of an upset win over Collingwood in the Qualifying Final today, but Peter Sumich kicked a behind instead of a winning goal for a draw and a replay next week. The scores were 13.12 (90) each.

There was never a lot in it, with Collingwood leading by five points at quarter time and two goals at half time. Eagles' running players, such as Chris Lewis, troubled the Magpies' midfielders.

The typical intense tackling of West Coast disturbed Collingwood. Down to the wire, Collingwood could not clear the ball, opening the way for Karl Langdon to snap for goal. Chris Waterman and Sumich followed with points, to eliminate the Pies' eight-point lead with only six seconds to go.

Coach Leigh Matthews opened with Brian Taylor at full-forward and Gavin Brown in the pocket.

Taylor was taken off 21 minutes into the second quarter, returning 10 minutes into the last. He then goaled twice in four minutes.

Peter Daicos produced one of his goals of genius late in the day, a banana kick from the boundary line in the wrong pocket. Many watchers said it was the best they had ever seen.

Daicos had shaken the Eagles with an early goal, as had Taylor with two. The Eagles had their chances with an attempt by Chris Waterman and the Sumich shot from within 15 metres.

Brilliant Chris Lewis and slogging Dwayne Lamb matched Collingwood's midfield and showed the potency of the Eagles' forward line, with four-goal Sumich and the elusive Brett Heady.

Mick Malthouse dragged captain Steve Malaxos midway through the first term. Now to next week.

After 32 years, the Collingwood dream comes true

Oct. 6. In February, an entertaining article on world heavyweight boxing in the Melbourne *Sunday Age* quoted the sage of the New York Yankees, Yogi Berra, saying: 'In baseball, you don't know nuttin'.'

Just a month later, in the same paper, Mike Sheahan explained why Collingwood had no players regularly taking control of the game in the style of a long list of big hitters from other clubs.

Neither Peter Daicos nor Darren Millane could produce sustained brilliance, he complained. Gavin Brown's worth had been exaggerated. Other Magpies were similarly dismissed.

Flash to October 7 and the same writer is explaining how Collingwood's first Flag in 32 years was the culmination of a strategy that began in 1985 with an approach to Leigh Matthews to be coach.

Collingwood had finished second in the home-and-away series, drawn with the Eagles in the Qualifying Final, then won three on the trot.

The leader for the MCG battle against Essendon was Tony Shaw, who that day became the first captain to win the Norm Smith Medal for best on the ground.

The Bombers had started strongly, with Paul Salmon taking charge of the forward line and kicking two goals in the opening few minutes. But the Magpies were superb in the second quarter, scoring five goals in the first nine minutes to set up a 34-point advantage.

Then with ruckman Damian

A Premiership at last. The Collingwood supporters swamp Victoria Park to rejoice over the victory.

Monkhorst leading the charge and beating Simon Madden and Salmon, Collingwood built on their dominance. Scott Russell kept winning the ball from the centre and even goaled twice.

Craig Starcevich, who had come off the bench half-way through the first quarter, went on to kick a significant goal in the second quarter, to be followed by two each from Gavin Crosisca and Scott Russell.

A further 18 minutes were to pass before Doug Barwick got the Magpies' next goal.

Although Darren Millane was a bit of a slow starter, he too established supremacy, while Mick McGuane fully deserved the praise showered on him for his ruck roving. Shane Morwood was faultless, as was Craig Kelly across halfback.

As perhaps could have been expected, there were two moments of genius from Daicos. From tight on the boundary line he kicked Collingwood's first goal 21 minutes into the first quarter. Half-way into the third quarter he chipped in a banana kick while almost impossibly stuck between a pair of defenders.

Gavin Brown returned after being concussed to down Alan Ezard in defence, with a goal following to give the Pies a 40-point lead. The final siren went as the scoreboard showed 13.11 (89) to 5.11 (41), and the Magpies and their supporters erupted into a frenzy born of years of frustration.

A turbulent scene during the match after the felling of Gavin Brown.

Darren Millane swoops on the ball and avoids a lunge from his opposing winger, Essendon's Greg Anderson.

1990 Statistics

Leading Goalkicker:
John Longmire (N. Melb) 98
Brownlow Medallist:
Tony Liberatore (Foots)
Finals: Elimination Final Melb 10.13 (73) Haw 8.16 (64); **Qualifying Final** Coll 13.12 (90) W. Coast 13.12 (90); **Qualifying Final Replay** Coll 19.12 (126) W. Coast 9.13 (67); **First Semi-final** W. Coast 19.16 (130) Melb 15.10 (100); **Second Semi-final** Ess 7.12 (54) Coll 17.15 (117); **Preliminary Final** Ess 18.13 (121) W. Coast 8.10 (58); **Grand Final** Coll 13.11 (89) Ess 5.11 (41)

Ladder:	W	L	%	pts
Ess	17	5	139.2	68
Coll	16	6	130.2	64
W. Coast	16	6	118.4	64
Melb	16	6	113.2	64
Haw	14	8	120.6	56
N. Melb	12	10	114.0	48
Foots	12	10	99.3	48
Carl	11	11	104.1	44
St K	9	13	100.6	36
Geel	8	14	93.7	32
Rich	7	15	78.6	28
Fitz	7	15	78.4	28
Syd	5	17	70.4	20
Bris	4	18	71.4	16

How the Magpies made it happen, at last

Rarely can a Grand Final have been won without a significant move by one of the coaches.

That was the case, however, in the win by Collingwood, a Flag-grabbing effort that came from the Magpies' deep strength of desire.

There simply were no Magpies who played badly.

With a sensible forward line-up, Kevin Sheedy would have been pleased early on as Paul Salmon's great height was augmented by the skills of the smaller players, such as Michael Long, Darren Bewick, Alan Ezard and Tim Watson.

Midway through the first quarter Leigh Matthews replaced Damian Monkhorst, who had been in the square with Gavin Brown. The choice of the more mobile Craig Starcevich worked until he was injured in the third quarter.

Back into the ruck at the start of the second quarter, big 'Monkey' was soon the star big man.

Having been walloped in midfield by Collingwood in the Second Semi, the Bombers initially had Peter Cransberg on McGuane, but he was taken off and replaced 20 minutes into the second quarter by Kieran Sporn, who was later able to compete well with Graham Wright.

Rover Tony Francis soon toyed with a leaden Mark Thompson, so Ezard was summoned from the bench to the fray and soon the pair were scrapping.

Derek Kickett found Tony Shaw hard to contain in midfield and, similarly, Craig Kelly and Michael Christian were dominant as key defenders.

At the half-time break it was clear that Sheedy's options were very narrow. A shoulder injury to Greg Anderson closed them even further.

Only Watson, it seemed, would be capable of rallying the Bombers. He came out strongly in the third quarter but, like his team, did not have the capacity to get the goals that were needed.

Peter Daicos was troubled by Gary O'Donnell, who then slowed down Scott Russell. Gavin Crosisca managed to dominate defender Paul Hamilton in the second quarter, but was worried by him the rest of the time.

As a last effort, Sheedy moved Madden to full-forward where he missed two easy chances.

This reflected Essendon's inability to fight back. They also appeared unfit. The drawn Qualifying Final meant that they had missed three consecutive weeks.

An exception was Kickett, who took the mark of the day when he shot up on Shaw's shoulders. That was possibly the only glimpse of Bomber glory.

The Magpies came out determined to reverse the tide of football history.

Peter Daicos: the Macedonian Marvel and his miracles

Memories. The handball whizzes from the galloping Peter Daicos. Over the despairing head of Geelong's Ian Nankervis.

And here is Daicos again, almost impossibly, running on to gather the same ball and goal from 40 metres.

Another memory: he is flying through the air, feet first, like a soccer striker, and slams the ball on the volley on to his target.

Swerving, weaving and baulking on those often-damaged legs, he finds space where none seems to exist. 'Daics' has two players, their socks down, hanging off him while, with black socks proudly pulled up, he slots another.

As the Brisbane Bears' John Gastev was hurtling him off the ball near the point post he still goaled, and got 12 more.

In Australian sport there have been many outstandingly gifted players whose daring and dash were such that magnificent deeds were always expected.

So it was with Peter Stanley Daicos, born September 20, 1961, in Fitzroy, Melbourne, to parents who came to Australia as teenagers from Macedonia.

His father loved South Melbourne, so Daicos trained with the Swans' Little League. He was persuaded to join the Magpies only after his family moved to Collingwood territory at Preston.

Daicos' first senior game, in round four of 1979, when he was 17, is remembered because St Kilda lost at Victoria Park by 178 points, 31.21 (207) to 3.11 (29). He had 29 possessions.

In the 1980s his goal-finding feats became almost common. Nine goals against Richmond in 1981 included a wonder shot.

In a drawn Qualifying Final in 1990 he delivered, late in the day, with a banana kick from the boundary line in the 'wrong' pocket, to roll it in against the Eagles. And in Collingwood's Grand Final win he kicked two majors of breathtaking artistry.

Such a shot often sent the ball through from the forward pocket on the third bounce. Whether marking, slipping through tight packs or paddling the ball to a team-mate or himself, he was always exciting and in control.

His personality was less reliable than his football, however, for he loved a beer with his mates and a game of cards. His business upsets made headlines, but after his 250-game career of 549 goals ended in 1993 he went on to become a radio commentator.

The manner of his dumping by Collingwood brought no credit to the club in the eyes of his legions of fans.

Crows shock Hawks for first up win in Adelaide

March 22. Some of the worst worries of Victorian clubs came true tonight when Adelaide entered the national competition by comprehensively beating Hawthorn.

At Football Park, Adelaide, a sell-out crowd of 44,902 one-eyed fans saw their Crows win 24.11 (155) to 9.15 (69). Adelaide led by 51 points at half time, while the early Premiership favourites were easily pushed aside just a week after taking the pre-season championship.

Hawthorn's lapses at centre-half back were shown up by Peter McIntyre and John Klug, both kicking four goals. Dermott Brereton was reported by both field umpires after a clash with Crows captain Chris McDermott, who was stretchered off (→5/9/93).

A new-look team, and a huge crowd, as the Crows cruise to victory in Adelaide.

Now the Lions cry: 'Don't let us die'

April 14. 'This is not a fund-raiser,' Fitzroy chairman Leon Wiegard said today, 'this is a club-saver.'

Unless Fitzroy clear up a debt of $650,000, he said, 'the people of Victoria don't want Fitzroy'.

He said the club had already cut the debt from $2.6 million. An even keel could take them into the black.

During the rally at Princes Park the scoreboard still showed yesterday's defeat by Footscray. But the 3000 or so Lions supporters were a much smaller crowd than the estimated 10,000 at similar Richmond and Footscray rallies in the past.

A personal cheque for $250 was presented by Collingwood President Allan McAlister. Favourite son Kevin Murray said supporters should remember that the club had been through tougher times.

Blues' only goal

June 2. Carlton scored their lowest total in 87 seasons today. The 1.10 (16) at the Western Oval was their worst in 111 matches against Footscray. It was the worst score since the black season of 1904 when Carlton scored 1.8 (14) – twice.

Carlton were saved from embarrassment by a goal from a free kick to Mark Arceri with 33 seconds to go. Footscray kicked 8.9 (57).

Final Six: the new way of the AFL

March 11. And now for the Final Six. After 19 years of having a Final Five as the cut-off for teams to go into the Finals, the League has decided to expand it to six, with two Elimination Finals.

With the Adelaide Crows, it is now a 15-team competition.

Back in 1897 the top four clubs of the eight in the competition played each other after the home-and-away rounds. The Premiership was decided by a Finals Ladder.

Such a 'Round Robin' finals system was used again in 1924. Between 1898 and 1930 a range of play-off methods determined the Premiership. In 1931, Ken McIntyre's Final Four system commenced and continued until 1971. The McIntyre Final Five system was introduced in 1972 (→10/3/92).

Former Demon Brian Wilson got six goals for St Kilda in a win against his old club.

Bears' owner wilts after losing $3.3m

March 25. The Brisbane Bears owner, Reuben Pelerman, confirmed today that he is likely to give up ownership of the team at the end of the season.

Since taking control of the club in February last year he estimates he has lost $3.3 million. He bought the team in a deal worth $10 million over five years but now says the losses were an embarrassment.

'It's been a terrible, heavy burden to me,' he said. It is likely the team would attempt to copy the structure of Melbourne clubs – and move to a larger supporter base in Brisbane.

His losses have convinced him that private ownership of a team was not viable. 'It's crazy. You've got so many players to support, not like soccer or rugby league. Financially it's embarrassing.'

ADELAIDE CROWS

The citizens of Adelaide were engaged in some form of football from as far back as 1860. An advertisement in the *Adelaide Register* of April 25 1860 proposed forming a football club and on the next evening 16 men formed the Adelaide Football Club.

From the very start, football attracted members of high social standing in Adelaide and early newspaper reports concentrated more on the names of dignitaries than on the performances of the players. Rules of the early games were not noted, but teams could number 35 or more players. It has been suggested that they followed Victorian Rules, but Geoffrey Blainey says in *A Game of Our Own* that Adelaide football was more likely to have picked up points from English codes.

Port Adelaide Football Club was formed in 1870 and immediately exerted an influence and presence on the South Australian game that has extended to the present day. In 1873 there was an attempt to call all clubs together and agree on a uniform set of rules. The strongest clubs, Port Adelaide, Kensington and Adelaide, agreed, but not all teams went along with the notion.

For one winter in the mid-1870s it appears that a more rugby-related version of football was played, but it was soon overtaken by something that approximated Victorian Rules.

By 1877 the Adelaide teams were playing a form of football that was similar enough to Victorian football to enable teams to meet visiting Victorian sides Melbourne and St Kilda in the first intercolonial matches. Norwood was formed in 1878 and conceded just one goal in winning all of its 12 matches. Norwood won six Premierships in a row and in 1888 beat South Melbourne for the 'Championship of Australia'.

One of the prime objectives of the Victorian Football Association upon its formation in 1877 was to arrange games between Victoria and other colonies.

There were problems with finding the right venue in Melbourne and the proposed dates did not suit the South Australians. This was the first in a long catalogue of differences between the states.

Finally, representative sides met in the first true intercolonial clash on July 1 1879, and Victoria thrashed a South Australian team by 7.14 to 0.3 at East Melbourne Cricket Ground.

Despite many interstate encounters mistrust between the two states festered over the years. In the 1980s South Australians took delight in beating Victorian teams in State of Origin games.

With the advent of the national competition it was only natural that a major footballing state such as South Australia should be represented, but the SANFL refused to join. The $4 million licence fee was a sore point, but there was always the feeling that being part of the 'Victorian' Football League was equally galling.

In July 1990 the Port Adelaide club put out feelers to the AFL about the possibility of joining the National League. Within three weeks the heads of agreement had been drawn up.

Meanwhile South Australian clubs had started legal action to stop Port negotiating with the AFL for a month.

The SANFL set about forming its own proposal for a South Australian team, saying that it was prepared to enter a composite side in 1991.

On September 19 1990 a 13-1 vote by the clubs gave the all-clear to the AFL to sign a deal with the SANFL and soon the Adelaide Crows were in existence. For now, Port Adelaide had been left out in the cold. **Russell Holmesby**

Jakovich runs hot for Demons with 11 goals

Aug. 3. Allen Jakovich made the MCG his own today, booting 11 goals in Melbourne's 20.20 (140) to 13.10 (88) win over North.

His shots included one that was so freakish it seemed to belong to soccer. He stuck out his right boot as the ball came off the pack and it volleyed across his body into the goal as Jakovich fell over.

He also kicked Melbourne's first six goals and it seemed likely at one stage that he would emulate John Longmire's triumph of last season, beating the opposition alone.

In the second term Jakovich even had time to chat to his girlfriend, who was sitting behind the goals.

The first other scorer for the Demons was Jim Stynes in the third.

Longmire, meanwhile, kicked 7.0, showing greater accuracy than Jakovich, who also had seven behinds, one out on the full, and his number taken for abusive language.

Allen Jakovich shows his dashing style, as he marks over North fullback Michael Martyn during his goalkicking spree at the MCG.

He is not a big man, but North Melbourne half-forward Brett Allison can occasionally rise to the heights, as he shows with this outstanding mark.

Irish eyes are smiling 'Brownlow'

Jim Stynes gets the good news.

Sept. 23. Jim Stynes, the Melbourne ruckman who was one of the greatest Brownlow Medal favourites in years, has won it by five votes.

He polled 25 votes to become Melbourne's sixth medallist, beating West Coast winger Craig Turley.

Just seven years after he first kicked an Australian football in Dublin, 25-year-old Stynes was a hero.

As an 18-year-old about to start study to be a schoolteacher, Stynes answered a bold advertisement for recruits. His first kick in the Under-19s produced a behind, and a lesson in what the goals meant.

When about to be leased to the VFA club Prahran in 1986, Stynes decided to show Demons' officials just how well he could play.

He also bounced back after running over the mark in 1987, a mistake that helped end Melbourne's hopes that year.

David Cloke ends 333 games.

Hawks pluck Eagles in Waverley Final

A Grand Final with a difference. The scene at Waverley as Hawthorn and West Coast vie for the Flag.

Sept. 28. The Hawthorn side called 'too old and too slow' by critics won the 1991 Flag with a great victory over West Coast, 20.19 (139) to 13.8 (86), before 75,230 at Waverley Park, not the unavailable MCG.

The Eagles, who were accidentally introduced by the AFL at the pre-game lunch as the 'West Coast Egos,' jumped away to a four-goal lead. Darrin Pritchard's brilliant opening and two goals by Jason Dunstall kept Hawthorn in reach.

Then the young Hawks came of age. Steve Lawrence dominated in the ruck and James Morrissey on the backline. Paul Dear played the game of his life up forward.

Only West Coast's Guy McKenna seemed able to stop the old Hawthorn machine, as Michael Tuck, Gary Ayres, Chris Mew and Dermott Brereton outran the WA speedsters. Business as usual.

The Hawks piled on eight goals in the last term and finalised their summer T-shirt slogan: 'Too old. Too slow. Too good.'

John Platten lets go with a primal scream to celebrate the Hawks' win over the West Coast Eagles, to the amusement of all assembled for the after-match formalities. He played pretty well during the day, too.

1991 Statistics

Leading Goalkicker:
Tony Lockett (St K) 127
Brownlow Medallist:
Jim Stynes (Melb)
Finals: First Elim. Final Melb 17.11 (113) Ess 11.9 (75); **Second Elim. Final** Geel 15.14 (104) St K 14.13 (97); **Qualifying Final** W. Coast 15.11 (101) Haw 18.16 (124); **First Semi-Final** W. Coast 17.15 (117) Melb 12.7 (79); **Second Semi-Final** Haw 13.17 (95) Geel 13.15 (93); **Preliminary Final** Geel 8.16 (64) W. Coast 11.13 (79); **Grand Final** Haw 20.19 (139) W. Coast 13.8 (86)

Ladder:	W	L	D	%	pts
W. Coast	19	3		162.2	76
Haw	16	6		135.9	64
Geel	16	6		131.6	64
St K	14	7	1	120.4	58
Melb	13	9		110.9	52
Ess	13	9		109.2	52
Coll	12	9	1	115.5	50
N. Melb	12	10		91.2	48
Adel	10	12		89.4	40
Foots	9	12	1	87.9	38
Carl	8	14		88.9	32
Syd	7	14	1	85.0	30
Rich	7	15		87.4	28
Fitz	4	18		66.3	16
Bris	3	19		69.5	12

The wonderful, durable Michael Tuck

Michael Joseph Tuck, the fifth of Frank and Aileen Tuck's seven children, always seemed to last longer than the rest.

When Aileen called the Tuck mob in for tea, young Michael was the one who'd still be out in the paddocks, kicking a footy the way his Dad had taught him. He became an outstanding footballer at St Michael's in Berwick.

In 1970, while playing in the South Gippsland League, he was invited to train with Hawthorn. By then he had come to know the Ablett boys up Drouin way, and also their sister Fay, whom he would later marry.

Hawthorn thought he looked too skinny, so they sent him down to Brendan Edwards' gym to strengthen up. And when he came back he was still too skinny, but nobody questioned his strength or ball-handling skills.

He kicked 65 goals at full-forward for Hawthorn Reserves in 1971. When Peter Hudson injured his knee, Tuck had a chance to break into the senior side.

In a memorable debut on 20 May 1972, 18-year-old Tuck opened at full-forward and goaled with his first three kicks.

Hawthorn later used him in various positions but it was as a ruck rover that the man who came to be called Friar or Tucky first earned a place in football history.

Hawthorn's ruck combination of Don Scott, Leigh Matthews and Michael Tuck had no equal in the 1970s. Tuck showed the speed and stamina of a champion 400-metre runner. He had an instinctive ability to read the play, always tackled hard, and could kick the ball long and straight.

Mentally and physically he was as tough as the old clay-covered boots he used to wear into the training rooms after a hard day digging trenches at Berwick, where he worked as a plumber.

Between 1974 and 1980 he notched up the extraordinary total of 138 consecutive games.

In July 1984 Tuck was named captain of Victoria. WA won in a thriller, with Tuck seeming a little off his game. It later emerged that he had played with a serious eye injury because he didn't want to let anybody down.

After an operation to repair a partially detached retina, Tuck struggled to regain form, often preferring to take marks on the chest. The club thought he might

'Make my day', says Tucky.

only play another year or so.

But Tuck had a habit of coming good. In 1986 he succeeded Leigh Matthews as Hawthorn skipper. Perhaps his finest moment was holding the 1986 Premiership cup aloft, his first of four as captain.

At the end of every season the Press would ask if Tucky was coming back, and he'd say he'd talk it over with 'Mr Jeans'. And every year Tucky was back.

Younger players held him in awe. With his long-sleeved guernsey and beard flecked with grey, Tuck seemed like a relic from an earlier football era. Yet there he was among the best players, still able to catch the speedsters using all the guile of nearly two decades in the game.

Towards the end of his career Tuck became one of the most effective taggers in the League.

On the first day of spring in 1990 Tuck played his 404th senior game, breaking Kevin Bartlett's all-time League record. Hawthorn's 1991 Grand Final win was Tuck's 426th game and 39th Finals appearance. He played in 13 Premierships: 1976, '78, '83, '86, '88, '89, '91 (day); 1977, '85, '86, '88 (night); 1972 (reserves); and 1976 (NFL).

In October 1991 he again discussed his future with the Hawks. But this time Tucky wasn't coming back.

Hawthorn named a grandstand after him. His country bestowed an Order of Australia Medal (OAM) for 'service to Australian football'. And the AFL struck the Michael Tuck Medal for the best and fairest player in the summer competition Grand Final.

People still wonder if he stopped too soon.   **Damien Cash**

Collingwood and the football world mourn Darren Millane

Darren Millane is dead. The wild Collingwood boy died in Queens Road, Albert Park, at 3.30 on the morning of October 7 when his car hit a truck.

After a big night out with his mates at The Tunnel nightclub in the city, 26-year-old Millane had got behind the wheel. Police later said he was well above the legal limit of blood alcohol.

Just a year ago he was a hero of the Premiership-winning side, playing for a club that was lucky to get him. He came from Dandenong VFA and wanted to play for St Kilda, but that club was caught in the Foschini-Morwood clearance tussle and stayed clear. Millane trained at Hawthorn but found it not to his liking.

At Collingwood he demonstrated aggression on the wing, a strong mark and a high level of skill. The fans loved him.

His escapades and brushes with the law and footballing authorities added to the public perception of Darren Millane as a wild man. But in his eight years at Collingwood he played 147 games and kicked 79 goals, winning the Copeland Trophy in 1987.

The public outpouring of grief after his death was immense. One newspaper alone published more than 1000 bereavement notices and the Dandenong Town Hall was needed to cope with the number of mourners at his funeral, 8000 of whom waited outside, blocking the Princes Highway.

As with Les Darcy, and even Phar Lap, an Australian sporting idol was dead in his prime.

The public grief over the death of Darren Millane is all too apparent.

1992

March 14. Hawthorn defeat gallant Fitzroy in the Foster's Cup Grand Final, 19.14 (128) to 8.15 (63).

March 21. Jason Dunstall opens his account with 12 goals in Hawthorn's 21.15 (141) win over Geelong 18.13 (121).

March 22. Essendon defender Brad Fox 'turns blue' after a strangulating tackle from St Kilda forward Tony Lockett. The Saints win 18.20 (128) to Bombers' 17.9 (111) (→ 5/4/93).

March 25. Great Southern Stand at the MCG opened by Donald Cordner, President of Melbourne Cricket Club.

April 6. Daniel Metropolis kicks six goals in his first game for West Coast in their 16.17 (113) win over St Kilda 12.8 (80).

May 2. Adelaide's Andrew Jarman says he cannot understand why umpires are pinging his side for the so-called 'Crow throw'.

May 3. Geelong kick an AFL record 37.17 (239) to Bears' 11.9 (75). Bears' coach Robert Walls says to media: 'Be kind boys, and make it brief.'

June 6. Footscray defeat former possible merger partner Fitzroy 22.14 (146) to 11.18 (84) and are top of the Ladder after 12 rounds.

June 12. Collingwood back down on boycott threat over transfer of Footscray game to the MCG. A compromise gives Victoria Park one extra game this season or next.

July 10. AFL Players' Association President Justin Madden negotiates new collective bargaining agreement with AFL, says players' strike is 'possible' (→ 28/3/95).

July 29. St Kilda defeated Hawthorn 19.16 (130) to 7.13 (55). Wag advertises in *Herald Sun* 'Lost and Found': 'LOST – the plot at Waverley Park last Saturday. Finder kindly return to Hawthorn Football Club. Before September if possible'.

Debuts
Jason Ball (W. Coast)
Brad Boyd (Fitz)
James Hird (Ess)
Anthony Koutoufides (Carl)
Mark Mercuri (Ess)
Tony Modra (Adel)
Michael Voss (Bris)
Darryl White (Bris)

Retirements
Terry Daniher (Ess)
Simon Madden (Ess)
David Rhys-Jones (Carl)

Great Southern Stand rocks to game of century

There's new magic in the air as the Great Southern Stand is packed for the Carlton and Collingwood centenary clash.

May 7. The billing as The Game of the Century was overblown, but tonight's celebration match between Carlton and Collingwood at the MCG had enough skill to captivate 83,262 fans. But despite the football, star billing went to the newly completed Great Southern Stand.

That Carlton won, 16.9 (105) to 9.18 (72), at Collingwood's centenary is interesting, but so is the emergence of the Blues' prized recruit (ex-Geelong and Swans) Greg Williams, who gradually dominated Michael McGuane in the centre.

Carlton captain Stephen Kernahan was superb, kicking seven goals and earning best-on-ground, with another four from Stephen Silvagni.

The Blues' pressure on significant forwards struck at Collingwood's running players. Gavin Brown, a key Magpie, appeared off-colour, while Peter Daicos had trouble getting clear of Tom Alvin.

Then at time-on in the third quarter Daicos took a pass from McGuane in the forward pocket. Calmly he played on, then ran around to snap a masterly goal.

This was not enough, however. The MCG may have been awash with searchlights, booming music, laser beams and fireworks, but as a Magpie party it became just a wash-out.

Hawks to Waverley

March 10. Hawthorn will play all their home games at Waverley Park.

There was strong statistical support for such a move. At Glenferrie Oval, Hawthorn had averaged 17,200 spectators at each home game for the five years up to 1973.

In spite of great success in the 80s, average crowds at Princes Park dropped to 14,000 in the last five years of the decade, compared with 30,000 at Waverley Park.

Libba's 41 touches

May 17. Tony Liberatore shone in the wet at Carrara today, with 41 possessions as Footscray notched an 11.18 (84) to 6.6 (42) win over a depleted Bears side.

Last night Liberatore, at 164 centimetres and 73 kilograms, became the father of eight-pound Thomas Francis, just 113 centimetres shorter than his dad. His wife, Jane, went into labour at midday and Tony was determined to be at the birth.

And Brendan's 44

April 11. Brendan McCormack's 44 possessions, few of them wasted, helped Fitzroy to come back against Adelaide at Princes Park today.

Down by 23 points late in the first term, the Lions found determination and even ferocity, helped by deliveries from McCormack and Paul Roos.

The Lions were two goals behind after the first quarter, but won 19.16 (130) to 14.13 (97) (→ 17/5).

Full-forwards take the spotlight

Lockett gives Brad Fox a hug.

Jason Dunstall leads the team in after scoring 17 goals against Richmond.

Typical Lockett, out in front.

Aug. 15. Jason Dunstall's 12 goals in Hawthorn's 25.20 (170) win over Richmond, 13.8 (86), today continued his tremendous season of scoring in a a great year for goalkickers.

Dunstall must fancy the Tigers. Today's bag brings to 29 he's scored against them – this season. The 17 goals from Hawthorn's 25.22 (172) in the first game against Richmond, 14.9 (93), was just one goal short of Fred Fanning's tally for Melbourne against St Kilda in 1947.

Last month Tony Lockett brought up his 100 for the season when he kicked six goals in St Kilda's 19.16 (130) win over Hawthorn, 7.13 (55). His total actually lifted to 104 on that day, although Dunstall had beaten Lockett to the century mark three weeks earlier.

Dunstall's century came up on July 4 when, 54 minutes into the win over Geelong, he kicked his fifth goal. He ended that game with nine, for a total of 104 from 15 games.

At that stage he was ahead of schedule to beat the AFL record of 150 goals in a season, which is shared by Bob Pratt of South Melbourne (1934) and Peter Hudson of Hawthorn (1971). Oddly, in this round Lockett was held goal-less for the first time since 1988.

Lockett set a personal and club record on June 13, kicking 15 goals against the Sydney Swans at Moorabbin. He dominated this game, sending three forlorn opponents back to Sydney – Andrew Dunkley, Neil Cordy and Craig Nettlebeck.

After missing two games through injury, Lockett kicked six goals in term one, three in the second, three in the third and another trio in the final quarter.

It was an awesome performance (→1/5/93).

TV changes the football culture

March 22. The influence of television on football has become a subject of debate.

While cynics may see football as actually being run from Seven, the channel's sports boss, Gary Fenton, says that if the biggest criticism is that games now start at 2.08 or 8.38, 'someone's lost the plot'.

But the pre-season Foster's Cup was certainly made for TV, and as a cash source for clubs.

In recent years it's been a testing ground for innovations such as four interchange players, green lights to signal umpires to start play, 30-second breaks between goals and re-start and cameras in dressing rooms before games.

Seven paid some $10 million to the League last year, garnering 1.4 million national viewers and millions in advertising (→19/6/95).

Darren Jarman is an all round player and the Hawks prime mover from the centre, but he likes to take a mighty big mark like this one.

Dermie adjusts spectator's specs

Aug. 29. Melbourne supporter Frank Yeomans, 52, today accused Hawthorn star Dermott Brereton of assaulting him.

Brereton did not return to the ground after half time in the VSFL curtain-raiser at the MCG today. Mr Yeomans, of Alexander Road, East Ringwood, said as the Hawthorn players were leaving the field at half time he was calling out to him in an uncomplimentary fashion.

Brereton ran 30 metres to the fence, grabbed his bifocals from his nose, screwed them up in his hands and threw them into the crowd.

'I was just giving him a bit of verbalising at half time when he cracked,' said Mr Yeomans. 'I yelled out, "You're a has-been and a hack and you should go and join Daniher and Madden at the retirement village".'

Final Six battle goes to last round

Aug. 30. Geelong, Collingwood and Footscray filled the top three spots on the AFL Ladder at the end of the home-and-away season, but the rest remained in doubt until the last match, in which West Coast beat Carlton 18.12 (120) to 12.15 (87).

The win tipped the Blues out of the Six, making room for St Kilda, better on percentage only.

West Coast's win allows them to host next week's Elimination Final in Perth, and their opponent will be Hawthorn. The parochial crowd and West Coast's renowned home ground form have strongly reduced Hawthorn's chances of getting through the Finals series.

Collingwood held on to third spot yesterday after a dramatic win over Adelaide, 13.9 (87) to 11.16 (82). The great dread of Collingwood fans was that they would lose and meet their nemesis, Hawthorn, in a knockout match.

Geelong showed a glimpse of Finals form in beating Essendon 16.14 (110) to 9.10 (64). The Cats' run to the Finals was badly affected by a devastating loss to the Adelaide Crows, 24.25 (169) to 11.12 (78), in the second last round.

Hawthorn continue their long run of success, going into their 11th successive Finals campaign. This equals Melbourne's Finals run from 1954 to 1964.

Last flight of a great Bomber squadron

We hate to see you go. Essendon warhorses Simon Madden and Terry Daniher clown around before their last game.

Aug. 29. The farewell was far from fond. Two former Essendon captains, Simon Madden and Terry Daniher, failed to last their final match at Waverley Park today.

Madden came off injured nine minutes into the first quarter, while Daniher's injury-led departure was half-way through the third term.

Madden returned for the final minutes of the match, which was easily won by Geelong. But Daniher, dual Premiership captain, was not seen again.

After being four goals down at half time, Essendon surrendered in the last stanza to a seven-goal charge, making the final score 16.14 (110) to 9.10 (64).

Tim Watson joined Madden and Daniher in a lap of honour before the game, to a standing ovation from the large crowd.

Dons' fans were saying farewell to three of their favourite sons.

Daniher had been honoured earlier in the year. A medal for the best New South Wales player in State of Origin matches has been struck and will be called the Terry Daniher Medal.

Simon Madden had been the best ruckman in Australia and held the club record for the most number of games played (378) and most goals (575). (→ 25/9/93)

Scott Wynd wins another Bulldog Brownlow

Sept. 21. A great year for the Bulldogs was rounded off tonight when ruckman Scott Wynd won the club's ninth Brownlow Medal.

Wynd, 22, polled 20 votes to win from Hawthorn full-forward Jason Dunstall (18), Geelong defender Ken Hinkley (17) and St Kilda forward Stewart Loewe (16).

Footscray have now won two Brownlows in three years, with Tony Liberatore scoring in 1990.

The team made the Preliminary Final this year, something of a triumph since the club had faced extinction in 1989.

Wynd's consistency was shown by the fact that he received only three best-on-ground votes but polled in 10 games. Wynd missed the Qualifying Final through injury.

Scott Wynd handpasses in Footscray's First Semi win over St Kilda.

The Six system

March 10. The McIntyre Final Six system has been revised.

Week One. In the First Elimination Final, fourth on the Ladder will play fifth (loser omitted). In the Second Elimination Final third meets sixth (loser omitted). The two ladder leaders play the Qualifying Final.

Week Two. First Semi-Final. The Qualifying Final loser plays the lowest placed Elimination Final winner (loser omitted). Second Semi-Final. The Qualifying Final winner plays the highest placed Elimination Final winner.

The winner of the first Semi-Final mets the loser of the Second Semi-Final in a Preliminary Final, with the winner going on to the Grand Final against the winner of the Second Semi-Final. (→ 8/2/94).

Last Melbourne side out of Finals

Barnesy marks over Scott Wynd.

Sept. 19. No Melbourne team is in next Saturday's Grand Final after today's defeat of Footscray.

The hopes of Victoria are carried by Geelong against the West Coast Eagles, which is trying to make history by becoming the first out-of-State team to take the Flag.

Led by Essendon discard John Barnes, Geelong kicked 20 goals to Footscray's 10 in the last three quarters today, winning by 22.17 (149) to 12.13 (85).

Last season Hawthorn united Victorians anxious to keep the Flag flying where the game began.

Barnes and Billy Brownless run on to the MCG with their mates next week carrying Geelong's hopes for a Premiership after 29 years. Both country boys, Brownless is from Jerilderie and Barnes from Cobram. The towns are opposed in the Murray League. Brownless was reluctant to join Geelong and spent a year playing for Jerilderie before joining Geelong in 1986. Barnes went to Essendon in 1987 where injuries and an inability to comply with discipline saw him leave. He was drafted by Geelong in 1991.

Although beaten in the Second Semi by the Eagles, Geelong are capable of anything.

The Flag flies West

Sept. 26. The West Coast Eagles made history today as the first club outside Victoria to achieve the Premiership. Their victory over Geelong, 16.17 (113) to 12.13 (85), has placed Victoria's most sought-after sporting trophy in Western Australian possession for at least a year.

West Coast won by 28 points, but it was not until a blistering five goals in the third quarter that they looked like running ahead of Geelong by any margin.

Attacking hard from the start of the game, the Cats seemed likely to dominate the day. The Eagles looked nervous at this stage. But they, too, had the bitter experience of a Grand Final loss to spur them on, and the lesson of last year's drubbing by a ruthless Hawthorn gave the still-young side the determination to draw on everything they knew, or could do, to avoid feeling that same way again this year.

There were some tough physical contests, and the Eagles missed opportunities to score goals, until wingman Peter Matera came through with a running right-foot goal from 60 metres out that saw the beginning of fully skilled football by the Eagles.

The second quarter opened with a superb goal by the Cats' Gary Ablett, soon followed by a terrific Ablett torpedo kick marked superbly by Bill Brownless, near the point post. Although Brownless managed only a behind, Geelong had announced their intention to overpower the opposition in this term.

But West Coast rallied enough to make it a quarter of hard work for Geelong. Ablett had to scrabble for the ball and was held from goaling. Matera again scored a brilliant long-kicking goal for the Eagles, and Tony Evans booted a quick two. At half time the Eagles were 12 points down, but gaining.

West Coast made the third quarter their own in an electrifying display of eager, swift and accurate football. Adding five goals to Geelong's only one by Ablett, the Eagles raced to a 17-point lead.

The teams traded goals in the final term, but the pace and energy of the Eagles was taking a noticeable toll on the Cats. The star player remained Matera, who took out the Norm Smith Medal (→ 1/10/94).

The sight Victorians dreaded becomes a reality as Matera leads the charge.

1992 Statistics

Leading Goalkicker:	Ladder:	W	L	D	%	pts
Jason Dunstall (Haw) 145	Geel	16	6		145.6	64
Brownlow Medallist:	Foots	16	6		129.8	64
Scott Wynd (Foots)	Coll	16	6		114.9	64
Finals: First Elimination Final W.	W. Coast	15	6	1	125.9	62
Coast 14.16 (100) Haw 12.15	Haw	14	8		122.9	56
(87); **Second Elimination Final**	St K	14	8		120.2	56
Coll 12.11 (83) St K 13.13 (91);	Carl	14	8		112.3	56
Qualifying Final Geel 26.16 (172)	Ess	12	10		92.8	48
Foots 17.9 (111); **First Semi-final**	Adel	11	11		101.4	44
Foots 19.5 (119) St K 14.6 (90);	Fitz	9	13		90.3	36
Second Semi-final Geel 14.11 (95)	Melb	7	14	1	87.3	30
W. Coast 20.13 (133); **Preliminary Final** Geel 22.17 (149) Foots	N. Melb	7	15		89.5	28
ry Final Geel 22.17 (149) Foots	Rich	5	17		73.5	20
12.13 (85); **Grand Final** W. Coast	Bris	4	17	1	64.6	18
16.17 (113) Geel 12.13 (85)	Syd	3	18	1	74.1	14

Gary Ablett: the improbable on a regular basis

Gary Ablett was a figure from the mythological past of Australian football long before he became a legend.

Before ascending into video heaven with that mark of the millenium in 1994, flying higher than anyone had flown before, higher than the football itself, he was a bush champion, a certified match winner, a player capable of doing anything on the football field.

He was characterised not so much by flying in the air as working hard on the ground and with his body. Although he came to be known as 'god' he was no saint, having a number of suspensions for over-physical involvement. He even caused a sensation by pleading guilty at the Tribunal.

His Homeric status had long been confirmed – his deeds in 1989 included kicking 14.3 to break Doug Wade's record and then winning the Norm Smith Medal for nearly taking the 1989 Flag off his own boot.

That 9.1 would have been 11.1 and a win had the game gone another minute. Few Grand Finals before or since have been marked by the sheer will-to-win that Ablett displayed in that last quarter.

Before all this Ablett was a different kind of legend. He was the quintessential country footballer who found it difficult to adapt to the wiles of the city, and would rather pot rabbits than goals, ride a surfboard rather than the back of some opponent.

In the days when Ablett played for Hawthorn it seemed that he would be overshadowed by his brother Geoff, a marvellously lithe, long-kicking wingman who eventually played 229 games, 202 of them for Hawthorn, including the 1976 and 1978 Premierships.

Ablett played six games with the Hawthorn Seconds in 1980, was injured and went bush in 1981, was wooed back by Allan Jeans and made his senior debut in 1982 off the bench. He played just six games with the Hawks, five with his brother, but never settled in. Everyone thought he had the ability, but wondered about the commitment to the city and to the Hawthorn discipline.

Next season he played country footy with Myrtleford.

Bill McMaster, Geelong's long-time country recruiting officer, saw him play, and reported to Geelong: 'Ablett is the best player I've ever seen play country football. If he was available right now, next week, I'd place him straight in the centre. And I've never been able to say that about a player in my life before.'

After some to-ing and fro-ing with a clearance from Hawthorn, Ablett lined up with Geelong in the first round of 1984. He was best on the ground in No. 5, Polly Farmer's old number.

On the centreline with Ablett was another recruit, Greg Williams, and Geelong captain Michael Turner.

Ablett kicked three goals and also got three weeks for striking. He was also picked for Victoria, that year, kicking eight against WA, and was named All-Australian – a season after playing in the bush.

Ablett has had periods of trouble with some of his coaches and officials. Like many great sportsmen he has a great foundation of belief in himself, and that can sometimes rub the wrong way. John Devine, Geelong coach 1986-1988, knew Ablett was a 'football superman' but never quite harnessed his abilities.

Malcolm Blight, coach from 1989 to 1994, seemed better suited to the wayward genius, getting him back to the game in 1991 after a period of disillusion with it. Blight released Ablett's awe-

Ablett: among the football gods.

some power as a goalkicker – with centuries in 1993 and 1994, and again in 1995.

Ablett has played in four losing Grand Finals with Geelong including 1995, and that is an abiding disappointment.

But surpassing that are the images of the great man, impressions of the ball in flight bending to his will, his great strength of mind and body, and doing the improbable on a regular basis.

Not bad for a bush footballer.

Tony Lockett: the goal king may break all records

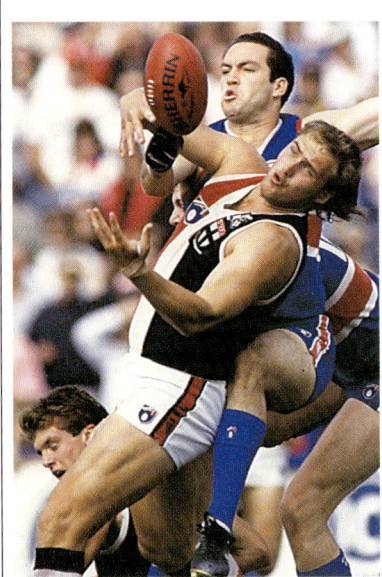

Tony Lockett: settled down to reach for the record.

Sometime in the next few years, an astonishing football record could well fall. Two players, Jason Dunstall and Tony Lockett, are approaching Gordon Coventry's longstanding career record of 1299 goals kicked between 1920 and 1937 for Collingwood.

Dunstall is ahead, but given Lockett's awesome performances, the race could be his.

The score is 1077 to 1008, with the retired Doug Wade on 1057. In spite of illness and injury, this year Lockett averaged 5.8 goals a match to Dunstall's 3.9.

The sometimes fiery Lockett kicked a goal in his first game of senior football, and it's been goals ever since, Considering that after kicking six goals for the Swans in round one in 1995 he was admit-

ted to hospital for five days with a duodenal ulcer, missing two rounds, the skill of this giant in a team that finished twefth becomes even more apparent.

He returned for his first appearance for the Swans at the Sydney Cricket Ground, before 11,000 fans, to boot seven in a 32-point win over Fitzroy.

Held to only three goals in a big from-behind win over Adelaide the following week, he missed Round Seven with a jarred knee, returning to kick eight in an amazing 72-point win over eventual Premiers, Carlton, six against Essendon and 16 straight against Fitzroy at the Western Oval.

Lockett kicked five against his former club, St Kilda, then seven against Fremantle for 103 for the

season and a career total of 1001. This is the fourth season in which he has kicked a century. His year finished with six after half time, making a total of seven, in the crushing of Collingwood's Finals fantasy.

Tony Lockett is a country boy, a lover of practical jokes who, by way of contrast, cannot eat and often vomits before a game, suffers from asthma and such groin pain that he has needed anaesthetic.

He has forgotten his boots for a State game, written off at least three cars driving between Melbourne and his home in Ballarat, trains and races dogs, loves his family, and shared the 1987 Brownlow Medal with John Platten of Hawthorn.

Adelaide gets bout of Modra mania

March 28. Richmond players played flat out but were flattened by Adelaide to the tune of 94 points. Tony Modra was in song.

Using his remarkable leap and quick leads, Modra outplayed all opponents to boot ten goals before going off in the final quarter, supposedly with sore shins – it was more likely a sore kicking foot.

Modra's blond glamour and charms at full-forward have made him a superstar in his football-mad one-team town.

Today's superb display by Modra has lifted the Crows to the top of the Ladder, and put the Tigers at the bottom. Adelaide's admiration for their champion knows no bounds.

Final scores: 28.10 (178) to 12.12 (84) (→ 27/3/94).

A sight to thrill South Australians. Tony Modra rises for a super mark.

24-goal shootout at the MCG

Paul Salmon against Geelong – 18 kicks and 10 marks to score 10.6.

May 1. 'It was one-for-one and who was going to break?' said Essendon coach Kevin Sheedy. 'I just kept sending a runner out, saying "The deal is we've just got to keep outscoring them"'.'

At one end of the MCG was the Bombers' Paul Salmon, at the other, the Cats' Gary Ablett. It was the full-forward match up made in heaven.

And at the end of an incredible afternoon Sheedy's wish came true. Salmon kicked 10.6 in Essendon's 23.18 (156) win over Geelong, 19.18 (132).

But in that loss Ablett kicked a phenomenal 14.7.

Ablett equalled his own club record, passed John Coleman's 13 goals in a game between these clubs in 1952 and registered the highest tally in a losing side (→ 15/4/95).

Bears' big day

May 16. Brisbane romped away from Sydney today, and took several records as souvenirs. Second last on the ladder, the Bears made such mincemeat of the Swans that at half time the score was 19.10 to 4 points. This is an AFL record half-time margin. Brisbane went on to set another AFL record with a three-quarter-time scoreboard of 27.17 to 2.6. Then at the finish, with 33.21 (219), the Bears set a new record for their club. Sydney were 8.9 (57).

Sydney have now suffered 22 defeats in a row. But coach Ron Barassi states: 'Not much point going berserk. I said when I came to Sydney we had a long way to go.'

Dermie's lip costly

Aug. 19. Hawthorn have fined Dermott Brereton a sum 'quite sufficient to put my nose out of joint', said the most influential footballer of the past decade. His crime was to publicly criticise the match committee, calling its recent selections 'bewildering'. The club regards this as a serious breach of solidarity. The size of the fine? It's known to be over $10,000.

Brereton admits that his remarks could not be tolerated. 'Those types of comments ... can really tear down what takes years to build up,' he said. 'Therefore I can only offer the club my sincere apology.'

Winmar stands against racism

May 2. When Nicky Winmar of St Kilda showed off the colour of his skin in defiance of the racist taunts he had heard all day from within the Collingwood crowd on April 17, he also laid bare the whole issue of racism in football. It was the start of a controversy that the AFL is now determined to settle.

'I'm black and I'm proud to be black!,' Winmar had yelled to the crowd.

In a television debate over the issue, Collingwood club President, Allan McAlister, inadvertently threw petrol on the flame when he said: 'As long as they (Aborigines) conduct themselves like white people – well, off the field – everyone will admire and respect them.'

Strongly denying accusations of racism, McAlister apologised to the President of the Aboriginal Advancement League for what was 'a slip'.

McAlister has announced that the Collingwood Football Club will consider taking action against their players who use racist taunts on the field.

In a survey of AFL players conducted by the *Sunday Age* last year, 36 per cent admitted having made racist remarks in a match.

Essendon club President David Shaw has said that the club's four or five Aboriginal players 'cop heaps' and has publicly criticised what he calls the 'ugly element' of racially based insults (→ 30/6).

An image that will last. Nicky Winmar shows pride in his heritage.

Magpies feel impact of Aboriginal curse

June 30. In retaliation for alleged racist remarks by the Magpies' club President, Allan McAlister, a Darwin Aboriginal man placed a 'curse' on the club last month.

McAlister flew to Darwin on a fence-building mission with Aboriginal people after it became clear his repeated apologies for remarks made on television were not adequate to undo the insult. Nor, it seems, was his visit.

Although McAlister has vowed to stamp out racism if it exists at Collingwood, John Kelly, a member of the Walpiri people from central Australia, performed a tribal ritual around McAlister, and said the curse thus created would adversely affect the performance of the Collingwood team.

The curse seems to have had its desired effect – the Magpies have lost four out of five since then including three in a row.

Coincidence? Are the sensitive psyches of footballers vulnerable to suggestion? Or do the Kelly curses really stick?

The Magpies are taking no further chances. Arrangements are now being made for Kelly, an entertainer, to fly to Melbourne and lift the so-called 'hoodoo' in another ceremony should he be satisfied that racism is purged from Collingwood. This will take place at the Magpies' next training session (→ 23/6/95).

Barassi's Swans end 26-game losing streak

June 27. After a year of pain and crises, the Swans today ended a 26-week losing streak, beating Melbourne by 40 points at the SCG, 23.11 (149) to 16.13 (109).

The lead changed about 10 times in the second quarter. With just a three-point lead at half time, the Swans fired up. Full-forward Richard Osborne, who received a severe head injury five weeks ago, kicked 10 goals.

The Swans opened the third stanza with a goal by Osborne, then by Leon Higgins, another from Osborne, Daryn Cresswell, David Murphy and Mark Bayes before Osborne got two more, Creswell and Murphy one each, followed by two more by Osborne (→ 16/7/94).

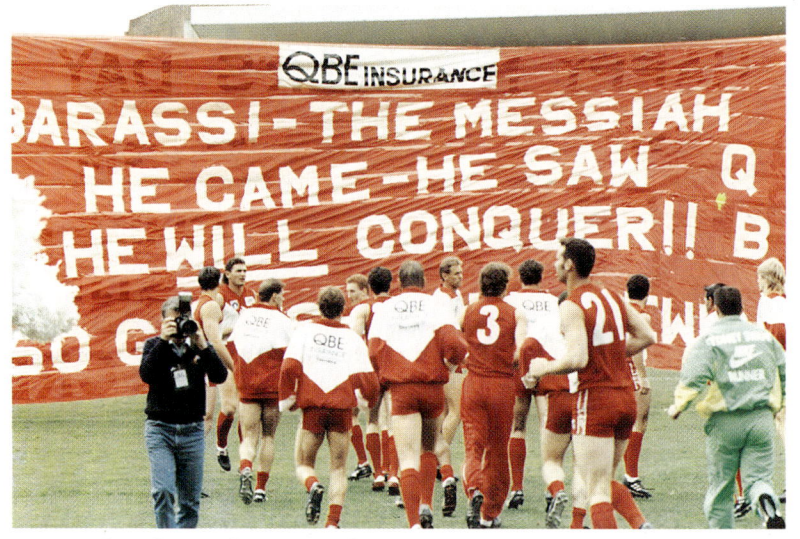

A Messiah and a prophecy. Now the Swans have come out of the wilderness.

Three get 100

Aug. 21. Jason Dunstall's 100th goal for the season today puts him up with the other century-getters Gary Ablett and Tony Modra.

Ablett's century came up at the end of last month when he kicked 10 against North Melbourne. In round six he kicked 14 of Geelong's 19 goals, but Essendon won by 24 points.

Oddly, Modra's 100th came in a losing game. Fitzroy, sitting on 12th, beat Adelaide by five points in Melbourne. In spite of this, Modra was mobbed by fans on his return to Adelaide.

Dunstall's fourth century in nine seasons with the Hawks was far from his easiest, but came in a 27-point win over the Crows.

Alan Schwab found dead in Sydney

Schwab: a life of football.

June 18. One of the most powerful and most loved figures in Australian football, Alan Schwab, was tonight found dead in a Sydney hotel.

Aged 52, Schwab was the AFL's Executive Commissioner and interim Sydney Chairman. He was found in his room after missing appointments today.

A post mortem will be conducted over the weekend. A police spokesman said: 'There did not appear to be any sign of violence.'

After being appointed interim Chairman of the revived Board of Directors of the Swans three months ago, Schwab had stayed at the Boulevard Hotel.

The Swans coach, Ron Barassi, was stunned. 'He was a great footy person, a friend, and all of a sudden he's not here,' he said.

The Chief Executive of the AFL, Ross Oakley, described Schwab as 'really the football engine room' of the AFL. He paid tribute to Schwab's work on the draft rules and the salary cap which helped keep the competition even.

Schwab leaves a widow, Lynn, and three children, including Cameron, who is General Manager at Richmond. He started as a junior clerk with the VFL in 1958, joining St Kilda as assistant to General Manager Ian Drake seven years later.

Two years later he moved to Richmond as General Manager, becoming crucial to the Tigers' most succesful era of four Premierships.

Adelaide invade Melbourne Finals

Its huge, it flies and its name is Shaun Rehn, Adelaide's grand ruckman.

Sept. 5. Adelaide fans swept into the MCG today, with a proud banner that said they 'crowed'.

And they had something to crow about as their side withstood the immense pressure of Hawthorn to make it into next Saturday's Second Semi-final against Carlton.

Up to 20,000 South Australians joined 35,000 plus locals to see the teams tied at 3.4 after the Crows' fierce three-goal opening.

Adelaide had fallen over the line with a 24-point win over Collingwood at Football Park last week, getting fifth spot on percentage.

The Crows had a four-goal advantage at half time, but slipped to seven points up going into the last lap.

Jason Dunstall and Paul Hudson goaled in the first five minutes, but then each kicked behinds, as did John Platten and Glenn Nugent.

One of the Hawks' best, Ben Allan, missed a half volley, leading to the loose ball being seized by Andrew Jarman who handpassed to Matthew Liptak for a bouncing 60-metre goal.

Nigel Smart snapped another to give the Crows the lead. Then Victorian reject Stuart Wigney kicked his third and Smart his fourth to put it out of doubt, 16.14 (110) to 13.17 (95).

Ominously for Victorians, there is now the prospect of an historic Crows and Eagles Grand Final.

AFL draft rules to lift cellar dwellers

Aug. 27. The AFL Commission has announced wide-ranging changes to draft rules, slanted heavily towards helping Sydney and Brisbane.

Restrictions on players from NSW and Queensland have been reintroduced. For three years Sydney (with a 50-player list) and Brisbane will have three pre-national draft selections from their states.

This has upset most other clubs, especially Richmond, Fitzroy and North Melbourne.

For the first time since the start of a national draft a Victorian club, Richmond, will get special pre-draft consideration.

Sheldon and Joyce get marching orders

Sept. 8. Three days after Hawthorn crashed out of the Finals, coach Alan Joyce has been sacked.

Yesterday St Kilda dismissed coach Ken Sheldon as the blood-letting continued at Moorabbin.

Hawks' President Trevor Coote phoned Joyce with the news. He said there was no immediate replacement, but preferred a Hawthorn person.

St Kilda finished 12th this year and four senior officials have gone recently. Sheldon said: 'At least I can walk away with dignity. I'm proud of what I put into St Kilda.'

Hawks in turmoil over $2m loss

Dec. 13. Hawthorn members took out their frustrations over their team's failures on the club administration tonight.

A fiery annual meeting included the replacement of two Directors and the Board kept having to defend itself under questioning by angry members among the 1000 present.

The club announced a $640,000 loss, making the loss for the last two years more than $1 million.

Club President Geoff Lord blamed renovation costs, the recession, unattractive home-and-away games and the opening of the Great Southern Stand at the MCG.

Exuberant Essendon's clean sweep of season

Michael Long, best on field and the Dons' inspiration, celebrates after a brilliant run and a long goal.

'Baby Bombers' James Hird and Joe Misiti in seventh heaven.

Sept. 25. At half time in the Preliminary Final last week, Carlton fans were counting their chickens, or Crows, before they hatched.

Adelaide were 42 points in front of the much-feared Essendon youngsters, and the Blues had their feet up, looking forward to an easy day against the Crows in today's Grand Final. But an 11 goal to two second half by Essendon soon ruined that happy scenario for the Blues. Essendon suddenly flicked the switch to 'rampant' against Adelaide, winning 17.9 (111) to Adelaide 14.16 (100).

And then they carried the feeling into the Grand Final, and won that 20.13 (133) to 13.11 (89).

At the end of the season, Essendon, the team which was 11th after round seven, won every trophy on offer except one – including Father of the Year by veteran of the year Tim Watson.

Aside from the Premiership, Gavin Wanganeen won the Brownlow, and the Michael Tuck Medal for best on field in the Foster's Cup Grand Final. Essendon won that too.

And Michael Long won the Norm Smith Medal for his stunning display of running, jumping, and standing still, in the Big One.

The only medal that Essendon didn't win was named after a Bomber legend. Gary Ablett took out the John Coleman Medal for goalkicking.

The night and day Premierships surely make up for that.

The Grand Final was won – and lost – in the first quarter. Essendon had 13 scoring shots to three, with the young Bombers exuberant all over the field. Seven Essendon players – Wanganeen, David Calthorpe, Dustin Fletcher, Rick Olarenshaw, Mark Mercuri, James Hird and Joe Misiti – were under 21.

The slightly older crew led by the dashing Michael Long, but including Gary O'Donnell, Mark Harvey and Paul Salmon were all terrific. Coach Kevin Sheedy's faith in youth, adaptability and joyful attack paid off in a spectacular way.

For Carlton only Stephen Kernahan, with seven goals from 13, was a winner on the day. The rest looked slow and as if modern football had passed them by.

Two champions of the Aboriginal race, and champions on the field, Michael Long and Gavin Wanganeen, acknowledge the cameras and the crowd after the Bombers' Grand Final victory. Long won the Norm Smith Medal for best in the Grand Final, while Wanganeen is this year's Brownlow Medallist.

1993 Statistics

Leading Goalkicker: Tony Modra (129)
Brownlow Medallist: Gavin Wanganeen (Ess)
Finals: First Elimination Final Haw 13.17 (95) Adel 16.14 (110); **Second Elimination Final** N.Melb 11.3 (69) W.Coast 17.18 (120); **Qualifying Final** Ess 14.14 (98) Carl 15.10 (100); **First Semi-Final** Ess 16.12 (108) W.Coast 11.10 (76); **Second Semi-Final** Carl 13.8 (86) Adel 8.20 (68); **Preliminary Final** Adel 14.16 (100) Ess 17.9 (111); **Grand Final** Carl 13.11 (89) Ess 20.13 (133)

Ladder:	W	L	D	%	pts
Ess	13	6	1	119.1	54
Carl	13	6	1	117.6	54
N.Melb	13	7		120.8	52
Haw	13	7		116.6	52
Adel	12	8		117.8	48
W.Coast	12	8		115.8	48
Geel	12	8		111.6	48
Coll	11	9		101.3	44
Foots	11	9		99.0	44
Melb	10	10		112.2	40
Fitz	10	10		99.5	40
St K	10	10		94.2	40
Bris	4	16		75.3	16
Rich	4	16		70.7	16
Syd	1	19		63.3	4

Black Magic

The contribution of Aboriginal players to Australian football in recent times is such that the game would now be inconceivable without them. Since 1990, two Norm Smith Medallists, Peter Matera and Michael Long, and one Brownlow Medallist, Gavin Wanganeen, have been players of Aboriginal descent.

In the same period, Essendon Football Club has placed itself at the cutting edge of the game – and, indeed, Australian society – by building a team around a core of Aboriginal players. That decision was instrumental in netting the club the 1993 Premiership, and the Grand Final of that year - with great Aboriginal players of the past like Polly Farmer and Maurice Rioli performing the ceremonial functions – made for a wonderful celebration of all-Australian football.

Of course, the history of Australian football has not always been so happy, particularly when it is considered that many believe one of the sport's sources is the ancient Aboriginal game of marngrook. Played with a possum skin stuffed with charcoal, marngrook was played along tribal lines with teams being organised on the basis of totems (it is likely, therefore, that the Eagles have been playing the Crows in this country for thousands of years). The greatest honour in marngrook was bestowed upon those who could kick the possum skin furthest into the air and leap highest to catch it.

This being the case there is a shameful lack of Aboriginal names in the honour roll of Australian football from the early years of its history until the 1960s. One of the outstanding football books of recent years, Steve Hawke's autobiography of Graham 'Polly' Farmer, solidly makes the case that the Western Australian ruckman should be regarded as the greatest player of all time. Farmer was a man of rigid application and towering but silent ambition.

The best known Aboriginal player from the period before World War 2, Fitzroy's Doug

Maurice Rioli, Richmond's champion centreman from the Northern Territory.

Nicholls, was an extraordinary individual who touched the lives of many people, black and white. At various stages of his impoverished youth, Nicholls boxed in Jimmy Sharman's fight tent and lived on what he could earn as a professional runner.

Later, during the premiership of Don Dunstan, Nicholls rose to be Governor of South Australia. Folklore has it that he was rejected from Carlton on racist grounds, but he was so respected by his team-mates at Fitzroy (among whom was triple Brownlow Medallist Haydn Bunton) that they participated in the 'football church parades' he organised. A committed Christian, Nicholls once remarked that a footballer can preach a sermon by the way he plays the game.

The next Aboriginal player of note was Norm McDonald, the so-called 'Black Bullet' who was a highly regarded member of Essendon's champion team of the 50s, playing in six Grand Finals and winning the club's best and fairest in 1951. In the 60s, Polly Farmer quietly established himself as one of the game's all-time greats during his relatively brief spell (only six seasons) with Geelong. Farmer was a great indivi-

dual player, but his visionary use of handball had a transforming effect on the Geelong team as a whole. The beguiling question for Farmer's Victorian fans is whether they ever saw the best of him, as he suffered a crippling knee injury in his first VFL game.

Sid Jackson played 136 games with Carlton between 1969 and 1976 and was a member of two Premiership sides. Brilliant, volatile and highly skilled, Jackson dragged the issue of race into the public spotlight when he alleged that he had been subjected to racist abuse from a Collingwood opponent in the 1970 Second Semi-final.

However, the players who made the Australian public think about the relationship between Aboriginal people and football as never before were Jim and Phil Krakouer who arrived at North Melbourne in 1982. Like a surprising number of great Aboriginal footballers, including Jackson and Farmer, the Krakouers were Nyungahs from southern Western Australia. Slight in stature but quick in mind and blessed with an uncanny mutual understanding, the Krakouer brothers undid opposition defences as simply as if they were shoelaces.

Responses ranged from delight to anger, and while the Krakouers received more media attention than any Aboriginal players before them, it seemed that they also received more abuse. While there had been Aboriginal footballers before them, none had played in such an obviously, and threateningly, Aboriginal way.

The issue of the relationship between the game and its Aboriginal players simmered inconclusively until the fourth round of the 1993 season when St Kilda enjoyed a rare victory over Collingwood at Victoria Park.

Walking from the ground, St Kilda's Nicky Winmar was subjected to racial abuse from a section of the Collingwood crowd. Stopping, he lifted his jumper and pointed proudly to his black skin. In his book *Obstacle Race – Aborigines in Sport*, Colin Tatz, the Professor of Politics at Macquarie University, wrote that the photograph which captured Winmar's lonely act of defiance 'may well become the most famous photo in football history'. Certainly, it threw the sport into uproar.

Australian football's great limitation is that it is not played internationally. Fans of the Australian game do not get to see the contrast in temperament and skills that are on display when, for example, England plays Tonga in rugby union or Australia plays the West Indies in cricket.

Our diversity must come from within, and, over the past decade, the most novel and exciting talents to come to our game have largely been players of Aboriginal descent – Matera, Lewis, Long, Cockatoo-Collins, Wanganeen, Kickett, Chisholm, Winmar, Mitchell.

Attributing special sporting qualities to people of a particular race can be a dangerous practice, but, as a summary of the Aboriginal contribution to Australian football, few would argue with the title chosen by the Nyungah people of Western Australia for the short film they made about football in the 80s – 'Black magic'.

Martin Flanagan

A fond farewell from fans for Peter Daicos

March 2. Peter Daicos has finished at Collingwood.

The end to a playing career full of enchantment and deeds almost beyond greatness came with a phone call today from Leigh Matthews telling Daicos he'd drop by his hotel for a chat. Matthews came to say it was time for Daicos to give it away, but the star said he would think about nominating for the draft.

In 250 games for 549 goals, Daicos could thread the ball through mere chinks. Knee surgery hampered his career, but he still topped Collingwood's goalkicking for five years, including 97 in 1990.

For so many supporters, a defining moment has been witnessing a Daicos goal that combined artistry, nerve and profound skill. Many think there is still a place in the Magpie nest for him.

Peter Daicos, with daughter Madison, does a lap of honour at the MCG.

Mickey McGuane bounces the MCG

Mickey McGuane on the run.

April 4. Mick McGuane took on the MCG and Carlton today. He beat both with a fine game and one brilliant solo effort.

In the second quarter, McGuane got the ball behind the centre and began a zig-zagging arc for the Punt Road goal, bouncing the ball seven times, darting, daring, as shepherds held a clearway. At the end he was in space to put the ball through. Collingwood went on to win 14.16 (100) to Carlton's 9.12 (66).

Three umpires

March 25. The three-umpires system will be used officially for the first time tomorrow.

Given a trial in Foster's Cup and pre-season matches, the system was today condemned by the new Hawthorn captain, Chris Langford.

He said the extra umpire would have a great impact on the tussles between full-forwards and full-backs and he feared over-zealous umpires would award easy kicks. However, it might also protect full-backs from some robust opponents.

Now a Final Eight

Feb. 9. The AFL today announced a Final Eight system.

Designed by Ken McIntyre, who has been working out Finals systems for the League since 1931, the new system means that Victorian clubs finishing on top could have to play finals interstate.

The main attraction of the change is a Second Preliminary Final, giving both eventual Grand Finalists a similar run in, nine Finals instead of seven and an overhaul of the way Finals tickets are sold.

It's that man again. The irrepressible Allen Jakovich celebrates a goal with a 'high five'. Others in the outer feel free to make their own gestures.

Modra fires up to kick 13 goals

March 27. Adelaide were awesome tonight in their destruction of Carlton, with Tony Modra kicking 13 in a new opening round record.

The Crows shot to the top of the Ladder by beating last year's Grand Finalists by 66 points at Football Park, 22.18 (150) to 13.6 (84).

Missing suspended captain Stephen Kernahan and injured Andrew McKay and Earl Spalding, Carlton nevertheless could only watch as Modra outclassed Stephen Silvagni, Mil Hanna and Michael Sexton.

Shaun Rehn rucked brilliantly and had an astonishing 16 handballs, all of them fast and skilful.

Wheels falls off out at Footscray

April 6. Coach of the year in 1992, when Footscray reached the Preliminary Final, Terry Wheeler is today out of a job.

Captain Scott Wynd asked his players not to dwell on Wheeler's departure, but to give new coach Alan Joyce a fair go.

Joyce has agreed to soften the tough attitude that contributed to his departure from Hawthorn.

Wheeler was an unlucky coach, losing key players through injury. 'I believe that I've been able to take a team that was on the brink of extinction back into the hearts of many, many football people,' he said.

Dermie's 7 makes 14 for season

Aug. 3. Dermott Brereton's career is in doubt after he was tonight suspended by the AFL for seven matches for a career total of 37, more than anyone else playing.

The Swans player said he would assess his playing future at the end of the season.

This was the eighth time that Brereton has been suspended and his second seven-game suspension this season. The Tribunal found that Brereton twice hit Richmond's captain Tony Free with an open hand.

Free has had a plate inserted in his broken jaw (→ 14/7/95).

Lockett charged with charge on Caven

May 11. St Kilda's Tony Lockett was tonight suspended for eight matches by the AFL Tribunal.

Lockett, who pleaded not guilty, was cited on video evidence and found to have struck Sydney defender Peter Caven in Sunday's game at the SCG. Lockett cannot play again until round 17 in July.

Caven marked, running with the flight of the ball in the first quarter and was met heavily by Lockett, who was running in the opposite direction. Caven received a compound fracture of the nose which will need plastic surgery and keep him out for six to eight weeks.

Caven said he could remember little of the clash. 'I was running to mark it and I sort of marked it and then felt a collision,' he said.

Lockett began his evidence by apologising to Caven for the injuries, which he had not intended.

Lockett had won the game, by a point, single handedly, kicking 11 goals after the Saints trailed by 38 points at the last break.

Lockett's football power contrasted badly with the incident. (→ 3/8).

Gary Ablett's grab over Gary Pert may be the greatest mark yet taken.

The brainwaves of Kevin Sheedy

June 19. Kevin Sheedy's suggestion of a $10 levy on all households to help save Victoria's AFL clubs is the latest in a series of brainwaves from the Essendon coach.

For instance, back in 1982 there was his idea, later adopted, of an apprentice school for young footballers. Then in 1986 he suggested expanding the competition to Brisbane before SA and WA.

Two years later he said the Brownlow should be expanded to include 'Cazaly' awards for the best players in each position, there should be a Final Eight and flags on goal posts to help kickers.

Blood rule new medical measure

Aug. 4. The AFL's new rules about bleeding players are gathering more criticism than support from those they are meant to protect. Today the AFL Players' Association joined others in protest against the rules, which have arisen from alarms about AIDS. The League's penalty ruling of $2,000 against players who refuse a blood test is the main complaint. The AFL's General Manager of Football Operations, Mr Ian Collins, responsible for drafting the rules, believes the League must protect players from possible infection. But doubts are now being raised about the rules' legality (→ 1/4/95).

Six clubs are talking mergers

Aug. 6. Six Melbourne-based AFL clubs are involved in merger talks, according to a Director of one of the clubs.

He named Hawthorn, Melbourne, Fitzroy, Richmond, North Melbourne and St Kilda as having held talks at a very early stage.

Merging teams are assured of help with money, fixtures, draft concessions and promotion by the AFL.

Talks between Melbourne and Fitzroy have been inconclusive, while Richmond has negotiated with several clubs (→ 8).

League unveils Five-Year Plan

Aug. 22. Victoria cannot sustain 11 professional teams. This is made clear by the AFL's strategic five-year plan, released today.

The 192-page document spells out the case for a 16-side competition, with the Fremantle Dockers coming in next season and a second Adelaide side possibly in 1996. The loss of a Victorian club is 'the most likely scenario'.

Clubs will have to meet a financial solvency criterion, meaning that each club must satisfy the AFL or a chartered accountant that it will be able to pay all debts.

The plan also revealed that:
* The AFL's debt increased 33 per cent from $13 million in 1986 to $17.3 million last year. The Chief Executive, Ross Oakley, said assets far exceed this debt.
* Effective enforcement of the salary cap is necessary because of past abuse.
* The AFL will not be a banker to clubs and guarantee debts.
* A special effort will be made to arrest an alarming decline in participation in football among juniors, partly through single mothers preferring non-contact sports and young Australians taking to fads such as skateboarding and video games.
* Papua New Guinea is a potential market of AFL players, with Africa and Russia considered growth areas.
* Hamstring injuries have soared since 1985, but the incidence of corked thighs and calves has dropped.

The report also places a heavier emphasis on State of Origin games and the creation of a Rest-of-Australia side to play Victoria, South Australia and WA.

There is a call for the re-establishment of chances for players to represent Australia, most probably against Ireland, an increase in player payments and an increased emphasis on Saturday night football, with six matches to be telecast exclusively on pay TV from next year.

The League said the gap between the financially strong and the weak clubs is widening. (→ 2/5/95).

Fantastic Final Eight Finals series

Sept. 25. The Final Eight has been a triumph, quietening after one season those who were unconvinced of its merits.

The Finals matches, with all their tension and drama showed the fairness – and the fierceness – of the Eight in a series of amazingly close games.

When in the Second Qualifying Final, North Melbourne slid home by 23 points in the first AFL game where extra time decided the result, against Hawthorn at Waverley Park, there was a celebration.

Then Geelong's Billy Brownless kicked a 35-metre winner after the siren to bury the Bulldogs at the MCG by five points.

Against Collingwood, the Eagles just survived a last-quarter attack at the WACA for a two-point win.

One of Geelong's greatest wins came when they bustled Carlton out of contention at Waverley Park. The Cats were without captain Mark Bairstow, Garry Hocking, Paul Couch and Michael Mansfield.

The next day Melbourne's Garry Lyon slotted in 10 goals to end Footscray's season. A 10-goal third quarter took Melbourne on to a 79-point win.

For Geelong, it was back from the near-dead again in week three. With the score against North Melbourne tied, Gary Ablett marked in the goal square with three seconds on the clock and booted the Cats into the Grand Final after the siren.

On the other side of the country at the WACA the awesome Eagles annihilated Melbourne by 65 points.

During the year just getting into the Eight was a desperate thing.

Finals fever began early for Bris-

A first in AFL football, when extra time is called for after a tie.

bane after the Bears ran over the top of a depleted Essendon in round 13.

For teams such as Richmond the Eight meant that a Finals chance beckoned for the first time since 1982, in round 15. Three rounds later, however, the Tigers sank beneath the fearful surge that seemed to mark the Eagles.

Geelong proved the sense of the system when they came back from the death seat in round 15 to begin a run with Gary Ablett's 10 goals at Kardinia Park the following week in a win over Melbourne, then a loss to Footscray, victories over the Blues, Adelaide, North and Fitzroy, a three-point loss to the Magpies, and then wins against Sydney and Richmond.

If just getting there was half the fun, those that survived the journey had an even more exciting ride. The Eight and great games have made this the most exciting Finals series in many seasons.

Billy Brownless gets the Cats home.

Hawks' record

Sept. 3. Hawthorn charged into the Finals for a history-making 13th year in a row today with a win over Adelaide, 9.12 (66) to 6.11 (47).

Hawk Jason Dunstall was held to just two goals by Nigel Smart. Injury-ridden, Dunstall has kicked a mere 33 goals in the last 11 games after scoring 64 in the first 11.

Coach Peter Knights said it had been a very hard road to the Finals, much of it made difficult because players handballed too often, using dry weather techniques in the wet.

Shaw resigns

Aug. 8. Fitzroy's woes worsened today with the resignation of coach Robert Shaw.

He told the club he would not continue beyond 1994 because he had lost his 'passionate commitment' of the past.

'Why continue and cheat the club and go through the motions?' he asked. Shaw, 39, will coach the Lions in the last four games of the season.

Under Shaw since 1991 the Lions have finished 14th, 10th and 11th and are now 13th.

Diesel's medal

Sept. 26. Carlton's brilliant centreman Greg Williams has won his second Brownlow Medal by two votes from West Coast's Peter Matera. Williams was also co-winner of the medal playing for Sydney in 1986.

His 30 votes were the highest under the single 3/2/1 voting system since the Matthews-Fothergill tie in 1940.

Williams' breathtaking hand and foot skills, and amazing football vision have overcome an alleged lack of leg speed.

FREMANTLE

FREMANTLE DOCKERS

Football has been strong in the WA port city of Fremantle for as long as there has been football in the state. Fremantle clubs dominated the competition winning 49 Premierships between 1885 and 1994 in the West Australian Football League.

Not surprisingly when the WA Football Commission came to decide what the second WA team would seek the AFL licence it favoured Fremantle.

There was some opposition from non Fremantle WAFL clubs at a meeting of presidents and general managers in April 1993, but it was as the Fremantle Dockers that the new team was launched on July 21, 1994.

Gerard Neesham, veteran of 247 WAFL games and nine for Sydney in 1982, was appointed coach, promising to bring the 'chip and draw' style of football to the AFL that he had practised with such success at Claremont. He coached Claremont to three Flags, and played in the two others for them in 1981 and 1987.

Neesham had to work with a restricted list of local players as many of them had already been snapped up by the West Coast Eagles. Fremantle will receive some draft concessions and look to acquire a number of experienced AFL players.

Fremantle also bring new colours to the AFL – becoming the first team to use purple and green in its innovative home and away uniforms, celebrating the working class 'Docker' connection of the area.

The Fremantle Dockers will play their first games in the AFL in 1995 with home grounds at the Subiaco Oval and the WACA.

Eagle supermen crush Cats

Oct. 1. The West Coast Eagles have today moved a step further towards becoming the most powerful club in the AFL by crushing Geelong 20.23 (143) to 8.15 (63).

With a second Premiership in three years, the almost robotic Eagles now talk of how they modelled themselves on Hawthorn, studying that club when they won their fourth Flag in seven years in 1989.

In an unattractive game, the Eagles today showed discipline and strength. The injury to Geelong's Garry Hocking in the opening minutes was also crucial, and while John Barnes pumped the ball forward it steadily returned from an Eagle's boot.

Without Barry Stoneham and, later, with Hocking hobbling, Geelong had no one who could tame a rampaging Glen Jakovich.

Pin-point kicking by the Eagles wreaked havoc, as did their defence which never strayed far from the boundary line, not risking a turnover through risky disposal.

Gary Ablett and Billy Brownless were starved of chances, while Tim McGrath struggled to keep up with Brett Heady. A brave 'Buddha' Hocking and mighty Michael Mansfield just kept on trying.

Geelong were caught, too, by the Eagles' zone defence set up for the kick-in, torturing Ken Hinkley and Stephen O'Reilly.

The Eagles' Dean Kemp won the Norm Smith Medal.

For Malcolm Blight, coach in three losing Grand Finals, the future is uncertain, as Geelong fail at the final hurdle once again.

Still trying. Billy Brownless flies over Eagle Ashley McIntosh.

A statement from the showers.

1994 Statistics

Leading Goalkicker:
Gary Ablett (Geel) 129
Brownlow MedalList:
Greg Williams (Carl)
Finals: First Qualifying Final Geel 15.16 (106) Foots 15.11 (101); **Second Qualifying Final** N. Melb 15.24 (114) Haw 13.13 (91); **Third Qualifying Final** Carl 14.12 (96) Melb 18.15 (123); **Fourth Qualifying Final** W. Coast 11.16 (82) Coll 12.8 (80); **First Semifinal** Melb 21.18 (144) Foots 9.11 (65); **Second Semi-final** Geel 15.15 (105) Carl 10.12 (72); **First Preliminary Final** N Melb 14.19 (103) Geel 16.13 (109); **Second Preliminary Final** W. Coast 16.21 (117) Melb 8.4 (52);

Grand Final W. Coast 20.23 (143) Geel 8.15 (63)

Ladder:	W	L	D	%	pts
W. Coast	16	6		132.2	64
Carl	15	7		132.5	60
N. Melb	13	9		129.0	52
Geel	13	9		114.2	52
Foots	13	9		110.6	52
Haw	13	9		109.1	52
Melb	12	10		116.6	48
Coll	12	10		99.9	48
Rich	12	10		93.8	48
Ess	11	11		97.9	44
Adel	9	12	1	86.9	38
Bris	9	13		88.4	36
St K	7	14	1	74.9	30
Fitz	5	17		70.3	20
Syd	4	18		78.1	16

Captain Courageous Tony Shaw leaves game in tears

Sept. 11. Collingwood died in Perth in the Qualifying Final, going down to the Eagles by two points. This ended their season, and also ended the career of the great battler Tony Shaw.

Shaw wept as his team-mates cheered him from the ground. After all the blood and sweat he has spilled for the club, the tears were justified.

For 17 years the little bloke with the mobile mouth and passionate determination to win had been around Victoria Park, even if he was first rejected as too slow, short and stocky and a dud kick.

His finest hour was captaining the 1990 Premiership side, and winning the Norm Smith Medal for best on the ground.

The kid who arrived from Essendon and failed in his trial with the Under-19s in 1977 had timed things badly. Tommy Hafey had just taken over as senior coach, Max Richardson had replaced Des Tuddenham as captain. Departing coach Murray Weideman had taken the club to their first

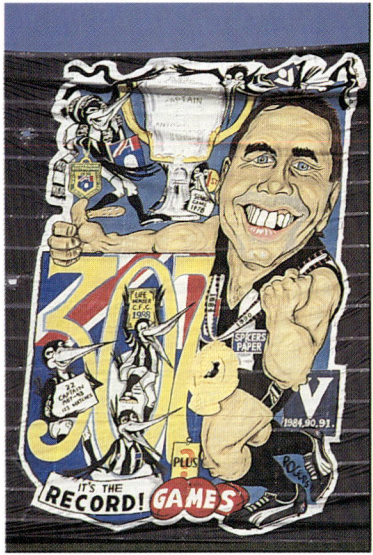

A salute to a milestone.

A tear from Tony and a consoling hand as the Magpies leave the field.

wooden spoon in the League.

But inside a year Shaw was the Reserves best and fairest and by 1978 played for the Seniors.

First as a rover then as a centreman, he had amazing courage, was a great getter of the ball, a constructive handballer and sel-

dom wasted his short kicks.

Running the Melbourne Marathon made him realise that the fruits of hard work were boundless. Sheer hard work earned him a State place and two Copeland Trophies.

The Reservoir boy who walked

two paper rounds, helped his brother clean the MCG and his father clean the Masonic Club in the city, became a Collingwood Council gardener, and also rose to become the King of Moomba.

Tony Shaw, 34, was Collingwood captain 1987-1993.

Footscray's favourite Doug Hawkins is on the wing

Who but Doug Hawkins would be cheered by Scraggers when he danced around the Doug Hawkins Wing playing for Fitzroy?

Hero of 329 Footscray games, he had stuck with the club when they were going under, rejected good money from Essendon and only left when the club no longer wanted him.

A year earlier a little aircraft had towed a sign over the same Western Oval expressing gratitude for Dougie's days from 1978 to 1994 doing battle on the patch of ground that was to carry his name.

The former Housing Commission boy, born in May 1960 and raised in Braybrook, became something of a legend both on and off the field. After his 300th game he told on television how after his knee injury in 1986 he went on a long binge, finally realising his fiancee was gone and he missed footy.

Even though at the end of the 1995 season he was publicly ma-

A salute to the grand stand.

Ted Whitten watches Doug Hawkins pass his record of 321 games.

king noises about giving it away, he had made new fans through TV's *Footy Show*.

He was perhaps best summed up by distinguished coach David Parkin, who said: 'There are no obvious flaws in his football make-up. Capable of marking against

the talls, outmanoeuvring the medium strongs, a quickness and agility to go with the athletes, and outstanding ground work to match any small, makes him a terribly difficult opponent to counter.'

He had many of the on-field

attributes of Footscray's greatest son, Ted Whitten. For a knockabout bloke Hawkins was a very good football dancer, displaying dazzling pirouettes and very grand jetes on the wing. He was the essence of the proud and skilful Bulldog.

Dockers dazzle dismal Lions for first win in the AFL

April 15. There was little celebration and Fremantle's players even had trouble starting the team song, but today's 43-point win over Fitzroy at the Western Oval was a milestone.

The Dockers' first AFL victory came just three weeks after their initiation in a match tagged the battle of the wooden spooners. Captain Ben Allan said his team had exceeded Melbourne expectations, basically because the amount of young talent from the WAFL had been under-estimated.

Coach Gerard Neesham said: 'It was good to win in Melbourne, and that's a different track for us; it's a pretty hard, boggy track. Our blokes are built for the fast tracks in the west.'

Fitzroy had much more possession but failed to finish, hampered by the lack of a strong full-forward. Only 7561 saw Fremantle score 18.13 (121) to 11.12 (78).

The Dockers, in their distinctive colours, warm up before their first game.

Big Sticks' ten

April 15. Unable to play against Fitzroy last week and hampered by a groin injury, Stephen Kernahan was superb at full-forward for Carlton at the MCG today, kicking 10.7 against Footscray.

The Blues skipper was unstoppable. First Barry Standfield, then Matthew Croft and Ben Sexton were tried on Kernahan, with Croft having another go, while Kernahan led and marked, picking up 12 marks and 25 possessions.

Carlton, 23.20 (158), won by 98 points, Footscray scoring 8.12 (60).

No Super League

April 15. Hanging over football, according to AFL Chief Executive Ross Oakley, is the spectre of a Rupert Murdoch-style Super League.

The AFL could be vulnerable, he warns. Collingwood President Allan McAlister believes a Super League coup is likely and Carlton President John Elliott said his club has been approached about such a league.

Writing in *The Age*, Peter McFarline says lack of appeal overseas could save the AFL because the game would not be attractive to a mass international TV audience.

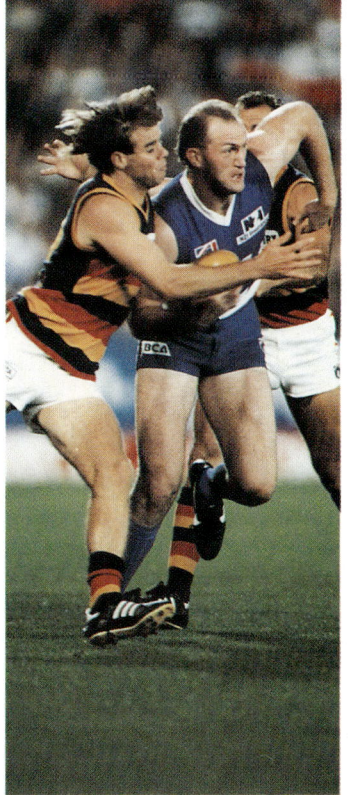

North Melbourne fullback Mick Martyn contests the ball as North march to an emphatic win over the Adelaide Crows in the Ansett Cup pre-season competition. North won by 30 points, 14.9 (93) to the Crows 8.15 (63), and are being tipped as Premiership winners.

Arafura football

April 15. An international Australian Rules football council has been set up to foster the game abroad.

And a study will be made of the game's following in PNG.

The council represents Japan, PNG, New Zealand, Singapore and Hong Kong. The winner of the gold medal for football at the Arafura Games, PNG wants a permanent development officer.

General Manager of Football Operations, Ian Collins said that in the 1960s and 1970s football was No. 1 in PNG, but rugby league had taken over.

Bernie's bad day

April 1. What a date for Fitzroy to fail for half the game. Not a behind, not even a rushed point was scored in Bernie Quinlan's first half as an AFL coach.

'We came up against a very good side,' he said of Essendon's 74-point win. Bomber Michael Long was the best on the ground, sharing the honours with centre half-forward James Hird and Gavin Wanganeen.

Brad Boyd, debuting as captain, got the Lions' first goal three minutes into the second half. Essendon won 16.16 (112) to 6.2 (38) (→ 6/5).

Dons and Pies play a classic draw before 94,825

April 25. It was an Anzac Day match of heroes. In a heart-stopping encounter before 94,825 rapt spectators, the second largest home-and-away crowd in history, Collingwood and Essendon drew at the MCG.

Saverio Rocca bagged nine goals for the Magpies, emerging from last season's inconsistencies to leap, mark and lead with inspiration.

His third term, when Collingwood kicked seven goals to two, travelling from 16 points down to 16 points up for the last quarter, had all the great elements.

But the Magpies did run flat in the second term and then half-way into the last quarter, letting the never-lie-down Bombers back in.

With four goals in eight minutes, the Bombers turned a 22-point deficit into a six-point lead. Only bad kicking then let them down, with the siren blowing on Collingwood's 17.9 (111) to 16.15 (111).

Kevin Sheedy tried three players on Rocca. All failed. New Magpie Dermott Brereton helped clear the way for Rocca, while Gavin Crosisca took care of James Hird.

As the second half got under way, Crosisca began to be helped by Mick McGuane, Alan Richardson, Brett James and Shane Watson.

Joe Misiti, whose great afternoon included 30 possessions, gained control of McGuane, however.

Che Cockatoo-Collins justified a $1500 club fine for his last minute inclusion in a final term of 12 touches, a great mark and goal.

Saverio Rocca flies over Ryan O'Connor to mark and bag another goal.

AFL tempts clubs with $4 million merger offer

June 13. AFL teams found unable to pay their way face deregistration under a scheme aimed at forcing mergers of some Melbourne clubs.

This is part of a package of merger incentives worth $4 million which went to the 16 clubs today.

For the first time clubs will have to raise a minimum amount of money or risk losing their licence. The amount generated and contributed must be at least up to the cost of taking part in the competiton.

In a carrot-and-stick scheme the AFL offered merging sides an extra $700,000 on the salary cap above the annual limit of $2.3 million over three years, guaranteed attendance and membership income worth $400,000, $450,000 in promotion over two years, $100,000 in general administration subsidies and $200,000 for severance payments, as well as $700,000 for ground and social club improvements.

The offer includes $1.2 million to repay debts and an increase in player numbers from 42 to between 44 and 50, depending on 'seedings' of merging clubs.

The 'stick' is that from 1998 the AFL would expel teams that cannot pay their way.

Only eight clubs would need to vote in favour of the merger incentive package, but 11 for the minimum financial criteria.

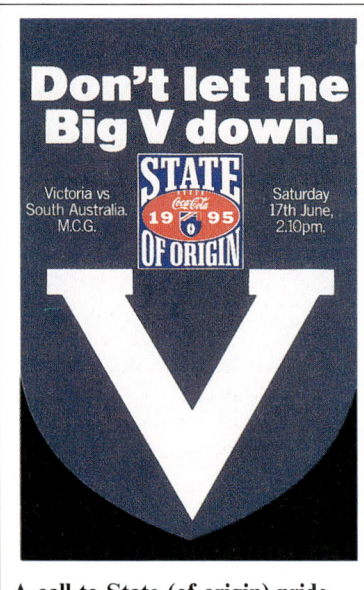
Tigers roar again, but Demons in hell

May 14. Richmond made it seven in a row with a struggling win over Adelaide on Friday, while Melbourne scraped a win over Brisbane today after six losses.

The Tigers were not attractive in their 14-point win, 10.12 (72) to 9.4 (58), but it is their best season opening in 75 years. Matthew Knights was outstanding, with 38 possessions. For the Crows, Tony Modra played almost a lone hand up forward, with five goals.

Angry supporters heckled Melbourne coach Neil Balme at three-quarter time. Then captain Garry Lyon turned in a magnificent term, with 11 touches and the Demons won 12.10 (82) to 10.15 (75).

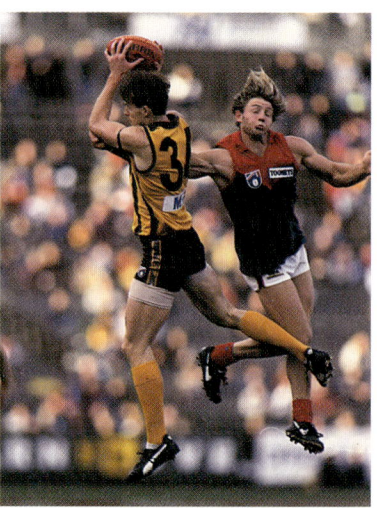

Michael Gale marks for the Tigers.

Mark Graham beats Stephen Tingay.

A plague of 'knees' cuts down footy stars

June 3. A shocked silence descended on the MCG when the crowd realised Melbourne forward David Schwarz had done his knee again, after a miraculous 16-week recovery from a serious injury to it.

Schwarz, who returned from a knee reconstruction to play last week, collapsed when attempting to switch direction half-way through the opening term.

Schwarz's injury is just one of a number which have afflicted AFL players this season in an unprecedented plague.

Questions are being asked not just about modern surgery and recovery times, but about such fundamentals as strapping of ankles and knees, the distance between boundary fence and line, and ground conditions.

Some of the victims so far include North Melbourne's Matthew Capuano, Richmond's Tony Free and Matthew Richardson, Essendon's Darren Bewick, Carlton's Rohan Welsh, and Brisbane's Ross Lyon and Steve Lawrence.

Just back from knee reconstruction, Demon David Schwarz is out again.

Blues back to best after seeming worst

June 4. After Carlton's second loss for the season, to St Kilda last week, coach David Parkin said: 'Take it on record that it was one of Carlton's saddest days, particularly on a day when Justin Madden played his 250th game for Carlton. We have gone from the best team in the competition to the worst team in two weeks.'

The Blues managed just 3.6 (24) against the rampaging Saints' 11.14 (80), and this followed an equally insipid 8.12 (60) loss to Sydney's 21.6 (132).

However, more than 27,000 Blues fans at Princes Park today watched the reversal of football fortunes in growing good cheer.

By the end of the afternoon Carlton were the best team in the competition again joyfully pounding Hawthorn by 102 points, 26.16 (172) to 10.10 (70).

Stephen Kernahan was back in town, kicking five, alongside speeding sensation Brad Pearce. So did Mil Hanna who exploded the game in the first quarter. Brett Ratten and Craig Bradley were dynamos.

Ted Whitten, keeper of the flame of interstate football, came to the MCG to say goodbye, and the crowd came too to salute him. Tony Lockett won the E.J. Whitten Medal as Victoria beat SA, 18.12 (120) to 8.9 (57).

Battling Saints send out an SOS

A distress signal from the Saints.

June 26. 'Everybody who loves the Saints, here is your go to make them survive and be successful,' said St Kilda President Andrew Plympton in launching the club's $1.5 million appeal. Plympton is seeking 15,000 adult members and a big cut in the $900,000 debt.

But a veteran St Kilda follower told the *Herald Sun* he would not be too disappointed if the club folded. 'I've been supporting them for 60 years,' he said. 'They've given me too much heartache.'

AFL signs with Seven in big TV rights deal

June 19. The AFL has knocked back a bid from the Nine Network of more than $200 million for broadcast rights to the national competition, re-signing with Seven for about $150 million.

The three-year deal from 1999 has some clubs believing that the extra income will enable them to continue in their own right.

The League has also raised the ante in the merger push by increasing the package's value from $4 million to $6 million. The deadline is October 31.

Eight clubs voted in favour of the merger package increase, but the League refused to put its controversial financial criteria plan to the ballot in case it was voted out.

The Age has revealed that the General Manager of Nine Melbourne, Ian Johnson, and Nine's Managing Director, David Leckie, had held talks with the AFL's Chief Executive, Ross Oakley.

Some years ago Nine tried to buy the rights to the League's major matches including pre-season games and State of Origin clashes.

Harry's 300th game disproves evolution

July 9. Justin Madden played his 300th League game today, against Richmond, cheered by 85,000 fans from both sides, in a Carlton win, 17.13 (115) to 12.13 (85).

He has often said that it was an indictment of the game that he is still playing, but the truth is that it is a tribute to the game, and to him as player and footy philosopher.

At Carlton in 1983 at first he was the 'wrong Madden', a beanstalk, a bit of a joke.

He played the first three games of 1985 in the 'twos' – yet by then had won the affection and respect of everyone, the best and fairest, came second in the Brownlow and had inherited the nickname 'Harry' from a departed player.

Behind the amiability and sheer size is a football brain that puts the hand on the ball 60 or 70 times a game, and sets the Carlton machine in motion, especially from the centre. Old-fashioned ruckwork is the secret of the team's success.

Behind the smile is a man who has things in perspective. An architect by profession, and President of the AFL Players' Association, to him the game is a source of enjoyment.

Robert Walls said: 'I loved coaching him because he would rarely miss a game and never complained ... He nodded agreement with every instruction given, and then went and did his own thing.'

Team-mates share the load.

Players' Code of Conduct introduced

AFL chief Ross Oakley confronts a racism row as the mediator between Damian Monkhorst and Michael Long.

June 23. The AFL Tribunal will get the power to punish players for on-field racial abuse.

Under the League's code of conduct, to be implemented next week, the penalties could range from fines to suspension. The code is due to be ratified by the Commission next week following months of deliberations.

Although mediation may be involved in hearings over racial abuse, the Tribunal, and not the AFL Commission, is expected to judge these cases.

Significantly, the League has also established a separate rule to penalise players who use illegal drugs or prohibited substances.

Initially the League proposed that players guilty of racial taunts on the field would be fined $1000 for the first offence and $5000 for subsequent offences. Later the AFL decided that mediation would be used as the primary way to settle a dispute.

The Age first revealed the code of conduct plan in March and since then Essendon's Michael Long has alleged that Collingwood's Damian Monkhorst racially abused him during a game. This led to a bungled attempt at mediation, but was later settled satisfactorily.

The AFL has promised to undertake a major advertising campaign as part of a drive to free the game of racial taunting, both on and off the field, by players and spectators.

Gallant Tigers hold Dons for night draw

July 14. In a sensational night game, Richmond and Essendon played a draw at the MCG.

A magnificent Tiger defence stopped dangerous attacks by Paul Salmon, Che Cockatoo-Collins, James Hird and Michael Long.

The Tigers suffered from the loss of the injured Matthew Richardson, with Stephen Jurica bravely trying to fill in.

Richmond officials are talking of taking action over an incident in which Stuart Maxfield had his jaw broken in an off-the-ball clash which no one actually saw. Maxfield is expected to be out for six weeks.

Richmond are still angry over the suspension last week of full back Scott Turner.

The Tigers' courage in matching Essendon with 15.11 (101) each has cost them dearly.

Michael Gale will have his collarbone x-rayed to help decide if it will need a pin (→2/9).

Tempers were high as players tangled at half time in the night match.

Goodbye, Mr Football

Aug. 22. Appropriately for a footballer who was a legend in his lifetime, Ted Whitten managed to have his death announced first on the top rating *Footy Show*.

Mr Football topped this today with live coverage of his State Funeral on television – a tribute to his role as emblem or epitome of a set of old and perhaps old-fashioned Victorian values.

Non-football fans and non-Victorians have been somewhat surprised at the outpouring of emotion for Whitten, following the TV announcement of his cancer on December 22 1994, and the televised ride around the sacred arena of the MCG before the State of Origin game against the hated Croweaters on June 17.

Who was he, this Ted Whitten, perhaps a king of football or a prince of punts? No, he was a simple Mister – Mr Football, representing the larrikin, working-class origins of the game before it became involved in marketing and going national, when it was played by 12 clubs on Saturday afternoon, when his suburb Footscray was redolent with the abattoirs and the boiling-down works and the hard life of working-class Melbourne after World War Two.

Perhaps that was why Ted became a TV star and character, almost as soon as the thing was introduced in 1956. He knew a way out when he saw it, through footy and TV, and a way of selling his product which was firstly Mr Football, and later Victorian and State of Origin football.

Whitten was a TV fixture as host, panellist, and commentator, one who could barely contain his urge to jump though the screen and do it all again.

Meeting Whitten was to have your hand crushed, your football soul peered into, and the hard question asked 'And what've you done for footy?' He'd done a lot.

His friend and fellow legend, triple Brownlow Medallist Bob Skilton, eulogised: 'EJ the footballer had everything; he was truly the complete package. He had wonderful skills, was tough as nails and a truly fierce competitor. He was a character who never lost his concentration. One minute it was a laugh, the next he had run right through you.'

Ted Whitten died on August 17, and St Patrick's Cathedral overflowed.

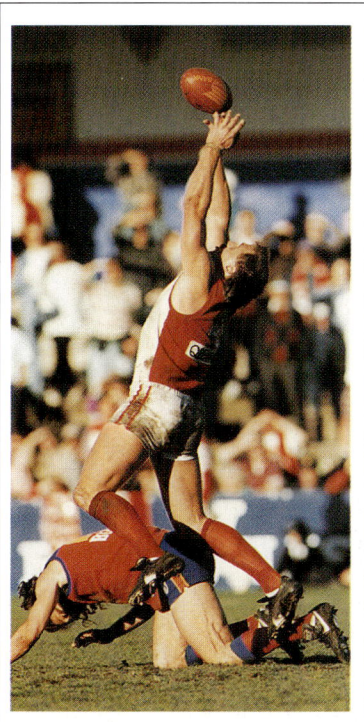

Tony Lockett is on his way to 16 goals against lowly Fitzroy.

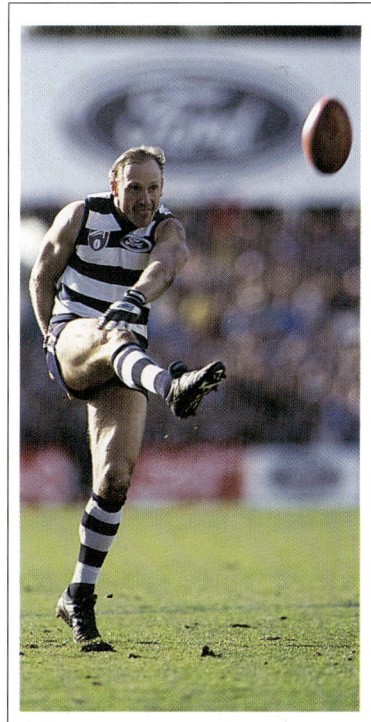

Superstar Gary Ablett kicks his 100th. goal for the season.

North champion Wayne Carey is the club's key to success.

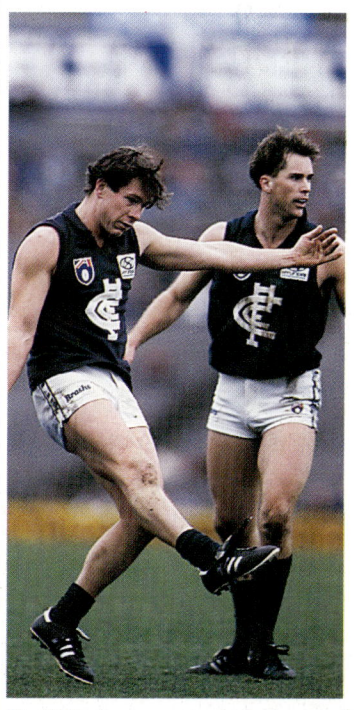

Brett Ratten – unsung, but one of the Blues' big possession winners.

Underdogs have their day at season's end

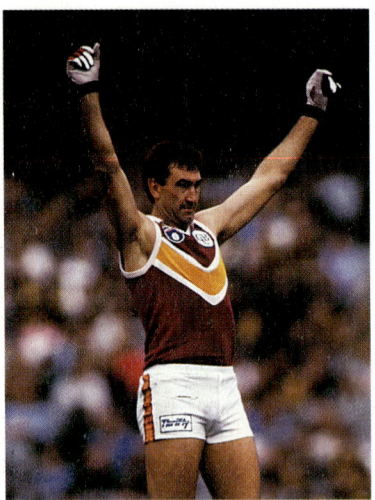

Roger Merrett brought Bears in.

Danny Frawley: tearful goodbye.

Sept. 3. Ron Barassi was kissed in Sydney, while in Brisbane Richard Champion was dampening a few team-mates' shoulders. The last games had been played in the home-and-away and, thanks to the Swans, Brisbane have made it into the Final Eight and a meeting with Carlton at the MCG.

To add to the emotional weekend retiring St Kilda captain Danny Frawley was spilling tears everywhere as he said goodbye after 12 hard years in defence. He, too, went out on a win, with the Saints finishing a good year by beating Footscray 20.12 (132) to 11.12 (78).

Elsewhere Carlton, Richmond, Geelong, North Melbourne and West Coast had easy tune-up wins before the Finals.

But the main action was interstate, where three of the contestants for the eighth spot, Brisbane, Melbourne and Collingwood, were engaged in cut-throat contests.

Melbourne dropped out in a Friday night match at the Gabba, in which they started well but were worn down by the team play and endeavour of the Bears.

Melbourne fans could only take away the imprint of an amazing feat by Shaun Smith, who took a chest mark in the goal square, about five metres above the ground.

The Bears were in, provided only that the Swans did the improbable and beat Collingwood in Sydney on Sunday. While the Bears watched at a bar in Brisbane, the Swans set about the task.

The Bears were groaning early, as Collingwood set up a handy lead, but the Swans began to work well and kept pegging away to be two goals down at three-quarter time.

An eight-goal last quarter, with Tony Lockett exerting his influence and finishing with seven goals, knocked the Magpies out.

The victory seemed like a Finals win for Swans supporters as well, as they swamped the players on the field, and retiring coach Barassi in the dressing room.

Season favourites Eagles crash in finals

Sept. 17. The unthinkable has happened. West Coast are not in the Grand Final.

It seemed this time last year that the Eagles were so strong that they might make up one half of the Grand Final equation for many years to come.

Their lapses through the year have been somewhat discounted, as they have seemed to cruise in other seasons, with coach Mick Malthouse bringing them to a peak for the Finals.

A hint of trouble came in round 21, when Carlton won a torrid encounter in the West by one point.

Then they lost the First Qualifying Final to Essendon. Today the West Coast ghost had been laid as North beat them all over the field to win 18.21 (129) to 10.11 (71). The Eagles have crashed, and the AFL competition seems balanced again.

A 'real goer' is popular Brownlow winner

Sept. 25. The atmosphere could scarcely have been more tense. As the Brownlow Medal count edged up, Sydney captain Paul Kelly twisted and turned, held his face, then looked up as he began to ease ahead of Michael Long of Essendon and Paul Couch of Geelong.

Kelly, an outsider, picked up two votes in round 20 to hit the front and stay there with two more in each of the next two rounds for a total of 21, three ahead of Hawthorn's Darren Jarman, who was, however, ineligible because he had been suspended, as was third placegetter, Garry Hocking of Geelong.

Kelly, a courageous, tireless player, could only express his disbelief as he spoke in the TV hook-up to his wife, Lyndelle, and team-mates with 1000 supporters at Randwick Racecourse in Sydney.

Among them was another medallist, Tony Lockett, who summed up: 'You little bloody ripper, mate!'

Kelly: a 'little ripper'.

Blues 20 wins a home-and-away record

Sept. 2. Carlton gladdened the hearts of statisticians and Blues fans by beating Essendon 16.12 (108) to 9.13 (67), becoming the first team in the history of the VFL/AFL to win 20 games in the home-and-away season.

The win also meant that Carlton finished four games in front of the other Finalists, the first time this has happened since the Coleman-powered Bombers of 1950, who finished 16 points ahead of North Melbourne – and went on to win the Grand Final.

The Essendon win was the Blues' 13th consecutive win, and was particularly meritorious after the tough, tight and tense one-point win over West Coast last week in Perth.

Essendon threatened once or twice but the storm never broke, Carlton showing that they had a complete and skill-laden team, with plenty of grit. Greg Williams was reported for abusing an umpire.

Super player and coach Ron Barassi announces that he is stepping back from the firing line, leaving the Swans in a strengthened position.

The Blues Brothers make it sweet 16

Sept. 30. This Grand Final was billed as the close one, Geelong's best chance since 1963, since a tick or two of the clock denied them in 1989.

After all, the pundits said, both sides came into the game having played a Preliminary Final, the Cats had an easy couple of Finals, which ought to balance out against Carlton's 15 wins in a row – and the home-and-away clash at Princes Park only ended with Carlton in front because that was when the siren sounded.

In prospect this game was going to be fought out to the wire. It would be a nail-biter if not a heart-stopper.

Instead it turned out to be a boilover, and a tear-jerker as far as Geelong was concerned.

For Carlton it was the pay back and the comeback after the Finals' humiliations of 1993 and 1994.

It was the Blues' 16th VFL/AFL Flag, the 16th win in a row by the team 16 points in front at the end of the home-and-away rounds. The final score was 21.15 (141) to 11.14 (80) – a margin of 61 points.

Carlton's win started in the engine room with Justin Madden, and a selection from Brett Ratten, Craig Bradley, Fraser Brown and Greg Williams.

Surprisingly, considering the devastating effect that quick clearances from this group had during the season, there was a defensive element to the set-up in the Grand Final. There were few instant goals created, but many goals worked forward by these footy engineers.

Up forward the captain, Stephen Kernahan, presented himself as a target out near the 50-metre line, before ducking back. Brad Pearce zipped closer to the goal square, Earl Spalding, Matt Clape and Dean Rice hit both packs and space.

Greg Williams was inventing a new position as a goalkicking centreman and forward. He often seemed to be getting and delivering the ball in the middle, then all of a sudden popping up from a hole at half-forward, to mark his own pass. He kicked five goals and gave away five more in a Norm Smith Medal-winning performance.

His rival for this honour was Anthony Koutoufides, a footballer who grew more astounding as the season

Grand Final favourites and determined to win, the Carlton team break the banner as they hit the ground running.

Silvagni wins a crucial contest.

Blues' captain Stephen Kernahan shows the cup off during a lap of honour.

progressed. 'Kouta' is a kind of wingman who plays in the ruck and at full-forward when required. He is tall, fast, strong, has a lovely pair of huge hands, and is a deft pass.

Carlton's backline, the most fraternal of the team of 'brothers', was impassable. For Geelong it was like trying to go up an avalanche.

Stephen Silvagni was just as strong as, and much too agile for Gary Ablett – who must have known

it wasn't his day when he missed three in the first quarter. He wasn't destined to be a match winner.

Peter Dean, Andrew McKay and Ang Christou roamed and hovered across the half-back line, cleaning up the sporadic forays by the Cats. Anything they missed was grabbed by Michael Sexton, as dependable as your favourite chair.

That most professional of sportsmen Craig Bradley hardly gave

Garry Hocking a smell of the footy, got by himself for 23 touches and kicked a couple of goals – including the all important 'undercoat' goal, the first one. He also kicked the traditional 'sealer' – the first goal of the last quarter.

The Grand Final wasn't the close one some had thought it would be, but it was a great day for the Blues, statistically the most successful team in 99 years of League football.

The man in white is not always right

Oct. 19. A report by the Umpires' Association puts a number on what long-suffering fans have always suspected – that umpires are right only some of the time. They're not right all the time.

To gain the real statistics, trained observers recorded all relevant incidents in a match on a computer. The game was then reviewed by a group including the three umpires, the emergency umpire, and the trained observer and umpires' coach David Levens.

The report noted that of 49 infringements in a game, 44 were penalised, but seven decisions were not warranted. That's an 'accuracy rating' of 75.5 %.

Put another way, an inaccuracy rating of 24.5 %.

The report stated: 'in our opinion, the standard of umpiring in the home-and-away matches on occasions did not meet our expectations. In the Finals series, however, when the best-performed 12 umpires were in action, we thought the overall standard of umpiring was good.'

But which 24.5 % were wrong?

No mergers, no Port Adelaide in 1996

Oct. 27. AFL Chief Executive Ross Oakley has announced, four days before the merger deadline, that there is no prospect of such a merger taking place this year.

The AFL's $6 million enticement for the first clubs to merge has not proved sufficient to overcome the Victorian clubs' desire to stand alone in the AFL's centenary year.

Oakley says the $6 million will remain on the table next year, and the option of additional inducements, such as the controversial club financial criteria, might be looked at.

Some 11 merger discussions had been held this year, and 'about six of them were very serious discussions,' said Oakley.

None of this is much consolation to Port Adelaide who are all dressed up in their bright new Port Power uniforms, but have nowhere to play in the AFL in 1996.

Oakley said he was disappointed. 'Anyone will get frustrated when they believe that something should occur ... but when you don't have the power or ability to make it happen, it's very frustrating.'

All aboard the coaching merry-go-round

Northey: off to the sunshine.

Matthews: on to the media.

Oct. 23. The appointment of Robert Walls as coach of Richmond has completed the circular coaching story begun by John Northey's resignation – or sacking – last month and his subsequent appointment to the job in Brisbane.

The acrimonious departure of Northey after such a successful season at Tigerland struck outsiders as bizarre, although there had been a number of newspaper reports of Brisbane's interest in him earlier in the season.

The Tiger tensions did not dissuade Walls from accepting a three-year contract with Richmond.

Walls, who had announced his resignation as coach of Brisbane, and from coaching, during the season, only to get the team into the Finals, was a hot property. He says he is looking forward to working back in Melbourne with a team of talented and dedicated young players who, in the end, finished third after a spirited run in the finals series.

Other moves were Tony Shaw replacing the self-sacked Leigh Matthews at Collingwood; Rodney Eade taking over at Sydney from Ron Barassi, Ken Judge scoring the task at Hawthorn following the sacking of Peter Knights, and South Australian Michael Nunan drawing the short straw at Fitzroy, after Bernie Quinlan's brief tenure.

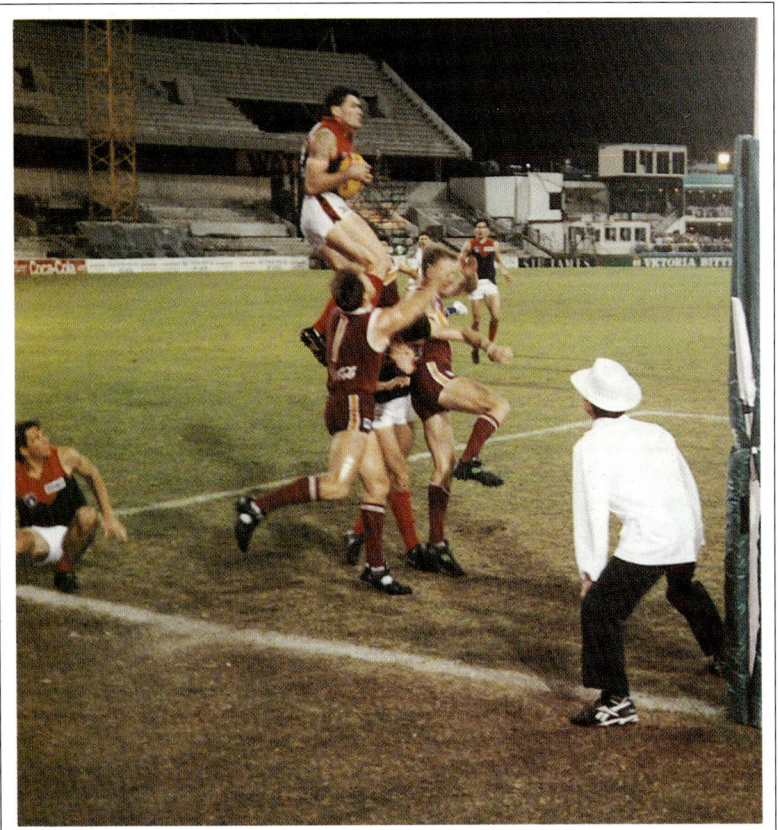
And the mark of the year award goes to Shaun Smith of Melbourne.

1995 Statistics

Leading Goalkicker:
Gary Ablett (Geel) 122
Brownlow Medallist:
Paul Kelly (Sydney)
Finals: First Qualifying Final Ess 11.8 (74) W. Coast 8.7 (55); **Second Qualifying Final** Rich 12.12 (84) N. Melb 17.12 (114); **Third Qualifying Final** Geel 24.11 (155) Foots 10.13 (73); **Fourth Qualifying Final** Carl 13.12 (90) Bris 12.5 (77); **First Semi-final** N. Melb 18.21 (129) W. Coast 10.11 (71); **Second Semi-final** Rich 12.14 (86) Ess 11.7 (73); **First Preliminary Final** Geel 20.9 (129) Rich 6.4 (40); Second Preliminary Final Carl 18.10 (118) N. Melb 8.8 (56); **Grand Final** Carl 21.15 (141) Geel 11.14 (80)

Ladder:	W	L	D	%	pts
Carl	20	2		137.8	80
Geel	16	6		131.9	64
Rich	15	6	1	107.9	62
Ess	14	6	2	127.6	60
W. Coast	14	8		122.9	56
N. Melb	14	8		114.8	56
Foots	11	10	1	91.5	46
Bris	10	12		95.3	40
Melb	9	13		100.7	36
Coll	8	12	2	96.8	36
Adel	9	13		80.1	36
Syd	8	14		100.7	32
Fre	8	14		92.8	32
St K	8	14		80.3	32
Haw	7	15		94.0	28
Fitz	2	20		58.2	8

Wheels turn full circle with new V.F.L.

Nov. 15. The Victorian Football League was formed 100 years ago, as eight clubs broke away from the Victorian Football Association.

Now the wheel has turned full circle, with the VFA moving into the naming space created when the Victorian Football League became the Australian Football League.

The VFA has re-named itself the Victorian Football League and restructured its competition. The new VFL ties the senior State football body more closely to the AFL, and brings country football back into the major State competition.

From the old VFA nine clubs have been selected as part of the elite State body, and two country clubs have been added, North Balla-rat and Traralgon. Werribee was a late inclusion. There is room for expansion in other country areas, possibly Bendigo or the Ovens and Murray League areas.

The senior State-based competition will have close links with the Australian Football League, as the Victorian State Football League under-18 competition will now be affiliated with VFL clubs.

Under 18 players have been a strong source of draft picks for the AFL, and they will now have the opportunity to nominate for the draft or continue their careers with their senior VFL Club.

The VFL also provides a back up competition to the AFL, in much the same way as the South Australian National Football League (SANFL) and the Western Australian Football League (WAFL) provide a system in which players who miss the AFL draft can stay under notice without moving interstate.

The VFL clubs are:

Box Hill: VSFL Feeder Club: Eastern Rangers.
Coburg: Calder Cannons.
Frankston: Dandenong Southern Stingrays.
North Ballarat: Ballarat Rebels.
Port Melbourne: Geelong Falcons.
Preston: Northern Knights.
Sandringham: Prahran Dragons.
Springvale: Oakleigh Chargers.
Traralgon: Gippsland Power.
Werribee: no feeder club.
Williamstown: Western Jets.

Trial Rules

Nov. 27. The AFL announced some trial rules for a three day $170,000 Lightning Premiership competition, held on February 9-11 as the opening football event of the centenary Year.

Trials include: Three points for a poster or a ball rushed across the scoreline by the opposition; a free kick against the last player to touch the ball before it goes out of bounds (but no shot for goal if the ball goes out of bounds within the 50 metre zone); six on the interchange benches; the ball thrown up instead of bounced; four goal umpires and four boundary umpires; defenders to kick in after a score without having to wait for the goal umpire to wave his flags.

Seven tops TV sports ladder, with huge ratings

If there are any lingering doubts about the media pulling power of football, they have been dispelled by the ratings of Melbourne's top 10 TV shows.

Football made five of the top 10, with (1) the *AFL Grand Final*, (3) an *AFL Preliminary* Final, (4) the *Brownlow Medal* telecast, (6) a night match between Adelaide and North Melbourne, (8) *The Footy Show* Grand Final Edition.

Channel 7 reaped the big benefits with its actuality telecasts, while Channel 9 laid some solid cement on new television ground with its knockabout *Footy Show*.

The battle for the 'football variety' crown will continue in 1996, as *4 Quarters* (7) on Friday nights, wrestles for supremacy with Thursday's *Footy Show* (9).

There are rival shows on Sunday too, as *The Footy Show* (9) and *Sportsworld* and *Gameday* (7) get into deep analysis of the weekend conflict. On Monday night it's on again with *Talking Footy* (7), with Bruce McAvaney et al.

The radio ratings battle also rages, with professional ABC team, led by an outstanding broadcaster in Tim Lane, competing with the 'football mouth' Rex Hunt on 3AW, and Magic 693 with Kevin Bartlett and his team, where one of the great attractions is listening to the verbal circumlocutions of Sam Kekovich.

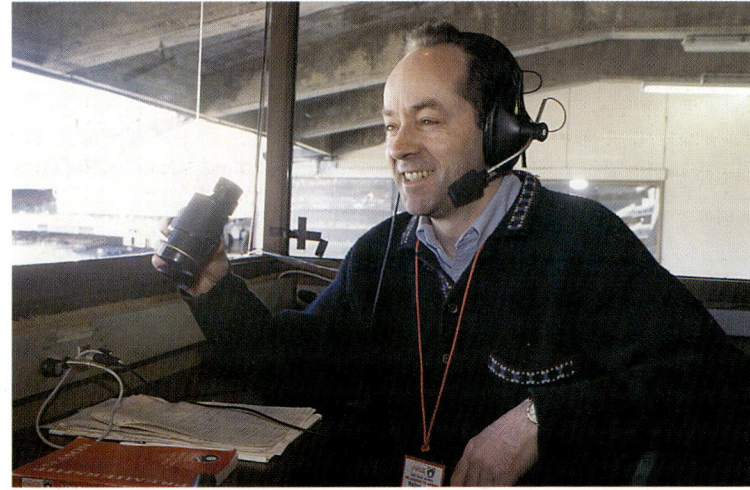

The commentators' commentator. Tim Lane heads up ABC football.

Tony Free, '4 Quarters' regular.

A late starter, Channel 7's '4 Quarters' built a big following.

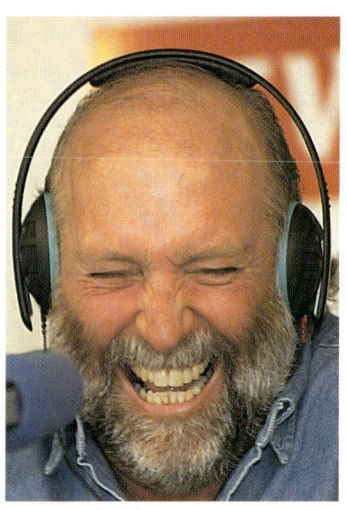

Rex Hunt, off the wall on 3AW.

Australia Post released the Centenary of the AFL stamps series in April, 1996. The stamps are sold in club booklets of 10. The booklets feature the club insignia, a portrait of notable player of the club, and facts about the club record.

BIBLIOGRAPHY

The Age, Melbourne, 1854-.

The Argus, Melbourne, 1846-1957.

Atkinson, Graeme, *Everything You've Ever Wanted to Know About Australian Rules Football*, The Five Mile Press, Canterbury, Vic., 1982; revised as Graeme Atkinson and Michael Hanlon, *3AW Book of Footy Records*, Matchbooks, South Melbourne, 1989.

Atkinson, Graeme, *The Book of VFL Finals*, The Five Mile Press, Canterbury, Vic., 1973 & 1981; revised as *The Book of Australian Rules Finals*, The Five Mile Press, Canterbury, Vic., 1983; and revised as *The Complete Book of VFL Finals*, The Five Mile Press, Canterbury, Vic., 1989.

The Australasian Sketcher, Melbourne, 1864-1957.

Aylett, Allen, *My Game: A Life in Football As Told to Greg Hobbs*, Sun Books, South Melbourne, 1986.

Barassi, Ron, with Peter McFarline, *Barassi: The Man Behind The Legend*, Simon and Schuster, Sydney, 1995.

Blainey, Geoffrey, *A Game of Our Own: The Origins of Australian Football*, National Australian Football Council, Information Australia, Melbourne, 1990.

Buggy, Hugh, *The Carlton Story: A History of the Carlton Football Club*, Eric White Associates, Melbourne, 1958.

Butler, Mark and Stephen Milne, *Sons of the 'Scray, Footscray's Finest 50*, Williamstown, Melbourne, 1993.

Christison, Darren, (ed.), *Football Yearbook, 1993*. GMG Sport, Woolahra, NSW.

Craven, John, ed., *Football the Australian Way*, Lansdowne Press, Melbourne 1969.

Delbridge, Noel, ed., *The Bulldog Book: sons of 'Scray (1883-1983)*, Footscray Football Club, West Footscray, Vic.

Dowling, Gerard P., *The North Story*, The Hawthorn Press, Melbourne, 1973.

Dunn, John, with Jim Main, *Australian Rules Football: An Illustrated History*, Lansdowne Press, Melbourne, 1974.

Dunstan, Keith, *The Paddock That Grew: The Story of the Melbourne Cricket Club*, Cassell, 1962, revised edn, Cassell, Melbourne, 1974.

Dyer, Jack as told to Brian Hansen, *'Captain Blood'*, Stanley Paul, London 1965.

Dyer, Jack, and Brian Hansen, *Captain Blood's Wild Men of Football*, Hansen, Cheltenham, 1993.

East, Alan, ed., *Eagles for the Flag*, Australian Sports Publications, North Perth, 1992, 1993.

Feldmann, Jules and Russell Holmesby, *The Point of It All: The Story of the St Kilda Football Club*, Playwright Publishing, Melbourne, 1992.

Fiddian, Marc, *The Pioneers*, Victorian Football Association, Melbourne, 1977.

Fiddian, Marc, *The Roar of the Crowd*, Victorian Football Association, Melbourne, 1987.

Fitzgerald, Ross and Ken Spillman, eds, *The Greatest Game*, William Heinemann Australia, Melbourne, 1988, repr. 1989, 1992.

Flanagan, Martin, *Southern Sky, Western Oval*, McPhee Gribble, South Yarra, 1994.

The Footballer: An Annual Record of Football in Victoria and the Australian Colonies. Ed. Thomas Power, Henriques & Co, Melbourne, 1875-.

Flower, Robert with Ron Reed, *Robbie*, Caribou Publications, Melbourne, 1968.

Football Life, Melbourne, 1968-1972.

Football Record, Victorian Football League, Melbourne, 1912-.

Gordon, Harry, *The Hard Way: The Story of the Hawthorn Football Club*, Lester-Townsend Publishing, Sydney, 1990.

Gordon, Kerrie and Alan Dalton, *Too Tough to Die: Footscray's Fightback 1989*, Self-published, Melbourne, 1990.

Handley, George, *The Great Grand Finals*, Walshe, Geelong, 1989.

Hansen Brian, *The Magpie Years '93* Brian Hansen Publications, Cheltenham, Vic.

Hansen, Brian, *Tigerland: The History of the Richmond Football Club from 1885*. Richmond Former Players and Officials Association, Melbourne, 1989.

Hansen, Brian, *The Magpies: The History of the Collingwood Football Club, from 1892 to 1992*, Semis Carla, Cheltenham, Vic., 1992.

Hart, Royce, *The Royce Hart Story*, Thomas Nelson Melbourne, 1970.

Hawke, Steve, *Polly Farmer: A Biography*, Fremantle Arts Centre Press, South Fremantle, 1994.

The Herald, Melbourne, 1839-

Hewat, T., *The Blues*, Carlton Football Club, Melbourne, 1982.

Hibberd, Jack and Garrie Hutchinson, *The Barrackers Bible - A Dictionary of Sporting Slang*, McPhee Gribble, 1983.

Hobbs, Greg, *125 Years of the Melbourne Demons*, Melbourne Football Club, Melbourne, 1984.

Holmesby, Russell, *Heroes With Haloes*, St Kilda's 100 Greatest, Playright Publishing, 1995.

Hopgood, Alan, *And the Big Men Fly*, Heinemann Educational, Melbourne, Vic., 1969.

Hunt, Rex, *The Football Bible '94*, Crossbow Publishing, Jolimont, 1993.

Hutchinson, Col, *Cat's Tales: Geelong Football Club, 1897-1983*, Geelong Advertiser, Geelong, 1984.

Hutchinson, Col (ed.), *1995 AFL Media Guide*, AFL Communications Dept., Melbourne.

Hutchinson, Garrie, *The Great Australian Book of Football Stories*, Currey O'Neil, Melbourne, 1983, repr. as *Great Australian Football Stories*, Viking O'Neil, Melbourne, 1989.

Hutchinson, Garrie, *From the Outer: Watching Football in the 80s*, McPhee Gribble, Fitzroy, Vic., 1984.

Hutchinson, Garrie, *Australian Rules Football: The Watcher's Guide*, William Heinemann Australia, Melbourne, 1988.

Johnston, Wayne, with Ron Reed, *The Dominator*, Caribou Publications, Melbourne, 1991.

Laurence, L, *History of South Melbourne Football Club*, South Melbourne Football Club, Melbourne 1963.

Linnell, Garry, *Football Ltd, The Inside Story of the AFL*, Ironbark Press, Sydney, 1993.

Lockett, Tony with Ken Piesse, *Plugger*, Sun Books, Melbourne, 1992.

Matthews, Leigh with Mike Sheahan, *Lethal*, Caribou Publications, 1986.

McDonald, John, *Football Year 94*, Pagemasters, Melbourne, 1994.

McGuire, Eddie and Jim Main, *Pants: The Darren Millane Story*, Celebrity Publishing, Melbourne 1994.

McHale, J. A.E. Chadwick and E. C. H. Taylor, *The Australian Game of Football*, C. G. Hartley & Co., Melbourne, 1931.

McKenna, Peter, *My World of Football*, Jack Pollard, North Sydney, c. 1972.

Main, Jim and Ken Piesse, *The A to Z of Football*, Wedneil Publications, Melbourne, 1982.

Main, Jim, ed., *1988 Football Year: The Year in Review*, Century Magazines, Melbourne, 1988.

Main, Jim and Darren Christison, eds, *1989 Football: The Year in Review*, Century Magazines, Melbourne, 1989.

Main, Jim and Russell Holmesby, *The Encyclopedia of League Footballers*, Wilkinson Books, Melbourne, 1992, rev. edn., 1994.

Mancini, A. and G.M. Hibbins, eds, *Running with the Ball: Football's Foster Father*, Lynedoch Publications, Melbourne, 1987.

Maplestone, Michael, *Flying Higher: The History of the Essendon Football Club 1872-1994*, Essendon Football Club, Melbourne, 1994.

Matthews, Brian, *Oval Dreams: Larrikin Essays on Sport & Culture*, McPhee Gribble, Ringwood, Vic., 1991.

Matthews, Leigh with Mike Sheahan, *Lethal*, Caribou Publications, 1986.

Mulvaney, D.J. *Cricket Walkabout: The Australian Aboriginal Cricketers on Tour 1867-8*, Melbourne University Press, Melbourne, 1967.

Nicholls, John, with Ian McDonald, *Big Nick*, Garry Sparke & associates, Hawthorn, Vic., 1977.

Palmer, Scott and Greg Hobbs, *100 Great Marks*, Sun Books, Melbourne, 1974.

Parkin, David, Ross Smith and Peter Schokman, *Premiership Football: How to Train, Play and Coach Australian Football*, Hargreen, North Melbourne, 1984.

Pascoe, Robert, *The Winter Game: The Complete History of Australian Football*, Text Publishing, Melbourne, 1995

Piesse, Ken, *The Complete Guide to Australian Football*, Pan Macmillan, Chippendale NSW, 1993.

Piesse, Ken, *Ablett: The Gary Ablett Story*, Wilkinson Books, Melbourne, 1994.

Powers, John, *The Coach: A Season with Ron Barassi*, Thomas Nelson, West Melbourne, 1978.

Richards, Lou and Tom Prior, *The Footballer Who Laughed*, Hutchinson of Australia, Richmond, Vic. 1981.

Richards, Lou with Stephen Phillips, *The Kiss of Death*, Hutchinson Australia, Sydney, 1989.

Richards, Lou with Stephen Phillips, *Shooting from the Lip*, Magenta Press, Scoresby, Vic., 1990.

Roberts, Michael, *A Century of the Best: The Stories of Collingwood's Favourite Sons*, Collingwood Football Club, Melbourne 1991.

Rodgers, Stephen, *Every Game Ever Played: VFL Results 1897-1989*, Viking O'Neil, Melbourne, 1983, rev. edn, 1990, 1992.

Sandercock, Leonie and Ian Turner, *Up Where, Cazaly? The Great Australian Game*, Granada, London, 1981.

Stremski, Richard, *Kill for Collingwood*, Allen & Unwin, Sydney, 1986.

Sutherland, Mike, Rod Nicholson and Stewart Murrihy, *The First One Hundred Seasons: Fitzroy Football Club, 1883-1983*, Fitzroy Football Club, Melbourne, 1983.

Taylor, E.C.H. *100 Years of Football: The Story of the Melbourne Football Club*, Melbourne Football Club, Melbourne, 1958.

Taylor, K, *Footystats 1993: Australian Football League Statistics, 1897-1992*, Fast Books, Sydney, 1992 (and 1993, 1994 updates).

Taylor, Kevin, *The Sydney Swans, The Complete History, 1874-1986*, Allen and Unwin, Sydney, 1987.

Victorian Football League, *League Football in Victoria*, VFL, Melbourne, 1972-1988.

Weightman, Dale with Bruce Eva, *Saving Our Skins, And Other Tiger Tales*, Floradale Productions, Kilmore, 1991.

Williams, Greg, *Diesel – The Greg Williams Story*, Ironbark, 1995.

Young, Ray and Dave Pincombe, *Footy Facts: All-Australia Guide to Aussie Rules, 1986-87*, Information Australia, Melbourne, 1987.

Photo Credit Index

The position of the pictures are indicated by two letters:
b = bottom, m = middle, l = left, r = right, x = middle left,
y = middle right, t = top, fp = full page, dp = double page.

Cover pictures by arrangement with the AFL, the Age, Sporting Pix and private collections.

General Index

Page numbers in roman type refer to articles,
those in italic to the chronology summaries and illustrations.

100 YEARS OF AUSTRALIAN FOOTBALL is the work of a team of researchers, writers, planners and production staff, in collaboration with a wider consulting group of historians, statisticians and writers.

Contributors and consultants include:

Professor Geoffrey Blainey, Geelong supporter and historian, author of *A Game of Our Own,* on the origins of Australian football.

Keith Dunstan, author of *The Paddock That Grew* and *Sports,* founder of the AFL (Anti Football League).

Martin Flanagan, author of *Southern Sky, Western Oval,* based on a year with the Footscray Football Club.

Harry Gordon, journalist and author, whose books include *The Hard Way,* a history of the Hawthorn Football Club. Member of the AFL Hall of Fame Committee.

Gillian Hibbins, co-author of *Running with the Ball,* the story of Henry Harrison and the beginnings of the Australian game.

Russell Holmesby, journalist, co-author of *The Encyclopedia of League Footballers* and the St Kilda Football Club History, *The Point of it All.*

Col Hutchinson, official Australian Football League statistician, author of *Cats' Tales.*

Garry Linnell, author of *Football Ltd,* the inside story of the AFL.

Noel Delbridge, Footscray Life Member, marketing consultant and football song lyricist.

Professor Robert Pascoe, author of *The Winter Game,* and Professor of History at Victoria University.

Professor Stuart Macintyre, Hawthorn supporter and Professor of History at the University of Melbourne.

Ross McMullin, Carlton supporter and historian.

Geoff Slattery, Managing Editor of *The Football Record.*

Robert Walls, former player and coach of Fitzroy, Carlton (four Premierships), and 1995 finalist, Brisbane.